A History of Scottish Child P

A History of Scottish Child Protection Law

Kenneth McK. Norrie

EDINBURGH
University Press

Edinburgh University Press is one of the leading university presses in the UK. We publish academic books and journals in our selected subject areas across the humanities and social sciences, combining cutting-edge scholarship with high editorial and production values to produce academic works of lasting importance. For more information visit our website: edinburghuniversitypress.com

First published in hardback by Edinburgh University Press 2020

Edinburgh University Press Ltd
The Tun – Holyrood Road
12 (2f) Jackson's Entry
Edinburgh EH8 8PJ

Typeset in New Caledonia by
Servis Filmsetting Ltd, Stockport, Cheshire,

A CIP record for this book is available from the British Library

ISBN 978 1 4744 4417 0 (hardback)
ISBN 978 1 4744 4418 7 (paperback)
ISBN 978 1 4744 4419 4 (webready PDF)
ISBN 978 1 4744 4420 0 (epub)

Contents

Expanded Table of Contents   vi

Table of Cases   xvi

Table of Statutes   xxi

Table of Statutory Instruments   xxxii

Foreword by The Hon. Lady Wise   xxxvi

Introduction   1

1   The Statutory Framework before 1968   7

2   The Statutory Framework after 1968   42

3   Child Protection through the Criminal Law   85

4   The Legal Process before 1968: The Juvenile Court   115

5   The Legal Process in the Modern Era: Scotland's Children's
    Hearing System   145

6   Home Supervision   176

7   Boarding-out and Fostering by Public Authorities   195

8   Institutional Care   232

9   Emergency and Interim Protection   280

10 Aftercare   299

11 Emigration of Children   312

12 Adoption of Children   336

    Index   387

Expanded Table of Contents

Table of Cases	xvi
Table of Statutes	xxi
Table of Statutory Instruments	xxxii
Foreword by The Hon. Lady Wise	xxxvi

INTRODUCTION	1

1 THE STATUTORY FRAMEWORK BEFORE 1968	7
Introduction	7
The Poor Law	10
Poor Law Jurisprudence	11
Reformatory and Industrial Schools	12
The Early Child Cruelty Statutes 1889–1908	13
The Prevention of Cruelty to, and Protection of, Children Act, 1889	14
The Prevention of Cruelty to Children Act, 1894	15
The Prevention of Cruelty to Children Act, 1904	16
The Children Act, 1908	17
Offences against children	18
Reformatory and industrial schools	19
Juvenile justice and juvenile courts	20
The Lead-up to the Children and Young Persons (Scotland) Act, 1932	21
The Children and Young Persons (Scotland) Acts, 1932 and 1937	24
The Post-war Period	26
The Clyde Report 1946	27
A substitute family	29
The Children Bill, 1948	31
The Children Act, 1948	32
Children's committees and children's officers	32
The boarding-out preference	33
Local authority duty to receive children into their care	34
Welfare as the guiding principle for local authority action	34

Local authority assumption of parental rights 35
The Children and Young Persons Act 1963 37
International Law Before 1968 38
  Early international declarations of the rights of the
    child 39

2 THE STATUTORY FRAMEWORK AFTER 1968 42
Introduction 42
The Kilbrandon Committee, 1961–1964 42
The Government's Response to Kilbrandon: The 1966 White
    Paper 44
The Social Work (Scotland) Act 1968 46
  An increased focus on preventive measures 46
  Greater involvement of the child's family 48
  The end of the boarding-out preference 49
  Clarifying and enhancing the role of the local authority 49
The Children Act 1975 51
The Lead-up to the Children (Scotland) Act 1995 53
  The Orkney Inquiry (the Clyde Report 1993) 53
  The White Paper: *Scotland's Children: Proposals for Child
    Care Policy and Law* 55
  Local Government etc (Scotland) Act 1994 56
The Children (Scotland) Act 1995 56
  Introduction 56
  Increased participation rights for children 57
  The new concept of the "looked after child" 59
  Duties of local authorities 60
  New orders 60
An Altered Landscape after the 1995 Act 61
  The changing face of "family" 63
  Constitutional changes 64
The Antisocial Behaviour Legislation 64
A New Regulatory Framework 66
  Limitations on who may work with children 67
  New oversight institutions 69
The Children's Hearings (Scotland) Act 2011 71
The Children and Young People (Scotland) Act 2014 72
  Giving effect to "GIRFEC" 72
  The "named person" scheme in the 2014 Act 74

International Law in the Post-1968 Period   77
The European Convention on Human Rights   77
     The Human Rights Act 1998 and the Scotland Act 1998   78
     Effects of the ECHR on domestic law   79
The United Nations Convention on the Rights of the Child   80
     The Children and Young People (Scotland) Act 2014   82
     The move to incorporation   83
Other International Treaties   83

3   CHILD PROTECTION THROUGH THE CRIMINAL LAW   85
Introduction   85
Sexual Offences   86
     Acts other than sexual intercourse   86
     Sexual intercourse   87
     Boys and the 1885 Act   88
     Twentieth-century legislation   88
     Exploitative sexual offences   89
     Other offences designed to protect children from sexual harm   93
The Crime of Child Cruelty or Neglect at Common Law   94
The Statutory Crime of Child Cruelty or Neglect   95
     The Prevention of Cruelty to, and Protection of, Children Act, 1889   96
     The Prevention of Cruelty to Children Acts, 1894 and 1904   97
     The Children Act, 1908   98
     Section 12 of the Children and Young Persons (Scotland) Act, 1937   99
Case Law on Section 12 of the 1937 Act   100
     Who may be charged   101
     Types of behaviour prohibited by s. 12   102
     The place of intent   103
     Likelihood of harm   105
The Parental Right of Chastisement   106
     The meaning of "reasonable chastisement"   106
The Right of School Teachers or Others to Inflict Corporal Punishment   108
     School teachers   108
     Persons acting in loco parentis   110
     Corporal punishment in residential establishments   111
     Corporal punishment in approved schools   112

Abolition of Corporal Punishment 112
In schools 113
In residential establishments 113
By foster carers 113
By parents and others 114

4 THE LEGAL PROCESS BEFORE 1968: THE JUVENILE
COURT 115
Introduction 115
The World-wide Juvenile Court Movement 117
Juvenile Courts in the USA 117
Juvenile Courts in Australia 120
Juvenile Courts in the UK 121
Dealing with juvenile offenders under the 1908 Act 122
Care and protection cases under the 1908 Act 124
The Juvenile Court under the Children and Young Persons
(Scotland) Acts, 1932 and 1937 127
Location of juvenile courts 130
Privacy and confidentiality 131
Jurisdiction of the Juvenile Court 132
Overview 132
The juvenile court's care and protection jurisdiction 134
Potential Outcomes in the Juvenile Court 137
Punitive disposals for offenders 138
Rules and Procedure at the Juvenile Court 140

5 THE LEGAL PROCESS IN THE MODERN ERA:
SCOTLAND'S CHILDREN'S HEARING SYSTEM 145
The Kilbrandon Report 145
The Social Work (Scotland) Act 1968 and the Children's
Hearing System 148
The Grounds of Referral to the Children's Hearing 150
Child beyond parental control 150
Bad associations or moral danger 151
Lack of parental care 152
Victim of scheduled offence 152
Female living with female victim of incest 154
Failure to attend school regularly 154
Commission of offence by child 155

Child absconsion   155
Grounds added subsequent to the 1968 Act   156
Overview of changing grounds   158
Qualification to the Welfare Test   159
A Missed Opportunity for England?   160
The World-wide Retreat from the Juvenile Court Ideal   166
Scotland the Different   169

6 HOME SUPERVISION   176
Day Industrial Schools   176
Supervision's Origins in Probation   177
Probation Prior to 1931   178
    Probation of Offenders Act, 1907   178
    Probation and the Children Act, 1908   181
The Probation of Offenders (Scotland) Act, 1931   181
The Role of Probation Officers in Care and Protection Cases
    After 1932   184
The Criminal Justice (Scotland) Act, 1949   186
The Kilbrandon Proposals for Probation and Supervision   188
Probation and the Social Work (Scotland) Act 1968   190
Supervision Requirements under the 1968 Act   193
Supervision under the Children (Scotland) Act 1995 and the
    Children's Hearings (Scotland) Act 2011   194

7 BOARDING-OUT AND FOSTERING BY PUBLIC
   AUTHORITIES   195
Introduction   195
A: Boarding-out under the Poor Law   197
The Old Poor Law   197
Boarding-out under the "New" Poor Law   198
The Poor Law (Scotland) Act, 1934   200
B: Boarding-out by Court Order 1889–1968   202
The Early Child Cruelty Statutes: "Fit Person Orders"   202
Committal to the Care of a Fit Person under the 1932 and 1937
    Acts   203
    Effect of a fit person order   205
    Variation and termination of fit person order   207
    Post-war pressure for change   209
Boarding-out after the Children Act, 1948   210

Boarding-out Regulations 1933–1959 213
  Choosing suitable foster parents 213
  Monitoring and visiting of boarded-out children 215
  The role of the foster parent 217
  Parents 218
The 1959 Memorandum on the Boarding-out of Children 219
C: Boarding-out and Fostering after 1968 221
The Social Work (Scotland) Act 1968 and the Children
  (Scotland) Act 1995 221
The Fostering Regulations 1985 and 1996 222
  Foster panels and fostering agreements 223
  Monitoring and termination of placement 225
Arrangements to Look After Children (Scotland) Regulations
  1996 226
Looked After Children (Scotland) Regulations 2009 227
Looking to the Future of Fostering: The National Foster Care
  Review 228
D: Kinship Care 229
Introduction 229
Kinship Care under the Looked After Children (Scotland)
  Regulations 2009 230
Kinship Care and the Children and Young People (Scotland)
  Act 2014 231

8 INSTITUTIONAL CARE 232
Introduction 232
A: Reformatory and Industrial Schools 233
The Growth of Reformatory and Industrial Schools 233
Reformatory and Industrial Schools Legislation 1854–1866 236
Later Nineteenth-century Legislation 239
Reformatory and Industrial Schools under the Children Act,
  1908 241
B: Approved Schools 1932–1968 243
Introduction 243
Approval of Approved Schools 245
Sending Children to Approved Schools 247
Length of Detention 247
Regulations Governing Approved Schools 249
  The managers 249

Premises, accommodation and food 250
Staffing 251
Education and training 251
Free time and home leave 252
Discipline and corporal punishment 253
Parental involvement 256
The medical officer 257
Inspection 258
C: Children's Homes 258
Voluntary Homes prior to 1948 258
Voluntary Homes after 1948 260
Local Authority Homes 261
Administration of Children's Homes (Scotland) Regulations,
    1959 262
D: The 1960s to the 1990s: Rethinking the Purpose of
    Residential Care 264
The Kilbrandon Report and the 1966 White Paper 264
Residential Establishments under the Social Work (Scotland)
    Act 1968 267
    Registration and visiting of residential establishments 268
Social Work (Residential Establishments – Child Care)
    (Scotland) Regulations 1987 269
    The statement of functions 270
    Discipline 270
    The role of the local authority and care authority 271
Further Rethinking of Residential Care in the 1990s 272
    The Skinner Report on Residential Care in Scotland 272
    The Fife Inquiry (The Kearney Report) 273
    The White Paper: *Scotland's Children: Proposals for Child*
    Care Policy and Law 274
Residential Establishments – Child Care (Scotland)
    Regulations 1996: The Current Rules 274
E: Secure Accommodation 275
Introduction 275
Criteria for Placing a Child in Secure Accommodation 276
Secure Accommodation (Scotland) Regulations 1983 277
Secure Accommodation (Scotland) Regulations 1996 and
    2013 278
Visitation and Inspection of Secure Units 279

 9 EMERGENCY AND INTERIM PROTECTION   280
    Introduction   280
    The Early Child Cruelty Statutes: 1889–1908   281
       Place of safety warrants   283
    Emergency and Interim Protection 1932–1995   284
       Place of safety warrants   287
       Interim measures   287
    The Orkney Case and the 1992 Clyde Report   288
    Child Protection Orders under the 1995 and 2011 Acts   290
       The Children (Scotland) Act 1995   290
       The Children's Hearings (Scotland) Act 2011   291
    Other Emergency Provisions in the 1995 and 2011 Acts   292
    Interim Orders Made by Children's Hearings under the 1995
       and 2011 Acts   294
       Warrants under the 1995 Act   294
       Interim compulsory supervision orders under the 2011 Act 295
    Definition of "Place of Safety"   296

10 AFTERCARE   299
    Introduction   299
    Early Aftercare Provisions   300
    Aftercare from 1932 to 1968   302
       Aftercare for other children and young persons
          1948–1968   305
    Social Work (Scotland) Act 1968   306
    Aftercare After 1995   307
    Corporate Parenting under the Children and Young People
       (Scotland) Act 2014   309

11 EMIGRATION OF CHILDREN   312
    Introduction   312
       Early emigration practices and motivations   312
       Where were children sent?   315
       Who arranged emigration?   316
       Why emigration was so dangerous   317
    The Legal Authority for Emigration   318
       Parental consent   318
       The child's consent   320
       Actings in loco parentis   322

Statutory Authority to Emigrate Children 1891–1932   323
    The Acts of 1891, 1894 and 1904   323
    The Children Act, 1908   325
Emigration under the Children and Young Persons (Scotland)
    Acts, 1932 and 1937   326
Emigration by Local Authorities under the Children Act, 1948   329
Emigration by Voluntary Organisations   332
Emigration of Children under the Social Work (Scotland)
    Act 1968   334

12 ADOPTION OF CHILDREN   336
Adoption of Children before the Adoption Acts   336
    Introduction   336
    Informal adoption   337
    Baby farming   341
    The pressure for change   342
The Debates on the Adoption of Children Act, 1926   344
The Adoption of Children (Scotland) Act, 1930   351
    The power to make an adoption order   352
    Restrictions on making an adoption order   352
    Consent to the making of an adoption order   353
    Matters in respect of which the court must be satisfied   356
    Terms and conditions   357
    Effects of an adoption order   358
    Interim orders and second adoption orders   359
    Existing *de facto* adoptions: adoption of adults   360
    The Adopted Children Register   362
    Conclusions on the Adoption of Children (Scotland) Act,
    1930   363
The Adoption of Children (Regulation) Act, 1939   364
The Adoption of Children Act, 1949   366
The Adoption Act, 1950   369
The Adoption Act, 1958   370
The Succession (Scotland) Act 1964   373
The Children Act 1975   374
The Adoption (Scotland) Act 1978   377
The Adoption and Children (Scotland) Act 2007   379
    Introduction   379
    Changes to the law of adoption   380

The Need for a New Form of Permanence 382
Permanence Orders 384
Adoption Statistics 385

Index 387

Table of Cases

SCOTLAND/ENGLAND AND WALES/UNITED KINGDOM

A, Petitioner 1936 SC 255...354
A & B, Petitioners 1932 SLT (Sh Ct) 37 358
A v Liverpool City Council [1982] AC 363 219
A v United Kingdom (1999) 27 EHRR 611 ....78, 107
AB v CB 1985 SLT 514..357
AB v Howman 1917 JC 23...26, 122, 170
ABC v Principal Reporter 2018 CSOH 81; 2019 SC 186..80
Airey v Ireland (1980) 2 EHRR 305..78
Aitken v Aitken 1978 SC 297...206
Andrew Lyall (1853) 1 Irv. 218...86–87
Application for a Child Protection Order 2015 SLT (Sh Ct) 9...............................281, 292
Armes v Nottinghamshire County Council [2018] AC 355...196–197
Attorney General ex rel. Tilley v Wandsworth London Borough Council [1981] 1 WLR
    854...34
Attorney General v Observer Ltd [1990] 1 AC 109...39
Authority Reporter v S 2010 SLT 765...80

B & B, Petitioners 1950 SLT (Sh Ct) 34 368
B & B, Spouses, Petitioners 1936 SC 256...352
B v C 1996 SLT 1370 358
B v Harris 1990 SLT 208..108
B v Kennedy 1992 SC 295 288
B v Murphy 2014 HCJAC 56...102
Baillie v Agnew (Thomas Baillie of Polkemmet v Sir Stair Agnew) (1775) 5 Brown's
    Supplement 526 ....8, 9
Barbara Gray or McIntosh (1881) 4 Couper 389...95, 342
Barnardo v McHugh [1891] AC 388 9
Beagley v Beagley 1984 SC(HL) 69 37
Boase v Fife County Council 1937 SC(HL) 28..129
Bowers v Smith [1953] 1 WLR 297..135
Brooks v Blount [1923] 1 KB 257...101
Brown v Hilson 1924 JC 1 109
Browne v Browne 1969 SLT (Notes) 15 206
Bute Education Authority v Glasgow Education Authority 1923 SC 675 354
Byrd v Wither 1991 SLT 206 108

C, Petitioners 1993 SCLR 14...349, 354, 370
C & C, Spouses, Petitioners 1936 SC 257...355, 357, 368
C v Harris 1989 SC 278 108
Campbell and Cosans v United Kingdom [1982] 4 EHRR 293...112
Campbell v Croall (1895) 22R 869...9, 341
Cartwright v HM Advocate 2001 SLT 1163...86
Chief Constable of Police Scotland v M 2016 SLT (Sh Ct) 148...93
Christian Institute v Lord Advocate [2015] CSOH 7; [2015] CSIH 64; [2016] UKSC 51 ....18, 73,
                                                                                                                                    75–76
Christian Institute v Scottish Ministers [2015] CSIH 64 74
Clark v HM Advocate 1968 JC 53 104–105
Conolly v Managers of the Stranraer Reformatory (1904) 11 SLT 638 240–241

Costello-Roberts v United Kingdom (1995) 19 EHRR 112..107, 255
Craig v Greig and McDonald (1863) 1 M 1172..320

D, Petitioner 1938 SLT 26..353
D v Sinclair 1973 SLT (Sh Ct) 47 172
David and Janet Gemmell (1841) 2 Swinton 552 95
David Brown (1844) 2 Broun 261 86–87
Demir v Turkey (2008) 48 EHRR 1272..81
Down Lisburn Health and Social Services Trust and Anor v H and Anor [2006] UKHL 36.........355
Dundee Corporation v Stirling County Council (1940) 56 Sh Ct Rep 189 247
Dunn v Mustard (1899) 1 F(J) 81..143, 202, 247

E and E, Petitioners 1939 SC 165...360
East Renfrewshire Council, Appellants [2016] SAC (Civ) 14...247
East Renfrewshire Council, Appellants 2015 GWD 35–564 247
Edinburgh EA v Perth and Kinross EA (1934) SLT (Sh Ct) 60..247
Ewart v Brown (1882) 10R 163 ....107, 109

F, Petitioner 1939 SC 166...360
F, Petitioner 1951 SLT (Sh Ct) 17..362
F v F 1991 SLT 357..206
Farquarson v Gordon (1894) 21R(J) 52...96
Fife Education Authority v Lord Provost etc. of Edinburgh (1934) 50 Sh Ct Rep 245..................247
Flannigan v Inspector of Bothwell (1892) 19R 909..321
Foreman v Advocate General for Scotland 2016 SLT 962..359

G, Petitioner 1939 SC 782...361
G & G, Petitioners 1949 SLT (Sh Ct) 60...372
G v Minister of Pensions 1950 SLT (Sh Ct) 79...208
G v Templeton 1998 SCLR 180..108
G v The Scottish Ministers 2015 GWD 36–577 68
Gibson (1845) 2 Broun 366...94
Gilmour v Ayr County Council 1968 SLT (Sh Ct) 41 206
Gray v Hawthorn 1964 JC 69...109–110
Guest v Annan 1988 SCCR 275...108

H, Petitioner 1960 SLT (Sh Ct) 3..353
H, Petitioners 1952 SLT (Sh Ct) 15 362
H & H, Petitioners 1944 SC 347...355, 357, 368
H & H, Petitioners 1948 SLT (Sh Ct) 37...358
H v H [1947] KB 463...356, 366, 367
H v Lees, D v Orr 1993 JC 238 ....103, 105, 106
Hamilton v Wilson 1993 SCCR 9..86
Harvey v Harvey (1860) 22D 1198..8
Hay v Duthie's Trs 1956 SC 511..359, 368
Henderson v Stewart 1954 JC 94 102
Heritors in the Parishes of Melrose and Stitchell v Heritors in the Parish of Bowden (1786)
    Mor. 10584...12
HM Advocate v K 1994 SCCR 499..90
HM Advocate v McKenzie 1970 SLT 81...368
HM Advocate v O'Brien & Ors (1845) 2 Broun 499 235
HM Advocate v Philip (1855) 2 Irv. 243...86, 93
Hope v Evered (1886) 17 QBD 338...283
Humphries v S 1986 SLT 683 (IH) 286
Humphries v X & Y 1982 SC 79...286

J v C [1970] AC 668 163
J v Children's Reporter for Stirling 2010 Fam. LR 140...277
Jamieson v Heatly 1959 JC 22 ....142, 171
JM v Brechin 2015 CSIH 58...104

JS, Petitioner 1950 SLT (Sh Ct) 3 352
JS v Mulrooney 2014 CSIH 70 103

K, Petitioner 1949 SC 140 361
K & K, Petitioners 1950 SLT (Sh Ct) 2..372
K v Authority Reporter 2009 SLT 1019 ....58, 79
Keltie v HM Adv. 2012 HCJAC 79...102
Kennedy v A 1986 SLT 358 172
Kennedy v A 1993 SLT 1134 108
Kennedy v S 1986 SC 43..103
Kerrigan v Hall (1901) 4F 10...339
Kincaid and Another v Quarrier (1896) 23R 676...319
Kirk Session of Coldinghame v Kirk Session of Dunse (1779) Mor. 10582........................12
Kirk Session of Inveresk v Kirk Session of Tranent (1737) Mor. 10552.............................12
Kirk Session of Rescobie v Kirk Session of Aberlemno (1801) Mor. 10589 12

L, Petitioner 1951 SLT 270 (IH)..362
L, Petitioners 1993 SLT 1310 and 1342..62
Lea v Charrington (1889) 23 QBD 272...283
Leeds City Council v West Yorkshire Metropolitan Police [1983] 1 AC 29 207
Liverpool Society for the Prevention of Cruelty to Children v Jones [1914] 3 KB 813....96, 101, 110
Locality Reporter Manager, Applicant [2019] SC Liv. 60 (10 July 2019, Livingston Sheriff
    Court)...102
Locality Reporter, Stirling v KR [2018] SAC Civ 30 ....106, 107, 108
Lord Advocate's Reference No 1 of 2000, 2001 JC 143 38

M, Appellant 2010 Fam. LR 152...80
M & M, Petitioners 1950 SLT (Sh Ct) 3 358
M v Aitken 2006 SLT 691 103
M v Hendron 2007 SC 556...269
M v Normand 1995 SLT 1284 105
M v Orr 1995 SLT 26 103
Mackay v Lamb 1923 JC 16...139
Macpherson v Leishman (1887) 14R 780 339
Magistrates of Edinburgh v Stirling County Council 1947 SLT (Sh Ct) 58 247
Marckx v Belgium (1979–80) 2 EHRR 330 78
Marshall v McDoual (1741) Mor 8930..321
Maxwell v HM Advocate 2017 HCJAC 64..93
McDonald v HM Advocate 1997 SLT 1237...87
McFadzean v Kilmalcolm School Board (1903) 5F 600.............................232, 318–319, 354
McGregor v H 1983 SLT 626 91
McGuire v McGuire 1969 SLT (Notes) 36 (OH) 37
McKenzies v McPhee 1889 16R (J) 53...143
McLaughlan v Boyd 1934 JC 19...87
McMichael v United Kingdom (1995) 20 EHRR 205...79
McShane v Paton 1922 JC 26 109
Mohamed v Knott [1969] 1 QB 1...91, 205
Morrison v Quarrier (1894) 21R 889...319, 321
Muckarsie v Dickson (1848) 11D 4...109
Munro v Munro (1840) 7 ER 1288..358

Nicol v Brown 1951 JC 87 170–171

Osborne v Matthan (No. 3) 1998 SC 682..52

P v Lothian Regional Council 1989 SLT 739...376
P v P 2000 SLT 781...206
P v Scottish Ministers 2017 CSOH 33 68
PQ & RQ, Petitioners 1965 SLT 93 367
Principal Reporter v K [2010] UKSC 56...80

R (G) v Barnet London Borough Council [2001] EWCA Civ 540 333
R (On the Application of P) v Secretary of State for the Home Department [2019] UKSC 3.........68
R (On the Application of SG & Ors) v Secretary of State for Work and Pensions [2015]
   UKSC 16...39, 81
R (On the Application of T) v Chief Constable of Greater Manchester [2014] UKSC 35..............68
R (Williamson) v Secretary of State for Education [2005] 2 AC 246...113
R v Boulden (1957) 41 Crim. App. Rep. 105..103
R v Connor [1908] 2 KB 26 ....98, 102, 103
R v Croydon Juvenile Court Justices ex parte Croydon LBC [1973] QB 426.........................207
R v Drury (1974) 60 Crim App Rep 195...102
R v Gibbons [1977] Crim LR 741 103
R v Hatton [1925] 2 KB 322 ....105, 106
R v Her Majesty's Advocate 1988 SLT 623..91
R v Liverpool City Justices ex p. W [1959] 1 WLR 149 353
R v Lyons [2002] UKHL 44...39
R v R (Parent and Child: Custody) 1994 SCLR 849 52
R v Senior (1899) 1 QB 283..98, 103
RB, Petitioners 1950 SLT (Sh Ct) 73 361–362
Re C (A Minor) (Adoption Order: Conditions) [1989] AC 1 358
Re D (An Infant) [1958] 1 WLR 197 354
Re D (An Infant) (Adoption: Parent's Consent) 1977 AC 602..224
Re Gilpin [1954] Ch 1..368
Re J (A Minor) (Adoption Order: Conditions) [1973] Fam 106..357
Re J (Children) (Care Proceedings: Threshold Criteria) [2013] 1 AC 680 290
Re M (An Infant) [1955] 2 QB 479 ....353, 354
Reilly v Quarrier (1895) 22R 879 319
Ridley v Little *The Times* 26 May 1960..102
Roy v Cruickshank 1954 SLT 217..141, 171

S v Authority Reporter 2012 SLT (Sh Ct) 89..102
S v L [2012] UKSC 30..381
S v Miller 2001 SLT 531 and 1304 ....58, 79, 159
S v N 2002 SLT 589..196
S v Sweden (2014) 58 EHRR 36 78
Saloman v Customs and Excise Commrs [1967] 2 QB 116..39
Sloan v B 1991 SC 412...288
Sloan v B 1991 SLT 530...54, 162
Spencer's Trustees v Ruggles 1981 SC 289 373
Stewart v Thain 1981 JC 13...255
Sutherland v Taylor (1887) 15R 224...338, 340
Sweenie v Hart 1908 SC(J) 81 ....234, 239

T, Petitioner 1997 SLT 724..381
TB, Petitioners 1950 SLT (Sh Ct) 74 352
Thomas Baillie of Polkemmet v Sir Stair Agnew (1775) 5 Brown's Supplement 526 ....8, 9
Thomson v Lindsay (1849) 11D 719 10
TM & PM, Petitioners 2017 CSOH 139..230
Tough, Petitioner 2015 CSIH 78...132

W v Clark 1999 SCCR 775 102
W v HM Advocate 2016 HCJAC 44..93
W v Kennedy 1988 SLT 583..171
Webster v Dominick 2005 1 JC 65...91
Weir v Cruickshank 1959 JC 94..129
West Lothian Council v MB 2017 SC (UKSC) 67...385
White v Jeans 1911 SC(J) 88..235
Williams v London Borough of Hackney [2018] UKSC 37...320
Windsor & Ors v CPS [2011] EWCA Crim 143 283
Woods v Ministry of Pensions 1952 SC 529..207–208

X and Y v The Netherlands (1985) 8 EHRR 235..78
X v United Kingdom [1982] 4 EHRR 188 276

UNITED STATES

Commonwealth v Fisher 213 Pa. 48 (1905)...118
Gault, Application of 407 P. 2d 760 (1965) 167
Gault, In Re 387 US 1 (1967)..166–168, 169–170, 172, 173
Holmes' Appeal 379 Pa. 599 (1955); 109 A. 2d 523...118–119
Mill v Brown 31 Utah 473, 88 Pac. 609 (1907) 119

Table of Statutes

SCOTLAND/ENGLAND AND WALES/UNITED KINGDOM

1567
Incest Act, 1567 (APS iii, 26, c. 15 (12mo. c. 14)) 90

1579
Poor Law, 1579 (For Punishment of the Strong and Idle Beggars and Relief of the Poor and Impotent) (APS iii 139, c. 12 (12mo. c. 74)) 10, 197

1617
Poor Law, 1617 (APS iv 542, c. 10 (12mo. c. 10)) 197–198

1661
Act against papists and priests etc., 1661 (APS vii 26, c. 37 (12mo. c. 8)) 7

1700
The Popery Act, 1700 (APS x 215, c. 3 (12mo. c. 3)) 7

1819
Cotton Mills and Factories Act, 1819 115

1829
Roman Catholic Relief Act, 1829 8

1833
Factories Act, 1833 115

1841
Act for Repressing Juvenile Delinquency in the City of Glasgow, 4 and 5 Vict. Cap. xxxvi, 1841 .... 233, 234–235

1845
Poor Law Amendment (Scotland) Act, 1845 .... 10–11, 198–200

1854
Reformatory and Industrial Schools (Scotland) Act, 1854 .... 13, 236–237
    s. 1 237
    s. 2 237
Youthful Offenders Act, 1854 .... 13, 237

1856
Reformatory Schools (Scotland) Act, 1856
    s. 10 237

1861
Conjugal Rights (Scotland) Amendment Act, 1861 8
Industrial Schools Act, 1861 13
Industrial Schools (Scotland) Act, 1861 238
    s. 9 .... 150, 151, 238
    s. 10 238
    s. 14 237–238

1864
Summary Procedure Act, 1864 96

1866
Industrial Schools Act, 1866 .... 13, 143, 176
    s. 5 239
    s. 8 238
    s. 10 238
    s. 26 176
    s. 28 .... 300, 323
    s. 41 238
    s. 49 238
Reformatory Schools Act, 1866 .... 13, 300
    s. 5 238
    s. 8 239
    s. 19 323

1872
Education (Scotland) Act, 1872 ... 115, 238, 242, 354
Infant Life Protection Act, 1872 .... 195, 342

1878
Glasgow Juvenile Delinquency Prevention and Repression Act, 1878 176

1883
Education (Scotland) Act, 1883 240

1885
Criminal Law Amendment Act, 1885. 19, 87–88
    s. 3 87
    s. 4 87
    s. 5 87
    s. 7 87
    s. 11 88
    s. 15 87

1886
Guardianship of Infants Act, 1886 8

1887
Probation of First Offenders Act, 1887 178
    s. 1 178

1889
Poor Law Act, 1889 36
Prevention of Cruelty to, and Protection of, Children Act, 1889 ... 14–15, 17, 30, 96–97, 202, 281
    s. 1 .... 14, 15, 18, 96, 97, 281, 282
    s. 2 .... 14, 96
    s. 3 .... 15, 115
    s. 3(a) 281
    s. 4(1) 281–282
    s. 5 .... 14, 125, 153

s. 5(1) 97, 282
s. 5(2) 15, 110, 202, 322
s. 14 .... 106, 109
s. 17 .... 282, 296
1891
Custody of Children Act, 1891 .... 9, 201,
340–341
Reformatory and Industrial Schools Act,
1891 .... 300, 319, 323–324
s. 1 .... 300–301, 323, 325
1893
Day Industrial Schools (Scotland) Act, 1893
.... 176–177
s. 4 240
Public Authorities Protection Act, 1893 241
Reformatory Schools Act, 1893 239
1894
Industrial Schools Acts Amendment Act,
1894
s. 1 240
Local Government (Scotland) Act, 1894 11
Prevention of Cruelty to Children Act,
1894 .... 16, 17, 94, 97, 143, 202, 282, 324
s. 1 .... 16, 18, 98
s. 5 16
s. 6 .... 98, 125, 153
s. 6(1) 324
s. 6(5) 324, 325
s. 7(1) 110
s. 9 16
s. 23(1) 97
s. 23(2) 16
s. 24 .... 106, 109
s. 25 296
Prevention of Cruelty to Children
(Amendment) Act, 1894 .... 15, 282
ss. 1 and 2 96
s. 17 96
1897
Infant Life Protection Act, 1897 .... 195, 342
1903
Employment of Children Act, 1903 115
1904
Prevention of Cruelty to Children Act,
1904 .... 16, 17, 98, 102, 202, 282, 322
s. 1 .... 18, 98
s. 6 .... 98, 125, 153
s. 6(1) 16, 203, 324
s. 6(5) 325
s. 7 110
s. 28 .... 106, 109
s. 29 296
sched. 2 16
1907
Probation of Offenders Act, 1907. 178–179, 181,
182, 186
s. 1 179
s. 1(1)(ii) 179
s. 2 181
s. 2(1) 183

s. 3(2) 179
s. 4 .... 179, 186, 301, 303
s. 6 179
1908
Children Act, 1908 .... 1, 16, 17–21, 31, 99,
121–126, 127, 130, 132, 133, 135,
160, 165, 170, 181, 205, 241, 247,
282, 328, 342, 351
Part I 195, 365
Part II 18, 125, 203
s. 12 ...... 18, 98, 98–99, 99, 101, 105, 125, 135
s. 13 .... 18, 99
s. 15 18
s. 16 19
s. 17 19
s. 20 .... 19, 284
s. 20(1) 283
s. 20(2) 282
s. 21 98
s. 21(1) 125, 153
s. 21(2) 135
s. 21(6) 325, 326
s. 22(1) 110
s. 24 .... 283, 284, 287
s. 24(1), (4) 284
s. 25(1), (3) and (4) 258
s. 37 .... 106, 109
s. 38 101
s. 38(2) 101, 110
Part IV 19, 126
s. 44 241
s. 45 241
s. 47 241
s. 52 242
s. 53 242
s. 54 242
s. 57 .... 19, 125
s. 58 .... 19, 125, 243
s. 58(1) 19, 244
s. 58(1)(a)–(c) 151
s. 58(1)(d) 152
s. 58(1)(e) 154
s. 58(1)(f) and (g) 151
s. 58(2) 126
s. 58(2) and (3) 20
s. 58(4) 126, 150
s. 58(7) 20, 126
s. 59 126
s. 60 20
s. 65(a), (b) 243
s. 70 .... 301, 325–326
s. 74(6) 26, 170
s. 75 241
ss. 77–83 177
s. 78(3) 177
Part V 20, 122–124, 126
s. 98 122
s. 99 122
s. 99(1) 138
s. 102 122

s. 102(3) 122
s. 103 122
s. 106 138
s. 107 243
s. 107(c) 181
s. 107(d) 122, 126
s. 107(e) and (f), (g) 122
s. 111 .... 21, 131
s. 111(1) 121, 123
s. 111(4) 123
s. 118 135
s. 131 .... 18, 122, 296, 353
s. 132 24
s. 132(9) 124, 283
sched. 19, 125, 135, 153, 283
Education (Scotland) Act, 1908 17
Old Age Pensions Act, 1908 17
1910
Children Act (1908) Amendment Act,
    1910 19
1911
National Insurance Act, 1911 17
1913
Mental Deficiency and Lunacy (Scotland) Act,
    1913 259
National Insurance Act, 1913 17
1918
Education (Scotland) Act, 1918
    s. 19 242
1922
Criminal Law Amendment Act, 1922
    s. 4 87
Empire Settlement Act, 1922 316
1925
Criminal Justice Act, 1925
    Part I 182
Guardianship of Infants Act, 1925 375
1926
Adoption of Children Act, 1926 ... 160, 338–339,
        344–351, 357, 358, 359, 360, 364, 366,
                                        369, 377
    s. 1 360
    s. 5(3) 358–359
    s. 6(2) 360
    s. 10 360–361
    s. 12(2) 351
Legitimacy Act, 1926 358
1929
Local Government (Scotland) Act, 1929 11,
                                        12, 133
    s. 3 204
1930
Adoption of Children (Scotland) Act,
    1930 .... 134, 160, 205, 350, 351–364,
                    357, 366, 367, 369, 377, 385
    s. 1 362
    s. 1(1), (3) 352
    s. 2 352
    s. 2(1) 352–353, 365, 366
    s. 2(2) 353

s. 2(3) 353–355, 355, 356
s. 2(4) 353
s. 3 356–357
s. 3(2) 355
s. 4 357
s. 5 .... 358, 359
s. 5(3) 358–359
s. 6(1) 359
s. 7 360
s. 9 .... 357, 365
s. 10 .... 360–362, 363
s. 11 362
Poor Law Act, 1930 330
    s. 52 36
1931
Probation of Offenders (Scotland) Act, 1931
    .... 181–184, 186
    s. 1(2) 183
    s. 3 183
    s. 4(2) 183
    s. 5(1) and (2) 183
    s. 5(3) 184
    s. 8(3), (4) 183
1932
Children and Young Persons Act, 1932 . 24, 160,
    165
    s. 15 171
    s. 89 24
Children and Young Persons (Scotland) Act,
    1932 .... 1, 2, 5, 17, 21–26, 30–31, 129,
            132–136, 148, 170, 201, 203–207,
            229, 244–245, 327, 329, 365
    Part I 25
    s. 1(1) 133
    s. 1(1) and (5) 25
    s. 1(1) and (6) 129
    s. 1(1)(i) 155
    s. 1(1)(ii) 154
    s. 1(4) 130
    s. 1(5) 134
    s. 1(6) 129
    s. 2 128–129
    s. 3(2) 131
    s. 6 .... 25–26, 134, 137, 185
    s. 6(1) 285
    s. 6(1)(d) 185
    s. 6(1)(i) 150, 151, 152
    s. 6(1)(ii)(a) and (b), (c) 153
    s. 6(1)(ii)(d) 154
    s. 7 .... 136, 150, 185
    s. 10(1), (3) 186
    s. 11 .... 284, 285
    s. 11(2) 285
    Part II 25
    s. 12 .... 25, 137
    s. 12(1) 137
    s. 12(2) 137, 185–186
    s. 14 133
    s. 15 .... 26, 138
    s. 16 .... 26, 137

s. 18 205
s. 19(2) 205
s. 19(6) 209
s. 19(7) 326–327
s. 19(8) 207
s. 20 204
s. 20(1) 203
s. 20(2) 204
s. 20(4) 206
s. 22(1) 204
s. 22(2) 208
s. 23(4) and (5), (6) 247
s. 25(1) 247–248
s. 25(2), (3) 248
s. 36 25
s. 37 .... 25, 245
Part IV 115
s. 40(3) 259
s. 41 258
s. 42 259
s. 64 .... 25, 98, 133, 284
s. 64(1) 248
s. 72 130
s. 75 131–132
s. 79(1)(i)(b) 204
sched. 1 245
sched. 1 para 1 245
sched. 1 para 2 245
sched. 1 para 7 245
sched. 1 para 15 248
sched. 1 para 15(2) 249
sched. 1 para 16 302
sched. 1 para 16(1) 303
sched. 1 para 16(5) 302
sched. 1 para 17(1) 302
sched. 1 para 17(2) 303
sched. 1 para 18 .... 303, 327–328
sched. 1 para 26 247
sched. 2 .... 98, 297
sched. 5 para 3 327

1933

Children and Young Persons Act, 1933 160,
                                    161, 207
  s. 1 102
  s. 61(1)(a) 135

1934

Poor Law (Scotland), Act 200–201
  s. 10 201

1937

Children and Young Persons (Scotland) Act,
  1937 .... 2, 17, 24–26, 29, 30–31, 32, 129,
        160, 187–188, 189, 203–207, 365, 368
  Part I 195
  s. 12 .... 14, 18, 99–106, 125, 135
  s. 12(1) 97, 100
  s. 12(2)(b) 99
  s. 12(7) 100, 106, 107
  s. 27 .... 101, 110
  Part III 115
  s. 39 130

s. 43 171
s. 43(2) 26, 138
s. 46 131–132
s. 47 287
s. 47(1) 290
s. 47(1A) 287
s. 49(1) 26, 137, 149
s. 49(2) 205
s. 50 .... 25, 133
s. 50(1) 140
s. 50(1) and (5) 129
s. 50(1)(i) 155
s. 50(1)(ii) 154
s. 50(3) 134
s. 50(4) 129
s. 52(1) 130
s. 55 133
s. 58 138
s. 59(1) 138
s. 61 .... 25, 137
s. 61(1) 137
s. 61(2) 137, 185–186
s. 65 .... 25, 99–100, 134
s. 65(1)(a) 150, 152
s. 65(1)(b)(i) and (ii), (iii) 153
s. 65(1)(b)(iv) 154
s. 65(2) 151
s. 66 .... 99, 137, 185
s. 66(2) 285
s. 66(2)(d) 149, 185, 187
s. 68 .... 136, 149, 150, 185, 187
s. 70(1), (3) 186
s. 71 285
s. 71(1) 284, 290
s. 71(2) 285
s. 72 247
s. 74(1), (2) 247
s. 75(1) 247–248
s. 75(2) 248
s. 77 248
s. 78 .... 302, 304
s. 78(1) 303
s. 78(5) 302
s. 79(3) 205
s. 79(4) 35, 110, 206, 304
s. 80 203
s. 80(1) 211
s. 83 245
s. 83(1) 245
s. 83(2) 245
s. 85 245
s. 85(1) 245
s. 88(3) 204
s. 88(4) 209
s. 88(5) 328
s. 88(6) 207
s. 88(7) 208
s. 96 259
s. 98 258
s. 99 259

s. 106 261
s. 107(1)(a)(ii) 204
s. 110 ....133, 248, 297
s. 110(1) 25, 354
sched. 1 ....99–100, 135, 152–153, 283
sched. 2 ....245, 304
sched. 2 para 5 248
sched. 2 para 6 248
sched. 2 para 6(2) 249
sched. 2 para 7 ....303, 327
sched. 2 para 12(1) 302
sched. 2 para 12(2) 303

1939
Adoption of Children (Regulation) Act, 1939
....364–365, 369
s. 1 364
s. 2 364
s. 2(3) 364
s. 6 364
s. 7 365
s. 9 365
s. 10 365
s. 11 ....364, 365
Custody of Children (Scotland) Act, 1939
s. 1(1) 352

1940
Law Reform (Miscellaneous Provisions)
   (Scotland) Act, 1940
s. 2 365
s. 2(1) 359

1946
Education (Scotland) Act, 1946
s. 1 252
s. 32(1) 133
s. 81 251
National Insurance Act, 1946 27

1947
National Health Service (Scotland) Act, 1947 27

1948
Children Act, 1948 .....27, 30–37, 46, 48, 49, 50,
                  147, 160, 203, 221, 260–261, 305,
                  329–332, 333, 368–369
Part I 34
s. 1 ....34, 47
s. 1(1), (2) 34
s. 1(3) 34, 37
s. 2(3) 37
s. 5 211
Part II 297
s. 12(1) 35
s. 13(1) 33, 211
s. 14(2)(b) 33
s. 15(1) 261
s. 15(2) 297
s. 15(4) 262
s. 15(5) 261
s. 17 ....331, 332
s. 19 305
s. 20 35
s. 20(1), (2) 306

s. 29 261
s. 29(6) 261
s. 31(1) 261
s. 31(1)(d) 264
s. 33 332
s. 38(2) 32
s. 39 32
s. 39(1), (2) 32
s. 40(5) 32
s. 41 32
s. 41(4) 32
s. 44 211
s. 51(1), (2) 297
s. 54 261
s. 54(3), (7) 261
s. 59 331
s. 60(2) 297
sched. 3 ....297, 328–329
Criminal Justice Act, 1948 139
National Assistance Act, 1948 27
s. 1 11

1949
Adoption of Children Act, 1949... 359, 366–369,
                                 369, 373
s. 2(1) 366
s. 3 367
s. 3(1) 366, 366–367, 371
s. 3(2) 367
s. 5 369
s. 7(2) 369
ss. 9 and 10 368
s. 11(1), (3) 368
s. 11(4) 369
s. 13 366
s. 14(1) 360
s. 15 367
s. 15(a), (e) 368
Criminal Justice (Scotland) Act, 1949 .. 186–188,
                                 189, 193–194
s. 2(1), (6) 186
s. 71(1), (2) 187
s. 72(1), (2) 187
s. 72(5) 188
sched. 3 para 4 187
sched. 11 171
Legal Aid and Solicitors (Scotland) Act,
   1949 27

1950
Adoption Act, 1950 ....369, 370, 377
s. 3(1) 356, 367

1958
Adoption Act, 1958 ....353, 357, 370–373, 377
s. 2(2) 372
s. 2(3) 376
s. 4 370–371
s. 4(1), (3) 371
s. 5(1) 356, 367, 371
s. 5(2), (4) 371
s. 7(1) 371
s. 7(2) 372

s. 22 376
s. 28 372
s. 28(2) 374
s. 29 375
s. 34 372
ss. 37–49 372
s. 38 372
s. 39 372
s. 41 372
s. 43 372
s. 50 376
s. 50(4)–(9) 376
Children Act, 1958
   Part I 195
1959
Mental Health Act, 1959
   s. 66(3) 276
1963
Children and Young Persons Act 1963 37–38,
                            161, 265, 306, 307
   s. 1 .... 37–38, 47, 161
   s. 3 .... 136, 151
   s. 46 .... 35, 306
   s. 47 .... 35, 306
   s. 57 132
   s. 58 .... 35, 306, 307
Criminal Justice (Scotland) Act 1963 306
   Part II 304
   sched. 2 para 1 304
   sched. 2 para 2 304
   sched. 2 para 5 304
   sched 2. para 7 305
1964
Succession (Scotland) Act 1964 .... 359, 373
   s. 2 373
   s. 23(1), (2), (3) 373
   s. 24 373
1968
Social Work (Scotland) Act 1968 .... 24, 37, 42,
               46–51, 56, 130, 136, 139, 140,
               148–156, 158, 160, 163–164, 171, 174,
               190–194, 221–222, 222, 266–269, 269,
                            270, 306–307, 334
   s. 1(4), (5) 50
   s. 2 .... 50, 56
   s. 2(2) 33
   s. 2(4) 33
   s. 3 .... 50, 56
   s. 5 222
   s. 12 .... 47, 55, 60
   s. 12(1) 47
   s. 15 .... 47, 59
   s. 15(3) 48
   s. 16 .... 36, 47, 53
   s. 16A 53
   ss. 17A to 17D 48
   s. 17E 48
   s. 20 .... 48, 52, 223, 271
   s. 20A 52
   s. 21 49

s. 23 .... 334, 335
s. 24 .... 48, 307
s. 25 .... 48, 308
s. 26 307
s. 27 192
Part III 52
s. 32(2)(a) 150
s. 32(2)(b) 151
s. 32(2)(c) 152
s. 32(2)(d) 100, 107, 153
s. 32(2)(dd) 153
s. 32(2)(e), (f) 154
s. 32(2)(g) 155
s. 32(2)(gg) 156
s. 32(2)(h) 155, 157
s. 34A 52
s. 36A 52
s. 37 286–287
s. 37(1A) 51
s. 37(2) 54, 285, 287, 288, 289
s. 37(3) 285
s. 37(4) 286
s. 37(5) 286
s. 37(5A) and (5B) 286
s. 38(1) 150
s. 40(7), (8) 288
s. 42(1), (2)(c) 148
s. 43(1) 148, 149, 159
s. 43(3) 287
s. 43(4) 288
s. 44 .... 48, 193
s. 44(1)(a), (b) 193
s. 44(5) 51, 149
s. 58A 276–277
s. 58A(3) 277
s. 59(1) 267
s. 59(2) 268
s. 59A 275
s. 61 .... 50, 268
s. 62 .... 50, 268
s. 62(3) 268, 271
s. 62(4) 268
s. 63 .... 50, 268
s. 65(1) 268
s. 67(1) 268
Part V 155
s. 68(1) 268
s. 94(1) 267, 297
s. 95 333
sched. 2 para 8 287
sched. 9 305
sched. 9 part I 333, 334
1969
Children and Young Persons Act 1969 163,
                                                    165
1973
Local Government (Scotland) Act 1973 .. 56, 190
   s. 161 56
1974
Rehabilitation of Offenders Act 1974 .... 67, 68

1975
Children Act 1975 .... 51–53, 363, 372, 374–377,
377, 383
   s. 1 374
   s. 3 375
   s. 4(2) 375
   ss. 10 and 11 376
   s. 12(2)(f) and (5) 376
   s. 14 375
   s. 27 376
   s. 28 375
   s. 32 376
   s. 47 52
   s. 53 376
   s. 66 52
   s. 72 275
   s. 74 53
   s. 75 53
   s. 79 .... 52, 223
   s. 80 52
   s. 82 52
   s. 83 287
   s. 83(a) 51
   s. 83(d) 286
   sched. 3 para 54(a) 151
   sched. 3 para 54(c) 153
   sched. 4 376
Criminal Procedure (Scotland) Act 1975 133,
171, 287
   sched. 1 .... 100, 153
1976
Adoption Act 1976 377
Sexual Offences (Scotland) Act 1976 88–91
   s. 2A 90
   s. 2B 90
   s. 2C 90
   s. 3 88
   s. 4 .... 88, 90
   s. 5 .... 87, 88
   s. 7 88
1977
Criminal Justice Act 1977 165
1978
Adoption (Scotland) Act 1978 ...... 367, 370, 376,
377–379, 381
   s. 3 378
   s. 6 .... 376, 378
   s. 6A 378–379
   s. 12 379
   s. 12(8) 356
   s. 14(1B) 379
   s. 15 379
   s. 18 383
   s. 24(3) 379
   s. 41(1) 368
   s. 45(5) 379
National Health Service (Scotland) Act 1978
   s. 13 73
1980
Criminal Justice (Scotland) Act 1980

   s. 80 89
   s. 80(7)(d) 89
Education (Scotland) Act 1980
   s. 48A 112–113, 113
1982
Civic Government (Scotland) Act 1982
   s. 52 .... 89, 94
   s. 52A 89
Criminal Justice Act 1982
   s. 25 276
1983
Health and Social Services and Social Security
   Adjudications Act 1983
   s. 7(2) 48
   s. 8 276
   s. 8(1) 156
   s. 8(2) 157
   s. 8(4) 277
   sched. 2 para 5(a) 52, 223
   sched. 2 para 6 334
Solvent Abuse (Scotland) Act 1983
   s. 1 156
1984
Foster Children (Scotland) Act 1984 ... 114, 195
Law Reform (Husband and Wife) (Scotland)
   Act 1984, s. 3(1) 352
1985
Child Abduction and Custody Act 1985 38
1986
Education (No. 2) Act 1986
   s. 48 112–113
Incest and Related Offences (Scotland) Act
   1986 90
   s. 1 90
   sched. 1(5) 368
Legal Aid (Scotland) Act 1986 59
1987
Registered Establishment (Scotland) Act 1987
   s. 3 268
1988
Civil Evidence (Scotland) Act 1988 171
1989
Children Act 1989 .... 165, 169, 377–378
   s. 53 297
   sched. 2 part II para 19 333
   sched. 10 para 33 378
   sched. 10(11) para 33 379
1990
Human Fertilisation and Embryology Act
   1990 385–386
1991
Criminal Justice Act 1991 165
1994
Criminal Justice and Public Order Act
   1994 165
   s. 145(2) 89
Local Government etc. (Scotland) Act 1994 ... 56
   s. 45 56
   Part III 56
   sched. 14 56

1995

Children (Scotland) Act 1995 ...... 24, 36, 53–63,
    64, 74, 79, 80, 82, 100, 156, 174, 222,
    267, 272, 274, 281, 287, 376
  Part I 61, 206
  s. 5(1) 322
  s. 11 231
  s. 11(3) 381
  s. 11(7) 378
  Part II 64, 148, 194
  s. 16 378
  s. 16(1) 58, 148, 159
  s. 16(2) 57
  s. 16(3) 173
  s. 16(5) 159, 160
  s. 17(1) and (2) 59
  s. 17(1)(a) 58
  s. 17(1)(c) 59–60
  s. 17(4) 57
  s. 17(6) 59
  s. 19 60
  s. 19(1) and (3) 60
  s. 21 .... 60, 73
  s. 22 .... 60, 231
  s. 25 60
  s. 26A 309
  s. 29 308
  s. 30 308
  s. 45(1)(a) 58, 62
  s. 51(5)(c)(iii) 149
  s. 52(2)(a) 151
  s. 52(2)(b) and (c) 152
  s. 52(2)(d) 100, 107, 153
  s. 52(2)(e) and (f) 153
  s. 52(2)(g) and (h) 154
  s. 52(2)(i) 155
  s. 52(2)(j) 157
  s. 52(2)(k) 156
  s. 52(2)(l) 157
  s. 52(2)(m) 157–158
  s. 55 61
  s. 57 .... 60, 290
  s. 57(1) 290
  s. 57(2), (4) 291
  s. 58 60
  s. 59 60
  s. 60 60
  s. 60(6)(e) 294
  s. 61(1)–(3) 292
  s. 61(4) 292
  s. 61(5), (6), (7) 293
  s. 61(8) 294
  s. 65(4), (7) 148
  s. 66 294
  s. 66(5), (8) 295
  s. 67 295
  s. 69 295
  s. 69(7) 294
  s. 70 194
  s. 70(10) 277

s. 71 51
s. 71(1) 194
ss. 76–80 61
s. 86 .... 61, 383–384
s. 87 61
s. 88 61
s. 89 61
s. 93 275
s. 93(1) 297
s. 93(2)(b) 63
Part III 378–379
s. 94 378
s. 95 .... 376, 378
s. 96 378
s. 97 379
sched. 2 para 16 379
sched. 2 para 22 379
sched. 2 para 25 376
sched. 5 .... 335, 376
Criminal Law (Consolidation) (Scotland) Act
  1995 92
  Part I 89
  ss. 1–7 91
  s. 2 93
  s. 3 92
Criminal Procedure (Consequential Provisions)
  (Scotland) Act 1995
  sched. 5 para 1 287
Criminal Procedure (Scotland) Act 1995 133,
  171
  sched. 1 .... 100, 153

1997

Police Act 1997 67

1998

Crime and Disorder Act 1998 .... 65, 165
Data Protection Act 1998 76
Human Rights Act 1998 .... 38, 64, 77, 78–79,
  80, 81
  s. 6(1), (3) 78
Scotland Act 1998 .... 64, 79
  s. 29(2)(d) 79
  sched. 5 para 7(1), (2) 79

2000

Sexual Offences (Amendment) Act 2000 . 91–92
  s. 1(3) 89
  s. 3 .... 91, 92
  s. 3(2) 92
  s. 3(5) 91
  s. 4 92
Standards in Scotland's Schools etc. Act 2000
  s. 16 113

2001

Regulation of Care (Scotland) Act
  2001 .... 69–70, 227, 268
  s. 1 69
  s. 2 .... 70, 279
  s. 10 70
  s. 12 70
  s. 18 70
  s. 25 70

s. 25(2), (3), (5), (13) 70
s. 26 70
s. 27 70
s. 74 298
sched. 1 69

2003

Commissioner for Children and Young People
    (Scotland) Act 2003
    s. 4 74
    s. 16 74
Criminal Justice (Scotland) Act 2003
    s. 51 .... 100, 106, 107–108
    s. 51(1), (3) 107
    s. 51(5) 100
    s. 51(5)(b) 107
Mental Health (Care and Treatment)
    (Scotland) Act 2003 267
Protection of Children (Scotland) Act 2003 .. 67,
                                                                    275

2004

Antisocial Behaviour etc. (Scotland) Act 2004
    64–66
    s. 4(4) 159
    s. 12(3) 157
    s. 13(1) 65
    s. 135 65
Children Act 2004 165
Civil Partnership Act 2004 .... 63, 92

2005

Protection of Children and Prevention of
    Sexual Offences (Scotland) Act
    2005 93–94
    s. 1 93
    s. 2 93
    s. 9 94
    s. 11 94
    s. 16 94

2006

Family Law (Scotland) Act 2006 63–64
    s. 21 63

2007

Adoption and Children (Scotland) Act 2007.. 64,
                                                            379–381, 385
    s. 1 380
    s. 4 380
    s. 9 380
    s. 12 380
    s. 14(3) 380
    s. 14(4)(d) 380
    s. 14(6) and (7) 378–379
    s. 29 381
    s. 29(1)(b) 379
    s. 30(1)(d) and (7) 379
    s. 31(3)(d) 381
    s. 32(2) 356
    s. 71 .... 376, 381
    Part 2 384
    s. 80 205
    s. 81 384
    s. 82 384

s. 83 .... 384, 385
s. 84(5)(c) 385
s. 97 281
s. 107 381
sched. 3 61
Protection of Vulnerable Groups (Scotland) Act
    2007 .... 67, 275
    sched. 2 67

2008

Human Fertilisation and Embryology Act
    2008 .... 64, 385–386

2009

Sexual Offences (Scotland) Act 2009 92–93,
                                                                    152
    s. 23 89
    s. 24 89
    s. 33 89
    s. 34 89
    s. 42 92
    s. 43 93
    s. 43(6) 93
    s. 45 93
    s. 52(a)(iii) 86

2010

Public Services Reform (Scotland) Act
    2010 .... 70–71, 227
    s. 44 70
    s. 47 71
    s. 47(1)(f) 279
    s. 53 71
    s. 59 71
    s. 60 71
    s. 62 71
    s. 63 71
    s. 64 71
    sched. 12 71
    sched. 12 para 6 279

2011

Children's Hearings (Scotland) Act 2011 66,
                        71–72, 80, 148, 152, 154, 158,
                                    159, 174, 291–292, 294
    ss. 1–13 72
    s. 25 .... 148, 159
    s. 26 160
    s. 28 173
    ss. 35–36 61
    ss. 37–54 60
    s. 38 291
    s. 39 291
    s. 54(a) 294
    s. 55 294
    s. 56 294
    s. 67 158
    s. 67(2)(a) 152
    s. 67(2)(b) 100, 107, 153
    s. 67(2)(c) 152, 153
    s. 67(2)(d) 153
    s. 67(2)(e) 154, 158
    s. 67(2)(f), (g) 152, 158
    s. 67(2)(h) and (i) 157

s. 67(2)(j)..155
s. 67(2)(k) and (l).....................................157
s. 67(2)(m)......................................156, 158
s. 67(2)(n)..151
s. 67(2)(o)..154
s. 67(2)(p) and (q)..................................158
s. 67(3)...153
s. 78(1)(a)..58
ss. 79–81..72
s. 81...279
s. 83...194
s. 83(2)(d)...66
s. 83(6)...277
s. 86...72, 281
s. 86(1)(a)..296
s. 86(3)...295
s. 90(1)...148
s. 91(3)(a)..295
s. 92(2)...295
s. 93...148
s. 93(5)...295
s. 94...148
s. 96(4)...296
s. 109(3) and (5)......................................296
s. 119(3)(a)..295
s. 120(3)..295
s. 120(5)..296
s. 122...58
s. 123...295
s. 126...72
s. 144(1)...51, 194
s. 156(3)(b)..149
s. 162...72
Part 19..59, 80
s. 200...279
s. 202...275, 298
Forced Marriage etc. (Protection and
    Jurisdiction) (Scotland) Act 2011..........158
s. 13(3)..158
2013
Crime and Courts Act 2013..........................165
2014
Children and Young People (Scotland) Act
    2014..........72–77, 228, 299, 308, 309–311,
380
Part 1..74
ss. 1–3...82
Part 2..74
Part 3..74
Part 4..74, 76
s. 19(1)...75
s. 19(5)...75
ss. 20–21..75
s. 22(2)...75
s. 23...76
s. 26...75, 76
Part 5..74
Part 9...309, 310

s. 58(1)..310
s. 59...310
s. 60..310–311
s. 60(2)..311
ss. 61 and 62..311
ss. 63 and 64..311
s. 65...311
s. 66...308
s. 66(2)(a)(i)...308
s. 67...309
s. 68...73
s. 71...231
s. 95...74
s. 96...74
s. 97(1)...74
sched. 4...310
Marriage and Civil Partnership (Scotland) Act
    2014..64
2018
Data Protection Act 2018.............................76
2019
Age of Criminal Responsibility (Scotland) Act
    2019..69
ss. 4–27..69
s. 78...133
Children (Equal Protection from Assault)
    (Scotland) Act 2019.............................114
2020
Disclosure (Scotland) Act 2020......................69

AUSTRALIA

New South Wales – Neglected Children and
    Juvenile Offenders Act 1905........120–121
Queensland – Children's Court Act 1907.....121
South Australia – Children's Protection and
    Young Offenders Act 1979...................169
South Australia – State Children Act
    1895..120–121
Tasmania – Children's Charter 1918...........121
Victoria – Children's Court Act 1906....120–121
Western Australia – State Children Act
    1907..121

CANADA

Young Offenders Act 1984...........................169

NEW ZEALAND

Children, Young Persons and Their Families
    Act 1989, Parts II and IV.....................169
Neglected and Criminal Children Act 1867 (31
    Vict. 1867 No. 14)................................236

UNITED STATES

Illinois Juvenile Court Act, April 21, 1899 (Ill.
 Laws 131)... 117

INTERNATIONAL CONVENTIONS

Convention on the Elimination of
 Discrimination Against Women
 (1981).. 84
 Art. 16 84
Convention on the Protection of Children
 Against Sexual Exploitation and Sexual
 Abuse (2010).. 83
Convention on the Rights of Persons with
 Disabilities (2008) 84
 Art. 7 84
Convention on Transnational Organised Crime
 (2003).. 84
Declaration of the Rights of the Child
 (1924).. 39
European Convention on Human Rights
 (ECHR) (1953)... 38, 41, 54, 64, 71, 77–80,
 81, 83, 108, 174, 381
 Art. 3 .... 78, 255
 Art. 5 .... 276, 277
 Art. 5(1)(d).. 41
 Art. 5(4)... 276
 Art. 6 .... 58, 79
 Art. 6(1)... 41
 Art. 8 .... 29, 68, 75–76, 78, 79, 289
 Protocol 1, Art. 2 112

Protocol 7, Art. 5 41
Hague Child Abduction Convention
 (1980).. 38
International Convention on Civil and Political
 Rights (1976) 84
 Art. 24 84
International Covenant on Economic, Social
 and Cultural Rights (1976)...................... 83
 Art. 10(3).. 83
 Art. 12(2).. 83
 Art. 13(2a).. 83
Minimum Age (Industry) Convention
 (1919)... 39
Night Work of Young Persons (Industry)
 Convention (1919)................................... 39
Rules for the Protection of Juveniles Deprived
 of their Liberty (1990)............................. 83
United Nations Convention on the Rights of
 the Child (UNCRC) (1991) 54, 57, 62,
 71–72, 74, 80–83
 Art. 3(2)... 82
 Art. 8 382
 Art. 12 57
 Art. 16 289
 Art. 18 81
 Art. 19 108
 Art. 19(1).. 82
 Art. 21 378
 Art. 33 157
United Nations Declaration of the Rights of
 the Child (1959) 40–41
Universal Declaration of Human Rights
 (1948)... 39–40
 Art. 25 40

Table of Statutory Instruments

SCOTLAND/ENGLAND AND WALES/UNITED KINGDOM

1890
General Rules for the Management and
  Discipline of Certified Reformatory
  Schools, 1890 239
1891
General Rules for the Management and
  Discipline of Certified Industrial Schools,
  1891 239
1920
Reformatory and Industrial Schools (Scotland)
  (Transfer of Powers) Order, 1920 (SR&O
  1920 No. 429 (S. 40)) 242
1921
Reformatory and Industrial Schools
  Regulations, 1921 242
  regs 1, 2, 3 242
  reg. 4 242–243
1931
Probation (Scotland) Rules, 1931 (SR&O 1931
  No. 1023 (S.53)) 183
1933
Children and Young Persons (Scotland) Care
  and Training Regulations, 1933 (SR&O
  1933 No. 1006 (S. 55)) 2–3, 222, 253
  reg. 2 249
  reg. 3 250
  reg. 4 250
  reg. 5 250
  reg. 7 251
  reg. 9 252
  reg. 10 252
  reg. 11 253
  reg. 12(4) 253
  reg. 13 .... 253, 254
  reg. 14 .... 112, 254
  reg. 15 .... 112, 254
  reg. 16 .... 112, 255
  reg. 17 .... 112, 255
  reg. 18 .... 112, 255
  reg. 19 .... 256, 328
  reg. 20 257
  reg. 21 257
  reg. 22 .... 248, 303
  reg. 24 258
  Part C 33, 213
  reg. 37 213
  reg. 40 .... 217, 303
  reg. 41 214

reg. 42 213
reg. 43 214
reg. 44 214
reg. 45 213
reg. 46 214
reg. 48 214
reg. 49 216
reg. 50 216
reg. 51 216
reg. 53 218
Children and Young Persons, Scotland
  (Transfer of Power) Order, 1933 (SR&O
  1933 No. 821 (S.44)) 327
Children and Young Persons (Voluntary
  Homes) Regulations, 1933 (SR&O 1933
  No 923 (S. 50)) 259
Juvenile Courts (Constitution) (Scotland)
  Rules, 1933 (SR&O, 1933 No. 984
  (S. 54))
  rule 4 140
  rule 13 .... 128, 140
  rule 15(1) 140
1934
Juvenile Courts (Procedure) (Scotland)
  Rules, 1934 (SR&O 1934 No. 641
  (S. 36)) 140
  rule 3 140
  rule 4(a) 170
  rule 8(1) 140–141
  rule 8(2) 141
  rule 9 141–143
  rule 9(1), (3), (5) 141
  rule 9(6) 141–142, 149
  rule 9(6)(b) 26, 138
  rule 9(7) 142
  rule 10 .... 143–144, 171
  rule 10(7) 149
  rule 10(7)(a) 26, 138
  rule 18 130
Poor Relief Regulations (Scotland), 1934
  (SR&O 1934, No. 1296 (S. 69)) 201
1947
Children (Boarding-out etc.) (Scotland) Rules
  and Regulations, 1947 (SI 1947/2146 (S.
  76)) 33, 201, 213
  Art. 2 214
  Art. 4 210
  Art. 7 214

Art. 8 214
Art. 9 214
Art. 10(1), (2), (3), (4) 214
Art. 11 214
Art. 14 216
Art. 15 216
Art. 16 216
Art. 17 216
Art. 18 216
Arts. 23–28 260
Art. 33 218
sched. 217
sched. para 5(f) 111
sched. para 10 218
1948
Voluntary Homes Registration (Scotland)
    Regulations, 1948 (SI 1948/2595) 260
1951
Juvenile Courts (Constitution) (Scotland)
    (Amendment) Rules, 1951 140
Juvenile Courts (Procedure) (Scotland) Rules,
    1951 (SI 1951/2228) 140, 141, 142
    rule 9 171
    rule 10 171
    rule 11(2) 141
1952
Voluntary Homes (Return of Particulars)
    (Scotland) Regulations, 1952 (SI
    1952/1836) 260
1959
Administration of Children's Homes (Scotland)
    Regulations, 1959 (SI 1959/834) 261,
                                            262–264, 269
    reg. 1 262
    reg. 2 262
    reg. 4 262
    reg. 6 263
    reg. 7 263
    reg. 10 263
    reg. 11 263
    reg. 13 262
    reg. 14 262
    reg. 17 264
    reg. 21 262
    reg. 21(1) 263
Boarding-out of Children (Scotland)
    Regulations, 1959 (SI 1959/835
    (S. 55)) 111, 114, 213, 218, 219
    reg. 1(1)(b) 213
    reg. 2 214
    reg. 5 214
    reg. 7 214
    reg. 11 111
    reg. 11(1) 219
    reg. 13 216
    reg. 15 219
    reg. 16 216
1961
Approved Schools (Scotland) Rules, 1961 (SI
    1961/2243 (S. 124)) 249, 252, 253, 269

rule 1 249
rule 2(1), (2)–4) 250
rules 6 and 7 250
rule 8 250
rule 10(1), (4) 251
rule 11(1) 269
rule 18 250
rule 19 251
rule 19(1) 251
rule 21 252
rule 22 252
rule 23 253
rule 24 252
rule 25 253
rule 28 255
rule 29 .... 112, 255
rule 30 .... 112, 256
rule 31 .... 112, 256
rule 31(c) and (d) 256
rule 31(e), (f) and (g) 256
rule 32 .... 112, 256
rule 34(1), (2) 275
rule 35 257
rule 36 256
rule 39 .... 256, 328
rule 40 257
rule 41 257
rule 42 257
rule 43 249
rule 44 303–304
rule 46 304
rule 47 304
rule 48 258
1971
Act of Sederunt (Social Work) (Sheriff
    Court Procedure Rules) 1971 (SI
    1971/92) 171
Children's Hearings (Scotland) Rules 1971
    (SI 1971/492) 172
1972
Raising of the School Leaving Age (Scotland)
    Regulations 1972 (SI 1972/59 (S. 6)) ... 133,
                                                        306
1975
Reporters (Conduct of Proceedings before the
    Sheriff) (Scotland) Regulations 1975 (SI
    1975/2251) 52
1982
Emigration of Children (Arrangements by
    Voluntary Organisations) Regulations 1982
    (SI 1982/13) 333
1983
Secure Accommodation (Scotland)
    Regulations 1983 (SI 1983/
    1912) 277–278
    reg. 2 278
    reg. 2(1) 277
    reg. 3 277
    reg. 4 278
    reg. 19 276

1985

Boarding Out and Fostering of Children
(Scotland) Regulations, 1985 (SI
1985/1799) 113–114, 222, 222–223,
224–225
reg. 4 223
reg. 6(1) 223
reg. 6(2) 224
reg. 7 224
reg. 8 .... 113, 224
reg. 14 224
reg. 18 225
reg. 19 225
reg. 21(3) 226
reg. 23 223
Foster Children (Private Fostering) (Scotland)
Regulations 1985 (SI 1985/1798) 114

1986

Children's Hearings (Scotland) Rules 1986 (SI
1986/2291) 172

1987

Social Work (Residential Establishments –
Child Care) (Scotland) Regulations 1987
(SI 1987/2233 (S. 150) 269–272,
274–275
reg. 2 .... 269, 271
reg. 4 269
reg. 5(1) 270
reg. 10 270
reg. 10(1), (2) 113
reg. 16 .... 271, 279
reg. 18 271
reg. 21 271
reg. 23 271
reg. 24 272
reg. 26 271
reg. 27(3) 271
sched. 1 270

1988

Secure Accommodation (Scotland)
Amendment Regulations 1988 (SI
1988/841)
reg. 3 278
reg. 4 278

1996

Adoption Allowances (Scotland) Regulations
1996 (SI 1996/3257) 381
Arrangements to Look After Children
(Scotland) Regulations 1996 (SI
1996/3262) 226, 227
reg. 3 226
reg. 4 226
reg. 5 226
reg. 6 226
regs 8 and 9 .... 226, 278
reg. 18 226
reg. 19 226
sched. 1 226
Children's Hearings (Scotland) Rules 1996 (SI
1996/3261 (S. 251)) 172

rule 5 79
rule 15(4) 58
Emergency Child Protection Measures
(Scotland) Regulations 1996 (SI 1996/3258
(S. 248)) 294
regs 3 and 4 293
regs 8 and 9 293
reg. 15 293
Fostering of Children (Scotland) Regulations
1996 (SI 1996/3263) 113–114, 222, 223,
224, 227
reg. 12(4) 224
sched. 1 224
sched. 2 paras 1 and 3 225
sched. 2 para 6 .... 114, 225
sched. 2 para 8 225
sched. 3 para 6 223
Residential Establishments – Child Care
(Scotland) Regulations 1996 (SI 1996/3256
(S. 246)) 275
reg. 8 275
reg. 10 113
reg. 16 279
Secure Accommodation (Scotland) Regulations
1996 (SI 1996/3255 (S. 245)) 278
reg. 4 278
reg. 15 278

1997

Act of Sederunt (Child Care and Maintenance
Rules) 1997 (SI 1997/291) 171, 172

2002

Children's Hearings (Legal Representation)
(Scotland) Rules 2002 (SSI 2002/63) 59
Regulation of Care (Requirements as to Care
Services) (Scotland) Regulations 2002 (SSI
2002/114)
reg. 2 70
regs 6, 7 and 9 70
reg. 10 70
reg. 12 70

2009

Adoption Support Services and Allowances
(Scotland) Regulations 2009 (SSI
2009/152) 381
Children's Hearings (Legal Representation)
(Scotland) Amendment Rules 2009 (SSI
2009/211) 59
Looked After Children (Scotland) Regulations
2009 (SSI 2009/210) 64, 227, 230–231
reg. 4(1)(h) 309
reg. 10 230
reg. 10(3) 230
reg. 11 231
reg. 27(2) 227
reg. 46 231
reg. 49 227
reg. 52 227
sched. 3 230
sched. 4 230–231
sched. 5 230–231

sched. 5 para 5 114
sched. 5 para 5(a) 231
sched. 6 para 6 114

2011

Children's Hearings (Scotland) Act
   2011 (Emergency Child Protection
   Measures) Regulations, 2012 (SSI
   2012/334) 280
Public Services Reform (Social Services
   Inspection) (Scotland) Regulations 2011
   (SSI 2011/185) 71
Social Care and Social Work Improvement
   Scotland (Registration) Regulations 2011
   (SSI 2011/28)
   reg. 3 71
Social Care and Social Work Improvement
   Scotland (Requirements for Care Services)
   Regulations 2011 (SSI 2011/2010)
   regs 6, 7 and 9 71
   reg. 13(1) 71

2012

Children's Hearings (Scotland) Act 2011
   (Child Protection Emergency Measures)
   Regulations 2012 (SSI 2012/334) 283,
   294

2013

Children's Hearings (Scotland) Act
   2011 (Implementation of Secure
   Accommodation Authorisation) (Scotland)
   Regulations 2013 (SSI 2013/212) 279
Children's Hearings (Scotland) Act 2011
   (Movement Restriction Conditions)
   Regulations 2013 (SSI 2013/210) 66
Children's Hearings (Scotland) Act 2011 (Rules
   of Procedure in Children's Hearings)
   Rules 2013 (SSI 2013/194) 172
   Part 6 79

Children's Legal Assistance (Scotland)
   Regulations 2013 (SSI 2013/200) 59
Secure Accommodation (Scotland) Regulations
   1996 (SSI 2013/205)
   reg. 4 279
   reg. 16 278

2015

Continuing Care (Scotland) Order 2015, SSI
   2015/158 309
Police Act 1997 and the Protection of
   Vulnerable Groups (Scotland) Act 2007
   Remedial (No. 2) Order 2015 (SSI
   2015/423) 68

2016

Children and Young People (Scotland) Act
   2014 (Relevant Services in Relation to
   Children at Risk of Becoming Looked
   After etc.) (Scotland) Order 2016 (SSI
   2016/44)
   Art. 2 73
Continuing Care (Scotland) Amendment Order
   2016 (SSI 2016/92) 309
Kinship Care Assistance (Scotland) Order 2016
   (SSI 2016/153) 231
   Arts. 3, 4, 9 231

2017

Continuing Care (Scotland) Amendment Order
   2017 (SSI 2017/622) 309

2018

Continuing Care (Scotland) Amendment Order
   2018 (SSI 2018/96) 309
Police Act 1997 and Protection of Vulnerable
   Groups (Scotland) Act 2007 Remedial
   Order 2018 (SSI 2018/52) 69

2019

Continuing Care (Scotland) Amendment Order
   2019 (SSI 2019/91) 309

Foreword

by The Hon. Lady Wise

We have embarked in recent years upon the most anxious and detailed scrutiny of the way in which our jurisdiction, in common with many others, failed to protect some of its most vulnerable children. The Scottish Child Abuse Inquiry has provided and continues to provide an essential forum for the examination of the past treatment of children in the care of all forms of residential establishments. Professor Norrie's involvement in reporting to that Inquiry on the evolution of the statutory basis for state intervention in the lives of Scottish children marked the inception of this remarkable and most erudite account of the history of child protection law.

The text as a whole takes the reader from the early reluctance by the courts to interfere with the *patria potestas* through to some initial protection by piecemeal legislation and then to the modern Children's Hearing system and beyond. Professor Norrie's extensive knowledge of the area is most in evidence when he explores the implementation of Kilbrandon's recommendations in 1968, the reforms introduced by the 1995 Act and the ongoing reminder of the need for a proportionate response in every individual case. He offers a thorough understanding of how Scots Law measures on child protection evolved to their current state both in terms of policy and its substantive implementation. This hugely informative study of the historical development of such measures also bestows a detailed comprehension of the various rationales given for state interference in the lives of young people, with appropriate critical analysis of each. All those with an interest in child care matters, whether practitioners, policy makers, front line workers, academics or decision makers, will benefit from reading this important book. We ignore history at our peril, but the pace of change sometimes allows us little time to reflect on the prevailing attitudes and concerns of previous generations. Such views provide an essential backdrop to any contemporary understanding of the place of the child in society. Professor Norrie's treatment of this complex topic is typically scholarly yet eminently readable and includes a wealth of fascinating little known debate and commentary.

This is a rich account of a subject that affects us all and while billed as a historical legal text will have a far broader reach. The author is to be congratulated on his evocation of many lesser known policies, provisions and influences behind the myriad of relevant legislative provisions.

I welcome and commend this authoritative book as an invaluable addition to our understanding of the history and context of modern child protection measures.

Morag Wise
September 2019

Introduction

In the summer of 2016, the Scottish Child Abuse Inquiry (SCAI) commissioned me to draw up a report on the legislative provisions regulating the various environments in which children were accommodated when they were, for whatever reason, not living with their own families. The overarching aim of that Inquiry was, through an examination of the experiences of children who had suffered while in the care of persons or bodies other than their parents, to seek to learn lessons from the past in order to make children safer for the future. It also sought to provide acknowledgement of the suffering of victims and to allow them "closure". Given the ages of the oldest of the presently surviving victims of child abuse, it was assumed that my Report would start with the Children and Young Persons (Scotland) Act, 1932. However, I soon realised that the 1932 Act, primarily an amending statute, could not be properly understood without exploring the earlier legislation which it amended. So that took me to the Children Act, 1908, which had substantially expanded the role of the state in the care of children. Yet like the 1932 Act, the 1908 Act did not start with a clean slate. It too built upon earlier foundations and to gain a full understanding of the 1908 Act I found it necessary to examine yet earlier legislation. And so the process, as is the nature of historical study, went on.

My Report to the SCAI was published on their website in November 2017, and it records the details of the various regulatory regimes applying over the past 150 years or so to various institutions, including industrial schools (later known as approved schools) and children's homes, Borstal institutions and foster care. The present book seeks to build upon that Report through an exploration of the political choices that were made at various points in the development of child protection law in Scotland, and a contextualisation of these choices within world-wide trends. It is no part of my task here to replicate the work of the SCAI by documenting the utterly heart-breaking extent to which individual children suffered because the rules and regulations being examined were subverted, ignored and breached with impunity. I seek only to set out what these rules and regulations were and to trace, in a way that has never been done before, how they developed over the course of time and why they did so in a particular way. Now, this risks presenting an unduly positive picture of our child protection laws and policies, for the developments I will describe are, for the most part, sensible and were motivated by sound political assessments. But the study of law is not a complete study of how society in fact operates. This is a book on the law, though I hope that by setting out the legal position and the policy choices underpinning that position at various points in time it will be easier to see the disconnection between the benign aims of the law and the actual experiences of all too many children and young people in care – and to see, indeed, the sheer illegality of many of the practices uncovered by the Scottish Child Abuse Inquiry.

There are, of course, more general reasons to study the history of any institution, process or phenomenon, in particular, that a full understanding of where we are now can be reached only with knowledge of how we got to the present situation. The original contribution that I hope to make with this book is to trace the development of child protection law in Scotland from its earliest manifestations to the present day, with the aim of enhancing not so much our understanding of how our contemporary processes operate, but why they do so in the way that they do. This has never been done before. Another purpose to be achieved through the exploration of historical development is that it gives us lessons that can be learnt for the future. We can discover which past initiatives were successful and which proved to be little more than blindalleys. Analysing long-term trends from the past puts us in a better position to assess whether it is now necessary to strike out in wholly new directions, or to recalibrate or build upon existing practices. It allows us to understand the pressures that led to change and to judge the long-term significance of contemporary concerns. The study of history is not only about understanding the past but also about making appropriate choices for the future.

Another motivation for writing this book has been to restore to memory many laws and practices that have simply vanished from our collective consciousness. Few people today are even aware of the existence of the Children and Young Persons (Scotland) Act, 1932 – far less the profound changes it effected – probably because it was quickly overshadowed by the much longer-lasting Children and Young Persons (Scotland) Act, 1937. The 1932 Act, in both its Scottish and English manifestations, is absent from the UK Government legislation website legislation.gov.uk (delivered by the National Archives), and only the English version may be found on Westlaw. It merits not a single mention in the leading contemporary exposition of child law *The Law Relating to Parent and Child in Scotland* (A.B. Wilkinson and K.M. Norrie, first edition 1993; third edition 2013). The 1933 Care and

Training Regulations deserve to be remembered if for no other reason than that they were the model for replacements that regulated both foster care and residential schools until the mid-1980s. Their influence on the current regulations ought not to be ignored.

A final reason for historical study is, quite simply, that it is fascinating to learn about our relatively recent past. I hope that readers of this book find enough to interest them even when they have no role in future policy-making.

One of the remarkable features that will be seen throughout this book is the long continuity in Scotland's response to children in trouble. At one level this is not surprising because the problems facing children who have been neglected or abused, or who have got into trouble with the police, have not fundamentally altered in the century or more that is our primary focus of attention here. While society around them has changed, the basic needs of children have not. Political structures and priorities change with the temper of the times, but the need of any child for a safe and secure childhood as a prerequisite for a contented and fulfilled adulthood remains a constant. The aim of any child protection measure has long been to provide that safety and security. More surprising, perhaps, is the longevity of the philosophy upon which the Scottish approach to child protection is based. The clear focus on the welfare of the child has been central for far longer than we tend to remember today, as indeed has been the belief that child-offending should be conceptualised as a failure in appropriate parenting rather than as a sign of punishment-deserving wickedness. Though it is often thought that this approach developed in the 1960s, in fact it has been followed in Scotland for almost ninety years, and even when it was formally adopted in the very different world of the inter-war years, it was designed as a development of rather than a radical departure from what had gone before. And it is not only the underlying approach that shows remarkable continuity. The creation of a wholly new tribunal in 1968, the children's hearing, has served to hide the continuities in the legal processes activated by child neglect and abuse: personnel and structures may on the surface be different but the processes that children's hearings follow were established long before the hearing system itself, as were the grounds for its jurisdiction. As well, the outcomes of these processes have barely changed for a century. What has changed, but only very recently, is how the placements in which child protection is provided are regulated, as we as a society have become much more conscious of – or, perhaps, less willing to ignore – the dangers that children face when placed outwith their family environment.

Some social attitudes have, of course, changed radically, and with them the legal rules that they reflect. Our willingness to accept corporal punishment of children has all but evaporated. And we are in today's post-Imperial world horrified at our earlier practice of forced emigration to the colonies as a "solution" to the problem of children in need. Perhaps most noticeably, attitudes towards the role of parents once children have been removed from their care has transformed. Until the 1960s the prevailing approach was to see the child protection process as a means of insulating children from bad parental influences, and there was very little provision made for children to keep contact with their parents and no provision at all for working with the parents to ease the child's eventual return to their care. That approach changed in the latter part of the twentieth century until, today, parental contact is protected in its own right and is indeed perceived (surely rightly) in all but the most egregious cases of bad parenting as a means of enhancing the child's welfare.

And some things come and go in cycles. The best example, as we will see, is the concept known today as kinship care. The late Victorian legislation that first allowed children to be removed from their parents sought to have these children placed with other family members, but in the early twentieth century that changed to reflect the increasingly held belief, mentioned in the previous paragraph, that damaged children should be insulated from their whole family backgrounds. However, early twenty-first-century legislation once again embraced the notion that there is an advantage in including the child's wider family in his or her care while being looked after away from home.

It is these ebbs and flows, these eddies and currents of thinking, that this book aims to tease out through a close examination of the governing legislation. It seeks to build upon the Report that I produced for the SCAI, by moving beyond the detail and to concentrate more on the policy aims behind the law as it evolved into today's system of child protection – though I still find room for the detail of the legislation, for that is crucial to understanding how effect is given to policy. And I go wider than the Report and examine the development of measures such as compulsory supervision orders, emergency orders and aftercare obligations. A major issue covered in this book but not in the Report is the law of adoption, the practice of which was explicitly excluded from the remit of the SCAI. Though this institution was originally designed to be – and technically remains – a private law action, adoption is today usually the final stage of a child protection process, and the story of how that transformation came about is very much worth recounting.

The sources that I have used include not only the primary legal materials (the primary and secondary legislation, and the case law) and the published studies of historians, but also government and other official reports and – invaluably – the parliamentary debates on the various Acts passed by Westminster, and latterly Holyrood, from the Prevention of Cruelty to, and Protection of, Children Act, 1889 to the Children (Equal Protection from Assault) (Scotland) Act 2019. Not only do these debates help us to understand the objectives of the legislation, but they illuminate as few other sources can the political and social attitudes of the day. From the fear of leaving children in front of open grates to the provisions allowing boys at residential schools to work in foundries, from the Admiral MP deprecating how few boys from industrial schools are sent to sea to the first SNP MP worrying that the new children's panels would be composed of amateur "do-gooders", these debates provide revealing snapshots of the attitudes, and experiences, of our law-makers in a by-gone age. These debates also illuminate how much the world changed in the middle decades of the twentieth century. It is hard to believe that only 42 years separated the contributions to the debates on the Adoption Bill, 1926 of that wounded survivor of Gallipoli, Major Attlee, and the contributions to the debates on the Social Work (Scotland) Bill 1968 of the man who later became Scotland's first post-Devolution First Minister, Donald Dewar. Case law also serves to reveal social circumstances at particular points in time, as well as legal developments, and from the law reports we will read about the flea-ridden Stranraer Reformatory at the turn of the twentieth century, and about the post-war mother seeking to retrieve her child from care by offering to provide him with a house that had an indoor lavatory.

Historical work always throws up facts that have little to do with the subject-matter at hand but which are arresting in their own right. For my understanding of the 1932 legislation, I have relied quite heavily on the eponymous textbook *The Children and Young Persons (Scotland) Act, 1932* by M.G. Cowan, which had sat on my bookshelf for many long years, being afforded little more than the occasional cursory glance. When drawing up my Report to the Scottish Child Abuse Inquiry, I took down the book and read it from cover to cover, only then realising from Lord Sands' preface, when he referred to the author as "Miss Cowan", that she was a woman. I know of no earlier legal textbook written by a woman, certainly not in Scotland. The author was Minna Galbraith Cowan, the daughter and granddaughter of sheriffs (her grandfather becoming the Senator Lord Cowan in 1851), an educationalist well-known in her day as the author of *The*

Education of Women in India (1912). Miss Cowan deserves to be remembered as the pioneer she was.

I hope, therefore, that readers will find the following pages informative legally, politically and socially. The need for legal processes to protect children from harm will, sadly, always be with us and future designs of these processes are more likely to be successful with an understanding of the past. My view of that past is what is offered here.

Kenneth McK. Norrie
Howwood, August 2019

1. The Statutory Framework before 1968

INTRODUCTION

The Court of Session, as the supreme court of equity in Scotland, has always claimed the right, traced through the Scottish Privy Council to the Crown itself, to superintend the upbringing of children within Scotland, though the earliest cases, from the seventeenth century, arose in one very particular context. As expressed by Wilkinson and Norrie[1] (citing Lord Fraser[2]):

> In the seventeenth century, when religious controversy and confidence in the rightness of sectional religious opinions ran high, robust views were sometimes entertained of state powers of interference in the religious upbringing of children. In 1665 the Scottish Privy Council, from which the Court of Session's jurisdiction in custody matters is derived, ordered that the children of Scott of Raeburn and his wife "being infected with the error of Quakerism" to be taken from them and, later in the same year, the young Marquis of Huntley was taken from the custody of his mother and guardians "they being Popishly inclined" and entrusted to the care of the Protestant Archbishop Sharp of St. Andrews under a direction that "no persons Popishly inclined have liberty to serve or attend him". By an Act of 1661[3] "All children under Popish tutors or curators" were taken from their care, and by an Act of 1700[4] not only professed Papists but also those suspected of Popery were declared incapable of the offices of tutory or curatory.

These were not, however, the true origins of Scottish child protection law. The concern underlying these cases and statutes was hardly the welfare of children as we understand that concept today. Saving children from "Popery" was far more to do with maintaining the ascendancy of the protestant religion, especially amongst the land-owning classes, than with saving the souls of the children involved.

Outwith the specialities of state favouritism towards a particular religious

---

1 Wilkinson, A. and Norrie, K. *The Law Relating to Parent and Child in Scotland* (W. Green, 1st edn 1993), p. 221.
2 *A Treatise on the Law of Scotland Relative to Parent and Child, Guardian and Ward* (W. Green, 3rd edn, 1906 by J. Clark), pp. 90–91.
3 APS vii 26, c. 37 (12mo. c. 8).
4 The Popery Act 1700, APS x 215, c. 3 (12mo. c. 3).

confession, the common law of Scotland gave strong, but not unlimited, protection to the *patria potestas*, that is to say, the power of the father of a legitimate child (and, to a lesser extent, the mother of an illegitimate child) to control the child's upbringing until puberty. The state, on its own initiative, had no power to interfere in that upbringing simply because the child was being cruelly mistreated. It was, however, accepted in *Baillie v Agnew*[5] in 1775 that, on the petition of the children's maternal grandfather (their mother having died), the Court of Session could order the removal of children from their father's care, he "having contracted unusual habits of drinking, in which he proceeded to high acts of ferocity and maltreatment, and terror to his children, so that, in their grandfather's apprehension, they were in danger of their lives". Fraser, writing over 100 years later, suggested that title to seek such a protective remedy would inhere only in relatives and not in either strangers or the Lord Advocate acting for the Crown as *parens patriae*.[6] If that was so, then the state itself had no power to take any protective action and could act only when someone with title brought the matter to the court's attention – commonly in the context of a custody dispute in which the father's *patria potestas* could be defeated by the court exercising its equitable jurisdiction and giving precedence to considerations of the child's welfare.[7] It is no surprise, therefore, that all the cases before the latter half of the nineteenth century involved children from families wealthy enough to have their disputes played out in court. Children from families of modest means, with neither land nor political influence at stake, were left to be brought up and treated or mistreated by their parents as the latter thought fit, irrespective of the vulnerabilities of the children's own situations and irrespective, after the Roman Catholic Relief Act, 1829, of the religious beliefs to which their parents adhered.

The courts' traditional reluctance to interfere with the *patria potestas* was modified by the Conjugal Rights (Scotland) Amendment Act, 1861 and the Guardianship of Infants Act, 1886, which permitted custody disputes to be resolved by taking into consideration the welfare of the child rather than on the basis of the father's absolute rights over his children. It is unlikely that this went any further than the Scottish courts had already

---

5 *Thomas Baillie of Polkemmet v Sir Stair Agnew* (1775) 5 *Brown's Supplement* 526.

6 Fraser, *A Treatise on the Law of Scotland Relative to Parent and Child and Guardian and Ward*, 93–94.

7 The best known nineteenth century example is *Harvey v Harvey* (1860) 22 D 1198, for a discussion of which see Marshall, K. in J. Grant and E. Sutherland *Pronounced for Doom: Early Scots Law Tales* (Avizandum, 2013), pp. 16–30.

gone in cases like *Baillie v Agnew*. A parent's right to the possession of his or her child remained stronger than that of anyone else, even a charitable body to whose care the child had been voluntarily surrendered. The House of Lords held in *Barnardo v McHugh*[8] that a child accommodated by Dr Thomas Barnardo in his eponymous children's home had to be restored to his mother's care notwithstanding Dr Barnardo's belief that the mother was wholly unsuited to the care of a child.[9] Partly as a result of this decision, Parliament enacted the Custody of Children Act, 1891 which allowed persons bringing up children other than their own to resist claims for their return by their parents: the effect was to place the onus on the parents to prove, "having regard to the welfare of the child", their fitness to resume the custody of their own children.[10]

The 1891 Act proved particularly useful for charitable organisations, which had stepped into the gap created by the state's reluctance to become directly involved in the upbringing of children beyond the confines of the Poor Law. Many such organisations had been established in the nineteenth century with the overt mission to "save" children from both vice and poverty – concepts that were widely assumed to go hand in hand. At its benign best these missions sought to improve the life prospects of vulnerable children by diverting them onto more productive paths than their family circumstances were leading them, by helping them acquire useful skills and offering them good influences; at its worst, they equiperated poverty with criminality and immorality and sought to split up indigent families with little or no regard paid to the emotional needs of the children they were seeking to save.

It was, therefore, the children of the poor who were the main focus of child protection law when statute for the first time gave courts the power to deal with the issue of cruelty to children other than through the criminal law or in the context of custody disputes (in both of which the child was peripheral to the adult issues directly before the court). Indeed, even before the early child cruelty statutes, the need to protect children from the dangers created by the very circumstances in which they lived had been recognised, and processes were in place in Scotland that, today, we would accept as a legitimate manifestation of the state's power and duty to protect its young citizens. The

8 [1891] AC 388.

9 A strong underlying current in this case was the mother's desire that the child be brought up in her own Roman Catholic faith, which was anathema to the good "doctor", an Irish Protestant of pronounced anti-Catholic views.

10 See for example *Campbell v Croall* (1895) 22R 869.

most important of these were the Poor Law, which from the middle ages had imposed obligations on the relevant authorities to provide for orphans and deserted children, and the industrial and reformatory schools legislation of the mid-nineteenth century, which sought to provide not only education but also food and accommodation for both needy children and children who broke the law. Because they influenced the development of child protection law in the narrower sense of state-instigated intervention in family life to protect children from harm, as well as being precursors to the much wider contemporary conception of child protection law, it is necessary to give brief consideration to both these processes.

THE POOR LAW

The earliest legal mechanism in Scotland by which the state took responsibility for providing accommodation to children whose home circumstances were unsuitable was the Poor Law, which offered some limited support to individuals who were unable to earn a living, and to their dependants. Relief under Scotland's Poor Law was traditionally restricted to those unable to work, rather than those for whom no work was available. From the fifteenth century, anyone other than the disabled were prohibited from begging for alms. In 1579, during the minority rule of King James VI, the Parliament of Scotland enacted legislation[11] that became the foundation of the old Scottish Poor Law,[12] and this applied until the radical changes brought about by the British Parliament in the Poor Law Amendment (Scotland) Act, 1845. The 1845 Act, drafted and carried through Parliament by Lord Colonsay, the then Lord Advocate,[13] swept away the older law and redesigned the provision of poor relief. Its substantive effect was to shift that provision, as had happened some years earlier in England, from one primarily based on "outdoor relief" (alms) to one predominantly based on "indoor relief",

---

11 "For Punishment of the Strong and Idle Beggars and Relief of the Poor and Impotent" APS iii, 139, c. 12 (12mo. c. 74).

12 For a detailed history of the "Old Poor Law", see Sir George Nicholls, *A History of the Scotch Poor Law* (John Murray, 1856) and Mitchison, R. *The Old Poor Law in Scotland: The Experience of Poverty 1574 – 1845* (EUP, 2000). The history of the Poor Law from biblical times is the subject of a long (anonymous) "Essay On the Poor law of Scotland" published in 1871 *Poor Law Magazine* 137. The author ascribes, if in part, the mid-century rise in the demand for poor relief to "the irruption of low Roman Catholic Irish into our towns" (p. 143). The most detailed judicial discussion of the 1579 Act is to be found in *Thomson v Lindsay* (1849) 11D 719, a decision of the Whole Court, in which a majority held that the father, being able-bodied (though without work) was not entitled to claim poor relief for either himself or his pupil children.

13 And from 1852 to 1867 Lord President of the Court of Session.

this to be effected by the extension of the system of poor houses that had existed to some limited extent in Scotland for at least one hundred years. Most children accommodated in poor houses were there as dependants of their parents, but the Poor Law authorities also had an obligation to care for orphans and deserted children.[14]

The 1845 Act also redesigned the structures under which the Poor Law was administered, by sweeping away the central role of the Kirk, an institution that had been substantially weakened in both its political and moral authority by the Disruption in 1843. Delivery of poor relief was still effected at the parish level, but instead of this being done by the Kirk itself, "parochial boards" were established to administer the Poor Law and to run poor houses. Oversight was provided at a national level, with the parochial boards being supervised by a central Board of Supervision based in Edinburgh,[15] which had the power to investigate the running of poor houses and to monitor the placements of children boarded-out from poor houses.

The Board of Supervision was replaced in 1894[16] by the Local Government Board for Scotland, a substantially more powerful body than its predecessor, with a membership that included *ex officio* both the Secretary for Scotland (a government minister, later of cabinet rank) and the Solicitor General. The 1894 Act also replaced the parochial boards with elected parish councils, which were themselves replaced by local councils established under the Local Government (Scotland) Act, 1929. Local authorities became, thereby, Poor Law authorities, and they remained so until the Poor Law, as a distinct legal doctrine, was abolished in 1948.[17] Locally elected bodies have therefore since at least 1894 had an important role in providing for needy children.

POOR LAW JURISPRUDENCE

After the cases in *Morison's Dictionary* under the heading "Poor Law",[18] later nineteenth-century decisions (mostly, as in *Morison*, on which parish

---

14 Macdonald, H.J. "Boarding-Out and the Scottish Poor Law, 1845 – 1914" (1996) 75 *Scottish Historical Review* 197, p. 198.

15 For a description of the operation of the Board of Supervision, see Blackden, S. "The Board of Supervision and the Scottish Parochial Medical Service 1845–95" (1986) 30 *Medical History* 145, pp.147–148.

16 Local Government (Scotland) Act, 1894.

17 National Assistance Act, 1948, s. 1.

18 The numerous cases in *Morison's Dictionary* involving the Poor Law as it applied to children are all concerned with determining the parish upon which liability for relief lay. See for example *Kirk*

was liable to pay relief) and commentaries on the Poor Law are to be found in the *Poor Law Magazine*, being the in-house magazine of the Society of Inspectors of the Poor for Scotland. This commenced publication in 1858 and ceased in 1929,[19] when the Local Government (Scotland) Act, 1929 transferred the responsibility for poor relief to local authorities. *Scots Law Times* carried a separate section of law reports – the *Poor Law Reports* – between 1932 and 1941, the vast majority of which again concerned the question of which local authority was liable to pay relief: decisions on that matter were made by the Department of Health for Scotland. Challenges to refusal of poor relief were taken to the sheriff court or the Outer House of the Court of Session.

REFORMATORY AND INDUSTRIAL SCHOOLS

Though the (new) Poor Law was designed to give preference to indoor relief, the practice of boarding-out the children of paupers into foster homes[20] meant that poor houses never developed into major providers of residential accommodation for children. But the nineteenth century did see the development of residential establishments for children who for different reasons were unable to remain at home, in the form of reformatory and industrial schools.[21] The distinction between the two was clear in theory but far less so in practice. Reformatory schools were originally designed for children who had committed offences and were direct alternatives to prison; industrial schools, on the other hand, were primarily schools for poor and vagrant children who were perceived to be at risk of falling into life-long indigence and were designed to divert them from a life of indolence to one of productive usefulness.

Both types of school found their origins in a developing nineteenth-century consciousness that juvenile delinquency was as much a social as a criminal problem, traced frequently to the harmful influences surrounding many children's upbringing, and from the consequences of which these children could with some state intervention be saved. The connection between crime, immorality and poverty was likely overstated but making that connec-

---

Session of Inveresk v Kirk Session of Tranent (1737) Mor. 10552; Kirk Session of Coldinghame v Kirk Session of Dunse (1779) Mor. 10582; Heritors in the Parishes of Melrose and Stitchell v Heritors in the Parish of Bowden (1786) Mor. 10584; Kirk Session of Rescobie v Kirk Session of Aberlemno (1801) Mor. 10589.

19 Heinonline carries the first fourteen volumes in electronic form.

20 See Chapter 7 below.

21 For details of the development of these institutions, see Chapter 8 below.

tion allowed the argument to gain purchase that an appropriate response to the juvenile offender was to seek to replace the offender's existing circumstances with a safe and secure environment which, through education in useful trades, would provide the opportunity to develop skills necessary to allow the child to become a productive member of society. Macdonald suggests that the same thinking was applied to justify removing poor children from parents "unfit" by reason of poverty "in the interests of controlling future pauperism".[22] The aim in both cases was to break cycles – either of poverty (caused by parental indolence) or delinquency (caused by parental immorality) – by replacing the bad familial influences over children with the good philanthropic influences that it was hoped these schools would provide. There was, therefore, little need to keep the two institutions structurally and conceptually separate.

Reformatory and industrial schools were put onto a statutory, and country-wide, basis by the Reformatory and Industrial Schools (Scotland) Act, 1854, the Youthful Offenders Act, 1854, and the Industrial Schools Act, 1861. It is from this point that we can understand them as being compulsory institutions, but government certification for their running was not required until the Reformatory Schools Act, 1866 and the Industrial Schools Act, 1866. These schools tended to operate on a residential as opposed to a day basis, a tendency furthered, as Ralston points out,[23] by the fact that government funding was available for certified institutions to which children could be compulsorily sent for keeping. Throughout the late nineteenth and early twentieth centuries, there was debate as to the advisability of schools taking both categories of children,[24] but the practice remained endemic and may well help to explain the ease with which Scots law later came to deal together both offenders and those offended against.

THE EARLY CHILD CRUELTY STATUTES 1889–1908

The origins of compulsion, a defining characteristic of state intervention in family life for the purposes of protection of children, may be found in a series of statutes from the late nineteenth and early twentieth centuries which conferred on the court the power to remove children from their existing

22 Macdonald, H.J. "Boarding-Out and the Scottish Poor Law, 1845 – 1914" (1996) 75 *Scottish Historical Review* 197, pp. 201–202.

23 Ralston, A.G. "The Development of Reformatory and Industrial Schools in Scotland 1832 to 1872" (1988) 8 *Journal of Scottish Historical Studies* 40, p. 48.

24 Ibid. p. 48

environments and to commit them to be cared for in a safer environment. These early statutes laid the foundations for the more modern law, and it will be seen throughout this book that the principles, and sometimes even the processes, established in the Acts between 1889 and 1908 have proved remarkably resilient and are to a surprising extent recognisable today.

The Prevention of Cruelty to, and Protection of, Children Act, 1889

The Prevention of Cruelty to, and Protection of, Children Act, 1889 was the first UK statute expressly designed to respond to parental mistreatment or neglect of children (beyond either punishing the criminal or activating the Poor Law). The protection offered was, however, dependent on the child having been the victim of a criminal offence. Section 1 rendered liable to punishment

> Any person over sixteen years of age having the custody, control, or charge of a child, being a boy under the age of fourteen years, or being a girl under the age of sixteen years, [who] wilfully ill-treats, neglects, abandons or exposes such child . . . in a manner likely to cause such child unnecessary suffering, or injury to its health . . .

This replaced an existing common law offence,[25] and the real innovation in the 1889 Act was that as well as punishing the offender, the court was authorised to remove the child from any perpetrator convicted of the crime under s. 1, or of any other offence "involving bodily injury to the child". Section 2 of the 1889 Act expanded state power substantially by authorising a constable to take a child against whom any of the offences specified in the Act had been committed to a "place of safety" where the child could be detained until "dealt with" by a court of summary jurisdiction.[26] More long-term provision could thereafter be made in respect of the child under s. 5, which provided that if a person with custody or control of a child was convicted, committed for trial, or bound over in relation to any offence under s. 1 the court "may order that the child be taken out of the custody of such person and committed to the charge of a relation of the child, or some other fit person named by the court". This later came to be known as a "fit person order" and was one of the roots of boarding-out (fostering) of children beyond the Poor Law. Oddly, these provisions passed

---

25 The history and meaning of this provision, and its final manifestation in the still extant s. 12 of the Children and Young Persons (Scotland) Act, 1937, are explored in Chapter 3 below.
26 This matter is explored more fully at Chapter 9 below.

almost without comment in the Parliamentary debates on the Bill, where far more time was spent on the issue of protecting children from harmful employments, with much dispute as to whether children performing in theatres was necessarily harmful.[27] Restrictions on employment of children formed the subject-matter of s. 3 of the 1889 Act.

Nothing in the Act authorised the state to take action to prevent foreseeable future harm: rather, it was designed to respond to harm that had already been suffered. Nor was the process one in which the child was taken "into care" as it later came to be understood, for it did not justify the removal of the child to an industrial school (which retained its focus on "vagrant" children): rather it was a mechanism for the transference of custody of a child from harmful parents to others who could provide the child with a better upbringing, one more likely to turn the child into a productive member of society. It was in essence state-mandated fostering of children, primarily with relatives in the context of what today would be called "kinship care". There were, however, no limitations expressed as to who would be a "fit person" for these purposes:[28] the matter was one for the court to judge and there seems to have been no prior approval provisions. Nor, at this point in time, was there any provision to oversee the relative or fit person into whose charge the child was committed, by visiting, inspection and the like. The person to whom the child was committed was given "the like control over the child as if he were its parent" and was made responsible for the child's maintenance.[29] So the state accepted no more responsibility for how the child was treated by the person to whose charge he or she was committed than it had for children being brought up by their own parents: so long as they committed no criminal offence in doing so, fit persons could bring up the child as they thought fit.

The Prevention of Cruelty to Children Act, 1894

The 1889 Act was amended by the Prevention of Cruelty to Children (Amendment) Act, 1894 by adding "assault" to the acts prohibited by s. 1, and by equalising at 16 the age at which both boys and girls stopped being within the term "child" for the purposes of the Act. The 1889 Act, as so amended,

27 See HC Deb. 19 June 1889, vol. 337 cols 227–266; HL Deb. 22 July 1889, vol. 338 cols 950–968.
28 Other than a requirement on the court to select "if possible" a person who was of the same religious persuasion as the child: Prevention of Cruelty to, and Protection of, Children Act, 1889, s. 5(2).
29 Prevention of Cruelty to, and Protection of, Children Act 1889, s. 5(2).

was then replaced by the Prevention of Cruelty to Children Act, 1894, which included a number of significant developments in the law. Within the s. 1 offence, mental harm (or "mental derangement" as it was – and was still in the second decade of the twenty-first century – termed) was for the first time explicitly recognised in addition to bodily harm. Section 5 dealt with the detention of children in places of safety and added a right of the child to seek refuge in such a place. An important development is found in s. 9, which provided that if any child was brought to court in circumstances authorising the court to deal with a child under the Industrial Schools Acts the court "in lieu of ordering that the child be sent to an industrial school, may make an order under this Act for the committal of the child to the custody of a relation or person named by the court". The effect of this was to bring the child protection legislation and the industrial schools legislation very close together, though it was not until the Children Act, 1908 that a single statute melded the processes into a unified whole. Also of note is s. 23(2), which provided that a failure to provide for the child by seeking maintenance under "the Acts relating to relief of the poor" was to be encompassed within the concept of "neglect" of the child for the purposes of s. 1 of the 1894 Act. Both s. 9 and s. 23 indicate an early realisation that a child's needs are seldom determined by the route through which he or she comes to the attention of the authorities. Scotland has held firm to this understanding ever since.

The Prevention of Cruelty to Children Act, 1904

The 1894 Act was repealed,[30] but substantially re-enacted, by the Prevention of Cruelty to Children Act, 1904. Perhaps the most significant development in the 1904 Act was s. 6(1), which provided that the concept of "fit person" into whose care a child might be committed was now to include "any society or body corporate established for the reception of poor children or the prevention of cruelty to children". This built upon the long-established fact that private charitable and religious endeavours, collectively known as "voluntary organisations", were at the forefront of providing services, including accommodation, for needy children, in addition to the public provision of the Poor Law. The importance of s. 6(1) was that it brought voluntary organisations within the system of state compulsion, for they could now receive children sent to them involuntarily by the courts as well as receiving abandoned street children and children given voluntarily by their parents into their care.

---

30 Prevention of Cruelty to Children Act, 1904, sched. 2.

THE CHILDREN ACT, 1908

The Children Act, 1908 constitutes a significant turning point in the legislative history of both child protection law and juvenile justice throughout the United Kingdom. Though substantially amended by the Children and Young Persons (Scotland) Act, 1932, it remained the principal Act for Scotland until its repeal in large part by the Children and Young Persons (Scotland) Act, 1937.

The 1889, 1894 and 1904 Acts had been written with a narrow (and necessarily retrospective) focus on the criminal law: children could be removed from their parents and committed to the care of others (not the state) if the person with their care or control was shown to have committed one of the various specified offences against them. This was in addition to, though overlapped with, the reformatory and industrial schools legislation that allowed for state-supported accommodation for young offenders and child vagrants. A much more unified approach was taken in the Children Act, 1908, the first Act to deal in the same statute with destitute children, children who were the victims of cruelty and neglect, and children who had committed offences. It was also the first Act to allow the state to remove children from their parents even when no crime had been committed. It is no coincidence that this Act was passed during the Liberal Administration that lasted from 1906 until the outbreak of the First World War, and which had set fundamental social reform as one of its main priorities. The 1908 Act may be seen as part of a series of Acts[31] that both laid the foundations of the modern welfare state and at the same time normalised the notion that the state's obligations to protect citizens might also involve significant interference in their lives. The Bill that became the 1908 Act was introduced in the House of Commons by the Under-Secretary of the Home Office, Herbert Samuel;[32] and moved at Second Reading by the Lord Advocate, Thomas Shaw.[33]

The Lord Advocate accepted that the Act entailed a significant increase in the power of the state over family life, but dismissed any concerns this raised as having little real purchase in contemporary society: "There may be in some persons' minds a doubt as to the advisability of the State interfering with the responsibility of the parents: but that is an argument more familiar

---

31 Notable social achievements of the Liberal Government other than the Children Act, 1908 included the Education (Scotland) Act, 1908 (introducing free school meals and medical inspection of pupils), the Old Age Pensions Act, 1908 and the National Insurance Acts, 1911 and 1913.
32 Later Leader of the Liberal Party between 1931 and 1935.
33 Later Lord Shaw of Dunfermline, Lord of Appeal in Ordinary.

in former days than now".[34] The 1908 Act changed the terms we use, and for the first time the law talked of "children and young persons" instead of, as before, "children" (defined in the earlier statutes as boys under 14 and girls under 16, then all persons under 16). Section 131 of the 1908 Act defined "child" to mean "a person under the age of fourteen years" (the school leaving age) and "young person" to mean "a person who has attained the age of fourteen years and is under the age of sixteen years" (later, seventeen years).

Offences against children

Part II of the Children Act, 1908, headed "Prevention of Cruelty to Children and Young Persons", replaced and expanded the provisions (described above) from the 1889 to 1904 Acts. The range of offences that could justify committing the care of a child to a fit person, or to an industrial school, was significantly expanded. The offence in s. 1 of the 1889, 1894 and 1904 Acts (the progenitor of s. 12 of the long-lasting Children and Young Persons (Scotland) Act, 1937) appeared as s. 12 of the 1908 Act, and in addition various other actions that had come to be recognised as harmful to children were explicitly made offences, most noticeably "overlaying" of children (suffocating children who were sleeping in the same bed as the adult, when the adult was "under the influence of drink"[35]), and exposing children to the risk of burning by allowing a child under seven to be "in any room containing an open fire grate not sufficiently protected".[36] Questioning whether criminalising bereaved parents was an effective response to family tragedies, Stewart[37] suggests that what was described as "overlaying" was really the phenomenon of unexplained deaths given a name,[38] which in the mind of the Government created worries about the alcoholic working-class and showed an attitude of official distrust of working-class mothers' ability to bring up children fit to defend the Empire. Indeed much of the Act was about improving children's health for that reason – a major concern in

---

34 HC Deb. 24 March 1908, vol. 186, col. 1259. Yet it was an argument that was resurrected in the modern era when some people were upset about state agencies sharing information with each other about their children: *Christian Institute v Lord Advocate* [2016] UKSC 51.

35 Children Act, 1908, s. 13. The Lord Advocate made the scarcely believable claim that in London alone there were 1,600 infant deaths attributable to this cause: HC Deb. 24 March 1908, vol. 186 col. 1255.

36 Children Act, 1908, s. 15. The Lord Advocate also stated that in one (unspecified) year there had been 1,600 infant deaths for this reason: HC Deb. 24 March 1908, vol. 186 col. 1254.

37 Stewart, J. "Children, Parents and the State: The Children Act, 1908", (1995) 9 *Children and Society* 90, pp. 95–96.

38 The name we might use today is "cot death", or sudden infant death syndrome.

Edwardian society, and the justification accepted by many who would otherwise be reluctant to afford the state any interest in family life afflicted by poverty. It was not only the offences created by the 1908 Act that would justify state interference in family life: in addition, the child being a victim of any offence listed in the First Schedule to the Act (from then on known as "scheduled offences") also allowed the court to deal with the child under s. 20 as well as to punish the offender. Scheduled offences included "bodily injury" to the child or young person and the sexual offences in the Criminal Law Amendment Act, 1885.[39] Even exposing children to a sexualised environment activated the 1908 Act's protective mechanisms, as when the accused had allowed a child or young person to be in a brothel, or had caused or encouraged the seduction, prostitution or unlawful carnal knowledge of a girl under 16.[40]

Reformatory and industrial schools

Part Four of the Children Act, 1908 further harmonised the child protection provisions with the regulation of reformatory and industrial schools. The primary aim of the 1908 Act was to bring these schools under better state control and, in the Lord Advocate's words, to "link together the whole scheme of reformatory and industrial schools in the most useful manner".[41]

Though the aims of, and regulatory mechanisms for, both types of school were now the same in the 1908 Act, the grounds upon which a child could be sent to each school remained different. A child over the age of 12 but under 16 convicted of an offence punishable by penal servitude or imprisonment could be sent to a reformatory school in lieu of prison.[42] In modern language, one might refer to this as "the offence ground". "Care and protection grounds", which justified the sending of the child to an industrial school, were more numerous.[43] Previously, a child could be sent to an industrial school if found begging or having been neglected. The 1908 Act set out seven distinct grounds in response to which a child could be sent to an industrial school,[44] most of which provided the origins

---

39 On the Criminal Law Amendment Act, 1885, see Chapter 3 below.
40 Children Act, 1908, ss. 16 and 17, as amended by the Children Act (1908) Amendment Act, 1910 (which added the reference to unlawful carnal knowledge).
41 HC Deb. 24 March 1908, vol. 186, col. 1257
42 Children Act, 1908, s. 57.
43 Ibid. s. 58.
44 Ibid. s. 58(1).

sixty years later for the (non-offence) grounds of referral to the children's hearing.[45]

Nevertheless, reformatory and industrial schools were perceived as performing substantially overlapping functions, and it was possible for children subject to one category of ground to be sent to the other category of school. Specifically, youthful offenders under the age of 12 could be sent to an industrial as opposed to a reformatory school.[46] The court retained the power to commit the child to the care of a relative or other fit person instead,[47] and if it did so the court could also order that the child be placed under the supervision of a probation officer:[48] as we will see later in this book this was one of the roots of compulsory supervision of neglected children.[49]

Juvenile justice and juvenile courts

Though it had been recognised from the early Victorian period (most notably in the field of employment) that children ought to be treated differently from adults, Part Five of the Children Act, 1908, marked the first occasion on which that was made a central feature of criminal justice. The Act embraced a recognition, which seems to have been first accepted in an official Report from 1896, that

> Nothing has been more certainly demonstrated in the practical development of the reformatory system than that juvenile crime has comparatively little to do with any special depravity of the offender, and very much to do with parental neglect and bad example . . .[50]

It was this insight that provided a foundation for the 1908 Act – and it is from this point that it is appropriate to talk of "juvenile justice" as a process for dealing with young offenders separate from and applying a different approach to adult offenders. The primary political objective of Part V of the 1908 Act was to ensure that children and young persons were no longer sent to prison. Even as late as 1909, 151 children under the age of ten years were sentenced to imprisonment in Scotland.[51] In addition to that policy, the 1908

---

45 See Chapter 5 below.
46 Children Act, 1908, s. 58(2) and (3).
47 Ibid. s. 58(7).
48 Ibid. s. 60.
49 See Chapter 6 below.
50 *Report of the Departmental Committee on Reformatory and Industrial Schools*, 1896 (Cmnd 8204), p. 22 (quoted in Kelly, C. "Continuity and Change in the History of Scottish Juvenile Justice" (2016) 1 *Law, Crime and History* 59, p. 76).
51 Morton Committee Report *Protection and Training* (1928), p. 12.

Act envisaged the child being dealt with by a "juvenile court". However, this "juvenile court" was not a new type of court separate from the adult court, but simply a court of summary jurisdiction (in Scotland, the sheriff or the justice of the peace court, or the police or burgh court) dealing with juvenile offenders, to which some special arrangements applied, including ensuring that juvenile courts sat at different places, or at least at different times, from adult courts, and sat in private.[52] But procedure applicable to juvenile cases was the same as that for adults, as was the court personnel.

Nevertheless, the Children Act, 1908 might be said to represent a radical reimagining of how the phenomenon of youth offending was to be responded to. There was more to this change than simply dealing with children in a separate, more child-friendly, process: the outcomes were deliberately designed to be different since it was recognised that the special position of children required a different response to that appropriate for adult offenders. The Lord Advocate in the Parliamentary debates declared that the objective of the juvenile court was "to treat these children not by way of punishing them – which is no remedy – but with a view to their reformation".[53] Half a century later, the Kilbrandon Report described the 1908 Act as having proceeded "on the footing that young offenders should be treated differently from adults, and that the aim should be to seek to educate and reform, rather than to punish".[54] The 1908 Act is, therefore, the precursor of all subsequent substantial Children Acts in Scotland dealing with both young offenders and victims of abuse and neglect: both categories of children would be dealt with in the same manner, for their needs were similar, and their difficulties often stemmed from similar failings in their upbringing.

THE LEAD-UP TO THE CHILDREN AND YOUNG PERSONS (SCOTLAND) ACT, 1932

In 1925 the Secretary of State for Scotland appointed a committee under the chairmanship of Sir George Morton, KC,[55] with a remit

> to enquire into the treatment of young offenders and of young people whose character, environment or conduct is such that they require protection and training, and to report what changes, if any, are desirable in the present law or its administration.

52 Children Act, 1908, s. 111.
53 HC Deb. 24 March 1908, vol. 186 col. 1257.
54 Kilbrandon Report, *Children and Young Persons, Scotland* (HMSO, 1964), para 41.
55 Later to find legal immortality by acting as counsel for Mrs May Donoghue when she sued after finding a snail in a bottle of ginger beer manufactured by the soft drinks firm Stevenson and Son.

This Committee reported in 1928,[56] and it concluded that the aspirations contained in the Children Act, 1908 had not come to pass, with juvenile offenders being dealt with through procedures much the same as had gone before and with the change of mindset underpinning the 1908 Act not having affected practice to any noticeable degree. The Morton Committee Report, therefore, recommended the proper establishment of juvenile courts as tribunals separate from the adult courts, subject to separate procedures and, crucially, manned with specially trained justices.

Other government reports on related matters appeared around the same time. In 1926 the Government published its *Report of the Departmental Committee on Sexual Offences against Children and Young Persons in Scotland.*[57] The 1908 Act had responded to concern in this area by criminalising the bringing up of girls in brothels, or otherwise in circumstances that exposed them to immorality, but increasing awareness of sexual abuse in non-sexualised environments was manifest in the 1926 Report. Writing in 1933, Cowan stated that the 1926 Report recognised "the heinous nature of some of the offences involved, and the psychological and moral effect even of those of a less serious character on the whole future of the child".[58] It is sometimes thought that our concern for the long-term emotional impact of sexual abuse of children, apart from the moral considerations, developed only late in the twentieth century, but both the Report and the commentary cited manifest a much earlier awareness of the psychological damage such abuse might cause.[59] Though the recommendations made in the 1926 Report for increased penalties for sex offenders were not given legislative effect, sexual offences against children did receive greater prominence in the legislation following the Morton Committee Report, as indicators of the need for compulsory measures of care and protection.

In response to the recommendations of the Morton Committee Report and its English counterpart,[60] and especially the idea that youth offending and young people needing care and protection were simply different manifestations of the same problem (or the same set of problems), the

---

56 *Protection and Training* ("the Morton Committee Report") (HMSO, 1928).

57 Cmnd 2592, 1926. The *Report of the Departmental Committee on Sexual Offences Against Young Persons* Cmnd 2561, 1925 is an equivalent report looking at the situation in England and Wales.

58 Cowan, M.G. *The Children and Young Persons (Scotland) Act, 1932* (W. Hodge & Co, 1933), p. 4.

59 See also the Parliamentary debate on the issue at HC Deb. 12 February 1932, vol. 261, cols 1224 et seq.

60 *Report of the Departmental Committee on the Treatment of Young Offenders* (the Molony Report), HMSO, 1927.

National Government led by Ramsay MacDonald drafted a Children and Young Persons Bill, which received its Second Reading on 12 February 1932. The Debate was led for the Government by Oliver Stanley, then Under-secretary in the Home Department,[61] and he emphasised that the Bill's major purpose was to amalgamate the treatment of juvenile offenders and that of neglected and deprived children. The underlying philosophy that drove the Government's policy was that the similarities between the two classes of children far outweighed any differences, that poverty and neglect were the main causes of juvenile criminality and that reducing exposure to deprivation was the most efficient way of reducing both child neglect and juvenile delinquency. Stanley said this:

> But the habitual criminal is often not born but made. His persistence in crime is far less due to inherent vices than to the circumstances of his life . . . We recognise that other conditions than mere inherent vice may have entered into an offence; that the child's upbringing at home, the discipline he receives in the home circle or the lack of it, the economic conditions under which he lives, the squalor and misery of his life, even the companions with whom he associates in school . . . or out of it, may have had much more to do in turning that child into an offender than any spirit of natural evil.[62]

He went on:

> Let me turn from the case of the young offender to that of the neglected child, which forms the other branch of the duties of the Juvenile Court. It was one of the most revolutionary proposals of the Act of 1908 which for the first time allowed a court in this country to entertain and consider cases in which no offence had been committed, but in which the circumstances made it desirable that the child should receive protection. The right was given to the Court in respect of children up to 16, under specific categories of home circumstances— begging, destitution, drunken parents, sexual offences, prostitution, or being found wandering without any parental control—to look into the circumstances of such children, and either send them to an industrial school or commit them to the care of a fit person. By this Measure we extend that principle. In the first place, we extend the age from 16 to 17, and we abolish these special categories, substituting one wide definition which we believe will be sufficient to bring in a number of cases which today are brought in only by greatly straining the law. I should like hon. Members to realise that when we are dealing with cases of this kind there is no question of ignoring the facts as regards substituting the State for the parents, or breaking up family life, because the fundamental basis in a matter of this kind is that parental control should be adequate, and that such action is legitimate when the proper parents or guardians are either unwilling or unable to exercise that parental control . . .[63]

61 And later Secretary of State for the Colonies, in Churchill's wartime Cabinet.
62 HC Deb. 12 February 1932, vol. 261, cols 1167–1168.
63 HC Deb. 12 February 1932, vol. 261, col. 1178.

Stanley also described the overall aim of the reforms as an "increased simplicity, to make [the court process] much more intelligible to the young person, and by being more intelligible, less frightening".[64] The radicality of this approach can be gleaned from the dismay that Lord Sands, writing extra-judicially, expressed at Stanley's hope that the court process might be made less frightening for young offenders. He offered the view, which is unlikely to have been unusual amongst the Scottish judiciary at the time, that for a "real offender . . . the more frightening one can make the Court the better".[65]

THE CHILDREN AND YOUNG PERSONS (SCOTLAND) ACTS, 1932 AND 1937

Today, we have rather forgotten the Children and Young Persons (Scotland) Act, 1932. It has been overshadowed, perhaps even obliterated from our minds, by the Children and Young Persons (Scotland) Act, 1937, passed a mere five years later and important sections of which remain in force to the present day. Yet the 1937 Act was a consolidating statute that did not fundamentally alter processes as they were then followed in Scotland nor their underlying principles. The 1932 Act did just that and may well be the most radical child law statute of the twentieth century, exceeding in that respect even such fundamental Acts (which of course we do remember today) as the Social Work (Scotland) Act 1968 and the Children (Scotland) Act 1995.

Not the least of its radicalities, the 1932 legislation marked a separation of Scottish from English child protection legislation. All the earlier Acts in this area had covered both jurisdictions, though with modifications for Scotland in the Children Act, 1908.[66] From 1932 there was to be quite separate legislation, though it was not until the 1960s that the two jurisdictions took noticeably different paths. By an unusual procedural mechanism, the 1932 Bill was passed as a UK statute[67] but applied to Scotland with a number of modifications set out in the fifth schedule and, under s. 89 (not printed in the "Scotland" version of the Act), the UK Act with these modifications was to be printed "as if it were a separate Act which had received the Royal Assent on the same day as this Act" and to be cited as the Children and Young

---

64 Ibid. col. 1172.
65 Lord Sands, Foreword to Cowan, M.G. *The Children and Young Persons (Scotland) Act, 1932* (W Hodge & Co. Ltd, 1933) at xiv.
66 Children Act 1908, s. 132.
67 Children and Young Persons Act, 1932, 22 & 23 Geo. V, c. 46.

Persons (Scotland) Act, 1932.[68] Another reason why the 1932 Act has faded from our consciousness is that, though it made many profound changes, it was in the main an amending Act, with the 1908 Act remaining the Principal Act until it and the 1932 Act were in large part repealed by the consolidating Children and Young Persons (Scotland) Act, 1937.[69]

The definitions of "child" and "young person", originally found in the 1908 Act, were amended in the 1932 Act[70] (to increase the age at which a "young person" reached adulthood from 16 to 17), and these definitions were replicated in the 1937 Act:[71] "child" since 1932 has been a person under 14 (at that time the school leaving age) and "young person" has been a person between the ages of 14 and 17.[72] And the formal (and increasingly irrelevant) distinction between industrial schools and reformatory schools was finally abolished[73] – all such schools were now to be approved (applying the same standards) by the Secretary of State for Scotland, and were known from this point as "approved schools". From then on the focus was firmly on the care children needed, rather than the reasons that brought them to court.

The 1932 Act expanded considerably the types of case that could be dealt with by the juvenile court under the 1908 Act. By s. 1(1) and (5),[74] the court was given jurisdiction over juvenile crime, school attendance cases, care and protection cases (which were themselves delineated much more expansively) and applications for adoption orders. Part I of the 1932 Act sought (though in the event mostly unsuccessfully[75]) to establish a proper juvenile court to be manned by specially training justices, while Part II went on to specify both those over whom the court had jurisdiction and the potential outcomes open to the court. Putting it in contemporary terms (which would not have misrepresented the position in 1932), s. 12[76] set out the offence ground for the juvenile court's jurisdiction, while s. 6[77] set out the grounds

---

68   22 & 23 Geo. V, c. 47. A detailed and valuable commentary on the 1932 Act is to be found in Cowan, M.G. *The Children and Young Persons (Scotland) Act, 1932.*

69   For a detailed commentary on the 1937 Act, see Trotter, T. *The Law as to Children and Young Persons* (W. Hodge & Co Ltd, 1938).

70   Children and Young Persons (Scotland) Act, 1932, s. 64.

71   Children and Young Persons (Scotland) Act, 1937, s. 110(1).

72   These remain the definitions for the purposes of the Children and Young Persons (Scotland) Act 1937 that survive today, notwithstanding that the school leaving age has changed.

73   Children and Young Persons (Scotland) Act, 1932, ss. 36–37.

74   Subsequently re-enacted as s. 50 of the Children and Young Persons (Scotland) Act 1937.

75   See further Chapter 4 below.

76   Subsequently re-enacted as s. 61 of the Children and Young Persons (Scotland) Act, 1937.

77   Subsequently re-enacted as s. 65 of the Children and Young Persons (Scotland) Act, 1937.

that needed to be established before the court could treat the child as being "in need of care or protection".

The potential outcomes for any child or young person who was found to fall into any of the "care" categories were virtually the same as the potential outcomes for a child or young person found guilty of an offence.[78] Perhaps the most interesting aspect of all of this was that for the first time a welfare test was explicitly applied in respect of both groups of children and young persons.[79] Also applicable to both groups was the rule that the education authority had to be notified of the child or young person being brought before a juvenile court[80] and (importantly) once notified was obliged to supply the court with such information about the child or young person's home surroundings, school record, health, character and of available approved schools as appeared to the authority as "likely to assist the court".[81] A holistic approach, taking into account the child's life circumstances and environment, was to be the hallmark of the Scottish approach from this time. Scottish child protection law, including within its embrace children and young persons who had committed offences, took on characteristics in 1932 that have defined it to the present day.

The Children and Young Persons (Scotland) Act, 1937 was the principal child protection statute in Scotland for the next 30 years (and remains at the time of writing the source of the primary crime of child neglect). Of course, the coming of War, within two years of the passing of the 1937 Act, severely inhibited both how child protection was practiced and the development of policy. But the end of the War brought a profound change in governmental attitudes to child protection law and practice, and the role of the state.

THE POST-WAR PERIOD

The Labour Government under Clement Attlee that took office in July 1945 is rightly recognised as the most socially transformative of all twentieth-century Governments, for it changed the very nature of the relationship between the state and its citizens. Until the Second World War, child protec-

---

78 See further, Chapter 4 below.
79 Children and Young Persons (Scotland) Act, 1932, s. 16; Children and Young Persons (Scotland) Act, 1937, s. 49(1). See also rules 9(6)(b) and 10(7)(a) of the Juvenile Courts (Procedure) (Scotland) Rules, 1934.
80 Failure to notify risked rendering the proceedings incompetent: *AB v Howman* 1917 JC 23 (dealing with the Education Authority's right to be heard under s. 74(6) of the Children Act, 1908).
81 Children and Young Persons (Scotland) Act, 1932, s. 15; Children and Young Persons (Scotland) Act, 1937, s. 43(2).

tion, though frequently instigated by the state, was for the most part left to be implemented by charitable endeavour. However, within a very few years of the end of the War child protection had become a duty that the state owed to its citizens. Though the state did not immediately displace voluntary organisations as the main provider of facilities for children in need of care and protection it did, through local authorities, become the central player not only in the instigation of processes to protect children but in the over-sight of providers of accommodation and other facilities for children. Local authorities have retained that central role ever since.

It was the Children Act, 1948 that substantially increased the involve-ment of the state in the running of the institutions, homes and placements upon which the child protection processes relied and, while it by no means "nationalised" child protection, the 1948 Act may properly be seen as belonging to a group of measures introduced by the Attlee Government predicated upon the acceptance that the state itself has responsibility for the wellbeing of its citizens, including the National Insurance Act, 1946, the National Health Service (Scotland) Act, 1947, the National Assistance Act, 1948, and the Legal Aid and Solicitors (Scotland) Act, 1949. As Professor Cretney put it:

> The notion that the community should charge itself with specific responsibility to provide care for all children deprived of a normal home life – and not merely to secure the subsistence of the destitute and, at the other extreme, to provide through the wardship jurisdiction for the affairs of the wealthy – was wholly novel; and in this respect the Children Act 1948 surely deserves to be remembered as one of the cornerstones of the post-war welfare State.[82]

The 1948 Act was the legislative response to two official reports, pub-lished two years earlier.

THE CLYDE REPORT 1946

One of the last acts of Churchill's War Ministry had been to establish, in April 1945, two separate committees of inquiry, one for Scotland and one for England and Wales, into the state's provision of accommodation for children in need. The Scottish *Committee on Homeless Children*, under the chairmanship of James L. Clyde, KC,[83] was given a remit (rather wider than

---

82 "The Children Act 1948: Lessons for Today?" (1997) 9 *Child and Family Law Quarterly* 359, p. 360.

83 Later Lord Advocate, and then Lord President of the Court of Session from 1954 to 1972.

its title suggests) "to inquire into the existing methods of providing for children deprived of normal home life, and to consider what further measures
should be taken to compensate them for lack of parental care". The last eight
words, curiously formulated, are to be noted: they do not, of course, refer to
monetary compensation, but (as we will see) presage the artificial replacement of "normal home life" as the main aim of state intervention in family
life. The Committee's Report was published in 1946,[84] at the same time as
the English equivalent, the *Report of the Committee on the Care of Children*
(the Curtis Report).[85]

The investigations of the Clyde Committee revealed that the existing position in Scotland was characterised by a variety of mechanisms through which
homeless children could be looked after, either by the state in its various
manifestations (central or local) or by private institutions (religious or philanthropic), each mechanism being subject to different regulatory regimes,
and with a bewildering range of different central government departments
with ultimate oversight. The Clyde Report identified the "three main solutions at present adopted in Scotland to meet the problem" of children and
young persons who cannot reside with their parents: (i) boarding-out the
child with foster parents, (ii) sending the child to a home run by a charity (a
"voluntary home") and (iii) maintaining the child in a home run by a local
authority. But these apparently limited options hid the diversity of service
provided, which was dependent not only on the nature of the home involved
but also on the legal route by which children came to be accommodated
there; also hidden were the different regulatory regimes, involving separately the Poor Law authorities, local education authorities, central government and local government, to which different types of accommodation of
children were subject. The Clyde Report concluded:

> We consider that the time has now come to sweep away the existing anomalies
> and to recognise the importance of the welfare of children as a distinct function
> of the Local Authority, and not as an incidental function of a group of separate
> committees of different Local Authorities primarily concerned at present with
> other functions.[86]

To achieve this, the Report recommended:

> [T]hat in each County and large Burgh [that is to say, in each local authority area in
> Scotland] there should be established a Children's Care Committee which would

---

84 *Report of the Committee on Homeless Children*, hereinafter "the Clyde Report", (Cmnd 6911,
   1946).
85 1946, Cmnd 6922.
86 Clyde Report, para 80.

administer the whole of this field. This Committee should have transferred to it all the functions at present exercised by the Public Assistance and Public Health Committees regarding these children. This would no longer then be regarded as an incidental matter in Poor Law or Local Health administration. Further, to the Town Councils of large Burghs and to the County Councils of Counties, and through them to their respective Children's Care Committee, would be transferred all the functions at present exercisable by Education Authorities in relation to care and protection cases under the Children and Young Persons (Scotland) Act, 1937.[87]

A substitute family

An overarching theme throughout the Clyde Report was the recognition of the concept of "family" as the ideal environment to bring up children. However, the Committee understood by that concept not "family life" as we today, steeped in the language of Art. 8 of the European Convention on Human Rights,[88] understand that term but simply as an environment away from "the large institution". In a paragraph headed "Value of the Family", the Clyde Report said this:

> The lesson which above all else the war years have taught us is the value of home. It is upon the family that our position as a nation is built, and it is to the family that in trouble and disaster each child naturally turns. It is the growing awareness of the importance of the family which has largely brought into prominence the problem of the homeless child. How then is the family to be re-created for the child who is rendered homeless?[89]

"Re-creation" of the family was not seen, as it would be today, in terms of maintaining contact between the child and the family into which he or she had been born in order to work towards the eventual rehabilitation of the child with that family. Instead, the Clyde Committee thought that the aim of the law should be the creation of a substitute family, in a private home, for the child who could not remain with his or her parents. In the words of the Clyde Report:

> The answer is certainly not to be found in the large Institution. That is an out-worn solution, and some of them have left a bad impression upon the Members of the Committee who have visited them. The uniformity, the repression,[90] the impersonality of these cold and forbidding abodes afford no real consolation to

---

87 Ibid. para 80
88 "Everyone has the right to respect for his private and family life, his home and his correspondence".
89 Clyde Report, para 43.
90 Frustratingly, this sinister word is given no further elaboration.

the children who grow up in them, and constitute a sorry preparation for entry into a world where the child must ultimately fend for itself.

Undoubtedly the solution of the problem is the good foster parent. By this means the child should get the nearest approximation to family life, and receive that individual treatment whereby it secures the necessary opportunity to build up its own personality and equip itself for the transition to independence and self-reliance in later years.[91]

State provision of substitute families, which would replace the unsatisfactory families from which children or young persons had been removed, was therefore presented as the primary solution to lack of parental care. The Report's preference for foster parents over institutional care was underpinned by a belief, which may strike the modern reader as naïve, that "parental affection"[92] would always be an inherent part of the care offered by those fostering children. But more noticeable throughout the Report is the assumption that a child once "homeless" (including through state removal of the child from its home due to parental inadequacy) will require to remain in the care of the state until adulthood. It is striking that there is little in the Clyde Report about working with the child's own family to allow its return, other than the unelaborated, and substantially qualified, assertion that "every encouragement should be given to . . . a reunion of the family (if the parents are satisfactory)".[93] Nor is there anything about parental contact with children accommodated away from their parents: the Report saw the purpose of child protection as being to insulate the child from the harmful environment from which he or she had been removed. This also explains why there is no indication in the Clyde Report that care within the child's wider (natural) family was a strategy to be considered, far less preferred. In fact, a change in attitudes towards kinship care had come about rather earlier than the Clyde Report. While committing the child to the care of "fit persons" had originally been conceived as boarding the child with other members of his or her own family,[94] that had disappeared with the enactment of the Children and Young Persons (Scotland) Act 1932, though it would reappear (in the slightly different guise of "kinship care") early in the twenty-first century. The aim of the 1932, 1937 and 1948 Acts was to ensure that the child would be provided with family life by the state: just not with

---

91 Clyde Report, paras 44–45.
92 Ibid. para 83.
93 Ibid. para 105.
94 As was seen above, the Prevention of Cruelty to, and Protection of, Children Act, 1889 created the "fit person" order that committed the child to the care of "a relation of the child, or some other fit person named by the court".

their own family. Many of the Clyde Report's recommendations focus, there-fore, on ensuring the highest quality of foster parents, while at the same time ensuring that foster parents were not subject to unnecessarily intrusive state supervision by the local authority. The Report recommended, for example, that the existing three-monthly visitation system be reduced to six-monthly, on the ground that this would be sufficient if the foster parents were well-chosen in the first place.[95]

Consistent with this desire to create a substitute family for the child, the Clyde Report showed a clear distrust of birth parents, and it was at pains to point out that irrespective of whether the child was placed with foster parents or in an institution, the child should be protected from arbitrary removal by their parents:

> The Committee consider that the boarding out Authority or the Authority in charge of the Home should have a discretion to retain the child, subject always to a right of appeal to the Secretary of State or to the Sheriff against a decision to retain.[96]

THE CHILDREN BILL, 1948

Both the Clyde and the Curtis Reports made substantially similar recom-mendations which to a large extent the Government accepted and made the basis of their Children Bill in 1948.[97]

The Children Bill was introduced in the House of Lords, and at Second Reading[98] the Debate was led by the Lord Chancellor (Viscount Jowitt), who commenced his speech with the recognition, which had underpinned the 1908, 1932 and 1937 Acts, that the child's environment was a primary factor in both neglect and delinquency cases.[99] The question then became: "how can we so arrange matters as to save those children who have not the benefit of a normal home life from suffering that disadvantage throughout their whole lives?"[100]

It was acknowledged in the Parliamentary debates that child protection too often lacked humanity in its application:

---

95 Clyde Report, para 69.

96 Ibid. para 105.

97 The lead up to the Children Act, 1948 is explored by Cretney, S. in "The State as Parent: The Children Act 1948 in Retrospect" 1998 *Law Quarterly Review* 419.

98 Curiously, forty years to the day after the introduction (in the House of Commons) of the Bill that became the Children Act 1908.

99 HL Deb. 10 February 1948, vol. 153, col. 917.

100 Ibid. col. 914.

There has been, on the part of too many voluntary bodies and public authorities, a failure to give to those under their care the personal sympathy and human understanding so necessary to the wellbeing of children who lack the love and affection of their parents.[101]

The two main recommendations of the Curtis and Clyde Committees were accepted: (i) the local authority was to be the primary state body for dealing with all such children, with each local authority being required to establish a children's committee and to appoint a children's officer and (ii) the boarding-out of children and young persons in foster homes should be statutorily recognised as the preferred solution for children and young persons requiring to be accommodated away from their parents.

THE CHILDREN ACT, 1948

Children's committees and children's officers

The bulk of the Children Act, 1948 deals with how child services, and not only those required as a result of court and other administrative decisions, were to be organised and delivered at a local level. Section 39 obliged all local authorities[102] to establish a children's committee for the purposes of their functions under the Children and Young Persons (Scotland) Act, 1937 and under the 1948 Act itself.[103] These committees were to have no function other than these (except with the consent of the Secretary of State).[104] A "children's officer"[105] was also to be appointed by each local authority,[106] and that person was not to be employed by the local authority in any other capacity.[107] The Lord Chancellor painted this attractive picture:

> It is for the local authorities to give the children's officer adequate staff. I should suppose that in many cases—I think I might say in most cases—the children's officer would be a woman, and she would require not merely academic qualifica-

---

101 HC Deb 7 May 1948 vol. 450 col. 1611.
102 In Scotland then defined as "the councils of counties and large burghs": Children Act, 1948, s. 38(2).
103 Children Act, 1948, s. 39(1). Two or more local authorities could organise a combined committee to serve each: s. 40(5).
104 Children Act, 1948, s. 39(2).
105 A history of the development of children's officers, and the early difficulties they found in establishing their position and fighting for resources in the austere post-war world, is offered by Parker, R. in "Getting Started with the 1948 Act: What Did we Learn?" (2011) 35 *Adoption and Fostering* 17.
106 Children Act, 1948, s. 41.
107 Ibid. s. 41(4).

tions, skill and administrative capacity but, beyond everything else, enthusiasm, fondness for children, and the type of personality which would enable her to be looked upon by the children as a real friend. Then she will be able to restore to the children the sense of being real members of the community and not unwanted members, as these children are so apt to feel they are. Of course, she cannot know all the children in care, and she must, therefore, have officers under her who will be allocated to specific groups.[108]

The children's committees, in the event, operated for only 20 years, before being subsumed into the wider social work departments of local authorities that were required to be set up in 1968;[109] the children's officers' role was at the same time taken over by the new Directors of Social Work.

The boarding-out preference

Boarding-out with foster parents had long been the most common means of accommodating children and young persons whose care fell to the state, though there had never been a statutory requirement that this be treated as the preferred solution. Following the recommendations of the Clyde and Curtis Reports, the Children Act, 1948 required that: "a local authority shall discharge their duty to provide accommodation and maintenance for a child in their care – (a) by boarding him out", or "(b) *where it is not practicable or desirable for the time being to make arrangements for boarding-out*, by maintaining the child in a home provided under this Part of this Act or by placing him in a voluntary home the managers of which are willing to receive him".[110] This made boarding-out the primary aim and placing a child in an institution, whether local authority or voluntary, was to be explored as an option only after boarding-out with a family had been assessed to be not practicable or not desirable. Even more importantly, regulations could be made to include provisions for ensuring that the household into which a child was boarded was approved.[111] Vetting of foster households had in fact been introduced very shortly before the 1948 Act was passed, when Part C of the Care and Training Regulations, 1933 was replaced by the Children (Boarding-out, etc.) (Scotland) Rules and Regulations, 1947.[112] This was a

---

108 HL Deb. 10 February 1948, vol. 153, cols 917–918.
109 Social Work (Scotland) Act 1968, s. 2(4) repealed the 1948 Act provisions on children's committees, with s. 2(2) requiring each local authority to have a social work committee to perform their functions.
110 Children Act, 1948, s. 13(1).
111 Ibid. s. 14(2)(b).
112 Details of both sets of Regulations are given at Chapter 7 below.

direct result of the recommendation in the Clyde Report that foster parents ought to be chosen with far more care than had happened in the past.

Local authority duty to receive children into their care

The enactment of a boarding-out preference did not represent a major sea-change in child care policy: rather, it merely built upon and strengthened existing practices. However, right at the start of the Children Act, 1948, there was just such a sea-change, because the effect of Part I of the Act was to impose on local authorities a wholly unprecedented duty to be proactive and not simply reactive in respect of vulnerable children. The state (through the offices of each local authority) was for the first time placed under a statutory obligation to receive into their care any child[113] who appeared to have no parents or guardians or who had been lost or abandoned, or whose parents or guardians were "prevented" for any reason from providing for the child's accommodation, maintenance and upbringing: in any of these cases, the intervention of the local authority was required whenever it was "necessary in the interests of the welfare of the child",[114] (as assessed by the local authority). Once the child was in the care of the local authority, that authority was obliged to keep the child in its care so long as his or her welfare – in the opinion of the local authority – appeared to require it or until the child attained the age of 18 years.[115] This did not, however, authorise the local authority to keep the child if the parent or guardian wished to take over the care of the child and they were obliged "where it appears to them consistent with the welfare of the child so to do" to endeavour to secure that the care of the child was taken over either by a parent or guardian or by a relative or friend.[116]

Welfare as the guiding principle for local authority action

The Children Act, 1948 made the child's welfare the guiding principle for local authority action in relation to children in their care. Previously, those

---

113 That is to say a person who appeared to the local authority to be under the age of 17.

114 Children Act, 1948, s. 1(1). The duty under s. 1 was later held by the Court of Appeal to impose a duty to examine each case individually – it was an unlawful fettering of discretion to make policy decisions as to when such advice and assistance was and was not to be offered: *Attorney General ex rel. Tilley v Wandsworth London Borough Council* [1981] 1 WLR 854.

115 Children Act, 1948, s. 1(2). Interestingly, the age of 18 as the limit of local authority obligation had been suggested by the Clyde Committee while the (English) Curtis Committee had suggested the age of 16: see HC Deb. 7 May 1948, vol. 450 col. 1685.

116 Children Act, 1948, s. 1(3).

looking after children under statutory authority would be vested with the rights and powers of a parent,[117] but parents were not (and, it is often forgotten, are not) under any statutory obligation always to act in their child's best interests. Under the 1948 Act, for any child in the care of a local authority, "it shall be the duty of that authority to exercise their powers with respect to him so as to further his best interests, and to afford him opportunity for the proper development of his character and abilities."[118] The courts, since at least 1925, had been required to regard the welfare of the child as their first and paramount consideration, but under the 1948 Act, this became also the guiding principle in relation to local authority decision-making over children in their care. This new obligation to further the child's best interests subjected local authorities to a higher level of care than the general law imposed on parents, and it is possible to see this as the means by which the Clyde Report's aim to "compensate" the child for lack of a normal upbringing was achieved. Development of character and abilities was further enhanced by the provision that permitted local authorities to meet the expenses of education and training of young persons under 21 who had previously been in the care of the local authority[119] and, later, to visit, advise, "befriend" and exceptionally give financial assistance to anyone between the ages of 17 and 21 who had previously been in their care.[120] All these provisions amounted to a substantial increase in state responsibility: local authorities, since the 1948 Act came into force, have been obliged to seek to further the child's best interests in all the decisions they make in respect of the child.

Local authority assumption of parental rights

A not altogether welcome development in the Children Act, 1948 – and one that reflected that distrust of parents manifest in the Clyde Report – was the creation of a procedure whereby parental rights in respect of any child in the care of a local authority could be assumed by that local authority simply on its passing a resolution to this effect (the so-called "parental rights resolution"). There had been antecedents in English law, but none in Scots law, to

---

117 Children and Young Persons (Scotland) Act, 1937, s. 79(4).
118 Children Act, 1948, s. 12(1).
119 Children Act, 1948, s. 20, amended by s. 46 of the Children and Young Persons Act 1963. Section 47 thereof authorised local authorities to guarantee deeds of apprenticeship and articles of clerkship.
120 Children and Young Persons Act 1963, s. 58. See further Chapter 10 below.

public institutions taking over parental rights without court process.[121] The Poor Law Act, 1889 had allowed guardians of Poor Law unions (which did not exist in Scotland) who maintained a deserted child to "resolve that such child shall be under the control of the [Poor Law] guardians until it reaches the age, if a boy, of 16, and if a girl of 18 years". Parents could seek to over-turn this resolution by making a "complaint" to a court and showing that the child was not deserted or that "it is for the benefit of the child that it should be either permanently or temporarily under the control of such parent, or that the resolution of the guardians should be determined", and if so the court "may make an order accordingly . . . and the guardians shall cease to have the rights and powers of the parent as respects the child". This process, re-enacted as s. 52 of the (English) Poor Law Act, 1930 which transferred the power to pass such resolutions to local authorities, is clearly the model used for the parental rights resolution, which was applied to Scotland as well as England and Wales in the Children Act, 1948. Interestingly, it was not a model that had impressed the (English) Curtis Committee:

> We do not favour the assumption of parental rights by a local authority under Section 52 of the Poor law Act, 1930, by mere resolution, without an initial application to a Court. We think it objectionable (even though in practice the Section may have worked satisfactorily or at any rate without criticism) that the rights of a parent or other guardian should be extinguished by a mere resolution of a Council. Even if extra publicity and work were involved in court proceedings, we are of opinion that they would be more than counterbalanced by the value of an impartial and detached judicial inquiry at the outset directed to the paramount welfare of the child.[122]

The process, being restricted to England and Wales at that time, was not discussed by the Clyde Committee and the rejection of the Curtis objections in the debates on a UK statute meant that this process, conceptually inde-fensible in England,[123] became part of Scots law in the Children Act, 1948. For almost fifty years, therefore,[124] all local authorities in Scotland had the power to assume parental rights over children in their care simply by making a resolution to that effect. Parents could oppose this resolution, though only subsequent to its passing, and on parental opposition being intimated in

---

121 See Cretney, S. "The Children Act 1948: Lessons for Today?" (1997) 9 *Child and Family Law Quarterly* 359. Parliament was fully aware that it was imposing an English process on Scotland: HL Deb. 10 February 1948 vol. 153 cols 919 and 982; HC Deb. 7 May 1948 vol. 450 col. 1691.

122 Curtis Committee Report, para 425(ii).

123 See also the rather muted criticism by Younghusband, E.L. "The Children Act 1948" (1949) 12 *Modern Law Review* 65.

124 The process was re-enacted, with only minor modifications, in the Social Work (Scotland) Act 1968, s. 16, before being abolished by the Children (Scotland) Act 1995.

writing (within one month), the resolution (which took effect immediately) would fall 14 days after that intimation unless the local authority sought the sheriff's authority for the resolution to continue. The sheriff could allow the resolution to continue only if he were

> satisfied that the child had been, and at the time when the resolution was passed remained, abandoned by the person who made the objection or that that person is unfit to have the care of the child by reason of unsoundness of mind or mental deficiency or by reason of his habits or mode of life.[125]

If the parents consented to the resolution or did not challenge it on time, parental rights were transferred to the local authority even in the absence of any court order, and the parents lost the right to resume the care of their child under s. 1(3) (and indeed the right to claim custody).[126]

THE CHILDREN AND YOUNG PERSONS ACT 1963

Just as the Children and Young Persons (Scotland) Act, 1932 was over-shadowed five years after its passing by the Children and Young Persons (Scotland) Act 1937, so too the Children and Young Persons Act 1963 fell from our consciousness (at least in Scotland)[127] after the passing five years later of the Social Work (Scotland) Act 1968. Nevertheless, the importance of the 1963 Act must not be under-estimated. Following a recommendation of the Ingleby Committee[128] and in what was described by the Home Secretary of the time as "far and away the most important clause" in the Bill,[129] s. 1 of the Act imposed for the first time an obligation on local authorities to take preventive action: local authorities were required "to make available such advice, guidance and assistance as may promote the welfare of children by diminishing the need to receive children into and keep them in care". Commenting on the Act, it was said that

> the stronger and more progressive local authorities have, it is understood, for some time past been taking these preventive measures with the tacit support of the Home Office, but the legislation of this enlightened action represents

---

125 Children Act, 1948, s. 2(3).

126 *McGuire v McGuire* 1969 SLT (Notes) 36 (OH); *Beagley v Beagley* 1984 SC(HL) 69. For a full description of the process as it applied under the Social Work (Scotland) Act 1968, see Wilkinson, A. and Norrie, K. *The Law Relating to Parent and Child in Scotland* (W. Green, 1st edn 1993), pp. 418–444.

127 The Children and Young Persons Act 1963 contained far more sections applicable to England and Wales than to Scotland, and some of these remain in force today.

128 *Report of the Committee on Children and Young Persons* (1960) Cmnd 1191, para 50.

129 HC Deb. 15 July 1963 vol. 681 col. 292.

another of the hard-won but crucial extensions of the law into the field of social health.[130]

The aims of s. 1 were fulfilled, and the 1963 Act changed social work practice significantly. It was reported in 1968:

> This preventive aspect of child care work has developed steadily and now forms an important function of local authorities.
>
> Close co-operation in preventive work continues to develop between local authorities, the Department of Health and Social Security, and the voluntary organisations. Co-ordination between different social services provided by local authorities has also increased; the practice of housing departments informing children's departments of families liable to eviction orders is spreading . . . [M]ore gas and electricity authorities are informing children's departments when there is a danger that gas or electricity supplies will be cut off because of non-payment of bills. Children's departments have thus been given more opportunities to investigate cases . . . and to help the families concerned.[131]

INTERNATIONAL LAW BEFORE 1968

International law, when derived from an international treaty, is not directly enforceable in Scottish courts unless made part of our domestic legal system by statute;[132] customary international law,[133] on the other hand, is automatically part of our legal system.[134] In either case, the effect of international law is to impose upon the state – and the agencies through which the state acts – those obligations embodied in either customary international law or the treaties signed by the executive on behalf of the state. Customary international law has added little to the principles of child protection but, for the past century, there have been formal international agreements containing provisions relating to the protection of children. None of the international treaties with that aim was given legislative force in Scotland in the pre-1968 period, but that does not mean that they were without effect in the development of our law. They would be used as a guide to the interpretation of

---

130 Stone, O.M. "Children and Young Persons Act 1963", (1964) 27 *Modern Law Review* 61, pp. 61–62.

131 *Child Care in Scotland, 1968* (Cmnd 4069), paras 20–21.

132 As for example the Child Abduction and Custody Act 1985, which "incorporated" the Hague Child Abduction Convention, and the Human Rights Act 1998, which "incorporated" the European Convention on Human Rights.

133 Defined by Wex Legal Dictionary (Legal Information Institute) as "a general and consistent practice of states that they follow from a sense of legal obligation".

134 "A rule of customary international law is a rule of Scots law": *per* High Court of Justiciary (Lords Prosser, Kirkwood and Penrose) in *Lord Advocate's Reference No 1 of 2000*, 2001 JC 143, para 23.

statutes, because of the long-standing presumption that Parliament does not intend to legislate in a way that is incompatible with the international obligations undertaken by the United Kingdom and embodied in Treaty.[135]

Early international declarations of the rights of the child

The earliest international treaty that recognised and protected children's rights was in the field of labour law,[136] but the League of Nations adopted in 1924 a much more general *Declaration of the Rights of the Child*, which had been drafted in 1923 by the International Save the Children Union. It was brief:

1. The child must be given the means requisite for its normal development, both materially and spiritually.
2. The child that is hungry must be fed, the child that is sick must be nursed, the child that is backward must be helped, the delinquent child must be reclaimed, and the orphan and the waif must be sheltered and succoured.
3. The child must be the first to receive relief in times of distress.
4. The child must be put in a position to earn a livelihood, and must be protected against every form of exploitation.
5. The child must be brought up in the consciousness that its talents must be devoted to the service of its fellow men.

The second of these principles, by obliging states to "reclaim" the delinquent child and to shelter and succour any child who, for whatever reason, was not being looked after sufficiently by their own family, recognised the legitimacy – and necessity – of states adopting compulsory measures of care over children. Such compulsion had of course been possible in the UK since the late nineteenth century, and there is no indication from the Parliamentary debates on any of the various Children and Young Persons Acts of the 1930s that the 1924 Declaration influenced their design. Nevertheless, the aims of that legislation were to a very large extent consistent therewith.

The League of Nations was replaced at the end of the Second World War by the United Nations, and one of that organisation's earliest acts was to adopt, in 1946, the 1924 Declaration. It subsequently adopted, in 1948, the Universal Declaration of Human Rights, which included an article

---

135 *Saloman v Customs and Excise Commrs* [1967] 2 QB 116; *Attorney General v Observer Ltd* [1990] 1 AC 109; *R v Lyons* [2002] UKHL 44; *R (On the Application of SG & Ors) v Secretary of State for Work and Pensions* [2015] UKSC 16.

136 The International Labour Organisation has promulgated a number of conventions dealing with children and young persons in the workplace, starting with the Minimum Age (Industry) Convention, 1919 (No. 5), and the Night Work of Young Persons (Industry) Convention, 1919 (No. 6) both of which were ratified by the UK in 1921.

recognising that "Motherhood and childhood are entitled to special care and assistance. All children, whether born in or out of wedlock, shall enjoy the same social protection".[137] Then in 1959, the General Assembly of the United Nations adopted a much-expanded version of the 1924 Declaration, in the UN Declaration of the Rights of the Child 1959.[138] This is in the following terms:

THIS DECLARATION OF THE RIGHTS OF THE CHILD to the end that he may have a happy childhood and enjoy for his own good and for the good of society the rights and freedoms herein set forth, and calls upon parents, upon men and women as individuals, and upon voluntary organizations, local authorities and national Governments to recognize these rights and strive for their observance by legislative and other measures progressively taken in accordance with the following principles:

1. The child shall enjoy all the rights set forth in this Declaration. Every child, without any exception whatsoever, shall be entitled to these rights, without distinction or discrimination on account of race, colour, sex, language, religion, political or other opinion, national or social origin, property, birth or other status, whether of himself or of his family.

2. The child shall enjoy special protection, and shall be given opportunities and facilities, by law and by other means, to enable him to develop physically, mentally, morally, spiritually and socially in a healthy and normal manner and in conditions of freedom and dignity. In the enactment of laws for this purpose, the best interests of the child shall be the paramount consideration.

3. The child shall be entitled from his birth to a name and a nationality.

4. The child shall enjoy the benefits of social security. He shall be entitled to grow and develop in health; to this end, special care and protection shall be provided both to him and to his mother, including adequate pre-natal and post-natal care. The child shall have the right to adequate nutrition, housing, recreation and medical services.

5. The child who is physically, mentally or socially handicapped shall be given the special treatment, education and care required by his particular condition.

6. The child, for the full and harmonious development of his personality, needs love and understanding. He shall, wherever possible, grow up in the care and under the responsibility of his parents, and, in any case, in an atmosphere of affection and of moral and material security; a child of tender years shall not, save in exceptional circumstances, be separated from his mother. Society and the public authorities shall have the duty to extend particular care to children without a family and to those without adequate means of support. Payment of State and other assistance towards the maintenance of children of large families is desirable.

7. The child is entitled to receive education, which shall be free and compulsory, at least in the elementary stages. He shall be given an education which will

137 Universal Declaration of Human Rights (General Assembly Resolution 217A (III), 10 December 1948, Art. 25.

138 UN General Assembly Resolution 1386 (XIV), 20 November 1959.

promote his general culture and enable him, on a basis of equal opportunity, to develop his abilities, his individual judgement, and his sense of moral and social responsibility, and to become a useful member of society. The best interests of the child shall be the guiding principle of those responsible for his education and guidance; that responsibility lies in the first place with his parents. The child shall have full opportunity for play and recreation, which should be directed to the same purposes as education; society and the public authorities shall endeavour to promote the enjoyment of this right.

8. The child shall in all circumstances be among the first to receive protection and relief.

9. The child shall be protected against all forms of neglect, cruelty and exploitation. He shall not be the subject of traffic, in any form.

10. The child shall not be admitted to employment before an appropriate minimum age; he shall in no case be caused or permitted to engage in any occupation or employment which would prejudice his health or education, or interfere with his physical, mental or moral development.

11. The child shall be protected from practices which may foster racial, religious and any other form of discrimination. He shall be brought up in a spirit of understanding, tolerance, friendship among peoples, peace and universal brotherhood, and in full consciousness that his energy and talents should be devoted to the service of his fellow men.

It is fair to say, however, that the 1959 Declaration had little direct influence on the way cases were decided or child care agencies acted. Nor, for its first four decades of operation, did the European Convention on Human Rights (ECHR), which came into force in 1953. The ECHR was drafted with a strong focus on adults and has few provisions directly referring to the special needs of the young.[139] In any case, direct petition to the European Commission and Court of Human Rights at Strasbourg was permitted for British citizens only in 1965.[140] Thereafter, as we will see at the end of the following chapter, the influence of the ECHR became ever stronger.

---

139 The only references to the child in the ECHR are in Art. 5(1)(d) and Art. 6(1) ("juveniles" in the context of court proceedings against them) and Art. 5 of Protocol No. 7 ("the interests of the child" in private law disputes between parents).

140 HC Deb. 7 December 1965, vol. 722, col. 235, oral answer by the Prime Minister, Mr Harold Wilson.

2. The Statutory Framework after 1968

INTRODUCTION

We will see elsewhere in this book that the Social Work (Scotland) Act 1968 was less radical in its effects than is often assumed, but it would be wrong to deny that it marked a significant milestone. 1968 was a watershed year, before which our law was based on Acts from the 1930s; since then our law has developed the contemporary structures it maintains to this day. We remember the 1968 Act primarily for giving effect to the recommendation of the Kilbrandon Report, discussed immediately below, to establish a new tribunal for dealing with children who previously would be dealt with through the juvenile court. But the Act did far more than that. In particular, it restructured the way that social services, and not only for children, were delivered. The substantive legal changes since 1968 have all built upon the framework established in the Social Work (Scotland) Act 1968.

THE KILBRANDON COMMITTEE, 1961–1964

In May 1961, John Maclay, the Secretary of State for Scotland,[1] appointed a Committee whose remit was "to consider the provisions of the law of Scotland relating to the treatment of juvenile delinquents and juveniles in need of care or protection or beyond parental control". Its chairman was CJD Shaw who, as a Senator of the College of Justice (and later Lord of Appeal in Ordinary), was known by the judicial title of Lord Kilbrandon. Kilbrandon himself described the makeup of the Committee as follows:

---

1 Though a member of the National Liberal and Conservative Party, he served as Scottish Secretary in Harold Macmillan's Conservative Government (before losing his post in the "Night of the Long Knives" on 13 July 1962).

There were two judges of the sheriff court . . . One of them was a woman.[2] There were three magistrates experienced in juvenile court work, two of them being women, an expert in probation work, a professor of law,[3] an approved school manager, a clerk to a juvenile court, a very distinguished child psychiatrist,[4] a well-known secondary headmaster and a senior county chief constable.[5]

He went on to describe the broad basis upon which the Committee's conclusions were based: it was to move "the treatment authority" responsible for children from being a small and specialised part of the criminal justice system to being a "small but important part of the system of social service". In other words, the focus of the judicial process was no longer to be on children and young persons who had offended, with the same court having jurisdiction over those who needed care and protection. Instead, the focus was to be on providing care and protection to every child and young person who needed it, including those whose need was manifested by their offending behaviour. In Lord Kilbrandon's own words:

> First of all, then, we are dealing with something much wider than the problem of delinquency. We have to consider the children in need of care and protection who, through the neglect, the malice or the vice of those to whose guardianship they have been confided, are running into some kind of moral or physical danger. Then again there is the child who is described as refractory or beyond parental control. This may be a manifestation of inadequacy on the part of his parents, but is more likely a manifestation of some form of maladjustment in the child himself. In any case there is no place here for the criminal law. Lastly, although this class was not expressly mentioned in the terms of reference, there is the persistent truant.[6]

The Kilbrandon Report, *Children and Young Persons, Scotland*, was published in 1964.[7] Its continuing influence cannot be overstated, and the literature it has generated has made it, without doubt, the single most studied document in Scottish child care law and practice.[8]

---

2 The woman was the perennially interesting Dame Margaret Kidd, Scotland's first female advocate and the United Kingdom's first female KC. The other sheriff was Sheriff Allan G. Walker, co-author of Walker and Walker on *Evidence* (W. Hodge & Co, 1964).

3 This was Professor Ronald Ireland, then Professor of Scots Law at the University of Aberdeen, and subsequently sheriff at Edinburgh and later Sheriff Principal of Grampian, Highlands and Islands.

4 Professor Fred Stone, who led the development of child psychiatric services in Scotland from the 1960s to the 1980s. The last surviving member of the Kilbrandon Committee, he died in 2009.

5 "Children in Trouble" (1966) 6 *British Journal of Criminology* 112, pp. 113–114.

6 (1966) 6 *British Journal of Criminology* 112, p. 114. Though failure to attend school had been a ground of jurisdiction for the juvenile court since 1932, the Kilbrandon Committee found that this was not treated seriously, and Lord Kilbrandon here described the prevailing view of truancy as being "only a kind of amiable weakness".

7 Scottish Home and Health Department/Scottish Education Department, 1964 HMSO.

8 As representative of that literature, see A. Lockyer and F. Stone, eds, *Juvenile Justice in Scotland: Twenty-Five Years of the Welfare Approach* (T&T Clark, 1998); Hallett, C. "Ahead of the Game

THE GOVERNMENT'S RESPONSE TO KILBRANDON:
THE 1966 WHITE PAPER [9]

In 1966 the Labour Government published its response to the Kilbrandon proposals, in the form of a White Paper. Most of the recommendations contained in the Kilbrandon Report were accepted by the Government, in particular, those relating to the establishment of children's panels to take over the dispositive role of juvenile courts. However, responsibility for implementation of the decisions of children's hearings was, in the Government's view, better placed on local authority departments with responsibilities far wider than had been envisaged by the Kilbrandon Report. Instead of the "social education departments" with an exclusive focus on children favoured by Kilbrandon, the White Paper suggested that every local authority should establish a broad social work department which would be responsible for a wide range of social functions, including but by no means limited to children. The social work skills needed in dealing with children were not considered substantially different from the skills needed in dealing with adults in difficulties, and in any case, children could not be seen in isolation from their families and communities. The White Paper said this:

> In order to provide better services and to develop them economically it seems necessary that the local authority services designed to provide community care and support, whether for children, the handicapped, the mentally and physically ill or the aged, should be brought within a single organisation. As it would be undesirable to separate the administration of support in the community from that of residential care, this organisation should be responsible also for residential establishments which are intended to provide personal care, support and rehabilitation.[10]
>
> . . .
>
> The Kilbrandon Committee recommended that the child care services should be amalgamated with other services for children. They thought that the resulting new service could be the "centre and core" of a wider service in the future which might cater "for the needs of adults of all ages as well as those of the children in the family". It is just such a wider service that is now proposed, and child care seems to be an appropriate function for it to have. The present duties and

or Behind the Times? The Scottish Children's Hearing System in International Perspective" (2000) 14 *International Journal of Law, Policy and the Family* 31; Waterhouse L. and McGhee, J. "Children's Hearings in Scotland: Compulsion and Disadvantage" (2002) 24 *Journal of Social Welfare and Family Law* 279. The Report itself was republished by HMSO, with an insightful Introduction by Professor Fred Stone (one of the members of the Kilbrandon Committee), in 1995 and is available at <http://www.gov.scot/Resource/Doc/47049/0023863.pdf> (last accessed 24 June 2019).

9 *Social Work and the Community* (Cmnd 3065) 1966.
10 *Social Work and the Community* (1966), para 10.

powers of the local authority in regard to deprived children, including the duties of providing advice, guidance and assistance to children and parents who seek it, will therefore become the responsibility of the social work department. This department will undertake also the supervision and care of children who are subject to decisions of the children's panel which is to be set up.[11]

The White Paper's proposals on the implementation structures are not in fact wholly inconsistent with the Kilbrandon Report. For one thing, it was the clear view of the Kilbrandon Committee that all the various outcomes possible for children in need should be the responsibility of a single agency:

> The evidence before us has led us to the conclusion that the need for residential training facilities can be met only by a comprehensive approach by a single agency exercising statutory responsibility both for children's homes and residential schools of all kinds provided within the public field.[12]

Indeed, it could be argued that making the single agency responsible both for children and for all others in need of social assistance better reflected the Kilbrandon approach of seeing the child within the context of his or her own family and community, allowing better the development of services to tackle the family's problems rather than those of the child in isolation. And it built upon the acceptance by the Kilbrandon Report that removal of the child from his or her home and the creation of a substitute home should not be seen as the primary (and long term) solution, but should instead be regarded as an option that would be suitable only in some cases and even when used should be seen as one (temporary) part of an integrated process rather than the whole solution in itself. This was all the more reason, the White Paper concluded, to ensure that all aspects of state support for families fall within the responsibility of one agency.

> The proposal to merge the children's department into a new local authority department with much wider responsibilities will be a departure from the recommendations of the Committee on Homeless Children (the Clyde Committee) in 1946 that deprived children should be the responsibility of a separate local authority department. But there have been many developments in social work since then, and some of the most important of these have stemmed from the work done and experience gained by the children's departments set up then. At that time, the care of deprived children was seen as mainly concerned with the provision of substitute homes. In the last fifteen years increasing emphasis has been placed on efforts to prevent deprivation by securing adequate care of the child in his own home whenever that is practicable. This change of emphasis has involved child care workers to an increasing extent in work with the parents, relatives

11 Ibid. para 19.
12 Kilbrandon Report, para 187.

and communities to which the children belong, and the nature of this work has developed into the provision of guidance and support for a wide range of people who are in emotional or social difficulty. Largely from this experience has grown the recognition that this kind of support and guidance is of the essence of social work, for deprived children as for other members of the community.[13]

The single agency became the social work departments which in 1968 Scottish local authorities were required by law to establish.

THE SOCIAL WORK (SCOTLAND) ACT 1968

The Social Work (Scotland) Act 1968 that followed represented a major development point both in the law and in the practice of child protection in Scotland. The primary aims of this legislation were set out by Lord Hughes when he introduced the Bill in the House of Lords on 21 March 1968:

[The Bill] seeks to do two broad things. One is to integrate all the existing services of local authorities which are concerned with the social support of individuals and of families. This is to be achieved by bringing together the existing welfare and child-care services and by giving the new organisation powers which are more general and a little wider than those which they possess under existing legislation. The new organisation will also include the probation service.[14] The other main effect of the Bill will be to set up a new kind of body to deal, under some measure of compulsion, with children who, because they are delinquent or for some other reason, are in need of care and protection. This body is closely based upon the recommendations of the Kilbrandon Committee, although we have decided to call it a children's panel rather than a juvenile panel as the Kilbrandon Committee recommended.[15]

The establishment of the children's hearing system, based on the model proposed in the Kilbrandon Report, is considered in detail in Chapter Five of this book. The other changes to practice, and to mindset, contained in the 1968 Act, are considered in the immediately following paragraphs.

An increased focus on preventive measures

It has justly been said of the Children Act, 1948 that it:

provided a new administrative structure and a new sense of purpose in dealing with deprived children, but it had little to say about the families they came from, or about ways in which the deprivation might be prevented.[16]

---

13 *Social Work and the Community* (1966), para 57.
14 This was a matter of sustained criticism throughout the parliamentary passage, in both Houses, of the Bill: see further, Chapter 6 below.
15 HL Deb. 21 March 1968 vol. 290 col. 793.
16 Packman, J. *The Child's Generation: Child Care Policy in Britain* (2nd edn, 1981), p 52.

The first statutory preventive, as opposed to responsive, obligation on local authorities had been contained in s. 1 of the Children and Young Persons Act 1963, but it was the Social Work (Scotland) Act 1968 that made addressing the root causes of child deprivation a central feature of child care law and practice. This was consistent with the well-established approach of seeing "deprivation" in the widest possible terms – including material deprivation caused by poverty, being deprived of a safe and secure upbringing, and being deprived of the moral and social guidance necessary to prevent the child falling into antisocial or offending behaviour.

The 1948 Act's imposition of a general duty on local authorities to receive children into their care when this was necessary in the interests of their welfare[17] was re-enacted as s. 15 of the Social Work (Scotland) 1968.[18] The preventive approach first enshrined in the 1963 Act was significantly enhanced by s. 12 of the 1968 Act, which imposed an obligation on local authorities "to promote social welfare" by providing advice, assistance and facilities "on such a scale as may be appropriate for their area".[19]

> Though this was a duty on the local authority as a whole, it was interpreted, and indeed enacted, as a duty that rested heavily on the shoulders of the social work department. The social work profession has used the statute imaginatively – at times pushing it to the limit by relying on it to support families experiencing enforced poverty.[20]

Section 12(1) remains in force today.

"Community care" became a general trend, and not only with troubled children, in the 1970s. It had obvious attractions for resource-constrained local authorities, but if treated as a policy without due regard to the needs of individuals then its pursuit risked authorities being found in breach of their statutory duty to provide and maintain such residential and other establishments as may be required for their functions under the 1968 Act.[21]

17 Children Act, 1948, s. 1.
18 Receiving a child into care under s. 15 was done without sanction of any court or tribunal and was therefore often presented as "voluntary care". Section 16 of the 1968 Act, however, maintained the local authority's power to assume parental rights in respect of children in their care under s. 15; and while care became compulsory thereby it would be wrong to see lack of compulsion as the equivalent to voluntariness. The Kearney Report (*Report of the Inquiry into Child Care Policies in Fife* (HMSO 1992) pointed out at pp. 213–218 that the relationship between s. 15 and the children's hearing system was always somewhat ambiguous.
19 Social Work (Scotland) Act 1968, s. 12(1).
20 Gilmour I. and Giltinan, D. "The Changing Focus of Social Work" in A. Lockyer and F. Stone, *Juvenile Justice in Scotland: 25 Years of the Welfare Approach* (1998) at p. 153.
21 See the *Report of the Inquiry into Child Care Policies in Fife* ("The Kearney Report"), HMSO 1992, discussed below.

Also repeated from the Children Act, 1948 were (i) the provision that

> where a child is in the care of a local authority under any enactment, it shall be
> the duty of that authority to exercise their powers with respect to him so as to
> further his best interests, and to afford him opportunity for the proper develop-
> ment of his character and abilities[22]

and (ii) the provisions allowing the local authority to make educational grants
or guarantee indentures and apprenticeships.[23]

Greater involvement of the child's family

The 1960s were characterised by increasing recognition that the child's original family ought usually to be involved in his or her care even while subject
to compulsory protective measures. Rehabilitation was becoming the ultimate goal. Section 15(3) of the Social Work (Scotland) Act 1968 required
local authorities to endeavour (so long as consistent with the welfare of the
child) "to secure that the care of the child is taken over either (a) by a parent
or guardian of his, or (b) by a relative or friend of his". This showed that the
aim of child protection (where the child had been removed from his or her
home) after 1968 was no longer the creation of an ersatz family to replace
the harmful influences of the child's own family: rather the aim was now
to be to work with the child's own family to effect sustained change and
thereby improve the child's life chances and if the child had to be removed,
to enhance the chances of a speedy return home. Both the decision-making
and implementation structures put in place by the 1968 Act made that aim
the central feature of child care practice, as it has been ever since.

The focus on families also had implications for parental contact ("access",
in the pre-1995 language). We saw earlier that parental contact with children accommodated with foster carers or in a children's home was previously actively discouraged, and the 1968 Act itself said nothing about access.
However, s. 7(2) of the Health and Social Services and Social Security
Adjudications Act 1983 inserted into the 1968 Act a new s. 17E,[24] requiring
the Secretary of State to prepare, and keep under revision, "a code of practice with regard to access to children who are in care or who are subject to
a supervision requirement under section 44 [of the 1968 Act]".[25] The Code

---

22 Social Work (Scotland) Act 1968, s. 20, as originally enacted.
23 Ibid. ss. 24 and 25.
24 See also ss. 17A to 17D which dealt with parental access to children subject to parental rights
    resolutions under s. 16.
25 See the explanation of this new provision by the Under Secretary of State for Scotland (John
    MacKay) at HC Deb. 11 May 1983, vol. 42 cols 854–855.

of Practice Access to Children in Care or Under Supervision in Scotland was laid before Parliament on 16 December 1983, and it stated as a general principle:

> [A]uthorities should put a high priority on arranging and maintaining close links between the child and his parents (and other close members of his family) while he is in care. This aim should be modified only where there are clear signs that restriction of contact is necessary either to protect the child from real physical or emotional harm, or to ensure the success of a longer-term plan for the child's future which has been agreed, after the most careful consideration, as being in his best interests.[26]

The end of the boarding-out preference

Consistent with the new focus on families, and in a substantial (if unremarked at the time) shift in policy from what had gone before, the boarding-out preference and its aim of providing the child with a replacement family that had so marked the Children Act, 1948 disappeared. Instead, s. 21 of the Social Work (Scotland) Act 1968 simply listed as alternatives the ways by which the local authority could discharge its duties to provide accommodation and maintenance for children in their care: by boarding the child out with foster carers or by maintaining the child in a residential establishment, or by other unspecified means. It was then left to either the local authority or the children's hearing to determine which option better served the individual child's interests, without any official preference one way or the other. It is worth noting, however, that some local authorities adopted their own policies which had the effect of re-establishing an institutional preference for one outcome over another.[27]

Clarifying and enhancing the role of the local authority

The Second Reading Debate on the Social Work (Scotland) Bill in the House of Commons was opened by the Secretary of State for Scotland, Mr William Ross, who said this:

> As the House knows, in 1964 the [Kilbrandon] Committee recommended that juvenile courts should be replaced by new juvenile panels with continuing responsibility for the children brought before them. The Committee recommended,

---

26 *Code of Practice*, para 4.
27 See *Sheriff Kearney's Report of the Inquiry into Child Care Policies in Fife* (HMSO 1992), p. 175.

also, that all the public services for children should be formed into one social education department as part of the education authority.

In June, 1964 it was decided to accept the recommendation on juvenile panels. A little later it was accepted that the services for children should be reorganised but it was thought that the Committee's recommendation did not necessarily offer the best way of doing it.[28] This doubt about the form of reorganisation came from the second stream of opinion. There was an increasing feeling that the various welfare services—those for elderly people, for the handicapped and for the support of the sick as well as for children—should be reorganised in a more coherent way.

These services were set up and developed in a piecemeal way at different times and, apparently, in response to different needs. We can see now that they have a great deal in common, because they draw on the same groups of people for their staff, and these staffs are trained in similar ways. In addition, they are often concerned with members of the same families. I think that the same can be said of the probation service.[29]

The children's committees established under the Children Act, 1948 were therefore replaced by the new social work committees, which had far wider responsibilities than children alone. The 1968 Act required local authorities to establish social work committees to carry out their statutory functions.[30] Just as the 1948 Act had required local authorities to appoint children's officers, so the 1968 Act required them to appoint, instead, directors of social work.[31]

As well as the creation of a single agency within local authorities to perform functions that different local authority departments had previously performed, the 1968 Act also effected a significant shift of responsibility from central to local government. Local authorities had long been responsible for identifying, vetting and overseeing foster carers with whom children could be boarded-out, but prior to the 1968 Act, it was the Secretary of State who "approved" schools for children sent to them and who vetted and registered voluntary homes. That approval and registration, with consequent monitoring duties that involved inspecting and visiting homes and those accommodated therein, now largely passed to local authorities.[32]

The creation of the children's hearing system also carried with it new obligations for local authorities. Most obviously, it was on local authorities

---

28 See the White Paper *Social Work and the Community* (1966) discussed above.

29 HC Deb. 6 May 1968, vol. 764 cols 49–50.

30 Social Work (Scotland) Act 1968, s. 2 and s. 1(4). Section 1(5) also transferred to the local authority the functions of education committees in relation to what until then had been called approved schools.

31 Ibid. s. 3.

32 Ibid. ss. 61–62. Under s. 63 registration was sometimes still required with the Secretary of State.

that the duty to "give effect" to supervision requirements made by a children's hearing was imposed,[33] a duty they have had ever since.[34] This duty required local authorities to take over the existing role of the probation service in relation to young offenders. Local authorities also became crucial to the investigations carried out by the reporter, and not only because of the various sources of information under their control (within their social work and education departments). This was especially so after local authorities became obliged to cause enquiries to be made in relation to any child they considered might be in need of compulsory measures of care and to pass on the information they discovered thereby to the reporter.[35] This, together with local authorities' preventive obligations, rendered them a central player not only in the provision of services but also in the investigation of possible child abuse, neglect and offending. As well as that, their employment of reporters and their obligations to support and maintain individual children's panels gave local authorities a multi-faceted role in the quasi-judicial process that determined the outcomes for individual children. Local authorities were now involved in investigation, disposal and the provision of services to children deprived of an appropriate upbringing. It has justly been said that the 1968 Act marked the start of an important shift in the very nature of social work: "Child and family welfare has moved from being concerned with the provision of services to individuals and families to a powerful interventionist authority with the law placing limits on its actions".[36]

THE CHILDREN ACT 1975

The Social Work (Scotland) Act 1968 was significantly amended by the Children Act 1975. That Act

> started life as a modest Private Member's Bill designed to give effect to the recommendations of the Houghton committee.[37] In the course of its precarious parliamentary career, it picked up a mass of subordinate clauses, but the main aim, as its sponsor, Dr David Owen,[38] made clear, was 'to provide more and better

33 Ibid. s. 44(5).

34 Children (Scotland) Act 1995, s. 71; Children's Hearings (Scotland) Act 2011, s. 144(1).

35 Social Work (Scotland) Act 1968, s. 37(1A), as inserted by s. 83(a) of the Children Act 1975.

36 Gilmour I. and Giltinan, D. "The Changing Focus of Social Work" in A. Lockyer and F. Stone, *Juvenile Justice in Scotland: 25 years of the Welfare Approach* (1998), p. 144.

37 *Report of the Departmental Committee on the Adoption of Children* (1972, Cmnd 5107).

38 Shortly thereafter to become Foreign Secretary in James Callaghan's Labour Government. Perhaps he is best remembered for leaving the Labour Party as part of the "Gang of Four" who

chances of a secure substitute home for children whose parents cannot give them a home' . . .[39]

The duty in the 1968 Act on local authorities to exercise their powers to further the best interests of children in their care, was replaced in the 1975 Act by a somewhat stronger requirement to focus on the child's welfare:

> Where a child is in the care of a local authority under any enactment [or of a voluntary organisation, they][40] shall, in reaching any decision relating to the child, give first consideration to the need to safeguard and promote the welfare of the child throughout his childhood; and shall so far as practicable ascertain the wishes and feelings of the child regarding the decision and give due consideration to them, having regard to his age and understanding.[41]

That focus was sharpened further by the imposition of a new requirement on local authorities to review the child's case at least every six months.[42] The 1975 Act also gave title to foster parents to apply for the custody of children of whom they had had "care and possession" for stated periods, or on cause shown.[43] Making a custody order would have the effect, similar to that of an adoption order, of transferring responsibility for the child from the local authority to the foster parent.

The children's hearing system was amended by the insertion of a new s. 34A into Part III of the 1968 Act, which allowed the hearing to appoint a person for the purpose of safeguarding the interests of the child in the proceedings under Part III because of a potential conflict of interests between the child and the parent.[44] This came into effect on 30 June 1985 and the person appointed quickly became known as a "safeguarder"[45]. And a new s. 36A permitted the Secretary of State to make regulations authorising any reporter to conduct proceedings in the sheriff court irrespective of whether or not he or she was a solicitor or advocate.[46]

---

established the Social Democratic Party, and resisting thereafter its merger with the Liberal Party. After leaving Parliament in 1992 he supported, and then opposed, the UK's membership of the European Union.

39 Jackson, S. "The Children Act 1975: Parents' Rights and Children's Welfare" (1976) 3 *British Journal of Law and Society* 85.

40 These words were added by the Health and Social Services and Social Security Adjudications Act 1983, sched. 2 para 5(a).

41 Social Work (Scotland) Act 1968, s. 20, as substituted by the Children Act 1975, s. 79.

42 Social Work (Scotland) Act 1968, s. 20A, inserted by the Children Act 1975, s. 80.

43 Children Act 1975, s. 47. "Cause" had to relate to the welfare of the child: *Osborne v Matthan (No. 3)* 1998 SC 682. See also *R v R (Parent and Child: Custody)* 1994 SCLR 849.

44 Children Act 1975, s. 66.

45 See McDiarmid C. et al. *The Role of the Safeguarder in the Children's Hearing System* (Scottish Government, June 2017).

46 Children Act 1975, s. 82. See Reporters (Conduct of Proceedings before the Sheriff) (Scotland) Regulations 1975 (SI 1975 No. 2251).

The 1968 Act had re-enacted the provisions from the Children Act, 1948 allowing local authorities to pass a resolution assuming parental rights and powers in respect of a child in their care,[47] and the 1975 Act extended that power by allowing them to pass a resolution vesting in any voluntary organisation (that was either an incorporated body or a trust) parental rights and powers in respect of any child being cared for by the organisation.[48] The power of local authorities to pass such a resolution, in its own favour or in favour of a voluntary organisation, disappeared, unmourned, with the coming into force of the Children (Scotland) Act 1995.

THE LEAD-UP TO THE CHILDREN (SCOTLAND) ACT 1995

The early 1990s, by which time the children's hearing system had been in operation for two decades, saw a number of policy developments and, in particular, the publication of various official reports that suggested that the whole system for looking after children unable to be cared for by their parents required a substantial overhaul. The Skinner Report on residential care[49] and the Kearney Report on the Fife Inquiry[50] are examined elsewhere in this book.[51] These, together with Lord Clyde's Report following the Orkney Inquiry and the contemporaneous White Paper *Scotland's Children*, all contributed to the development of the Children (Scotland) Act 1995, which was presented as a fundamental overhaul of child law in Scotland, in both its private law and its public law aspects. None of these reports, however, challenged the principles underlying the children's hearing system, and nor did the 1995 Act itself.

The Orkney Inquiry (the Clyde Report 1993)[52]

In February 1991, nine children from four families, aged between 8 and 15, were removed from their homes in Orkney under place of safety

---

47 Social Work (Scotland) Act 1968, s. 16.
48 Ibid. s. 16, as substituted by Children Act 1975, s. 74. Where it subsequently appeared to be necessary in the welfare of the child that parental rights and powers should no longer be vested in a voluntary organisation the local authority had to pass a resolution vesting such rights and powers in themselves: 1968 Act, s. 16A, as inserted by the 1975 Act, s. 75.
49 *Another Kind of Home* (Scottish Office, HMSO, 1992).
50 *Report into Child Care Policies in Fife* (HC Papers 1992–93, No. 91).
51 See Chapter 8 below.
52 *Report of the Inquiry into the Removal of Children from Orkney in February 1991* (HC Papers 1992–93, No. 195).

orders granted in terms of s. 37(2) of the Social Work (Scotland) Act 1968, as a result of investigations into another family which led social workers to believe that the nine children were victims, or members of the same household as victims, of schedule 1 offences of a highly serious nature. The original investigations were subsequently shown to be flawed, but children's hearings were held to deal with these children, the procedure at which was also flawed. On applications to the sheriff for proof of grounds of referral, the sheriff dismissed the applications as incompetent and required the return of the children to their homes. On appeal by the Reporter, the Court of Session overruled the sheriff,[53] though the Court's reasoning was itself highly suspect.[54] By the time the Court of Session delivered its judgment, the Reporter had abandoned the case. Every stage in this process was followed by a highly critical press, and as a result of media pressure, a Public Inquiry into the events and the underlying law was set up. This Inquiry was chaired by Lord Clyde,[55] who identified a number of problematical issues in both law and practice. He concluded that any future reform of the law needed to take full account of the UK's obligations under both the European Convention on Human Rights and the UN Convention on the Rights of the Child.[56] His recommendations included the following:

(i)   allegations made by a child of sexual abuse should be treated seriously though not necessarily accepted as true;[57]

(ii)   agencies should share with each other the whole information relevant to their areas of responsibility;[58]

(iii) local authorities should draw up guidelines for the management of cases of child abuse consistent with national guidelines;[59]

(iv)   the legal process for removal on an emergency basis of children to places of safety should be completely restructured,[60] and placed under the control of sheriffs rather than children's hearings;[61]

(v)   reasonable access by parents and family should be allowed to children in

---

53 *Sloan v B* 1991 SLT 530.

54 Substantial flaws in the way the Inner House dealt with the case were identified by Wilkinson A. and Norrie K. *The Law Relating to Parent and Child in Scotland* (W. Green, 1st edn, 1993), pp. 464–466.

55 Then a Court of Session judge; subsequently a Lord of Appeal in Ordinary. This Lord Clyde was the son of the Lord Clyde whose 1946 *Report on Homeless Children* is discussed in Chapter 1 above.

56 Clyde Report 1993, paras 15.2–15.3.

57 Ibid. para 15.23.

58 Ibid. paras 15.30–15.31.

59 Ibid. paras 15.57–15.66.

60 Ibid. paras 16.1–16.42. See Chapter 9 below.

61 Ibid. paras 18.8–18.38.

places of safety, restrictions being imposed only when there are compelling reasons to do so;[62]

(vi) interviewing of children should be planned and executed with the greatest of care;[63]

(vii) a three year qualification course for social workers should be introduced as quickly as possible;[64]

(viii) no social work department should be without a sufficient proportion of its staff adequately skilled and knowledgeable in the identification, investigation and management of problems of child protection;[65] and

(ix) local authorities should have the same responsibilities towards children removed to places of safety as they have to other children in their care.[66]

The White Paper: *Scotland's Children: Proposals for Child Care Policy and Law*[67]

Around the same time as the Clyde Inquiry, the White Paper, *Scotland's Children: Proposals for Child Care Policy and Law* was published. This recommended that the local authority duty under s. 12 of the 1968 Act to "promote social welfare" be replaced with a duty to support the care of the child in the community, to assist in keeping families together and, most importantly, to provide advice, services and assistance for rehabilitation after a period in care.[68] While family placement was to remain the "preferred option for most young people", the changing role of foster carers was recognised:

> The role of foster carers has evolved and the demands and expectations have increased. The task is no longer simply to provide a caring and nurturing environment for a child. While this remains the primary contribution, foster parents are now often expected to observe and record a child's behaviour and note aspects of the child's development. They are regularly involved in child care reviews and children's hearings. For many carers their role is a much more explicit and contractual one of partnership, not only with the local authority but also with parents. Increasingly, they have an important role in informing the planning for children.[69]

Two important shifts in thinking are evident here: a reconceptualisation of foster care as part of a process towards the resolution of the child's

---

62 Ibid. paras 17.23–17.24.
63 Ibid. paras 17.47–17.78.
64 Clyde Report 1993, para 19.8.
65 Ibid. para 19.14.
66 Ibid. paras 17.1–17.2.
67 Scottish Office, HMSO 1993, Cm 2286.
68 *Scotland's Children*, para 3.3.
69 *Scotland's Children*, para 3.21.

difficulties, and not as a solution in itself, and a new perception of foster parents as performing a quasi-professional role.

Local Government etc. (Scotland) Act 1994

A substantial reorganisation of local government was effected by the Local Government etc. (Scotland) Act 1994. This abolished the existing regional and district councils which had been established by the Local Government (Scotland) Act 1973 shortly after the children's hearing system came into effect and replaced them with unitary authorities. The Act also removed the requirement for local authorities to have a social work committee,[70] and replaced the requirement under the 1968 Act for each local authority to appoint an officer "to be known as the director of social work" with a requirement that each local authority appoint an officer "to be known as the chief social work officer".[71] Though the 1994 Act did not list "social work" as one of the functions of the new unitary authorities,[72] most of the responsibilities that local authorities had under the 1968 Act (and other Acts) remained. The 1994 Act also removed from local authority control the reporter to the children's panel, who had been a local authority employee (though a semi-independent one) since the establishment of the children's hearing system. Building upon some of the recommendations in the Finlayson Report,[73] the 1994 Act transferred the functions of reporters and the administration of the children's hearing system from local authorities to the newly-established Scotland-wide Scottish Children's Reporter Administration.[74]

THE CHILDREN (SCOTLAND) ACT 1995

Introduction

Gilmour and Giltinan say this:

> The longevity of the [Social Work (Scotland) Act 1968] is a testament to its strength and to the forward thinking of its creators. However, by the late 1980s there was beginning to be a radical rethinking of the way the social work profes-

---

70 Local Government etc. (Scotland) Act 1994, sched. 14, repealing s. 2 of the 1968 Act.
71 Local Government etc. (Scotland) Act 1994, s. 45, inserting a new s. 3 into the 1968 Act.
72 Local Government (Scotland) Act 1973, s. 161 had listed "social work functions".
73 *Reporters to Children's Panels: Their Role, Function and Accountability* (Scottish Office, 1992).
74 Local Government etc. (Scotland) Act 1994, Part III.

sion specifically and society in general were responding to the needs of children and families. From the later 1970s child protection became a central activity of the social work profession, with a high priority being given to the initial investigation of allegations of child abuse . . . The evolution of knowledge and the growth of experience relating to child protection, combined with the changing economic environment and a greater emphasis on the rights of children arising out of Britain's commitment to the United Nations Convention on the Rights of the Child, led to the need for a redefinition of the public and private law relating to children in Scotland. The Children (Scotland) Act 1995 is not a retuning of previous law. It is a major new body of law on the care of children which has evolved from an examination of existing law and reflects the values and principles of the society it serves.[75]

The Children (Scotland) Act 1995 is in two substantive parts. Part One deals with private law matters (residence, contact and the like) and was based on the recommendations of the Scottish Law Commission in its 1992 *Report on Family Law*.[76] Part Two, based to a large extent on the recommendations in the 1993 White Paper considered above, deals mostly with public law matters such as local authority responsibilities towards children in need and the children's hearing system.

Increased participation rights for children

The Children (Scotland) Act 1995 gives a much-increased focus on listening to children, to a large extent in response to the international requirement under Art. 12 of the United Nations Convention on the Rights of the Child, briefly discussed at the end of this chapter.

Since 1968, the principle that children would have an opportunity to speak had been a central feature within the children's hearing system, and one of the major innovations in the 1995 Act was the extension of that principle to the court system.[77] Even more radically, s. 17(4) provided that local authorities in making decisions with respect to any child whom they are either looking after or proposing to look after must have regard so far as practicable to the views (if the child wishes to express them) of the child concerned, taking account of his or her age and maturity. But neither of these provisions, requiring only that the child's views be taken into account, qualifies the paramount consideration for courts, children's hearings and

---

75 Gilmour I. and Giltinan, D. "The Changing Focus of Social Work" in A. Lockyer and F. Stone, *Juvenile Justice in Scotland: 25 Years of the Welfare Approach* (T & T Clark, 1998), p. 155.

76 Scot. Law Com. No. 135 (1992).

77 Children (Scotland) Act 1995, s. 16(2).

local authorities exercising their functions under the Act: the welfare of the child.[78]

The imposition of an obligation to listen to children was intended to be more than a simple statement of principle. It was given practical effect in the 1995 Act, for one of the very few substantive "rights" granted by the Act to children was a right to attend at all stages of their own children's hearing.[79] The children's hearings rules made provision for children giving their views in person, through a representative or by audio or visual recording.[80] Nevertheless, there remained practical difficulties in ensuring every child's right to give views was effective in every case. Research commissioned by the Scottish Executive and published in 2006[81] identified a number of issues that children and young people found served to restrict their ability to participate fully, including the use of language that they did not understand, the tendency to talk over rather than directly to the children and young people, as well as unavoidable personal feelings such as fear of the unknown, embarrassment and suspicion of adult motives. The Report called for an advocacy service for children and young persons which it saw as complementary to participation rights: this recommendation found legislative endorsement in s. 122 of the Children's Hearings (Scotland) Act 2011, but that provision has not (at the time of writing) yet been brought into force.

The 1995 Act made no change to the position that legal aid, though available when grounds of referral were being established before a sheriff and when decisions of the hearing were appealed to the sheriff, was not available at children's hearings themselves. This position was held, at least in some circumstances, to be contrary to the child's rights under Art. 6 of the European Convention on Human Rights[82] and, subsequently, to be contrary to the parents' equivalent rights.[83] In the latter case, indeed, lack of any statutory provision for legally aided attendance of solicitors at hearings was described by the Inner House as "an inbuilt systemic flaw in the legal aid scheme as it applied to the children's hearing system".[84] An "interim" scheme, outwith the legal aid scheme, to provide paid legal representation

78 Ibid. ss. 16(1) and 17(1)(a).
79 Ibid. s. 45(1)(a). See now Children's Hearings (Scotland) Act 2011, s. 78(1)(a).
80 Children's Hearings (Scotland) Rules 1996 (SI 1996/3261 (S. 251)), r. 15(4).
81 Creegan, C., Henderson G. and King C. *Big Words and Big Tables: Children and Young People's Experience of Advocacy Services and Participation in the Children's Hearing System*, Scottish Executive 2006.
82 *S v Miller* 2001 SLT 531 and 1304.
83 *K v Authority Reporter* 2009 SLT 1019.
84 Ibid. para 56.

for children at hearings was established in 2002,[85] and this was extended in 2009 to paid legal representation for relevant persons.[86] The interim scheme was repealed and replaced by Part 19 of the Children's Hearings (Scotland) Act 2011 and the Children's Legal Assistance (Scotland) Regulations 2013,[87] which amend the Legal Aid (Scotland) Act 1986 so that the child and relevant person (and some others) may in specified circumstances access legal aid funds to pay for a solicitor to attend hearings with them.[88]

The new concept of the "looked after child"

Children who were being accommodated either by voluntary organisations in charity-run children's homes or by local authorities in any residential setting were, prior to the Children (Scotland) Act 1995, commonly referred to as "children in care". The language of "care" reflected the words of the legislation from the earliest period when children were committed to the care of fit persons, and it continued to be used in the Social Work (Scotland) Act 1968 where, for example, local authorities were obliged to "receive the child into their care" in certain circumstances.[89] But there was no universal definition of "children in care", for the phrase was not a term of art, nor any statement of the general duties that were owed to such children. The duties were severally to be found in the rules and regulations governing the particular type of care to which the child was made subject. The 1995 Act changed the language from "child in care" to "looked after child" and by providing a universal definition[90] made that designation a term of art. In addition, the Act laid down general duties on local authorities to all children they look after, under whatever provision, which duties are enhanced, rather than determined, by the particular rules and regulations governing their placement.[91] Of particular note is s. 17(1)(c) which obliges local authorities to take steps to promote, on a regular basis, personal relations and direct contact between the child and any person with parental responsibilities and parental rights.[92] Contact, which before 1968 had been actively discouraged

---

85 Children's Hearings (Legal Representation) (Scotland) Rules 2002 (SSI 2002/63).

86 Children's Hearings (Legal Representation) (Scotland) Amendment Rules 2009 (SSI 2009/211).

87 SSI 2013/200.

88 For details, see Norrie, K. *Children's Hearings in Scotland* (W. Green, 3rd edn, 2013), pp. 8–12.

89 Social Work (Scotland) Act 1968, s. 15.

90 Children (Scotland) Act 1995, s. 17(6).

91 For details of these duties, see Wilkinson A. and Norrie K. *The Law Relating to Parent and Child in Scotland* (W. Green, 3rd edn 2013), paras 15.07–15.17.

92 Children (Scotland) Act 1995, s. 17(1) and (2).

and since 1983 was encouraged in terms of a Code of Practice, now became a statutory component of the care provided by local authorities to children they look after.

Duties of local authorities

Section 19 of the Children (Scotland) Act 1995 requires local authorities to prepare and publish, and keep under review, their plans for the provision of relevant services for or in respect of children in their area.[93] The 1995 Act also imposed a new obligation on local authorities to co-operate with each other: whenever one local authority considers that another local authority could help it carry out its functions under the Act, it can request that help, which then has to be provided unless the provision of help would unduly prejudice the other local authority's own functions.[94]

Additional to the still extant duty of local authorities under s. 12 of the Social Work (Scotland) Act 1968 to promote social welfare by providing assistance, the 1995 Act imposes duties on local authorities both to safeguard and promote the welfare of children in their area who are in need and also (so far as consistent with that duty) to promote the upbringing of such children by their families.[95] The Act also obliges local authorities to provide accommodation on a non-compulsory basis to any child in their area who requires it because no-one else can do so: this might include accommodation with foster carers, with relatives, or in a residential establishment.[96] Overall, the focus of the 1995 Act is even more on helping children within their own families than it was under the 1968 Act. However, the fact that the duty to do so exists only so far as is consistent with the overarching duty to safeguard and promote the welfare of children recognises that sometimes a child's welfare will require its removal from their family.

New orders

The Children (Scotland) Act 1995 created various new orders that could be made for the protection of children.

The child protection order[97] replaced (more or less) the old "place of

---

93 Ibid. s. 19(1) and (3).
94 Ibid. s. 21.
95 Ibid. s. 22.
96 Ibid. s. 25.
97 Ibid. ss. 57–60; thereafter Children's Hearings (Scotland) Act 2011, ss. 37–54.

safety order" and is designed to address the concerns identified by Lord Clyde in his 1993 Report in respect of that old order. The child protection order, and its antecedents, is considered more fully later in this book.[98]

The "parental responsibilities order", also introduced by the 1995 Act,[99] replaced the old parental rights resolutions under which a local authority could assume to itself, without court process, the parental rights of a parent whose child was in local authority care. The new order required to be made by a sheriff and had the effect of transferring to the local authority all parental responsibilities and parental rights except the right to agree (or decline to agree) to the making of an adoption order. Parental agreement was required, though it could be dispensed with on the same grounds as parental agreement to adoption could be dispensed with. The provisions relating to parental responsibilities orders were repealed by the Adoption and Children (Scotland) Act 2007,[100] which created (partly in place of that order) the new "permanence order", briefly discussed elsewhere in this book.[101]

The Children (Scotland) Act 1995 also created the child assessment order, which authorises an assessment to be made of a child's health, development or of the way in which he or she has been treated, even in the absence of parental consent to that assessment, and if necessary the removal of the child to the place where the assessment is to be carried out;[102] and the exclusion order,[103] which allows a sheriff on the application of a local authority to make an order to exclude a suspected abuser from the family home as an alternative to removing the child from that home. The latter is rarely used.

AN ALTERED LANDSCAPE AFTER THE 1995 ACT

And yet: for all the important changes that the Children (Scotland) Act 1995 made, it is difficult to regard its public law provisions as representing a significant change of direction in the way that the Children Act, 1908, the Children and Young Persons (Scotland) Act, 1932, the Children Act, 1948 and the Social Work (Scotland) Act 1968 were.[104] Though it ensured a greater focus on due process, the 1995 Act is, with hindsight, better seen

98 See Chapter 9 below.
99 Children (Scotland) Act 1995, ss. 86–89.
100 Adoption and Children (Scotland) Act 2007, sched. 3.
101 See Chapter 12 below.
102 Children (Scotland) Act 1995, s. 55; thereafter Children's Hearings (Scotland) Act 2011, ss. 35–36.
103 Children (Scotland) Act 1995, ss. 76–80.
104 Part I of the Children (Scotland) Act 1995, dealing with private law, is much more radical.

as marking the end of an era in which traditional understandings of family life held sway within an established legal framework rather than as a radical restructuring of the law. There is something of a paradox here, for the 1995 Act was passed at a time when the ideological underpinnings of child protection were changing. Up until then, both society and the law reflected a paternalistic response to child neglect and abuse. The welfare state that emerged in the late 1940s was built upon an understanding that the state could provide a better environment for the upbringing of children than neglectful or abusive parents, and its reliance for delivery on voluntary organisations did not diminish that belief. Social work became increasingly professionalised in the second half of the twentieth century, and both adoption and child care processes came to view inadequate parents as the sources of difficulty, rather than as struggling families who required help. The concept of child abuse gained a far higher profile and with it an increased willingness to apportion blame. Child neglect might often have been seen as a result of poverty and lack of education, but child abuse could find no such excuses. By the early 1990s, however, faith in the child care system was seriously shaken by a series of cases, including the Orkney case considered above and the Ayrshire case which in many respects was far worse.[105] In addition, the concept of children's rights had come to be accepted by the UK's ratification of the United Nations Convention on the Rights of the Child and paternalism came increasingly to be seen as an unsatisfactory underpinning of child protection.

Yet the 1995 Act made little attempt to reflect any new ideology: though lip-service was paid to children's rights the Act itself conferred only one right on the child – the right to attend his or her own children's hearing.[106] Social work practice had changed, the work of voluntary organisations had moved away from the provision of large institutions to house needy children to far more preventive activities including but not limited to working with troubled children at home. This happened irrespective of the legal framework. The real change at the end of the twentieth century came not in how the underlying child protection legislation was structured but from social changes, together with constitutional changes that affected family life but did not have that area of law primarily in view.

---

105 The so-called Ayrshire case culminated in the decision of the Inner House in *L, Petitioners* 1993 SLT 1310 and 1342. While in the Orkney case most actors up to and including the Inner House made errors in law, in *L, Petitioners* the process operated exactly as it was designed to act and no single actor could be criticised for the decisions they took – yet children were seriously harmed at the hands of the state which acted when no action was needed.

106 Children (Scotland) Act 1995, s. 45(1)(a).

The social change that was occurring around the time of the coming into force of the 1995 Act was that the very concept of "family" itself was undergoing profound reimagining; not unconnected, the constitutional background against which child protection operates shifted and became significantly more rights-based.

The changing face of "family"

The 1993 White Paper *Scotland's Children: Proposals for Child Care Policy and Law*[107] had acknowledged that family life was changing, and had, in fact, come to be led in Scotland in a great diversity of forms:

> The more traditional images of the family are being challenged by the very fact that many of our children now experience very diverse forms of family life as their parents cohabit, separate, marry and remarry. Increasingly, children are being asked to adjust to living in a family with one parent absent, usually the father, or to living with a step parent, again usually a stepfather. Despite these changes families remain and will remain the foundation of care for children and the development of young people. In this changing world families will need support in ensuring a consistently high quality of care.

However, the Children (Scotland) Act 1995 (passed at the tail-end of a long period of Conservative Government) did little to reflect that diversity and, as originally passed, continued to make distinctions between families based around marriage on the one hand, and non-marital families on the other;[108] the question did not even arise of giving any recognition to families based around same-sex couples. In the first decade of the twenty-first century, legislation transformed the law's understanding of family, as the law increasingly eschewed any attempt at providing a model for family life as it should be led: family law today aims to reflect how family life actually is led, with no political or moral preferences given to one form of "family" over another. So the Civil Partnership Act 2004 allowed same-sex couples to register their relationship and acquire thereby virtually all the rights and responsibilities open to opposite-sex couples through the institution of marriage (including the establishment of "step" relationships). The Family Law (Scotland) Act 2006 finally abolished the status of "illegitimacy"[109] and at last allowed fathers to have full parental responsibilities and parental rights from

---

107 Scottish Office, HMSO 1993, Cm 2286, para 1.10.
108 So for example the unmarried father was excluded from the definition of "relevant person" for the purposes of participation in children's hearings: s. 93(2)(b).
109 Family Law (Scotland) Act 2006, s. 21.

the birth of their children even when not married to the mother, provided new remedies to unmarried couples, and extended existing cohabitation rules to same-sex cohabiting couples. The Adoption and Children (Scotland) Act 2007 allowed unmarried couples and same-sex couples to make joint applications for adoption; the Human Fertilisation and Embryology Act 2008 extended parental orders after surrogacy to unmarried couples and same-sex couples; and the Looked After Children (Scotland) Regulations 2009 belatedly removed the prohibition on placing children for fostering with anyone other than a man and a woman acting together or a man or a woman acting alone. A little later, of course, the Marriage and Civil Partnership (Scotland) Act 2014 rendered marriage itself a gender-neutral institution.

Constitutional changes

The second reason why the Children (Scotland) Act 1995 can be seen as belonging to an earlier era is that it was passed in the twilight of a constitutional settlement that had seemed at the time immutable. Yet within three years of its passing – and only one year after the majority of Part II was brought into force – there occurred two transformative constitutional developments that rendered the background structures against which the law must operate very different from what had gone before. First, the Scotland Act 1998 (re-)established the Scottish Parliament and virtually all the matters considered in this book were brought within the legislative competence of that devolved legislature. Secondly, the Human Rights Act 1998 incorporated into Scottish domestic law the European Convention on Human Rights (ECHR), discussed further at the end of this chapter, since when both the interpretation and the application of the law of child protection (and much else) has required to be consistent with that Convention. The concepts of children's rights, proportionality of interference and participation in process, both in domestic and international law, have thereby acquired a far higher profile in legal disputes.

THE ANTISOCIAL BEHAVIOUR LEGISLATION

The early 2000s saw at least one attempt to give the state more punitive options when dealing with children who exhibit disruptive behaviour. That attempt sat very uneasily with the established framework since it tended to focus on behaviour and blame rather than circumstance and need, but in practice, its effect has been very limited and it has not proved to be a useful addition to the state's armoury in dealing with children. The Antisocial Behaviour etc. (Scotland) Act 2004 aimed to give local authorities more power to tackle antisocial behaviour, that is to say, sub-criminal or petty criminal behaviour that nevertheless causes alarm or distress to others, possibly out of proportion to the behaviour itself. Though antisocial behaviour orders had been introduced by the Crime and Disorder Act 1998, it was not until the 2004 Act that it was possible to make such an order in respect of a person under the age of 16 years (and over 12). The making of an antisocial behaviour order, at the behest of the local authority, has potential implications for the children's hearing, for much the same behaviour can be used to found either an application to the children's hearing for a compulsory supervision order or an application to the sheriff for an antisocial behaviour order. The 2004 Act also created the so-called "parenting order" which can be made in respect of any parent who fails to take reasonable steps to prevent their child from committing offences or being involved in antisocial behaviour.[110] And a new ground of referral to the children's hearing, based on antisocial behaviour, was created. Cleland, writing shortly after its enactment, strongly criticised this legislation on the ground that it (i) shifted decision-making over children with behavioural issues from the hearing to the court, (ii) downplayed the central focus on the welfare of children and (iii) encouraged a more punitive approach by hearings in determining the terms and conditions to be attached to a compulsory supervision order.[111] That punitive approach (and perhaps policy intendment) was revealed by the introduction of a new power by which the hearing could add a "movement restriction condition" to its order,[112] which could be enforced by "tagging" – that is to say, by requiring the child to wear an electronic tracking device.

In fact, the 2004 Act (at least in its application to children between the ages of 12 and 16)[113] has proved to be something of a dead letter. Local authorities, who have the choice of process to instigate in relation to children whose behaviour they have concerns over, have generally chosen to follow the familiar and long-established route of bringing matters to the attention of the reporter rather than going to the sheriff under the 2004 Act for an antisocial behaviour order. Movement restriction conditions, re-enacted

---

110 Antisocial Behaviour etc. (Scotland) Act 2004, s. 13.
111 Cleland, A. "The Antisocial Behaviour etc. (Scotland) Act 2004: Exposing the Punitive Fault Line Below the Children's Hearing System" (2005) 9 *Edinburgh Law Review* 439.
112 Antisocial Behaviour etc. (Scotland) Act 2004, s. 135.
113 Most antisocial behaviour orders in Scotland are made with the aim of dealing with unneighbourly behaviour of local authority or other social housing tenants.

in s. 83(2)(d) of the Children's Hearings (Scotland) Act 2011,[114] are only rarely imposed and, though occasionally mentioned in decided cases, have not been subject to any judicial discussion. Parenting orders do not appear in the law reports at all. The new ground of referral based on a child's antisocial behaviour was circular and ultimately meaningless and did not survive the Children's Hearings (Scotland) Act 2011.[115] The welfare philosophy that has long underpinned the child protection system has proved sufficiently robust that any outcome that could be perceived as punitive has not been embraced by any of the actors within the system, even while it remains technically available.

A NEW REGULATORY FRAMEWORK

Much more successful than the failed attempt to render children's sub-criminal behaviour into a justification for punitive state intervention was the shift in focus around the same time (the first decade of the twenty-first century) towards regulating who had access to children. From its earliest days in the late nineteenth century, the statute law on child protection has primarily been a reaction to that most unhappy of truths, that children are most vulnerable where they ought to be safest, that is to say within the care of their own families. Since the turn of the millennium, however, a great deal of legislative activity has been focused on ensuring children's safety from persons outwith their family circle but with whom they come into contact. That this was sorely needed has been amply shown by the evidence presented to the Scottish Child Abuse Inquiry, established in 2016 to look at claims of historic child abuse within care settings, and sitting still as this book goes to press. That evidence has brought to the public attention the disheartening extent to which children in the care of the state are vulnerable to mistreatment, abuse, emotional deprivation and sexual exploitation.

Statutory changes in the early years of the twenty-first century sought to reduce the risk to children from persons they come into contact with on a professional or quasi-professional basis, and not only in a child protection context, by creating mechanisms to identify persons who ought not to be allowed to work with children due to their previous behaviour. Around the same time, new institutions independent of local authorities were cre-

---

114 And see Children's Hearings (Scotland) Act 2011 (Movement Restriction Conditions) Regulations 2013 (SSI 2013/210).
115 See below at chapter five.

ated to conduct the registration and inspection of services for vulnerable children.

Limitations on who may work with children

The Rehabilitation of Offenders Act 1974 allowed individuals who have been convicted of offences not to disclose the existence of their convictions after the passing of certain periods of time. The policy behind this has always been to allow people to "move on" from their offending behaviour and to avoid having events from the past destroy their chances of living a (law-abiding) life with the same opportunities as anyone else. This is especially important when the offence was committed by a young and immature individual whose employment chances well into adulthood might be blighted by youthful bad judgments. But that important policy counteracts another policy, of ensuring that those who continue to pose a risk to vulnerable groups are identified and prohibited from working in any environment in which the risk might eventuate. The Police Act 1997 established a system of official certification of the existence (or non-existence) of offences, as employers in particularly sensitive fields began to request potential employees for proof of lack of previous convictions.

That system was significantly enhanced by the Protection of Children (Scotland) Act 2003, and then the Protection of Vulnerable Groups (Scotland) Act 2007, which required the Scottish Ministers to establish and maintain a list of individuals considered unsuitable to work with children (and, after 2007, with all vulnerable persons) and made it a criminal offence (i) for any person who knew he or she was on this list to work in a "child care position" (then, after 2007, "regulated work") and (ii) for any organisation to offer such a position to such an individual. Organisations involved with vulnerable groups (including children) now require potential employees or volunteer workers to provide a "Disclosure Certificate", first created by the Police Act 1997, and now a "PVG[116] disclosure", which is issued by Disclosure Scotland, an executive agency of the Scottish Government, which will disclose whether the individual is on the "unsuitable" list, and reveal any criminal convictions on the individual's record. Inclusion in the list of persons unsuitable to work with either children or vulnerable adults means that all "regulated work"[117] is closed to them, and that inclusion is

---

116 "Protecting vulnerable groups".
117 As defined in sched. 2 to the 2007 Act.

revealed with all higher-level disclosures.[118] The focus of this legislation is on identifying and protecting against risks, and it pays less heed to the objective behind the Rehabilitation of Offenders Act 1974 of allowing individuals to escape from their past.

The tension between these two policy objectives has led to a number of challenges being made to the PVG scheme, on the ground that it does not allow for any assessment to be made of the suitability of the individual in respect of the type of work that the individual wishes to undertake and is based solely on the existence of the offence: that it may operate, in other words, disproportionately to its legitimate aims. Judges have been singularly unpersuaded that a system cannot be developed that eschews a blanket ban approach in favour of one that allows for some degree of judgment and discretion to be exercised where no real risk of harm to vulnerable groups exists. In 2014 the Supreme Court[119] held the equivalent disclosure scheme in England and Wales to be incompatible with Art. 8 of the European Convention on Human Rights because it failed to draw any distinction on the basis of the nature of the offences to be disclosed, the disposal of the case and the time elapsed between when the offence took place and the employment was sought.[120] The Scottish Government, accepting that the Scottish system was vulnerable to challenge on the same grounds, made the Police Act 1997 and the Protection of Vulnerable Groups (Scotland) Act 2007 Remedial (No. 2) Order 2015[121] under which certain spent convictions need not be disclosed but which gave no right to challenge the inclusion of convictions that continued to require disclosure. The Outer House subsequently held that even the amended disclosure scheme, which required disclosure of an offence that had founded a reference to a children's hearing, was not a reasonable balance of competing interests since it contained no safeguards to allow the proportionality of the interference in Art. 8 to be evaluated objectively and fairly.[122] In one earlier case in the sheriff court, the sheriff simply removed a person from the list since her conviction for dishonesty created no risk to her acting as a kinship carer.[123] A further remedial order

---

118 The PVG Scheme allows for four levels of disclosure, depending on the purpose for which disclosure is required.

119 *R (On the Application of T) v Chief Constable of Greater Manchester* [2014] UKSC 35. See also *R (On the Application of P) v Secretary of State for the Home Department* [2019] UKSC 3.

120 See especially Lord Reed, para 119.

121 SSI 2015/423.

122 *P v Scottish Ministers* [2017] CSOH 33.

123 *G v The Scottish Ministers* 2015 GWD 36–577.

then followed[124] which gave the sheriff authority to remove certain offences from a person's disclosure certificate and PGV scheme record and the result is that spent convictions for serious offences will require to be disclosed unless a sheriff orders otherwise.

In June 2020 a new Act, the Disclosure (Scotland) Act 2020, was passed by the Scottish Parliament to restructure the PVG scheme, the most significant provision being one that will end the automatic disclosure of offences committed by persons under 17. Instead, Disclosure Scotland will assess whether convictions ought to be disclosed, their decision being subject to review, with an appeal to the sheriff. It aims, in other words, to strike a better balance between the two policies mentioned above than the current law achieves. 2019 also saw the passing of the Age of Criminal Responsibility (Scotland) Act 2019, which raised the age to 12, with the consequence that behaviour by persons under that age is never recorded as a criminal matter and so will not need to be disclosed; the new rules are retrospective.[125]

New oversight institutions

By the end of the twentieth century, it had become clear that the oversight of social care, in the sense of monitoring its safety and effectiveness, and its adherence to rules and regulations, was fragmented and inconsistent. Some but not all forms of social care required to be registered, with either the local authority or the Secretary of State (after Devolution in 1999, with the Scottish Ministers); the duty of inspection would often lie with the local authority, but sometimes it lay with health boards or the Social Work Services Inspectorate – and sometimes was not required at all. There was clear potential for conflict of interest, with local authorities having duties both to provide services and at the same time to monitor how well they were run, often in comparison (and indeed in financial competition) with similar services provided by voluntary organisations.

The Regulation of Care (Scotland) Act 2001 restructured the whole system of registration and inspection of all care services in Scotland, by creating the Scottish Commission for the Regulation of Care[126] ("the Care Commission"). That body was charged with registering and inspecting

---

124 The Police Act 1997 and Protection of Vulnerable Groups (Scotland) Act 2007 Remedial Order 2018 (SSI 2018/52).

125 Age of Criminal Responsibility (Scotland) Act 2019, ss. 4–27.

126 Regulation of Care (Scotland) Act 2001, s. 1 and sched. 1.

all care services, including residential child care and fostering, offender accommodation services, care and welfare in boarding schools, as well as non-NHS health care services.[127] Registration would be granted only if the care service were provided "in a manner which promotes and respects the independence of service users and, so far as it is practicable to do so, affords them choice in the way in which the service is provided to them."[128] Regulations specified persons who were not fit to provide, manage or be employed in a care service[129] and made provision as to fitness of premises[130] and the equipment and facilities to be provided in a care home service.[131] The Care Commission could issue improvement notices to any care service provider,[132] and registration could be cancelled if the improvements were not made.[133] In addition, the Care Commission could make summary application to the sheriff for an order immediately cancelling registration or imposing or varying conditions for registration if it appeared that there was a serious risk to some other person's life, health or wellbeing.[134]

Inspection of care services also rested with the Care Commission,[135] which had the power to require the provision of information and to enter and inspect premises.[136] Residential services required to be inspected at least twice a year, at least one of these being without any prior notification,[137] and fostering services were to be inspected at least once a year.[138] It was made an offence to obstruct inspection.[139]

The Care Commission was replaced in the Public Services Reform (Scotland) Act 2010 by Social Care and Social Work Improvement Scotland (SCSWIS), commonly known as "the Care Inspectorate".[140] The range of care services subject to regulation by the Care Inspectorate includes care home services; school care accommodation in a place in or outwith a public,

127 Ibid. s. 2.
128 Regulation of Care (Requirements as to Care Services) (Scotland) Regulations 2002 (SSI 2002/114), reg. 2.
129 SSI 2002/114, regs 6, 7 and 9.
130 Ibid. reg. 10.
131 Ibid. reg. 12.
132 Regulation of Care (Scotland) Act 2001, s. 10.
133 Ibid. s. 12.
134 Ibid. s. 18.
135 Ibid. ss. 25–27.
136 Ibid. s. 25(2).
137 Ibid. s. 25(3).
138 Ibid. s. 25(5).
139 Ibid. s. 25(13).
140 Public Services Reform (Scotland) Act 2010, s. 44.

independent or grant-aided school; secure accommodation; offender accommodation services; and fostering services.[141]

All providers of care services are today required to register with the Care Inspectorate,[142] and registration can be refused, granted, or granted subject to conditions.[143] Regulations specify persons who are deemed unfit to make an application for registration and also specify persons who are not fit to provide, manage or be employed in a care service.[144] In addition, no person listed in the children's list kept under the Protection of Vulnerable Groups (Scotland) Act 2007 may provide, manage or be employed in a care service for children.[145] Once a service has been registered, the Care Inspectorate may serve an improvement notice on a care service[146] and registration may be cancelled if after an improvement notice has been issued the relevant requirements are still not being met.[147]

The Care Inspectorate may inspect[148] any social service (which includes care services) in order to review and evaluate the effectiveness of the provision of the services being inspected, to encourage improvement, to investigate any cause for concern, and to give consideration to the need for an improvement notice.[149]

THE CHILDREN'S HEARINGS (SCOTLAND) ACT 2011

The children's hearings provisions in the Children (Scotland) Act 1995, together with those relating to child assessment orders and child protection orders, were replaced by the Children's Hearings (Scotland) Act 2011. This Act did not effect any fundamental change, but it was designed to strengthen the existing system and make it more consistent with both the European Convention on Human Rights and the United Nations Convention on the

---

141 Ibid. s. 47 and sched. 12.
142 Ibid. s. 59.
143 Ibid. s. 60.
144 Social Care and Social Work Improvement Scotland (Registration) Regulations 2011 (SSI 2011/28), reg. 3; Social Care and Social Work Improvement Scotland (Requirements for Care Services) Regulations 2011 (SSI 2011/210), regs 6, 7 and 9.
145 SSI 2011/210, reg. 13(1).
146 Public Services Reform (Scotland) Act 2010, s. 62.
147 Ibid. s. 64. Special provision is made for local authorities in relation to services which they are obliged under statute to provide and for which registration cannot therefore be cancelled: s. 63 requires Scottish Ministers to be notified of any improvement notice.
148 In accordance with the rules in the Public Services Reform (Social Services Inspection) (Scotland) Regulations 2011 (SSI 2011/185).
149 Public Services Reform (Scotland) Act 2010, s. 53.

Rights of the Child. New grounds of appeal, in particular against the implementation of secure accommodation authorisations, were created.[150] More (if not particularly effective) protection was given to the right of contact[151] and new interim orders were created.[152] A new process was created to allow anyone who did not fall within the definition of "relevant person" to apply to be deemed to be a relevant person and acquire thereby full participation rights in the children's hearing process.[153] Greater emphasis was placed on the support offered to both the child and his or her family to participate effectively in the decision-making process, in particular (but not only) by making legal aid available at some children's hearings. The most important structural change in the 2011 Act was the establishment of a new national body, Children's Hearings Scotland, a non-departmental public body charged with arranging and supporting the holding of children's hearings, and bearing responsibility in relation to the appointment, training and support of panel members.[154] Its chief executive is a new officer, the National Convener. The establishment of Children's Hearings Scotland acts to some extent as a counter-weight to the Scottish Children's Reporter Administration which is now completely separate from the organisational and dispositive role of the hearing.

THE CHILDREN AND YOUNG PEOPLE (SCOTLAND) ACT 2014

Giving effect to "GIRFEC"

The most far-reaching development in Scottish child protection law and practice in the twenty-first century has been the recognition of the merits of early state intervention in family life as a means of avoiding, or at least reducing the risks of, compulsory intervention later on. In 2004 the Scottish Executive published "Getting it Right for Every Child: A Report on the Responses to the Consultation on the Review of the Children's Hearing System", which identified the need to intervene earlier as one of the strategies that would help improve outcomes, and this led to *Getting it Right for Every Child*, or "GIRFEC", being developed as a framework of guidance and legislation informing all agencies working with vulnerable children and their families.

150 Children's Hearings (Scotland) Act 2011, s. 162.
151 Ibid. s. 126.
152 Ibid. s. 86.
153 Ibid. ss. 79–81.
154 Ibid. ss. 1–13.

The Children and Young People (Scotland) Act 2014 sought to give statutory effect to the GIRFEC approach of early intervention – not to be confused with compulsory intervention – by requiring local authorities to provide services such as family group decision-making services and support services in relation to parenting to children and their families in their area if these services would reduce the risk of the children becoming looked after children.[155] Insofar as referrals to the children's hearing is indicative of the need for compulsory measures to be implemented, a reduction of referrals since the mid-2000s suggests that the early intervention strategy is bearing fruit.[156]

The genesis of the 2014 Act may be traced to a Scottish Government consultation published in 2012.[157] Lady Hale, Lord Reed and Lord Hodge summarised the policy behind this Consultation Paper in a case that challenged part of the Act:[158]

> In general terms, two ideas underlay many of the proposals. The first was a shift away from intervention by public authorities after a risk to children's and young people's welfare had been identified, to an emphasis on early intervention to promote their wellbeing, understood as including all the factors that could affect their development. The second was a shift away from a legal structure under which the duties of statutory bodies to cooperate with one another (under, for example, section 13 of the National Health Service (Scotland) Act 1978 (cap. 29) and section 21 of the Children (Scotland) Act 1995 (cap. 36)) were linked to the performance of their individual functions, to ensuring that they work collaboratively and share relevant information so that "all relevant public services can support the whole wellbeing of children and young people" (para 73). In that regard, the consultation paper stated that it was "essential that information is shared not only in response to a crisis or serious occurrence but, in many cases, information should be shared about relevant changes in a child's and young person's life". There was, however, "no commonly agreed process for routine information sharing about concerns about wellbeing" (para 110). The establishment of a new professional role, that of named person, was proposed in order to address those concerns (para 111).

The "named person" scheme will be considered shortly, but a summary of the main provisions of the Children and Young People (Scotland)

---

155 Children and Young People (Scotland) Act 2014, s. 68; Children and Young People (Scotland) Act 2014 (Relevant Services in Relation to Children at Risk of Becoming Looked After etc.) (Scotland) Order 2016 (SSI 2016/44), Art. 2.

156 The statistics published by SCRA on their website show that in the year to 31 March 2019 there were 12,869 children and young people referred to them; in the year to 31 March 2013 (the first year these statistics were published on-line) the number was 22,561. The number of referrals has been decreasing annually for over a decade now ("Fact Sheet No. 2", August 2018, SCRA).

157 *A Scotland for Children: A Consultation on the Children and Young People Bill* (Scottish Government, 2012).

158 *Christian Institute v Lord Advocate* [2016] UKSC 51, para 1.

Act 2014 was given by the Inner House, earlier in the same case,[159] as follows:

> Parts 1 to 5 of the 2014 Act form a comprehensive scheme intended to pro-
> mote and safeguard the rights and well-being of children and young people.
> Part 1 requires the respondents to consider and, if appropriate, to take steps
> to secure better or further implementation ("effect") of the requirements of
> the UN Convention on the Rights of the Child (1990), reporting thereon to the
> Scottish Parliament triennially. Part 2 makes provision for the investigation, at
> the instance of the Commissioner for Children and Young People, of the extent
> to which any persons providing services for children and young people, excluding
> parents or guardians ("service providers": Commissioner for Children and Young
> People (Scotland) Act 2003 (asp 17), sec 16), have regard to the rights, interests
> and views of children and young people when making decisions, or taking action,
> that affect them. It remains the Commissioner's general function "to promote
> and safeguard the rights of children and young people." (2003 Act, sec 4.)
>   Part 3 provides for the preparation of three year "children's services plans" for
> local authority areas designed to secure, *inter alia*, that children's services are
> provided in a way which: best safeguards, supports and promotes the well-being
> of children; ensures that any action to meet their needs is taken at the earliest
> appropriate time; is most integrated from the point of view of recipients; and
> constitutes the best use of available resources. Part 4 requires service providers to
> make available, in relation to each child or young person, an identified individual
> ("named person"), whose general function is to promote, support or safeguard
> the well-being of the child or young person, on behalf of the service provider
> concerned. Part 5 provides for the preparation of a "child's plan" in respect of
> any child whose well-being is being, or is at risk of being, adversely affected by
> any matter and requires a targeted intervention beyond the services provided to
> children generally.
>   The "wellbeing" of the child or young person is to be assessed (2014 Act,
> sec 96) by reference to the extent to which he or she is or would be "Safe,
> Healthy, Achieving, Nurtured, Active, Respected, Responsible, and Included."
> (Described by the acronym "SHANARRI".) The [Scottish Ministers] must issue
> guidance on how the listed elements are to be used to assess well-being. The
> general principle, that functions should be exercised by local authorities in a way
> which is designed to safeguard, support and promote the well-being of children
> and young people, is extended (2014 Act, sec 95) to functions provided by them
> in terms of the Children (Scotland) Act 1995 (cap 36).

The "named person" scheme in the 2014 Act

By far the most controversial aspect of the 2014 Act was the named person
service. In summary, this sought to "make available" to all children (for the
purposes of the Act being persons under the age of 18 years[160]) and young

159 *Christian Institute v Scottish Ministers* [2015] CSIH 64, paras 2–4.
160 Children and Young People (Scotland) Act 2014, s. 97(1).

people (for the purposes of the Act being persons over 18 who remain in schooling[161]) an identified individual, known as the "named person",[162] to perform certain functions when he or she considers it appropriate to do so in order to promote, support or safeguard the wellbeing of the child or young person.[163] The functions are (i) advising, informing or supporting the child or young person, or a parent of the child or young person, (ii) helping the child or young person, or a parent of the child or young person, to access a service or support, and (iii) discussing, or raising, a matter about the child or young person with a service provider or relevant authority.[164]

There can be nothing objectionable in any of these aims, though they would only be fully achieved if information could be collated from a number of sources about individual children to allow properly informed decisions to be made as to whether support and guidance is necessary and whether the child is at risk of becoming a looked after child. Many tragedies in the past have been caused (at least partly) by the failure to bring together all the information held by different agencies about an individual child, depriving any single professional of the opportunity to see the whole picture.[165] The Children and Young People (Scotland) Act 2014, therefore, imposed duties on health boards, local authorities and the Scottish Ministers to share information with the service provider relevant to the named person's functions. The Act also required the service provider to share information with a wide variety of public authorities where it was likely to be relevant to an exercise of the named person functions unless to do so would be "in breach of a prohibition or restriction on the disclosure of information arising by virtue of an enactment or rule of law".[166]

In *Christian Institute v Lord Advocate* the whole named person scheme was challenged as being a disproportionate breach of the right to respect for family life, as protected by Art. 8 of the European Convention on Human Rights, and the information-sharing provisions in particular were challenged as being incompatible with the right to private and family life. If incompatible with the ECHR, the scheme would be outwith the legislative competence of the Scottish Parliament, and would not be law. The Outer House

---

161 Ibid. s. 22(2).
162 Ibid. ss. 20–21.
163 Ibid. s. 19(1).
164 Ibid. s. 19(5).
165 See the *Bichard Inquiry Report* (into the Soham Murders), The Stationery Office, HC 653, ordered by the House of Commons to be printed 22 June 2004.
166 Children and Young People (Scotland) Act 2014, s. 26 (as originally enacted but never brought into force).

and Inner House rejected both these challenges[167] but in the Supreme
Court,[168] the challenge to the information-sharing provisions was successful.
Lady Hale and Lords Reed and Hodge said this:

> [I]t can be accepted, focusing on the legislation itself rather than on individual
> cases dealt with under the legislation, that Part 4 of the 2014 Act pursues legiti-
> mate aims. The public interest in the flourishing of children is obvious. The aim
> of the Act, which is unquestionably legitimate and benign, is the promotion
> and safeguarding of the wellbeing of children and young persons. As the Dean
> of Faculty submitted, the policy of promoting better outcomes for individual
> children and families is not inconsistent with the primary responsibility of parents
> to promote the wellbeing of their children. Improving access to, and the coordi-
> nation of, public services which can assist the promotion of a child's wellbeing are
> legitimate objectives which are sufficiently important to justify some limitation on
> the right to respect for private and family life.[169]

However, while the named person scheme itself was legitimate and
benign – as must surely be obvious – and not in itself incompatible with the
European Convention, the information-sharing provisions that underpinned
that scheme were held to be incompatible with the rights of children, young
people and parents under Art. 8. The provisions were not "in accordance
with the law" because the interplay between the rules and the requirements
of the Data Protection Act 1998 made them inaccessible and because the
lack of safeguards meant that information sharing had the potential to operate disproportionately in practice even although not designed to do so.[170]

Following the Supreme Court's decision the Scottish Government
delayed the implementation of Part 4, and in July 2017 a new Bill was
introduced before the Scottish Parliament, the Children and Young People
(Information Sharing) (Scotland) Bill, which aimed to replace the original
duties under ss. 23 and 26 to share information with a duty, instead, to identify information the sharing of which could promote, support or safeguard
the wellbeing of the child or young person and to consider whether that
information could be shared in compliance with the Data Protection Act
(now 2018) and other relevant law. In addition, new ss. 26A and 26B were to
be inserted into the 2014 Act providing limitations on information sharing,
and requiring the Scottish Ministers to issue a Code of Practice on information sharing, compliance with which would be mandatory. Those responsible for drawing up that Code of Practice concluded that it was impossible

---

167 [2015] CSOH 7; [2015] CSIH 64.
168 [2016] UKSC 51.
169 Ibid. para 91.
170 Ibid. paras 79–101.

to reconcile the principles underpinning the named person scheme and the demands of the Supreme Court, and in September 2019 the Scottish Government announced it was abandoning the whole scheme. An opportunity for Scotland to lead the way in avoiding state intervention in the lives of vulnerable children was thus lost at the behest of those who continue to preference their own privacy interests over the wellbeing of other people's children.

INTERNATIONAL LAW IN THE POST-1968 PERIOD

The two sources of international law with the greatest impact on the development of law and practice of child protection in Scotland are the European Convention on Human Rights (ECHR), and the United Nations Convention on the Rights of the Child (UNCRC). In addition, a variety of other international treaties governing particular issues have been signed and ratified by the British Government.

THE EUROPEAN CONVENTION ON HUMAN RIGHTS

The ECHR was opened for signature on 4 November 1950 and, after the requisite number of ratifications (the first being by the United Kingdom on 8 March 1951[171]) it came into force on 3 September 1953. It was only after 1965, when individual petition to the European Commission and Court of Human Rights at Strasbourg was afforded to British citizens, that the ECHR became a factor in future policy-making; and only after the Human Rights Act 1998 that it became a decisive factor in judicial decision-making.

It has justly been said that a simple reading of the European Convention on Human Rights reveals that it is not a child-friendly treaty which, unlike the other main international and regional human rights instruments, does not even contain a general provision recognising the need for special protection and assistance to be given to the child.[172] The European Court of Human Rights for a long time had a habit of subsuming children's interests into those of their parents, but in the twenty-first century the Court began to be far more conscious of the interests of children, and more willing

---

171 Not without objection from such influential figures as Sir Stafford Cripps and Lord Chancellor Jowitt: see Wicks, E. "The United Kingdom Government's Perceptions of the European Convention on Human Rights at the Time of Entry" (2000) *Public Law* 438.

172 Woolf, M. "Coming of Age? – the Principle of 'Best Interests of the Child'" (2003) 2 *European Human Rights Law Review* 205, p. 205.

to accept that children's rights require protection in different ways from adults' rights.

Many of the articles, directly conferring rights on individuals, have been interpreted by the Strasbourg court to impose, as well, positive obligations on the state. In other words, not only must the state refrain from actions that directly breach the Convention, but it must also take positive steps to prevent others from doing so. So, for example, Article 3 provides, without qualification, that "no one shall be subjected to torture or inhuman or degrading treatment or punishment". Not only must the state itself not visit such treatment on anyone (including on children, for example by corporal punishment in state schools) but it must take effective measures to ensure that others are not able to visit such treatment on children.[173] Article 8, which by requiring respect for private and family life, protects physical integrity as well as personal privacy,[174] likewise imposes positive obligations on the state[175] and is indeed a more powerful protective instrument since the level of harm required to engage Art. 8 is significantly lower than that required to engage Art. 3. In *S v Sweden*[176] Art. 8 was held to be breached because Swedish law did not adequately protect a 14 year old girl from the voyeurism of her step-father.

The Human Rights Act 1998 and the Scotland Act 1998

The Human Rights Act 1998 greatly enhanced the position of the ECHR in the UK by making it unlawful for any public authority to act in a way that is incompatible with a convention right (unless it is required to do so by primary legislation).[177] "Public authority" is defined to include "any person certain of whose functions are functions of a public nature".[178] The care of children on behalf of the state, whether by a local authority, a voluntary organisation or a public health facility, is certainly a function of a public nature as is the decision-making of courts and tribunals in child protection proceedings. All child protection processes must therefore consist with the requirements of the ECHR.

---

173 See for example *A v United Kingdom* (1999) 27 EHRR 611.
174 *X and Y v The Netherlands* (1985) 8 EHRR 235, para 22.
175 *Airey v Ireland* (1980) 2 EHRR 305, para 32; *Marckx v Belgium* (1979–80) 2 EHRR 330, para 31.
176 (2014) 58 EHRR 36.
177 Human Rights Act 1998, s. 6(1).
178 Ibid. s. 6(3).

The Scotland Act 1998 too gave a special place to the ECHR, not-withstanding that (generally speaking) "international relations" were reserved to Westminster.[179] The implementation of international obliga-tions is devolved.[180] It is outwith the legislative competence of the Scottish Parliament to legislate inconsistently with the ECHR, [181] and the courts may write down any Act of the Scottish Parliament, where it is possible to do so, to make it consistent with the ECHR, or to strike down the legislation as "not law" where it is not so possible. Together with the Human Rights Act 1998, the Scotland Act 1998 makes the ECHR a major driver in the development of child protection law and there has been a greatly increased focus since their enactment on the central concepts of proportionality and participation.

Effects of the ECHR on domestic law

One of the most important principles that the European Court of Human Rights has extracted from Art. 6 (right to a fair hearing) and Art. 8 (right to respect for private and family life) is that of participation, that is to say, the obligation on the state to ensure that those whose civil rights may be affected by a legal process should have an effective opportunity to be involved in that process. Though participation has always been a central aim of the design of the children's hearing system, disputes about its correct application have generated significant case law in that context. Effective participation was held to be denied by the failure to permit the parents of a child referred to a children's hearing full access to the background papers drawn up by the social work department because a fair trial neces-sarily involves an opportunity to have knowledge of and comment on the observations of the other party.[182] That matter was resolved by regulations made under the Children (Scotland) Act 1995.[183] The ECHR has always been concerned with real as opposed to theoretical rights and the chil-dren's hearing's reliance on the child and parent arguing their own case (part of the original 1968 design, re-enacted in 1995) increasingly came under challenge[184] until eventually the Strasbourg Court's demand not just

---

179 Scotland Act 1998, sched. 5 para 7(1).
180 Ibid. para 7(2).
181 Scotland Act 1998, s. 29(2)(d).
182 *McMichael v United Kingdom* (1995) 20 EHRR 205.
183 Children's Hearings (Scotland) Rules 1996 (SI 1996/3261 (S. 251)), rule 5. The matter is spelt out in much greater detail in Part 6 of the Children's Hearings (Scotland) Act 2011 (Rules of Procedure in Children's Hearings) Rules 2013 (SSI 2013/194).
184 See *S v Miller* 2001 SLT 531 and 1304, and *K v Authority Reporter* 2009 SLT 1019.

for formal but "effective" participation led to legal aid being extended to (some) cases before children's hearings.[185]

The debate then turned to the definition of "relevant person" under the 1995 Act, which is the gateway to attendance at and the right to participate in children's hearings for persons other than the child. A series of cases extended the definition, through explicit reliance on the Human Rights Act 1998, to those who had contact orders in respect of the child but not full parental responsibilities and parental rights.[186] This series culminated in *Principal Reporter v K*,[187] where the Supreme Court held that a father who had no parental responsibilities and parental rights nor any contact order in his favour, but against whom allegations had been made and whose family life might be affected by any decision of the children's hearing, had to be brought within the definition of "relevant person" in other to ensure the 1995 Act's compatibility with the ECHR. That led to a (last minute) amendment to the relevant person provisions in the Children's Hearings (Scotland) Act 2011. But that Act did not grant participation rights (through the concept of "relevant person") to every person whose family life with the child might be affected. In *ABC v Principal Reporter*[188] it was held by Lady Wise in the Outer House that it was necessary to read down the relevant provisions in the 2011 Act so that the rights of participation of siblings of the child before a children's hearing could be protected, siblings having "family life" that might be affected by the hearing's decision. The decision was, however, reversed by the Inner House[189] on the ground that *Principal Reporter v K* did not require that everyone with family life with the child should be recognised as having the right of full participation at the children's hearing.

THE UNITED NATIONS CONVENTION ON THE RIGHTS OF THE CHILD

The United Nations Convention on the Rights of the Child (UNCRC) was adopted by the UN General Assembly and opened for signature on 20 November 1989:[190] it was ratified by the United Kingdom on 16 December 1991. Ratification requires signatory states to "take action to ensure the

---

185 Part 19 of the Children's Hearings (Scotland) Act 2011.
186 *Authority Reporter v S* 2010 SLT 765; *M, Appellant* 2010 Fam. LR 152.
187 [2010] UKSC 56.
188 2018 CSOH 81.
189 2019 SC 186.
190 UN General Assembly, session 44, resolution 25.

realisation of all the rights in the Convention for all children in their jurisdiction",[191] to keep under comprehensive review all domestic legislation and related administrative guidance to ensure full compliance with the Convention,[192] and to ensure "visible cross-sectoral coordination to recognize and realize children's rights across Government, between different levels of government and between Government and civil society – including in particular children and young people themselves".[193]

The effects of the UNCRC were described by Lord Hughes in *R (On the Application of SG and Ors) v Secretary of State for Work and Pensions*:[194]

[the UNCRC is] an international treaty ratified by the United Kingdom. It is binding on this country in international law. It is not, however, part of English law. Such a treaty may be relevant in English [or, he might have added, Scots] law in at least three ways. First, if the construction (ie meaning) of UK legislation is in doubt, the court may conclude that it should be construed, if otherwise possible, on the footing that this country meant to honour its international obligations. Second, international treaty obligations may guide the development of the common law. . . . Thirdly, however, the UNCRC may be relevant in English law to the extent that it falls to the court to apply the European Convention on Human Rights ("ECHR") via the Human Rights Act 1998. The European Court of Human Rights has sometimes accepted that the Convention should be interpreted, in appropriate cases, in the light of generally accepted international law in the same field, including multi-lateral treaties such as the UNCRC. An example is *Demir v Turkey* (2008) 48 EHRR 1272 which concerned the scope of article 11 (right of freedom of association).

The UNCRC recognises that the primary duty to look after children falls to parents:

State Parties shall use their best efforts to ensure recognition of the principle that both parents have common responsibilities for the upbringing and development of the child. Parents or, as the case may be, legal guardians, have the primary responsibility for the upbringing and development of the child.[195]

But in addition, it requires the state to have in place sufficient legal procedures that will allow the state to take such protective measures as are necessary:

States Parties undertake to ensure the child such protection and care as is necessary for his or her well-being, taking into account the rights and duties of his or her parents, legal guardians, or other individuals legally responsible for him

---

191 UN Committee on the Rights of the Child *General Comment No. 5* (CRC/GC/2003/527 November 2003), section I.
192 Ibid. section IV.
193 Ibid. section VI.
194 [2015] UKSC 16, para 137.
195 UNCRC, Art. 18.

or her, and, to this end, shall take all appropriate legislative and administrative measures.[196]

Further, there is a positive obligation on the state to take protective measures on behalf of any individual child at risk of harm:

States Parties shall take all appropriate legislative, administrative, social and educational measures to protect the child from all forms of physical or mental violence, injury or abuse, neglect or negligent treatment, maltreatment or exploitation, including sexual abuse, while in the care of the parent, legal guardian, or other person who has the care of the child.[197]

"Person" in that context can include manifestations of the state itself.

Though originally, the UK entered some Reservations to the UNCRC, these were all subsequently withdrawn.[198] One Reservation of relevance here allowed the United Kingdom to maintain in operation the children's hearing system in Scotland. The fear seemed to have been that the hearing's power to require a child to reside in a place of safety during an interim period might be held to be inconsistent with the UNCRC, but the new appeal mechanisms in the Children (Scotland) Act 1995 rendered the Reservation unnecessary for that purpose, and it was withdrawn shortly after the coming into force of the relevant parts of the 1995 Act.[199]

The Children and Young People (Scotland) Act 2014

The UNCRC's special position in Scots law was enhanced when the Children and Young People (Scotland) Act 2014 imposed an obligation on the Scottish Ministers to "keep under consideration whether there are any steps which they could take which would or might secure better or further effect in Scotland of the UNCRC requirements" and to report on these matters to the Scottish Parliament every three years; public authorities must also publish reports on the steps to the same end that they take.[200]

---

196 UNCRC, Art. 3(2).

197 UNCRC, Art. 19(1).

198 For details, see Norrie, K. *Legislative Background to the Treatment of Children and Young Persons Living Apart from their Parents: Report to the Scottish Child Abuse Inquiry* (2017), pp. 370–372.

199 Second Periodical Report (United Kingdom) to the UN Committee on the Rights of the Child (1999), at paras 2.12.1 and 2.12.2. Available at <http://www.togetherscotland.org.uk/pdfs/uncrc%20-%20uk%20second%20state%20report%201999.pdf> (last accessed 27 June 2019).

200 Children and Young People (Scotland) Act 2014, ss. 1–3. "Public authorities" are defined in sched. 1 to include local authorities, SCRA, CHS, health boards, and the Scottish Qualifications Authority.

The move to incorporation

Unlike the European Convention on Human Rights, whose substantive provisions were designed to be justiciable and which, consequently, could be incorporated into domestic law without difficulty, the UNCRC's substantive articles are a mixture of aspiration, governmental nudge and positive obligation. Nevertheless, the Scottish Government included in its 2018–19 Programme for Government a commitment to "incorporate" the substantive provisions of the UNCRC into domestic law with the overarching intention of embedding the rights in the UNCRC into the law of Scotland. As this book goes to press, the Scottish Government is consulting on how to give legislative effect to this policy objective. Whatever the form of the legislation that will eventually be enacted, the influence of the UNCRC, hitherto focused on policy-makers, is likely to become more and more significant for decision-makers (judicial and otherwise) and implementers of the law.

OTHER INTERNATIONAL TREATIES

The General Assembly of the United Nations adopted "Rules for the Protection of Juveniles Deprived of their Liberty" on 14 December 1990. The Council of Europe's Convention on the Protection of Children Against Sexual Exploitation and Sexual Abuse,[201] requires the screening of people working with children, programmes to support victims and the criminalisation of child prostitution, pornography, grooming and "sex tourism". Many other international treaties ratified by the United Kingdom, while they have a primary focus on adults, nevertheless contain special provisions relating to children. Among the most important of such treaties are the following:

(i) The International Covenant on Economic, Social and Cultural Rights[202] provides that "special measures of protection and assistance" should be taken on behalf of the young without discrimination and that they should be protected from economic and social exploitation.[203] States parties should aim for "the healthy development of the child"[204] and make primary education compulsory and free to all.[205]

---

201 CETS No. 201, entering into force on 1 July 2010, and ratified by the United Kingdom 20 June 2018.
202 Adopted by the United Nations General Assembly on 16 December 1966 and entering into force on 3 January 1976.
203 ICESCR, Art 10(3).
204 Ibid. Art 12(2).
205 Ibid. Art 13(2a).

(ii)   The International Convention on Civil and Political Rights[206] provides that "every child shall have, without discrimination as to race, colour, sex, language, religion, national or social origin, property or birth, the rights to such measures of protection as are required by his status as a minor, on the part of his family, society and the state".[207]

(iii)   The Convention on the Elimination of Discrimination Against Women[208] proscribes betrothal and marriage of children.[209]

(iv)   The Convention on the Rights of Persons with Disabilities[210] requires states parties to take all necessary measures to ensure that children with disabilities enjoy to the full all human rights and fundamental freedoms on an equal basis with other children, including the right to express views and to have assistance in doing so.[211]

(v)   The Convention on Transnational Organised Crime[212] was enhanced from 25 December 2003 by a Protocol to Prevent, Suppress and Punish Trafficking in Persons, especially Women and Children.

---

206   Adopted by the United Nations General Assembly on 16 December 1966 and entering into force on 23 March 1976.

207   ICCPR, Art 24.

208   Adopted by the United Nations General Assembly on 18 December 1979 and entering into force on 3 September 1981.

209   CEDAW, Art. 16.

210   Adopted by the United Nations General Assembly on 13 December 2006 and entering into force on 3 May 2008.

211   CRPD, Art 7.

212   Adopted by the United Nations General Assembly on 15 November 2000 and entering into force on 29 September 2003.

3. Child Protection through the Criminal Law

INTRODUCTION

The criminal law has a role to play, no less important for being indirect, in the protection of children and young people. It protects everyone in society from the harmful acts of others: the prohibitions on murder, rape or assault, or theft, fraud or dangerous driving are designed to secure benefit for everybody, whatever their age. But children and young people, being physically weaker and intellectually less developed than adults, are peculiarly vulnerable to harm and exploitation – particularly from those closest to them. They might suffer injury not just from the deliberate infliction of harm but also from the neglect of the care and attention that they need, or from the usages to which they are put by the adults who have the easiest access to them. The criminal law has long recognised that children and young people require more protection from harm than that offered to adults, and so makes punishable certain acts or omissions that would not be criminal if directed towards adults.

Yet the criminal law's protection is of necessity only very partial. Its focus is primarily on the criminal and not the victim. It seeks to reduce the overall incidence of harm by imposing sanctions on the criminal, and thus making the crime less attractive, to the benefit of all potential victims. The limitations of deterrence by the criminal law are well known, and an effective form of child protection came about only when the courts were given the power, in the late nineteenth century, not only to punish wrongdoing but also to take action in relation to child victims. Only then could we conceive of child protection law as being a body of law in its own right distinct from, if still activated by, the criminal law.

Other than with very specialist crimes such as *plagium*, which is an aggravated form of theft of a child under the age of puberty[1] (the victim being

---

1 Gordon, G.H. *Criminal Law* (3rd edn by M.G.A. Christie, 2001), para 14.26; Macdonald, J.H.A. *Criminal Law of Scotland* (5th edn by J. Walker and D.J. Stevenson, 1948), p. 39; Anderson,

the parent with the right to possession of the child), there are two major categories of crimes in respect of which children and young people, but not adults, may be the victim: certain sexual offences, and child neglect or cruelty.

SEXUAL OFFENCES

Acts other than sexual intercourse

The common law crime of "lewd, indecent and libidinous practice or behaviour",[2] which could be committed against any child, whether boy or girl, under the age of puberty, was aimed at acts performed for sexual gratification that did not involve sexual intercourse (understood to be constituted by – limited to – penile penetration of the vagina). The consent or otherwise of the child was irrelevant, for the crime was designed to prevent any such act being directed towards a person too young to understand its full implications. In the words of Lord Justice-Clerk Hope:[3]

> the law holds that under the age of twelve, however precocious may be the temperament – however much the girl has been familiar with scenes of vice and baseness of habits – she cannot give consent to the practices of any man upon her person, and cannot lawfully give the use of her person for any purpose he may have against her. Above the age of twelve, the case may be different.

Consent of a girl aged 12 or above or of a boy aged 14 or above was at common law a sufficient defence, though male-male sexual activity with post-pubescent youths, being suffused with an additional immorality lacking with female-male sexual activity, was vulnerable to charges being stretched to ensure punishment. So in *David Brown*[4] and *Andrew Lyall*[5] pleas of guilty were tendered to charges of lewd or libidinous behaviour though the boys in each case were described in the charge as "under or about" the age of

---

A.M. *Criminal Law of Scotland* (Bell and Bradfute, 2nd edn 1904), p. 175. See *Hamilton v Wilson* 1993 SCCR 9.

2 Abolished by the Sexual Offences (Scotland) Act 2009, s. 52(a)(iii).

3 *HM Advocate v Philip* (1855) 2 Irv. 243, p. 252.

4 (1844) 2 Broun 261.

5 (1853) 1 Irv. 218. The offence was regarded in this case as aggravated by the fact that the accused was a school teacher who committed the offences against two of his pupils in his schoolroom. The much later case of *Cartwright v HM Adv.* 2001 SLT 1163 also involved a school teacher, this time charged with shameless indecency by having sexual intercourse with a girl over 13 but under 16 (the time for prosecuting under the statutory offence having passed).

puberty; later, male-male sexual activity not involving anal penetration came to be charged as "shameless indecency".[6]

The Criminal Law Amendment Act, 1922 increased the scope of the offence of lewd, indecent or libidinous practices or behaviour in respect of girls by criminalising such acts with any girl over 12 and under 16 to the same extent as the common law criminalised these acts in respect of girls below the age of 12.[7] The age for boys remained 14.

Sexual intercourse

The legality of "sexual intercourse" (necessarily heterosexual, being penile penetration of the vagina) turned at common law on consent: without the consent of the girl, the act was one of rape. A girl under 12 could not (and cannot) give consent and so any act of sexual intercourse with her was necessarily rape.[8] The Criminal Law Amendment Act, 1885 – passed in large measure as a response to a series of revelatory articles published in the *Pall Mall Gazette*[9] on the extent of child prostitution in London – made "carnal knowledge" (that is to say sexual intercourse) with a girl under 13 a "high crime and offence", and with a girl over 13 and under 16 a "crime and offence" (with lesser penalties).[10] Consent was thereby rendered irrelevant to any statutory charge involving a girl under 16, for the primary aim of the Act was to protect young girls from exploitation and the obtaining of their consent by undue influence. This was reflected in some of the other offences created by the 1885 Act, such as procuring girls for prostitution by administering drugs, fraud or intimidation,[11] and abducting a girl under 18 for the purpose of having carnal knowledge with her.[12]

---

6 *McLaughlan v Boyd* 1934 JC 19; *McDonald v HM Adv.* 1997 SLT 1237.

7 Criminal Law Amendment Act, 1922, s. 4, re-enacted as s. 5 of the Sexual Offences (Scotland) Act 1976.

8 Hume, D. *Commentaries on the Law of Scotland Respecting Crime* (1797) i, 303; Alison, A. *Principles and Practice of the Criminal Law of Scotland* (1832) i, 213; Gordon, (3rd edn) para 33.12.

9 These articles have collectively come to be called "The Maiden Tribute of Modern Babylon", and are available today at <https://attackingthedevil.co.uk/pmg/tribute/mt1.php> (last accessed 18 December 2019).

10 Criminal Law Amendment Act, 1885, ss. 4 and 5, as applied to Scotland by s. 15.

11 Ibid. s. 3.

12 Ibid. s. 7.

Boys and the 1885 Act

The 1885 Act, with its focus very much on protecting young females, did not see the need to provide any additional protection to boys from any form of sexual exploitation by women, and the age remained 14 at which (hetero)sexual intercourse with boys could lawfully be had with their consent.[13] In relation to male-male sexual activity other than sodomy (which was a common law crime even when both parties consented[14]), the 1885 Act criminalised all and any such activity as "gross indecency":[15] the effect was not to protect young males from exploitation but to make them criminals themselves for having allowed themselves to be used in that way. So if a man of 25 had consensual sex with a boy of 14, or with a youth of 17 or with a man of 40, then both participants were guilty of the offence of either sodomy or "gross indecency" (anything other than penile penetration of the anus). If a woman of 25 had sex with a boy of 13, then the woman was guilty, and the boy was a victim; if she had consensual sex with a boy of 14, they were both innocent of any offence known to the law.

Twentieth-century legislation

The law remained thus until the Sexual Offences (Scotland) Act 1976, which made little substantive change. Sexual intercourse with a girl under 13 was an offence that attracted the same penalty as rape;[16] sexual intercourse with a girl over 13 but under 16 was an offence irrespective of consent but with lesser penalties;[17] lewd, indecent or libidinous practice or behaviour towards a girl between 12 and 16 was an offence irrespective of consent[18] and remained a common law crime for girls below 12 (and boys below 14) since they could not in law consent. Male-male sexual activity other than sodomy remained the offence of gross indecency,[19] and sodomy itself remained a crime at common law: neither consent nor age was relevant to

---

13 Without consent, the offence would be assault.

14 Hume *Commentaries on the Law of Scotland Concerning Crimes* i, 469; Alison, *Principles and Practice of the Criminal Law of Scotland* i, 566; Gordon *Criminal Law* (3rd edn 2001), para 34.01.

15 Criminal Law Amendment Act, 1885, s. 11: the section was given the heading "Outrages on Decency".

16 Sexual Offences (Scotland) Act 1976, s. 3.

17 Ibid. s. 4.

18 Ibid. s. 5.

19 Ibid. s. 7.

the charge in either case (though these issues would be highly relevant to both the decision to prosecute and the punishment on a finding or admission of guilt). The two so-called "homosexual offences" were substantially qualified by the Criminal Justice (Scotland) Act 1980,[20] after which no charge could be brought if the offence were committed in private, both parties were over the age of 21 and both had consented.[21] It would, however, be a mistake to see this as a provision protecting men under the age of 21 from predatory homosexuals – if the gay sex involved a consenting male under 21 then he would be as guilty as the other.[22]

Much of this was subsequently replicated in Part I of the Criminal Law (Consolidation) (Scotland) Act 1995, which remained the primary source of sexual offences in Scots law until the Sexual Offences (Scotland) Act 2009. The 2009 Act constituted a fundamental rethinking, following the work of the Scottish Law Commission,[23] and it explicitly sought to change the focus of the law (in relation to offences against children and young people) away from morality and gender differentiation to one of protection of all children. So all sexual acts with children under 16 are prohibited, with differential penalties depending on the age of the victim and the type of act, but without distinction in relation to gender or sexual orientation. In addition, a number of specific child-related sexual offences are created, such as causing a child to look at a sexual image[24] and indecent communication with a child.[25] Elsewhere, there are offences prohibiting the taking or keeping of indecent photographs of children.[26]

Exploitative sexual offences

Irrespective of both age and consent (and indeed of gender), the criminal law has for many centuries provided protection against sexual activity with close family members, not only to reflect society's perception of such acts being deeply, profoundly, immoral but also to recognise the greatly

---

20 Criminal Justice (Scotland) Act 1980, s. 80.
21 Rather oddly, none of this applied to acts committed on British merchant ships amongst crew members: Criminal Justice (Scotland) Act 1980, s. 80(7)(d).
22 The age of lawful male-male sexual activity was reduced to 18 by the Criminal Justice and Public Order Act 1994, s. 145(2) and then to 16 by the Sexual Offences Amendment Act 2000, s. 1(3).
23 Scottish Law Commission, *Report on Rape and Other Sexual Offences* 2007 (Scot. Law Com. 2007 No. 209).
24 Sexual Offences (Scotland) Act 2009, ss. 23 and 33.
25 Ibid. ss. 24 and 34.
26 Civic Government (Scotland) Act 1982, ss. 52 and 52A. "Child" in this context is a person under 16 years of age.

increased scope for sexual exploitation within the confines of family circles. Incest has been an offence in Scots law at least since the Incest Act 1567,[27] which criminalised sexual intercourse between parties whose relationship was within the long list of forbidden degrees found in Chapter 18 of the Book of Leviticus. The 1567 Act remained extant for over 400 years until it was repealed by the Incest and Related Offences (Scotland) Act 1986. This added incest into the Sexual Offences (Scotland) Act 1976[28] but reduced the categories of relationship subject to the prohibition. However, the main purpose of the 1986 Act was to address the fact that the crime of incest, previously too broadly drawn, was at the same time too narrow to protect children and young people from being persuaded into sexual activity by persons who were not their blood relatives but nevertheless had some form of quasi-familial influence over them. The Scottish Law Commission had pointed out in their 1981 *Report on the Law of Incest in Scotland*[29] that the crime of incest protected children from their own parents and a large number of remoter family members, but did not protect children from their step-parents or from their parents' non-marital partners. To address that gap new offences beyond incest were inserted into the Sexual Offences (Scotland) Act 1976 by the 1986 Act. A new s. 2B made it an offence to have sexual intercourse with a step-child or former step-child under the age of 21 (or any age, if the step-child had lived, before the age of 18, in the same household as the step-parent and been treated as a child of the step-parent's family). Also, a new s. 2C made it an offence for a person (aged over 16) who was in "a position of trust or authority" over a child (of either gender) under 16 to have sexual intercourse with that child, with somewhat higher penalties than for the existing offence under s. 4 of the 1976 Act of having sexual intercourse with a girl under 16. The offence was limited to situations in which the accused and the child were members of the same household,[30] for it was designed to protect against cohabitants and the like, though it was drawn broadly enough also to include some foster carers in whose household the child lived.[31] But limiting the offence to members of the same household meant that children in residential establishments, where

---

27   APS iii, 26, c. 15 (12mo. c. 14).

28   Sexual Offences (Scotland) Act 1976, s. 2A, as inserted by s. 1 of the Incest and Related Offences (Scotland) Act 1986.

29   Scot. Law Com. No. 69, 1981.

30   The rationale for this limitation is explained at Scot. Law Com. No. 69, para 4.33.

31   Cf *HM Adv. v K* 1994 SCCR 499 where a foster parent was charged with shameless indecency having had sexual intercourse with a girl he was fostering. He was unable to be charged under s. 2C since the girl was over 16 (and under 18).

it would be artificial to suggest that the child and carer were members of the same household,[32] would not be covered. Where the offence did apply, it was a defence for the accused to show that he or she believed on reasonable grounds that the child was over 16, or that the accused did not consent to the sexual intercourse, or that he or she was married to the child (having married abroad in a marriage recognised as valid in Scotland).[33] All of these offences, including incest itself, were limited to the act of sexual intercourse and did not cover other sexual activity. There would be a certain logic to this if the crime existed solely to protect against pregnancy, but if the legislation was aimed at the wider emotional harm caused by sexual exploitation, then it failed to address that sufficiently. However, the usefully flexible (but ultimately unsustainably flawed)[34] common law crime of shameless indecency was available in cases where the sexual activity did not include penile penetration of the vagina but would have been criminal if it did. So in *R v Her Majesty's Advocate*[35] a father's conviction for shameless indecency was upheld when he had non-penetrative sex with his 16 year old daughter.

The offences in the Sexual Offences (Scotland) Act 1976, as amended, were all replicated with no substantive change in ss. 1–7 of the Criminal Law (Consolidation) (Scotland) Act 1995.

A much broader, and more closely defined, offence was created by the (UK-wide) Sexual Offences (Amendment) Act 2000, that is to say, sexual activity by a person over 18 with a person under 18 while the former was in a position of trust in respect of the latter.[36] This new offence offered protection against any "sexual activity" (heterosexual or homosexual, penetrative or non-penetrative).[37] It also protected young people over 16 who were otherwise competent to consent to the full range of sexual activity – the rationale for the offence was the risk of exploitation by those in a position of trust in relation to the young person. "Position of trust" was expansively

---

32 In another context (the meaning of grounds of referral to the children's hearing) it was said that "the word 'household' . . . is plainly intended to connote a family unit or something akin to a family unit – a group of person, held together by a particular kind of tie who normally live together, even if individual members of the group may be temporarily separated from it": *McGregor v H* 1983 SLT 626 at p. 628.

33 Cf. *Mohamed v Knott* [1969] 1 QB 1.

34 See *Webster v Dominick* 2005 1 JC 65.

35 1988 SLT 623.

36 Sexual Offences (Amendment) Act 2000, s. 3.

37 "Sexual activity" was defined to mean any activity which a reasonable person would regard as sexual in all the circumstances, other than activity that could be so regarded only with knowledge of the intentions, motives or feelings of the parties: ibid. s. 3(5).

defined [38] to include anyone looking after persons under 18 in residential accommodation provided by a local authority or voluntary organisation, in a hospital or care home, or in full-time education. It was a defence if the accused could show that he or she did not know and could not reasonably have been expected to know that the young person was under 18 or was a person in relation to whom he or she was in a position of trust; it was also a defence that the accused was lawfully married to (or after 5 December 2005 in a civil partnership with) the young person.[39] The young person's consent, or ability to consent, was irrelevant to the offence.

The provisions in the Sexual Offences (Amendment) Act 2000 applicable to Scotland were repealed by the Sexual Offences (Scotland) Act 2009. This Act (rather oddly) did not replace the provisions in the Criminal Law (Consolidation) (Scotland) Act 1995 relating to incest and sexual intercourse with a step-parent (which will still be charged under the 1995 Act), but it did amalgamate and extend the two overlapping offences in s. 3 of the 1995 Act and s. 3 of the 2000 Act (both of which were repealed). Under the 2009 Act, it became, and remains, the offence of "sexual abuse of trust" for any person over 18 to engage in sexual activity with a person under 18 while in a position of trust over that person.[40] The rationale for this offence was explained by the Scottish Law Commission:

> Even if some instances of sexual contact with a person are wrong because of some characteristic of that person (such as age or mental condition), there is a separate and additional type of wrong where the perpetrator holds a position of trust over the victim. The existence of the trust relationship renders highly problematic any consent which the vulnerable person may give to sexual activity. But over and above the issue of the validity of consent, a person who holds a position of trust over another is acting inconsistently with the duties imposed by that position if he engages in sexual activity with that person.[41]

"Position of trust" is defined, similarly to the 2000 Act, to include the looking after of persons under 18 while they are detained by a court order or under an enactment in an institution, or are resident in a home or other place in which accommodation is provided by a local authority, or are accommodated and cared for in a hospital, care home service, residential establishment or accommodation provided by a school care accommodation service or secure accommodation service, and the looking after of persons under 18

---

38 Ibid. s. 4.
39 Ibid. s. 3(2), amended by the Civil Partnership Act 2004.
40 Sexual Offences (Scotland) Act 2009, s. 42.
41 *Report on Rape and Other Sexual Offences*, Scot. Law Com. No. 209 (2007), para 4.107.

who are receiving an education at a school or institution of further or higher education.[42] In addition, anyone who fulfils or exercises parental responsibilities or parental rights under an arrangement with a person who has such responsibilities or rights (private fosterers), or treats the person under 18 as a child of his or her family while being a member of the same household[43] is also in a position of trust.[44] The defences are (i) that the person over 18 reasonably believed either that the other person was over 18 or that he or she was not in a position of trust in relation to that person, and (ii) that the parties were married to or civil partners of each other or (giving further recognition to the legitimacy of non-marital sex) a sexual relationship already existed between them immediately before the position of trust arose.[45] Consent, or lack of it, is immaterial to this offence.[46]

Other offences designed to protect children from sexual harm

The Protection of Children and Prevention of Sexual Offences (Scotland) Act 2005 was a response to the increasing concern that children were vulnerable to "grooming", that is to say communicating with or meeting with a child with the intent of engaging in unlawful sexual activity with the child. Meeting, travelling to meet or making arrangements to meet with a child with the intention of having sex with that child, not reasonably believing them to be over the age of 16, became an offence even when no sexual activity, in the event, took place.[47] In addition, the Chief Constable was given the power to apply for a Risk of Sexual Harm Order, in respect of anyone whose previous behaviour indicates a risk that other children may be harmed: such an order will prohibit the subject from doing particular acts, such as communicating with children generally or being in the company of a specified child or children.[48] The 2005 Act also creates new offences such as paying

---

42 Sexual Offences (Scotland) Act 2009, s. 43. It is interesting to note that as long ago as 1855 the courts were particularly suspicious of sexual activity between a teacher and a pupil: see *HM Advocate v Philip* (1855) 2 Irv. 243 per Lord Justice-Clerk Hope, p. 247.

43 This would include step-parents and foster carers. "Sexual intercourse" by a step-parent continues to be covered by s. 2 of the Criminal Law Consolidation (Scotland) Act 1995.

44 Sexual Offences (Scotland) Act 2009, s. 43(6).

45 Ibid. s. 45.

46 *W v HM Advocate* 2016 HCJAC 44.

47 Protection of Children and Prevention of Sexual Offences (Scotland) Act 2005, s. 1. See, for example, *Maxwell v HM Advocate* [2017] HCJAC 64.

48 Protection of Children and Prevention of Sexual Offences (Scotland) Act 2005, s. 2. See for example *Chief Constable of Police Scotland v M* 2016 SLT (Sh Ct) 148.

for the sexual services of a person aged less than 18 years[49] and controlling the involvement of a person under 18 in the provision of sexual services or in pornography;[50] it also extends the offence of taking or distributing indecent photographs of children to include photographs of persons between the ages of 16 and 18.[51] This Act gives more attention to preventing sexual harm than the punishment of harm that has already been perpetrated on children and young people.

THE CRIME OF CHILD CRUELTY OR NEGLECT AT COMMON LAW

The second general type of crime against children and young people which the criminal law of Scotland recognised was child neglect, or exposing or deserting a child, or treating the child cruelly. Assaulting a child or young person was of course as criminal as assaulting an adult, but the common law also recognised that in some circumstances more passive behaviour towards a child or young person than actual assault would, too, amount to an offence – even when such neglectful behaviour directed towards (most) adults would not. As with sexual offences, this was because of the particular vulnerability of children to harm, but there was this additional factor justifying special offences: parents had legal duties of care towards their children, which they could not neglect with impunity.

Anderson, writing in 1904 and citing a series of Scottish cases from 1839 to 1868, says this:

> If a person has power over another, or a duty of taking care of another, and grossly neglects or cruelly ill-treats the dependent, he is guilty of an offence. Sick persons and children are peculiarly liable to neglect and ill-usage.[52]

After a discussion of the then extant Prevention of Cruelty to Children Act, 1894 (which will be discussed below) he goes on to describe exposure and desertion of infants as crimes at common law and states that "even placing the child in danger, without actual intent to desert, is criminal, as in sending the child in a basket by rail without informing the officials".[53]

---

49 Protection of Children and Prevention of Sexual Offences (Scotland) Act 2005, s. 9.
50 Ibid. s. 11.
51 Ibid. s. 16, amending s. 52 of the Civic Government (Scotland) Act 1982.
52 Anderson, A.M. *The Criminal Law of Scotland*, p. 167.
53 Ibid. pp. 171–172, citing the facts in *Gibson* (1845) 2 Broun 366.

Macdonald is to the same effect.[54] In *David and Janet Gemmell*,[55] parents pled guilty to a charge of "cruel and unnatural treatment" of their child whom they had locked in a cupboard and failed to afford wholesome food or decent clothing. In *Barbara Gray or McIntosh*[56] a baby farmer[57] had received a new-born "illegitimate" child from its mother, together with £22 for its upkeep, and after its death just over three months later was charged that she did

> culpably and wilfully neglect to supply the said child with wholesome and sufficient food and clothing . . . and keep or allow her to be kept in a dirty and damp condition, and expose her or allow her to be exposed to cold, and otherwise fail to give her such care and attention as were necessary to preserve the health of a child of such tender age; by all which, or part thereof, the said child was seriously injured in her health, and her constitution and vital powers were gradually destroyed . . .

Now, the essence of the common law crime was that the accused had some pre-existing obligation of care over the child, either as a parent or as a substitute-carer, and for that reason, there was no requirement to prove any intent to injure: the fault that justified punishment was neglect of duty rather than wicked intent. The pre-existing obligation of care meant that a charge, wider than a charge of assault, could be stated, if only in respect of a more restricted class of person than could competently be charged with assault.

There was, however, no mechanism within the common law, whether based on the *parens patriae* or not, that allowed the court before which an offender was brought to take on its own initiative directly protective action in relation to the victim of the offence – the child or young person. The removal of the offender to prison was the limit of the court's power before the enactment of the child cruelty statutes.

THE STATUTORY CRIME OF CHILD CRUELTY OR NEGLECT

The principle of the common law, that those with a pre-existing duty of care towards children could be prosecuted if they neglected that duty, was put onto a statutory basis in a series of statutes between 1889 and 1937.

---

54 Macdonald, J.H.A. *A Practical Treatise on the Criminal Law of Scotland*, p. 125, citing Hume *Commentaries on the Law of Scotland Respecting Crimes*, i, 299 and Alison, *Principles and Practice of the Criminal Law of Scotland*, i, 162.

55 (1841) 2 Swinton 552.

56 (1881) 4 Couper 389.

57 On this concept, see Chapter 12 below.

The Prevention of Cruelty to, and Protection of, Children Act, 1889

Section 1 of the Prevention of Cruelty to, and Protection of, Children Act, 1889 provided that:

> Any person over sixteen years of age who, having custody, control, or charge of a child, being a boy under the age of fourteen years, or being a girl under the age of sixteen years, wilfully ill-treats, neglects, abandons or exposes such a child, or causes or procures such child to be ill-treated, neglected, abandoned, or exposed, in a manner likely to cause such child unnecessary suffering, or injury to its health shall be guilty of [an offence] . . .[58]

Though there were statements in Parliament to the effect that this would extend to children the level of protection that already existed for animals[59] these were rhetorical flourishes since the protection of children existed previously through the common law crime discussed above. There is no common law crime of neglect of animals.

The Prevention of Cruelty to Children (Amendment) Act, 1894 added "assault" to the list of actions that amounted to the offence in the 1889 Act, and the ages for both boys and girls who were protected under the provision were equalised at sixteen.[60] Interestingly, this Act also expanded who might be held to have a duty of care towards the child, breach of which would render them criminally liable. By s. 17, "the provisions of [the 1889 Act and] this Act relating to the parent of a child shall apply to the step-parent of the child and to any person cohabiting with the parent of the child". It may well have been assumed that the person cohabiting with the parent of the child would be the (unrecognised, because unmarried) father,[61] but the terms were clearly wide enough to include cohabitants who had neither legal nor genetic relationship with the child. This may be the earliest statutory recognition of cohabiting couples and is probably evidence that it was children of the poor who were in the minds of the legislators.

In respect of the criminal law as such, this provision simply put into statutory form the pre-existing common law crime. The real innovation came with the granting for the first time to the criminal court of a power to

---

58   Penalties (listed under s. 2) were relatively severe: a fine of up to £100 or imprisonment for up to two years (if charged on indictment), or £25 or three months imprisonment (on summary conviction). A charge under this provision failed because it had not been prosecuted within the six months required for instituting complaints of statutory offences set down in the then extant Summary Procedure Act, 1864: *Farquarson v Gordon* (1894) 21 R (J) 52.

59   See for example Lord Herschell at HL Deb. 22 July 1889, vol. 338 col. 951.

60   Prevention of Cruelty to Children (Amendment) Act, 1894, ss. 1 and 2.

61   See *Liverpool Society for the Prevention of Cruelty to Children v Jones* [1914] 3 KB 813.

make an order to protect the victim of the crime in s. 1 as well as to punish the offender. The 1889 Act provided that if a person was convicted of an offence under s. 1, or of any offence involving bodily injury to the child, or was committed for trial for such an offence, then the court could "order that the child be taken out of the custody of [the offender] and committed to the charge of a relation of the child, or some other fit person named by the court".[62] This subsequently came to be known as a "fit person order", and the protection it offered was the separation of the child from the source of danger and his or her delivery to someone who (it was hoped) would provide the child with a safe and secure upbringing. It is notable that this new power to make a protective order was simply attached to an existing criminal process, and it did not create an independent child protection mechanism. Though it recognised for the first time that making orders for the protection of children was a legitimate role for the criminal court, the Act did not authorise the state, or its civil courts, taking action on its own initiative to protect the vulnerable.

The Prevention of Cruelty to Children Acts, 1894 and 1904

The provisions of the 1889 Act were re-enacted in the Prevention of Cruelty to Children Act, 1894, which contains an important development in that it offered an elaborated definition of "injury to health": this was now to include "injury to or loss of sight, or hearing, or limb, or organ of the body, and any mental derangement".

The reference to "mental derangement" within the concept of "injury to health" is significant as an early recognition that neglect and ill-treatment may cause harm to the mind as well as physical harm. However, the terminology of "mental derangement", which continues to be used today,[63] has not been subject to any judicial construction since its introduction, though it does suggest that something more than emotional neglect was envisaged by the drafters. Ill-treatment leading to unnecessary suffering is clearly wide enough to include suffering of the mind (even if short of a clinically recognised mental injury) as well as bodily suffering.

The word "parent" was further expanded to include "guardian and every person who is by law liable to maintain the child".[64]

---

62 Prevention of Cruelty to, and Protection of, Children Act, 1889, s. 5(1).
63 Children and Young Persons (Scotland) Act, 1937, s. 12(1).
64 Prevention of Cruelty to Children Act, 1894, s. 23(1).

Section 1 of the 1894 Act was replaced, without amendment, by s. 1 of the Prevention of Cruelty to Children Act, 1904. It was held in England that the omission by a non-resident father to contribute towards the support of his children could amount to an offence under the 1904 Act, even while the child was sufficiently supported by others.[65] Under s. 6 of both the 1894 and 1904 Acts, the criminal court continued to have and to exercise the power to remove the child from the offender's custody by making a fit person order.

The Children Act, 1908

Section 12 of the Children Act, 1908 re-enacted the crime in s. 1 of the 1904 Act, with additional words to give statutory force to the decision in *R v Senior*:[66]

> If any person over the age of sixteen years, who has the custody, charge or care of a child or young person[67] wilfully assaults, ill-treats, neglects, abandons, or exposes such child or young person or causes or procures such child or young person to be assaulted, ill-treated, neglected, abandoned, or exposed, in a manner likely to cause such child or young person unnecessary suffering or injury to his health (including injury to or loss of sight, or hearing, or limb, or organ of the body and any mental derangement), that person shall be guilty of [an offence] . . . and for the purposes of this section a parent or other person legally liable to maintain a child or young person shall be deemed to have neglected him in a manner likely to cause injury to his health if he fails to provide adequate food, clothing, medical aid, or lodging for the child or young person, or if, being unable otherwise to provide such food, clothing, medical aid, or lodging, he fails to take such steps to procure the same to be provided under the Acts relating to the relief of the poor.

The protective power of the court to commit a child under 16 to the care of a relative or other fit person was replicated without substantive change,[68] but as always it could operate only retrospectively, that is to say after the commission of an offence against the child or young person.

The Children and Young Persons (Scotland) Act, 1932 raised the age at which an individual was considered to be a young person to 17,[69] but the offence in s. 12 of the 1908 Act remained limited to victims under the age of 16. To achieve that, Schedule 2 to the 1932 Act amended the 1908 Act so

---

65 *R v Connor* [1908] 2 KB 26.

66 (1899) 1 QB 283. In this case failure to provide medical aid was held to be implicitly within the terms of the 1894 Act.

67 "Child" was a person below school leaving age, then 14, and "young person" was a person above that age but below 16.

68 Children Act, 1908, s. 21.

69 Children and Young Persons (Scotland) Act, 1932, s. 64.

that the accused under s. 12 would be a "person who has attained the age of sixteen years and who has the custody, charge or care of a child or young person under the age of sixteen years". These ages for both the offender and the victim of the statutory offence have remained in place ever since.

Section 12 of the Children and Young Persons (Scotland) Act, 1937

The Children and Young Persons (Scotland) Act, 1937 repealed most of the 1908 Act and replaced s. 12 thereof with a new and expanded s. 12, which is not substantially different from its predecessor. As enacted the new s. 12 read:

(1) If any person who has attained the age of sixteen years and has the custody, charge or care of any child or young person under that age wilfully assaults, ill-treats, neglects, abandons, or exposes him, or causes or procures him to be assaulted, ill-treated, neglected, abandoned, or exposed, in a manner likely to cause him unnecessary suffering or injury to health (including injury to or loss of sight, or hearing, or limb, or organ of the body, and any mental derangement), that person shall be guilty of an offence . . .
(2) For the purposes of this section –
(a) a parent or other person legally liable to maintain a child or young person shall be deemed to have neglected him in a manner likely to cause injury to his health if he has failed to provide adequate food, clothing, medical aid, or lodging for him, or if, having been unable otherwise to provide such food, clothing, medical aid, or lodging, he has failed to take steps to procure it to be provided under the Acts relating to the relief of the poor.
(b) where it is proved that the death of a child under three years of age was caused by suffocation (not being suffocation caused by disease or the presence of any foreign body in the throat or air passages of the child) while the child was in bed with some other person who has attained the age of sixteen years, that other person shall, if he was, when he went to bed, under the influence of drink, be deemed to have neglected the child in a manner likely to cause injury to his health.[70]
. . .
(7) Nothing in this section shall be construed as affecting the right of any parent, teacher, or other person having the lawful control or charge of a child or young person to administer punishment to him.

The commission of this offence was one of the bases upon which the child protection mechanisms set out in s. 66 of the 1937 Act (and discussed elsewhere in this book) could be activated. Section 65 of the Act defined a child or young person "in need of care or protection" to include a child or young person in respect of whom any of the offences listed in the First Schedule to

---

70 Section 12(2)(b) is repeated from s. 13 of the 1908 Act, the Parliamentary debates at the time being much concerned with "overlaying" as a cause of infant death. It was in 1908 far more common for babies and infants to share their parents' beds than is the case today.

the Act had been committed: the list included the offence contained in s. 12 and the sexual offences discussed earlier in this chapter. Since the children's hearing system was established under the Social Work (Scotland) Act 1968, being the victim of a "schedule 1 offence"[71] has amounted to a ground of referral to the children's hearing[72] and the offence in s. 12 remains today listed in schedule 1 to the Criminal Procedure (Scotland) Act 1995.

Almost sixty years after the passing of the 1937 Act, s. 12(1) was amended by the Children (Scotland) Act 1995 to take account of the abolition of "custody" and its replacement with the concept of parental responsibilities and parental rights: from then the potential offender was

> any person who has attained the age of sixteen years and who has parental responsibilities in relation to a child or to a young person under that age or has charge or care of a child or such a young person . . .

As it has always been, the essence of the offence is neglect of a pre-existing duty.

A more substantive amendment to s. 12 was made by s. 51 of the Criminal Justice (Scotland) Act 2003, which sought to tighten the defence of reasonable chastisement of children to a charge of assault (discussed later in this chapter). The word "assault" was removed from the list of actions that amount to the offence under s. 12(1) with the result that parents and others with responsibilities towards the child who assaulted their child would now be charged under the common law offence, in the same way as strangers to the child; in addition, subs. (7) was removed in its entirety.[73] These amendments (following the recommendations eleven years earlier of the Scottish Law Commission)[74] were designed to ensure that the defence of reasonable chastisement (as restructured by the 2003 Act) could be used only in respect of the common law charge of assault and could never be used by parents as a defence to a charge of neglect of parental duty under s. 12.

CASE LAW ON SECTION 12 OF THE 1937 ACT

The case law is generated by s. 12 of the Children and Young Persons (Scotland) Act 1937, and its statutory predecessors, from one of two appar-

---

71 Originally, sched. 1 to the 1937 Act, then to the Criminal Procedure (Scotland) Act 1975 and now to the Criminal Procedure (Scotland) Act 1995.

72 Social Work (Scotland) Act 1968, s. 32(2)(d); Children (Scotland) Act 1995, s. 52(2)(d); Children's Hearings (Scotland) Act 2011, s. 67(2)(b).

73 Criminal Justice (Scotland) Act 2003, s. 51(5).

74 *Report on Family Law* (Scot. Law Com. No. 135, 1992) para 2.105.

ently separate routes. Either the case is a directly criminal law matter brought to the court by a prosecutor seeking the punishment of the perpetrator of the offence, or it is the factual basis upon which child protection mechanisms over the victim (or the victim's siblings) are activated. The reported cases on s. 12 of the 1937 Act were mostly criminal cases before 1971 (when the children's hearing system came into operation) but since then have been more commonly concerned with grounds of referral to the children's hearing. However the case arises, the protective mechanisms that are the chief focus of this book become available.

Who may be charged

A number of the earlier cases – English, involving UK-wide legislation – dealt with who had caring responsibilities for the child and who, therefore, might be charged with an offence under s. 12. Section 38 of the 1908 Act, and thereafter s. 27 of the 1937 Act (for Scotland), provided that the parent or "lawful guardian" was presumed to have custody of the child or young person, that "any person to whose charge a child or young person is committed by any person who has the custody of him shall be presumed to have charge of the child or young person", and that "any other person having actual possession or control of a child or young person shall be presumed to have the care of him". In *Liverpool Society for the Prevention of Cruelty to Children v Jones*[75] Avory J said this:

> The very object of the last paragraph in s.38(2) [of the 1908 Act] is to provide that persons who are neither parents nor legal guardians nor legally liable to maintain the child may be subject to the obligations imposed by s. 12 . . .

He added that a gaoler would "undoubtedly have the custody of a child who was in the prison". It would follow that the managers of any approved school (or any other state-run institution for children or young persons, or any voluntary home) and foster carers would be subject to the same obligations, and liable to the same criminal charges. The question of who had charge, control or care of a child was held to be a matter of fact in *Brooks v Blount*,[76] where Salter J said: "a person who has actual possession or control of a child cannot be heard to say that he had not the care of the child" (for the purposes of a charge under s. 12 of the 1908 Act and subsequently the 1937 Act). In

75 [1914] 3 KB 813, p. 817.
76 [1923] 1 KB 257.

Ridley v Little[77] a headmaster was held to have been competently charged under s. 1 of the Children and Young Persons Act, 1933, the English equivalent to s. 12 of the 1937 Act (though the defence of reasonable chastisement was upheld); Kendrick and Hawthorn report a case from Fife in 1945 in which foster parents were convicted of wilful mistreatment of two boys in their care.[78] Under different legislation, the English Court of Appeal held that an accused who employed a 14 year old girl to baby-sit his children had "charge or care" of her.[79]

It must follow from the limitation to accused persons being over the age of 16 that only natural persons can be charged with this offence.

Types of behaviour prohibited by s. 12

More recent cases on s. 12 of the 1937 Act have considered the question of what type of behaviour might constitute an offence within its parameters, and what level of intent the accused must be shown to have possessed. In a decision that paid rather less attention to likelihood of harm than later cases have done, it was held in *Henderson v Stewart*[80] that the failure of a non-resident father to provide sufficient maintenance for his child could amount to "neglect" even although the child was well looked after by the mother (and the child's maintenance was partly borne by the National Assistance Board).[81] This suggests that s. 12 was at one time used as a mechanism to enforce child support. Other cases of neglect, which more clearly raise child protection concerns, have involved leaving three children under nine alone in a warm house with a barking and excreting dog from 11.30 in the morning until 8.30 in the evening,[82] failing to seek medical help for an injured baby,[83] deliberately overmedicating a sick child,[84] dangling a 13 month old child from the window of a multi-storey flat,[85] and leaving a child alone in a room with a pan of hot liquid.[86] A failure to protect the child from the

---

77 *The Times* 26 May 1960.
78 *National Confidential Forum for Adult Survivors of Childhood Abuse in Care: Scoping Project on Children in Care in Scotland 1930-2005*, para 2.7.2.
79 *R v Drury* (1974) 60 Cr App R 195.
80 1954 JC 94.
81 The same result had been reached in England under the Prevention of Cruelty to Children Act, 1904: *R v Connor* [1908] 2 KB 26.
82 *W v Clark* 1999 SCCR 775.
83 *S v Authority Reporter* 2012 SLT (Sh Ct) 89.
84 *Locality Reporter Manager, Applicant* [2019] SC Liv. 60 (10 July 2019, Livingston Sheriff Court).
85 *Keltie v HM Adv.* 2012 HCJAC 79.
86 *B v Murphy* 2014 HCJAC 56.

harmful acts of others was held to amount to "neglect" for the purposes of s. 12 in *Kennedy v S*.[87] The overall principle was identified by the Lord Justice-General, Lord Hope, in *H v Lees, D v Orr*,[88] where he said that what amounted to neglect was to be tested according to "what a reasonable parent, in all the circumstances, would regard as necessary to provide proper care and attention to the child". In the English decision of *R v Boulden*,[89] it was held that "to abandon" a child means to leave it to its fate. "Abandonment" was found to be established in *M v Orr*[90] where the accused, in order to free himself to go to the pub and get drunk, instructed his children to go to their grandmother's, or to school, but without doing anything to ensure their safety or that they followed his instructions. And "exposure" was established when a grandmother took the child to the house of a sex offender, got drunk there and allowed the child to share a bed with both grandmother and the offender, next to a bucket of excrement.[91]

JS v Mulrooney,[92] a children's hearing case, contains one of the few discussions of emotional abuse (though it involved s. 12 only obliquely). The sheriff had used the term "emotional abuse" to describe the "neglect" to which children had been subjected (a pattern of behaviour that seriously interfered with the child's cognitive, emotional, psychological or social development) and the Inner House said: "we cannot say that she was wrong to do so".[93]

The place of intent

Intent, in relation to the common law crime of child cruelty, concerned the action and not the consequences,[94] and this has always been the case under the statutory provisions also.[95] Trotter, writing in 1938, stated that "wilfully" meant that the act had to be done deliberately and not accidentally but that there was no need to establish intent to injure.[96] This was confirmed in the

---

87 1986 SC 43.
88 1993 JC 238, p. 245.
89 (1957) 41 Crim. App. Rep. 105.
90 1995 SLT 26.
91 *M v Aitken* 2006 SLT 691. Cf the English decision of *R v Gibbons* [1977] Crim LR 741 where it was held, construing the same word in the English statute, that "expose" did not include "expose to risk".
92 2014 CSIH 70.
93 Ibid. para 30.
94 Anderson, A.M. *The Criminal Law of Scotland* (1904), pp. 171–172.
95 *R v Senior* (1899) 1 QB 283; *R v Connor* [1908] 2 KB 26.
96 *The Law as to Children and Young Persons* (W Hodge & Co, 1938), pp. 21 and 25.

decision of the High Court of Justiciary in *Clark v HM Adv.*[97] where parents, who had failed to provide adequate food and medical aid as a result of which their daughter had died, were themselves so mentally disabled as to be unaware that their behaviour was harmful. The question to be decided was whether, in these circumstances, the parents could be said to have had the capacity for "wilful" neglect. The court held that capacity to understand the outcome was not necessary for a competent charge: "wilful" qualified the acts and not the harms listed in s. 12.

The matter was revisited in *JM v Brechin*,[98] which involved a ground of referral to the children's hearing that the father was guilty of "wilful ill-treatment" by lifting each of his twin children by one hand, exerting such force as to cause severe fractures to their ribs. The father contended (i) that the offence of wilful ill-treatment required proof of awareness either that his actions would cause unnecessary suffering or injury to health, or recklessness and (ii) that the word "wilfully" qualified both the actions (the neglect, ill-treatment etc.) and the consequences (the unnecessary suffering or the injury to health). These averments were rejected and, following *Clark v HM Adv.*, it was held that the word "wilfully" required only that the conduct be deliberate: the result was that the accused's awareness of the likely consequences of his or her actions was nothing to the point. Lord Carloway said this:

> "Wilful" ill-treatment requires deliberate or intentional conduct. "Wilful", as it is ordinarily understood in the context of the mental element in crimes, involves intention. Notwithstanding the origins of the statutory offence in legislation generally applicable throughout the United Kingdom, there is nothing to suggest that Parliament intended to restrict the common law position in Scotland. The pre-existing common law offences of child cruelty, loosely defined, paid little, if any, regard to either the motives or the state of mind of the perpetrator who put his child at risk or in danger, or caused the child to suffer injury. The relevant issue was whether harm would be likely to, or inevitably, arise from the deliberate act or omission in question.
>
> The scope of the requisite intention is sufficiently clear from the statutory purpose to improve the protection of children from cruelty (short of assault) at the hands of those who bear the responsibility of caring for them. The statute requires the assessment of ill-treatment or neglect, according to the objectively assessed likelihood of its harmful consequences, in order to give effect to that purpose. The offence strikes only at conduct at such a level of culpability that it is likely to cause the child suffering or injury to health. The imposition of criminal liability is circumscribed by the likelihood and significance of harm,

97　1968 JC 53.
98　[2015] CSIH 58.

and is restricted to the class of person in the position of responsibility for a child. The introduction of a subjective assessment of ill-treatment or neglect, involving a search for the carer's thinking at the relevant time, would remove the desired statutory protection otherwise afforded to children.

. . . [W]hat is required, first, is that the conduct be deliberate. Secondly, the court must be able to categorise the conduct as "ill-treatment", in the sense of involving what can reasonably be described as cruelty. The character or quality of conduct that will constitute ill-treatment is a matter to be determined objectively. The addition of the term "wilful" does not import a subjective element to that assessment. The proper threshold of criminal liability is fixed also by reference to the likelihood of sufficiently grave consequences arising from deliberate or voluntary action or inaction. The term "wilful" necessarily serves to exclude accidental or inadvertent conduct, as opposed to the accidental or inadvertent consequences of deliberate conduct, from the scope of the offence. It is unnecessary, and contrary to the statutory purpose, to restrict the scope of the offence by reference to the subjective awareness of the individual of the harmful nature of the conduct in question.[99]

Likelihood of harm

From the above, it is clear that likelihood of injury rather than intent to injure is of the essence of the s. 12 offence. It follows that conduct might be captured by s. 12 in one circumstance but not in another, depending upon whether, in these circumstances, the child was "likely" to be injured. So in *R v Hatton*,[100] a case decided under s. 12 of the 1908 Act, a conviction was quashed against a step-father who had committed an (unspecified) "act of indecency" (presumably, he masturbated) in the presence of his 11 year old step-daughter and had placed his hand over her mouth to stop her screaming, because his actions were not likely to cause unnecessary suffering but only agitation of mind. More recently it was held that for a father to leave his 20-month old child strapped in a car while shopping could not sustain a charge of "wilful neglect" without specification of likely risk.[101] In *H v Lees, D v Orr*[102] the lack of evidence that irresponsible parenting was likely to cause harm meant that no offence under s. 12 had been committed when a mother was drunk and incapable while in charge of her nine month old baby, nor when a father had left his 13 year old daughter alone in their house for six hours.

A likelihood of suffering may well exist even if, in the event, no suffering

---

99 [2015] CSIH 58, paras 49–51.
100 [1925] 2 KB 322.
101 *M v Normand* 1995 SLT 1284.
102 1993 JC 238.

occurs. In *Locality Reporter, Stirling v KR*[103] a four year old child had been
smacked in the head by her mother "with considerable force", but the child
did not seem to show any suffering, The sheriff had held that, therefore, he
could not find any likelihood of the ill-treatment causing unnecessary suffering, but the Sheriff Appeal Court overruled this on the ground that a blow
to the head, prohibited by s. 51 of the Criminal Justice (Scotland) Act 2003
(discussed below) was conclusive evidence of the likelihood of suffering.
The statute required no finding of suffering, but a finding of likelihood of
suffering. The court also suggested that likelihood of injury was more readily
to be inferred in cases like the present, which involved positive ill-treatment
than in cases like *H v Lees*, which involved neglect. That reasoning might
well have given a different result in *R v Hatton* (above).

THE PARENTAL RIGHT OF CHASTISEMENT

While assaulting children and young people, like assaulting any other person,
has always been either a common law or a statutory crime in Scotland, parents (and some others) were for a long time sometimes granted an immu-
nity from prosecution if their actions, which would otherwise amount to
an assault, came within the defence that came to be known as "reasonable
chastisement". This gave parents the right to visit corporal punishment upon
their children, certainly their pupil children and probably also their children
in minority.[104] When the common law crime of child neglect or cruelty was
put onto a statutory basis, the common law defence was also explicitly preserved.[105] The statutory formulation of this defence, latterly in s. 12(7) of the
Children and Young Persons (Scotland) Act, 1937, remained on the statute
book until its repeal in 2003; the defence itself survived until 2019.

The meaning of "reasonable chastisement"

The right of corporal punishment was never, however, unlimited in lawful
severity nor free from constraints on motive. According to Erskine (writing
in the eighteenth century) parents were allowed to exercise "that degree of

---

103 [2018] SAC Civ 30.
104 See Wilkinson A. and Norrie K. *The Law Relating to Parent and Child in Scotland* (3rd edn),
    para 7.36.
105 Prevention of Cruelty to, and Protection of, Children Act, 1889, s. 14; Prevention of Cruelty
    to Children Act, 1894, s. 24; Prevention of Cruelty to Children Act, 1904, s. 28; Children Act,
    1908, s. 37; Children and Young Persons (Scotland) Act, 1937, s. 12(7).

discipline and moderate chastisement upon them, which their perverseness of temper or inattention calls for".[106] The purpose of chastisement required to be educative and designed to further the welfare of the child which, in Fraser's words (writing in the nineteenth century), "while it sanctions, also limits the right".[107] Corporal punishment, then, was lawful but only when both (i) aimed at chastisement, in the sense of educative punishment, and (ii) within a moderate and reasonable level of severity. Going beyond this would expose the perpetrator to both criminal liability under s. 12 of the 1937 Act (and its predecessors), and to civil liability;[108] since 1971 (the offence in s. 12 being a scheduled offence for the purposes of the children's hearing system) punishing a child to a severity that is beyond reasonable chastisement has amounted to a ground for referral to the children's hearing.[109]

The concept of "reasonableness" is never static and always reflects the temper of the times, but cases from the earliest period indicate a judicial awareness of the dangers to vulnerable children of excessive physical punishment. The determination of what is "reasonable" today is influenced by the jurisprudence of the European Court of Human Rights, whose decisions on the matter[110] led directly to the passing of s. 51 of the Criminal Justice (Scotland) Act 2003 which, amongst other things, repealed s. 12(7) of the 1937 Act.[111] Section 51(1) lists the factors that the court must have regard to in determining whether the act amounts to "justifiable assault"; s. 51(3) provides that a blow to the head, shaking, or the use of an implement is never a "justifiable assault".[112]

Other than the imposition of an absolute prohibition on blows to the head of a child, shaking a child, or using an implement against a child, the factors listed in the Act and required to be considered all previously featured in the

---

106 Erskine, *An Institute of the Law of Scotland* (1773) I, vi, 53.

107 Fraser, *Parent and Child* (3rd edn) p. 83.

108 As for example in *Ewart v Brown* (1882) 10R 163.

109 Social Work (Scotland) Act 1968, s. 32(2)(d); Children (Scotland) Act 1995, s. 52(2)(d); Children's Hearings (Scotland) Act 2011, s. 67(2)(b). See for example *Locality Reporter, Stirling v KR* [2018] SAC Civ 30.

110 See especially *Costello-Roberts v United Kingdom* (1995) 19 EHRR 112 and *A v United Kingdom* (1999) 27 EHRR 611.

111 Criminal Justice (Scotland) Act 2003, s. 51(5)(b).

112 Previous attempts to restrict the defence of reasonable chastisement had failed. During the debates on the Children (Scotland) Bill in 1995 an amendment based on the Scottish Law Commission's proposal to that effect (*Report on Family Law* Scot. Law Com. No. 135, para 2.105) was defeated in the House of Commons by 260 votes to 193: HC Deb. 1 May 1995 vol. 259 col. 75, and then again in the House of Lords by 128 votes to 87: HL Deb. 5 July 1995 vol. 565 col. 1120.

case law, leading Wilkinson and Norrie to doubt "whether a radical change has been affected by the Criminal Justice (Scotland) Act 2003 to the law that applied before".[113] And while the 2003 Act may have sought to address ECHR concerns, there was an increasing acceptance that the Scottish position, even if compatible with the European Convention, breached Article 19 of the United Nations Convention on the Rights of the Child:[114] the UN Committee on the Rights of the Child more than once criticised the United Kingdom for not removing entirely from its law the parental defence of reasonable chastisement.[115]

THE RIGHT OF SCHOOL TEACHERS OR OTHERS TO INFLICT CORPORAL PUNISHMENT

School teachers

Most of the earlier cases on "reasonable chastisement" involved defenders who were teachers rather than parents.[116] In either case, however, the test for legality was the same: the striking of a child amounted to "reasonable chastisement" and provided, therefore, a defence to a charge of assault only when aimed at educative discipline, and only when reasonable force was used in all the circumstances. A teacher's power of chastisement, when it existed, was not traced to delegation by parents of their right to discipline but was a self-standing privilege arising from the obligation of the teacher

---

113 Wilkinson and Norrie, *Parent and Child* (3rd edn), para 7.41.

114 This is the obligation on Member States "to take all appropriate legislative, administrative, social and educational measures to protect the child from all forms of physical or mental violence, injury or abuse, neglect or negligent treatment, maltreatment or exploitation, including sexual abuse, while in the care of parent(s), legal guardian(s) or any other person who has the care of the child".

115 See Committee on the Rights of the Child, *Concluding Observations on the UK's Second Report*, 9 October 2002, CRC/C/15.Add.188; and Committee on the Rights of the Child, *Concluding Observations on the UK's Third and Fourth Report*, 3 October 2008, CRC/C/GBR/CO/4. The arguments are set out in detail in the Report *Equally Protected? A Review of the Evidence on the Physical Punishment of Children*, NSPCC Scotland, Children 1st, Barnardo's Scotland and the Children and Young Persons Commissioner Scotland (2015).

116 Indeed it was not until *Guest v Annan* 1988 SCCR 275 that a case appeared in the law reports in which a parent pled the defence (see also *Byrd v Wither* 1991 SLT 206 which involved the mother's cohabitant), though since then it has been vastly more common for parents to have been found to have committed an offence under s. 12 of the 1937 Act for the purposes of referral to the children's hearing: see for example *C v Harris* 1989 SC 278; *B v Harris* 1990 SLT 208; *Kennedy v A* 1993 SLT 1134; *G v Templeton* 1998 SCLR 180; *Locality Reporter, Stirling v KR* [2018] SAC Civ 30.

to maintain school-room discipline.[117] As early as 1848 the Lord President (Boyle) may be found saying:

> It is clear that a teacher of a public school, being bound to see that the pupils behave correctly, is entitled to administer chastisement when the pupils deserve it; but it must be moderate, and without any cruel or vindictive feeling or passion.[118]

In 1882 it was stated, "A schoolmaster is invested by law with the power of giving his pupils moderate and reasonable corporal punishment, but the law will not protect him when his chastisement is unnatural, improper, or excessive."[119] And in 1922 Lord Ormidale said this:

> we look in vain for anything in the evidence or in the complaint which indicates that the chastisement was cruel or savage, or anything more than a teacher, whether a head teacher or an assistant teacher, was entitled to inflict upon disobedient pupils in order to maintain discipline.[120]

This "entitlement" prevented the chastisement from being a common law assault, and the statutory offences contained first in the Prevention of Cruelty to, and Protection of, Children Act, 1889 and finally in s. 12 of the Children and Young Persons (Scotland) Act, 1937 all contained reservations explicitly preserving the right of teachers "to administer punishment".[121] There had been an attempt to limit this provision, when it first appeared in 1889, to punishment that was "reasonable and moderate", but the amendment failed.[122]

In the event, few cases against school teachers were actually successful, partly due to difficulty in establishing intent to cause injury,[123] and partly through a reluctance on the part of the courts to become involved in overseeing school-room discipline.[124] In *Gray v Hawthorn*[125] (one of the few cases in which a conviction against a teacher was sustained[126]) Lord Guthrie said this:

> There is no doubt that a school teacher is vested with disciplinary powers to enable him to do his educational work and to maintain proper order in class and in school, and it is therefore largely a matter within his discretion whether, and to

117 See Wallington, P "Corporal Punishment in Schools" 1972 *Juridical Review* 124.
118 *Muckarsie v Dickson* (1848) 11 D 4, p. 5.
119 *Ewart v Brown* (1882) 10 R 163, note, p. 166, per Sheriff Substitute Buntine.
120 *McShane v Paton* 1922 JC 26, p. 31.
121 See n. 105 above.
122 HC Deb. 3 July 1889, vol. 337 cols 1384–1386.
123 See for example *Scorgie v Lawrie* (1883) 10 R 610.
124 *McShane v Paton* 1922 JC 26.
125 1964 JC 69.
126 In *Brown v Hilson* 1924 JC 1 the charge of assault was held competent.

what extent, the circumstances call for the exercise of these powers by the infliction of chastisement. In general it is true to say that the court will not review the
exercise of these disciplinary powers by a schoolmaster, since it cannot interfere
with what falls within the scope of his discretion. If what the schoolmaster has
done can truly be regarded as an exercise of his disciplinary powers, although
mistaken, he cannot be held to have contravened the criminal law. It is only
if there has been an excess of punishment over what could be regarded as an
exercise of disciplinary powers that it can be held to be an assault. In other words
the question in all such cases is whether there has been dole on the part of the
accused, the evil intent which is necessary to constitute a crime by the law of
Scotland.[127]

A teacher's self-standing right of reasonable chastisement has, as we will
see below, now been removed by statute.

Persons acting *in loco parentis*

The "right" to inflict corporal punishment was recognised at common law to
inhere in more than simply parents and teachers. So too under the statutory
provisions discussed above, the right to administer punishment was held
not only by parents and teachers but also by any "other person having the
lawful control or charge of a child or young person". These words were to
be read with s. 38(2) of the 1908 Act and then with s. 27 of the 1937 Act,
which provided that "any person to whose charge a child or young person
is committed by any person who has the custody of the child or young
person shall be presumed to have charge of the child or young person".[128]
Persons having "lawful control or charge of a child or young person" would
certainly include foster carers with whom children have been boarded-out
by local authorities. Foster carers had long had all the rights and powers of a
parent,[129] which included the right of reasonable chastisement. The very aim
of boarding a child out with foster carers – to integrate the child fully into his
or her foster home – is consistent with the foster parents' power being the
same as they had over their own children. The only statutory modification
of this (before its outright prohibition, for which see below) is to be found

---

127 1964 JC 69, pp. 75–76. In this case, a series of punishments that amounted to what the Court
    described as "unjust persecution" of the pupil was held to go beyond the ambit of the teacher's
    disciplinary powers.
128 *Liverpool Society for the Prevention of Cruelty to Children v Jones* [1914] 3 KB 813 per Lord
    Avory, p. 817.
129 Prevention of Cruelty to, and Protection of, Children Act, 1889, s. 5(2); Prevention of Cruelty
    to Children Act, 1894, s. 7(1); Prevention of Cruelty to Children Act, 1904 Act, s. 7; Children
    Act, 1908, s. 22(1); Children and Young Persons (Scotland) Act, 1937, s. 79(4).

in the Schedule to the Children (Boarding-out etc.) (Scotland) Rules and Regulations, 1947[130] para 5(f), which stated that "The foster-parent shall not administer indiscriminate or harsh punishment": this does not, however, seem to add anything to the law of reasonable chastisement as applied to parents. Nothing similar appeared in the Boarding-out of Children (Scotland) Regulations, 1959,[131] but during their currency public foster parents could claim to act *in loco parentis* and so enjoy all the powers of corporal punishment (and its limitations) applicable to parents. It is worth noting that no case has been traced in which foster carers sought to rely on the reasonable chastisement defence in respect of children boarded-out with them.

Corporal punishment in residential establishments

The position of children in approved schools, remand homes, local authority homes and voluntary homes was very different, because secondary legislation long set down explicit, and often highly detailed, rules for the administration of corporal punishment, which superseded any common law power of reasonable chastisement inhering in those acting *in loco parentis*.

Prior to 1959, managers and staff of children's homes, whether voluntary or otherwise, could probably claim to be persons *in loco parentis* by virtue of having lawful control or charge of the children, and to have the right, therefore, to administer corporal punishment so long as that amounted to "reasonable chastisement" in the sense discussed above. The Administration of Children's Homes (Scotland) Regulations, 1959 recognised this right but did not constrain it any more than the common law did, other than to specify that corporal punishment was to be used only "exceptionally", and not against any child with physical or mental disability other than with the sanction of the medical officer.[132] Beyond that, the lawfulness of corporal punishment would be determined by the moderation of the force used, and the motives of the person administering the punishment. This was the case until the abolition of corporal punishment in children's homes (by then called residential establishments) from 1 June 1988 (see below).

---

130 SI 1947/2146 (S. 76).
131 SI 1959/835.
132 1959 Regulations, reg. 11.

Corporal punishment in approved schools

Teachers at residential schools, whether industrial or reformatory, could rely on the common law right of chastisement recognised in and preserved by the early child cruelty statutes. After the Children and Young Persons (Scotland) Act, 1932, the matter was regulated by secondary legislation. Corporal punishment by a "light tawse" was permitted in approved schools under the Children and Young Persons (Scotland) Care and Training Regulations, 1933,[133] though only "rarely" on girls. Details of the number of strokes permitted, varying according to the age and sex of the child, were laid down in the regulations, as was who could inflict the punishment; records were to be kept of punishments inflicted.[134] These rules, which superseded the common law position, were replicated in the Approved Schools (Scotland) Rules, 1961,[135] which applied until the abolition of corporal punishment in such schools from 1 June 1988 (see below).

ABOLITION OF CORPORAL PUNISHMENT

In schools

In *Campbell and Cosans v. United Kingdom*[136] it was held by the European Court of Human Rights that the use of corporal punishment in Scottish schools amounted to a breach of Article 2 Protocol 1 of the European Convention on Human Rights because it failed to respect the parents' philosophical conviction against corporal punishment. The Government (sensibly) considered it impractical to prohibit corporal punishment only in respect of children whose parents objected, and so instead, all pupils at public schools were granted protection from corporal punishment by their teachers. This was effected by s. 48 of the Education (No. 2) Act 1986, which inserted a new s. 48A into the Education (Scotland) Act 1980.[137] This provided that corporal punishment could never be justified on the ground that it was administered by a member of staff at a state (or other specified) school by virtue of his or her position as such. That provision did not cover

---

133 SR&O 1933 No. 1006 (S. 55).
134 1933 Regulations, regs 14–18.
135 1961 Rules (SI 1961/2243), rr. 29–32.
136 [1982] 4 EHRR 293.
137 For a description of the parliamentary history of this provision, see Marshall, K. "Spare the Rod" in J. Grant and E.E. Sutherland (eds) *Scots Law Tales* (2010), pp. 193–196.

independent schools, but it was repealed and replaced by the Standards in Scotland's Schools etc. Act 2000,[138] under which corporal punishment given by, or on the authority of, a member of staff to a pupil at any school "cannot be justified in any proceedings on the ground that it was so given in pursuance of a right exercisable by virtue of having a position as a member of staff". Teachers, acting as such, cannot visit corporal punishment on children even when authorised to do so by parents, and that rule does not breach parents' rights to their philosophical and religious views.[139]

In residential establishments

While the terms of s. 16 of the 2000 Act were carefully calibrated to ensure that they cover all staff, teaching or otherwise, at "schools", whether public or independent, they do not capture staff at institutions other than schools, such as children's homes or other residential establishments. Staff at such institutions had lost the power to chastise children physically some years earlier when the Social Work (Residential Establishments – Child Care) (Scotland) Regulations 1987[140] came into force. Regulation 10(1) thereof permitted "arrangements for discipline, relevant to the care and control of children resident in a residential establishment" to be determined by the managers, but this was qualified by Regulation 10(2) which stated that "the arrangements shall not authorise the giving of corporal punishment", which was given the same meaning as it had under s. 48A of the Education (Scotland) Act 1980.[141] This remains the law today.[142]

By foster carers

There was no statutory[143] prohibition on local authority foster parents visiting corporal punishment on the children they cared for until the Fostering of Children (Scotland) Regulations 1996.[144] These Regulations required

---

138 Standards in Scotland's Schools etc. Act 2000, s. 16.
139 *R (Williamson) v Secretary of State for Education* [2005] 2 AC 246.
140 SI 1987/2233.
141 "References . . . to giving corporal punishment are references to doing anything for the purposes of punishing the pupil concerned (whether or not there are also other reasons for doing it) which, apart from any justification, would constitute physical assault upon the person."
142 Residential Establishments – Child Care (Scotland) Regulations 1996 (SI 1996/3256), reg. 10.
143 It is possible that individual local authorities had policies requiring foster carers to refrain from corporal punishment, and such policies were expected to be followed by carers (Boarding Out and Fostering of Children (Scotland) Regulations, 1985, reg. 8).
144 SI 1996/3263. The matter was not mentioned in either the Boarding Out and Fostering of

that foster carer agreements[145] contain a provision recognising the foster carer's obligation not to administer corporal punishment to any child placed with them.[146] That obligation was repeated in the Looked After Children (Scotland) Regulations 2009.[147] Neither the 1996 nor the 2009 Regulations cover private foster carers[148] who, by acting *in loco parentis*, would seem therefore to remain governed by the same rules as parents themselves (set out above).[149]

By parents and others

In 2017 the Children (Equal Protection from Assault) (Scotland) Bill was published as a private member's bill, though it quickly gained the support of the Scottish Government. By 80 (cross-party) votes to 29 (Conservative) votes the Bill passed Stage One on 28 May 2019; Stage Two was completed on 20 June 2019; and stage three on 3 October 2019 (with a majority of 84 to 29, with the same political division as before). It received Royal Assent on 7 November 2019 and will come into force on the expiry of one year thereafter. The 2019 Act abolishes the defence of reasonable chastisement as an exercise of either a parental right or a right derived from having charge or care of the child, and it repeals s. 51 of the Criminal Justice (Scotland) Act 2003. Children now have the same level of protection from assault as adults.

Children (Scotland) Regulations 1985 or the Boarding-out of Children (Scotland) Regulations, 1959.

145 See Chapter 7 below.

146 1996 Regulations, sched. 2 para 6.

147 SSI 2009/210, sched. 6 para 6. The same rule applies to kinship carers: sched. 5 para 5.

148 Regulated under the Foster Children (Scotland) Act 1984.

149 The Foster Children (Private Fostering) (Scotland) Regulations 1985 (SI 1985/1798) does not mention corporal punishment.

4. The Legal Process before 1968: The Juvenile Court

INTRODUCTION

Children have had since the earliest days of the Scottish legal system a status different from and subservient to adults, certainly within the context of their own families. However, it was not until the nineteenth century that children, in their relations with the external world, came to be seen as requiring special treatment different from that accorded to adults. One of the earliest manifestations of the recognition that children, due to their physical weakness, ought to be dealt with differently from adults was in the realm of employment. As early as 1819 the Cotton Mills and Factories Act prohibited the employment in factories of children under the age of nine years and limited the working hours of nine to 16 year olds to 12 hours a day. The Factories Act, 1833 set up a system of factory inspectors to ensure the rules were adhered to.[1] The introduction of compulsory education of children[2] later in the century also recognised the special position of children, though that was predicated less on the need to recognise the limitations to children's physical capacities and more on the notion that children could and should be given the chance to develop their full capacities and that the state itself had a role in ensuring this.

The same thinking was applied to the legal process itself in the early years of the twentieth century. The idea that children who are brought to court as subjects of the process – as opposed to being the object of some dispute, typically between the parents – needing to be dealt with differently from adults grew out of a belief, increasingly accepted in the latter

---

1 The Employment of Children Act, 1903 extended these protections to non-factory work. Employment of children was frequently dealt with in the Prevention of Cruelty Acts, such as the Prevention of Cruelty to, and Protection of, Children Act, 1889 which by s. 3 prohibited children under 10 from being performers or sellers in places licensed for entertainment or the consumption of liquor. The mass of statutory materials were consolidated in Part IV of the Children and Young Persons (Scotland) Act, 1932 and then Part III of the Children and Young Persons (Scotland) Act, 1937.

2 Education (Scotland) Act, 1872.

half of the nineteenth century, in the specialness of children, that they were "corruptible innocents" who required to be protected from baleful influences. The science of child development was then in its infancy, but that specialness was assumed to encompass three separate but related ideas: that children, due to their inexperience and physical immaturity, were particularly vulnerable to the harmful influences of others, that notions of "guilt" played out differently with underdeveloped minds, and that children, much more so than adults, were capable of being "saved", that is of being moulded into good and productive citizens who obeyed the laws of man, and of God.

By the turn of the twentieth century, penal reformers were beginning to win the argument that young offenders ought to be dealt with in a rehabilitative rather than a punitive fashion; at the same time social reformers, seeing correlations between crime and poverty, and between poverty and neglect, began to argue in favour of intervening in children's lives even before any offences had been committed. Policies aiming to divert young people away from crime always require indicators of risk and all too often risk was identified by either sub-criminal behaviour or a sub-optimal home environment. Children who were being brought up in circumstances of neglect, poverty and lack of education, or were actively abused by their parents, were seen to be at a high risk of becoming offenders even before they (that is to say, some of them) had done so, and the legislation separating children from the adult criminal process went hand in hand with the civil processes for dealing with abused and neglected children.

It is, of course, one of the definitional features of the contemporary children's hearing system in Scotland that it deals with all children in need, including both offenders against the law and those who are victims of what may loosely be termed bad parenting. We in Scotland have a tendency to regard this approach as part of the genius of the Kilbrandon reforms in the 1960s, but in reality this feature applied in Scotland, indeed throughout the UK, for decades before the children's hearing system was legislatively brought into being. The early years of the twentieth century were marked, both here and abroad, by a growing belief that the categories of "offender" and "victim" were not entirely separate and it has long been regarded in Scotland to be a waste of intellectual energy to seek to classify any particular case as either a young offender or a care and protection case. All too often they are both, and to emphasise one aspect over the other would miss the inherent wholeness of the problems that children commonly face. Today, this is seen particularly clearly with children who show sexually harmful behaviour towards other children: these children (particularly pre-adolescent children who show such behaviour) very often themselves have suffered extensive abuse.[3] It is a political decision to regard such children as either victims themselves or (serious) offenders, but making such a decision obscures the reality that they are both. Any response of the law that institutionally emphasises one aspect over the other is, putting it at its mildest, less likely to be a successful response than one that recognises the inseparability of the child's back-history from his or her current behaviour patterns. The most effective institutional way of recognising that inseparability is to have the same legal process deal with all aspects of the child's or young person's life. That is the system that Scots law embraced almost a century ago and the reasons given then for this unity of approach continue to justify retaining that system today.

Yet it was not an original innovation in the United Kingdom to treat the two broad categories of children in the same legal process. The real puzzle is not so much why Scotland adopted such a system early in the twentieth century but how it has managed to retain it into the twenty-first century, by which time most other cognate jurisdictions that previously took a unitary approach have long since moved towards a separation between young offender cases and care and protection cases. Some consideration to that question will be given at the end of the next chapter.

THE WORLD-WIDE JUVENILE COURT MOVEMENT

Juvenile courts in the USA

The first court anywhere in the English-speaking world established for young offenders separate from adult offenders is generally recognised to be the Cook County Juvenile Court, established in Illinois in 1899.[4] The combined ideas of establishing special courts to deal with young offenders separately from adults and to include care and protection cases as a means of diverting potential offenders spread quickly across the United States.

> Within five years of 1899, eleven states had enacted statutes giving juvenile jurisdiction to either new or already existing tribunals. By 1909, the District of Columbia and twenty additional states had established juvenile courts. By 1927, all but Maine and Wyoming had some form of juvenile court in operation and

---

3 This matter is explored by Hackett, S. in *What Works for Children and Young People with Harmful Sexual Behaviours?* (Barnado's, 2004).
4 Illinois Juvenile Court Act, April 21, 1899 (Ill. Laws 131).

these latter two holdouts had enacted juvenile court acts shortly after the end of World War II.[5]

The typical design of these Acts followed that of Illinois in giving jurisdiction over all persons under the age of 16 suffering from either "delinquency" (that is to say those who had committed an offence) or "dependency and neglect" (that is to say those who were homeless or wanting in proper parental care). The common underlying legal rationale in the United States was that the state was entitled, indeed duty-bound, to exercise its *parens patriae* jurisdiction over all children within the state, which power superseded that of the parent.[6] This allowed the aim of the criminal legal process to be conceived not as punishment for wrongs committed but as rehabilitation and redemption of all those who needed it, whether offenders or those (through being homeless or in want of proper parental care) who were at risk of becoming offenders. As the Pennsylvania Supreme Court put it in 1905:

> [The object of the legislation] is to save, not to punish; it is to rescue, not to imprison; it is to subject to wise care, treatment and control rather than to incarcerate in penitentiaries and jails; it is to strengthen the better instincts and to check the tendencies which are evil; it aims, in the absence of proper parental care, or guardianship, to throw around a child, just starting in an evil course, the strong arm of the *parens patriae*.[7]

This was benevolent paternalism, in which the state, through the juvenile court, took over the role of the good, and the stern, parent seeking to ensure the child follows a path of righteousness rather than being tempted into criminality or indolence. Fifty years later the same approach continued to underpin the court's reasoning in *Holmes' Appeal*,[8] where it was said:

> The proceedings [at a juvenile court] are not in the nature of a criminal trial but constitute merely a civil inquiry or action looking to the treatment, reformation and rehabilitation of the minor child. Their purpose is not penal but protective . . . to check juvenile delinquency and to throw around a child, just starting,

---

5 Watkins, J.C. *The Juvenile Justice Century: A Sociolegal Commentary on American Juvenile Courts* (Carolina Academic Press, 1998), p. 45.

6 A history of the *parens patriae* jurisdiction as exercised by the Court of Chancery in England, and its translation into US jurisprudence, is given in Mack, J.W. "The Juvenile Court" (1909) 23 *Harvard Law Review* 104, and Rendleman, D.R. "*Parens Patriae*: From Chancery to the Juvenile Court" (1971) 23 *South Carolina Law Review* 205. More critical commentary is provided by Curtis, G.B. "The Checkered Career of *Parens Patriae*: The State as Parent or Tyrant?" (1976) 25 *De Paul Law Review* 895.

7 *Commonwealth v Fisher* 213 Pa. 48 (1905) at para 4. See also Holstein, S.B. "Slamming the Door on Prodigals: Changing Conceptions of Childhood and the Demise of Juvenile Justice" (1982) 9 *Northern Kentucky Law Review* 517.

8 379 Pa 599 (1955), pp. 603–604; 109 A. 2d 523, p. 525.

perhaps, on an evil course and deprived of proper parental care, the strong arm of the State acting as *parens patriae*. The State is not seeking to punish an offender but to salvage a boy who may be in danger of becoming one, and to safeguard his adolescent life . . . No suggestion or taint of criminality attaches to any finding of delinquency by a Juvenile Court.

In some states, parental failure in addition to the commission of an offence was a necessary precondition to the juvenile court exercising jurisdiction over the young offender. The Supreme Court of Utah, for example, held that:

Before the state can be substituted to the right of the parent, it must affirmatively be made to appear that the parent has forfeited his natural and legal right to the custody and control of the child by reason of his failure, inability, neglect, or incompetency to discharge the duty and thus to enjoy the right. Unless, therefore, both the delinquency of the child and the incompetency, for any reason, of the parent concur and are so found, the court exceeds its power when committing a child to any of the institutions contemplated by the Act.[9]

This was not necessary in all states, but the overall effect of founding the court's jurisdiction on *parens patriae* was to place a steadily increasing emphasis on parental failing and it was an easy step for such failing to become sufficient in itself, even without the commission of an offence, to justify the juvenile court taking over control of the upbringing of the child. In any case, it always assumed that good parenting (whether by parents or the state) would minimise offending behaviour.

Though we do not conceptualise the children's hearing in Scotland as exercising a *parens patriae* jurisdiction, it certainly assumes the form of state paternalism. The design of the early US juvenile courts was based on principles that will be very familiar to those working in the children's hearing system today. John C. Watkins described the thinking behind these courts at the turn of the twentieth century:

Behind both the Illinois law and the establishment of the Cook County Juvenile Court stood a cluster of ideas that served to promote a national movement for a separate juvenile justice system. In sum, there were at least five essential ideas or aims of juvenile justice. These were (1) the establishment of a tribunal that was organized to specifically avoid the stigma of criminalising the young; (2) a tribunal whose processes would largely avoid public scrutiny through closed-door proceedings and the judicial sealing of juvenile records; (3) a tribunal whose treatment ethos would attempt to reduce youth crime by eradicating delinquent behaviour in its "budding" stages; (4) a tribunal whose probation division would, in effect, open to the juvenile a "supermarket of social services" under the aegis

---

9 *Mill v Brown* 31 Utah 473, 88 Pac. 609 (1907).

of a new social science; and (5) a tribunal whose personnel, for the most part, held an almost pathological prejudice against adult criminal law and practice.[10]

The reference here to "budding stages" is revealing. It indicates that a central part of the juvenile court's role was to take jurisdiction over more than simply those young people who have committed offences: the language of "delinquent", because it encompasses socially disapproved as well as criminalised behaviour, was capable of capturing a significantly broader range of individuals than the language of "offender". There are of course dangers here in giving the court jurisdiction over sub-criminal behaviour, but if the aim is protection and the provision of help, then the dangers tend to be obscured by good motives. It was only some decades later that it came to be generally accepted that good motives in themselves are seldom if ever sufficient to justify state intervention in family life.

We can nevertheless see here the defining characteristics of a system of juvenile justice: a tribunal with wide jurisdiction beyond offenders and including those who show sub-offending behaviour and those who are neglected or abused; outcomes designed with the young person's welfare in mind; a process that eschews strict probative constraints to inquiry in favour of a wide examination of the young person in society. All of the characteristics mentioned by Watkins continue, with but little modification, to find reflection in the children's hearing system in Scotland today.

Juvenile Courts in Australia

The first decade of the twentieth century saw the establishment of specialist courts to deal with children and young people not only in the USA but across the English-speaking world, and beyond. Representative may be the position in Australia, which was succinctly described by Cuneen, White and Richards in *Juvenile Justice: Youth and Crime in Australia*:[11]

> In Australia, the major reason given for establishing children's courts was that they ensured that young people were tried separately from adults and were not subject to the harmful effects of contamination and stigma – particularly where the young person was before the court on neglect matters. Australian legislation establishing separate children's courts was introduced as follows:
>
> 1. South Australia – *State Children Act 1895*
> 2. New South Wales – *Neglected Children and Juvenile Offenders Act 1905*
> 3. Victoria – *Children's Court Act 1906*

10 *The Juvenile Justice Century: A Sociolegal Commentary on American Juvenile Courts*, pp. 49–50.
11 Cuneen, C, White, R, and Richards, K. (OUP, 5th edn 2015), pp. 12–13.

4. Queensland – *Children's Court Act 1907*
5. Western Australia – *State Children Act 1907*
6. Tasmania – *Children's Charter 1918*

The Australian legislation was based on child-saving rhetoric similar to that used in the USA. The courts were to be parental and informal, with correction administered in a 'fatherly manner' . . . Magistrates were to be specially selected, trained, and qualified to deal with young people; probation officers were to play a special role in supervising young people and preparing background reports.

The legislation establishing children's courts in Australia gave jurisdiction to the courts over criminal matters (juvenile offending) and welfare matters (neglected children and young people). The children's courts also had exclusive jurisdiction, which meant that other, lower courts could not hear cases involving children. The legislation also stipulated that the children's court had to sit separately from the other courts, and that special magistrates had to be appointed. In practice, most magistrates were simply designated as children's magistrates, and only in the major cities did anything like special courts exist.

This might have been describing the early years of the juvenile courts in the UK.

JUVENILE COURTS IN THE UK

It was the Children Act, 1908 that made the proposition that children ought to be dealt with differently from adults a central feature of criminal justice in the United Kingdom. New courts, similar to the models adopted around the same time in many jurisdictions, including the USA and Australia, were to be established under that Act to deal with children and young people, and they were to be known as "juvenile courts".[12]

Echoing the earlier views of the American reformers, the Lord Advocate in the Parliamentary debates on the 1908 Children Bill declared that the objective of the juvenile courts was "to treat these children not by way of punishing them – which is no remedy – but with a view to their reformation".[13] It was even recognised that youth offending was likely to be a consequence of parental influence, and for that reason alone, the young offender should not be subjected to the rigours of legal punishment. Stewart reports the Bill's sponsor, Herbert Samuel, Under-secretary at the Home Office, as expressing the view that the very fact of a child committing a crime was "an indictment of his upbringing by his parents".[14]

---

12 Children Act, 1908, s. 111(1).
13 HC Deb. 24 March 1908, vol. 186 col. 1257.
14 Stewart, J. "Children, Parents and the State: The Children Act 1908" (1995) 9 *Children and Society* 90, p. 95.

The 1908 Act dealt with far more than juvenile offenders, and it extended the jurisdiction of courts of summary jurisdiction beyond those who had already committed offences to include those at risk of falling into a life of criminality. The indicators of that risk were similar, as we will see below, to the indicators in the Illinois Act.

Dealing with juvenile offenders under the 1908 Act

Part V of the Children Act, 1908, headed "Juvenile Offenders", created a number of new rules that would apply to courts dealing with children (defined as those under the age of 14 years) and young persons (those aged 14 or above but under the age of 16 years)[15] accused of having committed offences. Children and young persons were no longer to be sent to prison, either on conviction or on remand.[16] Nor could any young person be imprisoned who had been fined or ordered to pay damages or costs and who defaulted.[17] Instead, on conviction, the child or young person could be committed to the care of a relative or other fit person,[18] sent to an industrial or reformatory school,[19] or be whipped[20] (presumably in a rehabilitative manner). In addition, the death penalty was abolished for any person under the age of 16 years.[21] But as well as these limitations on outcomes, new rules were also introduced in terms of the court process for dealing with children and young persons accused of committing offences. Perhaps the most important of these was that parents and guardians were to be involved in the process, as recognition of the responsibility for the child's good upbringing that rested ultimately with them. So they were required to attend the court hearing the case.[22] Indeed, the court had the power to order the parent or guardian to pay any fines, damages or costs in place of the child.[23]

Provision was also made to ensure that juvenile courts sat in different

---

15 Children Act, 1908, s. 131.
16 Ibid. s. 102. This was subject to qualification where the child was so unruly or so depraved that he could not be detained anywhere else: s. 102(3).
17 Ibid. s. 102(3).
18 Ibid. s. 107(d).
19 Ibid. s. 107(e) and (f). That this was genuinely intended as an educative outcome may be gleaned from *AB v Howman* 1917 JC 23 where the High Court of Justiciary suspended an order for detention in an industrial school because, contrary to the regulations, the local education authority had not been given a chance to be heard before the order was made.
20 Children Act, 1908, s. 107(g).
21 Ibid. s. 103.
22 Ibid. s. 98.
23 Ibid. s. 99.

court buildings, or on different days, or at different times, from adult tri-als.[24] The aim here was to prevent young people from being exposed to and contaminated by the criminal elements that frequented the corridors and waiting rooms of adult criminal courts, though that was difficult to ensure in practice given the architecture of individual court buildings and the difficul-ties of scheduling cases appropriately.

Another defining characteristic of American juvenile courts adopted in the 1908 Act was the requirement that cases involving children and young persons should not be heard in open court. Designed primarily to give the child privacy, its effect, if taken to the extreme, would be to insulate the workings of the court from public scrutiny. This was an issue that generated substantial criticism in the USA, but in the UK privacy was never confused with secrecy and the press could not be excluded from juvenile court pro-ceedings. The 1908 Act provided that:

> In a juvenile court no person other than the members and officers of the court and the parties to the case, their solicitors and counsel, and other persons directly concerned in the case, shall, except by leave of the court, be allowed to attend. Provided that bona fide representatives of a newspaper or news agency shall not be excluded.[25]

It is important to note that, notwithstanding the references in the 1908 Act to the "juvenile court" there was no structural difference between such courts and the normal criminal courts. Juvenile courts were not in the UK new bodies inserted into the judicial hierarchy, in the way that, sixty years later, children's hearings became new quasi-judicial tribunals. Rather, the juvenile courts were simply courts of summary jurisdiction (in Scotland, the sheriff or the justice of the peace court, or the police or burgh court) dealing with offenders below the age of 16, to which the above special arrangements applied.[26] They were not specialist courts staffed by specially qualified judges.[27] It was stated 24 years later in the House of Commons:

> The setting up of a different court to deal with the offences of children and young persons from the court which deals with the crimes of adults was one of the novel features of the 1908 Act. It was in principle revolutionary, but in form it was

24 Ibid. s. 111(1).
25 Ibid. s. 111(4).
26 Ibid. s. 111(1).
27 As late as 1928 the Morton Committee reported that "In no Scottish town, so far as we are aware, have arrangements been made to delegate the work of the juvenile court to one or perhaps two Magistrates specially chosen because they have experience of the difficulties of youth and under-stand the problem of juvenile delinquency" (p. 42) (quoted in Kelly, C. "Continuity and Change in the History of Scottish Juvenile Justice" (2016) 6 *Law, Crime and History* 59, p. 69).

rudimentary. The only practical difference that was made was that the juvenile court should sit either at a different time or in a different place from the ordinary adult court. They were the same magistrates in the juvenile and the adult court. It was the same procedure in the two courts, and in many cases it was the same place. In addition, the rights of the juvenile court were by no means unlimited. It was possible for the parent of a child charged before a juvenile court on an indictable offence to claim the right to have the child removed to an adult court, and it was the right of any young persons between 14 and 16 to claim the same right on his own behalf.[28]

Nor was the juvenile court under the 1908 Act one that itself dealt, except incidentally, with children and young people who were brought to court for reasons other than having committed a criminal offence: this was not, yet, a juvenile court on the American model described above in which the same process was used both for offenders and for care and protection cases. That was recognised by the American judge J.W. Mack, writing extra-judicially,[29] when he pointed out (in an article that quoted extensively from the Parliamentary debates on the Children Bill, 1908 including, incidentally, "the Lord Advocate of Scotland") that the UK model in the 1908 Act simply ensured outcomes for child offenders other than imprisonment, while the Illinois model embraced the notion that punishment for offenders under 16 was simply not appropriate and that a caring response was called for: and indeed was called for in respect of a broader class of children than simply offenders. Scots law (and English law) fully embraced that model only in 1932, as we will see later. But the 1908 Act did deal with care and protection cases and, as shown in the paragraphs below, there was substantial overlap in both the aims and outcomes of the two processes which remained, for the moment, technically distinct.

Care and protection cases under the 1908 Act

The new juvenile courts established under Part V of the Children Act, 1908 dealt explicitly with "offenders" and were therefore courts of criminal juris-diction. However, other parts of the 1908 Act granted the power to courts of summary jurisdiction[30] to deal with children who had not committed offences but for whom some measure of care had become necessary due to their home circumstances. Indeed, these parts were more substantial than

28 HC Deb. 12 February 1932, vol. 261, cols 1170–1171.

29 "The Juvenile Court" (1909) 23 Harvard Law Review 104, pp. 108–109.

30 In Scotland defined as the sheriff (for Parts One and Two) and as either the sheriff, magistrate or two or more justices of the peace (for the rest of the Act): Children Act, 1908, s. 132(9).

Part V and David Garland has pointed out that "from the first the court was empowered to intervene to rescue the child from the vagaries of working-class socialisation".[31] There were two primary mechanisms by which children could be removed from their families.

First, if a person who had the custody, charge or care of a child or young person was convicted of, or committed to trial for, an offence of child cruelty,[32] then the court (necessarily a criminal court) could order that the child or young person be committed to the care of a relative or other fit person named by the court.[33] This was not a new innovation in 1908, for there had been similar provisions in the earlier legislation.[34] Secondly, a child[35] could be sent to a certified industrial school.[36] The criteria for liability to be sent to such a school were listed in s. 58 of the 1908 Act, which allowed any person to bring before the court any child (apparently) under the age of 14 years who fell into one or more of various categories:

(a) The child had been found begging or receiving alms;
(b) The child had been found wandering without a settled place of abode or without a parent or guardian, or without a parent or guardian who exercised "proper guardianship";
(c) The child had been found destitute, his or her parent or parents being in prison;
(d) The child was under the care of a parent or guardian who by reason of criminal or drunken habits was unfit to have the care of the child;
(e) The child was the daughter of a father who had been convicted of an offence of unlawful sexual intercourse with any of his daughters;
(f) The child frequented the company of any reputed thief or prostitute;
(g) The child was living in a brothel or otherwise in circumstances "calculated to cause, encourage, or favour the seduction or prostitution of the child".[37]

These criteria did not necessarily require any offence either by or against the child to have been committed, but they were taken to indicate that the

---

31 Garland, D. *Punishment and Welfare: A History of Penal Strategies* (Gower, 1985), p. 223.
32 That is to say any of the offences in Part II of and the First Schedule to the Act, including assault, ill-treatment, neglect, abandonment or exposure of the child (all constituting an offence under s. 12 of the Children Act, 1908, which later became s. 12 of the Children and Young Persons (Scotland) Act, 1937), causing a child to beg, exposing a child to the risk of burning; any offence involving bodily injury to a child or young person.
33 Children Act, 1908, s. 21(1).
34 Prevention of Cruelty to, and Protection of, Children Act, 1889, s. 5; Prevention of Cruelty to Children Act, 1894, s. 6; Prevention of Cruelty to Children Act, 1904, s. 6.
35 Note that the provisions being discussed here applied only to children and not to young persons (that is, persons above the age of compulsory schooling).
36 Children could be sent to a reformatory school if they had committed an offence and were between the ages of 12 and 16: Children Act, 1908, s. 57.
37 Ibid. s. 58.

child was in need of protection from the risks their life circumstances had placed them in. We can see here substantial similarities with the criteria for bringing children before the juvenile court in Illinois: child deprivation and want of proper parenting. A child begging or receiving alms, or being destitute, indicates a child living in severe poverty and deprivation. A child whose parents or guardians are not exercising proper guardianship or whose habits make them unfit to have the care of a child – even when the parent had committed no criminal offence – is seen as being at risk of falling into delinquent behaviour. A child living in a sexualised environment, or with an incestuous father, is seen as being at risk of moral depravity. Poverty (at least if severe), depravity and neglect were all seen as justifying the state stepping in to take over the direction of the child's upbringing.

There was never a clear separation between the juvenile courts of Part V dealing with offenders and the courts of summary jurisdiction of Part IV dealing with care and protection cases, and in Scotland, in particular, the same courts (sheriff courts and justice of the peace courts) acted as both. Overlap is seen as well with the outcomes available to the court: while sitting as either a juvenile court or as a court of summary jurisdiction, the sheriff had the power to commit the child to an industrial school. The juvenile court could so commit a child under 12 who was charged (note: not convicted) with an offence.[38] The response to a younger child's potential offending behaviour was to be the same as the response to any child under 14 being the victim of any of the care and protection circumstances listed above. Another ground upon which a child could be sent to an industrial school was when the parent or guardian proved that he or she was unable to control the child and desired that the child be sent to such a school.[39] And in all of these cases (children who were victims of offences, or were liable to be sent to an industrial school,[40] or had been found by a juvenile court to have committed an offence[41]) the court could, instead of sending the child to an industrial school, commit the child to the care of a relative or other fit person named by the court.[42] This power applied to all children or young persons under the age of 16 years.[43]

---

38 Ibid. s. 58(2).
39 Ibid. s. 58(4).
40 Ibid. s. 58(7).
41 Ibid. s. 107(d).
42 Ibid. s. 58(7).
43 Ibid. s. 59.

THE JUVENILE COURT UNDER THE CHILDREN AND YOUNG PERSONS (SCOTLAND) ACTS, 1932 AND 1937

The Morton Committee had been established in 1925

> to inquire into the treatment of young offenders and of young people whose character, environment or conduct is such that they require protection and training, and to report what changes, if any, are desirable in the present law or its administration . . .

It published its Report "Protection and Training" in 1928.[44] To be noted, from the remit both of this committee and its English equivalent,[45] is the collocation of young offenders and young people who require protection and training – as indeed is the collocation of "protection" and "training". Yet the titles of the two reports indicate a difference in focus, which has in fact characterised the difference between Scottish and English policy-making ever since: from a remit that included both, the titles of the reports refers to the young offender in England and to the need for protection and training in Scotland. The Morton Committee made a fundamental connection in its deliberations between poverty and delinquency: it described the conditions in the slums of Glasgow, and asserted that "no solution to the problem of delinquency is possible without the removal of these conditions".[46] The Morton Committee concluded that the aspirations of the Children Act, 1908 had not fully come to pass. The later Kilbrandon Report summarised the findings in the Morton Committee Report as follows:

> The Committee found that throughout Scotland the general pattern was for juvenile cases to be heard by the Sheriff Courts or the Burgh Courts, and that, except in Lanarkshire, juvenile courts attached to the Justice of the Peace Courts were not functioning to any extent. The Committee recommended transfer of jurisdiction in the case of children and young offenders to specially constituted Justice of the Peace juvenile courts – the members of the court to be drawn from a panel of justices, appointed by the body of justices as a whole from their own number, and comprising persons who by knowledge and experience were specially qualified to consider juvenile cases.[47]

The central recommendation of the Morton Committee Report was, therefore, the proper establishment of tribunals, to be called juvenile courts,

---

44 Morton Committee Report, 1928 Cmnd 49–192.
45 The Molony Committee's *Report of the Departmental Committee on the Treatment of Young Offenders*, 1927 Cmnd 2831.
46 Morton Committee Report, p. 21.
47 Kilbrandon Report *Children and Young Persons Scotland* (1964), para 42.

separate from other courts, staffed by specialists and dealing with a broader range of child issues than merely offending behaviour.

The (English) Molony Report, had stated (with a startling mix of idealism and complacency) that what was needed in every magistrate who sat in a juvenile court was "a love of young people, sympathy with their interests, and an imaginative insight into their difficulties. The rest is largely common sense".[48] This was accepted by the Morton Committee, which saw the juvenile court as a place where persons with special knowledge and understanding of children would be invested with the necessary judicial powers to take suitable action in each case brought before them. Section 2 of the Children and Young Persons (Scotland) Act, 1932[49] therefore provided that "a panel of justices specially qualified to deal with juveniles" was to be set up in each district in Scotland. It may be noted that there were no criteria laid down as to what made a justice of the peace "specially qualified": contemporaneous comments explained this omission as follows: "it was thought best to leave this to the good sense and discretion of justices".[50] It is likely, from the comment of the Molony Committee quoted above, that what the drafters had in mind were informal qualities such as interest in and empathy with young people rather than any formal accredited qualification (which, in any case, did not exist at that time).

An interesting debate took place in Parliament on the constitution of juvenile court panels and, in particular, whether there should be a statutory requirement that women had to be included on the panel of justices. An amendment to secure such a requirement was defeated (by a large margin),[51] but an assurance was given that in the framing of the rules due regard would be given to this question,[52] and the following year Rule 13 of the Juvenile Courts (Constitution) (Scotland) Rules, 1933, provided that "Every juvenile court shall be constituted of not more than three justices from the juvenile court panel, of whom so far as practicable one shall be a man and one shall be a woman". Those familiar with the children's hearing system will note with interest the similarities with juvenile courts, which were envisaged to be panels of up to three justices, chosen from a juvenile court panel, formed for each county or burgh specified by order of the Secretary of State for Scotland as constituting an area in which the juvenile

48 *Report of the Departmental Committee on the Treatment of Young Offenders*, p. 25.
49 Subsequently re-enacted as s. 51 of the Children and Young Persons (Scotland) Act, 1937.
50 1933 *The Magistrate* p. 697.
51 HC Deb. 12 May 1932 vol. 265, col. 2230.
52 HC Deb. 12 May 1932 vol. 265, col. 2228.

court was to sit.[53] Localism was to be a defining characteristic of the juvenile court. Where juvenile courts were established, they were constituted as part of the justice of the peace courts, which meant that they were funded by local rates.[54]

It was never envisaged that the panels of justices to be established under s. 2 could be established throughout Scotland immediately, and instead the legislation was designed to allow progressive approval to be given area by area. The reason for this was explained by the Under-Secretary of State for Scotland:[55] unlike in England where the vast majority of juvenile cases were already dealt with by justices of the peace, only a small proportion were so dealt with in Scotland (the sheriff courts picking up the bulk of the work), so there was not the bank of justices of the peace from which specially qualified justices could be chosen.[56] This was a serious practical inhibition to achieving the aim of the 1932 and 1937 Acts as envisaged by the Morton Committee, and thirty years later the Kilbrandon Report pointed out that progress in establishing qualified panels was minimal and never covered much of the country:

> The Children and Young Persons (Scotland) Act, 1932 (later consolidated in the Children and Young Persons (Scotland) Act, 1937), provided for the setting up of such courts in any area where an order to that effect has been made by the Secretary of State. Only four such orders have been made – all prior to 1940 – applying to the counties of Ayr, Fife, Renfrew and the city of Aberdeen.[57]

But this is not to say that the principles of the juvenile court as envisaged by the 1932 Act were limited to these local authority areas. All the rules in the 1932 and 1937 Acts in respect of juvenile courts applied, in areas where juvenile courts had not been established, to all courts of summary jurisdiction (primarily the sheriff court) dealing with matters over which juvenile courts would have jurisdiction.[58] And even in the areas where juvenile court panels existed, the sheriff court retained concurrent jurisdiction in offender cases.[59]

---

53 Children and Young Persons (Scotland) Act, 1932, s. 1(6) and Children and Young Persons (Scotland) Act, 1937 s. 50(4).

54 *Boase v Fife County Council* 1937 SC(HL) 28.

55 HC Deb, 12 February 1932, vol. 261, cols 1218–1219.

56 This remained the case in 1964: Kilbrandon Report, para 47.

57 Kilbrandon Report, para 42.

58 Children and Young Persons (Scotland) Acts, 1932, s. 1(1) and (6) and Children and Young Persons (Scotland) Act, 1937, s. 50(1) and (5).

59 *Weir v Cruickshank* 1959 JC 94. Paras 44–46 of the Kilbrandon Report contain details of the various types of court in different parts of the country that could be constituted as juvenile courts, and of the distribution of business between them.

Location of juvenile courts

The Children Act, 1908 had required that the juvenile court be held either in a different building or room from ordinary sittings of the court, or on different days, or at different times. Section 1(4) of the Children and Young Persons (Scotland) Act, 1932[60] removed the possibility of juvenile courts sitting merely at different times from adult courts, and required that juvenile courts be held either in separate buildings entirely or at least in separate rooms from those used by adult courts. The same thinking (the need to isolate impressionable children from the shady characters who haunted criminal court buildings) was behind the provisions that required arrangements to be made to ensure that children and young people, while detained in a police station or being conveyed to or from any criminal court or waiting there, should be prevented from associating with any adult (other than a relative) charged with an offence; and in these circumstances, the child or young person was required to be in the care of a woman.[61] And there was differentiation even in sittings of the juvenile court itself. The Juvenile Courts (Procedure) (Scotland) Rules, 1934 required the Court in fixing sittings:

> to have regard to the varying ages of the children and young persons concerned, and to the different types of cases to be brought before it, and shall take the necessary precaution to prevent as far as possible young and comparatively minor offenders from mixing with older and more serious offenders. This may be done by holding Courts (a) on different days, or (b) at different hours; and in cases of smaller differences between the cases by (a) keeping the classes of offenders in separate rooms or (b) having a member of the Police Force or female attendant in the waiting room.[62]

The physical layout of many Scottish court buildings and the vagaries of scheduling judicial time meant that the aspiration of keeping children and young people apart from hardened criminals was rarely achieved in practice. It was not until the establishment of the children's hearing system by the Social Work (Scotland) Act 1968 that hearing rooms were made available (by local authorities) in entirely separate buildings.

---

60 Subsequently re-enacted as s. 52(1) of the Children and Young Persons (Scotland) Act, 1937.
61 Children and Young Persons (Scotland) Act, 1932, s. 74 and Children and Young Persons (Scotland) Act, 1937, s. 39.
62 Juvenile Court (Procedure) (Scotland) Rules, 1934, r. 18.

Privacy and confidentiality

Cowan[63] draws attention to another defining feature of the juvenile court.

> One of the main purposes of a separate Court is to secure in so far as possible an atmosphere in which the child can talk naturally, and to this end the presence of a large number of persons is to be avoided. Accordingly, under section 3(2) [of the 1932 Act], admittance is strictly limited to those directly concerned. The Court may, however, specially authorise others. . . . The question of the presence of the press was debated at great length.

The child's privacy and confidentiality had received some protection in s. 111 of the Children Act, 1908, and s. 3(2) of the 1932 Act[64] reflected that by providing that no person could be present at any sitting of a juvenile court except members and officers of the court, the parties to the case and their solicitors, counsel, witnesses and other persons directly concerned in the case, bona fide representatives of newspapers or news agencies, and such other persons as the court may specially authorise to be present. The major change was in the 1932 Act as this was now applied not only to the criminal proceedings to which juvenile courts were formally limited in the 1908 Act but to care and protection proceedings also.[65]

Another significant innovation in the 1932 Act was that reporting restrictions were introduced for the first time. The Morton Committee[66] had drawn attention to a resolution made by the Institute of Journalists urging "all newspapers to withhold the names of juvenile offenders tried or convicted in children's courts, as well as those of children innocently involved in criminal cases", but there was no statutory requirement to this effect until the 1932 Act. Section 75 provided that

> No newspaper report or any proceedings in a juvenile court shall reveal the name, address or school, or include any particulars calculated to lead to the identification, of any child or young person concerned in those proceedings . . . nor shall any picture be published in any newspaper as being or including a picture of any child or young person so concerned in any such proceedings as aforesaid . . .

This was replaced by s. 46 of the Children and Young Persons (Scotland) Act, 1937, which both widened the scope of the earlier legislation and narrowed

---

63 Cowan, M.G. *The Children and Young Persons (Scotland) Act, 1932* (W. Hodge & Co. 1933), pp. 17–18.

64 Subsequently re-enacted as s. 52(1) of the Children and Young Persons (Scotland) Act, 1937.

65 Children and Young Persons (Scotland) Acts, 1932, s. 3(2); Children and Young Persons (Scotland) Act, 1937, s. 52(1).

66 Morton Committee, p. 55.

its focus. Under the later statute the prohibition required a court direction and was applied to "any proceedings in any court" (as opposed to only
"a juvenile court") but at the same time limited to proceedings involving
"any offence against, or conduct contrary to, decency or morality".[67] Sheriff
Trotter assumed (if a little tentatively) that these words referred to offences
of a sexual nature.[68] The 1937 Act also allowed for a wider exception by
which the court permitted publication at its unlimited discretion than the
1932 Act, under which the court or Secretary of State could allow publication if satisfied that it was in the interests of justice to do so. (Section 46 of
the 1937 Act remains in force today.)[69]

JURISDICTION OF THE JUVENILE COURT

Overview

Probably the most important measure in the Children and Young Persons
(Scotland) Act, 1932 designed to enhance the position of the juvenile court
was the substantial expansion of the types of case that the court could deal
with. In particular, the juvenile court took over the care and protection cases
that, under the Children Act, 1908, had been dealt with by the ordinary
courts of summary jurisdiction. Of course, since juvenile courts, as such,
were in the event not established in many parts of Scotland, this change
might be characterised as in practice superficial. But conceptually the
change was significant. There was no longer to be any separation in structure between care and protection cases and young offender cases: whichever
court they came before was subject to the rules and procedures of juvenile
courts, and the outcomes were now virtually identical. So it was in 1932
that the characteristic feature of the contemporary Scottish way of dealing
with children in need came to full fruition. Bringing the two broad types of
cases together had another conceptual effect: that of turning the juvenile
court from a criminal tribunal into (primarily) a civil court. The juvenile
court even when dealing with offenders had always sought a welfare-based
outcome aimed at rehabilitation and now, for all categories of case that came
before it, the juvenile court would seek an outcome designed to further the
child's best interests.

---

67 That limitation was eventually removed by s. 57 of the Children and Young Persons Act 1963,
   which also extended the prohibition to sound and television broadcasts.
68 Trotter, T. *The Law as to Children and Young Persons* (W. Hodge & Co, 1938), p 83.
69 See for example *Tough, Petitioner* 2015 CSIH 78.

The 1932 Act[70] gave the juvenile court jurisdiction over:

(i) Juvenile crime. Juvenile courts could "hear charges against children and young persons". The 1932 Act also increased the court's overall jurisdiction from those under 16 to those under 17,[71] though this was achieved in the face of substantial political opposition.[72] In addition, and following a recommendation of the Morton Committee, the Act raised the common law age of *doli incapax* from seven to eight:[73] from then on no offence could be committed in law by a child under the age of eight, and that remained the case until the Age of Criminal Responsibility (Scotland) Act 2019 raised the age to 12.[74]

(ii) School attendance cases. Responsibility for ensuring school attendance had a few years earlier been transferred from the police to local authorities by the Local Government (Scotland) Act, 1929, and this had the effect, according to Cowan,[75] of removing school attendance cases from the police courts to the JP courts and the sheriff courts. Since these were to be juvenile courts in any case it was sensible and obvious that they took over such cases too, for school non-attendance was regarded as an effective indicator of deeper social problems. It remains today such an indicator and has always been a ground of referral to the children's hearing. These cases were, of course, limited to children below the school-leaving age, then 14.[76]

(iii) Care and protection cases. The criteria for a finding that a child or young person was in need of "care or protection" were substantially widened from what they had been under the 1908 Act and are discussed below. Under the 1908 Act, sending a child to an industrial school was possible only in respect of children under the age of 14 years, but now all children and young persons, defined to include all those under 17 years of age, were subject to the court's protective jurisdiction and all outcomes were possible. For young people above the school leaving age, the focus was on their training for future employment.

---

70 Children and Young Persons (Scotland) Act, 1932, s. 1(1), subsequently re-enacted as s. 50 of the Children and Young Persons (Scotland) Act, 1937.

71 Children and Young Persons (Scotland) Act, 1932, s. 64; the definition of "young person" was repeated in s. 110 of the Children and Young Persons (Scotland) Act, 1937.

72 HC Deb. 12 February 1932 vol. 261, col. 1173; 12 May 1932 vol. 265, col. 2207.

73 Children and Young Persons (Scotland) Act, 1932, s. 14. It is interesting to note that an amendment to raise the age to 14 was debated by the House of Commons but defeated by 168 to six votes: see HC Deb. 12 May 1932, vol. 265, cols 2234–2240. The age of eight was subsequently re-enacted in s. 55 of the Children and Young Persons (Scotland) Act, 1937 and repeated in the Criminal Procedure (Scotland) Acts 1975 and 1995.

74 In a provision added at Stage Three of the Scottish Parliament's consideration of this Act, it was required that after three years a review be held of the operation of the Act generally, and with a view to considering the future age of criminal responsibility: Age of Criminal Responsibility (Scotland) Act 2019, s. 78. That age may yet be increased further.

75 Cowan, *The Children and Young Persons (Scotland) Act, 1932*, pp. 12–13.

76 Raised to 15 by the Education (Scotland) Act, 1946, s. 32(1) and to 16 (where it remains) by the Raising of the School Leaving Age (Scotland) Regulations 1972 (SI 1972/59 (S. 6)).

In addition, the juvenile court was given jurisdiction to make adoption orders.[77] This gave the court jurisdiction over children and young persons up to the age of 21. Adoption had been introduced into the law of Scotland only two years earlier with the Adoption of Children (Scotland) Act, 1930, and initially only the Court of Session and the sheriff court could make adoption orders. The very fact that adoption was brought within the jurisdiction of the juvenile court indicates that the adoption order was, to some extent at least, perceived as a child protection mechanism.

The juvenile court's care and protection jurisdiction

Section 6 of the Children and Young Persons (Scotland) Act, 1932[78] set out the circumstances that would indicate that a child or young person was in need of care or protection. If any education authority, constable or any officer of a society authorised to bring proceedings (that is to say, a children's charity), had reasonable grounds for believing that a child or young person came within any of a number of stated circumstances (which today we would describe as "grounds of referral"), then it, he or she could bring the child or young person before a juvenile court or, in those areas of Scotland – most of them – in which juvenile courts had not been constituted separate from other courts of summary jurisdiction, before the sheriff. Three categories of child were specified in the Act as being in need of care or protection, though the first two might be broken down into sub-categories:

(a) "A child or young person who, having no parent or guardian, or a parent or guardian who is unfit to exercise care and guardianship or is not exercising proper care and guardianship, is falling into bad associations or is exposed to moral danger or is beyond control". The structure of this paragraph tends to opacity, but the essence of it is that the child either was "falling into bad associations or moral danger" or was "beyond control", as a consequence of either having no parent or guardian or of that parent or guardian being unfit or failing to exercise care. It would follow that a child or young person who had no parent or guardian, or a parent or guardian who was not exercising care and guardianship, but who was not falling into bad associations – for example, because someone else (such as another family member) was caring for him or her satisfactorily – would not come within this ground. Nor would the child come within this ground by falling into bad associations notwithstanding a decent standard of parenting by the parent or guardian. In the English case

---

77 Children and Young Persons (Scotland) Acts, 1932, s. 1(5); Children and Young Persons (Scotland) Act, 1937, s. 50(3).
78 Subsequently re-enacted as s. 65 of the Children and Young Persons (Scotland) Act, 1937.

of *Bowers v Smith*,[79] decided under the similarly worded s. 61(1)(a) of the Children and Young Persons Act, 1933, it was held that the ground was not established that three boys were falling into bad associations or moral danger by having, in each other's company, sexual intercourse with a girl when the parents were unaware that their sons knew the girl or were likely to indulge in such behaviour. There was no "blame" to be attached to the parents and therefore the complaint was not established that would justify the juvenile court taking action. This confirms that this ground was fundamentally concerned with parental failings rather than the child's behaviour.

(b) A child or young person in respect of whom certain specified crimes had been committed, or who was a member of the same household as the victim or perpetrator of such offence or, being female, was a member of the same household as a female in respect of whom an offence of incest had been committed by a member of that household.[80] The specified crimes were those in Part II of and the First Schedule to the 1908 Act and subsequently Schedule 1 to the 1937 Act (which included the offence of cruelty or neglect under s. 12 of both these Acts, residence in a brothel, begging, and specified sexual offences).[81] These provisions followed the recommendations of the *Report of the Departmental Committee on Sexual Offences*[82] and ensured a substantial extension of protection from the 1908 Act: the earlier Act had required a definite conviction[83] while in the 1932 and 1937 Acts that requirement was retained only in relation to residence in the household of the offender. There had been in the 1908 Act a special provision excluding from its operation children of prostitute mothers, but this was not repeated here and so such children could be brought before a juvenile court. This probably reflected a growing understanding that even although the harm might not come directly from the parent, the sexualised environment in which the parent lived was sufficiently harmful that it was believed better to separate the child from the sex-worker parent than to allow him or her to remain with her. Each case was, of course, different, but there must have been many circumstances in which applying the 1908 exception and allowing a child to remain with a prostitute mother represented a more enlightened and compassionate approach. The essence of this ground was the risk of future harm to the child or young person, though it included a response to harm already caused.

(c) Children of vagrants who were not receiving efficient elementary education.[84] This replaced the vagrancy ground that, under the Industrial Schools legislation, permitted children to be sent to such schools, and is one of the pre-cursors to the much wider "failure to attend school regularly" ground of

---

79 [1953] 1 WLR 297.
80 This last was a late addition by the House of Lords: HL Deb. 9 June 1932 vol. 84 col. 710 to ensure the age of the female victim of incest did not matter (the other scheduled offences being limited to victims under 16).
81 All of these related to persons under 16 notwithstanding that the general jurisdiction of the juvenile court was extended in the Children and Young Persons (Scotland) Act, 1932 to age 17.
82 Cmnd 2593 (1926).
83 Children Act, 1908, s. 21(2).
84 An offence created by s. 118 of the Children Act, 1908.

referral to the children's hearing, introduced in the Social Work (Scotland) Act 1968 and repeated in all subsequent children's hearings legislation.

There was one other way in which a child or young person could be brought before a juvenile court, and this was at the instance of his or her own parent or guardian, on the ground that the parent or guardian was unable to control the child or young person.[85] In such a case the only outcomes available to the court were that (with the consent of the parent or guardian who understood this outcome) the child or young person could be sent to an approved school or be placed under supervision of a probation officer or some other person for a specified period not exceeding three years. But the court could not send the child or young person to an approved school under this provision without the consent of the Education Authority because, as Trotter bluntly puts it, "A child in an approved school is a burden on the rates":[86] a parent could not therefore simply ask the court to relieve him or her of the burden of bringing up his or her child.[87]

Though these care and protection circumstances justified the court in taking action after 1932, it was found over 30 years later that it was relatively uncommon for this jurisdiction to be exercised. The Kilbrandon Report found that:

> Under existing law, children in need of care or protection are not a numerous class. We understand that in 1961–1962, 266 children were committed to the care of local authorities and 112 to approved schools on care or protection proceedings. Allowing for others who may have been committed to the care of other "fit persons" or placed under supervision, the annual total is probably not in excess of 500.[88]

This means that the great bulk of the work of the juvenile court, throughout its sixty-year history, was to deal with young offenders. It would, of course, be a mistake to infer from these figures that children before the 1960s were but rarely abused or neglected and they are better explained by a continued reluctance on the part of the state to get involved in the upbringing of children. Nevertheless, the important point remains that the process by which both broad categories of children and young persons were dealt

---

85 Children and Young Persons (Scotland) Act, 1932, s. 7; Children and Young Persons (Scotland) Act, 1937 s. 68. This happened only very rarely: see Kilbrandon Report, para 130 (which recommended the repeal of the provision).

86 Trotter, *The Law as to Children and Young Persons*, p. 126.

87 This provision was replaced by s. 3 of the Children and Young Persons Act 1963 which required the local authority to institute proceedings on this ground.

88 Kilbrandon Report, para 9.

with were substantially the same. So were the potential outcomes, though there were additional punitive outcomes for offenders.

POTENTIAL OUTCOMES IN THE JUVENILE COURT

If a child or young person was found to fall into any of the three "care or protection" categories, then the possible outcomes for the child or young person were:

(i)   To be sent to an approved school (as reformatory and industrial schools became under the 1932 Act),

(ii) To be committed to the care of any fit person (normally a voluntary organisation), or

(iii) To be made subject to the supervision of a probation officer.[89]

Each of these outcomes was also available in respect of any child or young person found guilty of an offence[90] (if punishable in the case of an adult with imprisonment), subject to the qualification that probation for offenders was available only in conjunction with committal of the child or young person to the care of a fit person and not as an outcome on its own.[91] Other than that relatively minor difference, however, the two groups of children and young persons were liable to the same outcomes. And importantly, in determining the appropriate outcome in any individual case, the welfare test was explicitly applied in respect of both groups:

> Every court in dealing with a child or young person who is brought before them, either as needing care or protection or as an offender or otherwise, shall have regard to the welfare of the child or young person, and shall in a proper case take steps for removing him from undesirable surroundings, and for securing that proper provision is made for his education and training . . .[92]

This gives no indication of the weight any tribunal was to attach to the welfare of the child or young person and suggests that it is merely a relevant factor, but there was an additional injunction in the Juvenile Court

---

89 Children and Young Persons (Scotland) Act, 1932, s. 6 and Children and Young Persons (Scotland) Act, 1937, s. 61 for juvenile offenders; 1932 Act, s. 12 and 1937 Act, s. 66 for children in need of care or protection. The court could alternatively order the parent or guardian to enter into a bond to exercise proper care and guardianship.

90 Children and Young Persons (Scotland) Act, 1932, s. 12(1); Children and Young Persons (Scotland) Act, 1937, s. 61(1).

91 Children and Young Persons (Scotland) Act, 1932, s. 12(2); Children and Young Persons (Scotland) Act, 1937, s. 61(2).

92 Children and Young Persons (Scotland) Act, 1932, s. 16; Children and Young Persons (Scotland) Act, 1937, s. 49(1).

Rules to "deal with the case in the child's best interests"[93] which comes close to making this the determining aim of the whole process. That the two groups were liable on the same considerations to the same outcomes was also emphasised with the rule that, in both cases, the education authority had to be notified of the child or young person being brought before a juvenile court and (importantly) once notified was obliged to supply the court with such information about the child or young person's home surroundings, school record, health, character and of available approved schools as appeared to the authority as "likely to assist the court".[94] This indicates that the child's needs were to be identified in a holistic manner, with the appropriate outcome being identified through an examination of more than simply the facts that brought the child or young person to the juvenile court. Unlike in an adult criminal case where the commission of the crime is the primary determinant of the outcome, in all types of case before the juvenile court the jurisdiction-founding fact (which today we would call the ground of referral) was only a small part of the determination of the outcome. This principle underpins the modern practice of the children's hearing system and has characterised decision-making over children in Scotland since 1932.

Punitive disposals for offenders

The 1932 Act did not prohibit any other disposals for offenders, and so it remained possible for the court to order that the child be whipped (if male and under the age of 16), pay a fine, damages or costs,[95] or be committed to a remand home.[96] The last mentioned was very uncommon[97] and, according to Cowan, used mainly to enforce a fine against a young person in paid employment who was not willing to pay the fine.[98]

The Children and Young Persons Bill as originally introduced in the House of Commons in 1932 had contained a provision for the abolition

---

93 Juvenile Courts (Procedure) (Scotland) Rules, 1934 (SR&O 1934 No. 641 (S. 36)), rr. 9(6)(b) (for offence cases) and 10(7)(a) (for care and protection cases).

94 Children and Young Persons (Scotland) Act, 1932, s. 15; Children and Young Persons (Scotland) Act, 1937, s. 43(2).

95 Children Act, 1908, s. 99(1); Children and Young Persons (Scotland) Act, 1937, s. 59(1). If the offender was a child (i.e. not yet a young person and so still at school) the fine, damages or costs had to be paid by the parent or guardian. The Kilbrandon Committee found in 1964 (paras 23–33) that such outcomes were ineffective and in most cases impracticable.

96 Children Act, 1908, s. 106, replaced by s. 58 of the Children and Young Persons (Scotland) Act, 1937.

97 Morton Committee Report, p. 177.

98 Cowan, *The Children and Young Persons (Scotland) Act, 1932*, p. 51.

of whipping, but the House of Lords (twice) removed the provision, and the Commons (after long debate and against the wishes of the National Government) eventually conceded the point.[99] Between 1908 and 1932 whipping was a relatively common punishment, even after the juvenile court had been established. Cowan reports the following statistics for whipping being ordered, in her 1933 book:

1925 – 255 cases
1926 – 266 cases
1927 – 197 cases
1928 – 127 cases
1929 – 176 cases
1930 – 155 cases
1931 – 196 cases

For comparison, this is roughly twice the number of children and young people who were in these years being sent to industrial or reformatory schools, though since whipping was probably perceived as a lesser outcome, these statistics likely reflect the seriousness of the offences committed. Only probation orders and fines outnumbered whipping as the most common outcomes.[100] It was reported shortly thereafter[101] that whipping was substantially more common in Scotland (where it was unanimously supported by sheriffs) than in England, being ordered in 1.63% of criminal cases against juveniles in Scotland while ordered in only 0.39% of such cases in England.

There was no call to abolish whipping in the 1937 debates, and though a bill was introduced in 1938 to do so,[102] this was not proceeded with as the threat of war began to dominate Parliamentary time. Corporal punishment was eventually abolished as a criminal punishment by the Criminal Justice Act, 1948.[103] The Kilbrandon Report in 1964, somewhat surprisingly, discussed corporal punishment as a potential outcome for children's hearings but only, it seems, to dismiss it as a public treatment measure.[104] In the event, the children's hearing, which took over the jurisdiction of the juvenile court in 1971, when the Social Work (Scotland) Act 1968 came into force,

---

99 See HL Deb. 9 June 1932, vol. 84 cols 721–729; HC Deb. 30 June 1932, vol. 267 cols 2069–2095. Whipping had long been recognised as a legitimate form of punishment (see *Macdonald's Criminal Law* 3rd edn, p. 17) for boys below the age of 16: *Mackay v Lamb* 1923 JC 16.

100 Cowan, *The Children and Young Persons (Scotland) Act, 1932*, p. 316.

101 *Report of the Departmental Committee on Corporal Punishment* (the Cadogan Report) 1938 Cmnd 5684, para 14.

102 Criminal Justice Bill, 1938, introduced by the Home Secretary, Sir Samuel Hoare.

103 Criminal Justice Act, 1948, s. 2.

104 Kilbrandon Report, para 34.

was given no power to impose any punitive outcome (though outcomes in individual cases are doubtless often perceived by the child and his or her family as having punitive effects).

RULES AND PROCEDURE AT THE JUVENILE COURT

The constitution of and process at the juvenile court were laid down in secondary legislation, and irrespective of the fact that juvenile court panels were actually established in only a few areas in Scotland, it is easy to see the blueprint for children's panels later adopted by the Kilbrandon Committee and enacted in the Social Work (Scotland) Act 1968. The Juvenile Courts (Constitution) (Scotland) Rules, 1933[105] provided in part as follows:

> 4: The justices for the county . . . shall, in accordance with these Rules, appoint from among their number justices specially qualified for dealing with juvenile cases to form a panel, hereinafter called the juvenile court panel.
> . . .
> 13: Every juvenile court shall be constituted of not more than three justices from the juvenile court panel, of whom so far as practicable one shall be a man and one shall be a woman.
> . . .
> 15(1) [T]he members of the juvenile court panel for each area shall immediately after their appointment select one of their number to act as chairman of the juvenile court throughout the period for which the panel is appointed.

In a similar vein, the Juvenile Courts (Procedure) (Scotland) Rules, 1934[106] (later substantially re-enacted as the Juvenile Courts (Procedure) (Scotland) Rules, 1951[107]) provide a precursor for procedure at children's hearings. It is important to remember that these Rules applied not only in fully constituted juvenile courts but also, in areas of Scotland where no such courts had been established, in any court of summary jurisdiction acting under the 1908 Act or (later) the 1937 Act.[108] Of particular interest are the following rules.

> Rule 8(1): The Court shall, except in any case where the child or young person is legally represented, allow his parent or guardian to assist him in conducting

---

105 SR&O, 1933 No. 984 (S. 54) (reproduced in Trotter *The Law as to Children and Young Persons*, pp. 323 – 325). The Juvenile Courts (Constitution) (Scotland) (Amendment) Rules, 1951 imposed an upper age limit of 65 for justices of the Juvenile Court Panel.

106 SR&O, 1934 No. 641 (S.36), and continued in force under sched. 3 para 1 to the 1937 Act. (Reproduced in Trotter, pp. 263–322.)

107 SI 1951/2228.

108 Juvenile Courts (Procedure) (Scotland) Rules, 1934, Rule 3, and Children and Young Persons (Scotland) Act, 1937, s. 50(1).

his defence to the complaint or opposition to the Petition including the cross-examination of witnesses for the prosecution or Petitioner.

Rule 8(2): Where the parent or guardian cannot be found or cannot in the opinion of the Court reasonably be required to attend, the Court may allow any relative or other responsible person to take the place of the parent or guardian for the purposes of these Rules.

Rule 9 set out the procedure to be followed when a child or young person was brought to the juvenile court on a charge of having committed an offence.

Rule 9(1): The Court shall explain to the child or young person the substance of the charge in simple language suitable to his age and understanding, and shall then ask the child or young person whether he admits the charge.[109]

. . .

(3) If the child or young person does not admit the charge the court may adjourn the case for trial to as early a diet as is consistent with the just interests of both parties, and in that event shall give intimation or order intimation to be given of such adjourned diet to such child or young person and his parent or guardian; but the Court may proceed to trial forthwith if the Court considers this to be advisable in the interests of the child or young person or to be necessary to secure the examination of witnesses who would not otherwise be available.

(4) (a) At the trial of the case the Court shall hear the evidence of the witnesses in support of the charge. At the close of the evidence-in-chief of each witness the witness may be cross-examined by or on behalf of the child or young person:

(b) If, in any case where the child or young person is not legally represented or assisted in his defence as provided by these Rules, the child or young person, instead of asking questions by way of cross-examination, makes assertions, the Court shall then put to the witness such questions as it thinks necessary on behalf of the child or young person and may for this purpose question the child or young person in order to bring out or clear up any point arising out of any such assertions.

(5) If it appears to the Court that a *prima facie* case is made out, the child or young person shall be told that he may give evidence or make a statement, and the evidence or any witness for the defence shall be heard.

(6) Where the child or young person is found guilty of an offence, whether after a plea of guilty or otherwise,

(a) he and his parent or guardian, or other person acting in accordance with these Rules, shall be given an opportunity of making a statement:

(b): The Court shall, except in cases which appears to it to be of a trivial nature, obtain such information as to the general conduct, home surroundings, school record and medical history of the child or young person as may enable it to deal

109 In a case decided under the Juvenile Courts (Procedure) (Scotland) Rules, 1951, an order to send the child to an approved school was quashed because he had not received notice as required by Rule 11(2), nor any explanation of the charge given to him: *Roy v Cruickshank* 1954 SLT 217.

with the case in his best interests, and shall if such information is not fully available consider the desirability of remanding the child or young person for such enquiry as may be necessary.

This particular provision is more important than its slightly hidden location might suggest: the court is required to obtain information to allow it to "deal with the case in [the child's] best interests". "Best" indicates the paramountcy of these interests, and the provision recognises that what is best for the child cannot be properly identified without this background information. That the information to be obtained from such reports and enquiries would affect the outcome of cases is made plain in *Jamieson v Heatly*,[110] where the Lord Justice-Clerk (Thomson) said of these provisions (as they appeared in the Juvenile Court Rules, 1951):

> No general rules can be laid down as to the amount, or even as to the source, of the information on these various topics which a judge ought to have before him. The judge here took a serious view of the case—and I am not surprised that he took a serious view of the case. In my view, if he was going to take a serious view of the case he ought to have had before him information about the home, or he ought to have continued the case in order that the necessary information should have become available. In these circumstances the judge did not have before him all the information which was available and desirable in order to enable him properly to assess the sentence. As we cannot be certain that he would, if he had had all that information, necessarily have reached the conclusions which he did reach, it seems to me that we have to quash the sentences.[111]

Rule 9(6) continues:

> The Court shall take into consideration any report which may be furnished by a Probation Officer or by an Education or Poor Law Authority . . .
>   (d) any written report by a Probation Officer, Education or Poor Law Authority, or registered medical practitioner may be received and considered by the Court without being read aloud:
>   Provided that
>   (i) the child or young person shall be told the substance of any part of the report bearing on his character or conduct which the Court considers to be material to the manner in which he should be dealt with;
>   (ii) the parent or guardian . . . shall, if present, be told the substance of any part of the report . . . which has reference to his character or conduct, or the character, conduct, home surroundings or health of the child or young person . . .
>   (e) if the Court . . . considers it necessary in the interests of the child or young person, it may require the parent or guardian, or other person acting in accordance with these Rules, or the child or young person, as the case may be, to withdraw from the Court.

110 1959 JC 22.
111 1959 JC 22, pp. 24–25.

(7) The Court shall thereupon, unless it thinks it undesirable to do so, inform the parent or guardian, or other person acting in accordance with these Rules, of the manner in which it proposes to deal with the child or young person and allow the parent or guardian, or other person acting in accordance with these Rules, to make a statement" . . .

Rule 10 governed procedure when the child or young person was brought before the juvenile court by petition (that is to say, by reason other than having committed an offence – on care and protection grounds, or for school truancy, or on the application for an adoption order). It provided:

(1) The Petitioner shall (except where he himself is the parent or guardian of the child or young person) serve upon the parent or guardian of the child or young person, if he can be found, a notice specifying the grounds on which the child or young person is brought before the Court and the time and place at which the Court will sit.[112]

(2) Before proceeding with the hearing, the Court shall inform the child or young person of the nature of the application.

(3) The Court shall hear evidence tendered by or on behalf of the Petitioner.

(4) (a) Where the nature of the case, or the evidence to be given, is such that in the opinion of the Court it is in the interests of the child or young person that the evidence, other than any evidence relating to the character or conduct of the child or young person, should not be given in his presence, the Court may hear any part of such evidence in his absence; and in that event his parent or guardian, or other person acting in accordance with these Rules, shall be permitted to remain in Court during the absence of the child or young person.

(b) The Court may exclude the parent or guardian, or other person acting in accordance with these Rules, while the child or young person gives evidence or makes a statement, if the Court is satisfied that in the special circumstances it is proper to do so: provided that the Court shall inform the parent or guardian or other person above mentioned of the substance of any allegation made by the child or young person, and shall give such parent or guardian or other person above mentioned an opportunity of meeting it by calling evidence or otherwise.

(5) If it appears to the Court after hearing the evidence in support of the application that a *prima facie* case is made out, it shall tell the child or young person and his parent or guardian, or other person acting in accordance with these Rules, that they may give evidence or make a statement and call witnesses.

. . .

Rule 10(7) then required the Court to obtain such information as to the general conduct, home surroundings, school record and medical history

112 See *McKenzies v McPhee* 1889 16R (J) 53, where committal of a child under the Industrial Schools Act, 1866 was held to be incompetent in the absence of any intimation (to the parents); and cf. *Dunn v Mustard* (1899) 1 F(J) 81 where in criminal proceedings for child cruelty against a father a child was removed without notice and this was held to be competent since the legislation then in force (the Prevention of Cruelty to Children Act, 1894) authorised the sheriff to make an order for custody of the child on his own initiative without notice to anyone.

of the child or young person as may enable it to deal with the case in the child's best interests, and to take that information into account, with provisos equivalent to those in Rule 9(6) set out above. The reference to the court dealing with the case in the child's best interests is once again to be especially noted. The outcome for any individual child, whether brought to the court for having committed an offence or because there were care and protection concerns relating to the child, was to be determined on an individualised basis that sought to improve the child's life. The court could require the child or young person, or the parent and guardian, to withdraw for the court and, unless it thought it undesirable or unnecessary to do so, had to inform the parent or guardian of the manner in which it proposed to deal with the child or young person.

The bare bones of the later structure of the children's hearing process – reading the basis (ground) upon which the child is brought before the court and seeking his or her acceptance thereon, adjourning to trial if there is a denial, taking account of a wide range of background circumstances, dealing with the case in the child's best interests, explaining the outcome – are all clear to see.

5. The Legal Process in the Modern Era: Scotland's Children's Hearing System

THE KILBRANDON REPORT

The significance of the Kilbrandon Report[1] will be clear throughout this book. It built upon the notion, which had earlier underpinned the parliamentary debates on the Children and Young Persons Bill in 1932, that the distinction that really mattered between children was not in terms of whether they were delinquents or offenders, or not, but the nature of their needs in terms of help to become productive members of society. Writing after the publication of the Report, Lord Kilbrandon said this:

> Of the four classes of children which we are now considering, only one class exhibits delinquency, yet all have this in common – that they are in trouble, something has gone wrong in the ordering of their lives, they have been deprived or they are depriving themselves – and the distinction is of no importance – of the opportunity to grow up in happiness and security. They are developing, so far as they are developing at all, along the wrong lines, and this feature they have in common is much more striking than any features which distinguish them.[2]

The Kilbrandon Report's crucial finding was that there was an identity of needs among various categories of children and young persons, with the result that that very categorisation was unhelpful in furthering the fundamental aim of prevention – either of harm to the child or young person or to others, and whether that harm was a result of offending behaviour or of circumstances inhibiting the child's proper development.

> [I]n terms of the child's actual needs, the legal distinction between juvenile offenders and children in need of care or protection was – looking to the underlying realities – very often of little practical significance. . . . From the standpoint of preventive measures, children in both groups could equally be said to be in

---

1 *Children and Young Persons, Scotland*, Scottish Home and Health Department, Scottish Education Department, 1964 HMSO.
2 (1966) 6 *British Journal of Criminology* 112, 115.

need of special measures of education and training – "education" being taken in its widest sense. The emphasis in these training measures might vary according to the circumstances of the individual case; in some the protection of the child would be of prime importance, in others the training regime might place more emphasis on discipline. Each case had, however, to be assessed on its merits, and the type of training, whether stressing the protective aspect, the disciplinary, or for that matter the need for special instruction in formal educational subjects on account of educational backwardness, had no necessary connection with the legal classification of children as delinquents or as children in need of care or protection.[3]

These were not the only groups of children whose needs were indistinguishable.

> The same is true of children brought before the courts as persistent truants or as beyond parental control. In the experience of the witnesses, persistent truancy is in many cases a manifestation of emotional disturbance often attributable to factors in the home and family background. So also the fact that a child is so refractory as to be beyond parental control calls in all cases for careful enquiry into the home and family circumstances and is likely to be attributable to factors personal to the child or to the parents themselves.[4]

The conclusion was inevitable:

> The consensus of experienced opinion which emerged from our discussions was that, for the purposes of treatment measures, these various classifications could not in practice be usefully considered as presenting a series of distinct and separately definable problems, calling in turn for distinct and separate principles of treatment. The basic similarity of underlying situation far outweighs the differences, and from the point of view of treatment measures the true distinguishing factor, common to all the children concerned, is their need for special measures of education and training, the normal up-bringing processes having, for whatever reason, fallen short.[5]

The Kilbrandon Report found that the existing juvenile court could not fully give effect to the preventive principle, for a number of reasons: its concentration on youth offending militated against early action being taken in respect of "potential delinquents"; it inhibited the court from ordering needed treatment because of the imperative to make the punishment fit the crime; punishment by its nature is a once and for all concept while treatment required to be moderated according to what progress is made.[6] The Report therefore recommended that the best way forward was to design a

---

3 Kilbrandon Report, para 13.
4 Ibid. para 14.
5 Ibid. para 15.
6 Ibid. para 54.

wholly new system where adjudication of the allegation and consideration of the measures to be applied were separated.[7] A "juvenile panel" should be established whose sole focus would be on determining the appropriate treatment, leaving the court process to adjudicate on disputes as to whether that treatment was needed (determined by the existence of various fact-scenarios including but by no means limited to the commission of an offence). It was also recommended that, as well as having an adjudication role, the sheriff should be the tribunal to which any appeal against the treatment decision of the juvenile panel could be taken.[8]

The proposed design and operation of the juvenile panel, and procedure before it, were described in Chapters IV and V of the Kilbrandon Report. As we saw in the preceding chapter of this book, much of the suggested process was modelled on the existing Juvenile Court Rules and, as we will see below, the circumstances that would justify a reference to the new tribunal largely built upon the existing jurisdictional bases of the juvenile court. Nor was the finding that child offending and child neglect required similar responses a radical departure from the approach under the Children and Young Persons (Scotland) Act, 1937. It was the personnel rather than the procedure in respect of which the Kilbrandon Report recommended the most substantial change. Building upon existing local authority personnel, and in particular the children's officers and children's committees introduced by the Children Act, 1948, the Kilbrandon Report recommended the creation of a "single executive agency" to deal with all child matters and in particular to take on responsibility for the implementation of decisions of the juvenile panel. The Report saw this role as encompassing "social education" of all children in need, not limited to those referred to the juvenile panel. In addition, a wholly new official, the "reporter to the children's panel", was suggested to take over the role of bringing the case to the panel, replacing the existing role of the police, local authorities and other authorised persons like the Royal Scottish Society for the Prevention of Cruelty to Children, in bringing cases to the attention of the juvenile court.

The continuing importance of the Kilbrandon Report is that the system it proposed has proved in the past half-century to be sufficiently robust to fend off, with truly remarkable ease, any suggestion that there is merit in classifying children and young people by any criteria other than their needs. Not for Scotland would the separation of care and protection cases from offender

7 Ibid. para 72.
8 Ibid. para 75.

cases – minimised by the Children and Young Persons (Scotland) Act, 1932 and obliterated virtually entirely by the creation of the children's hearing system – ever be restored.

THE SOCIAL WORK (SCOTLAND) ACT 1968 AND THE CHILDREN'S HEARINGS SYSTEM

It is for giving effect to the Kilbrandon Report's recommendation to establish the children's hearing (that is to say, the tribunal composed of three individual members of the children's panel attached to each local authority) that the Social Work (Scotland) Act 1968 is best remembered. The dispositive role of the juvenile courts was transferred by that Act to this new dispositive quasi-judicial tribunal. Juvenile courts, as such, ceased to exist.

The basic procedure set out in the 1968 Act has, if with ever greater specificity, survived the two complete re-enactments of the children's hearing system that subsequently followed.[9] What came to be known as the "grounds of referral" were to be read to the child and parent, in order to give them the opportunity to dispute the factual basis of the referral to the children's hearing.[10] If one or other did dispute, or did not understand, the ground or grounds, the matter would normally be sent off to the sheriff court for adjudication and determination of the facts.[11] If the ground or grounds were accepted, or the sheriff found them to be established, the children's hearing would then move to the dispositive stage. The paramount consideration of the hearing in determining the appropriate outcome of each individual case was the welfare of the child,[12] which the members of the hearing would identify through discussion of the various background reports with which they were presented, this discussion involving the child, parents, social work representatives and any other person the chairman of the hearing considered could bring value to the discussion.

That procedure, as we have seen, was modelled on juvenile court procedure, and the major change was the strict institutional differentiation between the probative and the dispositive stages. The court lost its role in

---

9 Children (Scotland) Act 1995, Part II; Children's Hearings (Scotland) Act 2011.

10 Social Work (Scotland) Act 1968, s. 42(1); Children (Scotland) Act 1995, s. 65(4); Children's Hearings (Scotland) Act 2011, s. 90(1).

11 Social Work (Scotland) Act 1968, s. 42(2)(c); Children (Scotland) Act 1995, s. 65(7); Children's Hearings (Scotland) Act 2011, ss. 93 and 94.

12 Social Work (Scotland) Act 1968, s. 43(1); Children (Scotland) Act 1995, s. 16(1); Children's Hearings (Scotland) Act 2011, s. 25.

determining the outcome, which has rested ever since exclusively with the children's hearing.[13] The sheriff court retained the power to adjudicate on disputes as to the existence of a ground of referral, and it gained a role hearing appeals from the disposition determined by the hearing.

While the power to decide on outcomes was transferred from the juvenile court to the children's hearing, the outcomes available to that new tribunal remained much as they were before: a child in appropriate circumstances might either remain at home and be placed under supervision (previously of a probation officer[14] and now of a local authority) or be accommodated away from home with foster carers or in a residential establishment ("approved" school or local authority or voluntary home).[15] Similarly, as we will shortly see below, most of the grounds upon which the hearing was given jurisdiction over any individual child were previously grounds of jurisdiction for the juvenile court. And the focus on the child's welfare, though enhanced,[16] was by no means new.[17]

However, the ongoing role of the children's hearing itself was far greater than that of the juvenile court, which, once it had made its decision, dropped out of the picture. The children's hearing, on the other hand, has always retained control of the child's progress even after its order is made: the hearing was (and is) required to review the child's case regularly until the supervision order is discharged or the child reaches the age of 18. Another change – perhaps the most important of all – was the substantially increased emphasis that the children's hearing system placed on the child and family participating in the decision-making process. The core of the hearing itself has always been the discussion, led by the hearing members, and involving all interested parties, of the whole case and not just the ground that brought the child to the hearing.[18]

13 The sheriff acquired a limited dispositive role in s. 51(5)(c)(iii) of the Children (Scotland) Act 1995 which allowed the sheriff to substitute his own disposal on a successful appeal. See now the more limited power in s. 156(3)(b) of the Children's Hearings (Scotland) Act 2011.

14 Children and Young Persons (Scotland) Act, 1937, ss. 66(2)(d) and 68.

15 Social Work (Scotland) Act 1968, s. 44(5).

16 Hearings were instructed to make decisions "in the best interests of the child": 1968 Act, s. 43(1).

17 The Children and Young Persons (Scotland) Act, 1937, s. 49(1), had required juvenile courts to "have regard to the welfare of the child or young person" and the Juvenile Courts (Procedure) (Scotland) Rules, 1934 (SR&O, 1934 No. 641 (S. 36)), rules 9(6) and 10(7) had required juvenile courts to "deal with the case in [the child's] best interests".

18 See further, Norrie, K. "In Defence of O v Rae" 1995 SLT (News) 353.

THE GROUNDS OF REFERRAL TO THE CHILDREN'S HEARING

Under the Social Work (Scotland) Act 1968, a child could be referred to the children's hearing by a reporter to the children's panel whenever the reporter was of the view that the child might be in need of compulsory measures of care.[19] This remains the case today. A child might be in need of compulsory measures of care if one or more of several fact scenarios, collectively known as the grounds of referral, are either accepted or established by proof. It is for the sheriff to determine whether the ground founded on by the reporter exists (if the ground is denied or not understood), and for the hearing to determine whether, in light of that ground existing and other background circumstances, the child does need compulsory measures of care (and to determine how best to meet that need). Under the 1968 Act, as originally passed, there were eight grounds upon which the reporter could refer a child to a children's hearing. Most of them reflected existing grounds upon which a child could be taken to a juvenile court.

Child beyond parental control

The first ground of referral was that the child was beyond the control of his or her parent.[20] This may be traced to two sources: (i) s. 6(1)(i) of the Children and Young Persons (Scotland) Act, 1932,[21] which gave the juvenile court jurisdiction over children who, being without parents or guardians or with unfit parents or guardians, were beyond control; and (ii) s. 7 of the 1932 Act, under which the juvenile court also had jurisdiction if, at the instance of the parent or guardian, it was shown that "he is unable to control the child or young person".[22] The latter had repeated an identical provision in the Children Act, 1908,[23] which was itself traced to s. 9 of the Industrial Schools (Scotland) Act, 1861, a provision that allowed the court to send a child to an industrial school if the parent "represents that he is unable to control him, and that he desires such child to be sent to an industrial school". This was always a slightly odd ground for the juvenile court's jurisdiction in that,

---

19 Social Work (Scotland) Act 1968, s. 38(1).
20 Social Work (Scotland) Act 1968, s. 32(2)(a).
21 Re-enacted as s. 65(1)(a) of the Children and Young Persons (Scotland) Act, 1937.
22 Re-enacted as s. 68 of the Children and Young Persons (Scotland) Act, 1937.
23 Children Act, 1908, s. 58(4).

before 1963,[24] it was one that had to be proved by the parent or guardian him- or herself (as opposed to any external agency). Under the 1968 Act, however, it became a ground, like all the others, to be proved (if challenged) by the reporter. This ground was re-enacted in both the Children (Scotland) Act 1995[25] and the Children's Hearings (Scotland) Act 2011.[26]

Bad associations or moral danger

The second ground in the 1968 Act was that through a lack of parental care the child was falling into bad associations or was exposed to moral danger.[27] Again, this is traced to s. 6(1)(i) of the 1932 Act which was worded in terms of the child falling into bad associations or being exposed to moral danger because he or she had no parents or guardians, or had unfit parents or guardians. Before that, the 1908 Act had listed a cognate ground as a justification for sending a child to an industrial school: that he or she "frequents the company of any reputed thief, or of any common or reputed prostitute", or resided in a house used for prostitution or otherwise lived in circumstances calculated to cause or encourage the seduction or prostitution of the child.[28] Frequenting the company of reputed thieves had even earlier been specified as one of the grounds for sending a child to an industrial school.[29] Moral danger was presumed under the Children and Young Persons (Scotland) Act, 1937 to exist when the child or young person was found destitute or begging,[30] but this was without prejudice to the generality of the concept. The original wording of this ground in the 1968 Act required a causal connection between the bad associations or moral danger and a lack of parental care, but the ground was restructured by the Children Act 1975, after which it was simply required to be established that the child was falling into bad associations or was exposed to moral danger.[31] The concept of "moral danger" was designed to be widely interpreted, though there are no reported cases under either the 1937 or 1968 Acts discussing what it might

---

24 The Children and Young Persons Act 1963, s. 3, required local authorities to initiate proceedings on the ground that the child was beyond parental control.

25 Children (Scotland) Act 1995, s. 52(2)(a).

26 Children's Hearings (Scotland) Act 2011, s. 67(2)(n).

27 Social Work (Scotland) Act 1968, s. 32(2)(b).

28 Children Act, 1908, s. 58(1)(f) and (g).

29 Industrial Schools (Scotland) Act, 1861, s. 9.

30 Children and Young Persons (Scotland) Act, 1937, s. 65(2). These were themselves grounds for sending a child to an industrial school under s. 58(1)(a)–(c) of the Children Act, 1908.

31 Children Act 1975, sched. 3 para 54(a), amending Social Work (Scotland) Act 1968, s. 32(2)(b).

encompass. It was re-enacted as a ground in the 1995 Act.[32] As society's notions of morality became less clear-cut, so the ground became more and more out of touch[33] (and more difficult to apply) as an indicator of the need for compulsory measures of care, and no ground based on morality appears in the Children's Hearings (Scotland) Act 2011. "Bad associations" does, however, have an afterlife in the 2011 grounds that the child has a "close connection" with a schedule 1 offender, or with a person who has carried out domestic abuse, or with a person who has committed an offence under the Sexual Offences (Scotland) Act 2009.[34]

Lack of parental care

The third ground of referral in the 1968 Act was that the child was likely to suffer unnecessarily or be seriously impaired in his or her health or development, this likelihood coming from a lack of parental care.[35] Though there was no direct predecessor to this ground in the earlier legislation, the roots of this "lack of parental care" ground may be traced to an analogous provision in the 1908 Act. The provision allowed a child to be sent to an industrial school if the parent, by reason of criminal or drunken habits, was unfit to have the care of the child.[36] That provision was widened by the 1932 Act which specified no reason for the parental unfitness but required the consequence to be that the child was falling into bad associations or moral danger, or was beyond control.[37] The ground of lack of parental care was repeated in the 1995 Act[38] and the 2011 Act,[39] which similarly focused on the damage that lack of parental care was likely to cause.

Victim of scheduled offence

The fourth ground was that any of the offences in schedule 1 to the 1937 Act had been committed either in respect of the child being referred to a

---

32 Children (Scotland) Act 1995, s. 52(2)(b).
33 As late as the 1990s it was commonly stated in children's panel training that the ground was aimed at children who associated with homosexuals or prostitutes.
34 Children's Hearings (Scotland) Act 2011, s. 67(2)(c), (f) and (g).
35 Social Work (Scotland) Act 1968, s. 32(2)(c).
36 Children Act, 1908, s. 58(1)(d).
37 Children and Young Persons (Scotland) Act, 1932, s. 6(1)(i), re-enacted as s. 65(1)(a) of the 1937 Act.
38 Children (Scotland) Act 1995, s. 52(2)(c).
39 Children's Hearings (Scotland) Act 2011, s. 67(2)(a).

children's hearing or in respect of any other child who was a member of the same household as the referred child.[40] This ground was an amalgamation of two distinct grounds (relating to the child victim and to the child who was a member of the same household as the child victim) in s. 6(1)(ii)(a) and (b) of the 1932 Act.[41] The first of these earlier grounds actually goes back further than 1932, for it appeared in the 1908 Act. This ground authorised the court to remove a child from the custody of a person who had committed one of the offences specified in the First Schedule to that Act against the child and commit the child to the care of a relative or other fit person.[42] Indeed, the 1908 provision can itself be traced to the earlier child cruelty statutes which gave the court a similar power.[43] The innovation in the 1932 Act was to give the juvenile court jurisdiction over children in the same household as the victim (typically, their siblings), and that was repeated in the 1968 Act. Oddly, and almost certainly accidentally, a related ground that appeared in the 1932 and 1937 Acts – that the child referred was a member of the same household as the perpetrator of the offence (as opposed to the victim of the offence)[44] – did not appear in the 1968 Act as originally enacted, notwithstanding that living with a perpetrator of a crime against children would often constitute a greater risk than living with a victim. It was not until an amendment to the 1968 Act was made by the Children Act 1975 that living with the perpetrator was reintroduced as a ground of referral[45] and (with changing references to the statutes where the applicable offences were located),[46] all three grounds (the child being a victim of a scheduled offence, or being a member of the same household as a victim, or being a member of the same household as the perpetrator) were re-enacted in both the Children (Scotland) Act 1995[47] and the Children's Hearings (Scotland) Act 2011.[48]

---

40 Social Work (Scotland) Act 1968, s. 32(2)(d).

41 Re-enacted as s. 65(1)(b)(i) and (ii) of the Children and Young Persons (Scotland) Act, 1937.

42 Children Act, 1908, s. 21(1).

43 Prevention of Cruelty to, and Protection of, Children Act, 1889, s. 5; Prevention of Cruelty to Children Act, 1894, s. 6; Prevention of Cruelty to Children Act, 1904, s. 6.

44 Children and Young Persons (Scotland) Acts, 1932, s. 6(1)(ii)(c) and 1937, s. 65(1)(b)(iii).

45 Social Work (Scotland) Act 1968, s. 32(2)(dd), as inserted by the Children Act 1975, sched. 3 para 54(c).

46 The Children Act 1975 changed the reference to offences in sched. 1 to the Criminal Procedure (Scotland) Act 1975; the Children (Scotland) Act 1995 changed that to offences in sched. 1 to the Criminal Procedure (Scotland) Act 1995.

47 Children (Scotland) Act 1995, s. 52(2)(d), (e) and (f).

48 Children's Hearings (Scotland) Act 2011, s. 67(2)(b), (c) and (d). Para (c) here was widened from its predecessors and now captures children with "a close connection" with the perpetrator of a scheduled offence. "Close connection" means living in the same household as or having significant contact with the offender: s. 67(3).

Female living with a female victim of incest

The fifth ground, that a female child was a member of the same household as a female victim of the crime of incest committed by another member of that household,[49] was taken from the 1932 Act,[50] distinct from members of the same household as a victim of a scheduled offence, in order to cover the case when the victim was not a child herself (scheduled offences being, primarily, offences against children). Such a scenario allowed state action even before 1932, for under the 1908 Act the court could send the daughter of an incestuous father to an industrial school (whether the victim was that daughter herself or one of her sisters).[51] Though re-enacted (in a slightly broader form[52]) in the 1995 Act,[53] this separate ground does not appear in the 2011 Act and there is no longer a ground of referral to the children's hearing when the victim of the crime of incest is an adult.[54]

Failure to attend school regularly

The sixth ground in the 1968 Act as originally enacted was that the child had failed to attend school regularly.[55] The juvenile court had taken over truancy cases from police and burgh courts in 1932,[56] and this ground transferred that jurisdiction to the children's hearing with truancy being an independent basis upon which the hearing can exercise its protective jurisdiction. The Kilbrandon Committee had therefore tapped into long-established thinking when it saw truanting as an indicator of some breakdown in the normal child-rearing process. The ground reappeared in both the 1995 Act[57] and the 2011 Act.[58]

---

49 Social Work (Scotland) Act 1968, s. 32(2)(e).
50 Children and Young Persons (Scotland) Act, 1932, s. 6(1)(ii)(d), re-enacted as s. 65(1)(b)(iv) of the Children and Young Persons (Scotland) Act, 1937.
51 Children Act, 1908, s. 58(1)(e).
52 The 1995 ground included offences related to incest: sexual intercourse with a step-child, or in abuse of a position of trust.
53 Children (Scotland) Act 1995, s. 52(2)(g).
54 In appropriate cases, where a risk to the referred child can be shown, the ground in s. 67(2)(e) – that the child is exposed to a person whose conduct makes it likely that the child will be abused or harmed – can be used.
55 Social Work (Scotland) Act 1968, s. 32(2)(f).
56 Children and Young Persons (Scotland) Act, 1932, s. 1(1)(ii), re-enacted as s. 50(1)(ii) of the Children and Young Persons (Scotland) Act, 1937.
57 Children (Scotland) Act 1995, s. 52(2)(h).
58 Children's Hearings (Scotland) Act 2011, s. 67(2)(o).

Commission of offence by child

The seventh ground was that the child had committed an offence.[59] From 1854 this occurrence had given the court the power to send a child to a reformatory school, and from 1861 it had permitted the court to send a child under 12 to an industrial school. That the child or young person had committed an offence was, of course, the original ground upon which the juvenile court, as established in the Children Act, 1908, exercised jurisdiction, becoming one of the grounds of its jurisdiction in the 1932 Act,[60] along with the care and protection grounds. Originally by far the most commonly used ground of referral to the children's hearing, the offence ground is today used in only a minority of cases.[61] It was, of course, re-enacted in both the 1995 Act[62] and the 2011 Act,[63] though the focus remains on the child's welfare.

Child absconsion

The eighth and final ground of referral in the 1968 Act, as originally enacted, was that the child was referred to the children's hearing under Part V of the Act.[64] This might be because he or she had absconded from a place of safety or person under whose control he or she had been placed by a supervision requirement, or from a residential establishment, or because he or she was currently subject to an order of the English court and was being transferred to Scotland. There was no antecedent to this in earlier legislation, and it is, therefore, the only truly original ground of referral to the children's hearing contained in the Social Work (Scotland) Act 1968. Yet it was mostly limited to children already subject to some form of state intervention in their lives (in Scotland or in England) and its effect was to give the reporter the opportunity either (i) to bring the child back to a hearing, after an absconsion, for

59 Social Work (Scotland) Act 1968, s. 32(2)(g).
60 Children and Young Persons (Scotland) Act, 1932, s. 1(1)(i), re-enacted in s. 50(1)(i) of the Children and Young Persons (Scotland) Act, 1937.
61 The Social Work Services Group *Statistical Bulletin for 1980*, published by the Scottish Office, shows that in 1972, the first full year of operation of the children's hearing system a full 87.5% of referrals were made on the offence ground, dropping gradually to 78.3 in 1980. The *Statistical Bulletin for 1988* reported a figure of 51%. By 2012, when the Scottish Children's Reporter Administration started to publish statistics on-line, there were 8,669 offence referrals out of a total of 36,298. In the year to 31 March 2019 there were 7,763 offence referrals out of a total of 23,140.
62 Children (Scotland) Act 1995, s. 52(2)(i).
63 Children's Hearings (Scotland) Act 2011, s. 67(2)(j).
64 Social Work (Scotland) Act 1968, s. 32(2)(h).

a variation of the existing terms of a supervision requirement or (ii) to trans-
late an existing English order into a Scottish order. It was more a ground to
review existing orders than a ground that would in itself lead to independent
measures, and it was not re-enacted in the Children (Scotland) Act 1995
which had more detailed provisions for the review of existing orders.

Grounds added subsequent to the 1968 Act

In many ways, the grounds of referral to the children's hearing reflect the
concerns that society has in respect of the risks to (and occasionally from[65])
children and young persons. These risks change as time goes by. As new
risks are recognised so new grounds have been introduced into the system.
The first new ground of referral to the children's hearing to be added after
the 1968 Act was contained in the Solvent Abuse (Scotland) Act 1983: that
the child had "misused a volatile substance by deliberately inhaling, other
than for medicinal purposes, that substance's vapour".[66] This was a response
to the new social problem of solvent abuse, which came to public prominence in the early 1980s. The practice of children "sniffing glue" in order
to achieve narcotic effects similar to that achieved by the misuse of illegal
drugs may have become less common – or at least less obvious – today
as other mind-altering substances have become more readily available to
young people, but it remains a highly dangerous activity.[67] The ground was
repeated in the Children (Scotland) Act 1995[68] but was absorbed under the
2011 Act into the rather broader ground that "the child's conduct has had, or
is likely to have, a serious adverse effect on the health, safety or development
of the child or another person".[69]

Section 8(1) of the Health and Social Services and Social Security
Adjudications Act 1983 inserted into the 1968 Act a further new ground: that
a child was in the care of a local authority and his or her behaviour was such
as to require "special measures" for his or her adequate care or control. The
concept of a child "in care" was broader than a child subject to a supervision
order, and so this new ground allowed a child in care to be brought before

---

65 See Cleland, A. "The Antisocial Behaviour etc (Scotland) Act 2004: Exposing the Punitive Fault
    Line Below the Children's Hearing System" (2005) 9 *Edinburgh Law Review* 439.
66 Social Work (Scotland) Act 1968, s. 32(2)(gg), as inserted by Solvent Abuse (Scotland) Act
    1983, s. 1.
67 It was reported in 2012 that the practice had killed more young people in the preceding 20 years
    than all the class A drugs together: *Druglink* November/December 2012, vol. 27. Issue 6, p. 18.
68 Children (Scotland) Act, 1995, s. 52(2)(k).
69 Children's Hearings (Scotland) Act 2011, s. 67(2)(m).

the children's hearing for the purpose of authorising "special measures" even when not presently subject to a supervision order. The somewhat recondite phrase "special measures" is a euphemism for the keeping of a child in secure accommodation, as is made plain in s. 8(2) of the 1983 Act. The ground was repeated in the 1995 Act in respect of children being accommodated by a local authority (a subset of children being "looked after" by a local authority, the successor concept to children "in care"), and who needed these special measures for his or her adequate supervision:[70] again, this close supervision indicated secure accommodation. The need for special measures, but this time "to support the child" again appeared in the Children's Hearings (Scotland) Act 2011,[71] and extended to include children subject to a permanence order who also needed special measures.[72] The evolving purpose of the special measures reflects the changing perception of the purpose of placing a child in secure accommodation.

When the Children (Scotland) Act 1995 replaced the provisions in the Social Work (Scotland) Act 1968 dealing with the children's hearing system with new provisions, most of the grounds of referral that existed immediately prior to the 1995 Act were replicated in s. 52(2).[73] However, one additional ground was added: that the child had misused alcohol or any drug, whether or not a controlled drug.[74] It was considered necessary to insert this new ground in order to fulfil Scotland's obligations under Art. 33 of the UN Convention on the Rights of the Child, which requires states to take all appropriate measures to protect children from the illicit use of "narcotic drugs and psychotropic substances". Under the 2011 Act, what had been a single ground in the 1995 Act became two separate grounds: that the child had misused alcohol, and that the child had misused a drug (whether or not a controlled drug).[75]

The Antisocial Behaviour etc. (Scotland) Act 2004 added a new, and somewhat circular, ground to the Children (Scotland) Act 1995:[76] if a sheriff made an antisocial behaviour order under the 2004 Act over a child he or she could require the reporter to refer the child's case to a children's hearing,

---

70 Children (Scotland) Act 1995, s. 52(2)(l).
71 Children's Hearings (Scotland) Act 2011, s. 67(2)(h).
72 Ibid. s. 67(2)(i).
73 The only ground to disappear was the absconsion or transfer ground in s. 32(2)(h) of the 1968 Act, discussed above.
74 Children (Scotland) Act 1995, s. 52(2)(j).
75 Children's Hearings (Scotland) Act 2011, s. 67(2)(k) and (l).
76 Children (Scotland) Act 1995, s. 52(2)(m), as inserted by Antisocial Behaviour etc. (Scotland) Act 2004, s. 12(3).

and the ground would be that the sheriff had so required. This awkward ground disappeared with the passing of the Children's Hearings (Scotland) Act 2011. Now, if the sheriff wishes to refer a child over whom he or she has made an antisocial behaviour order to a children's hearing, he or she must specify one of the substantive grounds listed in s. 67.

Finally, the Children's Hearings (Scotland) Act 2011, repealing the appropriate parts of the 1995 Act, restructured the children's hearing system (again without challenging its fundamental principles) and re-ordered the grounds of referral – now known as "the section 67 grounds". It also dropped some of the pre-existing grounds (as mentioned above) and created the following new grounds. Exposure of a child to a person whose conduct makes it likely that the child will be abused or harmed, or the child's health, safety or development will be seriously affected[77] is a new ground with no previous antecedents; so is the fact that the child has or is likely to have a close connection with a person who has carried out domestic abuse;[78] that the child has a close connection with a sex offender;[79] that the child's conduct has had or is likely to have a serious adverse effect on the health, safety or development of the child or another person;[80] and that the child has been, is being or is likely to be, subjected to physical, emotional or other pressure to enter into a marriage or civil partnership or is or is likely to become a member of the same household as such a child.[81]

Overview of changing grounds

Though the Social Work (Scotland) Act 1968 established the children's hearing system as a wholly new forum for dealing with children, seven of the eight original grounds of referral to the hearing contained in the 1968 Act were grounds upon which the juvenile court previously exercised jurisdiction. Six of these seven continue, if in slightly different guises, to found the jurisdiction of the children's hearing today. A substantial number of new grounds, often in response to new social problems (as for example with

---

77 Children's Hearings (Scotland) Act 2011, s. 67(2)(e).
78 Ibid. s. 67(2)(f).
79 Ibid. s. 67(2)(g).
80 Ibid. s. 67(2)(m).
81 Ibid. s. 67(2)(p). This last ground was subsequently separated into two: the existing "(p)" ground being restricted to marriage and the new "(q)" ground relating to civil partnership: this was necessary to tie the forced marriage ground to the new processes in the Forced Marriage etc. (Protection and Jurisdiction) (Scotland) Act 2011, which did not include forced civil partnerships (s. 13(3) making the appropriate amendments).

solvent abuse then drug or alcohol abuse) or the increased recognition of the harm caused by old social problems (as for example domestic abuse and forced marriages) have been added either from time to time or when the children's hearing system as a whole has been re-enacted. At the present time, the Children's Hearings (Scotland) Act 2011 contains 17 separate grounds of referral. The official statistics collected by the Scottish Children's Reporter Administration, published annually (and on-line since 2012), show the numbers of referrals and numbers of children referred under each ground.

QUALIFICATION TO THE WELFARE TEST

The children's hearing has, since its creation, been obliged to regard the child's welfare as its paramount consideration,[82] and even the decisions that appear most draconian are justified solely for that reason. In *S v Miller*[83] Lord President Rodger said that "it must be remembered that when a hearing makes an order for a child to be placed and kept in secure accommodation, it does so only because that is in the interests of the child's welfare."

The Children (Scotland) Act 1995 was the first to introduce a limited exception to the paramountcy of the child's welfare, for s. 16(5) thereof allowed the hearing to make a decision that was inconsistent with that so long as it was necessary to do so "for the purpose of protecting members of the public from serious harm (whether or not physical harm)". There were no court decisions discussing this provision which, it must therefore be supposed, was only rarely used. A potentially greater qualification to the paramountcy of the child's welfare was introduced by the Antisocial Behaviour etc. (Scotland) Act 2004, which allows local authorities to take a child to court instead of to a children's hearing, and to ask that the court subject them to an antisocial behaviour order. This may be granted if the sheriff finds it necessary in order to protect affected persons from further antisocial behaviour. If the order is sought over a child, the advice of the children's hearing as to whether it is necessary in these terms is to be sought.[84] But the decision is not made on the basis of the child's welfare. There have been no reported decisions in which an antisocial behaviour order has been sought against a child, and local authorities are clearly choosing to refer

---

82 Social Work (Scotland) Act 1968, s. 43(1); Children (Scotland) Act 1995, s. 16(1); Children's Hearings (Scotland) Act 2011, s. 25.

83 2001 SLT 531, p. 547.

84 Antisocial Behaviour etc. (Scotland) Act 2004, s. 4(4).

children exhibiting troublesome behaviour to reporters rather than take them to court.

The Children's Hearings (Scotland) Act 2011 repeated the rule in s. 16(5) of the 1995 Act, but added that when a hearing does make a decision inconsistent with giving paramountcy to the child's welfare for the purpose of protecting the child from serious harm it must nevertheless "regard the need to safeguard and promote the welfare of the child throughout the child's childhood as a primary consideration rather than the paramount consideration."[85] Again, there have been no cases in which this provision has been judicially discussed. The strength of the welfare test in the children's hearing system is located not only in the underpinning legislation but also in the very ethos of the system, which informs the mindset of all its players.

A MISSED OPPORTUNITY FOR ENGLAND?

It is well-known that the children's hearing system, established by the Social Work (Scotland) Act 1968, is uniquely Scottish and that reform of the legal process for dealing with children in trouble in England took a very different path from the 1960s onwards. Before then the two legal systems had developed hand in hand, with the Children Act 1908, which established juvenile courts, covering both jurisdictions, as did the structural and systemic amendments in the Children and Young Persons Act, 1932 and the Children Act, 1948. Even when the two legal systems acquired separate governing legislation – the Adoption of Children Act, 1926 and the Children and Young Persons Act, 1933 for England and the Adoption of Children (Scotland) Act, 1930 and the Children and Young Persons (Scotland) Act, 1937 for Scotland – the fundamental approaches in the two systems were designedly virtually identical. Practice, of course, developed differently, especially since the establishment of completely separate juvenile courts staffed by specially qualified justices of the peace occurred much more rapidly and more extensively in England than in Scotland.

As we saw above, the Kilbrandon proposals, and the Social Work (Scotland) Act 1968, which gave effect to them, were less radical than is often presented. In many ways these proposals were designed to give full effect to the philosophy of the juvenile courts that had existed across Great Britain since at least 1932. To a large extent they built upon existing principles, in particular the unitary nature of the process and its focus on the child's welfare. Yet

---

85 Children's Hearings (Scotland) Act 2011, s. 26.

an equivalent full effect was never achieved in England which, just as the children's hearing system was being established in Scotland, increasingly set its face against the approach that had governed for the previous 30 years in both jurisdictions. So in many respects it was English law that evinced a radical departure from the past, while Scots law built upon it. Nevertheless, policy-makers in England throughout the 1960s had toyed with the idea of adopting an approach based on similar principles to those that underlay the Kilbrandon proposals.

In 1961, just as the Kilbrandon Committee was established, the English equivalent, under the chairmanship of Viscount Ingleby, produced its *Report of the Committee on Children and Young Persons*.[86] The Ingleby Report suggested no radical change to the existing structures or processes in the (English) Children and Young Persons Act, 1933, but it did recommend increased emphasis on supporting families, and on preventing rather than curing child abuse and neglect.[87] It worried that the welfarist approach to youth offending could lead to children being kept away from home for long periods for minor offences, but nevertheless recommended that all children under 12 be dealt with as care and protection cases, which would be achieved by raising the age of criminal responsibility. Compared with the Kilbrandon proposals, the Ingleby proposals amounted to little more than tinkering at the edges, but they did nevertheless lead to some important changes in the law in the Children and Young Persons Act 1963, in particular the increased emphasis required by that Act on preventive social work.[88]

Around the same time, the Labour Party (about to come into power under Harold Wilson after 13 years of Conservative Government) commissioned Lord Longford[89] to examine the issue of juvenile offending. In 1964 he produced a report[90] that was more ambitious than the Ingleby Report but instead chimed with many of the recommendations in the Kilbrandon Report. The incoming Labour Government responded to the Longford Report with a White Paper[91] which seemed to endorse many of that Report's recommendations. It accepted that the main aim of criminal

---

86 HMSO 1961, Cmnd 1191.
87 Ingleby Report, paras 7–14.
88 Children and Young Persons Act 1963, s. 1.
89 A famous social reformer with deep interest in penal reform, he campaigned tirelessly in favour of the release of the child-murderer Myra Hindley, and in favour of laws prohibiting the "promotion of homosexuality" and against equalising the age of consent for gay sex.
90 Report of the Labour Party Study Group, "Crime: A Challenge to Us All" (1964).
91 *The Child, the Family and the Young Offender* (1965, Cmnd 2742). See commentaries on this White Paper at (1966) 6 *British Journal of Criminology* 105, 139 and 159.

justice should be to prevent rather than to respond to delinquency and to treat young people in trouble in a way that advanced their welfare. The most radical proposal was to remove all children under 16 from the criminal courts and to deal with them through the family welfare services. It recommended the establishment of "family councils", to be composed of social workers and others with knowledge and experience of dealing with children, which would determine outcomes while family courts would resolve disputes of fact (as well as dealing with other, more general, family issues). Juvenile courts would simply disappear, their fact-finding role being taken over by the family court and their dispositive role in care and protection cases by the family council. Supervision orders would be made instead of probation orders over young offenders, and they would last for a maximum of three years.

It will be seen that while there was some overlap, at least at the level of principle, between the proposals in England and in Scotland, there were also significant differences in detail. In fact, this White Paper met with such negative responses that the Home Office replaced it with a new White Paper[92] shortly after Roy Jenkins[93] became Home Secretary in 1968. The title, *Children in Trouble*, was deliberately chosen to indicate that its consideration included both children who caused trouble and children who suffered from trouble around them, but the 1968 White Paper was substantially more timid than its predecessor. It dropped many of the more radical proposals contained in the 1965 White Paper, such as those relating to family councils. Nevertheless, it accepted that juvenile offenders should if possible be dealt with outwith the court structure, preferably through agreements negotiated between the parents and social workers; disputes of fact were, however, still to be resolved by the juvenile court.

Both the separation of fact-finding and disposition, which Lord Hope a quarter of a century later would describe as the "genius" of the Kilbrandon reforms in Scotland,[94] and the focus on welfare-based solutions for all children and young people, were central to both the 1965 and the 1968 White Papers and looked as if they would become features of English process

---

92 *Juvenile Crime: Children in Trouble* (1968, Cmnd 3601).

93 Perhaps the most radical Home Secretary of the twentieth century. He later became President of the European Commission, returning to domestic politics by co-founding the Social Democratic Party, under whose banner he was elected to Parliament as the MP for Glasgow Hillhead in 1982. He lost that seat in the 1987 General Election and became a noted biographer of, amongst others, Gladstone, Roosevelt and Churchill.

94 *Sloan v B* 1991 SLT 530, p. 548.

too when the 1968 White Paper proposals were passed into law with the Children and Young Persons Act 1969. The Current Law Annotator of this Act[95] said this:

> This Act revolutionises the law relating to young people "in trouble", whether neglected, in moral danger, or delinquent. Inspired to a considerable extent by the recommendations in "Children in Trouble" ((1968) Cmnd. 3601), it provides that all such children should be treated, as far as possible, in the same way and by the same people, irrespective of fault. Misfortune is the single criterion for bringing anyone within the provisions of the Act: criminal behaviour is relegated to one category of misfortune.

Other than the reference to the English White Paper, this could have been describing the Social Work (Scotland) Act 1968. But for England it was not to be, for the Children and Young Persons Act 1969 was only very partially brought into force. That Act had been passed, while the Labour Government was in power, in the face of sustained (primarily party) political opposition,[96] which makes it all the more remarkable that the Social Work (Scotland) Act 1968, passed a year earlier by the same Parliament, had faced virtually no opposition.[97] Before either the Scottish 1968 Act or the English 1969 Act came into force, the Conservatives came to power and Quentin Hogg, who had led the opposition to the 1969 Act, became Lord Chancellor as Lord Hailsham and thus the minister primarily responsible for its implementation. The new Government had a very different ideological perception of youth crime to the defeated Labour Party, and the provisions removing young offenders from the English criminal justice system clashed with that ideology and so were never brought into force. The lack of opposition to the 1968 Act in Scotland, and the fact that its implementation was in the hands

---

95 Margaret Puxon, Barrister-at-Law (and counsel for the successful foster parents in *J v C* [1970] AC 668).

96 See the Second Reading debate at HC Deb. 11 March 1969 vol. 779 cols 1176–1303, where Quentin Hogg's amendment to reject the Bill outright was defeated by 200 to 140 votes (mostly along party lines). Sir Peter Rawlinson, QC, MP, for example, summing up for the opposition pointed out that taking a child's circumstances into account inevitably meant that "advantage is given to the offender whose circumstances are comfortable" (col. 1287). He concluded (col. 1290) that "The Bill offends against the major principle of fairness, it introduces unnecessary delays and cumbersome procedures, and is the fruit of a philosophy of penology which is unacceptable to the public".

97 The Scottish Peer Lord Ferrier was notably alone in his strong opposition to the whole of the Social Work (Scotland) Bill: HL Deb. 21 March 1968 vol. 290 cols 833–8. Mrs Winifred Ewing, the first and at the time sole Scottish National Party MP, welcomed the principle of the Bill but had deep concerns about the replacement of the juvenile court with a children's panel. The main concern of this representative of the socially conservative strand of Scottish Nationalism was the type of person who might be appointed to the panel: "do-gooders", she feared (HC Deb. 6 May 1968, vol. 764 col. 100).

of the Scottish Office, ensured that that Act did not suffer the same fate and it was fully brought into force in 1971.

It remains a matter of speculation why the 1968 Act survived the change in political climate while the 1969 Act succumbed. One explanation is that the original proposals made by Lord Longford and in the two White Papers were not warmly welcomed in England[98] while the Kilbrandon Report generally was in Scotland. The English proposals, emanating from a report by a Labour Peer, commissioned by the Labour Party, may have proved politically more vulnerable than the Scottish proposals, drafted by a judge of the highest repute for impartiality and appointed by a Conservative Government. Another explanation that has been suggested is that social work reorganisation in Scotland – the other major focal point of the Social Work (Scotland) Act 1968 – was already on the political agenda when the Labour Government came to power in 1964 and was not opposed when the Conservatives took office in 1970. In England, however, the children and young persons proposals stood (and fell) alone.[99] In addition, it may be that the English proposals – effectively to build upon and develop the well-established juvenile court system that existed across England – were seen as little more than disrupting court practices which were not generally thought to be operating dysfunctionally; the Scottish juvenile court system envisaged in 1932 had, on the other hand, failed to establish itself and so more fundamental changes were deemed necessary to "kick-start" the ideas on which the 1932 Act had been based.

Whatever the reason, and doubtless it was a combination of different things, the two jurisdictions from the end of the 1960s took increasingly separate paths. The English approach ultimately led to the rejection of the founding principle of the juvenile courts (in both jurisdictions) – the dealing in the same forum with the same range of available, welfare-informed, outcomes for both young offenders and children in need of care and protection. In Scotland that combination was embraced, indeed reinforced, with the establishment of the children's hearing system with its welfarist approach to all children in trouble, and continues to underpin the approach in this jurisdiction today.

98 See for example, the comment of Scott, P.D. on the 1965 White Paper in (1966) 6 *British Journal of Criminology* 105, and the more retrospective examination by Harris, R. in "Institutionalized Ambivalence: Social Work and the Children and Young Persons Act 1969" (1982) 12 *British Journal of Social Work* 247. The (English) Magistrates Association was a powerful opponent to the proposals in both White Papers; no such equivalent organisation existed in Scotland.

99 See Lockyer, A. and Stone, F. "The Kilbrandon Origins" in A. Lockyer and F. Stone, eds, *Juvenile Justice in Scotland: 25 Years of the Welfare Approach* (T&T Clark, 1998), p. 12.

Even when the Labour Party returned to power in 1974, its small (and ever-decreasing, eventually vanishing) majority meant that it had to seek consensus with its opponents and the chance that England would follow the Scottish lead (or rediscover its own unitary philosophy towards all children in trouble) was lost. The punitive powers of the juvenile court in England were increased by the Criminal Justice Act 1977, which raised the levels of fines and gave magistrates the power to send a young person to an "attendance centre" (generally run by the police) on default of payment. The complete separation of care and protection cases from criminal cases was effected by the Thatcher Government's Children Act 1989, which abolished welfare-based supervision orders and care orders in criminal proceedings and limited the jurisdiction of the juvenile court to offenders; the new family proceedings court[100] took over all care and protection cases. The Criminal Justice Act 1991 repealed the unimplemented parts of the 1969 Act and converted the juvenile court into the Youth Court. That criminal court became increasingly punitive in its approach, and the Criminal Justice and Public Order Act 1994 allowed it to impose custodial sentences on 12 to 14 year olds. By the time ("New") Labour returned to Government in 1997, there was no possibility of English law reverting to its roots, and the amelioration of the punitive approach to young offenders was slight. The Crime and Disorder Act 1998 stated that the primary aim of youth justice was to prevent offending behaviour, and the Children Act 2004 required co-operation between youth offending teams and child protection services. Ideologically, however, the two services were and remain quite separate: young offenders in England are treated as offenders and not as young persons in need of protection, guidance, treatment or control. The seed sown by the Children Act, 1908 became an established plant with the Children and Young Persons Act, 1932 whereby both offenders and the abused and neglected would be treated in the same tribunal, with a welfare response designed to tackle their underlying difficulties: that plant sent a sucker out from its rhizome into Scottish soil, where it flourishes today, but the parent plant itself withered and died in England in the last three decades of the twentieth century.

---

100 Later absorbed into the Family Court by the Crime and Courts Act 2013.

THE WORLD-WIDE RETREAT FROM THE JUVENILE COURT IDEAL

In many respects, the retreat in England from the unitary model that under-pinned the juvenile court as designed in 1932 followed contemporary inter-national trends, while it is the Scottish retention and enhancement of that model after 1968 that has for some years now been increasingly out of step in a world in which political imperatives have demanded more punitive responses to youth offending. A useful review, written in 2000, is provided by Christine Hallett,[101] who quotes the Australian writers Christine Alder and Joy Wundersitz as describing the distinction between the "welfare" model and the "justice" model as follows:

> the welfare model is associated with paternalistic and protectionist policies, with treatment rather than punishment being the key goal. From this perspective, because of their immaturity, children cannot be regarded as rational or self-determining agents, but rather are subject to and are the product of the environment within which they live. Any criminal action on their part can therefore be attributed to dysfunctional elements in that environment. The task of the justice system then, is to identify, treat and cure the underlying social causes of offending, rather than inflicting punishment for the offence itself. . . .
>
> [The justice model] assumes that all individuals are reasoning agents who are fully responsible for their actions and so should be held accountable before the law. Within this model, the task of the justice system is to assess the degree of culpability of the individual offender and apportion punishment in accordance with the seriousness of the offending behaviour. In so doing, the individual must be accorded full rights to due process and state powers must be constrained, predictable and determinate.

Hallett points out that different systems around the world combine each approach in different proportions, but the welfare model clearly dominated in both Scotland and England after 1932 and was affirmed in Scotland in 1968. Since then, however, English law has increasingly come to embrace the justice model. Hallett's conclusion is that Scotland has retained a much greater emphasis on the welfare model than most other countries.

The world-wide movement away from a unitary, welfarist, approach may well have started with – it was certainly boosted by – the important deci-sion of the US Supreme Court, *In Re Gault*.[102] That case involved a 15 year old youth, Gerald Francis Gault, who was alleged to have made a nui-

---

101 "Ahead of the Game or Behind the Times? The Scottish Children's Hearing System in International Context" (2000) 14 *International Journal of Law, Policy and the Family*, 31–44.

102 387 US 1 (1967). For a contemporary discussion, see Welch, T.A. "*Kent v United States* and *In Re Gault*: Two Decisions in Search of a Theory" (1967) 19 *Hastings Law Journal* 29.

sance phone-call in crude terms to a neighbour. The Arizona Juvenile Court adjudged him to be "delinquent" as a result of the allegation, without any of the constitutional due process protections accorded adults accused of a crime, and he was committed to a state industrial school until his 21st birthday – some six years away. Had he been charged with this minor offence as an adult, the maximum sentence would have been a fine of between $5 and $50 or up to two months' detention. Two months might be a proportionate response to the offence on a justice model, but the juvenile court considered that six years was by no means an unreasonable length of time to ensure this young person was properly rehabilitated into a productive member of society, which would clearly be for his own good.

On appeal, the Arizona Supreme Court[103] held that the rehabilitative aims of the juvenile court process – the welfare model – justified a procedure that was less adversarial, less technical and less "alienative" of the juvenile than normal criminal process. So the failure to provide the child and his family with any notice of the charges against him, and the failure to advise the child against self-incrimination, (both otherwise crucial elements in US due process) were justified as avoiding the stigma of criminality and reducing the adversarial atmosphere at juvenile court proceedings. On a further appeal, however, the US Supreme Court took a very different view, holding that the benevolent aims of the juvenile court process were not sufficient justification for the impairment of constitutionally-mandated procedural safeguards. The *parens patriae* approach that had previously provided the underlying rationale for juvenile court practice in the US was comprehensively, even contemptuously, dismissed. Justice Fortas, who delivered the lead judgement, listed all the benign aims of the juvenile court process but then went on:

> These results were to be achieved without coming to conceptual and constitutional grief, by insisting that the proceedings were not adversary, but that the State was proceeding as *parens patriae*. The Latin phrase proved to be a great help to those who sought to rationalize the exclusion of juveniles from the constitutional scheme; but its meaning is murky and its historical credentials are of dubious relevance.[104]

Given that Gerald Gault faced a loss of liberty, the *parens patriae* approach was found to be punitive in effect even if both its rhetoric and indeed its aim were benign. The Supreme Court simply did not believe that a child who

---

103 *Application of Gault* 407 P. 2d 760 (1965).
104 387 US 1, p. 16.

showed delinquent behaviour would be rehabilitated into a useful citizen by removing him from his home for upwards of six years.[105] Nor did the Court accept the normal justifications given for the informal procedures adopted by juvenile courts: denial of procedures frequently resulted in arbitrariness rather than "careful, compassionate, individualized treatment."[106] In stark language the Court said this:

> The fact of the matter is that, however euphemistic the title, a "receiving home" or an "industrial school" for juveniles is an institution of confinement in which the child is incarcerated for a greater or lesser time. His world becomes "a building with whitewashed walls, regimented routine, and institutional hours . . ." Instead of mother and father and sisters and brothers and friends and classmates, his world is peopled by guards, custodians, state employees, and "delinquents" confined with him for anything from waywardness to rape and homicide. . . . Under our Constitution, the condition of being a boy does not justify a kangaroo court.[107]

The case was, therefore, fundamentally a clash between the rhetoric of child-saving and the reality of incarceration.

Though few states in the United States have gone so far as to abolish completely the separate jurisdiction of the juvenile court, since *Re Gault* all states have had to ensure that procedures, at least at the adjudication stage, provide the constitutional protections afforded adults charged with criminal offences. This effected a profound shift in the balance between welfare and "justice". As Feld put it,

> *In Re Gault* began a "due process revolution" that substantially transformed the juvenile court from a social welfare agency into a legal institution. This "constitutional domestication" was the first step in the convergence of the procedures of the juvenile justice system with those of the adult criminal court . . .[108]

He goes on to describe how states in the US increasingly removed pre-offending behaviour and neglect cases from juvenile courts, and transferred serious or repeat offenders to adult criminal courts. In the 1990s, many states in the US substantially increased the range of criminal acts that were excluded from the jurisdiction of the juvenile court.[109]

---

105 At p. 22 Justice Fortas referred to recidivism rates which showed that, if rehabilitation was the aim of the juvenile justice process, it did not work and could not, therefore, be used to justify a more informal procedure.
106 387 US 1, p. 18.
107 387 US 1, pp. 27–28.
108 Feld, B.C. "Criminalising Juvenile Justice: Rules of Procedure for the Juvenile Court" (1984) 69 *Minnesota Law Review* 141.
109 Watkins, J.C. *The Juvenile Justice Century: A Sociological Commentary on American Juvenile Courts*, pp. 92–95.

The end result is that juvenile courts in the USA, even when they retain different outcomes for (the more minor) child offenders than for adults, and even when they cling to the hope of affording at least an opportunity for rehabilitation, no longer see child offenders as simply a sub-set of neglected children who need the state to provide the care and guidance their parents failed to provide. They are, in the USA today, criminal courts dealing with a particular (age-determined) class of criminal.[110]

Other countries followed the lead of the USA. The international trend since the 1960s has been to shift the balance between justice and welfare much more towards "justice". Citing various authors, Hallett summarises the position in the last two decades of the twentieth century:

> As Murray and Hill note: "if a general trend can be discerned in English-speaking countries it is towards the segregation of the processing of delinquents from that of care and protection cases". This change was evident in Northern Ireland in the separation of welfare considerations from criminal justice issues in 1982 (Curran *et al.*, 1995); in Ireland in 1991 (McGrath, 1997); in South Australia under the Children's Protection and Young Offenders Act 1979 (Wundersitz, 1996) and in Canada under the Young Offenders Act 1984 (Reitsma-Street, 1990). In New Zealand, the Children, Young Persons and Their Families Act 1989 (Part II) separated the care and protection of children and young persons who were placed under the jurisdiction of a Family Court from young offenders. Under provisions in Part IV for those aged fourteen to sixteen, this latter group came within the jurisdiction of the Youth Court (Ludbrook, 1992). In England and Wales, the Children Act 1989 excluded criminal proceedings against children from the new family proceedings court, leaving the juvenile (now youth) court with criminal jurisdiction. Although the Children Act places a duty on local authorities to take reasonable steps to reduce the need for criminal proceedings to be brought against children in their area, Anderson (1995: 58) notes that: "it is widely perceived among those working with young people in the criminal justice system, that their clients have effectively been excluded from many of the more positive provisions of the Children Act, because they are seen as offenders first and children second".[111]

SCOTLAND THE DIFFERENT

The really interesting question is how Scotland has managed to resist this clear international trend. An important part of the explanation is to be found in a crucial limitation to the US Supreme Court's judgment in *Re Gault*. Justice Fortas made it plain that:

---

110 Feld, B.C. "Juvenile Court Legislative Reform and the Serious Young Offender: Dismantling the 'Rehabilitative Ideal'" (1980) 65 *Minnesota Law Review* 167.

111 Hallett, C. "Ahead of the Game or Behind the Times? The Scottish Children's Hearing System in International Context" (2000) 14 *International Journal of Law, Policy and the Family* 31, pp.37–38 (full references omitted).

> We are not here concerned with the procedures or constitutional rights applic-
> able to the pre-judicial stages of the juvenile process, nor do we direct our atten-
> tion to the post-adjudication or dispositional process ... We consider only the
> problems presented to us by this case. These relate to the proceedings by which a
> *determination is made* as to whether a juvenile is a "delinquent" as a result of the
> alleged misconduct on his part, with the consequence that he *may* be committed
> to a state institution.[112]

In other words, the lack of due process safeguards, such as notice of the charges, the opportunity to prepare a defence, a warning against self-incrimination, was found to be unconstitutional in a process designed to determine whether the child was properly subject to the jurisdiction of the juvenile court. The decision did not find unconstitutional the process of determining the outcome, once the juvenile court's jurisdiction had been established: there would be no unconstitutionality in a juvenile court adopting rehabilitative aims in the determination of the outcome and *Re Gault* is simply authority for the proposition that these aims were not in and of themselves sufficient to cure any unconstitutionality in the adjudicatory part of the overall process.

In Scotland, it needs to be remembered that from the earliest days of the juvenile court and continuing throughout the history of the children's hearing, the adjudicatory stage has never been any less formal, or subject to fewer safeguards, than in normal criminal or civil process involving adults. The juvenile court, established under the Children Act, 1908 and enhanced by the Children and Young Persons (Scotland) Act, 1932, was a court of summary jurisdiction that conducted trials or proofs before moving on to the dispositive stage of the process. When dealing with offences, the juvenile court was required to deal with any complaint in respect of a child or young person "in accordance with the Summary Jurisdiction (Scotland) Acts".[113] There were a number of court decisions throughout the period in which the juvenile court operated where omissions of the normal safeguards led to successful appeals against the court's decisions. An example is found in *AB v Howman*[114] where an order for detention in an industrial school made by the sheriff was suspended by the High Court of Justiciary on the ground that the rule requiring the local education authority to be heard before any such order was made[115] had not been followed. In *Nicol v Brown*[116] the

---

112 387 US 1, p. 13, emphasis added.
113 Juvenile Courts (Procedure) (Scotland) Rules, 1934, r. 4(a).
114 1917 JC 23.
115 Children Act, 1908, s. 74(6).
116 1951 JC 87.

High Court of Justiciary allowed an appeal on the ground that the sheriff had not explained sufficiently to the child accused of an offence the charge he was facing. Notification of charges was required to be given to probation officers and education (then local) authorities by s. 15 of the Children and Young Persons (Scotland) Act, 1932 and by s. 43 of the Children and Young Persons (Scotland) Act, 1937;[117] notification to the parents and guardians was required by the Juvenile Court Rules.[118] In *Roy v Cruickshank*[119] an order that a 10 year old child be sent to an approved school was suspended due to a series of flaws, including failure to notify the child of the charge, failure to provide him with an explanation of the reason he had been brought to the juvenile court, and failure to ask whether he admitted the charge. And in *Jamieson v Heatly*[120] where two boys had pleaded guilty to assaulting another boy by placing a lighted squib in his pocket, the sentence of detention in a remand home was quashed since the juvenile court had not, as it was required to do under Rule 9 of the 1951 Juvenile Court Rules, obtained information about the boys' home life, school record and character: it could not make a decision about outcome in the children's best interests without that information.

When the children's hearing took over the dispositive role of juvenile courts under the Social Work (Scotland) Act 1968, the sheriff was given exclusive jurisdiction to determine whether a challenged ground of referral existed or not, and was required in doing so to follow normal civil (or, when an offence was alleged, criminal) process, with all the protections that entailed.[121] The leading of evidence today is governed by the Civil Evidence (Scotland) Act 1988, other than when the ground of referral is that the child has committed an offence, in which case procedure is governed by the Criminal Procedure (Scotland) Act 1995. It was stated by the Inner House in *W v Kennedy*[122] that the child's interests are not to be thwarted by an over-rigid application of the rules of evidence or procedure (in that case the evidentiary rules relating to hearsay), but the limits of flexibility had already

---

117 Subsequently reworded by the Criminal Justice (Scotland) Act, 1949, sched. 11 and then repealed by the Criminal Procedure (Scotland) Act 1975.
118 Juvenile Courts (Procedure) (Scotland) Rules, 1934 and 1951, r. 10.
119 1954 SLT 217.
120 1959 JC 22.
121 Procedure was originally governed by the Act of Sederunt (Social Work) (Sheriff Court Procedure Rules) 1971 (SI 1971/92), which was replaced after the Children (Scotland) Act 1995 by the Act of Sederunt (Child Care and Maintenance Rules) 1997 (SI 1997/291).
122 1988 SLT 583, p. 585.

been pointed out by Lord Justice-Clerk Ross in *Kennedy v A*:[123] "the principles of natural justice cannot be invoked to produce a result that would be
contrary to the clear provisions of a statutory instrument". These comments
were both made in relation to the application before the sheriff to establish
the ground of referral. Once the ground is established, or when it has been
accepted, the children's hearing determines the outcome following set rules
that, though designed to make the proceedings less formal and less adversarial than those in the sheriff court, are no less structured around statutory
requirements,[124] including notice of the hearing, explanation of the grounds
and notification of the right to call for review and to appeal. Failure to follow
the correct procedure at a children's hearing has always been a ground of
appeal.[125]

Given the procedural requirements at hearings and the fact that applications for proof of the ground of referral before the sheriff follow normal
court procedure, the concerns expressed by the US Supreme Court in *Re
Gault* would have no relevance to the Scottish children's hearing system.
And the earlier juvenile courts that had operated in Scotland since 1908
were never designed, in the way US juvenile courts often were, to operate
with procedural informality that tended to reduce the due process protections offered to the child brought to the court. Informality has never been an
issue that challenges the rights of the child or parent. This, however, cannot
be the whole explanation since English process is no less formal, yet English
law still abandoned the welfare response to juvenile offending.

Might the Scottish approach be more vulnerable to challenge than the
English approach on the basis of proportionality – that a minor act or a
marginally worrying state of affairs can lead to long-term and intrusive state
intervention? It needs to be remembered that proportionality does not operate in a void. The question must always be asked, proportionate to what?
An outcome may be determined by paying regard to either the act or the

---

123 1986 SLT 358, p. 362.

124 See Children's Hearings (Scotland) Rules 1971 (SI 1971/492); Children's Hearings (Scotland)
Rules 1986 (SI 1986/2291); Children's Hearings (Scotland) Rules 1996 (SI 1996/3261 (S. 251));
Children's Hearings (Scotland) Act 2011 (Rules of Procedure in Children's Hearings) Rules
2013 (SSI 2013/194).

125 Though the applicable primary legislation has never set down any grounds for appeal (other
than that the decision was not justified in all the circumstances of the case) it was from the
earliest days of the hearing system understood that "some flaw in the procedure adopted by the
hearing" would render the decision unjustified and, therefore, appealable: *D v Sinclair* 1973
SLT (Sh Ct) 47, per Sheriff Mowat, p. 48. "Irregularity in the conduct of a hearing" is assumed
to be a ground of appeal in r. 3.56(3)(a) of the Child Care and Maintenance Rules 1997 (SI
1997/291).

need, and a long-term removal of a child from his or her parent's care may well be a disproportionate response to a minor act, but a proportionate response to the child's needs. Proportionality operates differently, in other words, between the criminal process (where the sentence is designed to fit the crime) and the child protection process (where the outcome is designed to address the needs of the child). In any case, the range of options, even in the 1960s, was far wider in Scotland than seems to have been the case in Arizona. Sending a child to a residential school may be thought necessary if no other option is available, but in Scotland other forms of care and treatment, including home supervision, would be considered in determining what response was proportionate. And proportionality requires to be determined in light of the likelihood of the chosen response actually achieving its aims. In *Re Gault*, the US Supreme Court did not accept that Arizona provided sufficient rehabilitation in reality to justify incarcerating Gerald Gault in an industrial school until he was an adult. The Scottish system too would be flawed if the achievement of the benign aims of state intervention were implausible and its justifications no more than rhetoric. But a sufficient faith remains that the outcomes available to a children's hearing have the capacity to improve the lives of the children who appear before it. Modern legislation, indeed, prohibits the children's hearing from making an order unless persuaded that to do so would be better for the child than making no order,[126] which means that the hearing must be conscious of the true effects of any order it makes. English policy-makers, on the other hand, no longer believe that seeking to improve the lives of young offenders is an appropriate response to their offending behaviour. They may not believe that it is achievable.

It may be that the fact that child protection cases now make up the majority of the work of children's hearings has inclined that system to continue to see youth offending in the light of a breakdown of parenting, but in terms of the need for due process the dichotomy has always been false. The removal of a child from his or her home as a result of neglect or abuse is obviously a protective measure, but it can be as destructive of family life, and the neglectful or abusive parent – or indeed the child – may see it as being just as punitive as any removal due to the child's offending behaviour. That is why the Scottish system ensures appropriate due process, with protections and safeguards against arbitrary state action, in care and protection cases as much as with child offender cases. The need for this has become increasingly

126 Children (Scotland) Act 1995, s. 16(3); Children's Hearings (Scotland) Act 2011, s. 28.

recognised through the European Convention on Human Rights but was accepted even before that Convention gained the important place in our jurisprudence that it has today. Due process protections are afforded in both types of case in Scotland through the process for establishing disputed grounds of referral before the sheriff, with additional protections (in particular the requirement for proof beyond a reasonable doubt) when the ground of referral is that the child has committed a criminal offence.

These conceptual justifications for the Scottish system do not explain, however, why Scotland has been shielded from the winds of political change that, in most other English-speaking countries, have demanded a separation of young offenders from victims of child abuse or neglect, and a more punitive response to the former. English law is as conscious of the need to ensure due process as Scots law but succumbed to the calls for punitive responses to youth offending. In Scotland, on the other hand, there has been a truly remarkable lack of any political dimension to the debate as to the correct response to youth offending. A little-noted feature of the history of the Scottish children's hearing system is the extent to which it has been supported by politicians of all colours. It was a National Liberal Scottish Secretary (sitting in a Conservative Cabinet) who set up the Kilbrandon Committee in 1961, and a Conservative Scottish Secretary who presented it to Parliament in 1964. The Social Work (Scotland) Act 1968 was promoted by Willie Ross, MP, that long-serving Scottish Secretary in all of Harold Wilson's Labour Governments, and brought into force by a Conservative Scottish Secretary. The 1968 Act was replaced by the Children (Scotland) Act 1995 under the auspices of a Conservative Government, with Lord Fraser of Carmyllie being the Bill's promoter. After devolution in 1999, a Scottish Labour/Scottish Liberal Democrat Coalition oversaw the Antisocial Behaviour legislation amendments to the children's hearing system while Jim Wallace MSP was the Liberal Democrat Justice Secretary; then in 2007 a Scottish National Government achieved power in Scotland and amended the system into its current form with the Children's Hearings (Scotland) Act 2011. Scottish politicians of all creeds whether unionist-conservative, socialist, liberal or nationalist have consistently supported the children's hearings system and there has been no serious political challenge to its principles. That political support has found reflection in more general support. When the Scottish Executive consulted in 2004 on its developing policy GIRFEC,[127] it suggested that the needs of the individual child might be

---

127 "Getting it Right for Every Child": see Chapter 2 above.

balanced with the needs of family members and the wider community, but this proposition was rejected by "the vast majority of respondents [who] felt strongly that the children's hearing system should remain focused on meeting the needs of individual children".[128] It is this public support, perhaps more than anything else, that has allowed our politicians to let Scots law follow its own path, building upon its past and accepting the reality now politically denied elsewhere: children in trouble are, first and foremost, children. Once that is accepted, the state's primary responsibility becomes to deal with them as such, by tackling their troubles in a way that seeks to improve their life-chances, irrespective of how their troubles are manifested. Scotland may well do things differently from other jurisdictions but, in this field at any rate, it does them better.

---

128 *Summary Report on the Responses to the Phase One Consultation on the Review of the Children's Hearing System*, Scottish Executive, 2004.

6. Home Supervision

DAY INDUSTRIAL SCHOOLS

We saw in the first chapter of this book that both indigent and neglected children could be committed by a court to an industrial school under the terms of the Industrial Schools Act, 1866, in an effort to insulate them against bad influences and to provide positive influences in their place. This could only be achieved by removing the child or young person from his or her own home and requiring him or her to live in the industrial school as a residential establishment. However, when the cause of the child's difficulties was not bad parental influence, the school was able to permit a child "to lodge at the dwelling of his parent or of any trustworthy or respectable person".[1] In that case, the obligation remained on the school managers to feed and clothe the child, and the entirely benign effect of that arrangement was to provide some direct assistance to the parent bringing up the child and to provide some education to the child without in fact requiring the child's removal from the parent. Some industrial schools were unsuited to provide accommodation and had been set up as day schools. The earliest is generally recognised as having been established in Aberdeen in 1841.[2] In Glasgow, under the terms of a local Act, the Glasgow Juvenile Delinquency Prevention and Repression Act, 1878, there was established (on a site now occupied, curiously enough, by the University of Strathclyde) the Rotten Row Day Industrial School. Schools such as these usually started out taking voluntary admissions, but as day schools became progressively integrated into the industrial school system, the voluntary element evaporated. As well, the underlying welfarist ethos of day industrial schools tended in time to be subverted by the different ethos of residential industrial schools which had, in Kelly's words "a predominantly disciplinary character".[3]

Statutory regulation of day industrial schools first appeared with the Day Industrial Schools (Scotland) Act, 1893, which allowed the Secretary for

---

1 Industrial Schools Act, 1866, s. 26.
2 Kelly, C. "Reforming Juvenile Justice in 19th Century Scotland: The Subversion of the Scottish Day Industrial School Movement" (2016) 20 *Crime, History and Societies* vol. 2, p. 1.
3 Ibid. p. 1

Scotland to certify a school as a day industrial school for the purpose of both educating and feeding children sent to it: this still operated as a mechanism for the support of children who were permitted to remain at home. Most of the provisions of the 1893 Act were replaced by ss. 77–83 of the Children Act, 1908, under which the court was able to send to a day industrial school any child whom it could send to an industrial school: that included both the petty offender and the indigent or neglected child. It was indeed provided that the day industrial school had to be within a specified distance of the residence of the child sent to it.[4]

Now, none of this amounted to "supervision" of the child as it later came to be understood, for there was no individual nominated to watch over the child and his or her home circumstances. But it did allow the state to take action to ensure the education – and, of great practical importance, the feeding – of children whose sustenance and development would otherwise suffer from the poverty of their parents. Almost certainly a requirement to attend a day as opposed to a residential industrial school would be made over the indigent as opposed to the neglected child – for the aim of insulating children from malign influences would not be necessary in all cases of indigence. The "deserving poor" did not deserve to have their children removed from them. But nor were they subject to any oversight while the child remained in their care. State supervision of children who were permitted to remain in their own homes developed from very different origins.

SUPERVISION'S ORIGINS IN PROBATION

The most common outcome today of a child protection process in Scotland that leads to a legal order over the child is the imposition by a children's hearing of a compulsory supervision order, and the most common structure of that order involves the child remaining at home but being required to accept supervision of his or her life, or parts thereof, by the local authority. Supervision orders were not, however, introduced with the children's hearing system and, though they were used only infrequently before that system took effect, supervision orders as an outcome in child protection cases had been available since 1932. In relation to offenders, supervision as an alternative to incarceration has been available for rather longer in the form of probation, in which are found the main roots of today's compulsory supervision order.

4 Children Act, 1908, s. 78(3).

PROBATION PRIOR TO 1931

The origins of probation (though it was not then called that) are usually traced to 1875 when the Church of England Temperance Society established a system of "missionaries" who would work with drunkards appearing before the police courts in London, and who sought to persuade magistrates to offer early release to offenders who agreed to accept moral guidance from such missionaries. The motivation behind this movement was doubtless a mixture of religiously inspired humanitarianism and middle-class fears of an unruly and unproductive working class. The results of these efforts were sufficiently encouraging for Parliament to pass the Probation of First Offenders Act, 1887, which authorised courts across the country to engage with the practice. This was the first legislative use of the word "probation" in the technical legal sense of giving an offender the opportunity to escape punishment by proving that he or she had reformed (under the watchful guidance of some worthy person) – putting, that is, his or her behaviour to probation. Section 1 of the 1887 Act provided that any person convicted (for the first time) of an offence punishable by less than two years imprisonment could be "released on probation of good conduct" instead of being punished. This approach was consistent with a developing view in the late Victorian period that offenders could be "saved" by "seeing the light" and that it was a charitable act to show offenders and potential offenders the path to righteousness. However, the extent to which the Act was embraced across the country was highly variable, for it was permissive only and did not establish any national structure. Glasgow seems to have been the first place in Scotland to utilise, from 1905, a system of probation officers appointed by its police courts, though McNeill suggests that the motivation behind that initiative had more to do with addressing the undue levels of imprisonment of fine-defaulters rather than any religious mission to save the fallen.[5] Initially six police officers, together with three women to work with children, were appointed, all by the Chief Constable.[6]

The Probation of Offenders Act, 1907

The procedure was somewhat strengthened by the Probation of Offenders Act, 1907, which was the start of a recognisably modern system of proba-

---

5 McNeill, F. "Remembering Probation in Scotland" (2005) 52 *Probation Journal* 23, p. 27.
6 Ibid. p. 27.

tion.[7] As well as repeating the power to release offenders (and now not just first offenders) on probation,[8] the 1907 Act also gave the court itself the power to appoint probation officers – including, where the offender was under the age of 16, "children's probation officers"[9] – and also to name in the probation order an individual who was willing and suitable to act as such. The probation period was to be for not more than three years.[10] The duties of the probation officer were set down by the Act as follows:

(i) To visit or receive reports from the person under supervision at such reasonable intervals as may be specified in the probation order;
(ii) To see that he or she observes the conditions in the order;
(iii) To report to the court as to his or her behaviour;
(iv) To advise, assist and befriend him or her, and, when necessary, to endeavour to find him or her suitable employment.[11]

These duties make plain that the role envisaged for probation officers was a combination of supervision and guidance, the aim being that those placed on probation would learn from the probation officer what they were not learning otherwise: how to live a productive and law-abiding life. But there was a distinct iron hand beneath the velvet glove with the officer's obligation to report on the probationer's behaviour to the court, and the court's power of imprisonment if the terms of probation were breached.[12] Probation orders were considered particularly appropriate for young offenders because such offenders were seen as more open than adult offenders to guidance and reformation.

The power to appoint and control probation officers rested with Burgh Magistrates in the burghs, and with sheriffs in the counties. Remuneration of probation officers rested with Town and County Councils respectively, and no provision was made for any central governmental funding for the recouping of that expenditure. It is hardly surprising, then, that a variety of approaches across Scotland emerged both in relation to the extent to which these provisions were used and in relation to the sorts of person appointed as a probation officer.

A valuable study by Christine Kelly[13] explores the variety of approaches

---

7 A history of probation in Scotland is found in the Morton Committee Report (Scottish Office, 1928) at pp. 62–77.
8 Probation of Offenders Act, 1907, s. 1.
9 Probation of Offenders Act, 1907, s. 3(2).
10 Probation of Offenders Act, 1907, s. 1(1)(ii).
11 Probation of Offenders Act, 1907, s. 4.
12 Probation of Offenders Act, 1907, s. 6.
13 "Probation Officers for Young Offenders in 1920s Scotland" (2017) 9 *European Journal of Probation* 169.

adopted across Scotland to the identification and appointment of appropriate persons to take on the role of probation officer. In east coast towns, it was common for representatives of child protection organisations like the NSPCC to be appointed, but some courts would more typically turn to officers of civic organisations like the Boys Brigade, presumably in the hope that the activities arranged by such organisations would act as a suitable diversion from the behaviour, often little more than mischief, that led children into trouble with the police: this was "civil engagement as a route to reform".[14] Kelly concluded, from an examination of the evidence collected by the Morton Committee in the late 1920s, that many probation officers from these types of organisations perceived their role as being one of an "avuncular big brother" to their charges,[15] with citizen-building the clear aim of their activities. "Glasgow, on the other hand, prided itself on the organised efficiency of its probation services which were delivered with authority and thoroughness by criminal justice professionals, the police."[16] In other parts of the country, courts tended to rely on ministers of religion or members of temperance societies.

When the Morton Committee took evidence as to the characteristics that were thought desirable for probation officers the Chief Constables strongly preferred the role to be undertaken by police officers as opposed to what they perceived as unaccountable and untrained amateurs provided by charitable organisations.[17] Kelly identified some of the benefits that volunteerism had, however, particularly the fact that volunteers from civic organisations were much more likely than policemen to have wide business contacts who could help them in their role of finding employment opportunities for their charges.[18] But she also pointed out that the "lady child savers" who were usually appointed to supervise the behaviour of girls tended to have a much more judgmental approach to their charges that overemphasised the moral danger which they perceived girls of classes lower than their own faced from normal working-class life.[19]

14 Ibid. pp. 173–174. Writing in 1938, Sheriff Trotter in *The Law as to Children and Young Persons* (W. Hodge & Co, 1938), pp. 92–93 said this: "When the case is of a minor nature, a juvenile offender may be admonished and dismissed for a first offence, in which event an effort should be made to get him to join an organisation such as the Boys' Brigade or Boy Scouts, etc, where his energies can be turned to wholesome channels and his leisure time usefully and actively occupied".

15 Kelly, C. "Probation Officers for Young Offenders in 1920s Scotland" (2017) 9 *European Journal of Probation* 169, p. 178.

16 Ibid. p. 181.

17 Ibid. p. 174.

18 Ibid. p. 179.

19 Ibid. p. 179 On this point see (in the English context) Cale, M. "Girls and the Perception of Sexual Danger in the Victorian Reformatory System" (1993) 78 *History* 201, and (in the Scottish

Probation and the Children Act, 1908

When the Children Act, 1908 created the juvenile court that court was vested with the power to discharge an offender, on his entering into a bond, and to place him "under the supervision of a probation officer".[20] The terms, and length, of that probation continued to be governed by the Probation of Offenders Act, 1907, as did the duties of the probation officer. Though the Children Act, 1908 Act also made provision for children in need of care and protection, and gave to the juvenile court the power to deal with such children, supervision by a probation officer remained an option available only in the case of a juvenile offender: it was not (yet) one of the options open to the court in a care and protection case.

THE PROBATION OF OFFENDERS (SCOTLAND) ACT, 1931

The Probation of Offenders (Scotland) Act, 1931 enhanced and amended, but did not repeal, the 1907 Act. The concept was still at this moment in time limited to offenders, and in moving the Second Reading of the Bill that became the 1931 Act, the Secretary of State for Scotland, Mr William Adamson,[21] clearly regarded the benefits of probation as being particularly suitable for young offenders:

> In 1928 probation orders were made under Section 2 of the Probation of Offenders Act, 1907 in respect of 1,684 males and 500 females—a total of 2,184 persons, and there is no doubt that still fuller resort to probation could and should be made. There is reason to believe that, in present circumstances, many lads and girls are sent to prison who could have been dealt with more satisfactorily, from every point of view, in other ways. The whole subject was fully considered by the Scottish Departmental Committee on the Treatment of Young Offenders. In their report—published in 1928 under the title "Protection and Training"[22]— the Committee say, with reference to juvenile offenders between 16 and 21: Many, but not all, of these offenders—for there are differences in character and temperament—are plastic and at a receptive age. If it is suggested that some of them have little to learn and much to regret, we can only reply that we dare not admit permanent failure in any lad or girl between 16 and 21. Many of them

context) Mahood, L. and Littlewood, B. "The 'Vicious' Girl and the 'Street-corner' Boy: Sexuality and the Gendered Development of the Scottish Child-Saving Movement, 1850-1940" (1994) 4 *Journal of the History of Sexuality* 549.

20 Children Act, 1908, s. 107(c).

21 He was replaced as Secretary of State for Scotland five months later in that post when Ramsay MacDonald's Labour Government fell and the National Government (under Ramsay MacDonald) took over, by the Liberal MP for Caithness, Sir Archibald Sinclair.

22 That is to say, the Morton Committee Report.

are at a stage of development at which the tendency to crime can be diverted. They are very impressionable, and a prison, with its sad story of failure, makes a definite impression on them. This is inevitable, despite the devotion of governors and of their staffs. After a short sentence the offender is released. Prison has lost its terrors for him, and he has lost his repugnance for it. What is much worse, he may also have lost any sense of self-respect. The International Prison Congress, held in London in 1925, expressed the hope that every endeavour would be made to substitute other penalties for short terms of imprisonment; and to this end recommended inter alia, that the system of probation should be extended to the utmost extent. The annual report of the Prison Commissioners for Scotland for 1926 stated: It is very desirable that every expedient be tried before committing a young person to prison. There are bound to be cases where probation is inappropriate—for example, cases where the offence is so serious that a severe sentence is imperative in the interests of the community. As the Young Offenders Committee says: Probation is not a convenient substitute for committal to an institution, and it can never be a panacea for all forms of juvenile delinquency. None the less, Courts have before them a serious responsibility in determining what is the best treatment for the first offender and the young offender . . . One of the main defects of the Probation of Offenders Act, 1907, is that it contains no provision to ensure the existence throughout the country of an adequate number of duly qualified probation officers. It empowered, but did not require, burgh magistrates and sheriffs to appoint probation officers, and it threw the whole cost of any appointment made upon the local rates. The result is that in many areas no probation officer has been appointed, and an unduly heavy burden has, in general, been placed upon the voluntary workers who have engaged in probation services.[23]

A Scottish Office Circular published once the Bill was passed[24] described its effects:

In recent years a considerable development in the use of probation has taken place in England and Wales as a result of the provision made in Part I of the Criminal Justice Act, 1925, which applies to England and Wales only. The Act of 1931 makes somewhat similar provision for Scotland. It provides, in general, for the compulsory appointment of duly qualified salaried probation officers, and so affords more facilities for the exercise of probation by placing at the disposal of all Courts the services of suitable probation officers *whose duty it will be* to supervise cases when so required by the Courts; it establishes an Exchequer grant in aid of the expenditure incurred by Local Authorities in connection with this probation service; it enables, through the Rules which it authorises, a more systemic supervision to be maintained over persons put on probation; and it gives new powers to Court which will facilitate a more effective control over such persons.

The Secretary of State has no doubt that fuller use can, and should, be made of probation in Scotland. Many young persons and first offenders now sent to prison

---

23 HC Deb. 2 March 1931, vol. 249 cols 1081–1109.
24 Circular No. 2605, 11 December 1931, reproduced in Cowan, M.G. *The Children and Young Persons (Scotland) Act, 1932* (W Hodge & Co. Ltd. 1933), pp. 339–349.

might be better dealt with in other ways. It is very generally recognised that short sentences of imprisonment for minor offences, particularly where young persons and first offenders are involved, often have a definitely bad effect upon the delinquents.

The Probation of Offenders (Scotland) Act, 1931 provided that a probation order was to last for a minimum of one year,[25] established a right of appeal against its making[26] and, reflecting the 1907 provision relating to children's probation officers, required the court where possible to appoint a probation officer "experienced in dealing with children or young persons" when the offender was under 17.[27] The 1931 Act's greatest effect, however, was structural. The system became for the first time mandatory, with all local authorities being required to become probation areas, each with its own local Probation Committee.[28] One or more salaried probation officers had to be appointed by the Probation Committee for each probation area, and costs were to be shared for the first time with central government.

One of the most important policy objectives behind the 1931 Act, other than to increase the use of probation (particularly for young offenders) as an alternative to prison, was to strike an appropriate balance between a professionalised role of the probation officer and the voluntary work of the socially responsible amateur. The Act provided for two classes of probation officer:[29] salaried probation officers, appointed and paid by the local Probation Committees, and voluntary probation officers nominated in probation orders made by courts in individual cases but not paid by the state for the work. Voluntary probation officers had to be agents of (and might indeed be paid by) a voluntary society, which was defined as "a society carrying on mission work in connection with police courts or other work in connection with the supervision and care of offenders or in connection with social service".[30] This allowed the continuation of the existing philanthropic activities of voluntary organisations in offering supervision and guidance to children and young people who got into trouble with the police. But in a change to existing practice, at least in some parts of Scotland, the probation committees and courts were explicitly prohibited from appointing as either salaried or voluntary probation officers any person "who is or has at any

---

25 Probation of Offenders (Scotland) Act, 1931, s. 8(4), amending s. 2(1) of the 1907 Act.
26 Probation of Offenders (Scotland) Act, 1931, s. 8(3).
27 Probation of Offenders (Scotland) Act, 1931, s. 4(2).
28 Ibid. s. 3. These committees were constituted under the Probation (Scotland) Rules, 1931 (SR&O 1931 No. 1023 (S.53)).
29 Probation of Offenders (Scotland) Act, 1931, s. 1(2).
30 Ibid. s. 5(1) and (2).

time been a member of a police force".[31] This followed a recommendation of the Morton Committee, based on the fear that police officers would be perceived by probationers as too authoritarian to achieve the true purpose of probation.[32] Notwithstanding the continued use of voluntary officers, the 1931 Act represented a large step in the professionalisation of the role of the probation officer, with its increasing emphasis on efficiency, accountability and training. All of this was consistent with the professionalisation of a number of other roles in the period between the wars such as social workers, health visitors and child protection visitors.

Just as the Government had intended, probation was used substantially more often by juvenile courts than by adult criminal courts, and it has been reported[33] that probation was the outcome in 10.35% of juvenile court cases in 1932 and 13.47% of cases in 1945, which was very much higher than probation's use in the adult courts. As we will see immediately below the juvenile court could, after 1932, utilise probation officers in care and protection cases as well as offender cases, but that does not in itself explain the high number of probation orders over children and young people.[34] The supervision and guidance offered by probation made this outcome potentially appropriate for all children and young people before the juvenile court, whose needs were often traced to a lack of appropriate guidance, which could manifest itself in either offending behaviour or other difficulties.

THE ROLE OF PROBATION OFFICERS IN CARE AND PROTECTION CASES AFTER 1932

By the early 1920s, the benefits of probation were widely accepted, especially so for young offenders. It was recognised in a Scottish Office Circular dated 13 December 1923[35] that:

> Many juvenile offences are due to want of proper control or discipline, and the influence of a good Probation Officer is often effective in preventing a boy or girl from entering a dishonest or criminal life . . . Release on probation has this advantage over institutional treatment (apart from questions of economy) that

31 Ibid. s. 5(3).
32 Kelly, C. "Probation Officers for Young Offenders in 1920s Scotland" (2017) 9 *European Journal of Probation* 169, pp. 182–183.
33 Ibid. p. 187.
34 McNeill, F. "Remembering Probation in Scotland" (2005) 52 *Probation Journal* 23, looking at figures for Glasgow only, reports that in 1932 just under half and in 1954 just over half of all probationers in that city were under 16.
35 Quoted in Cowan, M.G. *The Children and Young Persons (Scotland) Act, 1932*, p. 25.

it does not remove the offender from his home or relieve the parents of their responsibility for his care and training.

Exactly the same thinking could be applied to children who suffered from a want of proper control or discipline but who did not go on to commit offences, as well as children who were neglected or exposed to bad influences or who were otherwise at risk of becoming unproductive members of society. In either case, relieving the parents of their responsibility to bring up the child was not necessarily an appropriate response. So it was no great innovation to extend the remit of probation officers beyond juvenile offenders and to include as well children and young persons in need of care or protection. This was effected by s. 6 of the 1932 Act, which provided that any child or young person brought to the juvenile court and found to be in need of care or protection could be placed "under the supervision of a probation officer, or of some other person appointed for the purpose by the court", this for a specified period not exceeding three years. The juvenile court could also make the same order at the behest of a parent or guardian on being satisfied that he or she was not able to control the child or young person.[36] Identical provisions were made in the Children and Young Persons (Scotland) Act, 1937,[37] when that Act replaced the 1932 Act. An order placing a child or young person in need of care or protection under the supervision of a probation officer was a self-standing order and could be made even if no other order was made,[38] unlike a probation order over an offender, which could be made only in conjunction with the committal of the child or young person to the care of a fit person.[39] This was designed to "secure for the juvenile [offender] the joint supervision of the 'fit person' and the probation officer, and also the continued concern of the court".[40]

Now, technically, an order under these provisions was not a "probation order", notwithstanding that the child was to be under the supervision of a probation officer, and notwithstanding that both types of order were specified to last for the same period of time. A probation order, properly so-called, contained the implication of a punitive response if its terms were

36 Children and Young Persons (Scotland) Act, 1932, s. 7. The parent had to consent to the making of this order, and the court had to be satisfied that it was expedient so to deal with the child or young person.

37 Children and Young Persons (Scotland) Act, 1937, ss. 66 and 68.

38 Children and Young Persons (Scotland) Act, 1932, s. 6(1)(d); Children and Young Persons (Scotland) Act, 1937, s. 66(2)(d).

39 Children and Young Persons (Scotland) Act, 1932, s. 12(2); Children and Young Persons (Scotland) Act, 1937, s. 61(2).

40 Trotter, T. *The Law as to Children and Young Persons* (W. Hodge & Co, 1938), p. 112.

breached, and so remained limited to juvenile offenders being dealt with under the Probation of Offenders Act, 1907. The order under the 1932 or 1937 Acts for children in need of care or protection was appropriately, and for the first time, referred to as a "supervision order". While probation orders, strictly, remained limited to offenders, for the purposes of the provisions in the Probation of Offenders (Scotland) Act, 1931 relating to salaries, remuneration and expenditure of probation officers "an order . . . placing a child or young person under supervision shall be deemed to be a probation order".[41]

The role of the probation officer acting under a supervision order was rather more focused towards guidance and advice than the role he or she had with offenders specified under s. 4 of the 1907 Act. Probation officers appointed to supervise the child were required to "visit, advise and befriend [the child or young person] and, when necessary, endeavour to find him suitable employment."[42] The advice was understood to be on how to lead a productive life, though the obligation to visit and befriend indicates that the probation officer would be expected to seek an understanding of the child or young person's whole circumstances. For young persons particularly, finding employment was an important aspect of that, though it had been hoped by the Morton Committee that what would be sought would be better than "blind-alley occupations and the higher wages offered them":[43] in other words what probation officers ought to seek were skilled apprenticeships.

THE CRIMINAL JUSTICE (SCOTLAND) ACT, 1949

The probation system in Scotland was restructured by the Criminal Justice (Scotland) Act, 1949, which repealed both the 1907 and the 1931 Acts. The 1949 Act extended the power of the criminal courts to use probation orders with offenders, in particular by extending the option of probation to all offences (other than those for which the penalty was fixed by law),[44] and by allowing the probation order to specify where the probationer was required to reside.[45] The Act set out the functions of probation officers acting under

---

41 Children and Young Persons (Scotland) Act, 1932, s. 10(3); Children and Young Persons (Scotland) Act, 1937, s. 70(3).
42 Children and Young Persons (Scotland) Act, 1932, s. 10(1); Children and Young Persons (Scotland) Act, 1937, s. 70(1).
43 Morton Committee Report, p. 112.
44 Criminal Justice (Scotland) Act, 1949, s. 2(1).
45 Ibid. s. 2(6).

both probation orders and supervision orders, in rather more detail than had gone before:

> It shall be the duty of probation officers to supervise the probationers and other persons placed under their supervision and to advise, assist and befriend them; to inquire, in accordance with any directions of the court, into the circumstances or home surroundings of any person with a view to assisting the court in determining the most suitable method of dealing with his case; to advise, assist and befriend, in such cases and in such manner as may be prescribed, persons who have been released from custody; and to perform such other duties as may be prescribed or may be imposed by any enactment.[46]

Though primarily a criminal justice Act focused mostly on probation orders, properly so-called, the 1949 Act also made certain adjustments to the Children and Young Persons (Scotland) Act, 1937 in relation to supervision orders made over children and young persons in need of care or protection. It allowed the court to make an order under s. 68 of the 1937 Act[47] committing the child to the care of a fit person either independently of or together with an order placing the child or young person under the supervision of a probation officer;[48] and if a fit person order were revoked under the 1937 Act it could be replaced with a supervision order.[49] Certain other changes were made to supervision orders which had the effect of bringing them much closer to the supervision requirements that would, after 1968, be made by children's hearings. First, any supervision order made under the 1937 Act could after the 1949 Act include a requirement as to the residence of the child or young person or as to the treatment for his or her mental condition, though only so long as he or she consented to that requirement.[50] Secondly, the length of time supervision orders would last was amended: the 1937 Act had provided that they were to last for a period specified in the order not exceeding three years,[51] but the 1949 Act provided that "a supervision order shall cease to have effect when the person to whom it applies reaches the age of eighteen".[52] (Since the three year provisions in the 1937 Act were not repealed, the age of 18 acted as a long-stop). And thirdly, a supervision order could now be amended on an application made by any

---

46 Ibid. sched. 3 para 4.
47 That is to say in respect of a child or young person beyond the control of the parent or guardian.
48 Criminal Justice (Scotland) Act, 1949, s. 71(1).
49 Ibid. s. 71(2).
50 Ibid. s. 72(1).
51 Children and Young Persons (Scotland) Act, 1937, s. 66(2)(d).
52 Criminal Justice (Scotland) Act, 1949, s. 72(2).

person.[53] Neither before nor after the 1949 Act, however, were supervision orders used particularly often.

THE KILBRANDON PROPOSALS FOR PROBATION AND SUPERVISION

The Kilbrandon Report's main underlying philosophy, which it found to underpin the existing law, was one of "social education" in which the child's parents would play a central role. The new structures it proposed were designed to build upon this idea, both for young offenders and for children in need of care and protection:

> The principle underlying the present range of treatment measures is, as we have indicated, primarily an educational one, in the sense that it is intended, wherever possible, not to supersede the natural beneficial influences of the home and the family, but wherever practicable to strengthen, support and supplement them in situations in which for whatever reason they have been weakened or have failed in their effect. Proposals for a more sweeping extension of coercive powers in relation to parents of juvenile delinquents are in our view not only unacceptable on general grounds (as implying the application of criminal sanctions against adult persons in circumstances in which no definable criminal offence has been committed); but are ultimately incompatible with the nature of educational process itself, more particularly in the context of the parent-child relationship. Such a process of education in a social context – or "social education" as we now describe it – essentially involves the application of social and family case-work. In practice, this can work only on a persuasive and cooperative basis, through which the individual parent and child can be assisted towards a fuller insight and understanding of their situation and problems, and the means of solution which lie to their hands. There is, we consider, already ample evidence that, to the extent that it is already applied, such an approach finds a ready response. This is especially so with parents, enlisting as it does their active commitment as participants in a process which for their part they are increasingly led to see as being in the true interests of their children. Such an approach seems to us to be a proper and appropriate one for the solution of the problems of the child within the family.[54]

The logical conclusion of this involvement of parents in the rehabilitation of the child or young person would be that he or she would remain at home far more frequently than was the case in the past. The Kilbrandon Report worried that removing a child from its family circumstances (the typical outcome at the time of child protection processes) gave the parents the impression that their own responsibilities were being extinguished, and they were "being

---

53 Criminal Justice (Scotland) Act, 1949, s. 72(5).
54 Kilbrandon Report (1964), para 35.

reduced to the role of passive spectators".[55] That would be avoided if more children were kept at home with their parents instead of being removed to approved schools, children's homes or foster carers, and a locally-based treatment plan involving the parent was put in place. To ensure the effectiveness of whatever treatment was identified, a substantial expansion of supervision of children in their own homes would be necessary. The existing system already allowed the juvenile court to authorise (amongst other things) "supervision (in the case of juvenile offenders under a probation order; in other cases, under a supervision order in which either a probation officer or some other supervising officer may be nominated)".[56] The Kilbrandon Report's major recommendation, to replace the juvenile court with a "juvenile panel" (which in the event became the children's hearing), was designed to ensure that the panel itself took on a role in monitoring and re-evaluating the child's development and his or her responses to the treatment being offered with, obviously, "that oversight, as a practical matter, being carried out on their behalf by the social education department [which became the social services departments of every local authority]".[57] Since "social education" was to be the key, it would follow that "in the great majority of cases [this education] will be carried on while the child remains within the home".[58]

If this were accepted, there would no longer be any need to distinguish, even at the formal level, between probation orders and supervision orders.

> Our proposals will, we consider, result in a substantially greater use of community measures of casework with children on the lines of the present probation, or of supervision under the 1937 Act, the case-work being carried out most commonly, under the juvenile panel's authority, by the social work staff of the social education department which we are recommending. One necessary consequence of our proposals is that the present distinction between supervision under the 1937 Act and probation [under the 1949 Act] as methods of treatment for juveniles would cease to exist. Probation as such is a method of treatment which has from the outset necessarily evolved in the closest association with the criminal courts. As such, it will, of course, continue in relation to persons dealt with by the criminal courts, but can of necessity have no place under the arrangements for the juvenile panels which we are recommending.[59]

The Report also made plain that the supervision on offer, while commonly given by the public social services of the local authority, might also in

---

55 Ibid. para 38.
56 Ibid. para 84.
57 Ibid. para 140.
58 Ibid. para 140.
59 Ibid. para 140.

appropriate cases be undertaken by voluntary organisations and other social agencies, both public and private.[60] There would remain, in other words, a place for volunteerism – what today we would refer to as "the third sector" – in the delivery of public services.

PROBATION AND THE SOCIAL WORK (SCOTLAND) ACT 1968

The Kilbrandon proposals in relation to probation and supervision for children and young persons raised the question, addressed in the White Paper *Social Work and the Community*,[61] whether all probation work should be placed within the remit of local authorities, or whether the existing Scottish Probation Service should be retained, but limited to adult offenders. The Government's conclusion was that, since "the main function 192 of the probation officer – personal social work with the offender and his family in the community – is basically similar to that of other social workers", "it would be better if all the functions of the probation service in Scotland were undertaken by the local authority social work department".[62] There were other practical considerations justifying this conclusion:

> A separate service for the adult offender would be a small service somewhat apart from the mainstream of social work, and this might well have adverse effects on career prospects, on the recruitment of staff of the calibre required and in the development of new social work skills by the service . . .[63]

When the Government brought forward the Social Work (Scotland) Bill to give effect to the Kilbrandon proposals, the bringing of all probation services within the remit of local authority social services caused more contention, debate and dissent than any other issue.[64] It was pointed out in the Parliamentary debates that the approach to probation and supervision suggested by the Kilbrandon Report and the White Paper was strenuously opposed by the existing Probation Service which feared losing its independence, as well as by the Sheriffs Substitute Association.

---

60 Ibid. para 141.
61 SED, SHHD, 1966, Cmnd 3065.
62 *Social Work and the Community*, paras 28–29.
63 Ibid. para 29.
64 The other issue that caused much debate (especially in the House of Commons) was the Bill's timing. Clearly substantial new roles were being given to local authorities, and it was considered by many to be ill-timed given that the Report of the *Royal Commission on Local Government in Scotland* was due within months: this appeared in September 1969 (Cmnd 4150) and the reorganisation of local government that it recommended was given effect to in the Local Government (Scotland) Act 1973.

Lord Hughes, in moving the Second Reading of the Bill, explained that the Government saw probation and aftercare as a specialised form of social work and that local authority social work departments should therefore take over that work from the existing Probation Service.[65] The underlying aim was to ensure the complete professionalisation of the probation service, and Lord Hughes saw no reason why existing probation officers would be any less likely than other social work staff to secure "posts which will offer both professional scope and material conditions at least as good as they now enjoy".[66] The preceding decades had in fact seen increasing use of professional probation officers, together with increased training and supervision, and the Government clearly saw an opportunity to complete that process, thereby removing the interested amateur who had been involved in probation since its earliest days. No speaker in Parliament sought a return to a reliance on volunteers, but many worried that control over probation officers would transfer from the Scottish Home Department to local authorities, with what they saw as an inevitable loss of independence, and that removing the conception of probation officers as officers of the court was a retrograde step. Lord Wells-Pestell, a member of the Inner London Probation Service, for example, said this:

> I believe that the Probation Service must remain a separate service for several reasons. In the first place, it must be independent, free from any local authority department, and must remain part of the court service, responsible solely to the court. Secondly, probation officers must be seen to be independent. If a probation officer is a servant of the local authority, he may find himself expressing a view or suggesting a course of action contrary to the policies or to the approval of his local authority department. As a probation officer, I have many times found it necessary, when a boy or a girl has absconded from a local authority home, to be critical in one's report of the local authority home. Can a probation officer do this if he is a member of a local authority? In my view, he must remain independent.
>
> I also believe that the efficiency of the Probation Service within a local authority department could well depend on the local authority's view of crime and the cost to the rates in providing the various treatment measures which may be necessary. The present structure protects the probation officer and the Probation Service from such possibilities. It makes him an officer of the court, and responsible to the court and to the magistrate. I also feel it is important that the offender should see the probation officer as an officer of the court, and that the offender should be responsible to the court through the probation officer. I think it would not help the relationship between the delinquent and the probation officer if

---

65 HL Deb. 21 March 1968 vol. 290 col. 795.
66 HL Deb. 21 March 1968 vol. 290 col. 796.

the delinquent felt that the probation officer was a local authority employee.[67] I believe this is essential as part of the treatment.[68]

At Committee Stage in the House of Lords, an attempt to remove the provision bringing probation services under local authority control was defeated, but only very narrowly, by 48 to 46 votes.[69] It was pointed out that the probation service would itself continue if with a remit that excluded children and young persons, adult offenders already taking up the majority of the work of probation officers.[70] Baroness Birk doubted that the idealised picture of the existing probation service being painted by those opposed to the change was realistic,[71] and she suggested that removing children and young persons from their remit would allow probation officers to widen and deepen their concern with released adult offenders, as local authority employees.[72]

When the Bill went to the House of Commons, many of the same objections were made. A number of MPs accepted that the work probation officers did with children should come within the remit of the social services department of local authorities, but opposed adult services being treated in the same way.[73] In response, the Government pointed out that clause 27 of the Bill (which became s. 27 of the 1968 Act) would require local authorities to prepare a probation scheme to ensure that (adult) criminal courts received the same sort of information and support that they presently did through the existing probation service.[74] That clause was then subject to a long debate at Report Stage,[75] notable for a contribution by Donald Dewar,[76] who rejected the idea that probation officers should be seen primarily as officers of the court: it would be better, he argued, to see matters from the point of view of the child, where the needs to have his or her home

---

67 In fact, as Lord Hughes later pointed out, probation officers were currently paid by local authorities: HL Deb. 9 April 1968 vol. 291 col. 201.
68 HL Deb. 21 March 1968 vol. 290 cols 8277–8828.
69 HL Deb. 9 April 1968, vol. 291 cols 214–215.
70 HL Deb. 9 April 1968, vol. 291 cols 179 (Lord Hamilton of Dalzell), 183 (Lord Balerno) and 195–197 (Lord Drumalbyn).
71 Ibid. cols 190–194.
72 See also Lord Drumalbyn at ibid. col. 198.
73 HC Deb. 6 May 1968, vol. 764 cols 64–66 (Michael Noble); 78–79 (Hector Monro); 140 (Ian MacArthur).
74 Ibid. cols 145–146 (Bruce Millan).
75 HC Deb. 17 July 1968, vol. 768 cols 1485–1521.
76 Later, of course, the first First Minister of Scotland. On losing his seat at the 1970 General Election Donald Dewar became one of the first reporters to the children's panel when the 1968 Act came into effect in 1971. He returned to Parliament in a by-election in 1978.

environment, family troubles etc. recognised would be the same irrespective of whether he or she had appeared before a (criminal) court or "had been within the ken of the social worker in some other way".[77] In the end, the Government prevailed and the probation service was absorbed as a whole within local authority social work services; the previous role of probation officers in respect of children and young persons was taken over by social workers whose new duties came within the terms of supervision requirements made by the newly established children's hearings, and the Scottish Probation Service, as such, disappeared. A necessary consequence of the 1968 Act's approach to probation and supervision was that there was no longer any space for the voluntary probation officer. And the punitive backstop inherent in the very concept of probation ceased (without, be it noted, any parliamentary comment) to be part of the outcome for young offenders.

SUPERVISION REQUIREMENTS UNDER THE 1968 ACT

Section 44 of the Social Work (Scotland) Act 1968 provided that when a children's hearing determined that a child or young person before it was in need of compulsory measures of care, it could make a "supervision requirement", which would either require the child to submit to supervision in accordance with such conditions as the hearing imposed or require the child to reside in a residential establishment named in the requirement and be subject to such conditions as the hearing imposed. The former, made under s. 44(1)(a), came to be known as a "home supervision requirement" while the latter, made under s. 44(1)(b), came to be known as a "residential supervision requirement". These terms, which never had statutory authority but were used widely by social workers, panel members and reporters, were inaccurate in that they suggested a limited choice between the child remaining at home or being sent to a residential establishment. In truth, a child might have been required to live somewhere other than his or her home under s. 44(1)(a), as a term of the supervision requirement, whether with another family member such as a grandparent or with a foster carer. The real distinction was between a requirement that the child reside in a residential establishment, and all other requirements: this was really a distinction in the terms and conditions of the order and hearings were free to design these terms and conditions however they considered would be best for the child. There was no longer any requirement, as there had been under the Criminal

---

77 HC Deb. 17 July 1968, vol. 768 col. 1493.

Justice (Scotland) Act, 1949, for the child to consent to the inclusion within the supervision requirement of a term requiring the child to reside at a particular place: all terms and conditions were to be determined according to the hearing's assessment of the child's welfare.

The role of the supervising social worker was not set out in statutory form, in the way that the role of probation officers had been. Given that the Kilbrandon Committee had made plain their expectation that the children's hearing itself would be the body that directed the form and extent of local authority involvement that was considered necessary in any individual child's life, statutory direction could only limit the flexibility necessary to allow the supervision requirement to be structured to meet the individual needs of every child or young person.

SUPERVISION UNDER THE CHILDREN (SCOTLAND) ACT 1995 AND THE CHILDREN'S HEARINGS (SCOTLAND) ACT 2011

The distinction between "home" and "residential" supervision requirements disappeared under Part II of the Children (Scotland) Act 1995 which replaced much of the 1968 Act. It was made plain that a supervision requirement made by a children's hearing could require the child to reside at any place or places specified in the requirement and to comply with any condition contained in the requirement.[78] Most supervision requirements made under the 1995 Act did not contain a requirement on the child to reside at a specified place away from home, and the only obligation on the child was to comply with the specified conditions. This necessarily involved some form of supervision and it was the local authority, through its social services department, that was obliged to "give effect" to any supervision requirement.[79]

The Children's Hearings (Scotland) Act 2011 changed the terminology from "supervision requirement" to "compulsory supervision order", but there was little change in the concept as it had been structured in the 1995 Act.[80] The local authority remains the "implementation authority" with duties to give effect to the order.[81]

---

78 Children (Scotland) Act 1995, s. 70.
79 Children (Scotland) Act 1995, s. 71(1).
80 Children's Hearings (Scotland) Act 2011, s. 83.
81 Ibid. s. 144(1).

7. Boarding-out and Fostering by Public Authorities

INTRODUCTION

Foster care of children has a remarkably long history in Scotland. As a social practice, it has doubtless occurred since time immemorial. Legally, however, the *patria potestas* (the almost unbridled power of the father over the "legitimate" child and, to a lesser extent, the mother over the "illegitimate" child) was in principle inalienable. Nevertheless, it included the power to determine on a day to day basis where the child was to be and some parents exercised this power by sending the child away to live with other relatives, or acquaintances, or with tradesmen who might teach the child an economic skill; other parents would pay others to bring up the child on their behalf and avoid thereby inconvenience (if for example, the mother had died) or embarrassment (if the child were "illegitimate"). At least to some extent, the law has attempted to regulate that type of practice for almost 150 years.[1] But the sending of a child to be brought up by someone other than his or her parents might also be done under the authority of the state and this practice has been subject to legal regulation in Scotland, if in rudimentary form, for almost half a millennium.

The practice of state authorities and charitable bodies sending children over whose care they had responsibility to be brought up by private individuals was by the mid-nineteenth century usually referred to as "boarding-out": a child was boarded-out with someone who, normally, received an allowance to cover the basic costs of feeding and clothing the child. The terminology of "fostering" began to take root between the two World Wars in the twentieth

---

1 Private fostering arrangements such as those came under increasingly close statutory regulation, starting with the Infant Life Protection Acts, 1872 and 1897, then Part I of the Children Act, 1908, Part I of the Children and Young Persons (Scotland) Act, 1937, Part I of the Children Act, 1958 and finally the Foster Children (Scotland) Act 1984. Full details may be found in Norrie, K *Legislative Background to the Treatment of Children and Young People Living Apart from Their Parents* (Report submitted to, and published by, the Scottish Child Abuse Inquiry, November 2017).

century but it was not until late in that century that the terminology of "fostering" completely replaced that of "boarding-out".

The legal regulation of fostering in Scotland has in the past 100 years or so been characterised, as we will see in this chapter, by a steadily increasing level of attention given to the identification and monitoring of suitable foster carers, and to how the child's welfare and progress are overseen and enhanced. But the very concept of fostering has also undergone profound change, particularly in the past fifty years. For most of the early centuries, the "carer" often hardly deserved that name (and was not given it). Then for much of the twentieth century fostering was seen as the replacement of one family with another: the gap between fostering and adoption was much narrower than it is now and both aimed to provide a loving parent for a child whose circumstances had tended to deny him or her of that advantage. Since the late twentieth century, however, while a child in a foster placement will be cared for in a private home, within a family setting, it is no longer true that the role of the foster carer is conceptualised as that of a substitute loving parent. The role has been increasingly professionalized and today foster carers, though not "employed" as such,[2] provide a quasi-professional service on behalf of the state which, through the local authority, owe duties of care towards children they look after. The relationship between local authorities and foster carers came under detailed scrutiny in *Armes v Nottinghamshire County Council*[3] where the Supreme Court held that a local authority was vicariously liable for the abuse inflicted on a child by foster carers looking after her. Lord Reed said this:

> Accordingly, although the foster parents controlled the organisation and management of their household to the extent permitted by the relevant law and practice, and dealt with most aspects of the daily care of the children without immediate supervision, it would be mistaken to regard them as being in much the same position as ordinary parents. The local authority exercised powers of approval, inspection, supervision and removal without any parallel in ordinary family life. By virtue of those powers, the local authority exercised a significant degree of control over both what the foster parents did and how they did it, in order to ensure that the children's needs were met.[4]

The abuse in that case occurred in the 1980s. The role of foster carer by then was becoming more about providing professional services under the direction of the local authority, and less about fitting a disadvantaged child

---

2 See *S v N* 2002 SLT 589.

3 [2018] AC 355.

4 Ibid. para 62.

into ordinary family life, and it may well be that the decision (or, at least, the reasoning) in *Armes* would have been rather different had it involved a fostering arrangement at a much earlier period of the development of the law of boarding-out and fostering.

A. BOARDING-OUT UNDER THE POOR LAW

THE OLD POOR LAW

In 1579 the Parliament of Scotland passed an Act "For Punishment of the Strong and Idle Beggars and Relief of the Poor and Impotent".[5] That Act substantially increased the existing penalties for begging, but it also contained this curious provision:

> If any beggar's bairns (male or female), being above the age of 5 years and within 14, shall be liked of by any subject of the realm of honest estate – such person shall have the bairn by direction of the provost and bailies within burgh, or judge in landward parishes, if he be a man-child to the age of 24 years and if a woman child to the age of 18[6] years . . .

It is at this distance in time difficult to imagine what the legislators hoped to achieve through this provision but, the overall thrust of the Act being the discouragement of begging, we may be fairly certain that the child's welfare was not at the forefront of their minds. The Act also allowed for the recovery of children who removed themselves from the service of the subject of honest estate, revealing the state of servitude in which children were thereby placed. The passage of time has also made it impossible to know the extent to which the provision was used to remove children from their indigent parents and to deliver them to the servitude of the subject of honest estate: certainly no reported cases have been traced where the provision was in play. Nevertheless, this is a remarkably early example of the Scottish state taking upon itself the power to remove children from their unworthy parents and to transfer custody and control of the child to a "better" person. The Parliament of Scotland returned to the matter in 1617,[7] having determined that notwithstanding the "divers worthy laws and statutes made by his Majesty and his predecessors for retraining of idle and masterful beggars" the number of beggars daily increases more and more and that their

---

5 APS iii 139, c. 12 (12mo. c. 74).

6 Oddly, Sir George Nicholls in his *History of the Scotch Poor Law* (John Murray, 1856), ch. 1 mistranscribed this age to 28.

7 APS iv, 542, c. 10 (12mo. c. 10).

children "doth contract such a custom and habit [of begging] that hardly they can be drawn thereafter to any other calling". The Parliament enacted that since, "if the said children were in their tender years put to work and employed and trained up in any commendable labour", it would be lawful for His Majesty's subjects to take, with the authority of the provost and baillies or by the Kirk Session, the children of poor and indigent parents "to be educated and brought up by them in their houses or to be put by them to such crafts, callings and vocations . . . as they please". The focus on education and training is to be noted, as is the fear that habits of idleness transmit down the generations. Whether or not either of these provisions were much used between the sixteenth and nineteenth centuries, they did set the pattern from the earliest days of the Poor Law for the preferred solution in Scotland to the problem of children whom the state deems ought not to be allowed to remain with their parents – the boarding-out or fostering of children. As we will see, throughout the history of Scottish child protection law, properly so-called, this was and remains the preferred option that the authorities seek to apply.

BOARDING-OUT UNDER THE "NEW" POOR LAW

The long-established practice of boarding-out destitute children with foster families proved to be a more economical means of providing for needy children than accommodating them in poorhouses,[8] which became the primary mechanism for poor relief after the restructuring of the Poor Law by the Poor Law Amendment (Scotland) Act, 1845. This led to boarding-out becoming more common under the new Poor Law than it had been under the old. It is worth noting, however, that it was a practice adopted by the parochial boards themselves and there was nothing in the 1845 Act itself that gave them statutory authority for doing so.[9] That gap was not filled until 1934.

How boarding-out under the Poor Law operated in practice was examined in 1876 by John S. Skelton, Advocate,[10] in *The Boarding Out of Pauper Children in Scotland*.[11] He suggested that the 1845 Act had been explicitly designed to increase the amount spent on the relief of the poor in order to reduce the incidence of begging in the streets, while at the same time chang-

8 See "On Boarding Out of Pauper Children" (1869) *Poor Law Magazine* 96.
9 See "Cottage Homes for Poor Children" (1869) *Poor Law Magazine* 612.
10 And prolific essayist, particularly for *Blackwood's Magazine*.
11 William Blackwood and Sons, 1876.

ing the traditional system of poor relief in Scotland to "indoor relief", or a place in a poorhouse (an uncommon institution in Scotland before 1845). However, outdoor relief was still encouraged, as being more economical, in relation to children.

Skelton noted that the parishes from which children were removed tended to be urban, and the parishes to which they were sent tended to be rural. As we will see, this remained the pattern until the second half of the twentieth century with the Isle of Arran, for example, having long received a significant number of boarded-out children from Glasgow and its surrounding towns.[12] In relation to who was likely to take in boarded-out children, Skelton said this:

> the class from which guardians are most frequently selected (a class in some respects peculiar to Scotland) is thus described by the Inspector of Greenock: 'Our children are chiefly boarded out with small farmers and crofters who have one or more cows and a portion of land' . . .[13]

Skelton speculates that it was the availability of smallholders and crofters who were willing to take children that made boarding-out so widespread in Scotland, while the relative lack of such a class in England inhibited the practice developing to the same extent there.[14] The aim was clearly that the boys would learn to be farm labourers and the girls to be domestic servants: in any case, the guardians obtained, as well as a small allowance to pay for upkeep, an additional pair of hands to help with the work on the land and in the house. The risk that these children would be used as cheap labour by their guardians, whose economic situation was invariably precarious was surely high.

Inspectors appointed by the parochial board would visit the children at frequencies the board itself determined, and this varied across the country from once a year to upwards of 8 times a year.[15] Skelton reported that the inspectors generally found the system worked well and believed that it certainly offered a better moral environment for the bringing up of

---

12 See "Pauper Children Boarded in Arran" (1863) *Poor Law Magazine* 309 where it was reported that at that time there were 130 children boarded-out in Arran. The Inspector's report reproduced there gives an interesting snapshot of both the time and of the care with which inspectors went about their duties.

13 Skelton, J. *The Boarding out of Pauper Children in Scotland*, pp. 81–82.

14 Higginbotham, P. *Children's Homes: A History of the Institutional Care for Britain's Young* (Pen and Sword History, 2017), pp. 219–223 traces the much more gradual adoption of boarding-out in England and Wales, where it had traditionally been resisted.

15 Skelton, J. *The Boarding Out of Pauper Children in Scotland*, pp. 95–101.

children than the poor house.[16] There was however the occasional – but only occasional – worry expressed by inspectors that in some cases the children did not attend school and were not treated as members of the guardian's family, but instead made to look after the family and treated as servants.[17] After reviewing these inspection reports, which may well have given a picture rather rosier than the reality for many children, Skelton offered a list of factors that contributed to successful boarding-out: (i) the taking of great care in selecting guardians, (ii) the thoroughness of inspection and supervision, (iii) the placing of a limit on the number of children in any one placement and (iv) the placing of a limit on the number of boarded-out children in any individual parish.[18] Of these, the most significant was identified to be inspection and supervision. Nevertheless, most of these factors have been repeatedly revisited by policy-makers up to the present day.

Skelton reported that on 1 January 1875 there were 5,985 orphans and deserted children chargeable to parochial boards in Scotland,[19] of whom 4,512 were boarded-out, which is well over 75% of the total. Macdonald, writing over 100 years later, says that "Between 1845 and 1914, 80-90% of children who came under the long-term care of the Scottish Poor Law were boarded-out", and she suggests as reasons why the practice developed (i) the fact that few poorhouses had in Scotland been built and (ii) boarding-out was a cheaper option than "indoor support".[20] As late as 1933, it was reported that 89% of children subject to the Poor Law were being boarded-out.[21]

THE POOR LAW (SCOTLAND) ACT, 1934

The practice of the Poor Law authorities boarding-out children for whom they were responsible finally received statutory sanction under the Poor Law (Scotland) Act, 1934. This allowed public assistance authorities[22] to make

---

16 Ibid. pp. 107–108.
17 Ibid. p. 113, quoting the Inspector of Dunfermline. Similar worries had been expressed, in rather stronger terms, earlier in "Boarding Out of Pauper Children" (1863) 6 *Poor Law Magazine* 60.
18 Ibid. p. 115.
19 Ibid. p. 76.
20 Macdonald, H.J. "Boarding-out and the Scottish Poor Law, 1845-1914" (1996) 75 *Scottish Historical Review* 197, pp. 198–199.
21 Abrams, L. *The Orphan Country: Children of Scotland's Broken Homes from 1845 to the Present Day* (John Donald Publishers, 1998), p. 39.
22 As the parochial boards established in 1845 had by then become. Parochial boards were quite separate from local authorities until 1894.

arrangements for the lodging, boarding, or maintenance otherwise than in a poorhouse of children under the age of sixteen years[23] who are orphans, or who have been deserted by, or are separated from, their parents, so however that any arrangements so made shall be subject to such regulations as the Department may make with respect thereto.[24]

In introducing the Bill, Lord Strathcona said of this provision:

> Clause 10 contains an important provision dealing with the boarding-out of children. The system of boarding-out with private persons children who have come under the control of authorities has long been a feature of poor law administration in Scotland, and it is generally recognised that the system has been amply justified by results. The system has developed without specific statutory authority. This clause is intended to give that authority and to secure that boarding-out will in all cases be under the best possible conditions. To that end it is proposed that all arrangements for boarding-out shall be made subject to regulations made by the Department of Health.[25]

The Poor Relief Regulations (Scotland), 1934,[26] required the child to be visited at least annually by the boarding-out authority – though in 1946 the Clyde Report noted[27] that during the War that requirement was often not fulfilled. A variety of government departments were responsible for visiting children boarded-out under the Poor Law.[28] The 1934 Regulations were replaced by the Children (Boarding-out etc.) (Scotland) Rules and Regulations, 1947, to be discussed below.

There seems to have been no provision conferring upon guardians receiving children under the Poor Law any parental powers, and children boarded-out under the 1934 Act could be retrieved by their parents at any time – subject only to the Custody of Children Act, 1891 which allowed guardians to resist such retrieval on proof that the parent could not show he or she was a fit person to have care of the child. Each public assistance authority decided itself which allowances to make to the person boarding a child on its behalf, and the amounts paid varied considerably across Scotland.[29]

---

23 This is a full two years below the age limit for young people in the same time-era being boarded-out under the authority of the court under the Children and Young Persons (Scotland) Act, 1932.
24 Poor Law (Scotland) Act 1934, s. 10.
25 HL Deb. 12 July 1934 vol. 93 col. 563.
26 SR&O 1934, No. 1296 (S. 69).
27 Clyde Report on *Homeless Children* (Cmnd 6911, 1946), para 17.
28 See Clyde Report, paras 18–21 for details.
29 Clyde Report, para 15.

B. BOARDING-OUT BY COURT ORDER 1889–1968

THE EARLY CHILD CRUELTY STATUTES: "FIT PERSON ORDERS"

The first of the series of statutes that sought to go beyond the criminalisation of child abuse and neglect and to provide, at the same time, some direct protection to the victims of such behaviour was, as we saw earlier in this book, the Prevention of Cruelty to, and Protection of, Children Act, 1889. This introduced what came to be known as "fit person orders", under which a child could be removed from the custody of a neglectful parent and delivered into the care of a relative or other person better fitted to bring up the child.[30] The identification of a suitable person to act as a "fit person" was left to the court, with no selection criteria laid down other than an injunction on the court to try to select a person who was of the same religious persuasion as the child.[31] Nor was there any monitoring mechanism established to ensure the child's continued wellbeing under the care of the fit person.

No provision was made for the relative or fit person to be paid an allowance to cover their expenses in bringing up the child (in the way that persons boarding children under the Poor Law were paid allowances to cover basic costs). Presumably, it was thought that a relative would gladly bear the expense, though the court could order that the parent contribute to the child's maintenance.[32] The state removed the child, but it did not itself pay for the child's future upkeep, nor have any role in directing how the child was to be brought up by the guardian.

These provisions were repeated in the Prevention of Cruelty to Children Act, 1894. In *Dunn v Mustard*[33] it was held competent for the High Court of Justiciary to review the making of a fit person order under the 1894 Act, notwithstanding that the custody of a child is normally a civil matter: child protection was not at this stage anything other than an adjustment of criminal procedure. The most important development in these early child protection statutes came in the Prevention of Cruelty to Children Act, 1904 which expanded the concept of "fit person" to whose care a child might be committed to include "any society or body corporate established for the reception of

---

30 See further, Chapter 1 above.
31 Prevention of Cruelty to, and Protection of, Children Act, 1889, s. 5(2).
32 Ibid. s. 5(2).
33 1899 1F (J) 81.

poor children or the prevention of cruelty to children".[34] Voluntary organisations like child welfare societies (though not the Poor Law authorities) could from this date be named as "fit persons" for these purposes. Fit person orders were no longer exclusively about boarding children out with families, for while voluntary organisations might exercise their powers by themselves accommodating the child in a private household, they might also accommodate the child in an institutional environment. The provisions in the 1904 Act were repeated and expanded in Part II of the Children Act, 1908.

COMMITTAL TO THE CARE OF A FIT PERSON UNDER THE 1932 AND 1937 ACTS

Notwithstanding the increasingly detailed legislation in these early years, it would seem that the committal powers under the Children Act, 1908 and its predecessors were in practice seldom used. Reporting in 1928, the Morton Committee suggested that

> This may have been due to the reluctance of a relative or other friend to undertake the responsibility, particularly when no financial assistance was available. Perhaps this is not altogether to be regretted – since direct financial assistance of this nature, without the intervention of any local authority, might attract relatives or friends who are not suitable for the task. In any case, machinery for finding a fit person was not provided under the [1908] Act.[35]

Whatever the reason for the under-usage of the power to commit children to the care of a fit person, the Children and Young Persons (Scotland) Act, 1932 (subsequently re-enacted as the Children and Young Persons (Scotland) Act, 1937) completed the transformation of fit person orders from a form of kinship care into (what we now call) fostering as a major component of state care. It did so in three ways. First, the reference to "relatives" to whom the child's care could be committed was dropped. It was now expected that the fit person chosen by the court would be quite independent of the child's immediate family. Secondly, the "fit person" in whose favour the order would be made was now to include the local education authority,[36]

---

34 Prevention of Cruelty to Children Act, 1904, s. 6(1).

35 Morton Committee Report *Protection and Training* (HMSO, 1926), p. 116.

36 Children And Young Persons (Scotland) Act, 1932, s. 20(1), subsequently re-enacted as s. 80 of the Children and Young Persons (Scotland) Act, 1937, provided that education authorities shall be deemed to be a fit person for this purpose and authorised them to undertake the care of children and young persons so committed. This was amended in the Children Act, 1948, after which local authorities rather than education authorities were deemed fit persons under s. 80 of the 1937 Act. That change made little difference in practice in Scotland since local authorities had

which would normally exercise its duty by boarding-out the children whose care had been committed to them with individuals they had identified as suitable. By this means, boarding-out became a financial burden on the state, which would pay the costs of feeding, clothing and housing the child while these services were actually performed by private individuals. There was no obligation on the education authority to accept the committal of any child to their care, but the fact that the Treasury bore the cost when the education authority was named as the fit person[37] gave the authority, as Cowan pointed out,[38] a direct incentive to do so – the costs of the only practical alternative (sending the child to an approved school) would fall on the education authority itself. The end result was that the power to choose a particular foster placement for the child rested ultimately with the education authority into whose care the child had been committed.[39] The public assistance (Poor Law) authorities were not similarly deemed to be "fit persons" for the purposes of court orders under the Children and Young Persons (Scotland) Act, 1932, but their long experience of boarding-out was tapped into: the 1946 Clyde Report[40] pointed out that education authorities tended to delegate the functions of identifying suitable foster parents to the public assistance authorities. In choosing individuals with whom to board-out children, education authorities were for the first time constrained by rules (considered below) as to the "fitness" of the foster parent. As before, they were also obliged, where possible, to choose a person of the same religious persuasion as the child or young person, or who was willing to give an undertaking that the child would be brought up in accordance with that religious persuasion.[41]

And thirdly, by substantially increasing the grounds upon which children and young persons could be found to be in need of care and protection, the 1932 Act also expanded the range of children over whom a fit person order could be made.[42] Children under ten could be sent to approved schools

---

exercised the functions of education authorities since s. 3 of the Local Government (Scotland) Act, 1929.

37 Children and Young Persons (Scotland) Act, 1932, s. 79(1)(i)(b); Children and Young Persons (Scotland) Act, 1937, s. 107(1)(a)(ii).

38 Cowan, M.G. *The Children and Young Persons (Scotland) Act, 1932* (W. Hodge & Co., 1933), p. 44.

39 Children and Young Persons (Scotland) Act, 1932, s. 20; Children and Young Persons (Scotland) Act, 1937, s. 88(3).

40 *Report of the Committee on Homeless Children* (1946, Cmnd 6911), para 22.

41 Children and Young Persons (Scotland) Act, 1932, ss. 20(2) and 22(1); Children and Young Persons (Scotland) Act, 1937, s. 88(3).

42 It was held in England that there was no reason why a fit person order could not be made over a

only in exceptional circumstances,[43] with the result that boarding-out was the default outcome for children of that age brought before the juvenile court. For older children also, boarding-out became the norm: the Clyde Report[44] recorded that in March 1945 of the 1,561 children then in the care of Scottish education authorities, 1,077 were boarded-out with foster parents.[45] These figures also illustrate that the making of a fit person order did not always lead to the child being boarded-out: the fit person, particularly if a voluntary organisation, could choose to fulfil its duty by accommodating the child in a children's home.

Effect of a fit person order

The analogy between boarding-out under a fit person order with modern-day fostering may be misleading, for boarding-out was perceived to make, and designed to make, permanent provision for the child's upbringing. Though it did not change the child's legal status, as the recently introduced adoption order did,[46] boarding-out involved a transference of parental rights and powers that would normally remain in effect for the rest of the child's childhood. An order made under the Children and Young Persons (Scotland) Act, 1932 or, later, the Children and Young Persons (Scotland) Act, 1937 for the committal of a child or young person to the care of a fit person lasted until the child or young person attained the age of 18 years,[47] (as opposed to 16 years under the previous law). This was, in today's terms, permanence planning and as such a fit person order is perhaps best seen as the precursor to the modern permanence order.[48]

Both the 1932 and the 1937 Acts provided that

child who was validly married (the marriage having been contracted abroad): *Mohamed v Knott* [1969] 1 QB 1.

43 Children and Young Persons (Scotland) Act, 1932, s. 18; Children and Young Persons (Scotland) Act, 1937, s. 49(2). Under the Children Act, 1908 there had been a power to board-out children under 10 who had been sent to a certified school but now the statutory expectation was that they would be boarded-out.

44 Clyde Report, para 23.

45 The Clyde Report, paras 34–35 also described the provisions under the War Pensions (Administrative Provisions) Act 1918 and the War Orphans Act, 1942, under which a small number of children who had lost parents during the two World Wars were boarded-out by the Minister of Pensions – including 23 who had been committed under the Children and Young Persons (Scotland) Act, 1937 to the care of the Ministry of Pensions.

46 Adoption of Children (Scotland) Act, 1930. See Chapter 12 below.

47 Children and Young Persons (Scotland) Act, 1932, s. 19(2); Children and Young Persons (Scotland) Act, 1937, s. 79(3).

48 Made under s. 80 of the Adoption and Children (Scotland) Act 2007.

the person to whose care a boy or girl is committed. . . . shall have the same rights and powers, and be subject to the same liabilities in respect of his maintenance, as if he were his or her parent, and the boy or girl shall continue to be in his care notwithstanding any claim by a parent or any other person . . .[49]

Responsibility therefore rested with the person or body named as a fit person by the order rather than, if different, the actual foster parent with whom the child lived. The position of the birth parent from whom the child had been removed was, however, left unclear. It was held in the sheriff court that the provision just quoted meant that the parents' rights and powers were vested in the fit person to the exclusion of the parents who lost, for example, their right of access to the child.[50] However, in the Outer House, it was held a year later that the more natural reading of the provision was simply that the fit person stood in the position of a parent and that it did not remove the actual parent's right to seek access.[51] Lord Fraser said:

[I]f the opinion expressed by the sheriff-substitute [in *Gilmour*] is well-founded, it would seem to imply that the jurisdiction of this Court and of the Sheriff Court is ousted by a committal order made by a juvenile court. Such a result would, in my opinion, be surprising and I would be unwilling to accept it unless it followed from very clear words in the statute. I do not find such words in this statute.[52]

This is an early precursor to the later debates in respect of the children's hearing system whether the making of a supervision requirement inhibited the court's power to make custody and access orders or, later, orders relating to parental responsibilities and parental rights.[53] Wilkinson and Norrie suggest as the guiding principle "that the effect of a section 11 order[54] is subject to such other lawful measures as may be taken in relation to the child".[55] If this were the principle applicable to fit person orders, then parents' rights would be suspended during their currency, and any inconsistent term contained in a private law order made by a court would not be given effect to while the fit person order was in effect.

---

49 Children and Young Persons (Scotland) Act, 1932, s. 20(4); Children and Young Persons (Scotland) Act, 1937, s. 79(4).
50 *Gilmour v Ayr County Council* 1968 SLT (Sh Ct) 41.
51 *Browne v Browne* 1969 SLT (Notes) 15.
52 1969 SLT (Notes) 15, p. 16.
53 See *Aitken v Aitken* 1978 SC 297; *F v F* 1991 SLT 357; *P v P* 2000 SLT 781.
54 That is to say an order regulating the exercise of parental responsibilities and parental rights made under Part I (the private law part) of the Children (Scotland) Act 1995.
55 Wilkinson, A. and Norrie, K. *The Law Relating to Parent and Child in Scotland* (W. Green, 3rd edn, 2013), para 8.52, citing the late Professor Thomson "Parental Rights and Children in Care: A 'Confusing Overview'" 1991 SLT (News) 379.

It had been held in England that when a child was committed to the care of a local authority under a fit person order that local authority became liable to pay any fines that a parent would be required to pay under the Children and Young Persons Act, 1933 (worded very similarly to provisions in the Scottish 1937 Act),[56] but this was overturned by the House of Lords some years later on the ground that the 1933 Act (and, implicitly, the 1937 Act) did not transfer all the obligations of a parent and that parents still retained some liability for their children.[57]

Variation and termination of fit person order

Though it would normally last for the whole of the child's childhood, it was possible to seek the order's variation or revocation before then, and under the statute "any person" could make an application to the juvenile court to vary or revoke the fit person order.[58] This general power was worded widely and does not specify the basis upon which variation or revocation would be ordered, though Trotter says that the person who sought variation or revocation had to show some interest, and sufficient reason for the application, and that "the welfare of the juvenile must be considered".[59] In *Woods v Ministry of Pensions*,[60] a mother was convicted of various offences and her eight year old child was committed to the care of the Minister of Pensions who boarded him out with foster parents, under whose care he thrived. Five years later the mother sought a revocation of the order on the basis that she had reformed her ways and was now in a position to offer the child (who was then 13 years old) a good home.[61] The sheriff refused the petition on the ground that it would not be in the child's best interests to revoke the order. The mother appealed, arguing that the sheriff had failed to give weight to a parent's "natural right of custody" which, she averred, could only be interfered with if there was a risk to the child's physical or moral welfare, which did not exist here. In dismissing the appeal, the Second Division concluded

---

56 *R v Croydon Juvenile Court Justices ex parte Croydon LBC* [1973] QB 426.

57 *Leeds City Council v West Yorkshire Metropolitan Police* [1983] 1 AC 29.

58 Children and Young Persons (Scotland) Act, 1932, s. 19(8); Children and Young Persons (Scotland) Act, 1937, s. 88(6).

59 Trotter, T. *The Law as to Children and Young Persons* (W. Hodge & Co, 1938), p. 160.

60 1952 SC 529.

61 The case affords a snapshot of life in the immediate post-War years: the mother, who had been widowed when her husband was killed in action, had clearly struggled with life's pressures, and her reformation consisted in remarrying, to a man who could provide her with a house with hot water and a lavatory.

that the appellant had failed to discharge the onus that she had of showing both that her own reformation was complete and that the advantages of the child's new life would not be destroyed or endangered if he were restored to her custody. The Lord Justice-Clerk (Thomson) said this:

> The consideration which particularly weighs with me on this aspect of the case is the moral and psychological condition in which the boy was when he was taken away from the petitioner and the fact that it was some considerable time before he began to benefit from his new environment. I feel that a sudden reversal of the policy presently in force might be fraught with risk. The task of nurturing him back to normality has been a difficult one. The situation might have been very different had he been a more or less normal boy when he was parted from his mother. But that is not the situation here. This is not a case of transferring a normal, self-reliant child from one environment to another, to which, after the initial upset, he might be expected to react favourably. This is a case where, in view of what we know of his history, to send the boy back even to an affectionate parent might have serious repercussions. I have great sympathy with the petitioner, who deserves every credit for the way in which she has reformed, but, if she has, as I believe she has, a genuine affection for her child, she will be the first to realise how important it is that nothing should be done to endanger the slow but steady improvement made by her son.[62]

That this is one of the very few reported cases in which revocation was sought[63] suggests that, for the vast majority of children and young persons committed to the care of a fit person, the order was effectively final and constituted permanent provision for their upbringing during the remainder of their childhood. This consisted with the underlying understanding of the very purpose of boarding children out – the replacement of their birth families with new, better, families who would bring them up in a more satisfactory environment from which they would emerge as adults able to take a productive place in society.

In addition to the general power to vary or revoke a fit person order, it was also provided that on the application of a parent, guardian or any near relative of the child or young person, the juvenile court could vary or revoke a fit person order on the ground that the child or young person was not being brought up in accordance with his or her religious persuasion.[64] The order could also be brought to an end before the young person's 18th birthday by

---

62   1952 SC 529, pp. 534–535.

63   The only other case in the Scottish law reports is *G v Minister of Pensions* 1950 SLT (Sh Ct) 79. Here, no reasons for refusing the petition for revocation were given by the sheriff, but it was held that the petition required to be served on the RSSPCC, which had originally sought the mother's prosecution for neglect, as well as on the Minister of Pensions.

64   Children and Young Persons (Scotland) Act, 1932, s. 22(2); Children and Young Persons (Scotland) Act, 1937, s. 88(7).

order of the Secretary of State, who had the power to discharge a child or young person from the care of the person to whose care he or she had been committed, either absolutely or conditionally.[65]

Post-war pressure for change

The 1946 Clyde Report,[66] examining the practice of boarding-out in Scotland at the end of the Second World War, came to much the same conclusions as those reached by Skelton in the context of the Poor Law, exactly seventy years previously.[67] The Clyde Report concluded as Skelton had done that boarding-out was far preferable to any other alternative, and in particular to the sending of a child to an approved school or children's home ("these cold and forbidding abodes"[68]). Like Skelton, the Clyde Report thought that the key to the success of any boarding-out scheme was the careful identification of appropriate carers within whose families the child or young person could be accommodated. However, the Clyde Report was far less sanguine than Skelton had been at city children being sent to unfamiliar rural environments which, due to underlying poverty, required them to work for their keep. Clyde identified one particular environment as being especially problematical, which Skelton had, in fact, commended:

> Many of the Local Authorities board out children on crofts. Some witnesses have condemned such a practice as unsuitable and we feel there is substance in their criticism. While fully appreciating what has been accomplished in the past through this valuable service, and the opportunity for home life which has been afforded to homeless children on some crofts, we think that, under modern conditions, radical changes are necessary. We strongly deprecate the boarding out of city children on crofts in very remote areas where they have no real contact with other children, where they have no facilities for learning a trade which is congenial to them, or where the living conditions are bad . . . Investigation of conditions in Highland crofts has shown that the lack of sanitation and the absence of facilities for training the children in cleanliness and personal habits make it inadvisable to board out children in remote crofts in the Highlands, where economic conditions are such that the practice of taking children seems to be regarded as an industry, and the labour obtained therefrom often enables the guardians to maintain their crofts. Instances were found where children on crofts were overworked by their foster parents.[69]

---

65 Children and Young Persons (Scotland) Act, 1932, s. 19(6); Children and Young Persons (Scotland) Act, 1937, s. 88(4).
66 *Report on Homeless Children* (Cmnd 6911, 1946).
67 Skelton, J. *Boarding Out of Pauper Children in Scotland* (William Blackwood and Sons, 1876).
68 Clyde Report, para 44.
69 Ibid. para 73.

The overall conclusion was, however, that boarding-out ought to be encouraged as the primary outcome to be sought for children removed from their families, whether for child protection reasons or because of the child's behaviour. But a much more robust mechanism for identifying suitable foster carers than had previously existed required to be established.

BOARDING-OUT AFTER THE CHILDREN ACT, 1948

The preference for boarding-out recommended in the Clyde Report (and in the English equivalent, the Curtis Report[70]) was given its first statutory recognition in Art. 4 of the Children (Boarding-Out etc.) (Scotland) Rules and Regulations, 1947. Also, during the debates on the Children Act, 1948, strong support was given to the notion that local authorities should pursue boarding-out in foster homes as the primary means by which they fulfilled their duty towards children in their care. Most speakers in Parliament saw boarding-out as a means by which needy children were supplied with a substitute family and all the benefits that flow from family life: it was seen as a solution of permanence, and one that would best set up the child for an independent life as an adult. Affirming the conclusion to that effect in the Clyde and Curtis Reports, the Lord Chancellor said this:

> I am glad to say that the conclusion has been reached, which I feel sure is right, that, of all the methods, the best is that of boarding the child out, if only a suitable home can be found in which the child can become a member of the family. So long as a suitable family is found, I feel quite certain that that method is a better one than placing the child in even the best form of institution. But if such a home cannot be obtained, then the local authority can use either their own residential homes or the homes of voluntary associations. As things are to-day, I am afraid that residential establishments will remain necessary for a long time. I think it regrettable, because I do not believe one can do better than arrange for the children to become members of an ordinary family, sharing the normal life of the community.[71]

A Scottish MP, Thomas Galbraith,[72] said this:

> Every child is entitled to a home. No matter how good an institution may be, it cannot supply the atmosphere and freedom which a home can give—where one can feel that one really has a place of one's own and an intimate place in the life

---

70 *Report of the Committee on the Care of Children* (Cmnd 6922, 1946).

71 HL Deb. 10 February 1948, vol. 153, cols 919–920. See also *HC Deb. 7 May 1948 vol. 450 col. 1614.*

72 MP for Hillhead, Glasgow between 1948 and 1982 (and so the immediate predecessor to Roy Jenkins in that constituency).

of the family. It may be that I am wrong, but so far as my researches have gone, it appears that the system of boarding out has been practised more freely in Scotland and been more fully developed there than in England. If I am right in my contention, the House will perhaps be interested to know that that system has been in existence in Scotland for over 170 years and that it is 103 years since, by the passing of the Poor Law (Scotland) Act, 1845, it received official recognition. It may also be of interest if I quote a few figures from my native city of Glasgow to show how much the system of boarding out is relied on in Scotland. At present the welfare committee of the Corporation of Glasgow has some 3,000 children under its care. No fewer than 2,600 of them are boarded out with foster parents and the remaining 400 are accommodated in children's homes.[73]

However, not all speakers quite bought into this ideal. The Earl of Scarbrough, for example, may be found saying:

The only other point I wish to touch upon in the general provisions of the Bill concerns the problem of boarding out. I agree with the views of the Curtis Committee up to a point, that at its best this is far and away the best method of caring for these children. But I think that "at its best" is a very important qualification. Once you begin to get below the best, you are exposing the child to very serious dangers . . . I do not place very great hopes on a sufficient number of the right type of families being found.[74]

But this was very much a minority view, and the provision passed easily that became s. 13(1) of the Children Act, 1948, giving first preference to boarding-out with institutional care only being permitted "where it is not practicable or desirable for the time being to make arrangements for boarding-out". Parker[75] rather tartly comments that

foster care was to be advanced because it was considered better for the children but also because the unit costs were less than residential care. There was, it seemed, the marvellous coincidence that what was best was also the cheapest.

The 1948 Act also removed the requirement that the local authority agree to be named as "fit person" for the purposes of the 1937 Act:[76] this was no longer to be a matter of choice for the local authority but one of statutory duty.

The 1948 Act set up the Scottish Advisory Council on Child Care,[77] and one of that Council's earliest reports came from its Boarding-Out

---

73 HC Deb. 7 May 1948, vol. 450 cols 1619–1620.
74 HL Deb. 10 February 1948, vol. 153 col. 960.
75 Parker, R. "Getting Started with the 1948 Act: What Did we Learn?" (2011) 35 *Adoption and Fostering* 17, p. 27.
76 Children Act, 1948, s. 5, amending Children and Young Persons (Scotland) Act, 1937, s. 80(1).
77 Children Act, 1948, s. 44.

Committee.[78] This report, published in 1950, repeated some of the concerns earlier identified in the Clyde Report:

> It has long been the practice of local authorities in Scotland to board out almost entirely in rural areas. In the past there was no doubt good reason for this . . . It is no longer possible to say that the advantage in this regard necessarily lies with the country . . . We feel that in future local authorities should not assume that boarding-out should be confined to country districts but should endeavour to secure suitable foster parents in urban areas as well . . . In several areas in Scotland the number of boarded out children may approach, or even exceed, the number of local children. We do not think it is desirable that any area should become a colony of boarded out children, since the aim of boarding out is to have the child absorbed into the community.[79]

There had been the power since 1933 to limit the number of children boarded-out in particular areas, but this comment suggests that it was not commonly used. Another issue that exercised the Council[80] was the appropriate frequency of official visitation of boarded-out children which, as noted below, had recently been cut from four times a year to two times. Noting that differing views had been offered to them, they concluded that "four visits a year to each boarded out child should not be necessary" if the foster parents "have been wisely chosen in the first place". The Council's major concern was to protect the privacy (and thereby, it was thought, willingness to serve) of foster parents, and very little attention was paid to the role of visitors investigating the wellbeing of the children being fostered – or indeed monitoring the performance of the foster parent. Their approach (and indeed conclusion) reflected that of the Clyde Report which likewise tended to look at matters from the perspective of the foster parents. The Council did conclude that "the possibility of returning the child to his parents, provided it is consistent with his welfare to do so, must always be present in the mind of the children's officer",[81] but that was said in the context of a discussion on the desirability of parental visits: such visits were not perceived as being particularly helpful and it was recommended that visits by parents or relatives or friends to a boarded-out child should not be allowed except at the discretion of the local authority acting through its children's officer.[82] All of this suggests that, throughout the 1950s, boarding-out was still being perceived as a permanent mechanism by which the child would be cut off from

---

78 Scottish Advisory Council on Child Care *Report of the Boarding Out Committee* (HMSO 1950).
79 Ibid. paras 8 and 9.
80 Ibid. paras 12 et seq.
81 Ibid. para 31.
82 Ibid. para 31.

the influences of his or her birth family, and be provided with a new and more suitable family.

BOARDING-OUT REGULATIONS 1933–1959

Throughout this period various sets of secondary legislation were made, governing the process for choosing foster parents and for monitoring and visiting foster children. These were, respectively, Part C of the Children and Young Persons (Scotland) Care and Training Regulations, 1933;[83] the Children (Boarding-out etc.) (Scotland) Rules and Regulations, 1947;[84] and the Boarding-out of Children (Scotland) Regulations, 1959.[85] A general trend towards more detailed regulation, and an increasing coverage, in these bodies of law, is clearly discernible. So, for example, the 1959 Regulations extended its application to boarding-out of children by voluntary organisations as well as by local authorities,[86] which had been the sole concern of the earlier Regulations.

Choosing suitable foster parents

Perhaps the most significant development in the 1933 Regulations was the setting out, for the first time, of criteria (albeit negative) to be applied in choosing suitable foster parents for children. Education authorities were required to keep a list of persons (who, incidentally, were referred to in the rules for the first time as "foster parents") who were "willing and fitted to undertake the care of boys and girls."[87] But instead of setting down qualities that ought to be sought in potential foster parents, the Regulations took the approach of specifying certain categories of individual who were barred from acting as a foster parent. Boarding-out was not permitted with persons in receipt of poor relief,[88] or who depended for a living mainly on payments received for boarding children.[89] Nor was boarding-out permitted with a person who had at any time been convicted of an offence that rendered them unfit to be a foster parent, or with a person occupying or residing in a

83 SR&O, 1933 No. 1006 (S.55) (reproduced in Trotter, pp. 335–347).
84 SI 1947/2146 (S. 76).
85 SI 1959/835 (S. 44).
86 1959 Regulations, reg. 1(1)(b). Boarding-out by the managers of approved schools was, however, excluded, being governed by the approved schools regulations considered in Chapter 8 below.
87 1933 Regulations, reg. 37.
88 Ibid. reg. 42.
89 Ibid. reg. 45.

house or premises which were licensed for the sale of any excisable liquor,[90] nor in a foster home in which a certified lunatic or mentally defective person was residing.[91] Even when none of these exclusions applied, no more than two children could be boarded-out at one address, unless of the same family "whom it is desirable to keep together"; and boarding-out was not permitted in foster homes where there were more than four other boys or girls resident.[92] Education authorities were able to board children in the areas of other authorities,[93] though some attempt was made to control the danger of too many boarded-out children being sent to particular areas: the Scottish Education Department had the power to inform local education authorities not to send children to specified districts.[94]

The 1947 Rules and Regulations repeated the exclusions in the 1933 Regulations and added some new ones. No child was to be boarded-out in a house that was unsanitary, did not have appropriate sleeping accommodation or was too far (taking account of transport facilities) from the school the child was to attend;[95] with a person in receipt of public assistance, or by reason of age or ill-health was not fit to care for a child;[96] or in a household that included a mentally defective person, someone suffering from pulmonary tuberculosis, or someone who had been convicted of an offence rendering the person unfit to have the care of a child.[97] And no child could be boarded-out in an environment that was "likely to be detrimental to the child".[98] The local authority had to satisfy itself through "all necessary enquiries" that any person whom it proposed to select as a foster parent for the care of boarded-out children was "of good character and [was] in all respects fit to look after the health, education and general well-being of children."[99]

Another exclusion was to be found in the new definition of "foster parent" in the 1947 Rules and Regulations: "a husband and wife, or a woman, with whom a child is boarded-out by a local authority".[100] This had the effect of excluding single men and unmarried couples from acting as foster parents.

90 Ibid. reg. 43.
91 Ibid. reg. 44.
92 Ibid. reg. 41.
93 Ibid. reg. 48.
94 Ibid. reg. 46.
95 1947 Rules and Regulations, art. 10(1).
96 Ibid. Art. 10(2).
97 Ibid. Art. 10(3).
98 Ibid. Art. 10(4).
99 Ibid. Art. 7.
100 Ibid. Art. 2.

The exclusion of single men may well be explained by official suspicion of a man's motives in wanting a child in his home, or perhaps by the social understanding of the time that caring for children was simply not man's work. The exclusion of couples who were unmarried probably reflected the belief that such couples were unlikely to be as stable as married couples, or that they would give the wrong moral message to impressionable children. Similar exclusions survived in the secondary legislation until 2009, though latterly limited to gay couples. The 1947 Rules and Regulations also required, again for the first time, that the local authority be satisfied as to the suitability of the chosen foster parents for the individual child.[101] The foster parent had where possible to be matched to the child's religious persuasion,[102] and so far as reasonably practicable, children of the same family were to be boarded-out in the same house.[103] Unless of the same family, no more than three children were to be boarded-out in the same house at the same time.[104]

The 1959 Regulations built upon this model, though with more detail being specified as to how the local authority or voluntary organisation were to assess prospective foster parents: this was to be done by making enquiries of persons to whom the prospective foster parent was known, in order to determine that he or she was of good character and in all respects suitable to look after the child.[105] Local authorities and voluntary organisations were also required to obtain and consider reports on the circumstances of the child's home and of the circumstances in which he or she came into care as well as a written report on the child's physical and mental health.[106] The proposed foster home had to be visited before the child was boarded-out to ensure that the home and the household were likely to be suitable for the child.[107]

Monitoring and visiting of boarded-out children

The 1933 Regulations required various officials of the local (education) authority to visit all the boarded-out children for whom they were responsible. The authority's medical officer was required to visit each child, in

---

101 Ibid. Art. 8.
102 Ibid. Art. 8.
103 Ibid. Art. 9.
104 Ibid. Art. 11.
105 1959 Regulations, reg. 5.
106 Ibid. reg. 2.
107 Ibid. reg. 7.

their foster home, every six months,[108] and an authority visitor was required to visit each child (again in their foster home[109]) within one month of the child's placement there and thereafter at least once every three months.[110] Half-yearly reports had to be submitted to the authority by the visitor.[111] A representative of the Scottish Education Department could visit the child at any time.[112] The 1947 Rules and Regulations imposed on local authorities an additional requirement to ensure that each child was allocated an officer who would supervise that child while he or she was boarded-out,[113] and that officer was obliged to visit the child and report to the local authority on a variety of stated matters, including the child's wellbeing and progress at school, his or her after-school activities and, interestingly, any complaint made by or concerning the child.[114] These visits had to be within one month of the boarding-out of the child and thereafter at intervals of not more than six months. This was a reduction in frequency from the previous requirement of three monthly visits, probably in response to the 1946 Clyde Report's suggestion that foster parents once (well) selected ought not to be burdened with too intrusive a visiting regime.

Under the 1959 Regulations, an officer of the local authority or voluntary organisation had to visit the child within two months of the initial boarding-out and thereafter at intervals of not more than three months, seeing the child, the foster home and foster parent, and writing a report thereon.[115] The local authority or voluntary organisation was obliged to terminate the boarding-out of a child with a particular foster parent "if it appears to them that it is no longer in the best interests of the child to be boarded-out with that foster parent."[116] This was much broader than the previous Regulations, where the local authority could bring the boarding-out to an end only on a foster parent's failure to satisfy the conditions in the Regulations. The new rule had the effect of requiring the local authority to take their on-going monitoring role far more seriously than before. And frequency of visitation, it will be noted, was restored to its pre-1947 level.

---

108 1933 Regulations, reg. 49.
109 Visiting the children at school was explicitly disallowed.
110 1933 Regulations, reg. 50.
111 Ibid. reg. 50.
112 Ibid. reg. 51.
113 1947 Rules and Regulations, Arts 14–15, 17.
114 Ibid. Arts 16 and 18.
115 1959 Regulations, reg. 13.
116 Ibid. reg. 16.

The role of the foster parent

The nature of the care and training expected to be provided by foster parents was set out in the 1933 Regulations in revealingly specific terms:

The foster-parents shall be required

(a) to give boys and girls the care and attention necessary for their proper training in habits of punctuality and thrift, of good manners and language, of cleanliness and neatness, of cheerful obedience to duty, of consideration and respect for others, and of honour and truthfulness to word and act,

(b) to notify the Education Authority of any material facts regarding the boys and girls (e.g. illness, accident) and

(c) to endeavour, in conjunction with the Education Authority, to find employment for the boys and girls when they leave school.[117]

The Schedule to the 1947 Rules and Regulations laid down a statement of principles that foster parents were expected to adhere to, in language that clearly assumed that boarding-out was a long-term arrangement for the upbringing and not merely the temporary care of the child:

In boarding children with foster-parents the object is to ensure that they are brought up in the atmosphere of a good and secure home. Foster-parents shall accordingly bring up a child placed by the local authority in their custody as one of their own children and devote to this duty the care which good parents give to their children. To this end, foster-parents should act in accordance with . . .

various listed principles, including the provision of wholesome and varied food, clothing in good repair, and appropriate sleeping arrangements.

Of particular note is Principle 5, which reads as follows:

5. *Training and Discipline.*
   a. Each child shall be brought up in accordance with his or her religious persuasion.
   b. The foster-parent shall train each child in habits of punctuality and thrift, of good manners and language, of cleanliness and neatness, of self-respect, of consideration and respect for others, and of honour and truthfulness in word and act.[118]
   c. Each child shall also be brought up in habits of industry, but shall be given adequate opportunity for play and recreation.
   d. Each child of school age shall, if his or her health permits, be sent regularly to school.
   e. Wherever possible each child shall be encouraged to join some juvenile organisation.
   f. The foster-parent shall not administer indiscriminate or harsh punishment. Persistent misconduct by the child shall be reported to the local authority . . .

---

117 1933 Regulations, reg. 40.

118 Much of this paragraph is repeated from the 1933 Regulations, r. 40, though the requirement there to train the child in "cheerful obedience to duty" was dropped.

Other principles required the foster-parent to co-operate with the local authority and to return the child to the authority whenever it demanded. Nothing equivalent appeared in the 1959 Regulations.

Parents

Throughout this period, there was little attempt in either the primary or the secondary legislation to engage with the parents or afford them a significant role in the life of their child while boarded-out. The twin assumptions were made that the very purpose of boarding the child out was to insulate him or her from bad parental influences and that in order to achieve that aim, the separation was for the long term. Under the 1933 Regulations, boarded-out children were allowed to receive letters from their parents, as well as visits from parents or guardians "at such reasonable intervals as the Education Authority may determine".[119] The matter was very much in the control of the education authority, who could "suspend the privilege in any particular case if they are satisfied that it is in the interests of the boy or girl to do so".[120] The conceptualisation of parental visits as a "privilege" is to be noted. Parents lost their rights on the making of the fit person order, and the concept of children's rights had, of course, yet to enter our consciousness. The rights of parents were weakened further by the 1947 Rules and Regulations, which reflected an increasing suspicion of parents where children had been removed from their care. Parents were allowed to require the local authority to furnish them with periodical reports as to the welfare and progress of the child while boarded-out with a fit person, but the onus was on the parent to ask; they were also permitted, unless (in the opinion of the local authority) it would be against the interests of the child, to communicate with their child or with the foster parent, either directly or through the office of the local authority.[121] The same article provided that "in exceptional circumstances the local authority may permit the parents to visit the child."[122] Under the 1933 Rules, visits could exceptionally be prohibited: now they were to be exceptionally permitted. Power remained with the local authority, whose discretion in the matter could not be challenged.[123]

---

119 1933 Regulations, reg. 53.
120 Ibid. reg. 53.
121 1947 Rules and Regulations, art. 33.
122 The foster parent was obliged to follow the local authority's instructions on this matter: 1947 Rules and Regulations, Schedule, para 10.
123 As late as 1982 the House of Lords affirmed that discretion to allow contact lay with local

Under the 1959 Regulations, boarding-out continued to be seen as a mechanism to provide the child with a substitute family for the rest of his or her childhood, and the only role for the parents specified was to be informed of the address of the foster home (unless the care authority or voluntary organisation considered that would be against the interests of the child)[124] and to be informed if the child died, ran away or fell seriously ill.[125] There was nothing in these Regulations about parental contact either direct or indirect, nor any requirement to attempt rehabilitation of the child with his or her birth family.

THE 1959 MEMORANDUM ON THE BOARDING-OUT OF CHILDREN

Shortly after the making of the 1959 Regulations, the Scottish Home Department published a *Memorandum on the Boarding-Out of Children*[126] in which it examined whether more changes were required. Many of the themes of the 1946 Clyde Report and the 1950 Scottish Advisory Council Report were repeated, which suggests that little on the ground had changed in the preceding decade. The Memorandum continued to view fostering as a long-term solution based on a family replacement model, as opposed to a short-term measure designed to give space for work to allow the child to be returned home:

> Boarding-out is a great deal more than the finding of a house in which the child may be given bed and board, kept reasonably clean, and sent regularly to school. It is, in its essential meaning, the creation of a home for the child. While by happy chance a foster home may sometimes so suit a particular child that the foster home quickly replaces, or largely replaces, his own, the normal experience is that the creation of a home is a slow, deliberate process in which child, foster-parent and boarding-out officer all play their different parts. It is not an easy task for any one of the three, and least of all for the child, whose reactions in a strange and bewildering situation must be understood sympathetically by the other two.[127]

authorities and that the court had no power to review the merits of their decision – except as being "*Wednesbury* unreasonable": *A v Liverpool City Council* [1982] AC 363. Writing of English law, see Masson, J. "Contact Between Parents and Children in Long-Term Care: the Unresolved Dispute" (1990) 4 *International Journal of Law and the Family* 97.

124 1959 Regulations, reg. 11(1).

125 Ibid. reg. 15.

126 HMSO, 1959: available at <https://archive.org/stream/op1266365-1001/op1266365-1001_djvu. txt> (last accessed 12 July 2019).

127 1959 Memorandum, para 6.

Nevertheless, the 1959 Memorandum is significant in being the first official statement that recognises a continuing role for the birth parents, and
there are signs of a weakening of the long-held perception that boarding-out
was a means of insulating the child from his or her birth family:

> The relationship of the boarded-out child to natural parents and relatives will
> present the boarding-out officer and the foster parent with delicate and difficult
> problems. In the light of the circumstances of the child, agreement will have to
> be reached between the boarding-out officer and the foster parents as to whether
> regular contact with the natural parents and relatives should be encouraged. It is
> frequently the impression of foster parents that, if contact is encouraged between
> the child and his parents and relatives, the child is likely to become unsettled
> and less responsive to their authority. It is vital that the foster parent should be
> guided by the boarding-out officer in this matter: such guidance should result
> in an understanding that their relationship to the child need not necessarily be
> impaired by the natural relationship to parents and relatives, which relationship
> is fundamental. It is recognised that in many cases it will be undesirable that the
> child should receive letters from his parents; but, wherever there is no reason for
> preventing this, such correspondence should be encouraged and the child trusted
> to maintain it. The boarding-out officer and the foster parent should exercise
> their discretion in scrutinising letters received and sent.[128]

The 1959 Memorandum also recognised that short-term boarding-out,
which was beginning to become more common by the late 1950s, would be
subject to very different considerations:

> Where the boarding-out is likely to be for a comparatively short period,
> and the return of the child to his own home almost certain, it is most desirable
> that regular contact with the natural parents and relatives should be maintained
> . . .
>
> An increasing proportion of children are received into care for short periods
> only, often until the mother returns from hospital or other domestic difficulties
> are overcome. These are normal children who have not been neglected. On
> coming into care they may be upset at first but will quickly recover their confi-
> dence if tactfully and sympathetically handled, and to this end suitable short-term
> foster homes, if they can be found, could make a very valuable contribution.[129]

Interestingly, the Memorandum suggested that boarding-out with a relative "is often to be preferred to boarding him [or her] out with strangers"
– though "the mere fact of relationship does not by itself make the relatives
good foster parents".[130] And it stated that children should never be brought
up to believe that the foster parents were their natural parents.[131] The con-

128 Ibid. para 26.
129 Ibid. paras 28–31.
130 Ibid. para 22.
131 Ibid. para 30.

ceptualisation of boarding-out as a permanent solution to a child's situation involving in all cases a replacement family was beginning to lose its grip.

The old fear of inappropriate motivations in those seeking to become foster parents resurfaced in the 1959 Memorandum:

> When a boarding-out officer is considering whether particular persons would make good foster parents, the first question which will arise in his mind is: "Why is a child wanted in this home?" The answer to that question is vital. If the boarding-out officer has reason to believe that the desire of the foster parents is to help a child by giving him a real home in which his life may develop naturally, then there already exists the basic condition from which a satisfying relationship of mutual affection and trust will grow. But if the boarding-out officer suspects that the potential foster parents have been prompted by a transient enthusiasm or by purely financial motives or by the idea of benefiting ultimately from the help a child might give in the house, on the farm or in the shop, he should exercise the greatest caution in coming to a decision. A foster child may be expected to help in the home or shop to the same extent as a child born in the home, but not to any greater extent. It would be an unwarranted risk to accept an offer of a home from foster parents whose uppermost thought was to make use of the child's services. A child exists in his own right and not as a means to an easier life for the foster parents.[132]

As a snapshot at the end of the period governed by the Children Act, 1948, the Secretary of State for Scotland reported that, on 30 November 1968, "6,207 children were boarded-out with foster parents (i.e., about 58 per cent of those in care)".[133]

C. BOARDING-OUT AND FOSTERING AFTER 1968

THE SOCIAL WORK (SCOTLAND) ACT 1968 AND THE CHILDREN (SCOTLAND) ACT 1995

The Social Work (Scotland) Act 1968 effected a substantial restructuring of the way that local authorities in Scotland provided social services. The children's hearing, created by the 1968 Act, had far more control than the previous juvenile court had in identifying the foster placement for the child. The juvenile court would simply name the local authority as a fit person to whom it was committing the child's care, leaving it to the local authority to board the child out if and as it saw fit. The children's hearing, on the other hand, acquired the power to place the child in a named foster home, though

---

132 Ibid. para 15.
133 *Child Care in Scotland, 1968* (Cmnd 4069), para 24.

it would do so only on the recommendation of the local authority, and only when satisfied that the foster parent and the placement of the child with him or her had been approved under the various Regulations considered below.[134] And the children's hearing never operated with a preconceived notion that boarding-out was better for the individual child in front of it than institutional care: the boarding-out preference that had so characterised the Children Act, 1948 was not repeated in the 1968 Act.

The Children (Scotland) Act 1995 made no substantive changes to the fostering regime, but the changes in both concepts and terminology effected by the 1995 Act required the replacement of the Boarding-out and Fostering of Children (Scotland) Regulations 1985 with the Fostering of Children (Scotland) Regulations 1996. As well as changing the language of "children in care" to "looked after children", the old terminology of "boarding-out", which had become "boarding-out and fostering" in the 1985 Regulations discussed below,[135] was finally replaced with, simply, "fostering". Also, the individual who had originally been the "guardian" in the legislation before the Care and Training Regulations, 1933, thereafter the "foster parent", was after 1996 to be known as the "foster carer". These changes are not to be dismissed as merely semantic, for they reflect the change in perception of the very nature of fostering. By the 1960s fostering no longer aimed at the creation of an ersatz family for a child, and by the 1990s it had become one of the range of mechanisms by which a child could be looked after by a non-parental carer, and could itself cover a range of temporary, long-term and even permanent placements. The language of "carer" instead of "parent" was also consistent with the increased professionalisation of the fostering role.

THE FOSTERING REGULATIONS 1985 AND 1996

Though the Social Work (Scotland) Act 1968 Act had given the Secretary of State power to make regulations governing how local authorities exercised their boarding-out functions,[136] new regulations were not made to replace the 1959 Regulations until the Boarding-out and Fostering of Children

---

134 As envisaged by the Kilbrandon Report, the Social Work (Scotland) Act 1968 had no place for "fit person" orders: both these orders and approved school orders were subsumed into the supervision requirement that might or might not contain provisions naming where the child was to live, and with whom: see Kilbrandon Committee Report, para 158.

135 Though the substantive provisions referred only to "fostering".

136 Social Work (Scotland) Act 1968, s. 5.

(Scotland) Regulations 1985.[137] These were themselves replaced by the Fostering of Children (Scotland) Regulations 1996,[138] which followed the Children (Scotland) Act 1995.

While the earlier Regulations had been based on the old perception of boarding-out as a long-term solution replacing one family environment with another, the 1985 and 1996 Regulations clearly saw fostering as a temporary placement, at least for most children. A continuing role in the child's life was now given to the child's birth parents: the care authority and foster parent were required to agree the arrangements to be made in respect of contact between the child and his or her family.[139]

Fostering panels and fostering agreements

As well as reflecting a shift in understanding of the very purpose of fostering, the 1985 Regulations introduced two major innovations. First, they regularised and strengthened the mechanism by which care authorities (that is to say local authorities and voluntary organisations who cared for children) identified and approved persons who would be suitable to act as foster parents. Previously it had been left to individual authorities and organisations to work out their own mechanisms, but the 1985 Regulations obliged each of them to establish fostering panels to perform that role.[140] The fostering panel's functions were to "consider every person referred to it by the care authority as a prospective foster parent" and to make recommendations to the care authority as to the suitability of such a person to act as a foster parent either for any child, any category of child or any particular child.[141] In considering the recommendations made by its fostering panel, the care authority had to have regard to its duties under s. 20 of the 1968 Act[142] to give first consideration to the need to safeguard and promote the welfare of the child throughout his or her childhood and to give due consideration to the ascertainable wishes and feelings of the child, having regard to his or

---

137 SI 1985/1799. These regulations were based to a large extent on *Proposals for Regulations on the Fostering of Children Under the Social Work (Scotland) Act 1968*, produced by the Social Work Services Group in December 1984.

138 SI 1996/3263.

139 1985 Regulations, reg. 23; 1996 Regulations, sched. 3 para 6.

140 1985 Regulations, reg. 4.

141 Ibid. reg. 6(1).

142 1968 Act, s. 20, as substituted by s. 79 of the Children Act 1975 and amended by the Health and Social Services and Social Security Adjudications Act 1983, sched. 2 para 5(a).

her age and understanding.[143] Bearing that in mind, the care authority could approve a person as a potential foster parent only if satisfied that that person was a suitable person with whom to place children.[144] The 1996 Regulations removed the role of voluntary organisations in fostering panels, which were now the sole responsibility of local authorities. They also added factors that had to be taken into account in determining whether to approve a person as a foster carer, including their previous experience in bringing up children and their motivations for wanting to be a foster carer.[145] The rule that foster carers had to be either married couples or single women was modified by the 1985 Regulations, and from then children could only be fostered in a household that comprised a man and a woman living and acting jointly together, or a man or a woman living and acting alone.[146] Though this opened fostering to unmarried cohabiting couples and (non-related) single men, the rule was structured to ensure that same-sex couples remained absolutely and in all circumstances barred irrespective of whatever they could offer any individual child. (Single gay men or lesbians were not excluded automatically but were unlikely to be approved as "suitable" given the mind-set of the time that regarded parenting by same-sex couples as axiomatically inimical to the interests of children.)[147]

The second innovation in the 1985 Regulations was to require the care authority (after 1996 the local authority alone) and approved foster parents to enter into a fostering agreement, dealing with (i) matters relating to the care to be provided for any children who might be placed with foster parents, including details of the financial arrangements; (ii) the care authority's policies and practice regarding the welfare of children for whom it had responsibility, the ways foster parents would be expected to follow these policies and practices and the assistance to be provided by the care authority to that effect; and (iii) the arrangements made by the care authority to review "at appropriate intervals" its approval of foster parents for the purposes of the regulations.[148] Foster parents were becoming thereby much more under the control of care authorities, not only in their initial selection but also in how they carried out their tasks as foster parents. It is from this

---

143 1985 Regulations, reg. 6(2).
144 Ibid. reg. 7.
145 1996 Regulations, sched. 1.
146 1985 Regulations, reg. 14. This was replicated in the 1996 Regulations, reg. 12(4).
147 It is not the place here to expose the fallacy inherent in this mind-set, but it is worth referencing the words, wise before their time, of Lord Kilbrandon in *Re D (An Infant) (Adoption: Parent's Consent)* 1977 AC 602, pp. 641–642.
148 1985 Regulations, reg. 8.

point that the role of foster parents starts to become a quasi-professional provision of services, as opposed to simply the altruistic opening of their family to a needy child. The reference to "financial arrangements" is consistent with this development and the earlier prohibition on boarding children out with persons who depend for their living mainly on payments received for accommodating children was not repeated in the 1985 Regulations. But allowances, rather than a salary, is what was envisaged. To these agreements the 1996 Regulations added details of the support and training to be given to the foster carer, the procedure for handling complaints against the foster carer and the foster carer's obligation to care for the child placed with the foster carer as if he or she was a member of that person's family and in a safe and appropriate manner and to promote his or her welfare having regard to the local authority's immediate and longer-term arrangements for the child.[149] The foster relationship had by now settled into one for the provision of services (the performance of the duties of the local authority), for which the carer was trained, albeit the level of care to be shown was that which the carer would show to his or her own children. But there were differences: in particular, a prohibition on the foster carer administering corporal punishment was to be included in the foster carer agreement.[150] Parents remained for another quarter-century able to visit corporal punishment on their own children.

Monitoring and termination of placement

The 1985 Regulations required the care authority to ensure that the child and foster parent were visited within one week of the placement (previously, it had been within two months) and thereafter at intervals of no more than three months, as well as "on such other occasions as the care authority considers necessary in order to supervise the child's welfare and to give support and assistance to the person caring for him".[151] The placement had to be terminated as soon as practicable where it appeared to the care authority that it was no longer in the child's best interests to be cared for by the person fostering him or her under the Regulations.[152] Likewise, if the local authority responsible for giving effect to a supervision requirement which contained a condition that the child reside with a person other than his or her parent

149 1996 Regulations, sched. 2 paras 1, 3 and 8.
150 1996 Regulations, sched. 2 para 6.
151 1985 Regulations, reg. 18.
152 Ibid. reg. 19.

or guardian came to the view that it was no longer in the child's interests to reside there, they had to refer the case to the reporter to arrange a children's hearing to review the child's case.[153] This imposed an important continuous overseeing role on local authorities even when a voluntary organisation was the care authority.

ARRANGEMENTS TO LOOK AFTER CHILDREN (SCOTLAND) REGULATIONS 1996

Children fostered by local authorities became "looked after children" under the Children (Scotland) Act 1995, and the Arrangements to Look After Children (Scotland) Regulations 1996[154] dealt with such matters as parental contact, care plans and visitation. They required the making of a care plan addressing both the immediate and the long-term needs of the looked after child, including the time when the child would no longer be a looked after child.[155] In determining an appropriate placement for the child, the local authority was required to consider the promotion of contact between the child and his or her family and others and the child's educational needs.[156] The child's case was required to be reviewed to ensure the care plan remained appropriate within six weeks of the placement, then three months later and thereafter every six months.[157] The child and the person with whom he or she was fostered, had to be visited by a representative of the local authority within one week of the placement, thereafter at least every three months, as well as whenever it was considered necessary to safeguard and promote the child's health, development and welfare, and whenever reasonably requested by the child or foster carer.[158] The local authority had to terminate the placement where for any reason it appeared to them no longer to be in the child's best interests to remain there.[159]

---

153 Ibid. reg. 21(3).
154 SI 1996/3262.
155 Arrangements to Look After Children (Scotland) Regulations 1996, regs 3–6 and sched. 1.
156 Arrangements to Look After Children (Scotland) Regulations 1996, reg. 5.
157 Ibid. regs 8 and 9.
158 Ibid. reg. 18.
159 Ibid. reg. 19.

LOOKED AFTER CHILDREN (SCOTLAND) REGULATIONS 2009

Both the Fostering of Children (Scotland) Regulations 1996 and the Arrangements to Look After Children (Scotland) Regulations 1996 were replaced by the Looked After Children (Scotland) Regulations 2009,[160] which continue to govern public fostering arrangements today.[161]

The 2009 Regulations finally removed the bar on same-sex couples acting as foster carers, so there is now no limitation on the type of family structure that potential foster carers must belong to: foster carers are assessed as suitable according to their own merits, without legally specified preconceptions about their lifestyles. Perhaps the most important development, however, in the 2009 Regulations is the provision that the local authority may not place a child with a foster carer unless it is satisfied that they have given full consideration to the possibility of entering into an arrangement for the child to be cared for by parents or persons with parental responsibilities and parental rights.[162] This creates a requirement to explore keeping the child at home and is designed to ensure that the local authority is convinced that removal of the child to foster care would be better for the child than the child remaining at home.

Voluntary organisations, which lost some of their monitoring role in 1996, may still be involved in fostering, but to do so they have to be a "registered fostering service", that is to say, an organisation registered as such under the Regulation of Care (Scotland) Act 2001, and subsequently the Public Services Reform (Scotland) Act 2010. Whenever a child is placed with a foster carer by a registered fostering service, the local authority must arrange for one of their officers to visit the child within 28 days of the placement; the local authority must also arrange to visit the child within 14 days of receiving representations from the registered fostering service that there are circumstances relating to the child which require a visit; and it must arrange to visit the child not later than three days from the day it is informed (by anyone) that the welfare of the child may not be or is not being safeguarded and promoted.[163]

---

160 SSI 2009/210, reg. 52.
161 For a detailed description of these Regulations, see Wilkinson A. and Norrie K. *The Law Relating to Parent and Child in Scotland* (W. Green, 3rd edn 2013), paras 15.36–15.41.
162 Looked After Children (Scotland) Regulations 2009, reg. 27(2).
163 Ibid. reg. 49.

LOOKING TO THE FUTURE OF FOSTERING: THE NATIONAL FOSTER CARE REVIEW

In December 2013 the Looked After Children Strategic Implementation Group published their *Final Report*,[164] which made a number of recommendations, including that there should be clear national descriptors of the various types of foster placement. Foster care by then had not for some decades been a single, invariable, outcome but now covered a variety of placements. The Report also recommended that foster carers should be required to undertake mandatory training (both initial and on-going). This goes a long way to foster care being recognised as a truly professional activity. Consistent with that development, allowances and fees should, the Review recommended, be examined, particularly in light of the increasingly complex needs of children in foster care. Especially contentious was the issue of whether fees (that is to say, payment for work performed) should be paid to foster carers, which would turn the existing quasi-professional role into a fully professional one and the Review itself set out the arguments without making a final recommendation one way or the other.

Many of these issues had been consulted upon by the Scottish Government as it prepared a new Children and Young People (Scotland) Bill.[165] But other than in relation to kinship care, discussed immediately below, the issues of training, allowances and fees were not dealt with in the Act that followed:[166] rather, statements of standards were published by the Scottish Government on training and core allowances.[167] What it means to be a foster carer remains at the time of writing in a state of some flux, and all that can be said with confidence is that the concept is today very different from what it was assumed to be less than fifty years ago.

---

164 Available at <https://www.celcis.org/files/5814/3878/4789/Foster-Care-Review-Final-Report. pdf> (last accessed 12 July 2019).

165 *A Scotland for Children: A Consultation on the Children and Young People (Scotland) Bill* (Scottish Government, July 3, 2012).

166 Children and Young People (Scotland) Act 2014.

167 See *The Standard for Foster Care* (Scottish Social Services Council, 2017); Button, D. *Research into Core Child Allowances for Foster Carers* (Scottish Government Social Research, 2014).

D. KINSHIP CARE

INTRODUCTION

The original "fit person order" made by the court under the pre-1932 legislation was designed to allow another, and more responsible, family member to take over the upbringing of the child. In the middle decades of the twentieth century, however, attitudes to unsatisfactory birth families hardened and the assumption developed that the best protection for children whose families had let them down was to insulate them from these families as much as possible. So, as we saw above, the Children and Young Persons (Scotland) Act, 1932 transformed fit person orders into a mechanism for the removal of children from their wider families. Towards the end of the twentieth century, however, much more emphasis began to be placed on the hope and expectation that children fostered by the state would be able to return to their own parents, and the need to remove familial influences was no longer a motivating consideration. At the same time, local authorities began to experience difficulties in attracting sufficient numbers of foster carers, a problem exacerbated by the increasingly diverse population in Scotland, which made placing children with carers of the same religious, ethnic and even linguistic background more and more challenging. So attention turned again to the possibility of other family members taking over the care of children who were the legal responsibility of the local authority. Many children with unsatisfactory parents have more stable grandparents, aunts and uncles, and even elder siblings, and in a significant number of cases an informal arrangement would be made for these other family members to step in, either on an emergency basis or on a more long-term basis.

However, there existed a number of inhibitions to accessing care offered by a child's wider family, notwithstanding the increasing acceptance that keeping a child within their family environment was actually good social policy. Such family members had seldom been through the formal process of becoming approved foster carers with the result that any such placement had to remain informal, even although the arrangement was frequently the best (or least worst) for the child. And of course, informal arrangements excluded the family carers from any fostering allowances that would be paid to approved foster carers, and from any support that local authorities provided to foster carers.

In 2007, therefore, the Scottish Government and the Convention of Scottish Local Authorities (COSLA) drafted a kinship and foster care strategy,[168] which included an agreement to pay an allowance to kinship carers of looked after children and to fund an advice service for kinship carers. The policy of encouraging kinship care seems to be working. It was reported in a SPICe Briefing published in 2016[169] that until the late 1990s less than 10% of all children looked after by local authorities were in kinship care placements; by 2012 that figure had risen to around a quarter; and by 2015 the figure was 27%. The Briefing also noted, however, that there were wide variations in the use of kinship care across different local authorities in Scotland.[170]

KINSHIP CARE UNDER THE LOOKED AFTER CHILDREN (SCOTLAND) REGULATIONS 2009

The 2009 Regulations provide for the approval by the local authority of (a) a person who is related to the child either by blood, marriage or civil partnership or (b) a person who is known to the child and with whom the child has a pre-existing relationship as a suitable carer for a child who is looked after by that local authority, that person to be known as a "kinship carer".[171] Before approving a person as a kinship carer the local authority must, so far as reasonably practicable, obtain and record in writing certain specified information,[172] including in respect of the prospective carer and other adults in the household, particulars of the accommodation, the standard of living and other matters relating to the capacity of the proposed carer to care for the child. Taking this information into account, the local authority must carry out an assessment of the person's suitability to care for the child.[173] The Scottish Government provides guidance on the process for approval.[174] The local authority must not place the child with a kinship carer unless it is satisfied that

(i)   placement is in the best interests of the child,
(ii)   placement with that kinship carer is in the best interests of the child,
(iii) the kinship carer is a suitable person to care for the child,
(iv)   the local authority has taken into account all the information available to it and
(v)   the kinship carer has entered into written agreements with the local authority concerning the matters listed in Schedules 4 and 5 to the 2009 Regulations.

---

168 "Getting it Right for Every Child in Kinship and Foster Care" (2007).
169 *Kinship Care*, Scottish Parliament Information Centre, November 2016, p. 12.
170 Ibid. pp. 13–14.
171 2009 Regulations, reg. 10.
172 Ibid. sched. 3.
173 Ibid. reg. 10(3).
174 See *Guidance on the Looked After Children (Scotland) Regulations 2009 and the Adoption and Children (Scotland) Act 2007*, Scottish Government, March 2011. For a discussion, see *TM & PM, Petrs* 2017 CSOH 139.

The matters listed in Schedules 4 and 5 include

   (i)   the obligation to provide support and training to the kinship carer,

   (ii) the procedure for review of the placement,

   (iii) the respective obligations of the local authority and the kinship carer,[175]

   (iv) agreements for any financial support to be provided for the child,

   (v) the arrangements for visits to the child by or on behalf of the local authority, contact arrangements with the parents and other persons and

   (vi) co-operation with the local authority by the kinship carer.[176]

The visitation requirements[177] on local authorities apply equally to children placed with kinship carers as to those placed with foster carers. Allowances must be paid by local authorities to approved kinship carers, or kinship carers who act under a kinship care order (see immediately below), and they may in the discretion of the local authority be paid to any other kinship carer or guardian of the child under s. 22 of the Children (Scotland) Act 1995.[178] There is, however, no national rate for payment of allowances, which remains a matter for each local authority.

KINSHIP CARE AND THE CHILDREN AND YOUNG PEOPLE (SCOTLAND) ACT 2014

The Children and Young People (Scotland) Act 2014 requires local authorities to offer "kinship care assistance" to any person who is considering applying for, or has obtained, a "kinship care order", that is to say an order under s. 11 of the Children (Scotland) Act 1995 applied for by a relative or friend of the child; assistance must also be given to the child.[179] The forms of assistance required are laid down in the Kinship Care Assistance (Scotland) Order 2016.[180] Assistance must be provided in a way that safeguards, supports and promotes the wellbeing of the child,[181] and it may include information and advice, as well as financial assistance both in making the application for the order and in fulfilling its terms.[182] The availability of this assistance must be publicised.[183]

---

175 These include an obligation not to administer corporal punishment: sched. 5 para 5(a).

176 2009 Regulations, reg. 11.

177 Ibid. reg. 46.

178 The provision of services to "children in need", as there defined.

179 Children and Young People (Scotland) Act 2014, s. 71.

180 SSI 2016/153.

181 2016 Order, Art. 3.

182 Ibid. Art. 4.

183 Ibid. Art. 9.

8. Institutional Care

INTRODUCTION

We have already seen that the preference in Scotland (sometimes legal, always factual) has long been for children who have had to be removed from their parents to be accommodated in domestic settings – in other words, boarded-out in a family environment with foster carers. Nevertheless, there have always been some cases in which it is necessary to accommodate children and young people in an institutional setting. But just as foster care offers individual children different experiences depending on the circumstances and character of the foster carer, so institutional care was and is composed of a wide variety of environments. Some set out to mimic as far as possible a family setting: the best known in Scotland was probably Quarrier's Homes, in rural Renfrewshire, which consisted of a number of detached houses each accommodating around 15 children and each house being

> under the charge of a lady or a married couple, who are known as the 'mother,' or the 'father and mother,' of the houses, and who exercise very much the same control over the children, in so far as their domestic life is concerned, as if they were their own.[1]

Other institutions, typically housing large numbers of children, were "cold and forbidding abodes".[2]

The nature of these institutions, their aims and philosophies, and the extent to which the state has been involved in their running, control or supervision, changed over time and the relationship between institutional care and the state today is very different from what it was 150 years ago. This chapter will look at the development of residential schools, before moving on to children's homes, and will end with an examination of how secure (locked) accommodation for children and young people evolved in Scotland.

---

1 *McFadzean v Kilmalcolm School Board* (1903) 5F 600, per Lord President Kinross, p. 610.
2 Clyde *Report of the Committee on Homeless Children* (1946, Cmnd 6911), para 45.

A. REFORMATORY AND INDUSTRIAL SCHOOLS

THE GROWTH OF REFORMATORY AND INDUSTRIAL SCHOOLS

The "reformatory movement" grew out of a number of disparate attempts across Europe to provide education and skills-training instead of punishment to children whose life circumstances had thrown them into criminality. In both France and Germany philanthropic societies and individuals had established institutions to accommodate such children from the early nineteenth century.[3] A small number of "schools of correction" were established in London in the 1820s and 1830s,[4] and in Scotland too. Ralston reports:

> The Dean Bank Institution for the Reformation of Female Delinquents was opened in Edinburgh in 1832 and Glasgow's House of Refuge for (male) Juvenile Offenders, which was founded in 1838, became the largest reformatory school in Britain and the only one to have a special Act of Parliament enabling it to finance its operations by a local assessment (Act for Repressing Juvenile Delinquency in the City of Glasgow, 4 and 5 Vict. Cap. xxxvi, 1841).[5]

Industrial schools, designed for the indigent rather than the offending child, appeared slightly later, and at the end of the nineteenth century it was said that "if London is regarded as the birth place of reformatory and industrial schools, Scotland claims to have been their cradle and nursery".[6] In 1841, at the instigation of the local sheriff, an industrial school was established in the city of Aberdeen for 20 boys who were involved in petty criminality, mostly begging: the attraction for the boys was to be the training in a trade, together with (or perhaps more especially because of) the hearty meals on offer to those who stayed at their lessons. Within two years the numbers of boys at the Aberdeen school had doubled and a similar establishment opened for girls.[7] The experiment was soon repeated in other

---

3 See Watson, J. "Reformatory and Industrial Schools" (1896) 59 *Journal of the Royal Statistical Society* 255. Holmes, H.T. *Reform of Reformatories and Industrial Schools* (Fabian Society, 1902), p. 5, describes some of the European equivalents. One of the best known was the *Rauhes Haus* (the "rough house") near Hamburg, established in 1833 and remembered today in the name of an underground railway station in Freie und Hansestadt Hamburg. So-called agricultural colonies were more common in France and Switzerland.

4 Watson, J. "Reformatory and Industrial Schools" (1896) 59 *Journal of the Royal Statistical Society* 255, p. 256.

5 Ralston, A. "The Development of Reformatory and Industrial Schools in Scotland 1832 to 1872" (1988) 8 *Journal of Scottish Historical Studies* 40, p. 42.

6 Watson, J. "Reformatory and Industrial Schools" (1896) 59 *Journal of the Royal Statistical Society* 255, p. 257.

7 Ibid. p. 258.

parts of Scotland,[8] typically through the efforts of philanthropic individuals, often connected to but by no means representing the state,[9] who were firm in the belief that children could be "saved" from the harmful influences that surrounded them. This thinking made little if any distinction between children of the indigent and children who offended, and though different schools had different focal points, there was from the start much overlap. Reformatory schools, which tended to be residential, were a manifestation of the growing belief that juvenile delinquency was as much a social as a criminal problem, from the consequences of which the youthful offender could with some intervention be saved;[10] industrial schools were designed to develop potential – and particularly employability – that indigent families could not themselves develop in their children and thereby to minimise the risk that the vagrant child would move from begging (a social problem) to stealing (a legal problem). At least in the early days, therefore, such institutions were driven by a desire to improve the lives of their inmates.[11] That they were responses to economic circumstances is clear from the comment by John Watson on the demographics of admissions to the Original Industrial School in Edinburgh in its first year of operation:

> Boys from Scotland 186; girls from Scotland 82
> Boys from England 11; girls from England 2
> Boys from Ireland 113; girls from Ireland 115

Writing in 1896 Watson says

> The disproportionate number of the Irish (nearly one half the whole) and the exceedingly small quantity (less than 3 per cent) of the English are noticeable features of this table, and are eloquent of the family circumstances of the two nationalities in the Scottish capital fifty years ago . . .[12]

The earliest legislation authorising such schools was the local Act of 1841, already referred to, "for repressing juvenile delinquency in the City of Glasgow". This Act vested the reformatory and industrial schools in that city

---

8 Ralston, A. "The Development of Reformatory and Industrial Schools in Scotland 1832 to 1872", (1988) 8 *Journal of Scottish Historical Studies* 40, p. 41.

9 Ralston, ibid. mentions a number of mid-nineteenth century sheriffs who were instrumental in setting up local schools for the sorts of children who commonly appeared before them.

10 Lord Low put it thus in *Sweenie v Hart* 1908 SC(J) 81, p. 82 "Reformatory schools have been established not only or mainly as a method of punishment, but for the better care and reformation of youthful offenders".

11 See Kelly, C. "Reforming Juvenile Justice in 19th Century Scotland: the Subvention of the Scottish Day Industrial Schools Movement" (2016) 20 *Crime, History and Societies* vol. 2, p. 1.

12 Watson, J. "Reformatory and Industrial Schools" (1896) 59 Journal of the Royal Statistical Society 255, p. 260.

in a board of commissioners to be appointed by the town council and gave authority to detain young persons for a term of years, so long as they consented. By this means, the young person avoided imprisonment. An application of the Act is shown in *HM Advocate v O'Brien & Ors*[13] where two young girls charged with theft had the proceedings against them discharged on their being admitted to the female "House of Refuge" in Glasgow, for three years in the case of one and five years in the case of the other. (A third accused went to trial and, on being found guilty, was sentenced to ten years deportation to Australia).

The reality of life in such schools, inevitably, was very varied. Industrial schools, in particular, were often established with a specific philosophy, whether religious or commercial, underpinning their operation. The Clyde Industrial Training Ship Association ran an industrial school on the *Cumberland*, and then the *Empress*,[14] both anchored in the Gareloch, while the *Mars*, an ex-Royal Navy ship anchored in the Tay at Wormit, was run by the Dundee-based Mars Training Ship Institution between 1869 and 1929. The aim of these was to train boys up for entry into the Royal Navy or the merchant marine.[15] Some schools (reformatory as well as industrial) were based on farms and provided agricultural training. Others, it was reported in a UK-wide survey published in 1902, provided out of date training of little practical value in the job market as it was developing then:

> Wood-chopping and gardening were considered sufficient for the boy, needlework and the washtub for the girl . . . Cheap tailoring and bootmaking, such as they generally teach, is useless as a means of livelihood, machine work in these industries having displaced hand labour . . .[16]

While the distinction between reformatory and industrial schools was clear in principle, it was less so in practice, particularly in Scotland where the boundaries between the two were from the earliest days porous.[17] This

13 (1845) 2 Broun 499.
14 The 13 year old Gilbert White was sent to this training school ship in *White v Jeans* 1911 SC(J) 88.
15 While this might have been the aim, the actuality was different. Watson, J. "Reformatory and Industrial Schools" (1896) 59 *Journal of the Royal Statistical Society* 255, p. 298 reports that in the years 1893 and 1894 of the 226 discharges from the *Empress* only 114 boys went to sea; of the 246 discharges from the *Mars* only 95 boys went to sea. He pointed out that the Royal Navy (unlike the Army) did not take boys from reformatories. In a House of Commons debate it was deprecated by the MP Admiral Field that "barely one-tenth of the whole go to sea": HC Deb. 23 March 1891 vol. 351 col. 1725.
16 Holmes, H.T. *Reform of Reformatories and Industrial Schools* (Fabian Society, 1902), pp. 8–9.
17 Ralston, A. "The Development of Reformatory and Industrial Schools in Scotland 1832 to 1872", (1988) *Journal of Scottish Historical Studies* 40, p. 42.

is unsurprising given that these schools were established as a result of local ad hoc initiatives which often designed their aims to include both, or at least made no distinction between children based on the cause of their need. There was throughout the nineteenth century a recuring debate as to the advisability of mixing the two types of child (the offender and the indigent) in the same institution[18] but the practical reality in a small country with limited means probably permitted no other approach. Though reformatories were clearly designed for those who had been convicted of offences, there were many more industrial schools and offenders were frequently accommodated there. Experience gained from this reality is likely to have shown that the needs of the two classes of children showed far more similarities than differences and Scotland's long experience of dealing with all children in the same way irrespective of what factor first justified state intervention may well be one of the reasons why we continue to be sanguine about doing so today.

REFORMATORY AND INDUSTRIAL SCHOOLS LEGISLATION 1854–1866

The earliest legislation which, interestingly, was limited to Scotland, reflected this overlap in the purpose of the existing reformatories and industrial schools. When the system was put onto a national basis in 1854, the terminology of reformatory school and industrial school was formalised, but the structure of the Act saw no clear distinction between the child needing reformation and the child needing a decent home. "Dunlop's Act", "An Act to render Reformatory and Industrial Schools in Scotland more available for the Benefit of vagrant Children"[19] carried the preamble: "WHEREAS it is expedient that Reformatory and Industrial Schools in Scotland should be made more available for the Education and Training of Vagrant Children. . . ." This allowed the sheriff to send to "any Reformatory School, Industrial School, or other similar institution within Scotland" a "vagrant child", that is to say a person under 14 years old who had been "found begging, or, not having any Home or settled Place of Abode or proper Guardianship, and having no lawful or visible Means of Subsistence, shall be found wander-

---

18 Ibid. pp. 48–49.

19 17 & 18 Vict. c. 74. Scotland was not alone in conflating the two categories of children at this time. In New Zealand industrial schools were established under an Act called the Neglected and Criminal Children Act 1867 (31 Vict. 1867 No. 14).

ing, and *though not charged with any actual Offence*.[20] Notably, it was the police who were charged with the task of bringing such children to court, making indigence as much a police matter as was crime, and making a reformatory school a place as suitable to send the vagrant child to as an industrial school. Attendance became enforceable for the first time and schools originally established as day schools became more and more residential.[21] Enforced detention at industrial schools[22] had little to distinguish it from enforced detention at reformatory schools, particularly since the aims remained the same: to effect a change in the life path of the child. In the same year Parliament passed, for the whole of the UK, the Youthful Offenders Act, 1854, which was more clearly limited to offenders. This gave the court power to send any offender aged under 16 to a reformatory school at the end of any sentence of more than 14 days, for a period of between two and five years. However, even although the institution may have been designed primarily to accommodate offenders, the length of detention clearly indicated an aim beyond punishment: it was designed to change the young person's life.

Watson reports a substantial increase in the total admissions to the Glasgow schools immediately following the passing of these Acts, for the system no longer depended on active co-operation from the bench.[23]

Later Acts attempted to draw a clearer line between the two types of school, but legislation never did so completely. The Reformatory Schools (Scotland) Act, 1856 provided that no school was to be certified as both reformatory and industrial,[24] but it did not prohibit offenders being sent to an industrial school, nor vagrants to a reformatory. The Industrial Schools (Scotland) Act, 1861 set out the categories of child liable to be sent to an industrial school by a court, and (completing the transformation of these schools into residential establishments) authorised the child's detention there until he or she reached the age of 15 years – after which the child could remain with their own consent[25] (suggesting the school could become

---

20 Reformatory and Industrial Schools (Scotland) Act, 1854, s. 1 (emphasis added).
21 Kelly, C. "Reforming Juvenile Justice in 19th Century Scotland: the Subvention of the Scottish Day Industrial Schools Movement" (2016) 20 *Crime, History and Societies* vol. 2, p. 1.
22 Wilfully leaving and refusing to return to the school to which the child had been sent under the 1854 Act attracted the penalty of whipping or imprisonment for up to 20 days: Reformatory and Industrial Schools (Scotland) Act, 1854, s. 2.
23 Watson, J. "Reformatory and Industrial Schools" (1896) 59 *Journal of the Royal Statistical Society* 255, p. 261.
24 Reformatory Schools (Scotland) Act, 1856, s. 10.
25 Industrial Schools (Scotland) Act, 1861, s. 14.

a refuge, or home, for a young adult). The categories listed included a child under 14 found begging or without a home or settled place of abode, a child under 14 who frequented the company of reputed thieves, and a child under 14 whose parent claimed to be unable to control him or her; in addition, the list included a child under 12 who had committed an offence.[26] So even when the boundary between the two types of school began to harden, a younger offender could still be sent to an industrial rather than a reformatory school. In both, the language of "detention" was deliberate. Another important development in the 1861 Act was that the child could be taken to the court by any person, whether a constable or not:[27] indigence was no longer to be seen as a police matter.

The UK-wide Industrial Schools Act, 1866 replaced the 1861 Act but retained most of the earlier rules. Any house of refuge for destitute children or industrial school "or other similar institution" was empowered (but not obliged) to receive children sent to it under the Act so long as it was certified as an industrial school.[28] The age at which a child detained in an industrial school was to be released increased from 15 to 16 years, though as before he or she could remain on giving written consent.[29]

The 1861 Act had provided that government certification for the running of an industrial school might be obtained if requested, though since government funding followed certification, there was a strong incentive for schools to make the request. Official certification was not, however, compulsory until the Industrial Schools Act, 1866 and the Reformatory Schools Act, 1866. As under the 1856 Act, a single school could not be certified as being both reformatory and industrial.[30] Government inspection was mandated for both[31] and schools lost thereby their wholly private character. "This was", in Kelly's words, "a prime example of philanthropic effort being co-opted by the state".[32] Nevertheless, they remained institutions mainly run by voluntary organisations, though after the Education (Scotland) Act, 1872 local schools boards established by that Act were permitted to establish and maintain certified industrial schools,[33] thereby making public pro-

---

26 Ibid. s. 9.
27 Ibid. s. 10.
28 Industrial Schools Act, 1866, s. 49.
29 Ibid. s. 41.
30 Ibid. s. 8.
31 Reformatory Schools Act, 1866, s. 5; Industrial Schools Act, 1866, s. 10.
32 Kelly, C. "Continuity and Change in the History of Scottish Juvenile Justice" (2016) 1 *Law Crime and History* 59, p. 64.
33 Education (Scotland) Act, 1872, s. 41.

vision for an endeavour which had before been almost entirely private and charitable.

As private institutions, reformatory and industrial schools were free to reject any child or class of child as they thought appropriate. This caused serious difficulties for certain types of child. Holmes, writing for the Fabian Society in 1902, reported that no school in Great Britain would take a mentally deficient child, nor an "immoral girl":[34] both categories of what today would be regarded as hugely vulnerable children were left, it seems, to their own devices. It may well have been felt that development of young people into productive citizens being the business of these schools, they had nothing to offer the mentally or morally deficient child. Society had not yet reached the point when child saving (which presupposes a capacity to be "saved") had become child protection (determined by the need for protection).

Under the 1866 legislation, an industrial school was defined as "a school in which Industrial Training is provided, and in which Children are lodged, clothed and fed, as well as taught".[35] Similarly, the managers of a certified reformatory school were obliged "to educate, clothe, lodge and feed" the inmates.[36] The duty to feed was a central element of industrial schools – and indeed, when non-residential, provided a strong inducement to the children of indigent parents to attend day schools regularly. In 1890 Rules and Regulations were drawn up which managers could use as models for their own schools and which had to be approved for certification:[37] these required "plain useful clothing" and "plain wholesome food" to be provided, as well as three hours daily of school education. "Industrial training" for boys was specified as "farm and garden work, and such handicrafts as can be conveniently practiced" and for girls was "needlework, washing and housework".

LATER NINETEENTH-CENTURY LEGISLATION

The Reformatory Schools Act, 1893 required that the period of detention be specified by the court as not less than three nor more than five years, but in no case for a period beyond the offender's 19th birthday.[38] The Day

---

34 Holmes, H.T. *Reform of Reformatories and Industrial Schools* (Fabian Society, 1902), p. 10.
35 Industrial Schools Act, 1866, s. 5.
36 Reformatory Schools Act, 1866, s. 8.
37 General Rules for the Management and Discipline of Certified Reformatory Schools, 1890; and General Rules for the Management and Discipline of Certified Industrial Schools, 1891.
38 In *Sweenie v Hart* 1908 SC(J) 81 a sentence of four years was quashed in respect of three boys already over 15 years old since it would take them beyond their 19th birthdays. Interestingly, the High Court of Justiciary speculated that it might have the power to modify the original sentence

Industrial Schools (Scotland) Act, 1893 allowed the court to send a child
to a day industrial school or to a residential industrial school on failure to
comply with an attendance order issued under the Education (Scotland)
Act, 1883:[39] this opened industrial schools to children who were not attending (normal) schools and is the first time school non-attendance was conceived as requiring an interventionist response. Finally, the Industrial
Schools Acts Amendment Act, 1894 provided that even after a child's
release from an industrial school he or she would remain under the supervision of the managers of the school until his or her 18th birthday. This
supervision allowed the managers to recall the child to the school if this was
"necessary for the protection of the child".[40] All this legislation had a place
for the protection of the interests of the child. Whether the residents took
comfort from that, or the staff kept the children's interests at the forefront
of their minds – or indeed whether the funding of the schools permitted
their aspirations to be achieved – were all different matters. Reformatory
and industrial schools were not comfortable or homely environments in
which to spend a part of one's childhood. Holmes[41] cites a Report of
HM Inspector from 1899, which contains this disturbing assessment of
Stranraer Reformatory:

> The general domestic arrangements of the school are not satisfactory: fleas
> appear to have got the upper hand, especially in the crowded attics. The school
> takes more boys than its buildings can justify, and in the struggle to make both
> ends meet the interests of the boys are apt to be lost sight of . . .

This is unlikely to have been a particularly uncommon situation in either
type of school. A few years later, Stranraer Reformatory appeared again in
the Law Reports, in a case in which the very nature of such an institution
was explored. In *Conolly v Managers of the Stranraer Reformatory*,[42] an
inmate of the school who had been put to work in a sawmill lost a finger
while operating a circular saw which he asserted was not properly fenced.
His action for damages would be time-barred if the defenders were a "public
authority", and that was the question before the court. The Lord Ordinary
held that the school was more closely analogous to a prison than a place for
the bringing up of children with the result that the institution was indeed

to conform with the time limits if satisfied that it was in the public interest to do so "and still more
in the interests of the offenders".

39 Day Industrial Schools (Scotland) Act, 1893, s. 4. See further, chapter 6 above.
40 Industrial Schools Acts Amendment Act, 1894, s. 1.
41 Holmes, H.T. *Reform of Reformatories and Industrial Schools* (Fabian Society, 1902), p. 5.
42 (1904) 11 SLT 638.

a public authority and the action, therefore, time-barred under the Public Authorities Protection Act, 1893.

By 1896, it was reported that there were 5,500 children kept as "inmates" in 43 certified institutions in Scotland.[43] Of these, in 1893, 33 were industrial schools.[44]

REFORMATORY AND INDUSTRIAL SCHOOLS UNDER THE CHILDREN ACT, 1908

The formal distinction between reformatory and industrial schools continued to be made by the Children Act, 1908, though by then, the practice of mixing children suitable for either in both being endemic, that distinction was becoming increasingly meaningless. One of the main policy objectives of the 1908 Act was to bring both types of school under the same regulatory regime. Both were defined effectively identically: s. 44 defined "industrial school" to mean "a school for the industrial training of children, in which children are lodged, clothed, and fed, as well as taught" and "reformatory school" to mean "a school for the industrial training of youthful offenders, in which youthful offenders are lodged, clothed, and fed, as well as taught".

Both types of school required state certification, and they were known, collectively, as "certified schools". Section 45 allowed the Secretary for Scotland to certify schools as fit for the reception of youthful offenders or children, without being limited to either reformatory or industrial: this marked the end of official efforts (never successful in Scotland) to keep the two types of school separate, and the previous prohibition on schools being certified as both was dropped. Schools, once certified, were to be inspected annually, and certification could be withdrawn, permanently or temporarily, if the Secretary for Scotland were dissatisfied with the condition, rules, management or superintendence of the school.[45] The state, both central and local government, paid for the maintenance of children in certified schools, and though parents could be required to contribute to the costs of maintenance,[46] it is unlikely that many did.

---

43 *Report of the Departmental Committee on Reformatory and Industrial Schools*, Cmnd 8204 (1896), pp. 8 and 132 (quoted in Kelly, C. "Continuity and Change in the History of Scottish Juvenile Justice" (2016) 1 *Law Crime and History* 59, p. 64).

44 Watson, J. "Reformatory and Industrial Schools" (1896) 59 *Journal of the Royal Statistical Society* 255, p. 276.

45 Children Act, 1908, s. 47.

46 Ibid. s. 75.

The managers of the certified school were statutorily obliged to "teach, train, lodge, clothe and feed" the child during the whole period of the child's residence.[47] Any child sent to a certified school who was under the age of eight years could be boarded-out with "any suitable person" until reaching the age of 10, and thereafter for such longer period (with the consent of the Secretary for Scotland) as the managers considered to be advisable in the interests of the child, though the managers retained responsibility for the child.[48] The managers had the power to make rules for the school but these required to be approved by the Secretary for Scotland.[49]

The overseeing power of the Secretary of State was transferred on 1 April 1920 to the Scottish Education Department (SED)[50] under s. 19 of the Education (Scotland) Act, 1918:[51] this served to emphasise the educational (reformative) as opposed to the punitive nature of the establishments. The SED made the Reformatory and Industrial Schools Regulations, 1921,[52] under which school premises were to be

> satisfactory as regards lighting, heating, ventilation, and sanitary condition, must provide adequate accommodation both for residential and instructional purpose, and must contain such equipment of workshops and special appliances as may be deemed necessary for securing the proper carrying on of the work of the institution.[53]

The (educational) qualifications of the school staff had to be approved by the SED, with teachers certified in particular subjects by the Department's normal regulations; staffing levels were required to be sufficient to meet the needs of the school.[54] The timetable and curriculum, both of education and general routine of the school, required to be approved by the Department.[55] Regulation 4 is, perhaps, the most significant for the oversight of reformatory and industrial schools. It provided that "An efficient Committee of Management must be appointed which should meet at the

---

47 Ibid. s. 52.
48 Ibid. s. 53.
49 Ibid. s. 54.
50 Established under the Education (Scotland) Act, 1872 (as the Scotch Education Department) then re-established (as the Scottish Education Department) under the Education (Scotland) Act, 1918.
51 Reformatory and Industrial Schools (Scotland) (Transfer of Powers) Order, 1920 (SR&O 1920 No. 429 (S. 40)).
52 These are reprinted in Roxburgh, R.W. *The Law of Education in Scotland* (Wm. Hodge, 1928), vol. 1 (no volume 2 ever appeared), pp.327–330.
53 1921 Regulations, reg. 1.
54 Ibid. reg. 2.
55 Ibid. reg. 3.

school at least once a quarter and arrange for some of the members to visit the school periodically". It is likely that the purpose of such visits was to allow the Committee to ensure the standards set out above continued to be met, and there was no specific obligation to inquire into the wellbeing of any individual child or to give them the opportunity to express concerns. The regulations concerned structural matters rather than care matters. And the qualifications of staff were educational rather than care qualifications (which at that point in time did not exist in any meaningful sense). It was recognised as early as 1928 that the quality of staff was a crucial element in the success of the institution, with the Morton Committee recommending that staffing at schools be considered carefully since the work "demands self-sacrifice, sympathy, unflagging energy and broad outlook".[56]

Whenever a child was sent to an industrial school, whether under s. 107 as an offender or under the care and protection provisions of s. 58, the period of detention was whatever to the court seemed proper for the teaching and training of the child, but in no case could extend beyond the child's 16th birthday.[57] That this was two years after the school leaving age suggests strongly that the child was expected to receive from an industrial school some form of industrial training, making him or her fit for the world of work. A youthful offender sent to a reformatory school would be kept there for a stated period of not less than three nor more than five years, and in any case not beyond the offender's 19th birthday.[58]

By 1931, it was reported that there were in Scotland "four reformatories containing 374 lads and nineteen industrial schools containing 1301 pupils".[59] This is a substantial decrease from the numbers reported in 1896.

B. APPROVED SCHOOLS 1932–1968

INTRODUCTION

Though the formal distinction between reformatory and industrial schools had been retained in the Children Act, 1908, in practice it had no effect, and in 1928 the Morton Committee Report recommended that the nomenclature of "reformatory school" and "industrial school" should no longer be

---

56 Morton Committee Report (1928), pp. 90–91.
57 Children Act, 1908, s. 65(b).
58 Ibid. s. 65(a).
59 Cowan, M.G. *The Children and Young Persons (Scotland) Act, 1932* (W. Hodge & Co, 1933), p. 61, citing the Education (Scotland) Statistical Lists, 1932, p. 92.

used but that some neutral term such as "training school" be used instead.[60] This suggestion was adopted by the Scottish Education Department in 1929 when it issued to all reformatory and industrial schools a circular[61] indicating its intention to cease using the terms "industrial" and "reformatory" schools in its official correspondence, and suggesting that school managers should adopt the same course, describing their establishments with neutral names such as "Aberdeen Oakbank School". Cowan, writing in 1932, suggested that this change in terminology reflected the reality on the ground:

> Changing social circumstances, an inspectorate, in touch with the general educa-
> tion of the country and a new nomenclature, have gradually tended to lessen,
> if not almost to obliterate, the distinction between the reformatory and the
> industrial school . . . No doubt it is true that the industrial schools contain many
> neglected children committed, under s. 58(1) of the Children Act [1908], through
> no fault of their own, but solely owing to the unsatisfactory condition of their
> homes, while all those in reformatories have been convicted. But the two catego-
> ries very often overlap, for the connection between neglect and delinquency is
> distressingly close.[62]

The distinction between the two types of school was formally abolished by the Children and Young Persons (Scotland) Act, 1932. This consisted with the overall thrust of that Act, which was to treat the two classes of children (the offender and the neglected or abused child) the same. From that starting point it logically followed that so too the two classes of residential school to which children could be sent should be the same. Opening the Second Reading Debate on the Bill that became the 1932 Act in the House of Commons, Oliver Stanley for the Government justified this approach as follows:

> After all, both classes of children, the neglected and the offenders, have had to
> suffer a withdrawal of their liberty, in the one case as a species of punishment,
> in the other purely for their own protection. The fact remains that they are both
> inside and, when they are inside, the object is the same in dealing with both,
> namely, when they get outside, to give them a good chance of making decent
> citizens. We have decided to abolish the distinction between these two types
> of schools, and to put them together in future under one heading of approved
> schools, to which the distinction which now exists will no longer apply.
>   I know that some people feel that it is unwise, and perhaps unfair, to mix up in
> the same school those who are there as punishment for an offence and those who

---

60 Morton Committee Report, pp. 94–95. In fact, this suggestion had been made in England as early as 1915 in the *Report of the Departmental Committee on Reformatories and Industrial Schools* (Cmnd 7886), p. 44.

61 SED Circular No. 80, 16 January 1929, reproduced in Cowan, *The Children and Young Persons (Scotland) Act, 1932*, pp. 327–332.

62 Cowan *The Children and Young Persons (Scotland) Act, 1932*, pp. 22–23.

are merely there for their own protection— that it means that the poor neglected child is contaminated by the bad young offender. The fact is that the distinction between the two is largely accidental. The neglected child may only just have been lucky enough not to have been caught in an offence. The character of the child who has been suffering from a long period of neglect at home, or a long period of evil surroundings, is much more likely to have been seriously affected than the character of the young offender who is perhaps in the school as the result of one short lapse into crime. We do not believe that either will suffer from being in the same school.[63]

APPROVAL OF APPROVED SCHOOLS

The First Schedule to the Children and Young Persons (Scotland) Act, 1932 and subsequently ss. 83 and 85 of, and Schedule 2 to, the Children and Young Persons (Scotland) Act, 1937 governed the approval of schools.[64] The system of approval was clearly designed to ensure that only schools suitable for their purpose, and safe for children and young persons to be sent to, received state funding. The managers of a school could

apply to the Scottish Education Department to approve the school for that purpose, and the Scottish Education Department may, after making such inquiries as they think fit, approve the school for that purpose and issue a certificate of approval to the managers . . .[65]

There were no statutory criteria set down by which the SED was to judge suitability for approval, but the SED, after having given approval, retained the power of oversight and could, if dissatisfied with the condition or management of the school, withdraw the certificate of approval.[66]

The SED was permitted to classify approved schools

according to the age of the persons for whom they are intended, the character of the education and training given therein, the religious persuasion of the persons for whom they are intended, their geographical position, and otherwise as they think best calculated to secure that a person sent to an approved school is sent to a school appropriate to his case . . .[67]

---

63 HC Deb. 12 February 1932, vol. 261, cols 1179–1180.
64 Existing certified reformatory and industrial schools were deemed to be approved by s. 37 of the Children and Young Persons (Scotland) Act, 1932.
65 Children and Young Persons (Scotland) Act, 1932, sched. 1 para 1; Children and Young Persons (Scotland) Act, 1937, s. 83(1).
66 Children and Young Persons (Scotland) Act, 1932, sched. 1 para 2; Children and Young Persons (Scotland) Act, 1937, s. 83(2).
67 Children and Young Persons (Scotland) Act, 1932, sched. 1 para 7; Children and Young Persons (Scotland) Act, 1937, s. 85(1).

In practice, however, they were approved only in relation to age and gender, and religious persuasion. Sheriff Trotter, in his book on the 1937 Act,[68] reproduces the list issued by the SED in October 1936 of the schools then approved. They were classified as follows:

1. Senior schools for boys between 14 and 17. This list included the Kibble School, Paisley, approved for 150 boys; Rossie Farm School, Montrose, approved for 80 boys; Springboig St Johns School, Glasgow for 90 Roman Catholic boys and Westthorn School, Glasgow, a Roman Catholic establishment which had the intriguing note appended: "further admissions to this school have been prohibited since 1st July 1936".[69]

2. Intermediate schools for boys between 12 and 14. This list contained Oakbank School, Aberdeen, approved for 150 boys (and a willingness to take Roman Catholic boys); Kenmure St Mary's, Bishopbriggs for 150 Roman Catholic boys; and Mossbank School, Glasgow, an education authority school for 150 boys.

3. Junior Schools for boys under 12. This included Balgowan School, Dundee for 150 boys; the Dale School, Arbroath for 20 boys; and St. Joseph's School, Tranent for 150 Roman Catholic boys.

4. Combined intermediate and senior schools for girls between 13 and 17. This list contained Dalbeth Girl's School, Glasgow for 100 Roman Catholic girls; and Dr Guthrie's Girl's School, Edinburgh for 75 girls.

5. Junior Schools for girls under 13. This included Balgay School, Dundee for 120 girls; Greenock Girl's Home for 30 girls; Kenmure St. Mary's Girls' School, Bishopbriggs for 40 Roman Catholic Girls; and Nazareth House School, Aberdeen for 140 Roman Catholic girls.

The list included a brief description of the skills the schools aimed to provide their residents beyond the normal school curriculum: mostly farming, joinery and tailoring for boys, and cookery and laundry work for girls. There are three points of particular note to the modern reader of these lists. First, the schools tended to be large establishments in which an institutional environment could hardly be avoided. Secondly, they were clustered in the main population centres with the result that many children would have been separated by some distance from their parents at a time when travel was much more troublesome, and expensive, than it is today. And thirdly, a remarkable number of the schools listed as approved in this 1936 document remained in operation (if with a different character) well into the twenty-first century.

---

68 Trotter, T. *The Law as to Children and Young Persons* (W. Hodge & Co, 1938), pp. 352–358.

69 The website Children's Homes available at <http://childrenshomes.org.uk> (last accessed 13 July 2019) has a history of this school (but no indication of what caused the "prohibition"). It opened in 1859 as a reformatory for 100 Roman Catholic boys.

SENDING CHILDREN TO APPROVED SCHOOLS

The criteria justifying the sending of a child to an approved school are considered in detail elsewhere.[70] The school selected was required to be (where practicable) a school for persons of the religious persuasion to which the child or young person belonged.[71] It was necessary for the order sending the child or young person to an approved school to specify the age and religious persuasion of the subject of the order,[72] and an error could, at least in some cases, amount to a fundamental nullity vitiating the order.[73] The order also had to specify the Education Authority of the area where the child or young person was resident, or if that was not known, the Authority in whose area the offence was committed or the circumstances that led to protective remedies arose:[74] on that identification rested the question of the authority's liability for the maintenance of the child in the approved school. This fundamentally financial question generated an extensive case law[75] (similar to that previously arising under the Poor Law). The same disputes arise today.[76]

LENGTH OF DETENTION

The Morton Committee Report had regarded the lengthy periods of detention permitted under the Children Act, 1908 as discouraging self-reliance and initiative[77] and their recommendation of a basic period of three years detention was given effect to by the Children and Young Persons (Scotland) Act, 1932. Thereafter the period of detention in an approved school for a child (that is to say a person under the age of 14 years) became three years

---

70 See Chapter 4 above.
71 Children and Young Persons (Scotland) Act, 1932, sched. 1 para 26; Children and Young Persons (Scotland) Act, 1937, s. 72.
72 Children and Young Persons (Scotland) Act, 1932, s. 23(4) and (5); Children and Young Persons (Scotland) Act, 1937, s. 74(1).
73 See *Dunn v Mustard* (1899) 1 F(J) 81. Here the error consisted in the interlocutor bearing to proceed under the wrong statute (admittedly a mere clerical, but fatal, error).
74 Children and Young Persons (Scotland) Act, 1932, s. 23(6); Children and Young Persons (Scotland) Act, 1937, s. 74(2).
75 See for example *Edinburgh EA v Perth and Kinross EA* (1934) SLT (Sh Ct) 60; *Fife EA v Lord Provost etc. of Edinburgh* (1934) 50 Sh Ct Rep. 245; *Magistrates of Edinburgh v Stirling County Council* 1947 SLT (Sh Ct) 58; and *Dundee Corporation v Stirling County Council* (1940) 56 Sh Ct Rep 189.
76 *East Renfrewshire Council, Appellants* 2015 GWD 35–564 and *East Renfrewshire Council, Appellants* [2016] SAC (Civ) 14.
77 Morton Committee Report (1928), p. 98.

or until the child was 15;[78] for a young person (that is to say a person over the age of 14 but under 17[79]) the period of detention was for three years if the young person was under 16 at the date of the order for detention, and was until the person's 19th birthday if he or she was 16 or over at the date of the order.[80] In either case the managers could extend the period by six months with the consent of the SED if they considered the person needed further care or training and could not be placed in suitable employment without it.[81]

These periods, though less than under the 1908 Act, were still rigid to modern eyes but that rigidity was mitigated substantially by the power of the managers to allow the child out on licence.[82] The circumstances of each child or young person detained in an approved school had to be reviewed after 12 months after the initial detention, and thereafter every six months, this was "in order that he or she may be placed out on licence as soon as he or she is fit to be so placed out."[83] The aim of detention in an approved school, therefore, was to prepare for release. After 12 months residence at the school, the managers could license the child or young person to live with the parent "or any trustworthy and respectable person (to be named in the licence) who is willing to receive and take charge of him" or her; while out on licence the child or young person remained under the formal care of the managers.[84] The effect of this, in Cowan's words, was that "The length of stay does not depend on the gravity of the case, but on the progress made. The discretion is thus taken from the magistrate and given to those who can watch the pupil's progress under training".[85] The operation of the licensing system therefore required school managers to keep each child's progress under regular review. The inspection regime had the same aim. The legislation provided that the SED "shall through their inspectors review the progress made by persons detained in approved schools with a view to ensuring

---

78 Children and Young Persons (Scotland) Act, 1932, s. 25(1); Children and Young Persons (Scotland) Act, 1937, s. 75(1).

79 Children and Young Persons (Scotland) Act, 1932, s. 64(1); Children and Young Persons (Scotland) Act, 1937, s. 110.

80 Children and Young Persons (Scotland) Act, 1932, s. 25(2); Children and Young Persons (Scotland) Act, 1937, s. 75(2).

81 Children and Young Persons (Scotland) Act, 1932, s. 25(3); Children and Young Persons (Scotland) Act, 1937, s. 77.

82 Children and Young Persons (Scotland) Act, 1932, sched. 1 para 15; Children and Young Persons (Scotland) Act, 1937, sched. 2 para 5.

83 Children and Young Persons (Scotland) Care and Training Regulations, 1933 SR&O 1933 No. 1006 (S. 55), reg. 22.

84 Children and Young Persons (Scotland) Act, 1932, sched. 1 para 15; Children and Young Persons (Scotland) Act, 1937, sched. 2 para 6.

85 Cowan, *The Children and Young Persons (Scotland) Act, 1932*, pp. 42–43.

that they shall be placed out on licence as soon as they are fit to be so placed out".[86] Inspection, therefore, was not limited to the suitability of the school but also included individualised assessments of the children and young persons accommodated therein, always with the aim of releasing the child or young person back into the community. There was, however, no provision to allow either child or parent to participate in any review of progress by either the managers or the inspectors. The Approved Schools (Scotland) Rules, 1961 similarly obliged the managers to release each pupil "as soon as he has made sufficient progress; and with this object in view they shall review his progress and all the circumstances of his case (including home surroundings) at least quarterly."[87] Again, there was no mechanism specified by which the parents (or indeed the child) could participate in the assessment of "sufficient progress" that might allow for release from the school.

REGULATIONS GOVERNING APPROVED SCHOOLS

Part A of the Children and Young Persons (Scotland) Care and Training Regulations, 1933[88] set out in some detail how approved schools were to be run, until their replacement by the Approved Schools (Scotland) Rules, 1961,[89] which applied until 1987.

The managers

Under the 1933 Regulations, the managers of each approved school, or a committee of them, were required to meet as often as was required for the efficient management of the school. "They shall arrange for some of their number to visit the school periodically . . . The headmaster or headmistress shall be responsible to the Managers for the conduct and discipline of the school."[90]

Under the 1961 Rules, the names of the managers of approved schools were required to be submitted to the Secretary of State,[91] and they were required to meet and to visit the school once a month in order to ensure that

---

86 Children and Young Persons (Scotland) Act, 1932, sched. 1 para 15(2); Children and Young Persons (Scotland) Act, 1937, sched. 2 para 6(2).
87 1961 Rules, r. 43.
88 SR&O, 1933, No. 1006 (S. 55) (reproduced in Trotter, T. *The Law as to Children and Young Persons*, pp. 335–347).
89 SI 1961/2243 (S. 124).
90 1933 Regulations, reg. 2.
91 1961 Rules, r. 1.

"the conditions of the school and the welfare, development and rehabilitation of the pupils under their care" were satisfactory.[92] Additional obligations, with a new focus on individual children, were imposed by the 1961 Rules: "A visiting Manager shall take opportunity to speak with individual pupils . . . A Manager shall discuss with the Headmaster any complaint made by a pupil."[93] Most importantly, the 1961 Rules for the first time explicitly required managers to "manage the school in the interests of the welfare, development and rehabilitation of the pupils".[94] Together, these provisions – and especially the opportunity for pupils to make complaints – gave rather more scope than had previously existed for visitors to uncover harmful regimes and unlawful practices. But since the managers were ultimately responsible for the running of the school, their visits to their own establishments could hardly be regarded as providing independent oversight.

Premises, accommodation and food

Both the 1933 Regulations and the 1961 Rules required the school premises to be maintained in a satisfactory condition as regards lighting, heating, ventilation, cleanliness, sanitary arrangements and safety against fire (with regular, then "frequent", fire-drills).[95] Adequate accommodation had to be provided both for residential and for instructional purposes, containing such equipment of workshops and special appliances as would be necessary for the proper conduct of the work of the school.[96] The number of children resident in a school was not to exceed the number for which the school was approved.[97]

Under the 1961 Rules, pupils were to be provided "with a separate bed in a room with sufficient ventilation and sufficient natural and artificial lighting" and with "easy access from every bedroom or dormitory to suitable and sufficient water closets and washing facilities"; suitable clothing was to be provided.[98] Provision was also made for pupils to receive

> sufficient, varied, wholesome and appetising food in accordance with a dietary scale adequate for the maintenance of health, to be drawn up by the Managers

---

92 Ibid. r. 2(1).
93 Ibid. r. 2(2)–(4)
94 Ibid. r. 4.
95 1933 Regulations, regs 3 and 4; 1961 Rules, rr. 6 and 7.
96 Ibid. reg. 3.
97 Ibid. reg. 5; 1961 Rules, r. 8 (which permitted the numbers to be exceeded "exceptionally").
98 1961 Rules, r. 18.

after consultation with the Headmaster and the Medical Officer and approved by an inspector.[99]

Withholding meals as punishment was explicitly forbidden[100]– which disturbingly suggests that this had earlier been a practice in at least some approved schools.

Staffing

The 1933 Regulations provided no more than that "the staff shall be sufficient for the needs of the school and, generally, the school-room instruction shall be given by teachers qualified under the [Scottish Education] Department's regulations".[101] That "generally" was an acceptance that qualified teachers could not always be guaranteed for approved schools.

The 1961 Rules contained rather more detailed requirements designed to ensure the quality of staff at approved schools. It was for the managers in consultation with the headmaster to determine the number, type and qualifications of staff to be employed by them;[102] suspension and dismissal lay with the managers but they had to act in accordance with s. 81 of the Education (Scotland) Act, 1946.[103] Teaching had to be provided by qualified teachers, except with the consent of the Secretary of State.[104] There remained throughout the period of approved schools no standards or qualifications in relation to the caring role of school employees. It was not in any case until the 1960s that professional courses in child care were established at institutions of further and higher education.[105]

Education and training

Education and training at approved schools were, on paper at least, designed to be more useful than that at the earlier reformatory and industrial schools. It aimed, as a minimum, to reflect the education provided at normal state

99 1961 Rules, r. 19.
100 Ibid. r. 19(1).
101 1933 Regulations, reg. 7.
102 1961 Rules, r. 10(1).
103 Which set out the procedure whereby Education Authorities (or, here, the governing body) could resolve that a certified teacher be dismissed.
104 1961 Rules, r. 10(4).
105 See *Child Care in Scotland, 1968* (Cmnd 4069), para 49: it was further reported at para 50 that in-service training courses for staff of approved schools "had to be curtailed in 1968", without explanation offered but perhaps a consequence of the sterling crisis in 1967.

schools, but with a greater emphasis on the practical skills that would fit the pupil for the job market. The 1933 Regulations sought a balance between "employment", education and leisure of children while resident at schools, prohibiting employment

> of such an amount as to interfere with further school-room instruction if such further instruction is required or is likely to be of benefit. Similarly, employment shall not interfere with the time needed for the boy's or girl's recreation or reasonable leisure.[106]

With a specificity that reveals a common practice, the same rule provided that "No boy or girl shall be employed on any work which may involve the risk of serious injury. Provided they are under adequate supervision, older boys in senior schools may assist in attending to furnaces".

Education rather than training for employment received a higher profile in the 1961 Rules and, reflecting the duty imposed on education authorities by s. 1 of the Education (Scotland) Act 1946, it was provided that education to be given in approved schools was to be such as "to secure the efficient full-time education suitable to the age, ability and aptitude of the pupils of compulsory school age and their further education thereafter as long as they remain in the school".[107] The "employment" of pupils, reduced from two hours to one hour a day, was specified in the 1961 Rules to be "light work such as making beds or cleaning boots" and any employment of older pupils was not to interfere with any further education that would benefit the pupil.[108] The reference to older boys "attending furnaces" did not reappear in the 1961 Rules.

Free time and home leave

The 1933 Regulations required reasonable provision to be made for free time and recreation: "generally, additional freedom shall be given towards the end of a boy's or girl's period of detention with a view to him or her returning to ordinary life".[109] Under the 1961 Rules pupils were to be encouraged

> in the right use of leisure and in healthy interests, and for this purpose as great a measure of liberty as possible shall be allowed during free time. Generally, additional freedom, including additional home leave when appropriate, shall be given towards the end of a pupil's period of detention with a view to facilitating his return to ordinary life.[110]

---

106 1933 Regulations, reg. 10.
107 1961 Rules, r. 21.
108 Ibid. r. 22.
109 1933 Regulations, reg. 9.
110 1961 Rules, r. 24.

At least one hour each day was to be spent in the open air (unless prevented by bad weather or illness).[111] If practicable, home leave of up to forty-two days, with no period more than fourteen days, was to be permitted each year:[112] it was left to the managers to determine practicality.

Discipline and corporal punishment

What to modern eyes is a disproportionate amount of space was devoted in both the 1933 Regulations and the 1961 Rules to the maintenance of discipline, and the regulation of corporal punishment. Under the 1933 Regulations, the discipline of the school was to be

> maintained by the personal influence of the headmaster or headmistress and of the staff. In the ordinary exercise of his or her responsibility for the general discipline of the school, the headmaster or headmistress shall endeavour to reduce all forms of punishment to the minimum. Punishment, where necessary, shall consist mainly of forfeiture of privileges or rewards; loss of conduct marks, recreation or liberty;[113] or degradation in rank. No boy or girl shall be deprived of recreation for more than one day at a time. The stopping of a period of home leave, i.e., leave extending to more than a day or two, is a severe punishment and should be resorted to only in the case of a serious offence.[114]

There was no specification of behaviour that justified punishment and the matter was left to the headmaster, headmistress and staff to determine. The only limitation to non-corporal punishment was that: "In no case shall the nature or the extent of the punishment be such as might be injurious to physical or mental health".[115] Psychological harm was probably not included in the concept of mental health as it was understood in 1933. But risks inherent in the punishment of isolation do seem to have been acknowledged with the following provision:

> For certain types of boys and girls isolation for a certain period may be the best method of correction and reform ... A period of isolation shall not exceed six hours and the room in which the offender is placed must be light, airy and safe for the purpose; it must not be a cell or even a room definitely set apart for such punishments. Some form of occupation shall be provided and the offender shall

111 Ibid. r. 25.
112 Ibid. r. 23.
113 It is unclear what "liberty" consists of in this context but may well implicitly have authorised locking a child or young person in a room within the school. See also reg. 13 of the 1933 Regulations which authorises "isolation".
114 1933 Regulations reg. 11.
115 Ibid. reg. 12.

be visited at frequent and regular intervals. In addition, some means by which the offender can communicate with the staff shall be furnished.[116]

Corporal punishment was subject to particularly detailed regulation. The 1933 Regulations provided:

> If corporal punishment is considered necessary a light tawse only may be used: a cane and any form of cuffing or striking are forbidden. No boy or girl who shows any sign of physical or mental weakness shall receive corporal punishment without the sanction of a medical officer. Corporal punishment should rarely be imposed on girls, whose treatment in other respects may differ from that required for boys, or be a modification of it.[117]

The rules varied according to the gender of the child being punished.

> In girls' schools, corporal punishment may be inflicted only on the hands and the number of strokes shall not exceed three in all on any one occasion. In boys' schools corporal punishment may be inflicted only on the hands or on the posterior over ordinary cloth trousers . . .

and the number of strokes varied according to age and where inflicted. [118] It would be implausible to suggest that girls' posteriors were considered to be physically more delicate than boys' and the limitation to belting girls' hands may well indicate an understated acknowledgement that sexual abuse was a possibility during corporal punishment. If so, this provision ignored the possibility of sexual abuse of boys which, we know today, was all too real. In any case, the specificity of corporal punishment in these rules indicates clearly an understanding of the risk that "legitimate" punishment might readily cross the line to physical abuse. Kendrick and Hawthorn[119] report a case from 1936 where the magistrate in the trial of a physical education instructor accused of assaulting boys at an approved school in Dundee expressed difficulty in knowing "where reasonable punishment ended and assault began". Though the accused, on conviction, was merely admonished the case does illustrate both that the limits to corporal punishment were real and that the state would take action when it was considered that they had been crossed. However, the additional comment of the magistrate on boys "whining to the police or to the medical officer grumbling about assault" serves to reveal the social realities which would substantially inhibit pupils

---

116 Ibid. reg. 13.
117 Ibid. reg. 14.
118 Ibid. reg. 15.
119 *National Confidential Forum for Adult Survivors of Childhood Abuse in Care: Scoping Project on Children in Care in Scotland 1930-2005* (June 2012, CELCIS/SIRCC), para 2.6.11.

at approved schools from bringing their ill-treatment to the attention of the appropriate authorities.

Minor punishments for "offences committed in the course of ordinary lessons in the school room" were to be administered by the principal and assistant teachers authorised to do so by the managers, who could also authorise the principal teacher to inflict corporal punishment on boys (not exceeding three strokes on the hands). Other than that, all punishment was to be administered by the headmaster or headmistress, or a person authorised to act in their absence, and by no other person.[120] Corporal punishment was not to be administered in the presence of other children, other than as punishment for minor school-room offences.[121] This suggests some level of awareness of the desirability of avoiding unnecessary humiliation for children deemed deserving of punishment.[122] A record was required to be kept by the headteacher of all punishments.[123]

Discipline and punishment were under the 1961 Rules likewise the responsibility of the Headmaster, who could give such instructions and delegate such responsibility as he saw fit.[124] Again, there was no list of offences that justified punishment, but the 1961 Rules did set down a comprehensive list of permissible punishments:

(a) reprimand;
(b) forfeiture of privileges or rewards;
(c) loss of conduct marks or reduction in rank;
(d) loss of recreation or liberty;
(e) performance of useful additional tasks;
(f) the disallowance of home leave, which could be used only in the case of a serious offence; or
(g) corporal punishment.[125]

The type of punishment to be used was to be determined "not only by the gravity of the offence but also by the age, temperament and physical condition of the offender." In no case was the nature or the extent of the

---

120 1933 Regulations, reg. 16.

121 Ibid. reg. 17.

122 Though it was some years later held that "humiliation" may be a legitimate part of reasonable punishment, so long as it was not degrading in the sense that would infringe Article 3 of the European Convention on Human Rights: *Stewart v Thain* 1981 JC 13, p. 18, per Lord Justice-Clerk Wheatley and *Costello-Roberts v United Kingdom* (1995) 19 EHRR 112.

123 1933 Regulations, reg. 18.

124 1961 Rules. r. 28.

125 Ibid. r. 29. Any other (unspecified) form of punishment could be inflicted only with the consent of the Secretary of State.

punishment to be such as might be injurious to physical or mental health.[126] Details were again given as to who could administer corporal punishment, and in what circumstances.[127] An important new provision in the 1961 Rules, which recognised the opportunity that the infliction of corporal punishment afforded for abuse (or, perhaps, which sought to reduce the risk of false allegations of excess punishment) was that "except when the punishment is inflicted in the presence of a class in a schoolroom, an adult witness must be present" and that no pupil could be called upon to assist the person inflicting the punishment.[128] As with the 1933 Regulations, girls could be hit only on the hands while boys could be hit on the hands or posterior,[129] and records were required to be kept when punishment was either corporal punishment or the stopping of home leave.[130]

Parental involvement

Neither the 1933 Regulations nor the 1961 Rules completely ignored parents, but parental involvement in the care and management of children resident in approved schools was minimal. This is likely to reflect the underlying assumption of the time that residents at approved schools were there in order to insulate them from detrimental familial influences. Visits by parents were permitted under the 1933 Regulations "at such reasonable intervals as the Managers may determine".[131] The 1961 Rules allowed pupils to receive visits from their parents, relatives or friends, though that was conceived as a "privilege", and it could be suspended "in the interests of the pupil or the school".[132] Frequency of visits was not specified, and it seems likely that individual schools followed their own practices in the matter. Consultation was required with parents whenever the managers proposed to place a boy in the Navy, Army or Air Force, or to emigrate him or her. It was further provided that "Managers shall not ignore an objection to disposal raised by parents (or guardians) unless the circumstances are such that it is definitely in the interests of the boy or girl that the objection shall be overruled".[133] Though this placed an obligation at least to attempt to secure the consent

126 1961 Rules. r. 30.
127 Ibid. r. 31.
128 Ibid. r. 31(c) and (d).
129 Ibid. r. 31(e), (f) and (g).
130 Ibid. r. 32.
131 1933 Regulations, reg. 19.
132 1961 Rules, r. 36.
133 1933 Regulations, reg. 19; 1961 Rules, r. 39.

of the parents, it is clear that the Managers had the power to make arrangements for the young person's future (including by emigration) even in the face of parental opposition.

Under the 1961 Rules pupils were to be encouraged to write to their parents at least once a week, and were allowed to receive letters: staff were, however, empowered to read these and the headmaster could withhold any letter, except one to the managers or the Secretary of State or his officers.[134]

The medical officer

A medical officer required to be appointed under the 1933 Regulations, who was to give medical examinations, to give "advice as to dietary and general hygiene", and to keep such records "as may be required" and keep the managers informed "as to the health of the school".[135] He also had to examine the punishment book and to call attention of the managers to any case of excessive punishment. The role of the medical officer seems therefore to have been a central element in external supervision of the safe operation of the school, though the role was ill-fitted to do this fully.

The role of the medical officer was set out with more specificity in the 1961 Rules: his duties included—

(a) a thorough examination of each pupil on admission and shortly before leaving the school;
(b) a quarterly inspection of each pupil;
(c) the examination and treatment of pupils as required;
(d) a visit to the school at least once each week;
(e) general inspection and advice as to dietary and general hygiene in the school;
(f) the keeping of such medical records as may be required;
(g) the furnishing of such reports and certificates as the Managers required; and
(h) the examination of the punishment book at each visit, drawing the attention of the Managers to any apparent case of excessive punishment.[136]

An interesting new provision in the 1961 Rules was that the managers, taking advice from the Medical Officer, had to "make full use of the preventive health measures at their disposal, including vaccination, immunisation and chest X-ray."[137] Dental care was also to be provided (and recorded).[138]

---

134 1961 Rules, r. 35.
135 1933 Regulations, reg. 20. Regulation 21 also required the appointment of a dentist.
136 1961 Rules, r. 40.
137 1961 Rules, r. 41.
138 1933 Regulations, reg. 21; 1961 Rules, r. 42.

Inspection

The school was to be open at all times to inspection by HM Inspector of Schools, and the managers had to give him all facilities for the examination of the books and records of the school, and under the 1961 Rules for the interviewing of staff or pupils.[139]

C. CHILDREN'S HOMES

VOLUNTARY HOMES PRIOR TO 1948

Schools, of course, were not the only form of establishment to which children could be sent by order of court and many children and young people would attend the local school run by the education authority while being accommodated in both institutional and non-institutional environments. Most of the institutions that provided children with residential accommodation before the Second World War were run by churches and voluntary organisations separate from (but often at least partly funded by) the state. They were "voluntary" not because they took in children subject to no legal order nor because children were there by the will of their parents rather than the state, but rather in the sense that they were funded through voluntary contributions rather than compulsory taxation. Voluntary homes of this nature remained entirely free from state control until the Children Act, 1908, and even that Act showed great reticence in requiring the state to become involved in how private charitable endeavours operated. It allowed, but did not require, the Secretary for Scotland to cause inspections of "any institution for the reception of poor children or young persons supported wholly or partly by voluntary contributions" which were not liable to inspection by any other government department.[140] The inspector, if so desired by the managers of the institution, had to be of the religious denomination of the institution (if it had one, and many did) or a woman if the institution was for the reception of girls only.[141]

This inspection regime was enhanced under the Children and Young Persons (Scotland) Acts, 1932 and 1937[142] but it remained effectively non-

---

139 1933 Regulations, reg. 24; 1961 Rules, r. 48.
140 Children Act, 1908, s. 25(1).
141 Ibid. s. 25(3) and (4).
142 Children and Young Persons (Scotland) Act, 1932, s. 41; Children and Young Persons (Scotland) Act, 1937, s. 98.

compulsory. A new requirement was imposed in 1932 on the managers of an institution[143] to notify the Secretary for Scotland of prescribed particulars, but these were limited to details of the persons responsible for the management of the institution, its religious denomination, the person in charge, the total number of beds, and whether annual reports and accounts were published.[144] Rather more substantially, the Secretary for Scotland acquired a new power to remove all children and young persons from a home found to be unsatisfactory.[145] The non-compulsory nature of this inspection regime meant that many smaller homes were able to avoid any form of official oversight. Cowan, in her commentary on the 1932 Act, pointed out that there was no official register of voluntary homes,[146] but she nevertheless offers some overview of the major providers of voluntary homes. She reported that in the first three decades of the twentieth century the Church of Scotland had founded or taken over "no less than six homes for destitute and homeless lads, two similar ones for older girls, eight hostels for working women and girls, and two orphanages for children of school age"; that the Episcopal Church in Scotland ran special homes for girls and young women and had a link to the Aberlour Orphanage which "provides for no less than 450 children"; that the Roman Catholic Church in Scotland "has an extensive scheme of some twenty-three different orphanages, homes, and hostels for children and young people"; and that there were large secular institutions such as that founded by Mr Quarrier at Bridge of Weir and a variety of "small homes containing perhaps a dozen girls or lads, which have been organised to meet a local situation by some special committee".[147]

Voluntary homes therefore provided a significant amount of the care of children and young persons living apart from their parents before the Second World War, but the legal regulation thereof was substantially less

---

143 "The institutions to which this Part of this Act [which was headed 'Voluntary Homes'] applies are homes and other institutions for the boarding, care and maintenance of poor children or young persons, being institutions supported wholly or partly by voluntary contributions" (except institutions certified under the Mental Deficiency and Lunacy (Scotland) Act, 1913): Children and Young Persons (Scotland) Act, 1932, s. 40(3). Under the heading "Homes Supported Wholly or Partly by Voluntary Contribution", the same definition is given in s. 96 of the Children and Young Persons (Scotland) Act, 1937.

144 See Children and Young Persons (Voluntary Homes) Regulations, 1933 (SR&O 1933 No 923 (S. 50)).

145 Children and Young Persons (Scotland) Act, 1932 Act, s. 42; Children and Young Persons (Scotland) Act, 1937, s. 99.

146 Cowan, M.G. *The Children and Young Persons (Scotland) Act, 1932* (W. Hodge & Co, 1933), p. 73.

147 Ibid. pp. 73–75.

than that governing the running of approved schools[148] (often managed by the same voluntary bodies that ran children's homes) and state-run institutions like Borstals and remand homes. They were, by and large, private (or church-based) charitable institutions which the state saw no role for itself in regulating unless (as with approved schools) they undertook the functions of the state (education, or the rehabilitation of offenders).

Local authorities had imposed on them a number of overseeing obligations in respect of children whom they themselves placed in "institutions" by articles 23 to 28 of the Children (Boarding-out etc.) (Scotland) Rules and Regulations, 1947.[149] The local authority, before placing the child, had to satisfy themselves that the institution selected was suited to the particular needs of the child;[150] that the institution was maintained for persons of the child's religious persuasion;[151] and that they could visit the institution and satisfy themselves as to the arrangements for the child's welfare.[152] The local authority was also obliged to visit each child they placed within one month of the placing of the child and thereafter at least once in every six months. The visitor was required to draw up a report on: (i) the child's health, well-being and behaviour, (ii) the progress of the child's education, and (iii) any other matters relative to the child's welfare which they considered should be reported.[153]

VOLUNTARY HOMES AFTER 1948

The state's hesitancy in regulating children's homes run by private institutions substantially weakened after the Second World War. Compulsory registration of voluntary homes was mandated by the Children Act, 1948, which for the first time imposed obligations on local authorities to provide for children in need. This Act required voluntary homes to be registered with the Secretary of State (though all existing homes were registered automatically),[154] and it

148 Both Cowan, p. 77 and Trotter *The Law as to Children and Young Persons*, p. 177 suggest that approved schools would be within the scope of the inspection provisions relating to voluntary homes if they received voluntary contributions, but if that is so then this would be in addition to the more extensive control such schools are otherwise under.

149 1947 SI/2146 (S. 76).

150 1947 Regulations, Art. 24.

151 Ibid. Art. 25.

152 Ibid. Art. 26.

153 Ibid. Art. 27.

154 The registration rules were contained in the Voluntary Homes Registration (Scotland) Regulations, 1948, SI 1948/2595. See also the Voluntary Homes (Return of Particulars) (Scotland) Regulations, 1952, SI 1952/1836.

was provided that no voluntary home could "be carried on" unless it was so registered.[155] The Secretary of State could, if the running of the home was not in accordance with Regulations or was in any other way unsatisfactory, remove the home from the register and "all or any" of the children resident therein could be received into the care of the local authority.[156] Section 54 of the 1948 Act extended the powers of inspectors appointed by the Secretary of State[157] to include the power to enter and inspect homes governed by the 1948 Act. In addition, a new duty to visit individual residents was placed on local authorities, with the aim of checking on their wellbeing,[158] and ensuring the continued suitability of the placement. It is noticeable that the structure of this obligation was one to visit the children, not the homes, which aimed to focus the visit on the individual child.

The Secretary of State was also given the power to make regulations "as to the conduct of voluntary homes and for securing the welfare of the children therein".[159] This could have been a substantial extension of state control of voluntary homes, but in the event, the power was not exercised until the making of the Administration of Children's Homes (Scotland) Regulations, 1959 which are discussed below. There was no attempt to set down minimum standards of the staffing of children's homes.[160]

LOCAL AUTHORITY HOMES

The Children Act, 1948 expanded the role of the state in other ways, in particular by enabling local authorities (or obliging them, if so directed by the Secretary of State) to provide, equip and maintain homes for the accommodation of children in their care.[161] Some had, of course, already done so. As with voluntary homes, the residents in local authority homes could be a mix of children and young people subject to court orders and those subject to no such orders. If the premises were unsatisfactory, the Secretary of State could close the home.[162]

---

155 Children Act, 1948, s. 29.
156 Ibid. s. 29(6).
157 Under s. 106 of the Children and Young Persons (Scotland) Act, 1937.
158 Children Act, 1948, s. 54(3). It was an offence to obstruct an inspector: s. 54(7).
159 Ibid. s. 31(1).
160 See HL Deb 10 February 1948, vol. 153 col. 937 where Lord Beveridge (the principal architect of the welfare state) expressed some concern that while the qualifications of children's officers were carefully prescribed no qualifications were prescribed for those running voluntary homes.
161 1948 Act, s. 15(1).
162 Ibid. s. 15(5).

The Secretary of State was given the power to make regulations as to the conduct of local authority homes,[163] but it was not until 1959 that he did so.

ADMINISTRATION OF CHILDREN'S HOMES (SCOTLAND) REGULATIONS, 1959[164]

These Regulations covered both local authority and voluntary homes, and they contained rules for the homes' administration, the welfare of children accommodated therein (irrespective of the basis upon which any individual child was there), and for oversight of both of these matters.

The 1959 regulations placed ultimate responsibility for the good running of the home on the "administering authority", that is to say the local authority providing, or the persons carrying on, the home.[165] That body was obliged to make arrangements for the home "to be conducted in such manner and on such principles as will secure the well-being of the children in the home."[166] The immediate focus on the child's "well-being" is to be noted. The administering authority had to appoint a person to be in charge of the home,[167] but neither the qualifications of this person nor criteria for selection were set down. Appropriate records were to be maintained,[168] but there was no requirement for any care plan to be drawn up for each of the residents. Nor was there any obligation to keep the parent or guardian informed of the child's day to day progress.[169]

Oversight of the running of the home was provided by a system of official visitation. The administering authority for any home had to ensure that the home was visited at least once a month by an authorised visitor who was obliged to "satisfy himself that the home is conducted in accordance with Regulation 1 of these Regulations"[170] (i.e. that the home was conducted in such a manner as to secure the well-being of the children). This "authorised visitor" was the local authority Children's Officer in the case of a local authority home or a person authorised by the person carrying on the home

---

163 Ibid. s. 15(4).
164 SI 1959/834.
165 1959 Regulations, reg. 21.
166 Ibid. reg. 1.
167 Ibid.
168 Ibid. reg. 14.
169 The parent or guardian had to be informed if the child died, ran away, was abducted, or suffered from any injury or illness likely to result in death or serious disability: 1959 Regulations, reg. 13.
170 Ibid. reg. 2.

in the case of voluntary homes.[171] This was self-regulation and did not, therefore, by any means provide independent scrutiny of children's homes, which clearly reduced the system's ability to identify institutional failings.

Another source, and perhaps more independent, of oversight of the running of the home was the medical officer, who had to be appointed to every children's home. This officer was responsible for the general supervision of the health of the children accommodated in the home and of the hygienic conditions of the premises and staff, and for the giving of advice to the person in charge of the home on these matters. The medical officer was obliged to attend at the home "with sufficient frequency to ensure that he is closely acquainted with the health of the children", to examine each child on admission and thereafter at least once a year and then immediately before discharge, to provide necessary medical attention, and to supervise the compilation of a medical record for each child. The medical officer also had to submit reports on these matters to the administering authority.[172]

Discipline was to be "maintained by the personal influence of the person in charge of the home".[173] Punishments, which had to be recorded, normally took the form of "a temporary loss of recreation or privileges", and if a child was punished with "abnormal frequency" the administering authority had to arrange for an investigation of the child's mental condition.[174] The assumption here was absolute that the punishment was in all cases justified. Corporal punishment was permitted "exceptionally", but could only be administered by a person specifically empowered by the administering authority to do so; if the child had any physical or mental disability the sanction of the medical officer was required before corporal punishment could be administered.[175] These rules were far less specific than for approved schools, and they made no distinction (as the rules for approved schools did) between boys and girls. Each administering authority may, however, have created their own more detailed rules.

There is nothing in the 1959 Regulations about the qualifications of the staff of the homes, nor the mechanisms for their selection, nor any exclusion criteria (even the most obvious, such as conviction of offences against children). That omission is all the more glaring given the express granting of the

171 Ibid. reg. 21(1).
172 Ibid. reg. 6. Dental care also had to be provided: reg. 7.
173 Ibid. reg. 10.
174 Ibid.
175 Ibid. reg. 11.

power to specify qualifications in the primary legislation itself.[176] The failure might be explained by a fear of excluding anyone willing to work in children's homes, but if so that suggests staffing was an ongoing problem. The Secretary of State for Scotland reported in 1968 that "one of the greatest difficulties in providing an adequate number and range of children's homes still lies in the recruiting and retaining of adequate and suitable staff".[177]

Another omission is that there is little about contact between the child and parents. The only reference is in a regulation limited to voluntary homes, where it was required that the administering authority provide information to the Secretary of State (if he required it) about the facilities for visits to and communication with children by their parents or guardians.[178] Contact was seen as a matter of appropriate (convenient) arrangements to be made by those in charge of the home, rather than as a right of either parent or child. Nor is there anything in the 1959 Regulations about preparing the child for return to his or her family: the Regulations are written on the assumption that the child's accommodation in the home would be long-term.

D. THE 1960S TO THE 1990S: RETHINKING THE PURPOSE OF RESIDENTIAL CARE

THE KILBRANDON REPORT AND THE 1966 WHITE PAPER

We have an understandable tendency today to concentrate on the Kilbrandon Report's role as progenitor of the children's hearing system, but doing so risks overlooking other crucial shifts in thinking that it represents, in particular the way that residential accommodation was reconceptualised. The relevant legislation in force at the time of the Kilbrandon Report had been based on the view that, since children were affected by their home environment, the best way to resolve the problem of children whose development was being inhibited or harmed was their long-term removal from that environment. The Kilbrandon Committee identified serious drawbacks to this approach: in particular, it focused on the child without tackling the underlying familial difficulties.

> Further, where the child's removal from home for residential training has to be ordered, the result in many cases at present cannot, it was suggested to us, fail

---

176 1948 Act, s. 31(1)(d).
177 *Child Care in Scotland, 1968* (Cmnd 4069), para 28.
178 1959 Regulations, reg. 17.

to appear to the parents as extinguishing their responsibility. With the child's removal from the scene they are still too often left largely to their own devices; and, while it is accepted that in most cases the child must eventually return to the home, official contact where maintained with the parents tends at best to be tenuous and intermittent. In such circumstances it is in many cases almost impossible, in the absence of any really close continuing relationship with the parents, to assist them to any informed understanding of the processes at work for their child; to persuade them that they have any immediate or future part in them; or to assist them in making the personal adjustments necessary either to overcome those factors, personal or external, which led to the child's removal, or which in the changed situation will equally be necessary if he is to settle down satisfactorily on his eventual return . . . [T]he parents for their part [are] reduced to the role of passive spectators.[179]

The key change in mindset may be traced to the Committee's finding that children were, in practice and irrespective of the statutory assumptions, usually returned home before adulthood and the Committee recognised that society continued to rely on parents to resume the care of their children. At the same time, social work practice had developed since its last major restructuring in the Children Act, 1948. By the 1960s there was a far greater emphasis than before on working with families to allow children to remain at home: this was especially the case after the move towards preventive strategies was given statutory impetus by the Children and Young Persons Act 1963. Yet the legal process for dealing with children found to be in need did little or nothing to address parental behaviour and it seemed instead actively to discourage social services from working with the parents to effect change. To the Kilbrandon Committee, a better approach was to see residential care not as a permanent solution to the difficulties faced by a child or young person but rather as a temporary measure during which intensive training could be given to the child or young person at the same time as offering support to the parents in order to increase the chances that the child's eventual return home would be successful. Seeing matters that way required close contact to be maintained not only with the child's parents but also with the social work staff who had supervised the child before (and would do so after) the period in residential care.

Throughout the period of residential training there should, it seems to us, be the closest contact with the staff of the social education department concerned, who will have reported on the child before the period of residential training was decided upon, and under whose supervision the child may already have been at an earlier stage. These officers should in our view throughout maintain contact

179 Kilbrandon Report *Children and Young Persons, Scotland* (1964), para 38.

with the child's home in preparation for his eventual return. In that way the period of residential training would be seen simply as a continuation of an existing process, to be followed naturally by a return to the same supervising agency on the child's release into the community. The existing arrangements, owing to the variety and division of statutory functions over the whole field of treatment of children, and the separate services created as a result, seem to us to militate unnecessarily against that continuity of treatment.[180]

The Government's response to the Kilbrandon Report was contained in the White Paper *Social Work and the Community*, published in 1966.[181] This accepted that care away from the family should no longer be regarded as the default response to children in difficulties, but that where it was still necessary its nature should be determined by need rather than administrative convenience. The White Paper also accepted that a variety of types of residential establishment would be required to meet the diverse needs of different children:

> It is increasingly recognised that for most people in social or emotional difficulty the best form of help, whatever their age and particular problem, is support in their own homes if that is practicable. . . . [However,] residential care on a short-term or long-term basis will continue to be necessary, and suitable establishments must be provided. There is scope for much improvement in this provision. More accommodation is needed over the whole range of establishments, from homes for old people to facilities for the care of babies and young children. More variety of types of establishment is also needed; for example, a child is sometimes placed in a home or school because nothing better is available, although all concerned recognise that the regime may not be entirely fitted to his particular needs.[182] There is too little flexibility of use between the various categories of establishment . . . The different forms of provision should be fitted to the needs of the users and not the other way round and, within the limits of administrative possibility, unnecessary or out-dated barriers between one form of provision and another should be taken down.[183]

The Social Work (Scotland) Act 1968 effected a substantial restructuring both of social work departments and of the residential and other institutions that they utilised to fulfil their duties to those in need of public assistance. The new approach to residential care, presaged in the 1966 White Paper, was explained by Lord Hughes, opening the Second Reading Debate in the House of Lords on the Social Work (Scotland) Bill:

---

180 Ibid. para 167.
181 Cmnd 3065 (1966).
182 *Plus ça change*: exactly the same comment was made in a Fabian Society publication over 60 years earlier: Holmes, H.T. *Reform of Reformatories and Industrial Schools* (Fabian Society, 1902), p. 13.
183 *Social Work and the Community* (1966), para 46.

Part IV of the Bill is concerned with the provision and regulation of the residential and other establishments which the local authority are given a duty to provide by Clause 12 of the Bill. Part IV makes no statutory distinction between different kinds of establishment, and it applies in exactly the same way to homes and day centres for children at one end of the scale and homes and centres for elderly people at the other. It applies to all establishments where they are provided and managed by the local authority themselves, by voluntary organisations or by private bodies or individuals, whether on a commercial basis or not. Any establishment carried on mainly to provide for people who could be assisted by the local authority under this Bill is required by Clause 62 to be registered with the local authority, who are given the powers of entry and inspection which will be necessary to ensure that the registration is effectively carried out. Part IV provides also for appeals against the refusal of a local authority to register any establishment.

In future there would be one set of rules – involving registration and oversight –governing all residential establishments in which the state accommodated children (other than for mental health reasons), whether these were schools or homes or both. All the institutions considered above in this chapter would come under the new rules. In the event, however, the existing separate rules continued to govern residential schools and children's homes for another twenty years after the passing of the 1968 Act.

RESIDENTIAL ESTABLISHMENTS UNDER THE SOCIAL WORK (SCOTLAND) ACT 1968

In a provision that remains in force today, the Social Work (Scotland) Act 1968 obliges local authorities to provide and maintain such residential and other establishments[184] as may be required for their functions under the Act (and, subsequently, under other Acts[185]), or to arrange for the provision of such establishments.[186] The state was no longer able to rely on charitable or religious bodies to provide this social service, though many such bodies continued (and continue) to do so under the ever-closer supervision of the state. Local authorities could and can fulfil their obligations under the Act to accommodate children by providing residential establishments themselves or with other local authorities, or by securing the provision of such

---

184 "Establishment" in this context means any establishment managed by a local authority, voluntary organisation or other person providing non-residential accommodation for the purposes of the Act, whether for reward or not; "residential establishment" means the same except that it involves residential accommodation: 1968 Act, s. 94(1).

185 Including the Children (Scotland) Act 1995 and the Mental Health (Care and Treatment) (Scotland) Act 2003.

186 Social Work (Scotland) Act 1968, s. 59(1).

establishments by voluntary organisations or other persons.[187] The existing categories of voluntary home, local authority home and approved school were subsumed by the Act into the new, single, category of "residential establishment", though each initially remained subject to their existing rules and regulations.

Registration and visiting of residential establishments

Any residential or other establishment the sole or main object of which was to accommodate persons for the purposes of the 1968 Act (other than those controlled or managed by a government department or a local authority) required to be registered with a local authority.[188] Registration could be refused on a number of grounds, relating to either the premises themselves or the staff.[189] So, for the first time, the fitness of those working in establishments where children resided came under state scrutiny – though no definition of "unfitness" was laid down. Registration, once granted, could be cancelled on specified grounds.[190] When registration was refused or cancelled, the local authority could remove all or any persons resident in the establishment forthwith.[191]

Any duly authorised officer of the local authority could enter any registrable establishment in the area of the local authority

> for the purpose of making such examinations into the state and management of the place, and the condition and treatment of the persons in it, as he thinks necessary, and for the purpose of inspecting any records or registers required to be kept therein . . .[192]

In addition, local authorities were obliged "from time to time to cause persons in establishments in their areas to be visited in the interests of the well-being of the persons in the establishment":[193] this mandated the visiting of each individual child accommodated in a residential establishment and,

---

187 Ibid. s. 59(2).
188 Ibid. ss. 61 (subsequently amended by the Registered Establishment (Scotland) Act 1987, s. 1) and 62. Registration was required with the Secretary of State if he specified that any establishment or class of establishment should be so registered: s. 63. These provisions were replaced by the Regulation of Care (Scotland) Act 2001.
189 Social Work (Scotland) Act 1968, s. 62(3).
190 Social Work (Scotland) Act 1968, s. 62(4), and as later amended by the Registered Establishment (Scotland) Act 1987, s. 3.
191 Social Work (Scotland) Act 1968, s. 65(1).
192 Ibid. s. 67(1).
193 Ibid. s. 68(1).

together with the obligation to examine the state and management of the premises, constituted the main mechanism by which local authorities monitored each child's wellbeing.

SOCIAL WORK (RESIDENTIAL ESTABLISHMENTS – CHILD CARE) (SCOTLAND) REGULATIONS 1987

More detail concerning the running of residential establishments was set out in the Social Work (Residential Establishments – Child Care) (Scotland) Regulations 1987,[194] which gave effect, after a nineteen-year delay, to the principle in the Social Work (Scotland) Act 1968 that all residential establishments for children were to be subject to the same level and nature of regulation by the state. They replaced both the Administration of Children's Homes (Scotland) Regulations, 1959 and the Approved Schools (Scotland) Rules, 1961 which had remained in effect after 1968. The 1987 Regulations imposed obligations primarily on the managers of residential establishments – that is to say the appropriate officers of the local authority or voluntary organisation providing the residential establishment.[195] The overarching obligation of these managers was to "make such provision for the care, development and control of each child resident there as shall be conducive to the best interests of each child".[196] The reference to "development" is particularly to be noticed:[197] children, by definition, are at a developmental stage, and their care needs to be focused on developing their capacities for the future. The regulations were designed, overall, to ensure that the running of residential establishments kept the welfare of the children therein the central focus of all activities. Evidence presented to the Scottish Child Abuse Inquiry in 2017–2019 suggests that the reality all too often fell woefully short of this ideal.[198]

---

194 SI 1987/2233 (S. 150).
195 1987 Regulations, reg. 2. That legal liability rests first and foremost with the managers of residential establishments was confirmed in *M v Hendron* 2007 SC 556.
196 1987 Regulations, reg. 4.
197 The Approved Schools (Scotland) Rules, 1961 had required the headmaster to run the school in the interests of the welfare, development and rehabilitation of the pupils (r. 11(1)) but the 1987 Regulation was more focused on the development of the individual.
198 The SCAI's Case Study No. 2 (May 2019) into the residential care of children provided by the Sisters of Nazareth, a religious group, in four locations throughout Scotland came to the following heart-breaking conclusion, p. ix: "The Nazareth Houses in Scotland were, for many children, places of fear, hostility and confusion, places where children were physically abused and emotionally degraded with impunity. There was sexual abuse of children which, in some instances, reached levels of the utmost depravity. Children in need of kind, warm, loving care and comfort did not find it. Children were deprived of compassion, dignity, care and comfort."

The statement of functions

An important innovation in the 1987 Regulations was the imposition on the managers of a requirement to prepare, and keep under review, a statement of functions and objectives for the establishment. This statement had to include the particulars specified in Schedule 1, which included the arrangements to meet the needs and development potential of the children resident in the establishment, including their emotional, spiritual, intellectual and physical needs; the arrangements to assist each child to develop his or her potential, and for formulating procedures in co-operation with the care authorities to deal with complaints from children, or their parents or relatives; the arrangements for visits by relatives and friends of the children; the establishment's policy on the involvement of children and parents in decisions about the child's future while in residential care; and the policy and practice in regard to the recruitment and training of appropriately qualified staff.

The reference to involving children themselves and their parents in decision-making and to allowing them to make complaints is one of the earliest provisions giving children in residential establishments or their families a voice. Involving parents in the care and future planning for children accommodated away from home had underpinned the thinking in the 1968 Act, and that is reflected here.

Discipline

Arrangements for discipline, relevant to the care and control of children resident in a residential establishment, were to be determined by the managers in accordance with the statement of functions and objectives formulated under regulation 5(1) but, in an important change to the previous law, these arrangements could not involve corporal punishment.[199] Corporal punishment in any context was coming under increasing attack throughout the 1980s,[200] and the decision was made that it was in all cases an inappropriate method to be employed in the care and control of vulnerable children.

---

199 1987 Regulations, reg. 10.
200 See further, Chapter 3 above.

The role of the local authority and care authority

The local authority that issued a certificate of registration under s. 62(3) of the 1968 Act was obliged by the 1987 Regulations to visit the residential establishment at least annually in order to satisfy itself "that the operation of the residential establishment continues to conform to the requirements for registration" and "that the safety and welfare of children resident within the establishment are being maintained".[201] A local authority could recommend to a children's hearing that a child be placed in a residential establishment only if, having carried out the procedure provided for in regulation 18, it was satisfied that it would be in the child's best interest to impose a supervision requirement with a condition to that effect.[202] And where the local authority came to the view that it was no longer in the interests of the child to remain in the residential placement named in the supervision requirement, it was obliged to refer the case to the reporter for a review of the supervision requirement.[203] There was, however, no sanction for the local authority's failure to do so.

The care authority (that is to say either the local authority or the relevant voluntary organisation[204]) had to ensure, so far as was consistent with its duty under section 20 of the 1968 Act and having ascertained so far as practicable the wishes and feelings of each child, that each child of the same family was placed in the same residential placement or, where that was not appropriate or practicable, that the placements facilitated as far as possible continued mutual contact and access.[205] This is a matter that has a direct impact on children being accommodated away from their families, but if the obligation was not fulfilled there was little that could be done to force the care authority to change its approach. The care authority had to take such steps as were necessary to satisfy itself that any placement continued to be in the interests of the child, by visiting the child (i) within one week of the placement being made; (ii) thereafter at intervals of not more than three months from the date of the last visit; (iii) on such other occasions as the care authority considered necessary in order to supervise the child's welfare; and by receiving and considering written reports on these visits.[206] The care authority was

---

201 1987 Regulations, reg. 16.
202 Ibid. reg. 26.
203 Ibid. reg. 27(3).
204 Ibid. reg. 2.
205 Ibid. reg. 21.
206 Ibid. reg. 23.

duty-bound to terminate the placement as soon as practicable where for any reason it appeared to it that it was no longer in the child's best interests to remain in the residential placement.[207] This required the care authority to keep the child's progress under constant review.

FURTHER RETHINKING OF RESIDENTIAL CARE IN THE 1990S

The early 1990s saw the publication of a number of reports, as policy-makers moved towards the drafting of the Children (Scotland) Act 1995. Some of these considered the use of residential care.

The Skinner Report on Residential Care in Scotland[208]

In 1991, after some years of declining use of institutional care for children and young people, the then Chief Inspector of Social Work Services, Mr Angus Skinner, was commissioned by the Secretary of State for Scotland to carry out a review of residential care in Scotland. This review:

> focused on the need for good-quality residential care in smaller units with spe-cialised functions. It also addressed key areas such as the training and qualifica-tions of staff, the rights of children, the need to safeguard children who were in residential care, the compatibility of a residential care regime and individual children's care plans, and the improvement of practice. The report recognised the central role of the local authority in providing residential care for children, but such recognition was not reflected in the allocation of guaranteed or ring-fenced resources . . . However, the place of residential care as an essential element in a comprehensive child-care provision became re-established.[209]

Skinner reported that the number of children and young people in homes or residential schools run by or registered with local authorities had fallen from 6,336 in 1976 to 2,161 in 1990, or from 4.2 per thousand to 2.0 per thousand,[210] though there were regional variations.[211] There were noticeable shifts in practice during that time, both from voluntary to compulsory care[212] and towards shorter stays in residential accommodation.[213]

---

207 Ibid. reg. 24.
208 *Another Kind of Home* (Scottish Office, HMSO, 1992).
209 Gilmour, I. and Giltinan, D. "The Changing Focus of Social Work" in A. Lockyer and F. Stone (eds) *Juvenile Justice in Scotland: 25 Years of the Welfare Approach* (1998), p. 152.
210 Skinner Report, para 2.2.
211 Ibid. para 2.6.
212 Ibid. para 2.9.
213 Ibid. para 2.10.

The Skinner Report recommended that residential care should not be seen as a last resort but as an option to be considered positively and that local authorities' policy statements explicitly identify residential care as part of a fully integrated child care strategy.

The Fife Inquiry (The Kearney Report)[214]

Residential accommodation was also at the heart of Sheriff Kearney's Report into child care policies adopted by Fife Regional Council. Though the legislative boarding-out preference had disappeared in 1968, it had long been suspected that some local authorities in Scotland nevertheless continued with that approach, often for financial reasons rather than through an individualised assessment of the needs of any particular child. Different local authorities adopted different policies with the result that the rates of accommodating children in residential establishments varied wildly across Scotland. Substantially the lowest rate was, by the 1980s, to be found in Fife, where in 1985 it stood at 5.9 children per thousand of population as opposed to 10.6 per thousand in mainland Scotland as a whole. By 1989 Fife's figure had fallen to 3.4 per thousand as opposed to mainland Scotland's total figure of 10.3.[215] (The lower figures given in the Skinner Report for roughly the same period relate only to local authority homes). Something had clearly changed in Fife and Sheriff Brian Kearney, a highly respected authority on child care law and practice, was appointed to examine the policies adopted by the local authority. Sheriff Kearney found that Fife Regional Council in the 1980s had a stated policy to give first preference to placements with foster parents, but he castigated as a "gross-oversimplification" any working assumption that home or a substitute home is in all cases better than residential care.[216] More problematical for the practice of child care was that, as a result of the council's policy, children's homes across Fife had been closed, limiting the possible outcomes available to children's hearings. Social workers employed by the council were encouraged to recommend home supervision to children's hearings in preference to any residential outcome and the Report questioned whether Fife Regional Council was acting inconsistently with its statutory duties or was undermining the authority of the hearing, by refusing to make recommendations for residential placements.

---

214 *The Report of the Inquiry into Child Care Policies in Fife*, (HC Papers 1992–93, No. 191).
215 Kearney Report, p. 30.
216 Ibid. p. 280.

The Inquiry concluded that the council's approach "was dangerous and inimical to good social work practice".[217]

A number of important recommendations were made in Part J, chapter IX of the Kearney Report, but the bulk of the Report related to practice in one region only. Its enduring importance was that it brought to public attention the dangers of local authorities applying in individual cases approaches based on generalised assumptions as to what was good for children.

The White Paper: *Scotland's Children: Proposals for Child Care Policy and Law*[218]

Acknowledging the findings of the Skinner Report, the 1993 White Paper *Scotland's Children* accepted that "the quality of care experienced by young people in many residential homes and schools needed to be improved".[219] But it was accepted that residential accommodation still had an important role to play in child care and protection.

> Residential homes and schools can offer special advantages in providing care and education by bringing together special skills to help young people, children and parents and by offering flexibility and creativity, for instance, in meeting the social and educational needs of older children through independent living schemes. Furthermore, it should be possible to develop shared care with families, and provide them with a wide range of support.
>
> Residential care, with or without education, will continue to meet important needs. Homes and schools need to be equipped to provide a good standard of care and education, looking after young people in a sensitive and positive manner, not least because some young people in care will continue to choose residential care, in preference to family placement, and their choice should be respected . . .[220]

RESIDENTIAL ESTABLISHMENTS – CHILD CARE (SCOTLAND) REGULATIONS 1996: THE CURRENT RULES

The Children (Scotland) Act 1995 itself had little to say about residential accommodation, but its passing necessitated a review of all secondary legislation underpinning local authority obligations towards children in their care – now to be referred to as "looked after children". The Social Work

---

217 Ibid. pp. 612–613.
218 Scottish Office, HMSO 1993, Cm 2286.
219 *Scotland's Children*, para 3.24.
220 *Scotland's Children*, paras 3.25–3.29.

(Residential Establishments – Child Care) (Scotland) Regulations 1987 were replaced by the Residential Establishments – Child Care (Scotland) Regulations 1996,[221] which remain in force today. The most significant development was the imposition of an obligation on the managers of a residential establishment to have in place appropriate procedures for the vetting of staff in relation to their suitability to work in the establishment both prior to their appointment and regularly thereafter.[222] Vetting of staff was later required to comply with the rules in the Protection of Children (Scotland) Act 2003 and the Protection of Vulnerable Groups (Scotland) Act 2007.[223]

E. SECURE ACCOMMODATION

INTRODUCTION

The earliest statutory authority in Scotland for keeping children under lock and key (other than in Borstal or Young Offenders Institutions) appears to have been a fairly obscure provision in the Approved Schools (Scotland) Rules, 1961 allowing the Secretary of State to approve the use of part of an approved school "as a special section for pupils who are abnormally unruly, or are persistent absconders".[224] There was no provision to govern how any individual child was determined to be "abnormally unruly" or a persistent absconder (or indeed to define these phrases), nor any mechanism to review that determination, and though the Secretary of State's authority was required for the initial placement in a special section both release and return to the special section were matters solely for the headmaster of the school.[225] The first use of the term "secure accommodation" would appear to be in s. 72 of the Children Act 1975, which inserted a new s. 59A into the Social Work (Scotland) Act 1968, authorising the Secretary of State to make grants to local authorities to provide "secure accommodation in residential establishments", "secure accommodation" being defined as "accommodation provided for the purpose of restricting the liberty of children". (This has remained the definition ever since.)[226] The provision allowing the use of a

---

221 SI 1996/3256 (S. 246).
222 1996 Regulations, reg. 8.
223 See Chapter 2 above.
224 Approved Schools (Scotland) Rules, 1961, r. 34(1).
225 Ibid. r. 34(2).
226 Children (Scotland) Act 1995, s. 93; Children's Hearings (Scotland) Act 2011, s. 202.

"special section" of an approved school was repealed in 1983 by the first set of regulations (considered below) dedicated to secure units.[227]

CRITERIA FOR PLACING A CHILD IN SECURE ACCOMMODATION

Since the United Kingdom acceded to the European Convention on Human Rights, any interference with a person's physical liberty has required to be compliant with Art. 5 thereof (right to liberty and security) and, in a different context from children in care, Art. 5 was held by the European Court of Human Rights to have been breached in *X v United Kingdom*.[228] That case involved s. 66(3) of the (English) Mental Health Act, 1959 which allowed the Home Secretary to recall to a secure mental hospital a patient who had been conditionally discharged therefrom, but which did not lay down any basis identifying when it would be appropriate for the Home Secretary to do so. An exercise of this unfettered discretion was challenged by a patient alleging a breach of Art. 5(4) of the European Convention, which requires the existence of "proceedings by which the lawfulness of [a detainee's] detention shall be decided speedily". The UK Government argued that the opportunity for recourse to the Mental Health Review Tribunal (MHRT) satisfied that requirement, but the European Court disagreed, pointing out that the MHRT had no power to determine the "lawfulness of [the] detention", nor to order the detainee's immediate release: rather its role was advisory only.[229]

There was, at the time, no obvious means to determine the lawfulness of detention of children and young persons in "special sections" of approved schools, and indeed no real process to determine whether the child or young person should be so detained. To pre-empt any challenge to detaining children and young persons in secure accommodation the UK Parliament enacted s. 8 of the Health and Social Services and Social Security Adjudications Act 1983.[230] This added a new s.58A into the Social Work (Scotland) Act 1968 allowing the children's hearing, when making a residential supervision requirement over a child, to add a condition that the child be

> liable to be placed and kept in secure accommodation in the named residential establishment at such times as the person in charge of that establishment, with

227 Secure Accommodation (Scotland) Regulations 1983, reg. 19.
228 [1982] 4 EHRR 188.
229 [1982] 4 EHRR 188, para 61.
230 See the discussion of the amendments at HC Deb. 11 May 1983, vol. 42 cols 856–857. See also, for England and Wales, s. 25 of the Criminal Justice Act 1982.

the agreement of the director of social work of the local authority required to give effect to the supervision requirement, considers it necessary that he do so . . .

Criteria for adding such a condition were specified as follows:

(a) [the child] has a history of absconding, and—
  (i) he is likely to abscond unless he is kept in secure accommodation; and
  (ii) if he absconds, it is likely that his physical, mental or moral welfare will be at risk; or
(b) he is likely to injure himself or other persons unless he is kept in secure accommodation.[231]

These criteria have not changed since.[232] Nor has the rule that attaching a secure accommodation condition to a supervision requirement does not impose any legal obligation to accommodate the child in secure accommodation but merely renders the child liable to be kept there. A decision requires to be made as to whether or not it is in the child's interests to implement that authorisation.[233] The use of secure accommodation in Scotland has always been about control in the child's own interests, and not punishment for the child's actions.

SECURE ACCOMMODATION (SCOTLAND) REGULATIONS 1983

The Regulations discussed above governing residential establishments and approved schools applied in whole to the secure parts of such establishments that provided secure accommodation. Additional rules were contained in the Secure Accommodation (Scotland) Regulations 1983,[234] applying to "accommodation provided in a residential establishment for the purpose of restricting the liberty of children".[235] No accommodation in any residential establishment could be used to restrict a child's liberty except with the approval of the Secretary of State.[236] The person in charge of a residential establishment providing secure accommodation was originally duty-bound to "ensure that a child placed and kept in such accommodation receives care

---

231 Social Work (Scotland) Act 1968, s. 58A(3), as inserted by s. 8(4) of the Health and Social Services and Social Security Adjudications Act 1983.
232 Children (Scotland) Act 1995 s. 70(10); Children's Hearings (Scotland) Act 2011, s. 83(6).
233 That it is not the children's hearing that makes that decision was held not to breach Art. 5 of the ECHR in *J v Children's Reporter for Stirling* 2010 Fam. LR 140.
234 SI 1983/1912.
235 1983 Regulations, reg. 2(1).
236 Ibid. reg. 3.

appropriate to his needs".[237] However, from 1 June 1988 responsibility for meeting the child's needs was shifted to "the managers", (that is to say the appropriate officers of either the local authority or voluntary organisation running the residential establishment providing secure accommodation[238]). Consequently, managers became obliged, in consultation with the person in charge of the residential establishment, to "ensure that a child placed and kept in such accommodation receives such provision for his care, development and control as shall be conducive to the child's best interests".[239]

SECURE ACCOMMODATION (SCOTLAND) REGULATIONS 1996 AND 2013

The 1983 Regulations were replaced by the Secure Accommodation (Scotland) Regulations 1996,[240] which were themselves replaced by the Secure Accommodation (Scotland) Regulations 2013.[241] The 2013 Regulations continue to apply today.

The 1996 Regulations repeated the 1983 obligation on the managers to ensure that the welfare of a child placed and kept in such accommodation was safeguarded and promoted.[242] Reviews of the case of a child kept in secure accommodation were required at greater frequency than with other accommodated children, and had to be conducted within seven days of the child being placed in secure accommodation and thereafter at least every three months, as well as at such times as appeared necessary or appropriate in light of the child's progress.[243] This was designed to monitor the keeping of the child in secure accommodation and to ensure that the child's liberty was restored as soon as detention was no longer necessary. (That did not, of course, necessarily involve sending the child home – merely that the child would no longer be kept in secure accommodation.)

The 2013 Regulations place an obligation on the managers to ensure that the welfare of any child placed and kept in secure accommodation is

---

237 Ibid. reg. 4.
238 Ibid. reg. 2, as amended by the Secure Accommodation (Scotland) Amendment Regulations 1988 (SI 1988/841), reg. 3.
239 1983 Regulations, reg. 4, as amended by the Secure Accommodation (Scotland) Amendment Regulations 1988, reg. 4.
240 SI 1996/3255 (S. 245).
241 SSI 2013/205, reg. 16.
242 Secure Accommodation (Scotland) Regulations 1996, reg. 4.
243 Ibid. reg. 15. Under the Arrangements to Look After Children (Scotland) Regulations 1996, regs 8 and 9, reviews were required within six weeks, then three months later and then at six monthly intervals.

safeguarded and promoted.[244] Reviews are dealt with under the Children's Hearings (Scotland) Act 2011 (Implementation of Secure Accommodation Authorisation) (Scotland) Regulations 2013,[245] which require the chief social work officer to review the child's placement in secure accommodation within seven days of the placement, and thereafter monthly (an increase from the three-monthly reviews under the 1996 Regulations), or whenever the child or relevant person[246] requests a review.

VISITATION AND INSPECTION OF SECURE UNITS

Visitation and inspection of secure accommodation were originally subsumed into the monitoring regime of all residential establishments,[247] which was the primary responsibility of local authorities. "Secure accommodation services" were later placed within the definition of "care services" for the purposes of the Regulation of Care (Scotland) Act 2001[248] as a result of which they became subject to registration and inspection by the Care Commission. Secure accommodation is today a "care service" under the Public Services Reform (Scotland) Act 2010[249] and so subject to the registration and inspection regimes of the Care Inspectorate.

---

244 Secure Accommodation (Scotland) Regulations 2013, reg. 4.
245 SSI 2013/212.
246 "Relevant person" in relation to a child within the children's hearing system is a parent, other person with parental responsibilities and parental rights, or a person deemed to be a relevant person because he or she has or has recently had significant involvement in the upbringing of the child: Children's Hearings (Scotland) Act 2011, ss. 81 and 200.
247 Social Work (Residential Establishments – Child Care) (Scotland) Regulations 1987, reg 16; Residential Establishments – Child Care (Scotland) Regulations 1996, reg. 16.
248 Regulation of Care (Scotland) Act 2001, s. 2.
249 Public Services Reform (Scotland) Act 2010, s. 47(1)(f) and sched. 12 para 6.

9. Emergency and Interim Protection

INTRODUCTION

It frequently happens that the state or its agencies feel obliged to take action in order to provide effective protection to children and young people on either an emergency or an interim basis. Emergency measures may be understood as those that need to be taken as a matter of urgency, even before anyone has had a chance to bring the matter to the attention of a legally constituted tribunal. Interim measures, whether following immediately after emergency measures or otherwise, are those authorised by an appropriate tribunal, but before it has had the chance to interrogate the case fully, or before plans have been put in place that would serve the child's long-term security. There is a significant degree of overlap between emergency measures and interim measures. Both are characterised by a perceived need for the state to act more quickly to protect the child's welfare than the normal child protection processes allow, to act indeed before it has been established that the child actually does need protective measures to be taken, or before appropriate measures designed to meet the needs of the child have been identified or put in place. Both are also characterised by their temporary nature, and they will have legal effect, in the case of emergency measures, only until the child or young person can be brought before an appropriate tribunal and, in the case of interim measures, only until that tribunal has had an opportunity to consider what long-term provisions are best suited, and are available, for the particular child in question.

The distinction between emergency and interim measures has never been clear-cut, and the point of division has shifted with the various statutory provisions that will be examined in this chapter. The current law adopts the nomenclature of "emergency child protection measures" to refer to both the removal by a constable of a child to a place of safety and the authorisation by a justice of the peace to any person to do the same;[1] at

---

1 Children's Hearings (Scotland) Act 2011 (Emergency Child Protection Measures) Regulations, 2012 (SSI 2012/334).

the same time, contemporary legislation allows for a variety of measures called "interim" orders.[2] In discussing the child protection order, created in 1995 as an interim order made by a sheriff, Sheriff Holligan[3] referred to "the emergency nature of the order" and pointed out that in the Children (Scotland) Act 1995 the relevant provisions appeared under the headnote "measures for the emergency protection of children" while in the Children's Hearings (Scotland) Act 2011 they appeared immediately before a headnote "other emergency measures". The terminology, however, reflects perception rather than substance, and the overlaps between the two categories justify them being treated here together: in any case, the one nearly always leads to the other.

THE EARLY CHILD CRUELTY STATUTES: 1889–1908

The design of the first statutory child protection provision that allowed for the summary removal of a child from a source of danger has proved remarkably resilient. In two sections, the Prevention of Cruelty to, and Protection of, Children Act, 1889 envisaged three separate stages, through which some (but not all) cases will go: (i) the immediate removal and keeping of a child from a source of danger without court involvement, (ii) the making by the court of temporary arrangements for the child's care while the suitability of long-term provision is explored, and (iii) the making by the court of more permanent arrangements. The first of these stages was to be found in s. 4(1) of the 1889 Act, which permitted a constable to take to a "place of safety"[4] any "child"[5] in respect of whom an offence under either s. 1 (ill-treatment, neglect, abandonment or exposure of a child) or s. 3(a) (causing or procuring a child to be in the street for the purposes of begging) had been committed. Though the wording of this provision allowed the constable to act only if he himself witnessed the commission of the offence, seeing a child in a situation of begging, or being alone, having been abandoned or exposed, or suffering from neglect, was almost certainly enough. The authority to detain the child in the place of safety under this provision lasted until he or she could be

---

2 For example, the interim child supervision order defined in s. 86 of the Children's Hearings (Scotland) Act 2011, or the interim order made during the permanence process under s. 97 of the Adoption and Children (Scotland) Act 2007.

3 *Application for a Child Protection Order* 2015 SLT (Sh Ct) 9, para 9.

4 The definition of this phrase is discussed later in this chapter.

5 Under the 1889 Act, a "child" was a boy under 14 or a girl under 16.

brought before a court of summary jurisdiction,[6] but it is noticeable – very much so, to modern eyes – that no timescale was laid down within which the child had to be brought before the court.

The second stage, also in s. 4(1), was that the court could, when the child was brought before it, take whatever further (interim) measures it thought fit "until the charge made against any person in respect of the said offence has been determined by the committal to trial, or conviction, or discharge of such person". The length of time such interim measures lasted would be dependent on the criminal process against the accused.

The third stage, set out in s. 5(1) of the 1889 Act, allowed the court to make more permanent provision, so long as the accused had not been discharged – when it had been shown, in other words, that the child did indeed require protection. It was assumed that the commission of the offence in the past indicated a need for protection in the future. Other than sending the child home, the court could, if satisfied that it was "expedient so to deal with the child", commit the child to the charge of a relation of the child or some other fit person named by the court, until the child's 14th birthday (if a boy) or 16th birthday (if a girl) or for such shorter period as the court specified.

The 1889 Act was amended by the Prevention of Cruelty to Children (Amendment) Act, 1894, by adding "assault" to the acts that would amount to an offence under s. 1 of the 1889 Act, and by equalising at 16 the ages for both boys and girls in respect of whom the Act applied. The procedure, as amended, was then re-enacted in the Prevention of Cruelty to Children Acts, 1894 and 1904, before being replaced by the Children Act, 1908, which further increased the range of offences against children or young people that would justify a constable taking a child or young person to a place of safety.[7] In addition, the 1908 Act permitted a child to be detained in a place of safety not only after having been taken there by a constable or other authorised person but also after the child him- or herself sought refuge there.[8]

More significantly, the 1908 Act dropped the requirement for the constable to have personally witnessed the offence before taking the emergency action, and the power summarily to take a child to a place of safety was for the first time activated if there was "reason to believe" that one of

6   That is to say, a sheriff or sheriff substitute: Prevention of Cruelty to, and Protection of, Children Act, 1889, s. 17.

7   For details, see Chapter 4 above.

8   Children Act, 1908, s. 20(2).

the specified offences had been committed.[9] This allowed constables to act on information received that an offence had been committed, so long as the information was credible. In the modern era, it was said that "The presence of uncertainties does not prevent there being reasonable cause to believe".[10] Further, the power of constables summarily to take children to a place of safety was extended to "any person authorised by a justice":[11] "justice" meant (in its application to Scotland) a sheriff or a justice of the peace.[12] This allowed other individuals and voluntary organisations (child protection societies and the like) to seek authorisation to remove children from situations of danger and detain them in a place of safety: such organisations became effectively constables for the purposes of these provisions. In a curious reflection of the 1908 position, the present-day power to act under the authority of a justice of the peace, together with the power of a constable of summary removal, are in the contemporary law described collectively as "emergency child protection measures".[13]

Place of safety warrants

Perhaps the most significant change made by the 1908 Act was its introduction of a new process to allow a sheriff or justice of the peace to issue a warrant to remove a child or young person to a place of safety in cases of suspected as opposed to actual harm.[14] The court required to be persuaded that the person seeking the warrant had "reasonable cause to suspect" that the child or young person (i) had been assaulted, ill-treated or neglected in a manner likely to cause him or her unnecessary suffering or to be injurious to his or her health, or (ii) was the victim of a scheduled[15] offence. Such a warrant could be sought by any person who, in the opinion of the court, was acting in the interests of the child or young person: this might be the police, a voluntary organisation such as the RSSPCC, the Salvation Army or a private individual.[16] This new warrant differed from the existing methods

9 Ibid. s. 20(1).
10 *Windsor & Ors v CPS* [2011] EWCA Crim 143 per Hooper LJ, para 53.
11 Children Act, 1908, s. 20(1).
12 Ibid. s. 132(9).
13 Children's Hearings (Scotland) Act 2011 (Child Protection Emergency Measures) Regulations 2012.
14 Children Act, 1908, s. 24.
15 Originally the First Schedule to the 1908 Act, and later the First Schedule to the 1937 Act.
16 The obtaining of a warrant disposed of any question of the applicant's good faith: so there was no civil liability for malicious prosecution or wrongful imprisonment (these actions being dependent on lack of probable cause): *Hope v Evered* (1886) 17 QBD 338; *Lea v Charrington* (1889)

of protection in that it was a measure requiring prior approval of a court, but it was as temporary as the summary removal by a constable acting on his reasonable beliefs. The warrant lasted only until the child or young person was brought before a court of summary jurisdiction which, if it felt further protective measures were appropriate, could commit the child to the care of a relative or other fit person.[17] As with the other 1908 provisions discussed above, there was no explicit time limit laid down within which the child had to be brought before a court on being detained under a warrant.

Before issuing a warrant under s. 24 the court had to be satisfied that the applicant had "reasonable cause to suspect" harm to the child. That constituted a lower standard than that which justified the constable acting on his own initiative without court authorisation, which was that the constable had "reason to believe" that the child was the victim of a specified offence. Over 100 years later, the same distinction was still being made in the legislation. Macfarlane et al.[18] put it thus:

> The standard of "reasonable grounds to believe" is more exacting than ... "reasonable suspicion" and entails that the applicant must be able not only sufficiently to specify the grounds but also to justify the contention that a reasonable person, on being given the information on which the belief is founded, would think "this situation puts the child at risk of significant harm and cannot be allowed to continue".

EMERGENCY AND INTERIM PROTECTION 1932–1995

The Children and Young Persons (Scotland) Act, 1932, which amended but did not repeal the 1908 Act, extended the definition of "young person" to 17,[19] thus extending the existing protection mechanisms to that age.

The emergency power in s. 20 of the 1908 Act of a constable or any person authorised by a justice to take a child to a place of safety was replaced by s. 11 of the 1932 Act (itself to be replaced by s. 71(1) of the Children and Young Persons (Scotland) Act, 1937, which repealed both the 1908 and the 1932 Acts). Though the emergency and interim procedures themselves did not change to any significant extent, the long-term options available to the juvenile court in dealing with children and young persons in need of care

---

23 QBD 272. The warrant could only be executed, however, by a constable, though the constable would be accompanied by the applicant: 1908 Act, s. 24(4).

17 Children Act, 1908, s. 24(1).

18 Macfarlane, K., Driscoll, M., Kearney B., and Anderson L. in *Greens Annotated Acts: Children's Hearings (Scotland) Act 2011* (W. Green, 2018), p. 46.

19 Children and Young Persons (Scotland) Act, 1932, s. 64.

and protection were substantially expanded by the 1932 Act. It was provided that if the juvenile court was not, when the child was first brought to it from a place of safety, in a position to decide which of the various options it now had available that it ought to make,[20] it could make

> such interim order as they think fit for [the child's] detention or continued detention in a place of safety, or for his [or her] committal to the care of a fit person, whether a relative or not, who is willing to undertake the care of him [or her] . . .[21]

In substance this was no different from what had gone before, but it does seem to have been the first time that the terminology of "interim order" was used for this temporary provision. Also for the first time, and more substantively, an explicit timescale was laid down by the legislation. An interim order made under s. 11 of the 1932 Act (and then s. 71 of the 1937 Act) was to remain in force for not more than 28 days, though if the court thought it "expedient" it could make a further interim order. The language of both the 1932 and 1937 Acts created an ambiguity (which, in the event, was never resolved) whether only one further interim order was envisaged.[22]

The Social Work (Scotland) Act 1968 replaced the emergency power previously contained in s. 71 of the 1937 Act of a constable or other authorised person to take a child to a place of safety and keep him or her there.[23] The major change concerned the length of time a child could be kept in a place of safety before being brought to a tribunal, for under the 1968 Act it was substantially shorter than previously. It was now to be the same as for children kept in places of safety under warrants, discussed below: that is to say, until either the reporter to the newly created children's panel came to the view that there was no need for any compulsory measures of care, or on the day after a children's hearing first sat to consider the case, or in any case at the end of seven days after the child was first taken to the place of safety.[24] The taking of a child to a place of safety under this provision obliged the reporter to consider whether that child needed compulsory measures of supervision and, if the reporter did so consider, to arrange a children's hearing where practicable on the

---

20 Under s. 6(1) of the Children and Young Persons (Scotland) Act, 1932, and subsequently s. 66(2) of the Children and Young Persons (Scotland) Act, 1937.

21 Children and Young Persons (Scotland) Act, 1932, s. 11(2), subsequently s. 71(2) of the Children and Young Persons (Scotland) Act, 1937.

22 Trotter, T. *The Law as to Children and Young Persons* (W. Hodge & Co, 1938), p. 130 suggests that it would not be an abuse of power if a further interim order were deemed necessary after the first making of a further order.

23 Social Work (Scotland) Act 1968, s. 37(2).

24 Ibid. s. 37(3).

first lawful day after the child's detention.[25] Since the children's hearing arranged for the first lawful day would be highly unlikely to be able to make a dispositive decision at that early stage, it was given the power to issue a warrant for the further detention of the child in a place of safety, so long as it was satisfied that this was necessary in the child's own interests or there was reason to believe that the child would run away during the investigation.[26] "The child's own interests" might include preventing the child from acting in such a way as would make his or her own position worse.[27] That warrant would last for 21 days but, resolving the doubt that had existed under the 1937 Act, it was provided that this warrant could be renewed for one further period of 21 days.[28] Even 42 days of interim detention proved in some cases insufficient time to allow the reporter to fully investigate the child's case, and the local authority to identify the best option for the child. Therefore, the Children Act 1975 allowed the reporter to apply to the sheriff, after the children's hearing's warrants were exhausted, for a warrant from the sheriff requiring the child's detention in a place of safety for a further 21 days, which could then be renewed once.[29] So a child could be kept in a place of safety for a maximum of 84 days, the legislation clearly envisaging that this would be ample time to allow the hearing to make a fully-informed dispositive decision. However, it was held by the First Division in *Humphries v X & Y*[30] that in exceptional circumstances[31] it would be competent to invoke the *nobile officium* of the Court of Session in order to keep the child in a place of safety for longer than these statutory periods permitted.

Another significant change made by the Children Act 1975 was that it greatly expanded the categories of children who could be taken to a place of safety under s. 37 of the 1968 Act. After 1975, the constable, as well as taking the child believed to be a victim of an offence to a place of safety, could now also take a child who was a member of the same household as the child victim, and any child who was or was likely to become a member of the same household as a person who had committed or was believed to have

25 Ibid. s. 37(4).
26 Ibid. s. 37(4).
27 *Humphries v S* 1986 SLT 683 (IH).
28 Social Work (Scotland) Act 1968, s. 37(5).
29 Ibid. s. 37(5A) and (5B), as inserted by Children Act 1975, s. 83(d).
30 1982 SC 79.
31 The exceptional circumstances in this case were that the father of the children being kept in a place of safety under warrant was awaiting trial for the murder of the children's younger sibling and the children's hearing was being postponed in order not to prejudice that trial.

committed such an offence; as well, the constable could now take to a place of safety any child "who is likely to be caused unnecessary suffering or serious impairment of health because there is, or is believed to be, in respect of the child a lack of parental care".[32]

Place of safety warrants

Section 24 of the 1908 Act, under which a place of safety warrant could be issued by a court, was re-enacted without substantive change as s. 47 of the Children and Young Persons (Scotland) Act, 1937. While interim orders had had time-limits since 1932, it was not until the Social Work (Scotland) Act 1968 that an explicit limit was laid down for how long a child could be kept in a place of safety under a warrant issued under s. 47. That new time limit was the same as that for warrants issued by the children's hearing. The authority to keep the child or young person in a place of safety would now come to an end when either the reporter came to the view that there was no need for any compulsory measures of care, or on the day after a children's hearing first sat to consider the case, or in any case at the termination of seven days after the warrant had been issued.[33] The amended s. 47 was replaced without substantive change by s. 14 of the Criminal Procedure (Scotland) Act 1975, which itself was repealed by the Criminal Procedure (Consequential Provisions) (Scotland) Act 1995[34] and the warrant process was subsumed into that contained in the Children (Scotland) Act 1995, shortly to be discussed.

Interim measures

Whether brought to a children's hearing after being detained by a constable or under a warrant issued by a court, the convening of the "first lawful day hearing" brought the existing authority to detain the child to an end and any further authority to detain the child away from home came from the orders that the hearing itself made. A children's hearing would seldom be able to make a long-term order at the "first lawful day hearing"[35] and would normally have to continue the case to a subsequent hearing, to allow for further investigation,[36]

---

32 Children Act 1975, s. 83, amending s. 37(2) of the Social Work (Scotland) Act 1968.
33 Social Work (Scotland) Act 1968, sched. 2 para 8, adding a new s. 47(1A) to the 1937 Act.
34 Criminal Procedure (Consequential Provisions) (Scotland) Act 1995, sched. 5 para 1.
35 It might, if the child was subject to a supervision order and his or her case well-known, before some emergency required his or her removal to a place of safety.
36 Social Work (Scotland) Act 1968, s. 43(3).

either into the child's circumstances or into the available options suitable for the child's future care; or the case would be continued while the grounds of referral to the hearing were sent to the sheriff for proof, having been denied or not understood. Continuing the case for these reasons could indeed happen in any case and not only those involving children currently in places of safety. If the hearing did continue the case to a subsequent hearing, it could require the child to attend or reside at a clinic, hospital or establishment for not more than 21 days,[37] and to secure the child's residence there (if there was a risk that the child would not remain there of his or her own volition) it could issue a warrant to last for that whole period.[38] Such a warrant could be renewed once.[39] Though the terminology of "interim" order had been dropped in the 1968 Act in favour of "warrant", that effectively is what these warrants were: they made interim provision for the child's safety until such time as a longer-term dispositive decision could be made by a children's hearing. Though temporary, it was possible to appeal against the issuing of a warrant under this provision.[40]

THE ORKNEY CASE AND THE 1992 CLYDE REPORT

The emergency and interim provisions of the 1968 Act, set out above, were central to that most contentious of all children's hearings cases, *Sloan v B*.[41] This case arose out of the removal in early 1991 of nine children from their homes in Orkney to places of safety on the mainland under the provisions contained in s. 37(2) – though it was neither the granting of the warrants nor their renewal that was challenged in the appeal.[42] Nevertheless, the publicity generated by the case led the Secretary of State for Scotland to appoint Lord Clyde[43] to conduct an inquiry into the whole circumstances. In his subsequent Report,[44] Lord Clyde said this:

---

37 Ibid. s. 43(4).
38 Ibid. s. 40(7).
39 Ibid. s. 40(8).
40 Ibid. s. 49(5)(a). See for example *B v Kennedy* 1992 SC 295.
41 1991 SC 412. For comment, see Thomson, J. "*Sloan v B* – the Legal Issues" 1991 *Scots Law Times (News)* 421; Sutherland, E. "The Orkney Case" 1992 *Juridical Review* 93; Norrie, K. "Excluding Children from Children's Hearings" 1993 *Scots Law Times (News)* 67.
42 The appeal to the Court of Session, by the reporter, was against the decision of the sheriff who had dismissed the application to establish grounds of referral (which were denied at the first lawful day hearing) as incompetent.
43 Then a judge in the Court of Session, later a Lord of Appeal in Ordinary; son of the Lord Clyde who wrote the 1946 Clyde Report discussed above at Chapter 2.
44 *Report of the Inquiry into the Removal of Children from Orkney in February 1991* (Ordered to be printed by the House of Commons, 27 October 1992, HMSO, Edinburgh).

The removal of a child from the immediate control or care of the parents constitutes a significant invasion of the rights of the parent and of the child. While
a power to remove a child requires to be available the limits of its exercise and
the definition of its purpose must be certain, must be clearly known and must be
appropriate to the seriousness of the course of action. Section 37(2) of the [1968]
Act fails to meet these requirements.[45]

. . .

The failure to specify the scope and limits of the power to remove a child with sufficient clarity to enable the citizen to appreciate the occasions on which the power
may be exercised may well run foul of Article 8 [of the European Convention on
Human Rights][46] if not also Article 16[47] [of the United Nations Convention on
the Rights of the Child].[48]

He concluded:

The only occasion on which the removal of a child to a place of safety should be
permitted by the law is where there is a real, urgent and immediate risk that the
child is otherwise going to suffer significant harm, whether physical, moral or
psychological.[49]

The major problem Lord Clyde identified with the existing law was that
while the circumstances in which emergency action was authorised were
clear, these circumstances did not in themselves indicate the urgency that
alone could justify emergency action: there was no condition for the granting of the order that justified in the individual case the removal by the
state of the child from his or her home and family. The fact that a child was
believed to be – or indeed was – the victim of a scheduled offence certainly
might, but equally might not, necessitate in the actual circumstances of the
case the removal of the child from his or her home: yet that removal would
be lawful under the 1968 Act (and the earlier legislation) irrespective of
that necessity. As such the process was susceptible to arbitrary application.
The existing system was also flawed in failing to allow an appeal against the
emergency removal of a child to a place of safety. Appeals could, of course,
be had against decisions of the children's hearing (including the issuing of
a warrant), but not against the initial removal before the children's hearing
sat at all: the system could not accommodate the wishes of the family who
were content to attend a tribunal that would explore whether any measures
of care were necessary but wished to challenge the keeping of the child who

45 Clyde Report (1992), para 16.1.
46 This protects the right to respect for private and family life.
47 This protects the child's right to privacy, including from attacks against their way of life, their
    good name, their families and their homes.
48 Clyde Report (1992), para 16.3.
49 Ibid. para 16.5.

had been removed by a constable until that tribunal could be convened. A further difficulty with the existing system was that the warrants were inflexible, allowing only the taking of a child to and keeping the child in a place of safety: no less intrusive protective action was possible.

Lord Clyde recommended, therefore, that Parliament introduce an entirely new order to replace the existing emergency and interim measures,[50] and this recommendation was accepted by the Government in its subsequent White Paper.[51] The Children (Scotland) Act 1995 created what was (and is) called the "child protection order".[52]

CHILD PROTECTION ORDERS UNDER THE 1995 AND 2011 ACTS

The Children (Scotland) Act 1995

Under the 1995 Act, a child protection order could be granted by a sheriff in two circumstances. First, the order could be made on the application of any person[53] where the sheriff is satisfied that there were reasonable grounds to believe that the child "(i) is being so treated (or neglected) that he [or she] is suffering significant harm or (ii) will suffer such harm if he [or she] is not removed to and kept in a place of safety" or kept in the place where he or she is then being accommodated; in either case it must also be shown that the order is necessary to protect the child from such harm.[54] Not only was this more focused than the previous law on the immediacy of the threat facing the child that the order seeks to avoid, but it also, for the first time, authorised emergency measures in response to a belief that there would be future harm to the child, as opposed to harm that was currently being suffered. Reference to past harm, as in the 1937 Act,[55] was no longer sufficient, and present or future harm was now to be the criterion that justified emergency measures. Future harm may, of course, be predicted as likely from proved harm in the past.[56] The previous law was based on that understanding but, by making the assumption that proved harm meant that there certainly

---

50 Ibid. paras 16.9 et seq.
51 *Scotland's Children: Proposals for Child Care Policy and Law* (Cm 2286, August 1993) paras 5.8–5.18.
52 Children (Scotland) Act 1995, s. 57.
53 In fact, most applications for a CPO are made by local authorities.
54 Children (Scotland) Act 1995, s. 57(1).
55 Children and Young Persons (Scotland) Act, 1937, ss. 47(1) and 71(1).
56 *Re J (Children) (Care Proceedings: Threshold Criteria)* [2013] 1 AC 680.

would be future harm, the previous law had failed to focus on how likely there was a need for action to be taken to protect the child in the future.

The second circumstance in which a child protection order could be made was (on the application by a local authority only) when (i) the local authority had reasonable grounds to suspect that the child is being or will be so treated (or neglected) that he or she is suffering or will suffer significant harm, (ii) the local authority was making enquiries to allow them to decide whether they should take any action to safeguard the welfare of the child, and (iii) these enquiries, which the local authority reasonably believed to be urgently required, were being frustrated by access to the child being unreasonably denied.[57]

The child protection order, if made and irrespective of the ground upon which it was sought, could authorise a range of actions designed to offer the child protection, which included but was not limited to removing the child to a place of safety.[58]

The Children's Hearings (Scotland) Act 2011

These provisions were slightly restructured under the 2011 Act, which repealed the relevant sections of the 1995 Act and replaced them with provisions that continue to apply today. A child protection order can be made, as before, in two circumstances. First, it may be made on the application of a local authority if the authority has reasonable grounds to suspect that the child has been, is being, or will be treated or neglected in such a way that he or she is suffering or is likely to suffer significant harm, but that the local authority's enquiries into these suspicions are being frustrated by access to the child being unreasonably denied.[59] The order in these circumstances acts as a mechanism to allow the local authority to conduct necessary inquiries, rather than being a measure of immediate protection. Secondly, a child protection order may be made on the application of either a local authority or any other person if there are reasonable grounds to believe that the child has been or is being treated or neglected in such a way that he or she is suffering or is likely to suffer significant harm and in any case the order is necessary to protect the child from that harm or from further harm.[60] In this circumstance, the order acts as an emergency response to the dangers

---

57 Children (Scotland) Act 1995, s. 57(2).
58 Ibid. s. 57(4).
59 Children's Hearings (Scotland) Act 2011, s. 38.
60 Ibid. s. 39.

believed to face the child. Likelihood of the child suffering significant harm is now the threshold test for the making of this order, and the onus rests with the applicant to show it. Sheriff Holligan pointed out that in practice the two predominant circumstances in which child protection orders are sought are, first, in respect of children whose circumstances are well-known to social services and who now face some crisis in their family lives that is putting them at risk and, secondly, in respect of new-born infants where the mother's circumstances have raised serious concerns before the birth.[61]

OTHER EMERGENCY PROVISIONS IN THE 1995 AND 2011 ACTS

Though the child protection order was designed to allow the authorities to act quickly on the establishment of a belief that the child is likely to suffer significant harm, there will be some circumstances in which the urgency of the situation means that it is not practicable to establish that belief in court before protective action needs to be taken. This might be because, for example, a child or young person is discovered in a filthy house occupied by adults in a state of drink or drug-induced unconsciousness or incapacity, or having been abandoned or been found wandering the streets at night unaccompanied. In circumstances such as these, the state or its agencies – and perhaps private individuals – are authorised to take such measures as are thought necessary to protect the child from the immediately threatened harm.

The 1995 Act provided that a justice of the peace could grant an authorisation to do the things that a child protection order authorised if the conditions for the granting of such an order were satisfied but it was not practicable for a sheriff to consider the application.[62] This was unlikely to occur in practice in the larger cities, where procedures are in place to ensure that one or more sheriffs are available around the clock, but could happen more commonly in rural parts of Scotland. The emergency nature of this process was emphasised by the facts that such an authorisation lasted for 24 hours and that it would lose its effect if no action were taken to implement it within 12 hours of its being given:[63] it was designed to authorise immediate action required to be taken as a matter of urgency and the failure of the authorised parties to act immediately to do so was likely to indicate that the urgency, if it existed,

---

61 *Application for a Child Protection Order* 2015 SLT (Sh Ct) 9, para 13.
62 Children (Scotland) Act 1995, s. 61(1)-(3).
63 Ibid. s. 61(4).

had abated. Once granted, the authorisation had to be notified to the child's family, the local authority and the reporter, together with the reasons for its granting.[64]

Even without any prior authorisation, a constable retained the power that had existed since 1889 to take steps immediately to protect a child from imminent harm. The 1995 Act allowed a constable to remove a child to a place of safety and to keep the child there if the constable had reasonable cause to believe – this is similar to the 1889 formulation – that the conditions for the making of a child protection order existed, that it was not practicable to apply for such an order and that, in order to protect the child from significant harm (or further such harm) it was necessary so to remove and keep the child.[65] Though its predecessors were latterly subject to time limits, the authorisation under the 1995 Act to keep the child was of an even more temporary nature: the child could be kept in a place of safety under this provision for a maximum of 24 hours from the time the child was removed.[66] The expectation was that this period would give an applicant (nearly always, a local authority) time to apply for a child protection order which, if disposed of before the end of the 24 hours, would bring the constable's authority to an end:[67] if the application failed the child would be returned home, if the application succeeded then the child protection order would be legal authority to keep the child away from home and in a place of safety. Once a child had been removed by a constable under these provisions, various persons (including the child's family, the local authority and the reporter) had to be notified that the child had been so removed, and of the reasons.[68]

If a child had been taken, under the authority of either of these provisions, to a police station, there was an obligation to take the child as soon as reasonably practicable to another type of place of safety.[69] And in both situations the reporter was obliged to keep a close eye on the situation and the authorisation to keep the child in a place of safety would come to an end even before the stated 12 hours or 24 hours if the reporter came to be of the view either that the conditions underpinning the authorisation did not exist

---

64 Emergency Child Protection Measures (Scotland) Regulations 1996 (SI 1996/3258 (S. 248)), regs 8 and 9.
65 Children (Scotland) Act 1995, s. 61(5).
66 Ibid. s. 61(6).
67 Ibid. s. 61(7).
68 Emergency Child Protection Measures (Scotland) Regulations 1996, regs 3 and 4.
69 Ibid. reg. 15.

or that it was no longer in the child's best interests to be kept in a place of safety.[70]

These provisions were replicated, with little substantive alteration, in the Children's Hearings (Scotland) Act 2011. Both s. 55, which deals with justice of the peace authorisations, and s. 56, which authorises a constable to remove a child to a place of safety, remain in force today.[71]

INTERIM ORDERS MADE BY CHILDREN'S HEARINGS UNDER THE 1995 AND 2011 ACTS

On the eighth working day after the granting of a child protection order, there must take place a children's hearing to consider the grounds of referral that the reporter has drawn up.[72] At that point typically, and indeed in any other case in which a child is brought before a children's hearing, it may happen that the hearing is unable to make a final decision on the case that day – either because the hearing needs more information or because the grounds of referral that have been drawn up are denied (or not understood) and the hearing refers the matter to the sheriff for proof of these grounds. The children's hearing may nevertheless be of the view that the child should continue to be kept away from home on a temporary basis – that is to say until such time as it is in a position to make a decision disposing of the case.

Warrants under the 1995 Act

The Children (Scotland) Act 1995 allowed the children's hearing to grant a warrant either when it sent the case to the sheriff for a finding of whether grounds of referral exist,[73] or when it continued the case after considering the grounds because it was unable at that point to dispose of the case.[74] Grounds were laid down for the granting of each of these warrants, the most important of which were (i) the risk of non-attendance at subsequent hearings, and (ii) the finding that it was necessary to keep the child in a place of safety in order to safeguard or promote his or her welfare. The warrant

---

70 Children (Scotland) Act 1995, s. 61(8).
71 The Emergency Child Protection Measures (Scotland) Regulations 1996 were replaced by the Children's Hearings (Scotland) Act 2011 (Child Protection Emergency Measures) Regulations 2012.
72 Children (Scotland) Act 1995, s. 60(6)(e); Children's Hearings (Scotland) Act 2011, s. 54(a).
73 Children (Scotland) Act 1995, s. 66.
74 Ibid. s. 69(7).

under s. 66 (granted when the reporter was directed to apply to the sheriff for proof of the grounds of referral) would last for an initial 22 days but, on cause shown, could be continued by the children's hearing for another 22 days,[75] and in no case could a child be kept for longer than 66 days.[76] Thereafter, the reporter could apply to the sheriff for a warrant for further detention,[77] though the legislation did not set down any time-limit for the sheriff's warrant nor indicate whether it could be renewed. The warrant under s. 69 (granted when the hearing continued the case for further consideration) would last until the expiry of 22 days, or until the next hearing, whichever was earlier, though that hearing, and any subsequent hearing, could grant a further warrant for the same period of time.

Interim compulsory supervision orders under the 2011 Act

The Children's Hearings (Scotland) Act 2011 restricted the hearing's power to grant warrants to situations in which they are needed in order to secure the child's attendance at a children's hearing.[78] In place of the other types of warrant under the 1995 Act a new power to make an interim compulsory supervision order (an "ICSO") was conferred on hearings by the 2011 Act. The children's hearing may make an interim compulsory supervision order whenever it has deferred making a dispositive decision but it considers that the nature of the child's circumstances is such that for the protection, guidance, treatment or control of the child it is necessary as a matter of urgency to do so.[79] This is, in fact, the same test as for the making of a compulsory supervision order itself,[80] other than the requirement that it is a matter of urgency. That additional requirement emphasises the emergency nature of the interim compulsory supervision order; its interim nature is shown not just by its name but by the time limits after which it will cease. An interim compulsory supervision order remains in force until the earliest of (i) the convening of the next children's hearing, (ii) the date specified in the order itself and (iii) the expiry of 22 days.[81] Further interim compulsory supervision orders may be made, on the same test except that there is no need to

---

75 Children (Scotland) Act 1995, s. 66(5).
76 Ibid. s. 66(8).
77 Ibid. s. 67.
78 Children's Hearings (Scotland) Act 2011, s. 123.
79 Ibid. ss. 92(2), 93(5) and 120(3).
80 Ibid. ss. 91(3)(a) and 119(3)(a).
81 Ibid. s. 86(3).

show continuing urgency.[82] There is no limit to the number of additional interim compulsory supervision orders that may be made by a children's hearing, except when made in conjunction with the referral to the sheriff for proof of grounds of referral, in which case a child may be subject to an interim compulsory supervision order for no more than 66 consecutive days.[83] An interim compulsory supervision order is more flexible than any of the previous warrants to remove a child to a place of safety, for it may contain any measure that a full compulsory supervision order is able to contain:[84] that might, but need not, involve the removal of the child from his or her home. But as Macfarlane et al. point out "the ICSO exists to address immediate and urgent needs, not long term needs, and therefore the measures included should be for the short term".[85]

DEFINITION OF "PLACE OF SAFETY"

The definition of "place of safety" has gradually developed throughout these various statutory provisions from 1889 to the present day. Originally, the concept was defined for the purposes of the Prevention of Cruelty to, and Protection of, Children Act, 1889 to include a poor house and any place certified by the local authority by byelaw under that Act.[86] That definition was widened substantially by the Prevention of Cruelty to Children Act, 1894 under which "place of safety" was defined to include "any place certified by the local authority under this Act for the purposes of this Act, and also includes any poorhouse or police station, or any hospital, surgery, or place of the like kind".[87] The 1894 definition was replicated in s. 29 of the Prevention of Cruelty to Children Act, 1904.

The Children Act, 1908 restructured the definition by removing the reference to local authority certification, and making it an exclusive rather than inclusive definition: from then on a place of safety was defined to "mean" (rather than, as before, to "include") "any poorhouse, or police station or any hospital or surgery, or any other suitable place, the occupier of which is willing temporarily to receive an infant, child or young person".[88] The concept

---

82 Ibid. s. 120(5).
83 Ibid. s. 96(4). The sheriff may, however, make an interim (or further interim) compulsory supervision order: s. 109(3) and (5).
84 Ibid. s. 86(1)(a).
85 Macfarlane et al. *The Children's Hearings (Scotland) Act 2011*, p. 121.
86 Prevention of Cruelty to, and Protection of, Children Act, 1889, s. 17.
87 Prevention of Cruelty to Children Act, 1894, s. 25.
88 Children Act, 1908, s. 131.

of "any other suitable place" rendered the definition open-ended, though it was, of course, to be interpreted according to its context: a suitable place would be a place suited to the reception of, and protection of, children. To this definition the Second Schedule to the Children and Young Persons (Scotland) Act, 1932 added "remand home", and the amended definition was repeated in the Children and Young Persons (Scotland) Act, 1937.[89] The Children Act, 1948 removed the reference in the 1937 Act to "poor house" (the Poor Law having been abolished) and added to the definition "any home provided by a local authority under Part II of the Children Act, 1948".[90] Each local authority was obliged to make provision, in the homes they provided, "for the reception and maintenance of children removed to a place of safety" under the 1937 Act,[91] this to be, so far as practicable, in accommodation for the temporary reception of children separate from that required under s. 15(2) of the 1948 Act to be provided for children in the care of the local authority.[92]

The Social Work (Scotland) Act 1968 defined "place of safety" as "any residential or other establishment provided by a local authority, a police station or any hospital, surgery or other suitable place, the occupier of which is willing temporarily to receive a child".[93] Both "residential establishment" and "establishment" were defined to mean a place "managed by a local authority, voluntary organisation or any other person, which provides [residential or non-residential] accommodation for the purposes of" the 1968 Act,[94] and any regulatory provisions governing such establishments would apply in relation to children taken to them as places of safety. The other named places, most obviously "other suitable place" would not be subject to specific provisions designed to ensure the wellbeing of children.

The Children (Scotland) Act 1995 defined "place of safety" to which children could be taken under various statutory provisions to mean

> (a) a residential or other establishment provided by a local authority; (b) a community home within the meaning of section 53 of the Children Act 1989; (c) a police station; or (d) a hospital, surgery or other suitable place, the occupier of which is willing temporarily to receive the child.[95]

89 Children and Young Persons (Scotland) Act, 1937 Act, s. 110.
90 Children Act, 1948, s. 60(2) and sched. 3.
91 Ibid. s. 51(1).
92 Ibid. s. 51(2).
93 Social Work (Scotland) Act 1968, s. 94(1).
94 Ibid. s. 94(1)
95 Children (Scotland) Act 1995, s. 93(1).

To this definition there was subsequently added: "(e) the dwelling-house of a suitable person who is so willing; or (f) any other suitable place the occupier of which is so willing".[96] Section 202 of the Children's Hearings (Scotland) Act 2011, though structured slightly differently, provides substantively the same definition. None of these definitions has been subject to judicial analysis.

---

96 Regulation of Care (Scotland) Act 2001, s. 74.

10. Aftercare

INTRODUCTION

It has long been recognised that children who have experienced state care tend to suffer disadvantage in comparison with children brought up by their own parents, this disadvantage can last well into adulthood and in some cases throughout their whole lives. A shocking picture of the contemporary position was revealed in the statutory guidance issued with the Children and Young People (Scotland) Act 2014.

> [D]espite the extensive framework of law and policy, many looked after children and care leavers experience some of the poorest personal outcomes of any group in Scotland. Low levels of educational engagement and achievement feed into high levels of poverty, homelessness and poor mental health. Rates of suicide and self-harm are higher than that of the general population. In 2013 a third of young offenders had been in care at some point in their childhood.[1]

In relation to care leavers' educational qualifications, the statistics make deeply depressing reading.

- 40% of looked after children leave school with one or more qualification at SCQF Level 5 or more; compared with 84% of all school leavers.
- 74% of looked after children who left school in 2013/14 were aged 16 or under; compared with only 27% of all school leavers.
- the exclusion rate for looked after children is over seven times that for all children.
- 73% of looked after children were in a positive destination nine months after leaving school, compared with 92% of all children.
- 6% of looked after children were in higher education nine months after leaving school, compared with 39% of all children.[2]

There is little possibility that these levels of disadvantage, which are likely to have life-long effects, were any less bad in the earlier periods of the development of Scottish child protection law. Some of the disadvantage

---

1 *Children and Young People (Scotland) Act 2014: Statutory Guidance on Part 9: Corporate Parenting*, para 9 (references omitted).
2 *A Blueprint for Fairness: Final Report of the Commission on Widening Access* (Scottish Government, March 2016), available at <https://www2.gov.scot/Resource/0049/00496619.pdf> (last accessed 8 July 2019).

will, of course, be traced to the very circumstances that required the state to intervene in the child's upbringing, but the disturbing fact remains that the intervention itself, though designed to protect the child from harm, is likely to have contributed not insignificantly to the lack of guidance and support, as well as the disruption of the child's education. That this has long been known explains why aftercare has always been an inherent part of the design of the statutory provisions authorising state intervention in family life.

By "aftercare" is meant the obligations on the state (and others) to make special provision for care leavers, that is to say, those young adults who had been, as children or young people, in the care of the state or had been brought up by foster carers or in the care of voluntary organisations. Ideally, it seeks to replicate (though in reality can only do so imperfectly) the continuing support, advice and practical assistance that young adults who spent their childhood at home can normally expect to receive from their own parents. Such assistance is not, in the normal case, traced to any legal obligation but reflects the desire of most parents (and even a moral imperative) to help ease their children's transition from dependent childhood to independent adulthood. Children who are looked after by the state are far less likely to receive such parental support as young adults and it behoves the state, therefore, to make up for the opportunities lost, at least partly, by its own actions.

EARLY AFTERCARE PROVISIONS

The first attempts at providing for young persons after they had left state or charitable care took the form of assistance in finding employment. This was not without sense, and though the types of employment considered suitable for children emerging from institutions were highly constrained, it consists with the notion that the purpose of state care was to turn a child into a productive (and law-abiding) member of society. Both the Industrial Schools Act, 1866 and the Reformatory Schools Act, 1866 allowed the managers of such schools to apprentice a child who had "conducted himself well" during time out on licence.[3] This was expanded upon in the Reformatory and Industrial Schools Act, 1891, which had the long title: "An Act to assist the Managers of Reformatory and Industrial Schools in advantageously launching into useful Careers the Children under their Charge". This provided that:

> If any youthful offender or child detained in or placed out on licence from a certified reformatory or industrial school conducts himself well, the managers

---

3 Industrial Schools Act, 1866, s. 28; Reformatory Schools Act, 1866, s. 19.

of the school may, with his own consent, apprentice him to, or dispose of him in, any trade, calling or service, including service in the Navy or Army, or by emigration,[4] notwithstanding that his period of detention or supervision has not expired; and such apprenticing or disposition shall be as valid as if the managers were his parents.[5]

The implication here is clearly that the managers would seek out a placement on behalf of the child or young person, or at the very least assist and advise him or her in doing so.

In an article published in 1896,[6] UK-wide statistics were reported for the "disposals" of young people discharged from reformatories and industrial schools up until the end of 1893. Of those placed in an employment situation, the figures were as follows:

From Reformatory Schools in Great Britain
To employment or [domestic] service: 15,008 boys and 5,329 girls
Sent to sea: 5,750 boys
Enlisted: 1,014 boys

From Industrial Schools in Great Britain
To employment or [domestic] service: 25,476 boys and 10,312 girls
Sent to sea: 9,952 boys
Enlisted: 2,024 boys

Significant numbers were, however, discharged without a place. The author of the article mentions that at one of the Glasgow industrial schools a "working boys home" had been established to accommodate boys discharged from the school and now in employment.[7] This indicates an early recognition by the voluntary organisation running the school that, having provided a protective (and training) environment to vulnerable young people, much of that effort would be rendered null by sending the young person out into the world without some continuing assistance.

The provisions of the 1891 Act were replaced by s. 70 of the Children Act, 1908, an Act which (as we saw earlier in this book)[8] brought together the treatment of both young offenders and children in need of care and protection. In addition, s. 4 of the Probation of Offenders Act, 1907, obliged probation officers to assist probationers' search for work.

---

4 Emigration is considered fully in the immediately following chapter.
5 Reformatory and Industrial Schools Act, 1891, s. 1.
6 Watson, J. "Reformatory and Industrial Schools" (1896) 59 *Journal of the Royal Statistical Society* 255, pp.295–296.
7 Ibid. p. 296.
8 See Chapters 1 and 4 above.

AFTERCARE FROM 1932 TO 1968

The aftercare provisions in both the Children and Young Persons (Scotland) Act, 1932 and the Children and Young Persons (Scotland) Act, 1937 were limited, as their predecessors had been, to those who had been detained in "approved schools" (as reformatory and industrial schools had become in the 1932 Act) but their focus expanded in these Acts beyond apprenticing the young person or placing him in the Navy or Army. After the expiration of the period of detention in an approved school, the child or young person was to remain under the supervision of the managers of the school. If the period of detention ended before the child or young person's 15th birthday this additional period of supervision lasted until their 18th birthday; if the period of detention ended after their 15th birthday, the supervision lasted for three years or until their 21st birthday (whichever was the shorter period).[9] It was not specified what form that "supervision" was to take, but the managers were given the power to recall any young person under 19 back to the school, if "it is necessary in his interests" to do so, this for a period of 3 months (or six months if the Scottish Education Department so directed) and in no case beyond the young person's 16th birthday. This suggests that the managers had to take steps to watch over the young person's progress after release and the implication is clear that they were to intervene in the young person's life whenever their lifestyle was reverting to earlier harmful patterns. During the period in which the young person was under the supervision of the school managers, he or she was deemed to remain under their care,[10] which meant that the managers continued to have all the rights and powers exercisable by law by a parent, which they would share with any parent with whom the young person was lawfully living.[11] This form of aftercare amounted to little more than a watching brief rather than the active provision of support for the young person.

The managers of approved schools retained the power that managers of reformatory and industrial schools had had for the previous 70 years to apprentice the child or young person or place him or her in any trade, calling

---

9 Children and Young Persons (Scotland) Act, 1932, sched. 1 para 16; Children and Young Persons (Scotland) Act, 1937, s. 78.

10 Children and Young Persons (Scotland) Act, 1932, sched. 1 para 16(5); Children and Young Persons (Scotland) Act, 1937, s. 78(5).

11 Children and Young Persons (Scotland) Act, 1932, sched. 1 para 17(1); Children and Young Persons (Scotland) Act, 1937, sched. 2 para 12(1).

or service, including in the Navy, Army or Air Force, so long as the young person "conducts himself well" during the period of supervision and so long as he or she provided written consent.[12] But the 1932 Act also included a significant innovation: it imposed, for the first time, a positive obligation on the managers of approved schools to provide active assistance to those under their supervision: they had to

> cause [the young person under their supervision] to be visited, advised and befriended and to give him assistance (including, if they think fit, financial assistance) in maintaining himself and finding suitable employment.[13]

These valuable support mechanisms could be called upon by the young person until their 18th or 21st birthday (depending on whether they had been released from the approved school before or after their 15th birthday).[14]

These aftercare provisions were supplemented by the Children and Young Persons (Scotland) Care and Training Regulations, 1933,[15] under which the

> managers shall make every effort to obtain suitable employment for a boy or girl on leaving [the school] and shall make arrangements for the proper discharge of their obligations under the Act in relation to the after-care of former pupils . . .[16]

The focus of these aftercare provisions remained on assisting the young person in finding work in the adult world. Obviously, in the early 1930s, this was difficult for the working population at large, and it was all the more important, therefore, that disadvantaged young people received as much help as possible in seeking work.

The aftercare provisions in the 1933 Regulations were restructured and widened by the Approved Schools (Scotland) Rules, 1961, but finding work was still the major focus of effort:

> 44. The Managers shall see that every effort is made to obtain suitable employment for a pupil over school age as defined in the Education (Scotland) Acts, who is fit for release on licence, and for this purpose they shall avail themselves where

---

12 Children and Young Persons (Scotland) Act, 1932, sched. 1 para 18; Children and Young Persons (Scotland) Act, 1937, sched. 2 para 7.

13 Children and Young Persons (Scotland) Act, 1932, sched. 1 para 17(2); Children and Young Persons (Scotland) Act, 1937, sched. 2 para 12(2). This seems to have been modelled on the duties of probation officers under s. 4 of the Probation of Offenders Act, 1907.

14 Children and Young Persons (Scotland) Act, 1932, sched. 1 para 16(1); Children and Young Persons (Scotland) Act, 1937, s. 78(1).

15 SR&O, 1933, No. 1006 (S.55).

16 1933 Regulations, reg. 22. Regulation 40 also required foster parents "to endeavour, in conjunction with the Education Authority, to find employment for the boys and girls when they leave school".

necessary of any help that can be obtained whether from public organisations or private individuals. Where the pupil's home is unsatisfactory they shall arrange for suitable accommodation.

. . .

46. The Managers shall ensure that a pupil on leaving has a sufficient outfit and, if necessary, a reasonable sum for travelling and subsistence, and they shall communicate with the pupil's parent and the education authority, if any, who have been contributing to his maintenance . . .

47. It shall be the duty of the Managers to ensure that adequate arrangements are made for the after-care of every pupil released from the school until the statutory period of supervision expires and they shall nominate for each pupil a suitable person to carry out after-care.

The nomination of a suitable person to perform aftercare functions was probably the single most effective addition to what had gone before, for it meant that there was now someone whose individual duty it was to build up a relationship with the young person and provide such support as was necessary to assist him or her in the transition to independent adulthood.

The Criminal Justice (Scotland) Act, 1963, Part II and schedule II, made further provision for the supervision of persons released from approved schools, replacing the supervision provisions in s. 78 of and schedule 2 to the Children and Young Persons (Scotland) Act 1937. That this was contained in criminal justice legislation, even although not all residents at approved schools were offenders, is worth noting. For the first time, aftercare was divorced from supervision. The person released from an approved school was to remain under the "supervision" of the managers of the school for a period of two years, or until his or her 21st birthday, whichever was the shorter period, and was to reside with a person named by the managers.[17] During that time the released person could be recalled.[18] While under supervision, the person remained "in the care of" the managers of the school,[19] which imposed on the managers the obligations of a parent and gave them the same rights and powers, and liabilities as respects maintenance, as a parent.[20] And then for three years after the period of supervision came to an end, the managers were required, but only if requested to do so and to the extent that they considered appropriate, to cause the person to be "visited, advised and befriended" and to give him or her "assistance (includ-

---

17 Criminal Justice (Scotland) Act 1963, sched. 2 para 1.
18 Ibid. sched. 2 para 2.
19 Ibid. sched. 2 para 5.
20 Children and Young Persons (Scotland) Act, 1937, s. 79(4).

ing, if they think fit, financial assistance)" in maintaining him- or herself and finding suitable employment.[21] These provisions were repealed in 1968.[22]

Aftercare for other children and young persons 1948–1968

It has already been noted that the aftercare provisions so far discussed were limited to children and young persons being discharged from approved schools. Yet only a minority of children subject to protective legal orders (or in care voluntarily) were accommodated in such schools, and most were boarded-out with foster carers or accommodated in children's homes run by voluntary organisations or local authorities, with a small number being supervised at home. These children too tended to find the transition to independent adulthood more difficult than children subject to no legal order at all. The disruption to their lives by state intervention was no less than the disruption caused by sending them to an approved school yet, with fostering being perceived as a mechanism to replace the original with an *ersatz* family, the assumption seems to have been made that there would be no need for the imposition of a legal responsibility to provide aftercare to children leaving a foster placement. The foster parents who looked after the child until adulthood were expected to feel under a moral obligation to offer support thereafter: just as there was no legal obligation on parents to support and assist their own children who had reached adulthood so too there was no need for a legal obligation to be imposed on foster parents in respect of persons they had brought up as children but were now young adults. In either case the support was thought likely to be voluntarily offered.

Though that underlying attitude towards fostering persisted beyond the passing of (and was indeed entrenched in) the Children Act, 1948, that Act did contain aftercare provisions for those children in the care of the state beyond those who had been detained in approved schools. Local authorities were authorised to provide hostels for young persons over the compulsory school age (then 15) but under the age of 21 who at any time after ceasing to be of compulsory school age had been in the care of a local authority.[23] Also, the local authority could make contributions to the costs of accommodation and maintenance of such persons who had attained the age of 18 years in a place near where he or she might be employed, was seeking employment, or

---

21 Criminal Justice (Scotland) Act 1963, sched. 2 para 7.
22 Social Work (Scotland) Act 1968, sched. 9.
23 Children Act, 1948, s. 19.

was undergoing education or training.[24] In addition and more comprehensively, the local authority could make grants for the education or training of any young person between the ages of 18 and 21 who had been in the care of a local authority immediately before their 18th birthday.[25]

The Children and Young Persons Act 1963 extended the education and training grants provision just mentioned to young persons who had been in care immediately before their 17th birthday.[26] That Act also sought to make available to all care leavers aftercare similar to that available to those discharged from approved schools and now governed by the Criminal Justice (Scotland) Act 1963. So local authorities were empowered, if requested by the young person, to visit, advise and befriend, and in exceptional circumstances give financial assistance to, anyone below the age of 21 who was or had been in their care on or after their 17th birthday.[27] This was not quite the same as under the Criminal Justice (Scotland) Act. First, there was, oddly, no reference here to assistance in finding employment; and secondly, the provision, unlike the equivalent in the Criminal Justice (Scotland) Act, was empowering only: it authorised without requiring local authorities to visit, advise and befriend the care leaver asking for help. The Children and Young Persons Act 1963 also gave local authorities power to guarantee apprenticeships or articles of clerkship in relation to any person in their care.[28]

SOCIAL WORK (SCOTLAND) ACT 1968

The earlier provisions were all repealed by the Social Work (Scotland) Act 1968. Aftercare was now to be available to all young persons who had been in the care of a local authority (irrespective of where they were accommodated while in care) on or after their attaining school leaving age (15 at the time the 1968 Act was passed but thereafter rising to 16).[29] The local authority was empowered, until the young person reached the age of 21, to make contributions to the costs of accommodation and maintenance of the young person in any place near the place where he or she might be employed or seeking employment or engaged in education or training; and

---

24 Ibid. s. 20(1).
25 Ibid. s. 20(2).
26 Children and Young Persons Act 1963, s. 46.
27 Ibid. s. 58.
28 Ibid. s. 47.
29 Raising of the School Leaving Age (Scotland) Regulations 1972 (SI 1972/59, S. 6).

to make grants to such young persons to enable them to meet expenses connected with their receiving suitable education or training.[30] Repeating the power they had acquired in the Children and Young Persons Act 1963, local authorities were authorised to guarantee indentures or other deeds of apprenticeship or articles of clerkship in respect of any person in their care, even although the period of apprenticeship would extend after the person left the care of the local authority. It may be noted that these were discretionary powers on the part of the local authority, which was not obliged to meet these costs or to give that guarantee. It is also to be noted that these powers applied only in respect of persons who were or had been in the care of a local authority – they did not apply to anyone in the care of a voluntary organisation.

Local authorities were, however, placed under a duty in respect of any person in its area under the age of 18 who had been when they reached school leaving age, but no longer were, in the care of either a local authority or a voluntary organisation: this was to advise, guide and assist that person until they reached 18 years of age.[31] This was similar to the obligation that had earlier appeared in s. 58 of the Children and Young Persons Act 1963, but the 1968 formulation omitted the reference to "befriending" the child, doubtless because it had by then come to be seen as professionally inappropriate for professional workers to become friends with young people who relied on them for the provision of services. And the 1968 Act differed from its predecessor in that it was not, as the 1963 provision had been, a matter of empowering the local authority to act when requested by the young person: it was now a matter of legal obligation. However, it is unclear the extent to which this duty amounted to a requirement to give practical assistance to a young person in need.

AFTERCARE AFTER 1995

The 1993 White Paper *Scotland's Children: Proposals for Child Care Policy and Law*[32] explained the continuing need for aftercare:

> The time when young people emerge from a period in care – whatever form it has taken – can be unsettling. They may emerge vulnerable and in need of support, particularly those of sixteen and seventeen who may move into a variety of situations – for example lodgings, private accommodation or a shared tenancy.

---

30 Social Work (Scotland) Act 1968, s. 24.
31 Ibid. s. 26.
32 HMSO 1993 (Cm 2286), paras 3.36 – 3.37.

A few may remain in foster placements or secure their own tenancy. However, many have had an interrupted education and as a result may have few, or no, qualifications. They may fail to obtain a training place or be unemployed. For them the transition from care is particularly difficult and may lead to homelessness and sleeping rough.

All these young people require assistance for the transition to independent living – for example getting accommodation and employment, and in budgeting and general support. The existing legislation does not adequately reflect their needs nor define the responsibilities of local authorities.

The Children (Scotland) Act 1995 which following this White Paper increased the aftercare responsibilities of local authorities: they remained obliged, as they had been since 1968, to advise, guide and assist young people who were looked after by a local authority at the time they ceased to be of school age[33] but a number of important changes were made. First, the age up to which such advice, guidance and assistance had to be given was raised from 18 to 19. Secondly, it was now explicitly stated that the assistance could be "in cash or in kind". And thirdly, between the ages of 19 and 21 local authorities were empowered (but not obliged) to give that advice, guidance and assistance. In 2014 that upper age was raised to 26,[34] in order to meet the policy objective of reflecting the fact that "ordinary families" in modern society tend to continue to provide support to young adults beyond the age of 21.[35] Likewise, the power under s. 25 of the Social Work (Scotland) Act 1968 to guarantee indentures and apprenticeships, which had become limiting and out of date, was replaced by a power to make grants to any young person under 21 who had been a looked after child to help them meet training and education expenses. The age of 21 here was also subsequently raised to 26.[36]

An entirely new form of aftercare was created by the Children and Young People (Scotland) Act 2014, which obliged local authorities to provide "continuing care" for all young people over 16 who have ceased to be looked after by a local authority. "Continuing care" is the provision to the young

---

33 Children (Scotland) Act 1995, s. 29. "At the time when [the child] ceased to be of school age" was later replaced with the more straight-forward age of 16: Children and Young People (Scotland) Act 2014, s. 66(2)(a)(i). (The precise delineation of "school age" was dependent upon school term dates – which might be different in different local authority areas – rather than the child's own birthday.)

34 Children And Young People (Scotland) Act 2014, s. 66.

35 See *Policy Memorandum* attached to the Children and Young People (Scotland) Bill 2014, paras 108–110.

36 Children (Scotland) Act 1995, s. 30, subsequently amended by Children and Young People (Scotland) Act 2014, s. 66.

person of the same accommodation and other assistance as was being provided immediately before the young person ceased to be looked after by the local authority, this until (a gradually increasing) age, now 21.[37] This allows young people to remain, for example, in the home (whether with foster carers or in a children's unit) where they had lived – possibly for some years – while they were being looked after.

The Looked After Children (Scotland) Regulations 2009 obliged local authorities to assess each looked after children's needs, including "the arrangements which require to be made for the time when the child will no longer be looked after by the local authority".[38]

CORPORATE PARENTING UNDER THE CHILDREN AND YOUNG PEOPLE (SCOTLAND) ACT 2014

A quite different approach to compensating young people for the reduction in their life chances that state intervention in their lives too often involves was taken in Part 9 of the Children and Young People (Scotland) Act 2014. This gave statutory force to the idea of "corporate parenting", which as a concept was first given governmental approval in "These are our Bairns: A Guide for Community Planning Partnerships on Being a Good Corporate Parent".[39] The Scottish Government explained what was meant by "corporate parenting":

> The term refers to an organisation's performance of actions necessary to uphold the rights and secure the wellbeing of a looked after child or care leaver, and through which physical, emotional, spiritual, social and educational development is promoted, from infancy through to adulthood. In other words, corporate parenting is about certain organisations listening to the needs, fears and wishes of children and young people, and being proactive and determined in their collective efforts to meet them. It is a role which should complement and support the actions of parents, families and carers, working with these key adults to deliver positive change for vulnerable children.[40]

---

37 Children (Scotland) Act 1995, s. 26A, as inserted by Children and Young People (Scotland) Act 2014, s. 67; Continuing Care (Scotland) Order 2015 SSI 2015/158 (which specified an upper age of 17), as amended by Continuing Care (Scotland) Amendment Orders 2016, SSI 2016/92 (increasing that age to 18), SSI 2017/62 (increasing that age to 19), SSI 2018/96 (increasing that age to 20) and SSI 2019/91 (increasing, finally, that age to 21 where it is intended it will remain for the foreseeable future).

38 Looked After Children (Scotland) Regulations, 2009, reg. 4(1)(h).

39 Scottish Government, 2008.

40 *Children and Young People (Scotland) Act 2014: Statutory Guidance on Part 9: Corporate Parenting*, para 11 (Scottish Government, 2014).

Unlike the "named person" scheme in the 2014 Act,[41] which was designed to apply to virtually every child in Scotland, corporate parenting is relevant only to looked after, and previously looked after, children and young people up to the age of 26. Schedule 4 to the Act lists the public bodies who are "corporate parents" for the purposes of the Act, including the Scottish Ministers, local authorities, health boards, the Care Inspectorate, the Scottish Police Authority, the Mental Welfare Commission for Scotland, the Scottish Legal Aid Board, the Scottish Qualifications Authority, Children's Hearings Scotland and the National Convener, the Scottish Children's Reporter Administration and the Principal Reporter, and all universities and colleges of further education. Each body will, of course, act as a corporate parent in its own relevant way. The University of Strathclyde, for example, waives all graduation costs for, and provides mentors to, all "care-experienced" students, with the aim of helping disadvantaged students to fit into and meet the demands of student life.[42]

The 2014 Act provides that, so far as is consistent with its other functions, it is the duty of every corporate parent:

    (a) to be alert to matters which, or which might, adversely affect the wellbeing of children and young people to whom Part 9 of the 2014 Act applies,

    (b) to assess the needs of those children and young people for services and support it provides,

    (c) to promote the interests of those children and young people,

    (d) to seek to provide those children and young people with opportunities to participate in activities designed to promote their wellbeing,

    (e) to take such action as it considers appropriate to help those children and young people—

        (i) to access opportunities it provides in pursuance of paragraph (d), and

        (ii) to make use of services, and access support, which it provides, and

    (f) to take such other action as it considers appropriate for the purposes of improving the way in which it exercises its functions in relation to those children and young people.[43]

The corporate parent must also prepare and keep under review its Corporate Parenting Plan,[44] setting out how it intends to fulfil its corporate parenting responsibilities. An important obligation is imposed by s. 60 of the 2014 Act, which requires all corporate parents to co-operate with each other,

---

41 See Chapter 2 above.

42 See *Corporate Parent Plan, University of Strathclyde*, available at <https://www.strath.ac.uk/media/ps/rio/docs/2019University_of_Strathclyde_CP_plan_FINAL.pdf> (last accessed 8 July 2019).

43 Children and Young People (Scotland) Act 2014, s. 58(1).

44 Ibid. s. 59.

in so far as reasonably practicable, while exercising their corporate parenting responsibilities: "co-operation" includes (but is not limited to) sharing information, providing advice and assistance, co-ordinating activities, sharing responsibility, funding activities jointly, and exercising functions under the Act jointly.[45] Each corporate parent (other than the Scottish Ministers) must report, at least every three years (and in whatever form is appropriate to its organisational structure), on how it has exercised its corporate parenting responsibilities, and provide such information on these matters to the Scottish Ministers as they reasonably require.[46] Corporate parents must have regard to the guidance on corporate parenting issued by the Scottish Ministers, who may also issue directions to particular corporate parents (except themselves, the Commissioner for Children and Young People in Scotland, and post-16 education bodies) about their corporate parenting responsibilities;[47] the Scottish Ministers must report to the Scottish Parliament every three years about how they have exercised their corporate parenting responsibilities during that period.[48] Designed to improve the long-term chances of children and young people who commence adult life from a disadvantaged position, it is at the time of writing too early to assess properly the success of this new strategy.

45 Ibid. s. 60(2).
46 Ibid. ss. 61 and 62.
47 Ibid. ss. 63 and 64.
48 Ibid. s. 65.

11. Emigration of Children

INTRODUCTION

Of all the outcomes in respect of children in Scotland over whom the state has assumed responsibility, the decision (previously but no longer available) to send the child to live permanently overseas – to emigrate the child, in other words – was the outcome that we now know to have been the most dangerous for any individual child. As well as being factually dangerous in the sense that it exposed the child to an increased risk of harm, it was problematical in legal terms not only because the decision, made in response to issues of upbringing, had effects far beyond childhood, but also because it was frequently a decision made on the basis of extremely dubious legal authority. It is apparent today – and could have been apparent when emigration of children from Scotland was common – that instead of providing protection to vulnerable children the practice very substantially increased the chances of them suffering even more abuse and neglect than they may already have faced.

Early emigration practices and motivations

The practice of sending vagrant children to the colonies was well-established long before Victoria came to the throne, but throughout that long and increasingly imperial reign, it became a conscious outcome sought both by individuals and by charitable organisations, some of which were established in the period solely to further that purpose. Part of the motivation for emigrating children and young people may well have been a genuinely held belief that a new life elsewhere in the British Empire would offer opportunities to improve their situation not available at home: it was suggested in 1867 that "Investigation will readily satisfy any candid mind that in the Colonies the children would have the same advantages for the present, and many more for the future than in England".[1] However, other motivations were also

---

1 Bracebridge, C.H. "Juvenile Emigration" (1867) 9 *Poor Law Magazine* 236. The author's major focus in this article was to show how the costs to the state would be significantly less than keep-

in play, including a desire to populate the Empire with white settlers, and to further the spread of Christianity, frequently of a particular confession. These motives, good and bad, all too often blinded individuals and institutions to the very real risks of removing vulnerable children from the spatial scope of the child protection legislation that began to appear towards the end of the nineteenth century. For too many children the "opportunities" offered by emigration failed to provide protection from neglect and exploitation, and offered nothing in return, in terms of the love and security that all children need.

Yet even when the practice was at its height, the potential dangers were well recognised. The Local Government Board in England[2] was concerned enough to commission in 1874 an investigation into the practices (then entirely unregulated) of two ladies, Miss Annie Macpherson and Miss Maria Rye. These individuals (with whom it is irresistible – though possibly unfair – to compare with Dickens' grotesque creation Mrs Jellyby in *Bleak House*) ran, separately, Homes for the reception of street children (known at the time variously as "waifs and strays", "gutter children" or "arabs") and pauper children (whose upkeep was presently a burden on the Poor Rate and whose passage would be paid for by the Poor Law authorities), with the aim of preparing these children for emigration to domestic service or farm labour in Canada. Similar homes, "in apparently direct connection with Miss Macpherson's mission" (she was herself Scottish) existed in Glasgow and Edinburgh as well as Liverpool and Dublin "from all of which considerable numbers of children of a similar character are sent out to Canada".[3]

The Report of this investigation (hereinafter "the Doyle Report") was published in 1875 and explained how the ladies had set up Homes for destitute children and prepared them, with a few weeks of work training, for a new life with domestic employers in Canada. The ultimate aim was to provide emigrating children with employment, not with new homes or families: it was to prepare them for the adult world of work rather than to restore to

ing a child in a workhouse and paying for his apprenticeship but, at p. 237, he accepts that this would only be so "if it be made clearly lawful for . . . [Poor Law] guardians to emigrate children" – which suggests doubt as to the lawfulness of the practice, even when in the control of the Poor Law authorities.

2 This was a body established in 1871 to take over, in England and Wales, the functions of (inter alia) the Poor Law Board. Its president was a Cabinet Minister. In Scotland the Local Government Board for Scotland took over in 1894 the functions of the Board of Supervision, the national body overseeing the operation of the Poor Law Amendment (Scotland) Act, 1845.

3 *Report to the House of Commons on Emigration of Pauper Children to Canada* by Andrew Doyle, Local Government Inspector, ordered by the House of Commons to be printed 8 February 1875, p. 6.

them their childhood. Conditions in receiving institutions in Canada were described in highly critical terms, though the Report did find that once children had been placed in domestic settings, their situations tended to improve somewhat (other than in terms of the education offered to the children). But there was no indication of any systematic supervision of the lives of children – nor indeed, in the Doyle Report, was there any suggestion that such a system was considered necessary. Placing a child in domestic or farm service was seen as the resolution of the problem for that child, whose case would now be closed. The very idea of the emigration of children to be used as labour in the harsh environment of the New World was subject to no sustained criticism. Few institutions in the nineteenth century created mechanisms to check whether or not the children they sent abroad were being afforded the better life they had been promised, and it is distress-ingly clear from much more recent official reports into the emigration of children[4] that uncountable numbers of vulnerable young people suffered severe deprivation, emotional and physical, by a practice that survived into the final decades of the twentieth century. Many experienced abuse, sexual or otherwise.

There was nothing peculiarly English about the activities of Miss Macpherson and Miss Rye. It is reported by the website of SurvivorScotland[5] that between 1869 and 1939 around 7000 children were sent from Scotland by Quarrier's Homes to Canada: other voluntary organisations, such as Barnardo's and the Salvation Army, were enthusiastic as well. The state too, though seldom directly responsible for arranging emigration, not only gave its imprimatur to the practice but encouraged it, primarily through the provision of funding under the Empire Settlement Acts, 1922–1972. Official reports such as the Morton Committee Report, published in 1928,[6] clearly perceived emigration as a desirable means of "disposing of" children in need. A 1929 Scottish Education Department Circular[7] to certified (reform-atory and industrial) schools brought to their attention the views laid out in the Morton Committee Report:

---

4 See especially *Report on Child Migration Programmes* (2018), published by the (English) Independent Inquiry into Child Sexual Abuse, and the *Report of the Northern Irish Historical Institutional Abuse Inquiry* (2017) vol. 2 Chapter 6: "Module 2: Child Migration Programmes: Australia".

5 Available at <http://www.survivorscotland.org.uk/are-you-a-survivor/child-migrants/> (last accessed 3rd November 2016).

6 *Protection and Training* (HMSO, 1928).

7 SED Circular No. 80, 16th January 1929, para 12, reproduced in Cowan, M.G. *The Children and Young Persons (Scotland) Act 1932*, (W. Hodge & Co, 1933), p. 331.

The Committee's remarks on migration as a method of disposal [of children and young persons committed to certified schools] should be carefully noted. In view of the attitude of the Dominions towards those who have been in certified schools, it is of supreme importance in the general interest that Managers should exercise scrupulous discrimination in selecting boys for submission to the migration authorities as suitable settlers. The Committee are of opinion that more might be done to make girls in industrial schools acquainted with the opportunities which await them abroad after a suitable training in this country.

To modern eyes, this does not read as placing children's welfare at the forefront of official consideration: it is a manifesto for settling the Empire (then at its absolute height) with suitable stock.[8] Three decades later, when the end of Empire was in the sight of those willing to see it, an Adjournment Debate on the practice was held in the House of Commons, during which Sir Archer Baldwin said this:

> The Australians are very anxious to fill the open spaces. They know full well that if we and they do not fill the open spaces the day will come when the overspill from the Asiatic countries will arrive. We should then have the same sort of trouble that we have recently had in Africa. Because of that the Australian authorities are anxious that Australia's population should be increased, especially with Britishers.[9]

The Under-Secretary of State for Commonwealth Relations spoke for the British Government when he said: "We are anxious to ensure that people of British Stock play a full part in the development of our great sister country in the Commonwealth".[10] "British Stock" was well-understood at that time to mean white people.

Where were children sent?

Canada was the major recipient of emigrated children until shortly after the First World War, and reception houses were established in various places in that country where children would be accommodated when they first arrived until permanent family (work?) placements could be found. Australia, New Zealand and Southern Rhodesia (Zimbabwe) became

---

8 The *Report on Child Migrants* (House of Commons, Health Committee, Session 1997–98, Third Report (1998)) explained the workings of the Inter-departmental Committee on Migration Expenditure (which oversaw the public costs of the Empire Settlement Acts) and reported that "between 1945 and 1954 approximately 2000 children were migrated to Australia in response to what the Committee called 'the Australian request for stock'".

9 HC Deb. 9 February 1959, vol. 599 col. 959.

10 Ibid. col. 964.

more favoured destinations between the Wars, as Canada's reluctance to receive unaccompanied children grew. The Empire Settlement Act, 1922 funded the emigration of a total of 2,259 children to New Zealand and it was reported that "the majority of migrants were juvenile males and were placed directly with farmers or in agricultural training",[11] probably because the very small population in New Zealand was insufficient to sustain large receiving institutions. From 1945 to the scheme's termination in 1953, children sent to New Zealand were placed with foster carers and not in institutions.[12] Southern Rhodesia took a small number but the bulk of children emigrated from the United Kingdom after the Second World War were sent to Australia. That country seems to have been particularly keen, after its vulnerabilities through low population became painfully apparent during the War, to receive children from the United Kingdom (perhaps to balance the official abandonment of its pre-war "whites only" immigration policy). While the hope always was that the children would find new homes in a family setting, it seems that in Australia large numbers of immigrants remained in the children's homes, often attached to farms, that initially received them and they never escaped institutional care until adulthood.

Who arranged emigration?

Voluntary organisations arranged the vast bulk of emigrations before the Second World War, and the managers of reformatory and industrial schools (usually run by voluntary organisations) were active in the practice even before they acquired the statutory authority to do so.[13] Shortly after the War local authorities acquired the power to arrange for a child's emigration but in practice most emigrations continued to be effected by voluntary organisations. The reluctance of local authorities to become involved may have been due, in part, to the lack of enthusiasm shown by the Curtis Committee[14] who suggested that high levels of care and supervision would have to continue to be given to children sent abroad, a standard that few local authorities could reach with children half a world away from their council offices. It

11 Appendix 1 to *Report on Child Migrants* House of Commons Health Committee (1998).
12 Ibid.
13 In a parliamentary debate on the inspection of industrial school ships in 1891 it was stated by Admiral Field that of the boys discharged from industrial schools each year "440 go to sea. The Army take 96 a year and 160 are emigrated": HC Deb. 23 March 1891 vol. 351, col. 1725.
14 *Report of the Committee on the Care of Children* (Cmnd 6922, 1946).

is noticeable that the Scottish equivalent to the Curtis Report, the Clyde Report[15] did not address the issue of emigration at all.

Why emigration was so dangerous

In 1998 the House of Commons Select Committee on Health published a study into the experiences of child migrants and found that many children had been subjected to harsh conditions, and physical and sexual abuse, even before being sent abroad, as well as while journeying to their new lives, and also in the institutions that received them.[16] This study was primarily descriptive and saw governmental responsibility as being moral rather than legal. Twenty years later the (English) Independent Inquiry into Child Sexual Abuse, in its own *Report on Child Migration Programmes*, put responsibility firmly on central government as it sought to identify the failings that led to so many children suffering so badly. Its conclusion was powerful and stark:

> [I]t is the overwhelming conclusion of the Inquiry that the institution primarily to blame for the continued existence of the child migration programmes after the Second World War was Her Majesty's Government (HMG). This was a deeply flawed policy, as HMG now accepts. It was badly executed by many voluntary organisations and local authorities, but was allowed by successive British governments to remain in place, despite a catalogue of evidence which showed that children were suffering ill treatment and abuse, including sexual abuse.[17]

The major failure identified in that Report on the part of most British bodies involved in the emigration of children was their failure to recognise the need to monitor the welfare of children and their progress once they had left the United Kingdom. This was made worse by the fact that, as was common at the time in relation to all children, no mechanisms were in place to allow children themselves to raise complaints – though even if there were any such mechanisms, the practical inhibitions on children doing so would be very difficult to get over.[18] Disturbingly, the 2018 Report records many instances in which abuse and neglect had been brought to the attention of the bodies responsible for emigrating children, but in response to which little if any systemic change followed. The Northern Irish Historical Institutional Abuse Inquiry[19] catalogued depressingly similar accounts of

---

15 *Report of the Committee on Homeless Children* (Cmnd 6911, 1946).
16 *Report on Child Migrants* House of Commons Health Committee (1998).
17 *Report on Child Migration Programmes*, (2018) p. vii.
18 Ibid. p. 14.
19 *Report of the Northern Irish Historical Institutional Abuse Inquiry* (2017) vol. 2 Chapter 6: "Module 2: Child Migration Programmes: Australia".

sexual abuse of child migrants, neglect, physical and psychological abuse, and an almost wilful disregard for young people's education. Though we easily recognise today the full extent of the risks child emigration subjected children to, perhaps the most disheartening findings are that the warning signs were all recognised at the time, but not effectively acted upon.[20] There is no reason to suppose that children emigrated from Scotland fared any better than those emigrated from other parts of the United Kingdom.

THE LEGAL AUTHORITY FOR EMIGRATION

No person or body can simply send another's child abroad, and in the absence of statutory authority for the practice of emigrating children, which did not appear until the end of the nineteenth century, the organisations and individuals involved in the practice would have had to rely on some other legal basis for giving them the power to do so. There are three possible bases that might be identified.

Parental consent

First, it might be argued that legal authority came from the consent of the parents or guardians of the children being emigrated. Miss Rye, operating primarily from England, was recorded in the Doyle Report as requiring the written consent of "widows" (probably a euphemism for unmarried mothers) in the following terms:

> I [. . .], aged [. . .] years, now living at [. . .] do declare that I am left a widow with [. . .] children, and that I am not able to provide for said children, and I now . . . give up my child [. . .] to Miss Maria S. Rye of Avenue House, High Street, Peckham, to be brought up by that lady in the knowledge and fear of God, her Saviour, and of her duty to her neighbour and to herself; and I give full permission for [. . .] my child, to be taken to Canada, America . . .[21]

In Scotland, the founder of what became known as Quarrier's Homes in Renfrewshire, Mr William Quarrier, seems also to have relied on parental consent. The Lord President in *McFadzean v Kilmalcolm School Board*,[22]

---

20 The *Report on Child Migration Programmes*, (2018) lists at pp. 20–21 a number of instances of official reaction to individual cases of sexual abuse, showing that an awareness of the dangers existed but without real institutional change following: perpetrators were regarded as rogue individuals whose wrongdoing gave no warning of underlying systemic failings.
21 Reproduced in Appendix 1, p. 37 of the Doyle Report.
22 (1903) 5F 600, p. 611.

a case involving a deed of trust dated 1876 designed "for the purpose of providing homes for, and upbringing and educating, destitute children" in Quarrier's Homes, pointed out that

> the form of agreement which persons desiring to have children received into the Homes are required to sign, bears that they are received with a view to being emigrated to Canada under the care of Mr Quarrier or his agents.

Lord Adam, in a later case,[23] expressed doubts as to whether the form, which he did not "altogether like", that Mr Quarrier required to be signed gave him any legal authority over the children. Even if parental consent was thought to provide sufficient legal authority, the obtaining of that consent was not assiduously sought, as is plain from the Doyle Report, where it is stated:

> In the case of infants, and of orphans or deserted children of the 'arab' class, it is alleged that the authority of the legal guardian is obtained. This, I apprehend, will be found to be done in a very loose and informal way.[24]

The author explores the matter no further, other than pointing out the danger of asking the child him- or herself – that he or she might refuse to go abroad, and so lose the chance of a bright future. In the Parliamentary debate on the Reformatory and Industrial Schools Act, 1891, which was the first to give explicit authority for school managers to emigrate their charges, it was stated that statutory authority was needed to circumvent parental refusal.[25] This strongly suggests an earlier reliance on both parental consent and its legal efficacy. However, the comment – indeed the whole motivation behind the 1891 Act (which started life as a bill applicable to England and Wales only) – was probably made from an English perspective where parental authority was different from, and young peoples' capacity far less, than in Scotland.

---

23 *Morrison v Quarrier* (1894) 21 R 889. This was one of a series of cases involving relatives of children seeking to remove them from Mr Quarrier's "unsectarian institution" to a Roman Catholic establishment instead. In *Kincaid and Another v Quarrier* (1896) 23R 676 Quarriers had received three children aged 13, 11 and 10 at the request of their dying mother and, by the time of the petition to remove the children to Smyllum Orphanage in order that they might receive a Roman Catholic upbringing, the two elder children were already in a Quarriers Home in Canada. In similar circumstances relatives persuaded the court to transfer custody of children from Quarriers to Smyllum in *Reilly v Quarrier* (1895) 22R 879. Even at this distance of time, one's heart sinks on reading of children being sent there. Conditions at Smyllum were condemned in the strongest terms by the Scottish Child Abuse Inquiry in its *Case Study No. 1* (October 2018), which found (p. 8) that "for many children who were in Smyllum and Bellevue, the homes were places of fear, coercive control, threat, excessive discipline and emotional, physical and sexual abuse, where they found no love, no compassion, no dignity and no comfort".

24 Doyle Report, p. 7.

25 HL Deb. 5 June 1891 vol. 353 col. 1698.

It is doubtful, at least in Scots law, whether parental consent was sufficient legal authority to the sending of children abroad. Parental responsibility in Scotland, as located in the *patria potestas*, was in principle inalienable,[26] and unless the parent were accompanying the child abroad, the practicalities of emigration in the nineteenth century would remove the child completely from the parent's power, and subject him or her to the practical power of others. Even if authority could be delegated, a requirement such as that demanded by Mr Quarrier that a destitute parent consent to the child's emigration before the child will be taken in for "upbringing and educating" can hardly be said to be freely given consent. In the modern era, and in a rather different context, Lady Hale, JSC, pointed out that "Helpless submission to asserted power does not amount to a delegation of parental responsibility or its exercise."[27] This was as true, though probably less recognised, in the nineteenth century as it is today.

The child's consent

A second source of legal authority for the emigration of children might be argued to have been the child's or young person's own consent. Many of the children involved (the street children, as opposed to children of paupers) had no parents or guardians to give consent, either because they were true orphans, or because they had been deserted by parents who could no longer be found. For such children the issue of consent to their emigration hardly seems to have crossed the minds of those who would send them abroad; insofar as it did the assumption seems to have been that the child, voluntarily submitting to the charity of the individual or organisation, was consenting to the plans made for their future. The Doyle Report contains this paragraph:

> Speaking of the class of children who compose the Scotch contingent to the army of young emigrants, Mr Quarrier writes, "We have been frequently asked how we get the children? We go out in the streets and invite those who are needy to come to the Home. We are known to most of the street children. Some come asking to get in, and others are brought by Bible women and missionaries . . . What sort of homes had the children before you took them in? is another question asked.

---

26 Smith, T.B. says, *Short Commentary on the Law of Scotland* (1962), p. 370: "The father's *patria potestas* cannot be transferred". This was true at least insofar as the *patria potestas* related to pupil children. Minor children (girls over 12 and boys over 14) were free to choose their own residence even while under the guardianship of curators (whose power was not traced to the *patria potestas* and was limited to consenting to deeds and transactions): *Craig v Greig and McDonald* (1863) 1 M 1172.

27 *Williams v London Borough of Hackney* [2018] UKSC 37, para 38.

I reply, the night asylum, the police office, cold stairs, haylofts and barrels and boxes along the harbour".[28]

Who were being referred to here were street children, that is those abandoned by their parents: the Poor Law authorities in Scotland are not mentioned as being particularly active in encouraging emigration of pauper children in the way that the Doyle Report suggests they were in England. However, it was elsewhere reported that, in the year 1859, 18 boys were "sent to Canada under free passage" from industrial schools in Glasgow,[29] which suggests that these schools took on the role in Scotland that the Poor Law authorities had in England. The same source later states that for the whole of the United Kingdom, the total number of children up to the end of 1893 emigrated by reformatory schools was 3,464 and by industrial schools was 2,269 (and for comparison, "sent to sea" were 5,750 boys from reformatories and 9,952 boys from industrial schools).[30]

There is no indication here of any limitation on the ages of the children being emigrated, but if the child's own consent was indeed the source of the legal authority to do so, then age becomes critical. The Doyle Report refers to a group of 150 children from Miss Rye's Homes that the author met before they set sail, two-thirds of whom were from workhouses, ranging in age between six and 14;[31] it is unlikely that children in the Scottish contingent were substantially older. But in Scots law at the time only minor children (that is to say girls over the age of 12 and boys over the age of 14) could determine their own residence since from that age their curator could neither claim custody nor require the child to reside in any particular place.[32] So in the aforementioned *Morrison v Quarrier*,[33] it was accepted that of twin children aged 13 in the care of Quarrier's Homes, the girl could decide herself whether to remain under the care of Mr Quarrier – and, implicitly, to be emigrated to Canada – while the boy could not. The incapacity of pupil children was radical, and it followed that the consent of girls younger than 12 or boys younger than 14 to their emigration would have had no legal effect at all.

---

28 Doyle Report, p. 5.
29 Watson, J. "Reformatory and Industrial Schools" (1896) 59 *Journal of the Royal Statistical Society* 255, p. 263.
30 Ibid, pp. 295–296.
31 Doyle Report, p. 7.
32 Erskine, i. vi. 14; *Marshall v McDoual* (1741) Mor 8930; *Flannigan v Inspector of Bothwell* (1892) 19 R 909.
33 (1894) 21 R 889.

Actings in *loco parentis*

The third possible source of legal authority for individuals or organisations to emigrate the children of other people may be said to be derived from their position *in loco parentis* to the child. It could be argued that, by undertaking in fact the care and guardianship of a child whose parents had, in effect, abandoned him or her, the charitable institution or person acquired thereby the power to act in the place of the parent. The Prevention of Cruelty to, and Protection of, Children Act, 1889, s. 5(2) gave to the "fit person" into whose charge a child had been committed by a court the "like control over the child as if he were its parent", which might have been interpreted to include the power to arrange for the child's emigration, on the ground that a parent certainly could make such arrangements. That Act was limited to children subject to court order and would not cover most children in the informal care of charitable institutions (which did not, in any event, become eligible to be named as "fit persons" until the Prevention of Cruelty to Children Act, 1904). In any case, neither the Act nor the concept of being *in loco parentis* removed the parental power of the parent. The doctrine is first and foremost a protective one, allowing a person who in fact has charge of or control over a child to take such actions as are necessary in the child's interests: it has never been one that conferred full parental rights with discretionary power.[34] With hindsight, it is perfectly obvious that children being emigrated were not being protected but were, in fact, being subjected to additional risks of harm. Arranging the permanent emigration of someone else's child could almost certainly not be regarded as a legitimate exercise of the *in loco parentis* role.

Nevertheless, a reading of the materials of the period (such as Mr Quarrier's statement quoted above) leaves the distinct impression that charitable persons and bodies operated on an unshakeable belief that, since their motives were (on their own assessment and, to be fair, probably of society in general at the time) pure and admirable, they must have the legal authority to further their plans. That they were long able to do so without challenge is probably explained by the fact that, when dealing with street children at least, there was no-one in a position to assert title or interest to raise a

---

34 See Wilkinson A. and Norrie K. *The Law Relating to Parent and Child in Scotland* (W. Green, 3rd edn, 2013), para 6.18. The modern manifestation of the *in loco parentis* relationship is found in s. 5(1) of the Children (Scotland) Act 1995 whereby any person over 16 who has the care or control of a child must do what is reasonable in all the circumstances to safeguard and promote the child's health, development and welfare.

challenge.[35] But the absence of anyone with title to question the legality of a practice does not in itself make the practice lawful, even when undertaken in good faith. The common practice of emigrating children without statutory authority rested, until the end of the nineteenth century, on very shaky grounds.

STATUTORY AUTHORITY TO EMIGRATE CHILDREN 1891–1932

The Acts of 1891, 1894 and 1904

There was, as we have seen, no explicit statutory authorisation of – and certainly no state control over – emigration of children when the practice was at its height in the nineteenth century. However, this changed with the Reformatory and Industrial Schools Act, 1891, though that applied only to the small class of children in the care of such schools. The 1891 Act granted to the managers of certified reformatory and industrial schools the power "to . . . dispose of . . . by emigration" any child or youthful offender, either detained in or placed out on licence from a reformatory or industrial school, who "conducts himself well", and who gives "his own consent".[36] The assessment of the child's conduct lay entirely with the school managers, and emigration was presented almost as a reward for good behaviour. This had been comprehensible in the context of apprenticing the child, which was where the reference to conduct originated,[37] but the extension in the 1891 Act of the available disposals of school residents to include "emigration" sat uncomfortably with that reference. Even more uncomfortable is that the emigration of juvenile offenders from reformatories had more than a whiff of transportation about it. In any case, the matter was not left entirely to the discretion of the school managers, and governmental oversight was provided by the fact that emigration was permitted only if the Secretary for Scotland consented. Though the child was required to consent there never would be in our law any requirement for parents to consent to the emigration (and,

---

35 Fraser, *A Treatise on the Law of Scotland Relative to Parent and Child and Guardian and Ward* (3rd edn W. Green & Sons, 1906 by J. Clark), pp. 93–94 points out that title to seek protective remedies over children inhered only in relatives and not in either strangers or the Lord Advocate acting for the Crown as *parens patriae*.

36 Reformatory and Industrial Schools Act, 1891, s. 1.

37 Industrial Schools Act, 1866, s. 28 and Reformatory Schools Act, 1866, s. 19 allowed the managers to apprentice a child who had "conducted himself well" during time out on licence.

in practical terms, loss forever) of their own children. The Parliamentary debate on the Bill that became the 1891 Act[38] indicates that this was a very deliberate policy and not a mere oversight.

A further group of children was subject to emigration regulation by the Prevention of Cruelty to Children Act, 1894, which made similar provision in relation to children committed by the court to the care of "fit persons".[39] Section 6(5) of the 1894 Act provided as follows:

> A Secretary of State, in any case where it appears to him to be for the benefit of a child who has been committed to the custody of any person in pursuance of this section, may empower such person to procure the emigration of the child, but, except with such authority, no person to whose custody a child is so committed shall procure its emigration.

The reference to "the benefit of the child" (absent, be it noted, from the provision relating to emigration by school managers) suggests a governmental obligation to undertake a welfare assessment, though how that assessment was to be made was left entirely unstated. No mechanism was created to allow the Government to assess the child's life-chances in one of the Dominions, as compared with remaining in Scotland. Unlike emigration by school managers under the 1891 Act, there was no statutory requirement in the 1894 Act to obtain the child's own consent – probably because the provision was aimed at younger children than those being discharged from the reformatory and industrial schools.

This provision became rather more powerful after the Prevention of Cruelty to Children Act, 1904 extended the concept of "fit person" to include any society or body corporate established for the reception of poor children or the prevention of cruelty to children.[40] For it was such voluntary organisations rather than private guardians that had long been at the forefront of the emigration movement in Scotland.

Now, there are two ways to look at both these provisions: either they made lawful that which had previously been unlawful, or they introduced governmental control to a practice that, though its legality had never been tested, was nevertheless an unchallenged mechanism for disposing of children. They were almost certainly at the time seen as providing control over an existing practice, for organisations like Quarriers had been arranging the emigration of children long before they became "fit persons" for the

---

38 HL Deb. 5 June 1891 vol. 353 cols 1696–1799.
39 Under s. 6(1) of the Prevention of Cruelty to Children Act, 1894.
40 Prevention of Cruelty to Children Act, 1904, s. 6(1).

purposes of the child protection legislation. Whatever the strict legal position, after 1891 no child under the care of the managers of an industrial or
reformatory school, and after 1894 no child subject to a fit person order,
could be emigrated without the involvement of central government, in the
person of the Secretary for Scotland. And in both cases, the applicable
provision amounted to the legislative supersession of the parents' rights
and responsibilities on the matter. The fact that the Secretary for Scotland
"empowered" fit persons to arrange for the emigration of children in their
care, while he "consented" to school managers disposing of the child by emigration suggests governmental involvement with the emigration of children
from schools came at a later stage, when all arrangements were in place,
than with the emigration of children in the care of fit persons. This distinction is likely to have gone unnoticed in practice.

It needs to be emphasised that the authority of the Secretary for Scotland
to emigration applied only in relation to children subject to such orders.
Given that many voluntary organisations (including Quarriers), even after
they became "fit persons" for these purposes, accepted into their care children subject to no court order, the question never was entirely theoretical
whether these legislative provisions amounted to statutory authorisation
of an otherwise unlawful practice, or merely the regulation of a common
practice in relation to one group of children. The practice of emigrating
children, therefore, remained unregulated at best and unlawful at worst in
respect of children in the care of fit persons in fact but not under any court
order.

The Children Act, 1908

Under the Children Act, 1908 emigration of children committed by the
court to the care of a fit person was governed by s. 21(6), which was in substantially similar terms to s. 6(5) of the 1894 and 1904 Acts:

> The Secretary for Scotland in any case where it appears to him to be for the ben-
> efit of a child or young person who has been committed to the care of any person
> in pursuance of this section, may empower such a person to procure the emigra-
> tion of the child or young person, but, except with such authority, no person to
> whose care a child or young person is so committed shall procure his emigration.

At the same time, emigration by school managers was dealt with under s. 70
of the 1908 Act, which was in similar terms to s. 1 of the Reformatory and
Industrial Schools Act, 1891. As before, and significantly different from
emigration by fit persons, as well as the Secretary for Scotland's consent, the

child him- or herself was required to consent to his or her own emigration arranged by school managers:

> If any youthful offender or child detained in or placed out on licence from a certified school, or a person when under the supervision of the managers of such a school, conducts himself well, the managers of the school may, with his own consent, apprentice him to, or dispose of him in, any trade, calling or service, including service in the Navy or Army, or by emigration, notwithstanding that his period of detention or supervision has not expired; and such apprenticing or disposition shall be as valid as if the managers were his parents:
>
> Provided that where he is to be disposed of by emigration, and in any case unless he has been detained for twelve months, the consent of the Secretary for Scotland shall also be required for the exercise of any power under this section.

That the child was required to consent almost certainly imported a limitation to the provision to children with the capacity to consent – which at that time in Scotland was gained at the age of 12 for girls and 14 for boys when children became minors and gained the power to determine their own residence. As Lorimer put it, a minor child "may marry, go abroad, and fix his domicile where he pleases, and no guardian or Court can restrain him".[41] Minor children had long been recognised as being able to determine their own domicile, while pupil children could not.[42] It is noticeable that there was a continuing lack of any regulation of emigration in respect of children who found themselves in the care of fit persons, including charitable organisations, but not under any court order.

EMIGRATION UNDER THE CHILDREN AND YOUNG PERSONS (SCOTLAND) ACTS, 1932 AND 1937

The provision in s. 21(6) of the Children Act, 1908 which had allowed the Secretary for Scotland to empower a fit person to arrange a child or young person's emigration was replaced by a similar power in s. 19(7) of the Children and Young Persons (Scotland) Act, 1932, but with two crucial additions to what had gone before. First, the child him- or herself was from now on required to consent, replicating the rule in relation to emigration arranged by school managers introduced by the 1908 Act, and incidentally limiting emigration of those subject to fit person orders to children with the capacity to consent, that is to say, boys over 14 and girls over 12. Secondly,

---

41 Lorimer, J. *Handbook of the Law of Scotland* (6th edn, 1894), p. 101.
42 Anton, A.E. *Private International Law* (1st edn, 1967), pp. 170–172; Clive, E. "The Domicile of Minors" 1966 *Juridical Review* 1.

the parents of the child were now to be "consulted", unless it was not practicable to do so – though as before parents were denied any right to prevent the emigration of their own child against their wishes. Both the child's consent and the consultation with the parents were matters that the Secretary for Scotland had to satisfy himself of before empowering the fit person to arrange for the child's emigration. Though the intent of this new formulation was clearly to enhance governmental oversight beyond what had gone before, not everyone was convinced that either the consultation process or indeed the aftercare likely to be available to the child once emigrated would in practice offer any more protection. Lord Banbury in the House of Lords debate on the 1932 Act may be found saying:[43]

> I pass to Clause 23. Subsection (7) of that clause says: The Secretary of State, in any case where it appears to him to be for the benefit of a boy or girl who has been committed to the care of any person, may empower that person to arrange for his or her emigration. The boy or girl may be sent abroad—of course at the expense of the ratepayer or the taxpayer. The Secretary of State of course will not do anything of this kind himself. He will appoint some official. The Secretary of State has to be satisfied that the boy or girl consents, and also that his or her parents have been consulted, or that it is not practicable to consult them. That, of course, makes the provision for consultation nonsense. The official will not take the trouble to consult the parents. He will say it is not practicable to consult them. And again we are dependent upon the Secretary of State or his official. If he chooses to send these children abroad he will have to pay a considerable sum to send them wherever they go. There will be the expense of the voyage and the expense of keeping them when they get there, wherever that is. And what they are going to do when they get there I do not know.

The "some official" became in 1933 the Scottish Education Department (the SED), for the powers of the Secretary of State for Scotland in this regard were transferred to the SED,[44] insofar as they related to children and young persons committed to the care of an education authority (a local authority).[45]

Reformatory and industrial schools became approved schools under the 1932 Act, the managers continuing to have the power to emigrate children under their care, with governmental consent given by the SED. Paragraph 18 of the First Schedule to the 1932 Act[46] was in the following terms:

43 HL Deb. 26 May 1932, vol. 84, cols 470–471.
44 Children and Young Persons, Scotland (Transfer of Power) Order, 1933 (SR&O 1933 No. 821 (S.44)).
45 See also sched. 5 para 3 of the 1932 Act, under which references in the Act to the Secretary of State were to be read as referring, in Scotland, to the Scottish Education Department.
46 And subsequently para 7 of the Second Schedule to the Children and Young Persons (Scotland) Act, 1937.

If a person under the care of the managers of an approved school conducts himself well, the managers of the school may, with his written consent, apprentice or place him in any trade, calling or service, including service in the Navy, Army or Air Force, or may, with his written consent and with the written consent of the Scottish Education Department, arrange for his emigration.

Before exercising their powers under this paragraph the managers shall, in any case where it is practicable so to do, consult with the parents of the person concerned.

There were two enhancements to what had gone before (as well as the addition of a reference to the Royal Air Force). First, the child's consent was now to be in writing (which was not explicitly the rule in relation to emigration arranged by fit persons); and secondly (as with emigration arranged by fit persons) the child's parents now had to be consulted. But the supplementary Regulations made plain the limitations to this consultation process. Regulation 19 of the Care and Training Regulations, 1933 provided in part:

[School] managers shall, as far as possible, consult the parents (or guardians) as to the disposal of a boy or girl and shall endeavour to secure the written consent of both parents (or guardians) in any case in which it is proposed to place a boy in the Navy, Army or Air Force, or to emigrate him. Managers shall not ignore an objection to disposal raised by parents (or guardians) unless the circumstances are such that it is definitely in the interests of the boy or girl that the objection shall be overruled.[47]

Section 88(5) of the Children and Young Persons (Scotland) Act, 1937 replaced the provisions in the Children Act, 1908 dealing with the emigration of children and young persons who had been committed to the care of fit persons (including voluntary organisations):

The Secretary of State[48] in any case where it appears to him to be for the benefit of a child or young person may empower the person to whose care he has been committed to arrange for his emigration, but except with the authority of the Secretary of State no person to whose care a child or young person has been committed shall arrange for his emigration:

Provided that the Secretary of State shall not empower such a person to arrange for the emigration of a child or young person, unless he is satisfied that the child or young person consents and also that his parents have been consulted or that it is not practicable to consult them.

After 1948, this provision was disapplied for children and young persons committed to the care of a local authority,[49] for whom the Children Act, 1948 made separate provision (discussed below). Where the provision con-

---

47 This was replicated in the Approved Schools (Scotland) Rules, 1961 (SI 1961/2243), r. 39.
48 Still, the SED for children and young persons committed to the care of an education authority.
49 Children Act, 1948, sched. 3.

tinued to apply, that is to say in respect of children committed to the care of voluntary organisations, the Children Act, 1948 added to the requirement that the child or young person consented the words "or being too young to form or express a proper opinion on the matter, is to emigrate in company with a parent, guardian or relative of his, or is to emigrate for the purpose of joining a parent, guardian, relative or friend."[50] This addition (the words of which are discussed below) suggests strongly that the requirement for the child's consent introduced in 1932 had acted to inhibit the ability of voluntary organisations to emigrate children who did not have the capacity to consent, or at the very least cast doubt on the legality of the practice. Emigration of pupil children, which had probably commonly occurred before, now became clearly lawful, if only in the specified circumstances.

EMIGRATION BY LOCAL AUTHORITIES UNDER THE CHILDREN ACT, 1948

The Children Act, 1948 substantially expanded the circumstances in which local authorities were obliged or empowered to receive children into their care. At the same time, local authorities were given the power themselves to arrange for the emigration of children in their care – always subject to the requirement to obtain the consent, in Scotland, of the SED. In the Parliamentary debates there was some disquiet expressed about both how children were selected for emigration, and the reception they were to receive when they reached their new homes. Henry Wilson Harris, MP for Cambridge University,[51] said this:

> It is not enough to ask whether a child is a suitable subject for emigration, and whether it is a boy or girl who is likely to face the new surroundings with equanimity and adapt itself to the new environment in which it finds itself. It is rather a question of whether emigration is the best thing which can be done for the child itself. It seems to me that the matter is not always put in that order.

He went on:

> First of all, a suitable subject is looked for, instead of looking to the best interests of the child itself. Let us assume that the selection is rightly made. What is going to happen when the child gets to Canada, Australia, Rhodesia, or wherever it may be? . . . Who is to take the place of the children's officer who is responsible for the after-care here and can be relied upon to carry it out efficiently? Who is to advise and befriend the child when it gets to the Dominions or to some foreign country?

50 Ibid. sched. 3.
51 And editor of the *Spectator* magazine between 1932 and 1953.

Who is to advise about its career? We know that far too often, girls sent overseas mechanically enter domestic service. Is there to be provision in the case of these emigrated children for their further education?

He doubted whether the requirement for the Secretary of State to be satisfied as to the child's welfare in the new country was sufficient, given that the matter would, in reality, be in the hands of the overseas government.[52]

Likewise, Mr Basil Nield[53] expressed doubts as to:

whether it is right, in the absence of parental consent and where the child is too young to form its own view, for it to be sent overseas as an emigrant. I hope this matter may be given further consideration, especially as I recall that in the report of the Curtis Committee there was no great enthusiasm demonstrated for such a system of assisted emigration.[54]

On the other side of the House Mr Somerville Hastings[55] worried that while Regulations (promised in the Bill but, as we will see below, not actually made until some decades later) would specify clearly the duties towards children emigrated by voluntary organisations after they had reached their new homes, there was nothing other than the Secretary of State's assessment to ensure the welfare of children emigrated by local authorities.[56] And he asked for a tightening of the consent provisions (which never happened):

I read in Clause 17 that emigration will only take place with the consent of the Secretary of State, and amongst other conditions he must see that the child consents or is too young to form or express a proper opinion on the matter. I am not at all happy about that. In the past Poor Law authorities have been rather too inclined to emigrate children to the Dominions and elsewhere, but by the Poor Law Act, 1930,[57] a child under 16 who is to be emigrated must give his consent before a petty sessional court. I feel that to be a stronger safeguard than that which is embodied in the phrase I quoted. I hope the Secretary of State will look into that point.[58]

In the end, the 1948 Act attempted to focus governmental attention more clearly than the earlier legislation had on the child's welfare, and for the first time there was included an obligation to assess the suitability of the arrange-

---

52 HL Deb. 7 May 1948, vol. 450 cols 1645-1646.
53 Later a High Court judge and author of *Fairwell to Assizes: the Sixty One Towns* (Garnstone Press, London, 1972) (subject of a distinctly lukewarm review in (1973) 32 *Cambridge Law Journal* 353).
54 HL Deb. 7 May 1948, vol. 450 col. 1653.
55 First President of the Socialist Medical Association and instrumental in persuading the Labour Party in the 1930s to support the development of a national health service.
56 HL Deb. 7 May 1948, vol. 450 col. 1627.
57 This Act did not apply to Scotland.
58 HL Deb. 7 May 1948, vol. 450 col. 1627.

ments in the overseas country for the child's future. Section 17 of the 1948 Act provided as follows:

> (1) A local authority may, with the consent of the Secretary of State, procure or assist in procuring the emigration of any child in their care.
> (2) The Secretary of State shall not give his consent under this section unless he is satisfied that emigration would benefit the child, and that suitable arrangements have been or will be made for the child's reception and welfare in the country to which he is going, that the parents or guardian of the child have been consulted or that it is not practicable to consult them, and that the child consents: Provided that where a child is too young to form or express a proper opinion on the matter, the Secretary of State may consent to his emigration notwithstanding that the child is unable to consent thereto in any case where the child is to emigrate in company with a parent, guardian or relative of his, or is to emigrate for the purpose of joining a parent, guardian, relative or friend.

For the first time, provision was made for the emigration of children too young to give their own consent, but the new proviso raised new questions. Though a narrow definition of "guardian" was given in s. 59 of the 1948 Act it has been suggested – presumably because at the time Scottish courts appointed tutors and curators rather than guardians – that there existed in official circles a fear that migration would dry up from Scotland unless the word were given the looser meaning that it apparently carried in England.[59] The word "friend" to whom a young child could be sent was even vaguer. Charitable organisations often presented themselves as "friends of the poor", though an *ejusdem generis* interpretation of the word in the context of the whole statutory list suggests the need for an existing personal connection.

It would be fair to say that local authorities throughout the United Kingdom were not particularly enthusiastic in their exercise of this new power. Indeed, they were criticised in the House of Commons for interpreting their duties under the 1948 Act "somewhat rigidly and without much imagination . . . They have ignored the immense opportunities which exist and which life in Australia presents for some of these children".[60] In the same debate, it was pointed out that the overall numbers of children

---

59 *Report of the Northern Irish Historical Institutional Abuse Inquiry* (2017) vol. 2 Chapter 6, para 56.

60 HC Deb. 9 February 1959 vol. 599 col. 950. This Adjournment Debate is hugely revealing of the blindly Utopian mindset adopted by some MPs on the topic of emigration. Nigel Fisher MP said this of children migrated to Australia: "These deprived children from bad homes, instead of drifting back, as they might very easily do, to their earlier and unsatisfactory environment, enter may be the Church, or the professions. The boys become farmers or doctors or lawyers or soldiers or businessmen. Any field of activity is open to them. The girls, perhaps, become teachers or nurses or farmers' wives": HC Deb. 9 February 1959 vol. 599 col. 951. Few did.

emigrated from the UK dropped from 388 in 1950 to 80 in 1958.[61] In the year before the Social Work (Scotland) Act 1968 came into force, it was reported that the Secretary of State for Scotland consented under the 1948 Act to the emigration of five children from Scotland.[62]

EMIGRATION BY VOLUNTARY ORGANISATIONS

Some children came (and come) into the care of both local authorities and voluntary organisations by means other than court order. Children informally in the care of local authorities were as much covered by s. 17 of the 1948 Act as were children in their care under court order. However, it would seem that children informally in the care of voluntary organisations could be emigrated without any government involvement, for they were covered by neither the provisions for children committed by court order to the care of fit persons (including voluntary organisations) nor s. 17 of the 1948 Act, which was limited to children in the care of local authorities. If children were informally cared for by voluntary organisations, then the legal authority for such organisations to emigrate them rested on the dubious grounds of the parent's or the child's own consent or an inherent power traced to the concept of in loco parentis. The lack of provision protecting this class of children from unregulated emigration was well understood as the 1948 Act was going through Parliament. Lord Scarbrough, who was connected with the Fairbridge Society (an organisation that had long been active in emigrating children from England to farms it operated in Australia), welcomed the provision in the Bill that became s. 33 of the Act giving the Secretary of State the power to make regulations to control the activities of voluntary organisations in this regard. He suggested[63] that most voluntary organisations would welcome regulation, "if only to prevent the possibility of enthusiastic individuals entering upon a field of which they have not had great experience", and suggested that, as a minimum, it should be provided that the sending institution should retain responsibility over every child they sent overseas until adulthood. He also asked that provision be made to ensure each child received an education and "opportunity to follow its bent", beyond the traditional fields of domestic service and farm work, and that aftercare should be provided for.

---

61 Ibid. col. 969.
62 Child Care in Scotland: A Report of the Secretary of State (Cmnd 4069, 1969), para 34.
63 HL Deb. 10 Feb 1948, vol. 153 cols 961–962.

In the event, however, difficulties in drafting regulations that would require the co-operation of both overseas governments and overseas voluntary organisations – as well as considerable expense in very large countries like Australia – meant that regulations were not made until 1982. There is evidence that organisations in Australia argued vigorously at the time that responsibility for on-going monitoring of children sent to Australia had to lie with those who undertook the responsibility of sending children there;[64] at the same time, the UK took the view that allegations of abuse could only be dealt with by the authorities on the ground.[65] Each side seemed to want the other to assume primary responsibility, with the inevitable result that no-one took any. In these circumstances it is hardly surprising that abuse and neglect flourished, and children and young people did not.

The practice of unregulated emigration continued after 1948 but increasingly "voluntary childcare societies could no longer recruit children to send or no longer wished to do so".[66] Ward LJ speaking of English law in 2001, said this:

> Paragraph 19 [of Part II of sched. 2 to the Children Act 1989] was enacted for the purpose of ending what many would regard as the scandalous child migration schemes that led to so many children in care being sent to the Colonies because the power under the Children Act 1948 given to the Secretary of State to control that emigration was never exercised in time. I believe the last group of children were sent out to Australia in 1967 but it was not until January 1982 that any regulations[67] were made to control this pernicious export.[68]

By 1982, however, the Social Work (Scotland) Act 1968 had replaced the 1948 Act in Scotland,[69] with the result that there never were Scottish regulations made under the 1948 Act controlling emigration by voluntary organisations. The matter instead was dealt with under the 1968 Act.

---

64 See the *Report on Child Migration Programmes* (2018), published by the (English and Welsh) Independent Inquiry into Child Sexual Abuse, p. 32, para 35. The same point was made in the 1998 Select Committee on Health *Report on Child Migrants*.

65 "The Inquiry concluded that several governments after 1970 failed to accept full responsibility for HMG's role in child migration. Sir John Major publicly stated that he 'was aware that there were allegations of physical and sexual abuse of a number of child migrants some years ago, but that any such allegations would be a matter for the Australian authorities'. This reflected a policy position that was maintained throughout the 1990s and 2000s." (Independent Inquiry into Child Sexual Abuse *Report on Child Migration Programmes* (2018) Executive Summary, p. ix).

66 *Report on Child Migration Programmes* (2018), p. 9.

67 The Emigration of Children (Arrangements by Voluntary Organisations) Regulations 1982 (SI 1982 No. 13) (England and Wales only).

68 *R (G) v. Barnet London Borough Council* [2001] EWCA Civ 540, para 31.

69 Social Work (Scotland) Act 1968 s. 95 and sched. 9, Pt 1.

EMIGRATION OF CHILDREN UNDER THE SOCIAL WORK (SCOTLAND) ACT 1968

The provisions discussed above governing emigration arranged by fit persons, by the managers of approved schools and by local authorities were all repealed by the Social Work (Scotland) Act 1968,[70] and replaced by a single provision applicable to all children in the care of a local authority or a voluntary organisation. Section 23 of the 1968 Act provided that:

> (1) A local authority or a voluntary organisation may, with the consent of the Secretary of State, arrange or assist in arranging the emigration of any child in their care.
> (2) The Secretary of State shall not give his consent under this section unless he is satisfied that emigration would benefit the child, and that suitable arrangements have been or will be made for the child's reception and welfare in the country to which he is going, that the parent of the child has been consulted or that it is not practicable to consult him, and that the child consents:
> Provided that where a child is too young to form or express a proper opinion on the matter, the Secretary of State may consent to his emigration notwithstanding that the child is unable to consent thereto in any case where the child is to emigrate in company with a parent or relative[71] of his, or is to emigrate for the purpose of joining a parent, relative or friend.

An amendment had been sought to the phrase "relative or friend" here, on the ground that there was no guarantee that such individuals were "desirable characters", but it was withdrawn on the assurance that local authorities would never recommend to the Secretary of State emigration to join undesirable relatives or friends.[72] (This assumes the existence of a mechanism to assess "desirability"). That this provision applied to "any child in their care" meant that the control of emigration now applied to all children irrespective of how they came into the care of either local authorities or voluntary organisations. Though it filled the gap in relation to children informally cared for by voluntary organisations, there were never to be any underlying regulations made under the 1968 Act either establishing a process by which the Secretary of State could satisfy himself of the matters he had to be satisfied about before he could give his consent, or specifying who had responsibilities, or the extent of these responsibilities, to the children once they had been emigrated. Half a world away, the children were now someone else's problem.

---

70 Social Work (Scotland) Act 1968, sched. 9 Part 1.
71 "Or friend" was subsequently added here by the Health and Social Services and Social Security Adjudications Act 1983 (c. 41), sched. 2 para 6.
72 HL Deb. 4 April 1968, vol. 290 cols 1381–1382.

The 1968 provision was seldom used, for the acceptability of emigrating children to the Dominions was evaporating as quickly as the British Empire itself. Nevertheless s. 23 of the 1968 Act remained in force in Scotland until 1 April 1997, when it was repealed by schedule 5 to the Children (Scotland) Act 1995. Since then, the state has not had the power to arrange, or to authorise others to arrange, or to regulate arrangements for, the emigration of children who would since 1995 be called "looked after" children.

12. Adoption of Children

ADOPTION OF CHILDREN BEFORE THE ADOPTION ACTS

Introduction

Roman law long recognised the institution of *adoptio* and *adrogatio*,[1] which was virtually complete in its effects in creating new family relationships that superseded the old. However, to the Romans adoption was not primarily a mechanism to ensure the good upbringing of children. Rather, it was used to ensure succession either to property or to position. Adoption was, within the Imperial Family, at least as common a mechanism by which Imperial power transferred as the assumption of power by *jure sanguinis*. (Both were, of course, less common than force of arms as the means by which new Emperors emerged.) Octavius, who as Augustus ruled as the first Emperor, gained most of his political power not from his blood-link to, but through his adoption by, his great-uncle Julius Caesar. He himself then adopted Tiberius, making his step-son his own successor. Nero, Hadrian and Marcus Aurelius were all adopted by the Emperors they succeeded (Claudius, Trajan and Antoninus). The same political use of adoption could be seen when Roman men were adopted into families to acquire a status necessary for a particular political office: the patrician Publius Clodius Pulcher, for example, was adopted (technically, "adrogated") in 59BCE by a plebeian family in order to be eligible to stand for the office of Tribune (a magistracy closed to patricians). Other than for political gain, adoption at Rome was most often used as a means of appointing successors to property or to keep a family lineage alive and so ensure the future veneration of the ancestors. Adoption was thus a mechanism to escape the severe limitations on testate succession.[2] The limitations in the Scots common law of succession, primarily the legal rights claimable by spouses and issue, were nothing like as severe as those in

---

1 The difference was this: *adoptio* was the process to transfer parental power from the existing holder of the *patria potestas* to the adopter; *adrogatio* was the process by which parental power was acquired over a person not presently subject to the *patria potestas* of anyone else.
2 Lindsay, H. "Adoption and Succession in Roman Law" (1998) 3 *Newcastle Law Review* 57. See also more generally Lindsay, H. *Adoption in the Roman World* (CUP, 2009).

classical Roman law and so there was no imperative for Scots law to develop adoption as a mechanism to open up succession to the will of the property owner. The idea that the law should step in to ensure the good upbringing of children, the modern purpose of adoption, developed long after the formative period of Scots law and so it is no great surprise that Scots common law, notwithstanding its Roman (or more accurately Roman-Dutch) heritage, did not develop the institution of adoption. More surprising, perhaps, was the lack of any legal protection afforded to fostering of children which, as we will see, was a common social phenomenon long unregulated by law.

Adoption as a legal institution was introduced into Scots law by statute in 1930. It is and always has been a private law action, but in the past 90 years it has developed – at least in practice[3] – far from its roots as a mechanism to provide security to private arrangements. In most cases today adoption is the endgame of a public law process.[4] Most children who are adopted today are at the time of their adoption being looked after by local authorities, having been compulsorily removed from their birth parents by some form of child protection process. Yet the applicants for the adoption order remain private individuals, and they can never be institutions. The common perception of adoption, the providing of a home for a baby whose parents (or mother) has reluctantly made her own decision that her baby would be better off being brought up by those more able to give it a good start in life, is far from the reality of the vast majority of cases. Throughout its 90 year history in this country, adoption had struggled to come to terms with its Janus-like character as a private law action to achieve public law aims, and its true nature is revealed only by exploring how the institution came to be introduced into our legal system and how it has developed since then.

Informal adoption

The history of adoption in Scotland cannot be fully understood without grasping the important point that, as a social phenomenon, adoption of

---

3 That the theory and practice of adoption have long since parted company has been pointed out often in the literature. See for example Lowe, N. "The Changing Face of Adoption – the Gift/Donation Model versus the Contract/Services Model" (1997) 9 *Child and Family Law Quarterly* 371; Ross, M. "Adoption in the 21st Century: Still Image Against a Moving Picture?" in J. Scoular (ed) *Family Dynamics: Contemporary Issues in Family Law* (Butterworths 2001), pp. 105–128; O'Halloran, K. "The Changing Face of Adoption in the United Kingdom", in K. O'Halloran (ed) *The Politics of Adoption: International Perspectives on Law, Policy and Practice* (Springer 2015), pp. 39–75.

4 See the statistics discussed at the end of this chapter.

children is far older than the legal institution of that name, and that the very word "adoption" was in common usage for many decades prior to that legal institution being created by statute. It is a word that, in its common understanding of "taking on" or "choosing", was frequently used to describe the social undertaking of the care of children by persons who were not their parents: such an arrangement, which was relatively unexceptional, came to be referred to as "*de facto*" adoption. Most commonly, what today we would call long-term foster care, arranged privately, was referred to (even in legal contexts) as adoption of children. So, for example, the facts in the 1887 case of *Sutherland v Taylor*[5] were described by the Lord President (Inglis) as follows:

> The mother delivered over the child to the respondent and his wife when it was two months old, and before it was baptised. This was done under an arrangement that the respondent and his wife were to adopt the child as their own, they being childless, and that the child was to remain permanently with them, the petitioner not being in a condition to support the child, and being apparently very willing to be quit of it.[6]

Likewise, Lord Mure put the facts thus:

> [The child] was delivered over to the respondent, upon his undertaking for a certain consideration, to adopt it, and a sum of money, amounting to £100, was provided for that purpose. That arrangement has been quite satisfactory in all respects, and the child appears to have been thoroughly well cared for by the respondent, who has, as I have said, been paid for its upbringing.[7]

This was not a case of a childless couple "buying" a child, but of them being paid to take on the burdens of raising the child as their own. Such arrangements were common and commonly referred to as adoption. In the Second Reading debate on what became the (English) Adoption of Children Act, 1926, the MP Major Attlee[8] was by no means misusing the word "adoption", for it was not then a legal term of art, when he described what had been happening for many years in his East London constituency.

> I rise only for the purpose of associating myself and my colleagues with support of the general principles of the Bill. It is a reform that is long overdue. I was amazed, when I first went down to East London, to find the extent to which adoption existed. We have had a good deal of reference to property and the idea of childless couples adopting children, but what we find in East London is

5 (1887) 15R 224.
6 Ibid. p. 227.
7 Ibid. p. 229.
8 Later, of course, Prime Minister Attlee.

that, where some misfortune befalls a family, there is nothing so common as the adoption of the children by neighbours—adoption frequently by a couple who already, one would think, had quite a heavy enough burden in looking after their own children.[9]

There was no question of such arrangements being treated by the law as enforceable contracts. The *patria potestas* being, in principle, inalienable, courts had long held that any private arrangements whereby a child was brought up by someone other than the parent were revocable and the natural parent could at any time reassert their parental rights including, in the case of a pupil child, the right to custody. So in *Kerrigan v Hall*[10] the foster carer was held not entitled to retain the child against the mother's demand for its return, as security for the unpaid maintenance that she had been promised. Lord McLaren recognised that "adoption" arrangements are by no means uncommon, and may indeed create enforceable obligations – but only of payment:

> With regard to the theory of adoption, it is hardly necessary to say that our law does not recognise any legal relation of adoption creating rights in the adopting parent and the adopted child independent of agreement, but as a matter of fact it is not uncommon for an arrangement to be made whereby a child lives with a relative of its parents, it may be with expectations or with a right to certain allowances. The law may be said to recognise such a form of adoption by not forbidding or discountenancing it. It may even lend its aid towards the enforcing of the pecuniary terms of the arrangement. But this is subject to the conditions which regulate all contracts involving the surrender of personal liberty for a limited time, and a contract will not be enforced to compel residence in a house after that residence has become distasteful to the person concerned, or his parent or guardian, according to the nature of the case.[11]

The arrangement was unenforceable even if its maintenance would be better for the child than the delivery of the child back to its parent. In *Macpherson v Leishman*[12] the mother of an "illegitimate" child (and therefore the only parent with parental authority in respect of the child) had arranged for it to be brought up in a "respectable household" with its father, but then she changed her mind nine months later. The Inner House held that though "the arrangement was a judicious one in the interests of the child" it could not be enforced against the mother unless there was a real and substantial risk of harm.[13]

---

9 HC Deb. 26 February 1926, vol. 192, cols 931–932.
10 (1901) 4 F 10.
11 (1901) 4 F 10, p. 16.
12 (1887) 14 R 780.
13 Ibid. per Lord Mure, p. 782.

However, if the matter went beyond merely providing the child with better chances and a more settled (even a happier) upbringing, then it was sometimes possible for the adopters to resist calls for the return of the child. Such resistance would not, however, be based on any "right" they had acquired to the child (by giving it a home or undertaking its upbringing) nor on any assessment that the child's welfare would be better served remaining where it was. The threshold was much higher. If the adopters could establish a real and substantial risk of harm to the child in being returned to its parent then the court would not order that return. *Sutherland v Taylor* provides an example, for that case came to court when the mother sought to have her child delivered back into her care and the carers refused her demand. While the court acknowledged that the petitioner, being the mother of the "illegitimate" child at the heart of the dispute, "has the only true legal title to custody and control",[14] it nevertheless refused her petition on the ground that the child's welfare and even life would be seriously imperilled by delivering her over to her mother and this was sufficient to "overcome the legal title of the petitioner".[15] This was a hard test to satisfy and the legal protection that it afforded to informal placements was, therefore, limited. Foster carers (at least those who were motivated by considerations other than money) must always have suffered an unsettling fear that the natural parents of a child would reclaim their children, a fear that may well have grown as the children came of age to earn wages and contribute to the family exchequer.[16]

In an attempt to reconcile the inalienability of the *patria potestas* with the desire to give some legal protection to those bringing up children, Parliament passed the Custody of Children Act, 1891, which gave statutory authority to the court to refuse a parent's demand to return the child, but only when the child had been abandoned or neglected, or the parent had otherwise acted in such a way that the court should refuse to enforce the parent's right of custody.[17] (Making arrangements for the upbringing of one's child by others was not in itself abandonment.) The protection provided by this Act went

14 (1887) 15R 224, p. 227.

15 Ibid. p. 229.

16 In proposing the Adoption of Children Bill, 1890, the Earl of Meath deprecated the iniquity of parents who allowed others to bring up their children, only to demand their return when the child reached a wage-earning age: HL Deb. 16 July 1889 vol. 338, col. 502. See also his comments at HL Deb. 25 April 1890 vol. 343 col. 1385.

17 In the two Parliamentary sessions before the 1891 Act was passed, Adoption of Children Bills (No. 101 of 1889 and No. 56 of 1890) foundered because they were perceived as too great an infringement on parents' rights: see HL Deb. 16 July 1889 vol. 338 cols 502–514, esp. Lord Halsbury, LC at cols 507–508 and Lord Fitzgerald at col. 512. See also HL Deb. 25 April 1890 vol. 343 cols 1385–1406.

little further than the Scottish courts, in the decisions discussed above, had already gone in any case.[18]

Baby farming

There was another story that acted as a counterpoint to the "good" foster-carer providing a respectable home for a needy child, who therefore "deserved" the law's protection from unreasonable and dangerous parental demands to return the child. The "bad" foster-carer was motivated not by love of children but by money, and she (for it was invariably a woman) went by the epithet, "baby-farmer". All too frequently, children were delivered into the care of those whose very livelihood was earned by this means, and who therefore had an incentive to take in as many children as they could and to spend as little on their care as possible. The practice of "baby farming", as this trade became known, was extensive and the risks, recognised from the early nineteenth century, legion. Normally involving "illegitimate" children, the parent would pay the baby farmer to relieve them of the practical care of the child. As a mechanism for hiding the progeny of illicit sexual unions, baby farming gave the plotline to many a nineteenth-century novel. Harriet Smith, Emma Woodhouse's protégé, had an experience so benign it is hardly recognised for what it was; Oliver Twist's early years "farmed" by the parish, were far harsher:

> The parish authorities magnanimously and humanely resolved, that Oliver should be 'farmed', or, in other words, that he should be despatched to a branch-workhouse, some three miles off, where twenty or thirty other juvenile offenders against the poor-laws, rolled around the floor all day, without the inconvenience of too much food or too much clothing, under the parental superintendence of an elderly female who received the culprits at and for the consideration of sevenpence-halfpenny per small head per week . . . She appropriated the greater part of the weekly stipend to her own use and consigned the rising parochial generation to even a shorter allowance than was originally provided for them . . . At the very moment when a child had contrived to exist upon the smallest possible portion of the weakest possible food, it did perversely happen in eight and a half cases out of ten, either that it sickened from want and cold, or fell into the fire from neglect, or got half-smothered by accident; in any one of these cases, the miserable little being was usually summoned into another world, and there gathered to the fathers it had never known in this.[19]

An exaggeration, certainly, but the vulnerability of such children in real life was illustrated in a number of notorious court cases in which the children

18 See *Campbell v Croall* (1895) 22R 869.
19 Dickens, C. *Oliver Twist*, chap. 2.

had been so neglected that they died,[20] or were even actively killed after the cash sum had been paid. Jenny Keating[21] refers to a case involving eleven babies found in such a state of total neglect that five of them subsequently died: this led to the setting up of the Select Committee on the Protection of Infant Life in 1871, followed by the first legislative attempt at regulating baby farms in 1872. This was the revealingly-named Infant Life Protection Act, 1872 which required baby farmers to register with the local authority, though it was limited to when they received children under the age of one year. The local authority was authorised, but not obliged, to appoint inspectors to satisfy themselves that the children were being properly maintained. The Infant Life Protection Act, 1897 raised the age to five years, made the appointment of inspectors obligatory, and allowed the local authority to limit the number of children under five who could be received for reward in any dwelling. By the turn of the twentieth century, there were increasing calls to tighten the rules,[22] and the Children Act, 1908 raised the age again to seven years and enhanced the inspection regime of what were now called "infant protection visitors".

The pressure for change

The First World War was a major catalyst for change in the field of child protection, not only because that catastrophe left many children orphans (as it did), but also because it increased the numbers of "illegitimate" children and, by leaving behind many war widows who could not afford the continuing upkeep of all their children, created an increasing demand for the services of baby farmers. At the same time, women who before the war had earned money by looking after children in informal fostering arrangements now gained new opportunities to earn more in factories and offices.[23] Shortly after the end of the War, the Government established a committee under the chairmanship of Sir Arthur Hopkinson on the Adoption of Children, and this Committee reported in 1921.[24] The push for such an investigation

---

20 See for example *Barbara Gray or McIntosh* (1881) 4 Couper 389.
21 Keating, J. "Struggle for Identity: Issues Underlying the Enactment of the 1926 Adoption of Children Act" (2001) *University of Sussex Journal of Contemporary History*, issue 3, pp.1–2. See also by the same author, *A Child for Keeps: the History of Adoption in England, 1918–1945* (Palgrave Macmillan 2008).
22 See for example (1906) *British Medical Journal* 17 Feb 1906, 396–7.
23 Keating J. "Struggle for Identity: Issues Underlying the Enactment of the 1926 Adoption of Children Act" (2001) *University of Sussex Journal of Contemporary History*, issue 3, p. 1.
24 1921 Cmnd. 1254. A useful discussion of the conclusions contained in the Hopkinson Report,

had come primarily from long-established child protection societies such as Barnardo's and the NSPCC, and also from more recently formed "adoption societies", which had been set up during the war to find suitable families with which to place war orphans (and, quickly, to deal with unwanted "illegitimate" children).

The major work of adoption societies during the First World War, such as the National Children's Adoption Association and the National Adoption Society, was to find long-term foster placements, referred to – as the names of these societies suggests – as adoption. But the coming of peace and more settled social circumstances allowed them to turn their attention from casework to policy development, and in the early 1920s these societies began to call for better regulation not only of the sort of placements they themselves arranged (which, they doubtless assumed, were the benign sort) but also of the reward-based placements that were characterised as "baby farms". Legal adoption, which had been introduced in many European and North American countries since the mid-nineteenth century,[25] seemed the ideal means to regulate such placements, as it would give the court a large measure of control over the whole process. So, when the likes of Barnardo's and the NSPCC gave their support to legislation on "adoption", they were, in essence, calling for the better regulation of long-term care of children by individuals rather than calling for the creation of a new legal institution that today we would recognise as being entirely different from fostering (however long-term). There may also have been the hope that the introduction of "proper" adoption would substantially reduce the numbers of children being placed with unsuitable private fosterers whose main motivation was financial gain: if the parents' motivation was to relieve themselves of the burden of bringing up their child, then it would be better for the child (as well as cheaper for the parent, the cynic might add) that the child be placed with someone whose motivation was a desire to have a child to show love and affection to rather than with someone looking for profit.

and of the slightly later Tomlin Reports (Cmnd 2401 and Cmnd 2469, 1924–5) may be found in Lowe, N. "English Adoption Law: Past, Present and Future", in S. Katz, J. Eekelaar and M. Maclean (eds) *Cross Currents: Family Law and Policy in the US and England* (OUP, 2000), pp. 309–312.

25 See Brosnan, J.F. "The Law of Adoption" (1922) 22 *Columbia Law Review* 332.

THE DEBATES ON THE ADOPTION OF CHILDREN ACT, 1926

Though the social practices of informal adoption and baby farming were much the same in both Scotland and England and baby farming was regulated on a UK-wide basis, the formal concept of adoption was introduced into the two legal systems at different moments in time. Legislation was enacted for England first,[26] perhaps because the official reports that recommended adoption as a legal institution had been commissioned by the Home Office rather than any government department with responsibility for Scotland also.

The road to the English legislation was described by the Conservative MP, Mr James Galbraith, as he moved the Second Reading in the House of Commons of his Private Member's Bill, the Adoption of Children Bill, 1926:

> So long ago as 1920 the then Secretary of State for Home Affairs (Mr. Shortt) appointed a Committee, which was presided over by Sir Alfred Hopkinson, to consider whether it was desirable to make legal provision for the adoption of children in this country and, if so, what form such provision should take. That Committee held numerous sittings, and examined a large number of witnesses, and in the year 1921 it issued a Report, in which it expressed the opinion very clearly that it was desirable that provision should be made for legalising the adoption of children in this country. The Committee stated that in their opinion the question was an urgent one, and they proceeded to give many reasons for coming to that conclusion. As a result and in consequence of that Report no less than six private Members' Bills were from time to time presented containing differing provisions in regard to this matter, and I think several of those Bills proceeded to a Second Reading. Having regard to the variance of opinion expressed, in April, 1924, the Labour Home Secretary, the right hon. Gentleman now the Member for Burnley (Mr. A. Henderson), as it seems to me very wisely, desired to have the matter further considered, and in April, 1924, he appointed another Committee presided over by a distinguished judge, Mr. Justice Tomlin, and the reference to that Committee was: To examine the problem of child adoption from the point of view of possible legislation, and to report upon the main provisions which, in their view should be included in any Bill on the subject. Shortly before that Committee made their first Report early in April, 1925, this matter again came before the House. Two private Members' Bills had been presented in that year dealing with the matter, and one of them, that presented by the hon. Member, now the senior Member for Cambridge University (Sir. G. Butler) was discussed on the 3rd April, 1925, and on that occasion the Under-Secretary of State for the Home Department took part in the discussion, and pointed out that although in the opinion of His Majesty's Government the matter was almost ripe for legislation, yet having regard to the fact that a Committee was still sitting dealing with this question, it was undesirable that legislation should be brought in until that Committee had reported, but the Government gave a very definite and clear

26 Adoption of Children Act, 1926.

pledge that as soon as that Committee had reported they would have the matter dealt with.

The Tomlin Committee made two reports the first on the 6th April, 1925 in which they expressed the view that a case had been made for giving legal effect to the adoption in this country of children, subject to proper safeguards, and the second in July, 1925, in which the Committee recommended a draft Bill dealing this question. It is that Bill which I now have the honour to submit to the House. I think that everyone who has studied this question must come to the conclusion that the opinion expressed by the Hopkinson Committee that the matter is an urgent one is the right and correct view. When I tell the House that since September, 1917, no less than 2,050 cases of adoption[27] have been arranged and carried out by one society only, namely, the National Children Adoption Association, and when I also tell the House that I am informed by the secretary of that Association that there are no less than 12 of these adoption cases arranged by this society every week, the House will see that the matter is a substantial one, and also an urgent one. Let me also remind the House of one other fact. The Hopkinson Committee stated—and I believe it is the fact—that this country has rather lagged behind other countries in dealing with this important problem. In practically every other country in the world, including our own Dominions and the United States of America, legislation has been passed in recent years for the purpose of dealing with this matter.[28]

This last point was picked up by the Home Secretary, Sir William Joynson-Hicks,[29] giving the Government's support to Mr Galbraith's Private Member's Bill. He pointed out that most states in Europe, the United States of America, and the Dominions of Canada, Australia and New Zealand had over the course of the past fifty years introduced legal adoption which was "working admirably"[30] and he quoted the senior magistrate of Wellington, New Zealand who said this:

> Speaking from my experience as a magistrate, exercising jurisdiction in the capital city of New Zealand, I can say with confidence that the system of adoption practised in New Zealand has been a success from every point of view. There is no doubt about its benefits both to the infant adopted and to the adopting parents, while the State gains in this way, that the burden of maintaining destitute persons is lightened, and its liability to care for and educate the unfortunate child is lessened, through the aid of private persons. It is agreed by all associated with the maintenance, care and guidance of destitute children that the conditions and training found in receiving homes, although excellent in many ways, fall short of those found in decent family life.[31]

27 Here using the word to refer to long-term foster placements.
28 HC Deb. 26 February 1926, vol. 192, cols 917–919.
29 This great prohibitionist had entered Parliament by defeating Winston Churchill in a by-election in 1908, requiring the then (Liberal) President of the Board of Trade to find another seat in Dundee (which he held until defeated by another prohibitionist in 1922).
30 HC Deb. 26 February 1926, vol. 192, col. 934.
31 Ibid. col. 934.

Though the Adoption of Children Bill was limited in its extent to England and Wales, it is worth exploring the issues that caused concern as that Bill was being debated for, as we will see, there was virtually no Parliamentary discussion when, four years later, the Adoption of Children (Scotland) Bill made substantially similar provision for lawful adoption in Scotland.

The most commonly expressed reason MPs gave for supporting the introduction of a system of formalised adoption of children was to protect long-term foster carers who had been bringing up children from the risk that the birth parents might demand the children's return. Mr Rentoul, for example, seconding the motion, urged support for the Bill for this reason:

> It proposes further to remove from those who have adopted children the unceasing dread that at some time or other the actual parents will turn up and claim the child, and unfortunately the danger of his doing so is almost automatically increased in proportion to the devotion and attention which has been showered on the child by the adopted parents. The marketable value has been thereby increased, and if the natural parent can claim the child with the entire weight of the law on his side, all the love and devotion and sacrifice of the adopted parent may count for naught.[32]

Major Attlee also found this a powerful reason to support the Bill:

> I have known of many cases of hardship where, after years of care, some parent, possibly an undesirable parent, has stepped in to take the child away, probably at the age of fourteen. I am not stressing the financial aspect, but the extraordinary hardship on the family that has adopted the child and has learned to love it, to have it taken away from them.[33]

Another MP, Mr Hurst,[34] agreed:

> In the past, one of the great deterrents in the way of the adoption of children has been the haunting sense of its insecurity. Under this Bill anybody who adopts a child will feel safe from all interference.[35]

Mrs Philipson said:

> It has been my experience to meet many women who have adopted children for the love of those children. I have many such women in my own constituency. One woman came to me the other day in great distress. She had adopted a child when it was only a few weeks old, and she lived in daily dread of the parents coming to reclaim that child.[36]

---

32 HC Deb. 26 February 1926, vol. 192, col. 927.
33 Ibid. col. 932.
34 Later Sir Gerald Hurst, author of the Report of the Hurst Committee on Adoption of Children (1954).
35 HC Deb. 26 February 1926, vol. 192, col. 953.
36 Ibid. col. 957.

There are two aspects that are worth noting about this part of the debate. First, all of these MPs were using the word "adoption" in its factual and non-legal sense and were primarily giving support to the regularisation of existing fostering arrangements. Secondly, the focus was to a startling extent (at least to modern eyes) much more on the adults involved than the children. MPs were seeing the major benefit to be achieved by the introduction of legal adoption as giving a sense of security to the long-term carers – rather than to the child.

Though the principle behind the Bill received virtually unanimous support, not all the details of the Bill were uncontentious. One issue that led to some debate was succession: as Mr Galbraith explained there had been a disagreement between the Hodgkinson Committee (which favoured succession rights of adopted persons in the estates of the adopters) and the Tomlin Committee (which did not).[37] Mr Rentoul said this:

> This Bill does not touch the question of succession rights. But I think there is a good deal to be said for giving an adopted child certain rights in this regard. It is a matter to which, perhaps, further consideration might be given when this Bill goes before a Standing Committee. In many respects the law of France with regard to adoption may be taken as guidance when we are framing our own system. In France the adopted child has exactly the same rights as the legitimate child. That may possibly be going a little too far, but I do feel that some definite right of succession ought to be given.[38]

The Home Secretary saw no need for the Bill to deal with succession because, he suggested, adoptive parents would be likely to make wills containing appropriate provision for the children they adopted.[39] Mr Hurst, however, pointed out[40] that adoptions were most common amongst the poor and that intestacy was, therefore, likely: he called for succession rights to be granted to adopted children – and indeed to the adopting parents.[41] In the end, succession was dealt with in both the 1926 Act and its later Scottish iteration only very partially by declaring that adoption did not deprive the adopted child of any succession rights from the estates of his or her birth parents. The question of the conferral of succession rights in the estates of the adoptive parents was left unanswered, which meant that no such rights were granted.

37 Ibid. cols 921–922.
38 Ibid. cols 930–931.
39 Ibid. cols 935–936.
40 Ibid. col. 955.
41 Ibid. col. 956.

Another point of concern was the place to be afforded to the voice of the child, and the weight to be given to the child's views. This led to some Parliamentary disagreement (and, subsequently, to a substantial difference between the laws of England and Scotland). The 1926 Bill (and then the Act) required the (English) court to have "due consideration" to the child's views on adoption. The Home Secretary said this:

> I was struck by a remark of the Seconder (Mr Rentoul) to the effect that the child should be given a reasonable opportunity of expressing an opinion before adoption. I should like to see every possible opportunity of that kind given, because the real object of this Bill is first, second and last the interest of the defenceless and orphan child. If a child for any reason takes a dislike to the father or mother proposed as its adopting parent, that child's view may be an instinctive one which we older people cannot understand, and it should weigh heavily and paramountly with the Court which has to deal with the question.[42]

This was not strong enough for some. Mr Pethick-Lawrence pointed out that:

> The actual words in the Bill are not nearly as strong as the words used by the Home Secretary with regard to this matter. He spoke of the "reasonable wishes of the child" and said that the "wishes of the child should be paramount." The actual words of the Bill are "the order if made will be for the welfare of the infant, due consideration being for this purpose given to the wishes of the infant, having regard to the age and understanding of the infant." The words "that the wishes of the child should be paramount" are much stronger, and if it is not possible to use the word "paramount" in the Bill I hope some stronger words will be found than those which are actually in the Bill at the present time.[43]

That hope was to prove vain. Also vain was Sir Robert Newman's call for the introduction of a provision into the English Bill requiring the positive consent of the older child (which he saw, tentatively, as the child 14 years of age or above).[44] He was supported in this by Sir John Pennefather, if only in the situation of a second adoption of an already adopted (older) child.[45] In Scotland, children have always acquired capacities to act earlier than their English counterparts, and as we will see the Scottish legislation conferred on the minor child (that is to say the girl aged 12 or above and the boy aged 14 or above), a right of absolute veto to the making of the adoption order. No such provision has ever appeared in the English adoption legislation.

---

42 Ibid. col. 935.

43 Ibid. cols 946–947.

44 Ibid. col. 962. Interestingly, the Hopkinson Report at para 32 had also made this recommendation, but it had not appeared in the 1926 Bill (which had been drafted by the Tomlin Committee).

45 Ibid. col. 975.

Another concern expressed by many MPs was the issue of secrecy. Informal adoptions, being outwith the law, could not stand against a requirement of the parent for the child's return and for that reason adoption societies had fallen into the habit of withholding information about the adopters from the birth parents in order to minimise the risk to the adopters that the birth parent would appear and demand the child's return. The matter caused further disagreement between the Hopkinson and Tomlin Committees, as explained by Mr Galbraith:

> The practice of adoption societies up to now has been this. They have taken every step to prevent the natural parents knowing where the child has gone. Their practice has been shortly as follows: Before the child is adopted they have, quite properly of course, given to the person who proposes to adopt the child the fullest information they can procure with regard to its parentage, its surroundings and, so far as they can ascertain, its hereditary tendencies. But all that the person who is giving up the child is told is that it is going to a home where the society is satisfied, as the result of its inquiries, that it will be adequately and properly and carefully maintained and looked after. That programme of secrecy was, I believe, essential so long as there was no legal ratification or sanction of the adoption, because as the law now stands these arrangements do not prevent, subject always to the overriding welfare of the infant, the natural parent reclaiming the child after he has parted with it for many years. The two Committees have come to different conclusions. The Hopkinson Committee recommended that, when the adoption order is made, notice should be given to the Registrar-General that such an order had been made, but that no notice should be given to him which would enable the identification of the adopting parent to be ascertained. On the other hand the Tomlin Committee has come to the conclusion that the necessity of secrecy is done away with once legal effect and force is given to adoption, and although this is a matter obviously as regards which there may be considerable difference of opinion, I have come to the conclusion that that is the right view, and that once you give legal effect to adoption in the way proposed, the necessity and the desirability of secrecy goes too.[46]

Mr Rentoul had this to say:

> We mean [when we talk of secrecy] that the actual parties to the transaction should be unknown to each other and that the identity of the natural parent should not be disclosed to the adopters, and vice versa. That is a point on which I think most adoption societies have up to now attached considerable importance, for two reasons, because of possible interference by the natural parent, and also because of the definite advantage to the child itself. One has to remember that over 75 per cent. of the children adopted are illegitimate and it has been thought that if you are giving them a start in life, as it were, it is better to veil from them the facts of their origin.[47]

---

46 Ibid. cols 925–926.
47 Ibid. col. 929. "Protecting" children from knowledge of their backgrounds was still sometimes considered appropriate as late as the 1990s: see C, Petitioners 1993 SCLR 14.

The chivalrous Lieutenant Colonel Headlam, who said that he had adopted a child (he meant in the non-legal sense), urged secrecy as a means of protecting the reputation of unmarried women who had given birth.[48]

Again, all of this debate on secrecy revolved around the effects on the adults and the effect on the child was all but ignored by most speakers. At the end of the day, both the 1926 and 1930 Acts allowed adoption orders to be made even when the birth parents were unaware of the identity of the persons adopting their child.

Few MPs talked about the limitations on who may adopt, but it is of some interest to note that Mr Palin, a man behind even his own times (and a trade unionist and former Lord Mayor of Bradford), felt that an injustice was being done to "maiden ladies and bachelors":

> I do not see why two maiden ladies should not adopt a child, and probably prove the very best foster parents. I have seen cases where such women have adopted a little waif of this description, and very good results have followed both to the foster parents and to the child. In the same way, I do not see why two bachelors should be debarred from taking the responsibility of training up a boy. They may have been unfortunate in the matrimonial mart, and I think they should have some compensation given them.[49]

Few commented on the one facet of the Bill that differentiated it from most other adoption regimes around the world and which indeed moved it far beyond the protection of existing placements: the power to make adoption a compulsory order granted against the wishes of the birth parents. Mr A.L. Kennedy wanted the Bill to go further in allowing adoption to be used as a compulsory child protection mechanism. He considered that the grounds in the Bill for dispensing with parental consent were not strong enough and ought to include the child who was being brought up in circumstances "highly and obviously injurious to its physical and moral welfare".[50] He was more concerned, however, by the fact that the Bill dealt with what he described as "the best class of adoption"[51] while at the same time failing to address "the real problems" of children being handed over to people who will keep them for reward (the baby farmer), and the failure of the state to keep a register of all "adopted" children (using the phrase widely to include all children kept long term by those not their parents).[52] This was one of

48 HC Deb. 26 February 1926, vol. 192, col. 944.
49 Ibid. col. 942.
50 Ibid. col. 948. The grounds were extended from the Bill as originally drafted during the Parliamentary process. Mr Thurtle at col. 958 urged caution in drawing the grounds too widely.
51 Ibid. col. 947.
52 Ibid. cols 949–950.

the few contributions that focused on the welfare of the child. Sir Henry Cautley also adopted that focus, but he came to the opposite conclusion. He strongly opposed ever allowing the court to dispense with parental consent. In his view, danger to the child was properly dealt with under the Children Act, 1908, and he made the unchallengeable point that forcing parents to give up their children is a very different thing from consensual adoption.[53] Most other MPs, however, seemed content to allow the new process to deal with both these situations. (In the event, it was many years before compulsion became a common feature of adoption practice.) The Bill passed with no real opposition and, as the Adoption of Children Act, 1926, it came into effect on 1 January 1927.[54]

THE ADOPTION OF CHILDREN (SCOTLAND) ACT, 1930

The First Reading of the Bill that became the Adoption of Children Act, 1930 was on 15 April 1930.[55] It was introduced by Mr Mathers, MP, who said: "The Bill which I am asking leave to bring in is identical with the English Act of 1926". This was not quite accurate, even if limited as he did to terminology and court process: the most notable differences were the requirement in the Scottish legislation, entirely absent from the English, to obtain the consent of the older child to the making of an adoption order, and the ability of persons adopted in Scotland to gain access to their birth records. Mr Mathers cited, as an example of why adoption should be formalised, the case of a widow who was unable to obtain the additional widow's allowance in respect of a child she and her husband had "adopted" at two years of age. Though slightly different from the primary concerns expressed in the English debate, as discussed above, it is equally notable that the sole justification given for introducing the legal process of adoption in Scotland (other than harmonising the law in the two jurisdictions) was to serve adult interests and needs. There was no debate at Second Reading and it may be assumed that the discussion four years earlier on the English Bill was considered to have provided a sufficient airing of the issues. The Bill passed without dissent and came into force on 1 October 1930.

The terms of the Adoption of Children (Scotland) Act, 1930 are worth examining in some little detail.

---

53 Ibid. cols 974–975.
54 Adoption of Children Act, 1926, s. 12(2).
55 HC Deb. 15 April 1930, vol. 237 col. 2738.

The power to make an adoption order

Section 1(1) of the 1930 Act allowed the court to make an adoption order, that is to say, an order authorising the applicant to adopt a "child under the age of 21 years"[56] who had never been married. This is immediate confirmation that adoption envisaged more than simply the transference of custody of the child because custody was a matter that related at common law only to pupil children (boys under 12 and girls under 14) and after the Custody of Children (Scotland) Act, 1939[57] to children under 16. The adoption order transferred the curatorial power over minor children, as well as the tutorial power over pupils. Married minors were excluded because marriage had the effect of forisfamiliating[58] the minor from the curatory of anyone.[59] An application could be made by two spouses jointly, but other than in that circumstance, no adoption order could be made authorising more than one person to adopt a child.[60] This was to remain the case for almost 80 years.

Restrictions on making an adoption order

Section 2 dealt with both (i) the limitations on who may adopt a child and (ii) the rules on consent to adoption. Subsection (1) contained two limitations. First, an adoption order could not be made where the applicant was under the age of 25 years, or in the case of a joint application where both applicants were under that age.[61] Secondly, no adoption order could be made if the applicant was or both applicants were less than 21 years older than the child. This suffered an exception if the applicant (or one of them) and the child were within the prohibited degrees of consanguinity: in other words, when the adoption was by close family members. This allowed, say, an aunt to adopt a nephew or niece even when she was less than 21 years older than the child; more commonly it was used to allow a young mother[62] (or young

---

56 The adoption order could, in fact, be made after the child's 21st birthday so long as the application was made before that date: *TB, Petitioners* 1950 SLT (Sh Ct) 74.

57 Custody of Children (Scotland) Act, 1939, s. 1(1).

58 As the English might say, emancipating.

59 See Wilkinson, A. and Norrie, K. *The Law Relating to Parent and Child in Scotland* (1st edn, 1993, pp. 44–45 for the common law authority; then s. 3(1) of the Law Reform (Husband and Wife) (Scotland) Act 1984.

60 Adoption of Children (Scotland) Act, 1930, s. 1(3). A petition was refused in *JS, Petitioner* 1950 SLT (Sh Ct) 3 having been made by the cohabiting parents of an illegitimate child.

61 Oddly, the reference to joint applications did not appear in the 1926 Act.

62 *B & B, Spouses, Petitioners* 1936 SC 256. Here the mother and her second husband were per-

father)[63] to adopt her (or his) own child. A further limitation on who was allowed to adopt was found in s. 2(2), which prohibited the adoption of a female child by a single male, unless the court was satisfied that there are special circumstances justifying the adoption "as an exceptional measure". The thinking behind this provision is fairly obvious, though nowhere in the very few cases on this provision is there any discussion of what might be special circumstances.[64] Sheriff Trotter suggested that consanguinity alone would not suffice as a special circumstance.[65]

A married person was able to make a sole application for an adoption order, but only with the consent of the other spouse, though that consent could be dispensed with either because the other spouse could not be found or was incapable of giving consent or the spouses were living apart, and the separation was likely to be permanent.[66]

Consent to the making of an adoption order

It was assumed from the start that the parents would be asked to consent to the adoption order, since it involved the surrender of their rights as parents, and was initially designed to give legally enforceable effect to informal arrangements, consensually entered into. Who was required to consent was set out in the important s. 2(3), in which may be found probably the most significant difference between Scots and English law. Consent to the adoption had to be given by every person – or, interestingly, "body" – who was in any of the following categories:

(i) A person or body who was a parent or guardian of the child. "Parent" was undefined but was understood to exclude "reputed" fathers (that is to say fathers of "illegitimate" children) who had no rights to give up.[67] "Guardian" too was undefined but the word was probably to be interpreted consistently with the definition of "guardian" contained in s. 131 of the Children

mitted to adopt the mother's child by a previous marriage even although both petitioners were less than 21 years older than the child (then nine years of age).

63 *D, Petitioner* 1938 SLT 26.
64 In *H, Petr* 1960 SLT (Sh Ct) 3 a married couple received into their care a month old baby girl, whom they intended to adopt, but the wife died before they could do so. In these circumstances, the test for allowing a single man to adopt a female child (by then contained in s. 2(3) of the Adoption Act, 1958) was held to be satisfied. See also *R v Liverpool City Justices ex p. W* [1959] 1 WLR 149 where the adoption order was made in favour of a single man who had married the mother of the child shortly before the mother died (the order was, however, quashed for other reasons).
65 Trotter, T. *The Law as to Children and Young Persons* (W. Hodge & Son, 1938), p. 226.
66 Adoption of Children (Scotland) Act 1930, s. 2(4).
67 *Re M (An Infant)* [1955] 2 QB 479.

Act, 1908 (and subsequently s. 110(1) of the Children and Young Persons (Scotland) Act, 1937), to include any person who had for the time being the charge of or control over the child or young person. "Person" within that definition could include a non-natural person such as a corporation or a charity, hence the reference to "body" consenting to the adoption.

(ii) A person or body who had the "actual custody" of the child. The Court of Session held, in a case turning on the definition of the phrase "actual custody" as it appeared in the Education (Scotland) Act, 1872, that the person who exercised complete control over a charity to provide homes for children was the person with "actual custody" rather than the "fathers and mothers" of the houses (the residential units) in which the children resided.[68] So the organisation that exercised care and control over a child living apart from his or her parents would require to consent to the child's adoption and not necessarily the individual with whom the child was actually living.[69]

(iii) A person or body who was liable to contribute to the support of the child. This would not normally include the unmarried father, since the point was to consent to the removal of parental rights, which the father of an "illegitimate" child did not have.[70] However, if the unmarried father was obliged to contribute to maintenance through an alimentary decree, or by enforceable contractual arrangement, then his consent would indeed be required under this provision, but not otherwise.[71]

(iv) The child him- or herself, if a minor. From the first introduction of legally sanctioned adoption in Scotland, the minor child's consent has been required, and if a girl 12 years of age or over or a boy 14 years of age or over (and under the age of 21) refused consent, then the adoption order could not be made. There was (and is) no equivalent rule in the English legislation. It was subsequently held that the child's consent must be based on a full understanding of his or her own background.[72] (Interestingly the court precisely one year later held that the parent could give valid consent

---

68 *McFadzean v Kilmalcolm School Board* (1903) 5F 600.

69 In *Bute Education Authority v Glasgow Education Authority* 1923 SC 675 the Lord President at p. 682 said this: "A natural parent may find it expedient to commit the care and charge of a child to someone other than himself or his own servants, or to board it in some family establishment other than one maintained by himself, or even in some institution. The head of such establishment or institution will, in general, have what the statutory definition calls the 'actual custody' of the child – by which I understand to be meant the *de facto* custody, not necessarily as a matter of any legal right."

70 *Re M (An Infant)* [1955] 2 QB 479.

71 Unmarried fathers who voluntarily made payments for their children's upkeep were not under an obligation and so their consent would not be sought: *Re D (An Infant)* [1958] 1 WLR 197 (commented on at [1958] 21 MLR 413).

72 In *A, Petitioner* 1936 SC 255 a child had been brought up since birth believing (falsely) that he was the legitimate child of a deceased married couple. The petitioner, who had brought him up and now wished to adopt him, did not want him to discover that he was, in fact, "illegitimate". The First Division of the Court of Session, however, required the child (by then 19 years old) to be informed of the whole circumstances before seeking his consent. (He consented on being informed about the truth of his background.) But cf. *C, Petitioners* 1993 SCLR 14, which involved a younger child.

even in ignorance of the identities of the adopters.)[73] It is tempting to see the Scottish requirement to obtain the minor child's consent to the making of an adoption order as an indication that such an order is one that goes far deeper than regulating and protecting the adopter's right of custody. But it needs to be remembered that, in 1930, the concept of custody applied only to pupil children. The requirement for the minor child's consent to adoption reflects, rather, the position of the minor child at common law, since that child was able to enter into transactions on his or her own behalf (subject to the consent of their curator, or father if "legitimate") and could indeed, with the consent of the father, choose their own curator.[74] The power of the adoptive parent of a minor child was originally one of curatory only.

Though adoption was initially perceived to be a consensual matter, the legislation has always permitted the court to do what few other countries in Europe had then permitted or today permit their courts to do:[75] that is to say, dispense with the required consent, and make the adoption order in the face of parental opposition. The existence of this provision confirms that, from its earliest statutory manifestation, the adoption process in both Scotland and England has had the potential for being a compulsory process to be used against a parent unwilling to give up his or her child: it is and always has been a child protection mechanism as well as a process by which birth parents (typically mothers) are able to allow others to care for their children. The grounds for dispensation appeared in the grammatically confusing proviso to s. 2(3) of the 1930 Act, which seemed to allow the court to dispense with consent when the person whose consent was otherwise required:

(i)   had neglected or treated the child with cruelty,
(ii) had abandoned or deserted the child,
(iii) could not be found or was incapable of giving consent,
(iv) being liable to contribute to the support of the child had persistently neglected or refused to do so, or
(v)   was "a person whose consent ought, in the opinion of the court and in all the circumstances of the case, to be dispensed with."

There were at least two matters that were very unclear from this proviso (which appeared as one continuous sentence rather than being broken down in the way it is presented above). First, it was unclear whether the last, catch-all, clause was a self-standing ground that applied generally, or

---

73 *C & C, Spouses, Petitioners* 1936 SC 257. This point was affirmed by a Court of Seven Judges in *H & H, Petitioners* 1944 SC 347 (if with a strong dissent by Lord Moncrieff). The matter was given statutory authority under the Adoption of Children Act, 1949, s.3(2), discussed below.

74 Stair, I, v. 12 and Erskine 1, iv, 54.

75 See the comment to this effect of Baroness Hale in *Down Lisburn Health and Social Services Trust and Anor v H and Anor* [2006] UKHL 36, para 34.

was an aspect of the immediately preceding ground and therefore applied only to persons liable to contribute to the support of the child. However, the English court held on an interpretation of the identically structured English provision that these words applied generally as a separate ground for dispensation.[76] The breadth of the ground seemed to confer on the court an almost unlimited discretion, though in the event it was seldom used. As Trotter said: "This clause gives the court a wide power, but, of course, there must be some cogent reason for dispensing with the consent".[77]

The second doubt was the question of whether it was possible to dispense with the child's consent. The wording in the Scottish proviso to s. 2(3) is not precisely the same as the wording in the English equivalent, for the first-mentioned ground for dispensing with consent in the 1930 Act does not appear in the 1926 Act. Yet the question of dispensing with the child's consent, not relevant in the English proviso, is simply ignored in the Scottish proviso. It seems from the wording of the grounds of dispensation that Parliament did not contemplate the dispensation in Scotland of the child's consent, for most of the grounds would be factually inappropriate. However, that the child was "incapable of giving consent" could clearly have been used in an appropriate case to dispense with the child's own consent (though no case has been traced in which it was). Later legislation made plain that dispensation was available only to the consent of parents and guardians,[78] but the Adoption (Scotland) Act 1978 changed this and provided that the child's consent could be dispensed with if he or she were incapable of consenting to the making of the order.[79]

Matters in respect of which the court must be satisfied

Section 3 set out certain matters about which the court had to be satisfied before it could make an adoption order. First, the court had to be satisfied that every person whose consent was necessary (but not dispensed with) had consented to, and understood the nature and effect of, the adoption order, and in particular that any parent understood that the effect of the adoption

76 *H v H* [1947] KB 463.

77 Trotter, T. *The Law as to Children and Young Persons*, p. 229.

78 Adoption Act, 1950, s. 3(1) and Adoption Act, 1958, s. 5(1).

79 Adoption (Scotland) Act 1978, s. 12(8). See now the Adoption and Children (Scotland) Act 2007, s. 32(2) which sensibly avoids the language of dispensation, instead disapplying the requirement to obtain the child's consent where the child is incapable of consenting to the order.

order would be permanently to deprive him or her[80] of his or her parental rights. Secondly, the court had to be satisfied that the order would be for the welfare of the child, giving due consideration to the wishes of the child having regard to the child's age and understanding. And finally, the court had to be satisfied that the applicant had not received or agreed to receive, and no person had made or agreed to make, any payment or other reward in consideration of the adoption, except such as the court sanctioned. Section 9 reinforced this by making it unlawful for the adopter or parent or guardian to receive any payment or other reward in consideration of the adoption (though no penalty was specified). The power of the court to sanction the reward (which still exists today) is, however, to be noted.

Terms and conditions

Section 4 of the Adoption of Children (Scotland) Act, 1930 allowed the court to attach to an adoption order such terms and conditions as it thought fit, in particular by requiring the adopter "by bond or otherwise" to make such provision for the adopted child as the court considered "just and expedient". Specifying this particular condition was the compromise position between those MPs who had expressed doubts about the lack of succession consequences of adoption and the Government position that including succession consequences would be inappropriate: both the 1926 and 1930 Acts left succession rules untouched while at the same time allowing the court to require the adopter to make financial provision for the child on the adopter's death.

It may be noted that conditions were not assumed to include conditions relating to contact between the child and birth parent, a matter that received no consideration in Parliament. This was entirely consistent with the notion of the adoption order being, in essence, a mechanism to protect long-term fosterers from the claims of the birth parents. So there was nothing surprising about keeping the adopters' identity from the birth parent.[81] It was not until some decades later that a condition relating to contact was held to be within the terms of the statute.[82]

---

80 This is a rare statutory use of "him or her" as opposed to the normal reliance on the masculine including the feminine.

81 *C & C, Spouses, Petitioners* 1936 SC 257; *H & H, Petitioners* 1944 SC 347.

82 In *Re J (A Minor) (Adoption Order: Conditions)* [1973] Fam 106 the Family Division in England held that while the general expectation was that after adoption the child should have no contact with his or her birth parents, it was competent to add a condition of contact (under what was by then the Adoption Act, 1958) if this was in the best interests of the child. It is worth noting that in *AB v CB* 1985 SLT 514 a Scottish sheriff held that it was incompetent to attach a condition of

Effects of an adoption order

The effects of the adoption order were specified in s. 5 of the 1930 Act and
they were significantly less than an adoption order would carry today. All
rights, duties, obligations and liabilities of the parents or guardians in relation to custody, maintenance and education were extinguished and they
were vested in and exercisable by the adopter as though the adopted child
was a child born to the adopter in lawful wedlock. This had a double effect.
First, the legal role of parent transferred from the birth parents to the
adoptive parents, who thereafter had the authority to bring up the child as
if they were his or her parents. Secondly, the child (if "illegitimate") would
be treated as the legitimate child of the adopter.[83] This was less radical
in Scotland, where means of legitimating "illegitimate" children had long
existed,[84] than in England which had adhered to the notion of the indel-
ibility of bastardy[85] until the Legitimacy Act, 1926 passed four months after
the Adoption of Children Act, 1926. Though it had hardly been in the
contemplation of the legislators, this legitimation effect was deliberately
sought (and achieved) in the first reported decision on the 1930 Act.[86] This
illustrates that the adoption process has always, from its very inception, had
the capacity to deal with situations other than those for which it was primarily designed.

The effect of an adoption order on succession, which had been contentious in the Parliamentary debates on the 1926 Act, was dealt with in s. 5(3)
of both that Act and the 1930 Act, but in a negative manner only. Adopted
children were not excluded from succession to the estate of their birth

contact on an adoption order. The Inner House did not decide the point (indeed Lord Hunter
explicitly expressed reservations about the English cases where this had been done) but held that
the father's refusal of consent unless the order maintained his contact with the child was unreasonable and dispensed with his consent on that basis. The House of Lords in *Re C (A Minor)
(Adoption Order: Conditions)* [1989] AC 1, p. 17 affirmed the competency of contact conditions
attached to an adoption order and in *B v C* 1996 SLT 1370 the First Division held that the law of
Scotland was the same as that of England on the matter, and affirmed a contact condition made
by the sheriff.

83 See *M & M, Petitioners* 1950 SLT (Sh Ct) 3 where it was held that parents who had married
subsequent to the birth of their child could not then adopt the child, she having been legitimated
by their marriage. On the other hand, such parents were able to adopt their natural child in *H &
H, Petitioners* 1948 SLT (Sh Ct) 37 because the child, having been conceived when the mother
was married to another man, was not legitimated by her parents' subsequent marriage.

84 See Wilkinson, A. and Norrie, K. *The Law Relating to Parent and Child in Scotland* (1st edn,
1993), pp. 5–26.

85 See *Munro v Munro* (1840) 7 ER 1288.

86 In *A & B, Petitioners* 1932 SLT (Sh Ct) 37 a husband and wife adopted the "illegitimate" child of
the wife.

parents and could only be included in testamentary provision made by their adoptive parents if included explicitly or by necessary implication.[87] The result, unstated but clear, was that adopted children were not brought within the intestate succession to the estates of their adoptive parents. This remained the case in Scotland until the Succession (Scotland) Act 1964.

The view was expressed in the Hurst Report in 1954 that all s. 5 achieved was to create a form of "special guardianship".[88] Other effects which to the modern mind are inherent in the very concept of adoption were not dealt with in either the 1926 or 1930 Acts. Trotter concluded his annotations to s. 5 with the comment:

> It would seem, although it is not quite clear, and the point has not yet been judicially determined, that the Act does not prohibit marriage between an adopter and an adopted child, as the adopting parent really only holds the position of a special guardian . . .[89]

Such a prohibition, which had been recommended by the Hopkinson Committee back in 1921,[90] was introduced only with the Adoption of Children Act, 1949. The 1930 Act was also silent on the issue of any claim the adopted child might have for damages or solatium on the wrongfully caused death of the parent. This was dealt with by s. 2(1) of the Law Reform (Miscellaneous Provisions) (Scotland) Act, 1940 and since then not only may an adopted child claim on the negligently caused death of his or her adoptive parent, but the adoptive parent may claim on the negligently caused death of their adopted child.[91] The adoption order only gradually took on the characteristics of a transference of parenthood itself, losing at the same time its identity as a protection of long-term fostering arrangements.

Interim orders and second adoption orders

The court was permitted to make an interim order instead of a full adoption order: the effect of this was to give custody of the child to the applicants for a probationary period not exceeding two years.[92] Trotter explained that "Such

---

87 That implication could not be drawn from evidence (incompetent in any case) that the testator had always treated the adopted child as his own. The implication needed to come from the testament and not the testator's actions: *Hay v Duthie's Trs* 1956 SC 511.

88 *Report of the Departmental Committee on the Adoption of Children* Cmnd 9248 (1954), para 196, leading ultimately to the Adoption Act, 1958, discussed below.

89 Trotter, T. *The Law as to Children and Young Persons*, p. 236.

90 Hopkinson Report, para 56.

91 As an example, see *Foreman v Advocate General for Scotland* 2016 SLT 962.

92 Adoption of Children (Scotland) Act, 1930, s. 6(1).

a course may be expedient when there is a doubt as to the desirability of the proposed adoption order".[93] The same consents as were needed for the making of an adoption order (including, in Scotland, that of the child) were needed before the court could make such an interim order.[94]

Section 7, included for the avoidance of doubt on the issue, permitted the court to make an adoption order over a child who was already subject to an adoption order. The original adopter would have to give consent to the subsequent adoption, but the birth parents would not.[95] One of the common purposes to which this section was put was to allow the adoption in Scotland of a child who had previously been adopted in England.[96]

Existing *de facto* adoptions: adoption of adults

Section 10 of the Adoption of Children (Scotland) Act, 1930 is a peculiar and revealing provision. As we have already seen, the major concern of MPs debating the Adoption of Children Bill in 1926 had been to provide security to persons who were bringing up children not their own. Many such arrangements were already in place, and it would be possible for these people to seek an adoption order by the normal process. But it was considered appropriate to allow the court to deal with pre-existing arrangements by a simplified process, which would effectively give retrospective legal effect to *de facto* adoptions that had been in existence on the day formal legal adoption was made available by statute. Since the informal arrangement was consensual, its ratification needed no further consent. However, the main advantage of this process was that such retrospective authorisations could be obtained, as an adoption order under s. 1 could not, even after the child had become an adult.

Section 10 allowed the court to make an order authorising the adoption of any person who had been at the date of commencement of the Act (1 October 1930) in the custody of and being brought up, maintained and educated by any person or two spouses as his, her or their own child, so long as, on that date, the child was under the age of 21. In moving the Second

---

93 Trotter, T. *The Law as to Children and Young Persons*, p. 237.
94 Adoption of Children (Scotland) Act, 1926, s. 6(2).
95 See *F, Petitioner* 1939 SC 166 where it was held that intimation to the birth father was not required when a child was being adopted, having previously been adopted.
96 See for example *E and E, Petitioners* 1939 SC 165. Automatic recognition between Scotland and England was not attained until the Adoption of Children Act 1949, which for the first time defined an adoption order as one made under either the Scottish or the English legislation: 1949 Act, s. 14(1)

Reading of the Adoption of Children Bill, 1926, which contained an identical provision, Mr Galbraith described the effect and justification for this clause as follows:

> Clause 10 enables the Court to authorise and to sanction *de facto* adoptions, and in effect it comes to this, that in any case where a child has in fact been adopted and kept and maintained by any person for two years, the Court can authorise and ratify that adoption without obtaining the consent of the person who has given up the child in a case where the Court is satisfied that it is unnecessary or desirable that the consent of that person should be obtained. I believe, so far as my experience is concerned, this is a most desirable provision. I have received, since I put down the Bill, a considerable number of letters from persons who have in years past adopted children, who speak of the way in which they have come to feel great affection for the children, and the children have begun to feel great affection for them, and they have pointed out the haunting fear they have had lest the natural parents, who have taken no interest in the children, may interfere and attempt to take the children away, and I believe the Clause which enables *de facto* adoption to be sanctioned is a good and desirable provision.[97]

There was a surprising number of cases under s. 10 of the Scottish Act and, curiously enough, none at all (at least, none reported) under the English Act. In *G, Petitioner*[98] a petition was presented to the Court of Session under s. 10 of the Scottish Act craving authority

> to adopt a child who had been in the custody of, and *de facto* adopted, brought up, maintained and educated by, the petitioner, since a date more than two years prior to the commencement of the Act, and was at the date of the petition still residing with, and being maintained by, the petitioner.

The "child" in this case was over 21 at the date of the application, and the court granted the adoption order craved, without issuing any judgment. The same result followed in *K, Petitioner*[99] where the person being adopted was 37 years old. The effect of such orders, given that there were no succession consequences carried by an adoption order and no upbringing powers any longer necessary, tended to be psychological or social, such as the perceived legitimation of the adopted person. But in *K, Petitioner*, the benefit was more substantial as the adoption order gave access to the benefits in a superannuation scheme which included adult children. One unsuccessful case was *RB, Petitioners*[100] where the petition was refused because the child had not resided with the petitioners for the two years before the commencement

97 HC Deb. 26 February 1926, vol. 192 col. 925
98 1939 SC 782.
99 1949 SC 140.
100 1950 SLT (Sh Ct) 73.

of the 1930 Act, she coming into their care on 11 November 1928 and the Act commencing on 1 October 1930. She was six weeks short of the requisite period.

The procedure under s. 10 constituted a quite separate code from that contained in the rest of the Act, and many of the conditions applicable to adoption orders under s. 1 (as well as the age condition) were held inapplicable to orders under s. 10. That the adoptee be unmarried was not a requirement and so in *L, Petitioner*[101] a 31 year old married man with four children of his own was able to be adopted under the terms of s. 10 by his mother (who had given birth to him while unmarried). Also, the requirement that the parties be resident in Scotland at the date of the order was held not to apply to s. 10 adoptions.[102] And the court could make an order under this provision even if the applicant were male and the person to be adopted female, and even without the consent of the parent or guardian (if it was considered by the court to be just and equitable and for the welfare of the "child" not to require that consent). Section 10, copied as it was from the English s. 10, unsurprisingly contains no mention of the consent of the person to be adopted, notwithstanding that the section was more typically used for the retrospective adoption of adults but the matter was not raised in any of the cases.

The Adopted Children Register

Section 11 of the 1930 Act established the Adopted Children Register, and required the Registrar-General for Scotland to mark the register of births in relation to the child with the word "adopted". The Registrar-General was required to make such entries as was necessary "to record and make traceable the connection between any entry in the register of births . . . and any corresponding entry in the Adopted Children Register". That connection was not to be publicly available without a court order, though in another major difference from the English Act it was to be made available on request to an adopted person who had attained the age of 17 years to whom the entries related.

---

101 *L, Petitioner* 1951 SLT 270 (IH), overruling *F, Petitioner* 1951 SLT (Sh Ct) 17.
102 *H, Petitioners* 1952 SLT (Sh Ct) 15.

Conclusions on the Adoption of Children (Scotland) Act, 1930

In many ways, the 1930 Act was less radical than it might appear, given that it created an entirely new legal institution. The key to understanding its true effect is the identification of its aim of providing security to long-term foster-carers: the 1930 Act provides, in essence, a form of protected custody and guardianship for such carers. Neither custody nor guardianship, of course, were new legal institutions but the additional protections afforded by the adoption order were innovative. To modern eyes, this was not a model that substituted one set of parents for another but was first and foremost a means of regulating the child's upbringing. The 1930 Act dealt with what today are called parental responsibilities and parental rights but did not purport to have any effect on parenthood itself. It took a series of statutes, culminating (as we will see below) with the Children Act 1975, before adoption could be regarded as a transference not only of upbringing powers but of parenthood itself.

Though adoption was not, at this stage, an institution that was intended to create a life-long legal relationship, there is little doubt that it created life-long social relationships. However, ambiguities remained as to adoption's true effect. It was never entirely clear that treating the child as born in lawful wedlock actually achieved lifelong legitimacy as opposed to treating the child for that purpose during its upbringing,[103] though that subtlety probably escaped most parties seeking to use adoption to legitimate, at least in their own eyes, the child they were bringing up. And though the primary aim of adoption was to secure the child's upbringing, the retrospective adoptions permitted under s. 10, considered above, show a common desire to have the law's imprimatur on social relationships, even after the time for bringing up the child had long since passed.

The design of the new order was very much in the private law mould. The adopters were the ones who, as private individuals, had to (and still have to) make the application for an adoption order. The role of the state in the 1930s was limited to registering the adoption order and ensuring that there was a mechanism to tie together the original birth registration with the registration of the adoption. Local authorities, which came to dominate the practice of adoption in the second half of the twentieth century, were entirely absent from the Adoption of Children (Scotland) Act, 1930, but the private law process was too useful a means to achieve public law ends and local authorities

---

103 See Wilkinson, A. and Norrie, K. *The Law Relating to Parent and Child* (1st edn 1993), p. 519.

were given a role within ten years; thereafter with each passing Act, that role grew and became pre-eminent.

THE ADOPTION OF CHILDREN (REGULATION) ACT, 1939

An important addition to the adoption legislation, passed weeks before the outbreak of the Second World War, was the Adoption of Children (Regulation) Act, 1939, which substantially increased the regulation of the practice of adoption, especially by adoption societies. The Act followed the recommendations of the Horsburgh Committee's *Report on Adoption Societies and Agencies*,[104] which had highlighted the lack of regulation of adoption societies. These societies had increased substantially in number – and in activity – since the passing of the Adoption of Children Act, 1926 and the 1939 Act required that arrangements for adoption, when made by bodies of persons, be made only by registered adoption societies and local authorities.[105] This meant that existing adoption societies, which had been established long before the 1926 Act or its Scottish equivalent in order to facilitate informal adoptions, and other charities which did so as part of their work with children, were now required to register under s. 2 with a "registration authority" (i.e. the appropriate local authority). The registration authority could refuse registration on a number of grounds, including that any person employed or proposed to be employed by the society was "not a fit and proper person to be so employed".[106] Placing of children with prospective adopters by registered adoption societies was governed by the rules in s. 6, which included a prohibition on placing a child with persons unable to adopt, a prohibition on placing a child with a person resident abroad unless a special licence to do so had been obtained under s. 11, and provisions under which the society could require the return of the child from the person with whom he or she had been placed. In order to discourage the practice of avoiding court approval by simply placing a child with carers and making it hard for birth parents to trace the carers (an old practice of adoption societies), the Horsburgh Committee also recommended that prospective adopters should have to inform local authorities of any placement. This was given effect to but only partially. The placing of children before the age of

---

104 *Report of the Departmental Committee on Adoption Societies and Agencies* Cmnd 5499 (1937).
105 Adoption of Children (Regulation) Act 1939, s. 1. The prohibition applied only to "bodies of persons" and so individuals (ministers and priests, GPs and the like) were still able to "make arrangements for the adoption of a child".
106 Adoption of Children (Regulation) Act 1939, s. 2(3).

nine with persons who were not the parent, guardian or relative of the child required to be notified to the child protection authorities (local authorities). Child protection visitors (who had been required to visit privately fostered children since Part I of the Children Act, 1908) were now also required to visit children who had been so placed until such time as they were either adopted or they reached the age of nine years[107] (the age at which, under the Children and Young Persons (Scotland) Acts, 1932 and 1937, child protection visits ceased for privately fostered children). The close identity between private fostering and adoption as originally conceived is once again revealed.

The 1939 Act amended s. 2(1) of the 1930 Act to qualify its proviso in order to allow an applicant or applicants to adopt even before reaching the age of 25, so long as the applicant, or one of them, was the mother of the child; it also allowed adoption when the age gap between adopter and adopted child was less than 21 years when, in the case of a joint application, one of the applicants was the parent of the child. It was made a criminal offence for any person (not being a local authority) to make or receive any payment or reward in connection with the making of arrangements for the adoption of children unless such payments were for the maintenance of the child or were authorised by the court.[108] This extended the prohibition beyond that contained in s. 9 of the 1930 Act, which was limited to adopters, parents and guardians receiving (but not making) payment. And the 1939 Act also made provision for the first time for the restriction (i) of advertising that a parent or guardian was willing to cause their child to be adopted, that a person was willing to adopt a child, or willing to make arrangements for the adoption of a child[109] and (ii) of sending children for adoption abroad.[110] A year earlier, as previously noted, another change of some significance had been effected, when s. 2 of the Law Reform (Miscellaneous Provisions) (Scotland) Act, 1940 extended the right to recover damages or solatium in respect of the death of a person caused by the fault of another to adopted children. This was the start of a process, not brought to its full fruition until the 1970s, whereby the adopted child progressively came to be treated in the same way for more and more purposes of law as the "legitimate" child of the adopter or adopters.

---

107 Ibid. s. 7.
108 Ibid. s. 9.
109 Ibid. s. 10.
110 Ibid. s. 11.

THE ADOPTION OF CHILDREN ACT, 1949

The Adoption of Children Act, 1949 amended both the 1926 and 1930 Acts, but it did not repeal them. Section 2(1) of the 1930 Act was repealed and replaced with a simpler set of rules relating to the age of the applicant or applicants. The previous rule that the applicant or both applicants had to have attained the age of 25 years and be at least 21 years older than the child to be adopted was replaced with the rule that the applicant or one of the applicants had to satisfy these requirements.[111] In addition, that rule was completely disapplied where the applicant or one of the applicants was the parent of the child; in relation to "relatives"[112] of the child, the only rule was that the applicant or one of them had to be at least 21 years old.[113] Section 3(1) of the 1949 Act replaced the 1930 Act's rules on whose consent was required before an adoption order could be made and the grounds for dispensing with any such consent. Under the new rules, an adoption order could not be made without the consent of every person or body who was a parent or guardian or was liable to contribute to the child's maintenance by court order or agreement. The continued reference to "person or body" meant that institutions might still have to be asked to consent to a child's adoption but the removal of the reference to "actual custody" meant that this would be so only if they were the child's guardian[114] or were liable to contribute to the child's maintenance.

The changes to the grounds upon which consent to adoption could be dispensed with was a response to a decision of the English court in 1947 which had highlighted the ambiguity in the existing law as to whether the catch-all ground (that the consent ought, in the opinion of the court and in all the circumstances of the case, be dispensed with) applied generally to everyone whose consent was required, or only to persons whose consent was required because they were liable to contribute to the child's maintenance.[115] The new rules provided that the necessary consent could be dispensed with:

(i)   In the case of a parent or guardian of the child, if they had abandoned, neglected or persistently ill-treated the child;

111 Adoption of Children Act, 1949, s. 2(1).
112 That is to say grandparent, sibling, aunt or uncle, whether of full-blood or half blood or by affinity, and including anyone who would be so treated as if the child were legitimate, and the father: Adoption of Children Act, 1949, s. 13.
113 Ibid. s. 2(1).
114 It was far more common in England than in Scotland for an institution to be appointed a child's guardian.
115 *H v H* [1947] KB 463.

(ii)   in the case of a person liable to contribute to the child's maintenance by
       virtue of a court order or an agreement to do so, if they had persistently
       neglected or refused so to contribute; and
(iii) in any case, if the person could not be found or was incapable of giving
       consent – or (in a formulation that appears in the law for the first time) that
       "his consent is unreasonably withheld".[116]

This last (and newest) ground was a deliberate attempt to narrow the
court's discretion from the formulation that had appeared until then (that
the consent ought, in the opinion of the court, be dispensed with), which in
England in *H v H* had been held to give the courts an unfettered discretion.
Paradoxically, however, while judges had been reticent before 1949 in dispensing with parental consent, it became progressively much more common
for them to do so thereafter. This almost certainly reflected not the change
itself in the wording of the ground to dispense with consent but the increased
use of adoption, particularly from the 1960s, as a mechanism for the compulsory permanent removal of children from resisting parents.[117] The new
ground became, because it was more evaluative than factual, the primary
source of dispute in the majority of contested adoption applications for the
next sixty years.[118]

The Scottish version of s. 3 of the 1949 Act also made plain that none
of the grounds for dispensing with consent applied to the consent of the
child,[119] which clarified a matter left in some doubt under the 1930 Act, as
discussed above. The end result was that the minor child's consent could
never be dispensed with at all.[120]

Section 3(2) of the 1949 Act also allowed the parents' and guardians' consent to be given subject to conditions relating to the child's religious upbringing, and without knowing the identity of the adopter(s).[121] Adoption orders
had previously been made in Scotland without the birth parent knowing

---

116 Adoption of Children Act, 1949, s. 3(1), proviso.
117 Lowe points out that there was a five-fold increase in adoptions from public care between 1952
     and 1968 – the type of adoption that was much more likely to be contested: Lowe, N. *Cross
     Currents: Family Law and Policy in the US and England*, S. Katz, et al. (eds), p. 318.
118 For a discussion of the major cases on this ground for dispensing with parental consent, see
     Wilkinson, A. and Norrie, K. *The Law Relating to Parent and Child in Scotland* (2nd edn,
     1999), paras 4.44–4.50.
119 Adoption of Children Act, 1949, s. 15. This was followed by the Adoption Act, 1950, s. 3(1) and
     the Adoption Act, 1958, s. 5(1).
120 In *PQ & RQ, Petitioners* 1965 SLT 93, the Inner House held that the requirement for the minor
     child to consent was absolute and since the child in the case was mentally incompetent the
     order could not be made. This remained the law until the Adoption (Scotland) Act 1978.
121 It was made plain, in the Scottish version of s. 3, that this applied only to the consent of the
     parent or guardian, and not to the consent of the child: 1949 Act, s. 15.

the adopters' identities,[122] but this provision seems to have been new for England. Stephen Cretney deprecated the fact that

> consent could now be given to an adoption by a person about whom the mother knew nothing; and the emphasis originally placed on the need for her to take a personal decision about the adopters' suitability had disappeared . . .[123]

The control of adoption was more and more shifting from the birth parents into the hands of the state.

The 1949 Act is notable for adding to the differences between the Scots and the English law of adoption, for while ss. 9 and 10 of the 1949 Act provided that adopted children would now be treated as children of the adopters for the purposes of succession, these provisions were not extended to Scotland.[124] It would be another 15 years before Scottish succession rights were affected by adoption.

There were a number of other, more or less important, amendments to the law contained in the 1949 Act. The adopter and adopted child were brought within the forbidden degrees of marriage, though the validity was preserved of any marriage solemnised contrary to the new rule before the 1949 Act was brought into force[125] (1 January 1950). This did not bring the child within the forbidden degrees in relation to persons who traced their relationship to the child through the adoptive parent such as the adoptive parent's other children – birth or adoptive – who became (social) siblings of the adopted child: the child remained (and remains) free to marry such persons. Nor did this bring the child within the forbidden degrees for the purposes of the crime of incest.[126] And the making of an adoption order was stated to terminate any existing order made under the Children and Young Persons (Scotland) Act, 1937 by which the child was committed to the care of a fit person,[127] as well as a resolution under the Children Act, 1948 by

---

122 *C & C, Spouses, Petitioners* 1936 SC 257; *H & H, Petitioners* 1944 SC 347.

123 Cretney, S. *Law, Law Reform and the Family*, Clarendon Press, 1998, p. 192.

124 Adoption of Children Act, 1949, s. 15(e). Compare *In Re Gilpin* [1954] Ch 1 where the adopted child was held entitled to share in an English succession with *Hay v Duthie's Trs* 1956 SC 511 where the adopted child was not in a Scottish succession. And see *B & B, Petitioners* 1950 SLT (Sh Ct) 34 where the adopted child died leaving property and the surviving adoptive parents were not entitled to any part of it.

125 Adoption of Children Act 1949, s. 11(1).

126 *HM Advocate v McKenzie* 1970 SLT 81. It was not until 1986 that the adopted child and adoptive parent were brought within the forbidden degrees for the purposes of the crime of incest: Incest and Related Offences (Scotland) Act 1986, sched. 1(5), amending the legislation then in force, the Adoption (Scotland) Act 1978, s. 41(1).

127 Adoption of Children Act, 1949, ss. 11(3) and 15(a).

which a local authority assumed parental rights over the child.[128] This was the start of the private law adoption order being given precedence over any existing public law order. This is based on the pervasive (but often false) assumption that the child's problems, which had previously justified public law intervention in his or her life, are "solved" by the making of an adoption order.

Perhaps the most important change in the 1949 Act was the increased involvement of local authorities. The Curtis Report[129] had noted that less than a quarter of adoptions in 1944 (in England and Wales) had been arranged by an adoption society and therefore regulated by the Adoption of Children (Regulation) Act, 1939. They recommended that a probationary period be introduced for all adopters with local authority supervision during that period. This recommendation was given effect by s. 5 of the 1949 Act, which required that the child to be adopted had been in the continuous care and possession of the prospective adopters for a least three months prior to the date of the order and that the applicant notify the local authority at least three months before the date of the order of his or her intention to make an application for an adoption order. During this period, the provisions in the 1939 Act for local authority supervision (discussed above) would apply in respect of all children to be adopted who were not of school leaving age. Local authorities were also given the explicit power (stated to be for the removal of doubt) "to make and participate in arrangements for the adoption of children".[130] Altogether, the Adoption of Children Act, 1949, therefore, represents the beginning of ubiquitous local authority involvement in what started life as a private law process and has since 1949 become increasingly a matter of public law.

THE ADOPTION ACT, 1950

The Adoption Act, 1950 was a consolidating Act[131] that repealed the 1926 and 1930 Acts, as well as the 1939 and 1949 Acts. It made little substantive amendment to the law as contained in these earlier Acts but became, for both Scots law and English law, the principal Act under which children were adopted throughout most of the 1950s.

---

128 Ibid. s. 11(4).
129 *Report of the Committee on the Care of Children* 1946, Cmnd 6922.
130 Adoption of Children Act, 1949, s. 7(2).
131 See HL Deb. 13 June 1950, vol. 167 col. 644.

THE ADOPTION ACT, 1958

The 1950 Act was replaced by the Adoption Act, 1958, which remained the governing legislation until the Adoption (Scotland) Act 1978 came into force on 1 September 1984. This meant that it was this legislation under which adoption orders were made during the period when numbers were at their absolute highest.[132]

The 1958 Act followed to some extent the recommendations of the Departmental Committee on the Adoption of Children, set up in 1953 under the chairmanship of Sir Gerald Hurst and reporting in 1954.[133] Some of the recommendations of that Committee were, however, not taken up. The suggestion, for example, that every adopted child be brought up in the knowledge of the adoption[134] was rejected, which elicited the following from a commentator writing in the *Modern Law Review*:

> The ludicrous coyness on this point of many otherwise sensible people has fre-quently had disastrous effects when the child discovers the truth, as he invari-ably will. It is deplorable that no mention of this important and very necessary recommendation appears in the new Act or any of the supporting statutory instruments.[135]

No such requirement has ever appeared in the adoption legislation,[136] but in fact the changing practice of adoption has made it a matter of little con-sequence in the vast majority of cases. Another recommendation contained in the Hurst Committee Report but not taken up by the 1958 Act was that children adopted in England, once they reached the age of 21, should be able to have access to records detailing their origins and that the Scottish rule allowing this be amended by raising the age from 17 to 21.[137]

The 1958 Act did, however, make a number of significant changes to the existing law. Importantly, s. 4 amended the rules on whose consent to the adoption was required, by removing from the list any person liable to main-tain the child – this had the effect of excluding from the adoption process

---

132 During the five year periods 1961–65, 1966–70 and 1971–75, the annual average number of adoption orders made (1,775, 2,129 and 1,768 respectively) was substantially higher than in any other five year period between 1931 and 2015: National Records of Scotland *Vital Events Reference Tables 2016*, Table 2.01.

133 *Report of the Departmental Committee on the Adoption of Children* 1954 Cmnd. 9248.

134 Ibid. paras 22 and 150–154.

135 Stone, O.M. "The Adoption Act 1958" [1959] 22 *Modern Law Review* 504.

136 As late as 1993 a sheriff was content that a six year old child be brought up in ignorance of the fact that she had been adopted: *C, Petrs* 1993 SCLR 14.

137 *Report of the Departmental Committee on the Adoption of Children*, para 201.

those unmarried fathers who had a financial obligation to the child: now, no unmarried father needed to be asked to consent to the adoption of their child. Section 4(3) also removed the references to "bodies" consenting, so that local authorities who had assumed parental rights, boards of managers of approved schools to which the child had been committed, and fit persons (voluntary organisations) to whom the child's care had been committed were no longer required to give their consent to the adoption (or have that consent dispensed with). Consent was now to be sought only from parents or guardians (and in Scotland from the minor child him- or herself), as well as, in appropriate cases, the spouse of an applicant who made a sole application while married.[138] In the case of parents, their consent had to be based on an understanding that the effect of the adoption order would be to deprive them permanently of their parental rights.[139]

The grounds for dispensing with consent were amended to reflect the reduction in those who were required to consent. Dispensation remained possible when the parent or guardian had abandoned, neglected or seriously ill-treated the child, could not be found or was incapable of consenting, or was withholding consent unreasonably.[140] Interestingly, the Hurst Committee Report[141] had recommended the deletion of the "unreasonable withholding" ground, but that did not happen in the 1958 Act. The old ground of persistent neglect or failure to fulfil financial obligations to the child (applicable to persons whose consent had previously been required on the basis of being liable to maintain the child[142]) was replaced by a wider ground: that the parent or guardian had persistently failed without reasonable cause to discharge the obligations of a parent or guardian.[143] The consent of a spouse of a sole applicant could also be dispensed with if the spouse could not be found or was incapable of consenting or was permanently separated from the applicant.[144]

The minimum age gap between adopter and adopted child, which had been a feature of the law since the first statutory introduction of adoption, was dropped in the 1958 Act, and no minimum age at all was set down for an adopter who adopted his or her own child; nor was there a minimum

138 Adoption Act, 1958, s. 4(1).
139 Ibid. s. 7(1).
140 Ibid. s. 5(1).
141 *Report of the Departmental Committee on the Adoption of Children*, para 120.
142 Adoption of Children Act, 1949, s. 3(1).
143 Adoption Act, 1958, s. 5(2).
144 Ibid. s. 5(4).

age for either when spouses adopted the child of one of them.[145] The 1958 Act required for the first time the court to take account of the health of the applicants.[146]

The role of local authorities in the adoption process was further strengthened. In placing children for adoption, local authorities were made subject to the same rules as adoption societies, even when they were placing children over whom they had not assumed parental rights.[147] Also, new rules were introduced to protect the placement of a child to be adopted during the process[148] and to increase the level of local authority involvement after placement. Previously, children placed for adoption by an agency were treated in the same way as privately fostered children (which required child protection visitors to visit them regularly but was limited to children of school age); now the Adoption Act 1958 replaced this with the concept of the "protected child", which included all children in respect of whom notice had been given of an intention to adopt.[149] The Act imposed the duty on local authorities to visit every protected child in their areas, and their officers were given the power to inspect the premises in which the child was kept;[150] these officers had also to satisfy themselves as to the child's wellbeing and could give advice as to the child's care and maintenance.[151] The local authority could prohibit any non-agency placement if it would be detrimental to the child,[152] and they could ask the court to order the removal of a child from any unsuitable surroundings.[153]

Overall, the effect of the Adoption Act 1958 was to restructure adoption law into a form that is to twenty-first-century eyes increasingly familiar. Local authority involvement increased, as did the distance between adop-

---

145 Ibid. s. 2(2). A minimum age nevertheless applied, being the age of marriage, which was and is 16.

146 Ibid. s. 7(2). But even before this, the applicants' health was a matter that was taken into account: in *G & G, Petrs* 1949 SLT (Sh Ct) 60 an adoption petition was refused on the ground that one of the applicants was suffering from tuberculosis; in *K & K, Petrs* 1950 SLT (Sh Ct) 2 the petition was granted notwithstanding that one of the applicants was suffering from tuberculosis. The requirement to take the applicants' health into account disappeared from primary legislation with the Children Act 1975, when all such considerations were subsumed into the requirement to regard the need to safeguard and promote the child's welfare as the first consideration.

147 Adoption Act, 1958, s. 28.

148 Ibid. s. 34.

149 Ibid. ss. 37–49.

150 Ibid. s. 39.

151 Ibid. s. 38.

152 Ibid. s. 41.

153 Ibid. s. 43

tion and long-term fostering. There were, however, still one or two steps that the law had to take before the contemporary model of a complete transference of parenthood from birth to adoptive parents was in place.

THE SUCCESSION (SCOTLAND) ACT 1964

The first of these steps was to allow adopted children succession rights in the estates of their adoptive parents and to remove succession rights in the estates of their birth parents. This had been achieved in English law by the Adoption of Children Act, 1949 but, as we have seen, the relevant provisions were not extended to Scotland. The Succession (Scotland) Act 1964, which effected a radical redesigning of the succession law of Scotland, finally made provision for adopted children in this jurisdiction. The 1964 Act provided that for all purposes relating to the succession of a deceased person (whether testate or intestate) who died on or after 10 September 1964 "an adopted person shall be treated as the child of the adopter and not of the child of any other person".[154] The adopted child, therefore, acquired the right to claim legitim from the moveable estate of a deceased adoptive parent and to represent the adoptive parent in any claim for legitim that parent would have had; the adopted child now also had the same rights on intestacy under s. 2 of the 1964 Act as the natural children of the deceased. At the same time, adopted children lost any equivalent claim in the estates of their birth parents. Any reference to children in a deed in which property was conveyed or succession arose, if made after the date of the adoption order, was to be construed as including the adopted child and any reference to children of the birth parent of an adopted child was to be construed as excluding the adopted child – all this unless the contrary intention be expressed or necessarily implied.[155] If the child was adopted jointly by two spouses, then he or she is treated as a brother or sister of the whole blood in relation to the spouses' other children (adopted or birth), and if adopted by a sole applicant is treated as a brother or sister of the half blood.[156] These rules continue to apply today.

---

154 Succession (Scotland) Act 1964, s. 23(1).
155 Ibid. s. 23(2). The contrary intention was implied in *Spencer's Trustees v Ruggles* 1981 SC 289 where the phrase "lawful issue" had been used in the deed and it was held that an adoption order did not render the child "issue". Property devolving along with a title, honour or dignity was excluded: s. 23(3).
156 Succession (Scotland) Act 1964, s. 24.

THE CHILDREN ACT 1975

The 1972 *Report of the Departmental Committee on the Adoption of Children*[157] was a major strand in the policy development that led to the Children Act 1975. This Report represents an important change of focus in adoption law and policy, for the Houghton Committee recognised that adoption had moved a long way from its origins in the protection of long-term foster carers who had received children from parents voluntarily entrusting their children to the care of others: by the 1970s adoption was primarily a major component of the wider child protection system. Also influential in the development of policy in the early 1970s was Rowe and Lambert's important book *Children Who Wait*,[158] which was a study of children in the care system who were experiencing difficulty in moving to long-term placements. These authors were among the first (but by no means the last) academic researchers to show that the longer children were in care the less likely rehabilitation with their birth families was and the more need, therefore, they had of permanent placement. The Children Act 1975 was the first to deal with adoption by explicitly locating that process within the field of child care, where it has remained ever since. The role of the local authority, which had been increasing with each Adoption Act passed after 1930, was substantially enhanced.

Section 1 of the Children Act 1975 imposed a duty on every local authority to provide a comprehensive adoption service, which the authority could do either by providing such a service itself or by making use of the services offered by approved adoption societies. Taken collectively, these services were to be referred to as the Scottish Adoption Service. Previously, local authorities merely had the power to provide adoption services,[159] but it now became an essential role that they were required to perform. Also, adoption societies, which previously simply had to be registered with, now required to be approved by, a local authority. This gave local authorities much more control over the standards and practices of adoption societies, for they could provide such approval only on being satisfied that the society would make

---

157 Known as the Houghton Committee Report (1972, Cmnd 5107), after its original chairman Sir William Houghton. In fact, he died during the committee's working and his position as chairman was taken over by Judge F.A. Stockdale.

158 Rowe, J. and Lambert, L. *Children Who Wait: A Study of Children Needing Substitute Families* (Association of British Adoption Agencies, 1973). This study was cited by the Lord Chancellor, Lord Elwyn Jones, opening the Second Reading debate on the Children Bill at HL Deb. 21 January 1975, vol. 356, col. 18.

159 Adoption Act 1958, s. 28(2).

an effective contribution to the Scottish Adoption Service.[160] The aim here was to ensure that adoption societies followed the standards of professional care required of local authorities. Adoption was to be seen primarily in terms of a social service governed by the good practice developed by social work departments. The "amateurs" in adoption societies became increasingly professionalised. Following on from this, private placements were criminalised and no one other than an adoption agency, whether local authority or adoption society, could either make arrangements for the adoption of a child or place a child for adoption (other than with relatives).[161] No longer was the minister or priest, GP or maternity home matron to be allowed to place "unwanted" children for adoption. These matters were to be exclusively in the hands of social work professionals.

The 1975 Act contained a number of other important amendments to adoption law, beyond those relating to local authorities:

(i) A new process, "freeing for adoption" was introduced which allowed the most contentious issues to be dealt with separately from (and earlier than) the final making of the adoption order.[162] Primarily, this process was designed to deal with parental consent – or more accurately, the dispensation of parental consent. In child protection cases consent was increasingly likely to be withheld and this new process became a major aspect of child protection practice in Scotland.

(ii) The need to safeguard and promote the welfare of the child throughout his or her childhood became the "first consideration" for the court reaching any decision in relation to adoption.[163] This placed the child's welfare at the centre of the decision-making process, if not the very purpose of the order. Previously welfare was merely a relevant factor in the decision that was originally designed, as we saw above, to serve adults' interests. However, quite deliberately the test was not the same as under the Guardianship of Infants Act, 1925, that the child's welfare was the first and paramount consideration. Lord Hailsham, speaking in the Second Reading Debate, justified this distinction on the basis that adoption destroys the parental relationship and so the interests of the birth parents (and indeed of the adoptive parents) are to be taken into account just as much as the child's interests. But he did not see the new provision as making much substantive difference since courts had always taken all of these interests into account in any case.[164] Lord Wigoder was not impressed by this reasoning and found the new test "insipid almost to the point of being ineffective".[165]

160 Children Act 1975, s. 4(2).
161 Ibid. s. 28, amending s. 29 of the Children Act 1958.
162 Children Act 1975, s. 14.
163 Ibid. s. 3.
164 HL Deb. 21 January 1975 vol. 356 cols 33–34.
165 Ibid. col. 37.

Baroness Bacon called for welfare to be the paramount consideration[166] but Scots law had to wait until 1995 for that to happen.[167] Until then, "first consideration" had lesser weight than "paramount consideration".[168]

(iii) The limitation on a single man adopting a female child was removed.[169] Any fear that that limitation was designed to address became subsumed into the need to safeguard and promote the child's welfare throughout her childhood.

(iv) A new ground for dispensing with parental consent to adoption was added to the already existing grounds: that the parent or guardian had seriously ill-treated the child and rehabilitation of the child with the parent or guardian was unlikely.[170] This differed from the existing grounds, none of which required rehabilitation to be shown to be unlikely.

(v) The age at which a person could make an application for an adoption order, which had previously differed for parents, for relatives and for anyone else, was simplified to be 21 for any applicant or applicants.[171]

(vi) A new rule was introduced to the effect that an application by a relative of the child (and in particular by a step-parent of the child) for an adoption order should be treated as an application for a custody order if the child's welfare would not be better safeguarded and promoted by making an adoption order.[172] In other words, a presumption was created that step-parents wishing some involvement in the child's lives were more appropriately dealt with by a custody than an adoption order.[173]

(vii) Children who sought information about their birth parents (which they had long been entitled to do) became entitled to counselling which local authorities were obliged to provide.[174]

(viii) Adoption agencies were permitted to submit to the Secretary of State for approval schemes by which they paid allowances to adopters or prospective adopters.[175] This acted as a qualification to the prohibition of payments in relation to adoption contained in s. 50 of the 1958 Act. The power to prepare an adoption allowance scheme became a duty on local authorities (but remained a power for adoption societies) after amendments made to the Adoption (Scotland) Act 1978 by the Children (Scotland) Act 1995.[176]

In sum, by 1975, a series of amendments to the original 1930 design of adoption had moved it from a protected form of custody and guardianship

---

166 Ibid. col. 49. So did the Bishop of Leicester at col. 58.

167 Children (Scotland) Act 1995, s. 95, amending s. 6 of the Adoption (Scotland) 1978 as discussed below.

168 See *P v Lothian Regional Council* 1989 SLT 739.

169 Children Act 1975, sched. 4, repealing s. 2(3) of the 1958 Act.

170 Ibid. s. 12(2)(f) and (5).

171 Ibid. ss. 10 and 11.

172 Ibid. s. 53.

173 This rule was repealed by the Children (Scotland) Act 1995, sched. 5 and replaced by a more general requirement on adoption agencies to explore alternatives to adoption.

174 Children Act 1975, s. 27, amending s. 22 of the Children Act 1958.

175 Ibid. s. 32, inserting new s. 50(4)–(9) into the Adoption Act 1950.

176 Children (Scotland) Act 1995, sched. 2 para 25. See now Adoption and Children (Scotland) Act 2007, s. 71.

of children to a complete parental relationship that lasted well beyond childhood. At the same time, the purpose to which adoption was put had altered, from the state sanctioning an initially private fostering arrangement to a state means of permanently separating a child from his or her birth family. There is a clear paradox here. If adoption has become primarily a child protection mechanism to ensure the good upbringing of a child, then the effects after the child gains adulthood ought logically to have diminished rather than increased, for the purpose of adoption will then have been achieved and its effects spent. The model that has been embraced, of ensuring a complete and permanent transference of parenthood, is predicated on the belief that the child's welfare can only be fully served by a lifelong transference. That belief sits ill with the contemporary practice of open adoptions, which recognises the reality of social relationships established by children before they are adopted at a typically older age today than in previous decades.

THE ADOPTION (SCOTLAND) ACT 1978

The Adoption of Children (Scotland) Act, 1930, though a separate statute from the earlier English legislation, modelled itself very closely upon the Adoption of Children Act, 1926. The Adoption Acts, 1950 and 1958 and the Children Act 1975 were all UK statutes which, in places, made special provision for Scotland.[177] The Adoption (Scotland) Act 1978 once again gave Scotland its own self-contained legislation though, as in 1930, the Scottish Act mirrored closely its English counterpart (the Adoption Act 1976). The 1978 Act repealed both the Adoption Act, 1958 and the parts of the Children Act 1975 dealing with adoption, replacing these with a complete statutory code for adoption in Scotland. That new code was not, however, noticeably different from the law as it had stood since 1975.[178]

The 1978 Act was amended a number of times subsequent to its passing. The Children Act 1989 amended the age requirements for applicants so that where a married couple adopted the child of one of them, the parent spouse had to be 18 or above while the non-parent spouse was required to be 21 or

---

177 In the Second Reading Debate on the Children Act 1975 the Bishop of Leicester deprecated the fact that there was not a separate Bill for Scotland: HL Deb. 21 January 1975 vol. 356 col. 57. Lord Wells-Pestell, summing up for the Government, answered that adoption had been in a UK-wide statute since 1950 and that now creating a separate Bill for Scotland would delay matters: col. 97.

178 The changes to existing law were in the main technical, designed to address issues raised by the Scottish Law Commission in its *Report on Adoption* (SLC No. 50, 1978): see the (short) Second Reading Debate in the House of Commons: HC Deb. 10 July 1978 vol. 953 cols 1202–1205.

above.[179] Rather more significant were the changes made to the 1978 Act by Part III of the Children (Scotland) Act 1995. This solely Scottish Act heralded an increasing separation between Scots law and English law in relation to adoption and the changes it made mostly reflected an increased focus on the welfare of the child:

(i)   Adoption societies were allowed to seek approval for the provision of specific services rather than a complete adoption service.[180] This allowed separate bodies to be maintained as part of the Scottish Adoption Service that did not carry out all the functions necessary for that service but which provided specialist services in limited areas only.

(ii) The welfare of the child under s. 6 of the 1978 Act was upgraded from "first" to "paramount" consideration for both the court and adoption agencies.[181] The primary motivation for this amendment was to bring Scots law into line with the UN Convention on the Rights of the Child, which required that the child's best interests be the paramount consideration in adoption proceedings.[182] But in any case, the views of policy-makers hardened against inadequate parents and the argument that the birth parents' interests ought to be balanced with the child's lost whatever purchase it previously had. As well, the timescale within which welfare was to be considered was increased from "throughout [the child's] childhood" to "throughout [the child's] life". It is, of course, virtually impossible for a court of law to assess accurately a person's welfare far into the future. Nevertheless, the new timescale was designed to reflect the fact that adoption had been for the past twenty years a relationship not just for the upbringing of children but one that reflected as far as it could the fact that a new family relationship had been created, with legal and social consequences that would last far beyond the childhood of the adopted person. The role in the court's decision-making process of the child's views was also restructured and s. 6 now obliged courts and adoption agencies to have regard so far as practicable to the views of the child (if the child wished to express views) taking account of his or her age and maturity, and also to the child's religious persuasion, racial origin and cultural and linguistic background. This reflected factors specified throughout the Children (Scotland) Act 1995[183] that had to be taken into account in various judicial and quasi-judicial processes.

(iii) A new section 6A was added into the 1978 Act which required adoption agencies, whether local authority or private, before making adoption arrangements to "consider whether adoption is likely to best meet the needs of that child or whether for him [or her] there is some better, practicable, alternative; and if it concludes that there is such an alternative it shall not proceed to make those [adoption] arrangements".[184] This was a deliberate

---

179 Children Act 1989, sched. 10, para 33.
180 Children (Scotland) Act 1995, s. 94, amending s. 3 of the 1978 Act.
181 Children (Scotland) Act 1995, s. 95, substituting s. 6 of the 1978 Act.
182 UN Convention on the Rights of the Child, Art. 21.
183 Children (Scotland) Act 1995, ss. 11(7) and 16.
184 Ibid. s. 96. This provision was repeated (in rather stronger language) in the Adoption and Children (Scotland) Act 2007, s.14(6) and (7)

attempt to ensure that adoption is used only when lesser interventions in a family will not suffice to meet the best interests of the child, by requiring agencies to explore the existence and feasibility of alternatives to adoption and to utilise these alternatives where possible. With the same aim, a new s. 24(3) was inserted into the 1978 Act[185] providing that the court could not make an adoption order unless it considered that it would be better to make the order than not to make the order.

(iv) Step-parent adoption could now be effected without the parental spouse having to join the application and give up their parental rights in order to reacquire them under the adoption order.[186] Both spouses could still, if they wished, adopt in a joint application[187] and it was not until the 2007 Act, considered immediately below, that such joint applications became incompetent.[188]

(v) The age at which adopted persons could seek access to their birth records was reduced from 17 to 16.[189]

THE ADOPTION AND CHILDREN (SCOTLAND) ACT 2007

Introduction

The Adoption and Children (Scotland) Act 2007, which replaced in its entirety the 1978 Act, is the first piece of Scottish adoption legislation that is entirely indigenous, having been passed by the Scottish, as opposed to the UK, Parliament and following the recommendations of the Adoption Policy Review Group (hereinafter the APRG), which was the first official review of adoption looking specifically and solely at Scots law. The Scottish Executive (as the Scottish Government was then known) had set up the APRG in April 2001, and as its very title makes plain, the work of this Group focused not only on the detailed rules of Scottish adoption law but also on the policy objectives behind this most radical of court orders. The APRG divided its work into two phases: Phase I looked at adoption within the broad spectrum of child protection services available to "looked after" children, and examined such matters as the recruitment, selection and assessment of prospective adopters, as well as the provision of post-adoption support for families;

---

185 Children (Scotland) Act 1995, sched. 2 para 16.

186 Ibid. s. 97, amending ss. 12 and 15 of the 1978 Act.

187 Adoption (Scotland) Act 1978, s. 14(1B), as inserted by the Children Act 1989, sched. 10(11) para 33.

188 Adoption and Children (Scotland) Act 2007, s. 29(1)(b). A sole application by a birth parent to adopt his or her child remains competent, but only if certain conditions are satisfied: s. 30(1)(d) and (7).

189 Children (Scotland) Act 1995, sched. 2 para 22, amending s. 45(5) of the Adoption (Scotland) Act 1978.

Phase II subjected to critical analysis long-established rules such as those limiting who may be adopters and it examined the legal framework for children who needed permanent placement away from their parents whether by adoption or otherwise. In both phases, the idea of "permanence" was at the heart of the work, for it was recognised that children invariably suffer if their future is uncertain and subject to constant change. "Permanence" of course was recognised to include sustainable rehabilitation with their birth parents of children presently being looked after by a local authority.

Changes to the law of adoption

The Adoption and Children (Scotland) Act 2007 imposed various new duties on local authorities to create and review their plans for the provision of adoption services,[190] to extend pre-adoption services and to undertake assessments of the needs of persons for adoption support services.[191] New duties in relation to post-adoption services were imposed, extending these services to all those involved in the adoption process, including the child, birth families and adoptive parents.[192] This was designed to recognise both the increasingly open nature of adoption (almost unavoidable when adoption is a child protection mechanism) and the continuing needs of all parties for support, advice and assistance, even after the formal legal process had come to an end. Adoption, though still a private law process, is one in which the state is profoundly involved, and now remains so even after the court process is over. Local authorities were given the power to make payments instead of providing the service directly.[193] The welfare of the child throughout life remains the court's paramount consideration,[194] but other factors have to be taken into account too, including in particular "the likely effect on the child, throughout the child's life, of the making of an adoption order".[195]

The categories of persons who are eligible to adopt were substantially extended. This was a matter of great contention in the press, which had a marked tendency to misdirect its attention away from the needs of looked after children and towards those family forms which, it was considered in

---

190 Adoption and Children (Scotland) Act 2007, s. 4, subsequently replaced by duties under the Children and Young People (Scotland) Act 2014.
191 Adoption and Children (Scotland) Act 2007, s. 9.
192 Ibid. s. 1
193 Ibid. s. 12.
194 Ibid. s. 14(3).
195 Ibid. s. 14(4)(d).

some quarters, the law should continue to encourage – through the tactic of disadvantaging other forms. Single persons and married couples had always been eligible to adopt, and to these categories was added "relevant couples", defined to be cohabiting couples in enduring family relationships and irrespective of their gender mix, married couples and civil partners: the major change in the law coming out of this was to extend eligibility to adopt to unmarried and same-sex couples.[196]

In addition, Scottish Ministers were given the power to make regulations on the preparation by local authorities of schemes for the payment of adoption allowances in relation to persons who have adopted a child through an adoption agency.[197] Another change, which heralded a slight shift back towards the interests of the birth parents, was that they were now allowed, after the making of an adoption order, to seek a contact order in relation to their previous child.[198]

Perhaps the most important change in the 2007 Act that affects how the court process in adoption operates was the restructuring of the grounds for dispensing with parental consent. The ground based on unreasonable withholding of consent was dropped for fear that its potential breadth might not survive a challenge under the European Convention on Human Rights. In its place, a welfare ground was introduced,[199] though that only applies in limited circumstances. Doubts were initially expressed as to whether the new ground was sufficiently robust to withstand ECHR scrutiny,[200] but the Supreme Court held that the new ground could only be used when dispensation was required as an imperative, that is to say in circumstances in which "nothing less than adoption will suffice":[201] giving the ground that interpretation was sufficient, they held, to satisfy the demands of the European Court of Human Rights for state interference in family life to be proportionate to its aims.

---

196 Ibid. s. 29. A (legally) single gay man had earlier been allowed to adopt in *T, Petitioner* 1997 SLT 724.

197 Adoption and Children (Scotland) Act 2007, s. 71. See the Adoption Support Services and Allowances (Scotland) Regulations 2009 (SSI 2009/152), replacing the Adoption Allowances (Scotland) Regulations 1996 (SI 1996/3257), made under the Adoption (Scotland) Act 1978.

198 Adoption and Children (Scotland) Act 2007, s. 107, amending s. 11(3) of the Children (Scotland) Act 1995. Previously birth parents were denied title to seek contact with children who had been adopted away from them.

199 Adoption and Children (Scotland) Act 2007, s. 31(3)(d).

200 See Norrie, K. "Adoption and the New Grounds for Dispensing With Consent" 2008 SLT (News) 213.

201 *S v L* [2012] UKSC 30. See also Norrie, K. "The Welfare Ground for Dispensing with Consent to Adoption: The Supreme Court Decides" 2013 SLT (News) 117.

THE NEED FOR A NEW FORM OF PERMANENCE

In policy terms, the more important Phase of the work of the APRG was Phase II, the conclusions and recommendations of which were published in 2005.[202] The Group, which had always seen adoption as a child protection mechanism, made the important – and often ignored – point that adoption is by no means suitable for all children who have had to be removed from their families and for whom a return to these families is, for whatever reason, simply not possible. It was coming to be recognised that the interests of children whose welfare requires that they remain permanently away from their families is not in all cases best served by severing all ties with their parents for all time coming, which from the start has been an underlying assumption and since 1975 had been the legal effect of an adoption order. Maintaining, even if only in formal legal terms, existing relationships may provide a child with a sense of continuity and of belonging, of history and identity, which sense it may be important to nurture even, or perhaps especially, in light of circumstances that have led to the child being looked after by a local authority.[203] Children other than those who are very young when they are removed from their families are likely to have formed bonds which can, and often should, be kept alive through, at a minimum, appropriate contact arrangements; older children may entirely understandably harbour the ambition to return to their families once they have grown up. In these, and many other, circumstances adoption as traditionally understood may be a disproportionate response to the child's current needs and circumstances. But children who have no realistic prospect of being reintegrated with their birth families, no less than any other child being looked after by local authorities, need permanent provision to be made for their upbringing. Taking these factors into account, the APRG concluded that there was a gap in the legal options available to children for whom neither adoption by a new family nor sustainable rehabilitation with their birth family was suitable.

Before the 2007 Act, there were two quite different orders that a court might make in relation to children who, having been removed from their birth families were unlikely ever to be able to be returned to them, but for whom an adoption order was not, or was not immediately, suitable. The

---

202 *Adoption: Better Choices for Our Children. Report of Phase II*, Adoption Policy Review Group, Scottish Executive, June 2005.

203 The United Nations *Convention on the Rights of the Child*, Art. 8, provides that a child has a right to preserve his or her identity, name and family relationships without unlawful interference.

APRG saw serious problems with both. First, the freeing order, created by the Children Act 1975 and latterly made under s. 18 of the Adoption (Scotland) Act 1978, effected a transference of parental responsibilities and parental rights from the birth parents to the local authority. The implication of an order freeing a child for adoption was of course that, in the foreseeable future, the child would indeed be adopted. However, the freeing order had many disadvantages, even beyond the obvious point that it promised something that there was no guarantee would be delivered. The order effected a complete break from the child's birth family, and there was no means of protecting contact between the child and the birth family during the time the child was free for adoption but not actually adopted – even although contact might subsequently be made a term of the adoption order itself. In addition, pending the making of an adoption order, the child was in "an adoption limbo" with no-one other than a local authority having responsibility for his or her wellbeing. And, perhaps worst of all, if an adoption order was not ultimately made, there was sometimes "no way back" for the child's legal status since revocation was a remedy available only in limited circumstances and the freeing order could not be converted into a parental responsibilities order.[204]

The second order that might achieve some form of permanent placement was the parental responsibilities order, granted under s. 86 of the Children (Scotland) Act 1995 (which itself replaced the old process of local authorities passing resolutions to assume parental rights). As with a freeing order, the effect of a parental responsibilities order was to transfer parental responsibilities and parental rights to the local authority. While freeing orders were designed for children with a chance of being adopted, parental responsibilities orders were designed for children who required to be kept permanently away from their birth families but in respect of whom the making of an adoption order was, for whatever reason, unlikely. The APRG identified a number of problems with this order also: (i) the statutory test for the order was not that the child needed to remain away from home permanently, though achieving that was nearly always the intent of those who sought it; (ii) parental responsibilities and parental rights were vested in a local authority and not in a substitute family, even if the child was living with a substitute family; (iii) there was no flexibility to allow transfer of some, as opposed to all, parental responsibilities and parental rights to the local authority, or to share them with the substitute family; (iv) the birth family had no right

---

204 APRG *Report of Phase II*, para 5.6.

to seek a contact or residence order in relation to the child, and the only option was the cumbersome one of returning to court to seek a variation of the order under the 1995 Act. In sum, local authorities were often left trying to justify in court a degree of transfer of parental responsibilities and parental rights that might not be in the best interests of the child, and which the authority might not want, to achieve a purpose that was not clear from the legislation.[205]

Given these problems, the APRG concluded that both these orders should be abolished, and replaced with a single order that would secure children in a long-term placement away from home and which was flexible enough that its terms could be structured in such a way as took account of the different needs of individual children. Flexibility was necessary in order to recognise that there are varying degrees of contact that will be appropriate between children in permanent placements and their birth families; some children will be awaiting adoption and some will not; the substitute families with whom children are placed may require a full transference of parental responsibilities and parental rights, or they may require only some degree of transference; for some children, it will be appropriate that the local authority retain some level of control over their upbringing while for other children this will be less appropriate. To this end, the APRG recommended that "there should be a new court order to be known as a Permanence Order."[206] The substance of this recommendation was given effect to in Part 2 of the Adoption and Children (Scotland) Act 2007.

PERMANENCE ORDERS

Permanence orders are orders that (i) always contain a mandatory provision giving the local authority the right to determine the child's residence and imposing on it the duty to provide guidance appropriate to the child's age and development; (ii) may contain ancillary provisions specifying contact arrangements and allocating different parental responsibilities and parental rights between different parties, including the people actually bringing up the child as long-term foster carers or kinship carers, the birth parents, and the local authority itself; and (iii) may contain a further provision giving authority for the child to be adopted.[207] Before it can make a permanence

---

205 Ibid. para 5.9.
206 Ibid. para 5.14.
207 Adoption and Children (Scotland) Act 2007, ss. 81–83.

order, the court must be satisfied either that there is no person with the right to regulate the child's residence or, if there is such a person, the child's residence with that person would be seriously detrimental to the welfare of the child:[208] this is the threshold condition that must be satisfied before the court is able to move on to any consideration of whether it should make a permanence order, and on what terms.[209]

The process to be followed in making a permanence order bears striking similarities to the process for making an adoption order. If the permanence order is to contain authority for the child's adoption then the parents and guardians, understanding the effect of an adoption order, must consent thereto, or have their consent dispensed with on the same grounds as consent to adoption itself may be dispensed with.[210] But a permanence order, even when it contains authority to adopt, is not an adoption order and the legal relationship with the birth parent survives the making of a permanence order, which has no effect on succession rights or forbidden degrees of marriage, or any other life-long consequence.

ADOPTION STATISTICS[211]

In 1931, the first full year of the operation of the Adoption of Children (Scotland) Act, 1930,[212] 347 adoption orders were made by Scottish courts, and thereafter the numbers rose steadily for the next decade and a half. 1946, the first full year of peace after the War when people were trying to get their lives back in order, is notable for being the year in which more adoption orders were made in Scotland, at 2,292, than in any other year before or since. Between then and 1978 the annual numbers of adoption orders made remained remarkably steady at just above or just below the 2,000 mark; after around 1978 numbers dropped gradually but remained in the high hundreds until the mid-1990s since when numbers dropped below 500; since 2009 (when the 2007 Act came into force) numbers have fluctuated between c. 450 and 550 per year.[213] There seems little correlation between

---

208 Ibid. s. 84(5)(c).
209 *West Lothian Council v MB* 2017 SC (UKSC) 67.
210 Adoption and Children (Scotland) Act 2007, s. 83.
211 All figures in this section are taken from National Records of Scotland *Vital Events Reference Tables 2018* Table 2.01.
212 The 1930 Act came into force on 1 October 1930, and between then and the end of that year 3 adoption orders were made.
213 The number in 2002 was 385, the lowest since 1931. The latest figure given is for 2018, when 471 adoption orders were made. (These figures include, since 2003, the small number – never

the numbers of orders made and the terms of the legislation governing the process. Social developments are likely to have a much more potent effect on overall numbers. So the decreased stigma attached to illegitimacy and unmarried motherhood doubtless reduced the numbers of children available for adoption, but that reduction was matched by an increase in the number of children affected by compulsory state intervention, which rose steadily after the end of the Second World War. Once adoption became primarily the outcome of child care and protection processes, social work practice became the single most important determinant of the number of adoption orders sought and made. National Records of Scotland do not record where children who have been adopted come from, nor why children are subject to adoption applications, but they do break down the figures from 1999 according to the type of adopter – joint opposite-sex couple, joint same-sex couple since 2010, single male and single female.[214] These figures show a gradually decreasing percentage of adoptions by single people, from around half in 1999 to around one third in 2018. The Table notes that "the vast majority of 'one adopter' cases are people who have become step-parents of their spouses or partners" and it may be assumed that the vast majority of the two adopter cases involve children presently looked after by a local authority. The number of adoption orders made in favour of couples in 2018 was 279 or around 60% of the whole.

more than 18 – of "parental orders" made under the Human Fertilisation and Embryology Acts 1990 and 2008.)
214 *Vital Events Reference Tables 2018* Table 2.03.

Index

Aberdeen
  approved schools, 246
  industrial schools, 176, 233
  juvenile court, 129
absconders, 155–156, 275–277
Adam, Lord, 319
Adamson, William, 181–182
adoption, 336–386
  Adopted Children Register, 362
  adoption orders, 134, 143–144, 352,
      356–360
  baby farming, 341–342
  as child protection mechanism, 374,
      377, 382
  consent, 353–357, 362, 366–368,
      370–371, 375, 376, 381
  debates on 1926 Act (England and
      Wales), 344–351
  eligibility to adopt, 352–353, 365, 366,
      371–372, 376, 377–378, 380–381
  freeing orders, 375, 383, 384
  informal (pre-1930), 337–341, 342–343
  introduction into Scots law, 134, 337,
      351
  legislation
    1930 Act, 337, 351–364
    1939, 1949 and 1950 Acts, 364–369
    1958 and 1964 Acts, 370–373
    1975 and 1978 Acts, 374–379
    2007 Act, 379–381
  as private law action, 337, 363–364, 369
  retrospective, 360–362, 363
  in Roman law, 336
  secrecy, 349–350, 367–368, 370
  societies and agencies, 364–365, 372,
      374–375, 376, 378–379
  statistics, 369, 370n132, 385–386
  and succession rights, 336–337, 347,
      358–359, 368, 373
  welfare of child, 375–376, 377,
      378–379, 381, 382

Adoption Policy Review Group (APRG),
    379–380, 382–384
aftercare, 299–311
  approved schools, 302–305
  corporate parenting, 309–311
  following emigration, 329–330,
      332–333
  in foster care and children's homes,
      305–306
  by local authorities, 305–309
  meaning of, 300
  reformatory and industrial schools,
      300–301
alcohol misuse
  by adults, 8, 18, 99, 292
  by children, 157
Alder, Christine, 166
Anderson, A.M., 94
Anderson, Lindsey (Macfarlane et al.),
    284, 296
antisocial behaviour orders, 64–66,
    157–158, 159–160
approved schools, 243–258
  and adoption, 371
  aftercare, 302–305
  approval system, 245–246, 248
  caring responsibilities, 101
  categories of, 246
  and children's hearing system, 149
  corporal punishment, 111–112
  court orders and juvenile court rules,
      136, 137, 138, 141n109, 247
  discipline and punishment,
      253–256
  education and training, 246, 248, 251,
      251–252
  and emigration, 327–328
  food, 250–251
  free time and recreation, 252–253
  home leave, 253
  inspection system, 248–249, 258

approved schools (*cont.*)
   legislation under 1932 and 1937 Acts,
      25, 26, 204–205, 247–249
   length of detention, 247–249
   managers, 249–250
   medical officers, 257
   parental involvement, 256–257
   premises and accommodation,
      250
   secondary legislation, 249–258
   "special sections", 275–276 *see also*
      secure accommodation
   teachers and staff, 251, 255
   see also industrial schools; reformatory
      schools; residential establishments
      (from 1968)
Army, enlisting of boys, 235, 256, 301,
   303, 316n13, 326, 328
Arran, boarded-out children, 199
Attlee, Clement, 5, 26, 27, 338–339,
   346
Augustus, Emperor, 336
Australia
   emigration to, 315–316, 329, 331, 332,
      333
   juvenile courts, 120–121, 169
Avory, Sir Horace, 101

baby farming, 341–342
babysitters, 102
Bacon, Baroness, 376
bad associations, 151–152
Baldwin, Sir Archer, 315
Banbury, Lord, 327
Barnardo's, 9, 314, 343
begging, 10, 19, 23, 125, 126, 197–198
   see also child vagrants
best interests of child
   in adoption cases, 378
   in boarding-out and fostering, 216, 225,
      226
   in international law, 40–41, 378
   and juvenile courts, 132, 138, 141–142,
      144, 149n16–17
   in kinship care, 230
   and local authorities, 34–35, 48, 52,
      226, 230, 384
   and parents, 35, 49
   and permanence orders, 384

and residential establishments, 269,
   271–272
   and secure accommodation, 278
Birk, Baroness, 192
birth parents
   and adoption
      consent, 353–354, 356–357, 366–368,
         370–371, 375, 376, 381
      contact orders, 381
      knowledge of adopter identity,
         349–350, 357, 367–368
      succession rights, 358–359
   and boarding-out, 201, 206, 207,
      218–219, 220
   and permanence orders, 385
birth records, searching for, 376, 379
boarding-out, 195–222
   aftercare, 305–307
   and birth parents, 201, 206, 207,
      218–219, 220
   changes in terminology, 222
   Clyde Report recommendations, 28–32,
      201, 204, 205, 209–210, 212, 216
   legislation
      Poor Law, 197–201, 204
      1889, 1894, 1904 and 1908 Acts,
         202–203
      1932 and 1937 Acts, 203–209
      1948 Act, 33–34, 210–211, 305–306
      1968 Act, 49, 50, 221–222
      1995 Act, 222
      Rules and Regulations, 210, 213–219
      Memorandum on the Boarding-Out of
         Children (1959), 219–221
   monitoring of children, 215–217
   see also foster carers (from 1996); foster
      parents (to 1996); fostering (from
      1985)
Boyle, Lord, 109

Canada
   emigration to, 313–314, 315–316, 318–
      319, 321, 329
   juvenile courts, 169
care authorities *see* local authorities;
   voluntary organisations
Care Commission, 69–70, 279
care homes, 70, 92
Care Inspectorate, 70–71

care leavers
  aftercare provisions, 300–311
  educational qualifications, 299
Carloway, Lord, 104–105
Cautley, Sir Henry, 351
certified schools *see* industrial schools;
  reformatory schools
charitable organisations *see* voluntary
  organisations
chief social work officers, 56, 279
child abuse cases, 53–55, 62
child assessment orders, 61, 71
child cruelty or neglect, 94–106
  approach of National Government in
    1932, 23–24
  caring responsibilities, 101–102
  intent and meaning of "wilful," 103–105
  and juvenile courts, 135
  legislation
    1889 Act, 14–15, 96–97, 281–282
    1894 and 1904 Acts, 15–16, 97–98,
      282
    1908 Act, 18–19, 98–99, 125–126,
      282–284
    1937 Act, 26, 99–106
  likelihood of harm, 105–106
  types of behaviour, 102–103
child migration *see* emigration of
  children
child prostitution, 19, 83, 87, 93–94, 125,
  151
child protection orders, 60–61, 71,
  290–294
child protection visitors, 365, 372
child vagrants, 12, 15, 17, 135–136, 234,
  236–238, 312
children, statutory definitions, 18, 25,
  89n26
"children in care" terminology, 59
children's committees, 28–29, 32–33
children's hearings, 145–160
  antisocial behaviour, 65
  and antisocial behaviour orders,
    157–158, 159–160
  basic procedure, 148–149
  blueprint in juvenile court rules, 140,
    144, 147, 148–149
  child protection orders, 294–296
  and child's best interests, 138, 149

comparison with England, 160–165
  emergency removal of children (Clyde
    Report 1993), 54
  establishment of, 46
  family participation in, 149
  and fostering, 221–222
  grounds of referral, 148–159
    and antisocial behaviour orders,
      157–158
    bad associations or moral danger,
      151–152
    child absconsion, 155–156
    child beyond parental control,
      150–151
    commission of offence by child, 155
    failure to attend school regularly, 154
    female living with female victim of
      incest, 154
    forced marriage/civil partnership,
      158
    lack of parental care, 152
    in local authority care requiring
      "special measures," 156–157
    misuse of drugs or alcohol, 157
    new grounds in 2011 Act, 152, 158
    overview of current position,
      158–159
    procedure, 148–149
    solvent abuse, 156
    victim of scheduled offence,
      152–153
  and Kilbrandon Report
    recommendations, 46, 145–148
  link to 1908 Act, 19–20
  no punitive powers, 139–140
  ongoing role, 149
  outcomes, 149
  participation rights, 57–59, 72, 79–80
  place of safety orders, 285–286,
    287–288
  reporters *see* main entry
  role of local authorities under 1968 Act,
    50–51, 271
  safeguarders, 52
  "schedule 1 offences" (from 1937),
    99–100
  school attendance, 133
  and secure accommodation, 276–277
  and state paternalism, 119–120

children's hearings (*cont.*)
   supervision requirements, 48, 50–51,
      193–194, 206, 222n134, 271,
      276–277
   unitary approach, 116–117, 171–175
   welfare test, 159–160
Children's Hearings Scotland, 72
children's homes *see* local authority
      homes; residential establishments
      (from 1968); voluntary homes
children's officers, 32–33, 262
children's panels *see* children's hearings
children's reporters *see* reporters
Churchill War Ministry, 27
civil partnerships, 63, 158
Cleland, Alison, 65
Clyde, James L., 27
   see also Clyde Report (1946)
Clyde, Lord, 54, 288
   see also Clyde Report (1993)
Clyde Industrial Training Ship
      Association, 235
Clyde Report (1946)
   acceptance of recommendations, 31, 32
   on boarding-out and fostering, 28–32,
      33–34, 201, 204, 205, 209–210,
      216
   and emigration of children, 316–317
   establishment and remit, 27–28
   on local authority involvement, 28–29,
      31, 32, 34n115, 35–36, 45
   overview of findings, 28–31
   on substitute families, 29–31
Clyde Report (1993), 53–55, 61, 288–290
Code of Practice Access to Children in
      Care or Under Supervision in
      Scotland (1983), 48–49
cohabitation, 63–64, 90, 96, 224, 381
Colonsay, Lord, 10
community care, 47
Conservative Governments, 163–164,
      165, 174
Cook County Juvenile Court, Illinois, 117,
      119–120
corporal punishment
   abolition of, 112–114, 139
   in approved schools, 112, 254–256
   defence of reasonable chastisement,
      100, 106–112

in loco parentis, 110–111, 113–114
   by parents, 114
   in residential establishments, 111, 113,
      263, 270
   in schools, 108–110, 112–113
   whipping, 138–140
corporate parenting, 309–311
cot death, 18
Cowan, M.G., 5–6, 22, 131, 133, 138, 139,
      244, 248
Cretney, Stephen, 27, 368
criminal responsibility, age of, 133
cruelty *see* child cruelty or neglect
Cunneen, Chris, 120–121
Curtis Report (1946)
   acceptance of recommendations, 31,
      32
   on adoption, 369
   on boarding-out and fostering, 210
   on emigration of children, 316
   on local authority involvement, 34n115,
      36
   publication, 28
custody orders, 52, 376

death penalty, 122
deprivation, emphasis on, 23, 45, 46–77,
      125–126
Dewar, Donald, 5, 192–193
Dickens, Charles
   Bleak House, 313
   Oliver Twist, 341
directors of social work, 33, 50, 56
disclosure certificates, 67–69
doli incapax, 133
Doyle Report (1875), 313–314, 318, 319,
      320–321
Driscoll, Morag (Macfarlane et al.), 284,
      296
drug misuse
   by adults, 292
   by children, 156, 157
Dundee
   approved schools, 246, 254
   industrial and reformatory schools, 235

Edinburgh
   approved schools, 246
   and emigration of children, 313

industrial and reformatory schools, 233, 234

education authorities
  and boarding-out, 213, 214, 215–216, 218
  delegation of duties, 204
  as fit persons, 203–204
  and juvenile courts, 26, 122n19, 134, 136, 138
  transfer of powers to local authorities, 28–29, 203n36

educational qualifications of care leavers, 299

emergency protection, 280–298
  child protection orders, 60–61, 71, 290–294
  Clyde Report (1946) findings, 288–290
  emergency and interim measures, distinction between, 280–281
  legislation
    1889–1908 Acts, 281–284, 287
    1932 and 1937 Acts, 284–285, 287
    1968 Act, 285–286, 287, 288–290
  place of safety, 53–54, 60–61, 281–290, 293–294, 296–298

emigration of children, 312–335
  abuse suffered, 317–318
  aftercare, 329–330, 332–333
  consent
    of child, 320–321, 323, 325–326, 328, 329
    of parents, 256, 318–320, 323–324
    of persons acting in loco parentis, 322–323, 324–327, 331
  destinations, 315–316
  early practices, 312–315
  legislation
    1891, 1894 and 1904 Acts, 323–325
    1908 Act, 325–326
    1932 and 1937 Acts, 326–329
    1948 Act, 329–332
    1968 Act, 333–335
  motivations for, 312–315
  statistics, 316, 321, 331–332
  and voluntary organisations, 316

emotional abuse, 103

employment of children, 15, 115, 186

Erskine, John, 106–107

exclusion orders, 61

Feld, Barry C., 168

Fife Inquiry, 53, 273–274

Finlayson Report, 56

Fisher, Nigel, 331n60

fit person, concept of, 202–203

fit person orders
  and adoption, 368, 371
  and emigration of children, 322, 324–327, 328
  legislation
    1889, 1894, 1904 and 1908 Acts, 15, 16, 97, 98, 202–203, 322
    1932 and 1937 Acts, 30, 203–209
  origins of, 14
  as outcome in juvenile court, 137
  and probation orders, 185, 187
  and supervision requirements, 222n134

Fortas, Abe, 167, 168n105, 169–170

foster carers (from 1996)
  allowances and fees, 228, 229–230, 231
  fostering agreements, 224–225
  kinship carers, 229–231
  monitoring and termination, 225–226, 226, 227
  relationship with local authority, 196–197
  role, 196–197
  suitability and approval, 223–224

foster parents (to 1996)
  aftercare, 303n16, 305–306
  caring responsibilities, 101
  changes in terminology, 213, 222
  and children's hearing system, 149
  corporal punishment and reasonable chastisement, 110–111, 113–114
  crofters as, 199, 209
  custody orders, 52
  eligibility and vetting, 33, 204, 213–215, 223–224
  as focus of 1946 Clyde Report, 29–31, 33–34
  and fostering agreements, 224–225
  informal adoption (pre-1930), 337–341, 342–343
  monitoring and termination, 225–226
  motivations, 221
  perception under Scotland's Children (White Paper), 55–56

foster parents (*cont.*)
  relatives as, 220
  roles, 217–218
fostering (from 1985)
  abuse cases, 196–197
  care plans, 226
  changes in terminology, 222
  fit person concept, 14, 15, 16
  fostering agreements, 224–225
  fostering panels, 223–224
  kinship care, 229–231
  monitoring and termination, 225–226, 226
  national review (2013), 228
  overview, 195–197
  secondary legislation, 222–227
Fraser, Lord (1969), 206
Fraser, Lord (*A Treatise on the Law of Scotland Relative to Parent and Child, Guardian and Ward*), 7
Fraser, Lord (of Carmyllie), 174
future harm, 15, 135, 290–292

Galbraith, James, 334–335, 347, 349, 361
Galbraith, Thomas, 210–211
Garland, David, 125
Getting it Right for Every Child (GIRFEC), 72–73, 174–175
Gilmour, Iain, 56–57
Giltinan, Donal, 56–57
Glasgow
  approved schools, 246
  boarded-out children, 199, 211
  and emigration of children, 313, 321
  industrial and reformatory schools, 176, 233, 234–235, 237, 301, 321
  poverty and delinquency, 127
  probation system, 178, 180, 184n34
Greenock
  approved schools, 246
  boarded-out children, 199
guardians, definitions and use of term, 222, 331, 353–354

Hailsham, Lord, 163, 375
Hale, Lady, 73, 76, 320
Hallett, Christine, 166, 169
Hastings, Somerville, 330
Hawthorn, Moyra, 102, 254

Headlam, Cuthbert, 350
Hoare, Sir Samuel, 139n102
Hodge, Lord, 73, 76
Holligan, William, 292
Holmes, H.T., 239, 240
Hope, Lord (1855), 86
Hope, Lord (1991, 1993), 103, 162
Hopkinson Report (1921), 342–343, 344–345, 347, 349, 359
Horsburgh Committee Report (1937), 364
Houghton, Sir William, 374n157
Houghton Committee Report (1972), 51, 374
Hughes, Lord, 46, 191, 266–267
Hurst, Sir Gerald, 346, 347, 370
Hurst Report (1954), 346, 359, 370, 371

illegitimacy, 63
imprisonment of children, 20, 95, 96n58, 122, 179, 181–183, 237
incest, 90, 91, 92, 154
industrial schools, 233–245
  aftercare, 300–301
  aims, 13, 19
  care and protection grounds, 19–20
  day schools, 176–177
  duties and obligations, 239, 242, 300–301
  education and training, 235, 239, 242
  and emigration of children, 314–315, 316, 323–326
  establishment of, 233–235
  ethos, 176
  grounds for sending, 18, 19–20, 150–151, 152, 155, 236–237
  legislation
    before 1908, 16, 236–241
    1908 Act and beyond, 18–20, 122, 125–126, 241–243
  length of detention, 243
  origins, 12
  oversight of, 242–243
  reformatory schools, overlap with, 12–13, 19–20, 25, 235–236, 237, 241
  statistics, 241, 243, 301, 316n13, 321
  see also approved schools
infant protection visitors, 342
Ingleby Report (1960), 37, 161

Inglis, Lord, 338
inspection of care services, 69–71
interim protection, 280–281, 285, 287–288, 294–296
International Labour Organisation, 39n136
Ireland, Ronald, 43n3

Jenkins, Roy, 162
Jowett, Viscount, 31, 32–33, 210
Joynson-Hicks, Sir William, 345
justices of the peace
  and emergency measures, 280, 283, 292–293
  qualifications for serving on juvenile courts, 127–128
juvenile courts, 115–144
  adoption orders, 134, 143–144
  age limits, 133–134
  approach of National Government in 1932, 23–24
  in Australia, 120–121
  care and protection cases, 25–26, 124–126, 132–138, 143–144
  cases at instance of parents, 136
  child beyond parental control, 150–151
  and child's best interests, 138, 141–142, 144
  comparison with England, 160
  grounds for action, 150–151, 152–155
  justices, 128–129, 140
  juvenile offender cases, 122–124, 132, 133, 138–143, 155
  Kilbrandon Report findings, 146–147, 188–189
  legislation
    1908 Act, 20–21, 121–126
    1932 and 1937 Acts, 25–26, 128–139
  Morton Committee recommendations, 22, 123n27, 127–128, 131, 133
  outcomes, 137–140, 181, 184
  privacy and confidentiality, 123, 131–132
  and probation, 137, 142, 181, 184
  replaced by children's hearings, 148
  rules and procedure, 140–144
  school attendance cases, 133, 143–144, 154
  separation from adult courts, 122–124, 130
  unfit parents, 152
  unitary approach, 132, 138, 162–163, 166–171, 173
  in United States, 117–120, 123, 124
  victims of scheduled offences, 152–153
  "welfare" and "justice" models, 166–169
juvenile delinquency, early ideas of, 12–13, 234

Kearney, Brian, 273, 284, 296
Kearney Report (1992–93), 53, 273–274
Keating, Jenny, 342
Kelly, Christine, 176, 179–180
Kendrick, Andrew, 102, 254
Kennedy, A.L., 350
Kidd, Dame Margaret, 43n2
Kilbrandon, Lord, 42–43, 146
Kilbrandon Report (1964)
  on care and protection cases, 136
  on Children Act, 1908, 21
  composition of committee, 42–43
  on corporal punishment, 139
  "genius" of, 162
  government response, 44–46
  importance of, 43
  on juvenile panels, 146–148
  on Morton Committee Report, 127
  on needs of children, 145–146
  on panels of justices, 129
  on probation and supervision, 188–190, 194
  remit, 42–43
  on residential care, 264–266
  on single agency for child care services, 44–45
kinship care, 4, 15, 30, 229–231
Kirk, and poor relief, 11

Labour Governments, 26–27, 44, 161–162, 163, 164, 165, 174
Lambert, Lydia, 374
legal aid, 58–59, 72, 79–80
Leicester, Bishop of, 376n166, 377n177
Liberal Government reforms 1906-14, 17

local authorities
  and adoption, 337, 363–364, 368–369,
    371, 372
    duties under 1975 and 1978 Acts,
      374–375, 376, 378–379, 383
    duties under 2007 Act, 380, 381, 384
    freeing orders, 383
    parental responsibilities orders, 61,
      383–384
    permanence orders, 384
  aftercare, 305–309
  and antisocial behaviour, 65
  antisocial behaviour orders, 159–160
  and baby farming, 342
  child protection orders, 290n53, 291,
    293
  and children's hearing system, 149
  children's homes
    local authority homes, 261–264
    oversight of voluntary homes,
      260–261, 262–263
  Clyde Report (1946) recommendations,
    28–29, 31, 32, 34n115, 35–36,
    45
  Clyde Report (1993) recommendations,
    54–55
  directors of social work, 33, 50, 56
  and emigration of children, 316,
    328–332, 334–335
  and fit person orders, 207, 211, 215
  as fit persons, 203n36
  and fostering, 196–197, 223–226, 227,
    229–231
  Kilbrandon Report recommendations
    and 1966 White Paper, 44–46
  kinship care, 229–231
  position of trust, 92
  and probation/supervision, 183,
    189–193
  removal of juvenile court
    responsibilities, 147
  reorganisation under 1994 Act, 56
  and residential establishments,
    267–269, 271–272
  responsibilities and powers, 32–37,
    47–53, 59–60
  and school attendance cases, 133
  Scotland's Children (1993 White Paper)
    recommendations, 55–56
  and secure accommodation, 277–279
  social work committees, 33, 50, 56
  social work departments, 44–46, 46–51,
    55
  and views of child, 57–58
local authority homes, 111, 261–264
  see also residential establishments
    (from 1968)
Longford, Lord, 161
Longford Report, 161–162, 164
"looked after children", 59, 274
Lorimer, James, 326

Macdonald, Helen J., 13, 95, 200
MacDonald, Ramsay, 22–23
Macfarlane, Katy, 284, 296
Mack, J.W., 124
McLaren, Lord, 339
Maclay, John, 42
Macpherson, Annie, 313–314
Major, John, 333n65
Mathers, George, 351
medical officers, 257, 263
Memorandum on the Boarding-Out of
    Children (1959), 219–221
Molony Report (1927), 127, 128
moral danger, 151–152
Morton, Sir George, 21
Morton Committee Report (1928)
  on approved schools, 247
  on care and protection, 22
  on emigration of children, 314–315
  on fit person orders, 203
  on industrial and reformatory schools,
    243–244, 247
  on juvenile courts, 22, 123n27,
    127–128, 131, 133
  on probation system, 179n7, 180,
    181–182, 184, 186
  remit, 21–22
Mure, Lord, 338

named person scheme, 73, 74–77
National Government (1931-35), 22–23,
    181n21
Navy, and going to sea, 235, 256, 301, 303,
    316n13, 326, 328
Nazareth Houses, 269n198
neglect see child cruelty or neglect

New Zealand
   adoption system, 345
   emigration to, 315–316
   industrial schools, 236n19
   juvenile courts, 169
Newman, Sir Robert, 348
Nield, Basil, 330
"normal home life", concept of, 28
Norrie, Kenneth McK., 2, 7, 108, 206
Northern Irish Historical Institutional
   Abuse Inquiry (2017), 317–318
NSPCC (National Society for the
   Prevention of Cruelty to
   Children), 180, 343

offence ground, 19, 25, 155
Orkney Inquiry, 53–55, 288–290
Ormidale, Lord, 109
overlaying, 18
Owen, David, 51–52

Palin, John, 350
parens patriae, 8, 95, 118–120, 167–168
parental contact, 4, 29–31, 45–46, 48–49,
   54–55, 59–60, 264
parental responsibilities orders, 61,
   383–384
parental rights resolutions, 35–37, 61
parenting orders, 65, 66
parents
   and best interests of child, 35
   and boarding-out, 201
   chastisement and corporal punishment,
      100, 106–108, 114
   child beyond parental control, 150–151
   and children in residential
      establishments, 270
   at common law, 94–95
   and emigration of children, 318–320,
      323–324, 327, 328
   involvement with children in approved
      schools, 256–257
   and juvenile court hearings, 122,
      140–141, 142–143, 144
   lack of parental care, 152
   participation rights under international
      law, 79, 80
   patria potestas, 8–9, 195, 320, 339,
      340

primary responsibility for children
      (UNCRC), 81
   and probation/supervision, 185–186,
      188–189, 206
   religious beliefs, 7, 8, 9n9
   rights for unmarried fathers, 63–64
   as sex-workers, 135
   unable to control child, 136, 150
   unfit, 13, 37, 71, 125–126, 134–135,
      151, 152
   see also birth parents
Parker, Roy, 211
parochial boards, 11, 198, 198–199, 200
patria potestas, 8–9, 195, 320, 339, 340
Pennefather, Sir John, 348
permanence orders, 61, 157, 384–385
Pethick-Lawrence, Frederick, 348
Philipson, Mabel, 346
place of safety, 53–54, 60–61, 281–290,
   291, 293–294, 296–298
plagium, 85–86
police
   indigence as police matter, 237, 238
   as probation officers, 178, 180, 183–184
   removal of juvenile court
      responsibilities, 147
   taking of child to place of safety,
      281–283, 284, 285, 286–287,
      293–294
Poor Law Acts (England), 36
Poor Law Magazine, 12
Poor Law (Scotland), 10–12, 197–201,
   204
poverty
   and delinquency (Morton Committee
      Report), 127
   "deserving poor", 177
   indoor and outdoor, 198–199
   role of Kirk, 11
   "saving" children from, 9–10
press reporting, 123, 131–132
prison see imprisonment of children
privacy and confidentiality, 123, 131–132
probation officers
   in care and protection cases, 137,
      185–186
   and children's hearing system, 149
   children's probation officers, 179, 183
   funding, 179, 183

probation officers (*cont.*)
  identification and appointment,
    179–180, 183–184
  introduction in Glasgow, 178
  in juvenile offender cases, 142, 181,
    181–185, 184
  professionalisation of role, 191
  roles and duties, 179, 181, 186,
    186–187, 190
  and search for work, 301
  voluntary, 183–184, 191, 193
probation system, 178–193
  Kilbrandon Report proposals, 188–190
  legislation
    from 1907 to 1949, 20, 178–188
    1968 Act and beyond, 51, 190–194
  probation orders, 183, 185–186, 189
prostitution
  by children, 19, 83, 87, 93–94, 125, 151
  by mothers, 135
Publius Clodius Pulcher (Clodius), 336
Puxon, Margaret, 163
PVG (Protection of Vulnerable Groups)
  Scheme, 67–69, 71

Quarrier, William, 318–319, 320–321
Quarrier's Homes, 232, 259, 314,
  318–319, 320–321, 324–325

Ralston, Andrew G., 13, 233
reasonable chastisement, 100, 106–112
Reed, Lord, 73, 76
reformatory schools, 233–245
  aftercare, 300–301
  aims, 13, 19
  duties and obligations, 239, 242,
    300–301
  education and training, 235, 239, 242
  and emigration of children, 314–315,
    316, 323–326
  establishment of, 233, 234–235
  grounds for sending, 19–20, 155,
    236–237
  industrial schools, overlap with, 12–13,
    19–20, 25, 235–236, 237, 241
  legislation
    before 1908, 236–239, 239–241
    1908 Act and beyond, 122, 125n36,
    241–243

  length of detention, 237, 239, 243
  origins, 12
  oversight of, 242–243
  statistics, 241, 243, 301, 321
  see also approved schools
regulation of care services, 69–71
religious organisations *see* voluntary
  organisations
religious upbringing of children
  and adoption, 367
  and approved schools, 247
  boarding-out and fostering, 202, 204,
    215, 229
  in early law, 7, 8
  remand homes, 111, 138
  see also residential establishments
    (from 1968)
Rentoul, Gervais, 346, 347, 348, 350
Report of the Departmental Committee on
  Sexual Offences against Children
  and Young Persons in Scotland
  (1926), 22, 135
Report on Child Migration Programmes
  (2018), 317
reporters
  administration, 56, 72
  and antisocial behaviour, 65
  conducting court proceedings, 52
  Kilbrandon Report proposals, 147
  and local authorities, 51, 56, 271
  place of safety orders, 285–286,
    293–294
  referrals to children's hearing, 73n156,
    150, 159
residential establishments (from 1968)
  best interests of child, 269, 271–272
  and children's hearing system, 149
  corporal punishment, 111–112, 113
  definition, 267n184
  discipline and punishment, 270
  obligations of managers, 269–270,
    275
  registration, 268
  secondary legislation, 269–272,
    274–275
  statistics, 272, 273
  vetting of staff, 275
  visits and monitoring of children,
    268–269, 271

see also approved schools; local authority homes; remand homes; voluntary homes
Richards, Kelly, 120–121
Rodger, Lord, 159
Ross, Lord, 172
Ross, William, 49–50, 174
Rowe, Jane, 374
Royal Air Force, enlisting of boys, 256, 303, 328
Royal Scottish Society for the Prevention of Cruelty to Children, 147
Rye, Maria, 313–314, 318, 321

safeguarders, 52
Salter, Sir Arthur, 101
same-sex couples, 63–64, 224, 227
Samuel, Herbert, 17, 121
Sands, Lord, 24
Scarbrough, Earl of, 211, 332
"schedule 1 offences" (from 1937), 99–100
"scheduled offences" (1908), 19
school attendance cases, 133, 143–144
Scotland's Children (1993 White Paper), 53, 55–56, 57, 274
Scottish Adoption Service, 374–375, 378
Scottish Advisory Council on Child Care, 211–213
Scottish Child Abuse Inquiry (SCAI), 1–2, 4, 66, 269, 319n23
Scottish Children's Reporter Administration (SCRA), 56, 72, 73n156, 159
see also reporters
Scottish Commission for the Regulation of Care (Care Commission), 69–70, 279
Scottish Education Department
and aftercare, 302
and approved schools, 245–246, 248–249
and boarding-out, 214, 216
and emigration of children, 314–315, 327–328
and industrial and reformatory schools, 242, 244
Scottish Government and Scottish Executive, 72, 174

Scottish Law Commission, 57
Scottish Privy Council, 7
Scottish Probation Service, 190–193
secure accommodation, 275–279
sexual offences against children, 86–94
1926 Report, 22, 135
under child neglect legislation, 105
and corporal punishment, 254
grooming, 93
gross indecency, 88, 88–89
incest, 90, 91, 92, 154
indecent photographs and images, 89, 94
in international law, 83
lewd, indecent and libidinous practice or behaviour, 86–87, 88
in position of trust, 90, 91–93, 154n52
and press reporting, 132
at residential establishments, 269
"scheduled offences" (1908), 19
sexual exploitation, 89–93
sexual intercourse, 87, 88, 91, 92
shameless indecency, 91
sodomy, 88, 88–89
treatment of allegations (Clyde Report), 54
Shaw, Lord, 17–18, 19, 21
Skelton, John S., 198–200, 209
Skinner, Angus, 272
Skinner Report, 53, 272–273
Social Care and Social Work Improvement Scotland (Care Inspectorate), 70–71
"social education", 188–189
Social Work and the Community (1966 White Paper), 44–46, 266
social work committees, 33, 50, 56
social work departments, 44–46, 46–51, 55
social workers, qualification course, 55
solvent abuse, 156
Southern Rhodesia, emigration to, 315–316, 329
"special measures", 156–157
Stanley, Oliver, 23–24, 244–245
Stewart, John, 18, 121
Stone, Fred, 43n4
Stranraer Reformatory, 240–241

Strathcona, Lord, 201
supervision
   Kilbrandon Report proposals, 188–190,
      222n134
   orders, 177, 185–189
   requirements, 48, 50–51, 193–194, 206,
      222n134, 271, 276–277
surrogacy, 64

teachers
   in approved schools, 251, 255
   caring responsibilities, 102
   and corporal punishment, 108–110,
      112–113
   in industrial and reformatory schools,
      242
Thomson, Lord, 208
Tomlin Reports (1925), 342n24, 344–345,
   347, 349
Trotter, Thomas (*The Law as to Children
   and Young Persons*), 103, 132,
   136, 180n14, 207, 246, 353, 356,
   359–360
truancy, 133, 143–144, 154

unitary approach
   of children's hearings, 116–117,
      171–175
   of juvenile courts, 132, 138, 162–163,
      166–171, 173
United States, juvenile courts, 117–120,
   123, 124
University of Strathclyde, 310

vagrancy, 12, 15, 17, 135–136, 234,
   236–238, 312

voluntary homes, 28, 50, 111, 149,
   258–261, 262–264
   see also residential establishments
      (from 1968)
voluntary organisations
   caring responsibilities, 101
   and "children in care", 59
   emergency measures, 283, 297
   and emigration of children, 316, 329,
      332–335
   as fit persons, 16, 203, 205
   and fostering, 223–226, 227
   growth of, 9
   parental rights and powers, 53
   position of trust, 92
   and probation/supervision, 189–190

Walker, Allan G., 43n2
Wallace, Jim, 174
Ward, Sir Alan, 333
Watkins, John C., 119–120
Watson, John, 234, 237
welfare state, 17, 27, 62
wellbeing of child (2014), 73, 74, 75,
   76–77
Wells-Pestell, Lord, 191–192, 377n177
whipping, 138–140
White, Rob, 120–121
Wigoder, Lord, 375
Wilkinson, Alexander B., 2, 7, 108, 206
Wilson Harris, Henry, 329–330
Wise, Lady, 80
Wundersitz, Joy, 166

young persons, statutory definitions, 18,
   25, 284